CRIMINAL JUSTICE ETHICS

4TH EDITION

For James

SAGE was founded in 1965 by Sara Miller McCune to support the dissemination of usable knowledge by publishing innovative and high-quality research and teaching content. Today, we publish over 900 journals, including those of more than 400 learned societies, more than 800 new books per year, and a growing range of library products including archives, data, case studies, reports, and video. SAGE remains majority-owned by our founder, and after Sara's lifetime will become owned by a charitable trust that secures our continued independence.

Los Angeles | London | New Delhi | Singapore | Washington DC | Melbourne

CRIMINAL JUSTICE ETHICS
THEORY AND PRACTICE
4TH EDITION

Cyndi Banks

Northern Arizona University

Los Angeles | London | New Delhi
Singapore | Washington DC | Melbourne

⑤SAGE

FOR INFORMATION:

SAGE Publications, Inc.
2455 Teller Road
Thousand Oaks, California 91320
E-mail: order@sagepub.com

SAGE Publications Ltd.
1 Oliver's Yard
55 City Road
London, EC1Y 1SP
United Kingdom

SAGE Publications India Pvt. Ltd.
B 1/I 1 Mohan Cooperative Industrial Area
Mathura Road, New Delhi 110 044
India

SAGE Publications Asia-Pacific Pte. Ltd.
3 Church Street
#10–04 Samsung Hub
Singapore 049483

Acquisitions Editor: Jerry Westby
Editorial Assistant: Laura Kirkhuff
Production Editor: Veronica Stapleton Hooper
Copy Editor: Amy Harris
Typesetter: Hurix Systems Pvt. Ltd.
Proofreader: Jeff Bryant
Indexer: Jean Casalegno
Cover Designer: Alexa Turner
Marketing Manager: Amy Lammers
eLearning Editor: Nicole Mangona

Printed in the United States of America

Library of Congress Cataloging-in-Publication Data

Names: Banks, Cyndi, author.

Title: Criminal justice ethics : theory and practice / Cyndi Banks.

Description: Fourth edition. | Thousand Oaks, California : SAGE, [2016] |

Includes bibliographical references and index.

Identifiers: LCCN 2015038683 | ISBN 9781506326054 (pbk.: alk. paper)

Subjects: LCSH: Criminal justice, Administration of—Moral and ethical aspects.

Classification: LCC HV7419 .B36 2016 | DDC 172/.2—dc23 LC record available at http://lccn.loc.gov/2015038683

This book is printed on acid-free paper.

SFI Certified Sourcing
www.sfiprogram.org
SFI-00453

16 17 18 19 20 10 9 8 7 6 5 4 3 2 1

BRIEF CONTENTS

Preface   xv

Acknowledgments   xvii

About the Author   xviii

PART I: THE INTERACTION BETWEEN ETHICS AND THE CRIMINAL JUSTICE SYSTEM

1. The Importance of Ethics in Criminal Justice   3

2. Police Ethics: The Nature of Policing and Police Corruption   18

3. Police Ethics: Use of Force, Investigations, Interrogations, and Lying 64

4. Racial Discrimination in the Criminal Justice System   98

5. Judges, Lawyers, and Ethics   126

6. The Purpose of Criminal Punishment   154

7. Ethics in Corrections: The Nature of Corrections   178

8. Ethics in Corrections: Guarding Ethically   217

9. The Ethics of Criminal Justice Policy Making   248

10. Ethics and the "War on Terrorism"   285

11. Media Ethics and Criminal Justice   312

PART II: THE APPLICATION OF ETHICAL THEORIES TO THE CRIMINAL JUSTICE SYSTEM

12. Duty and Principle   341

13. Considering the Consequences   352

14. The Importance of Character   365

15. Egoism, Pleasure, and Indifference   379

16. A Sense of Justice   389

17. Caring for Others   396

References   412

Index   439

DETAILED CONTENTS

Preface   xv

Acknowledgments   xvii

About the Author   xviii

PART I: THE INTERACTION BETWEEN ETHICS AND THE CRIMINAL JUSTICE SYSTEM

1. The Importance of Ethics in Criminal Justice   3
   - The Meaning of Ethics   3
   - The Value of Ethics   4
     - CASE STUDY 1.1 POLICE BRUTALITY IN NEW ORLEANS   5
     - CASE STUDY 1.2 POLICE BRUTALITY DURING KATRINA   6
   - Normative Ethics   6
   - Ethical Relativism   6
     - CASE STUDY 1.3 DEATH ROW INMATE SET FREE   7
   - Cultural Relativism   7
   - Ethical Absolutism   8
   - Ethical Pluralism   9
   - Religion and Ethical Standards   10
     - *Conduct Is Right Because God Commands It*   10
     - *God Commands Right Conduct Because It Is Right*   10
   - Ethics and Natural Law   11
   - Ethics and Law   12
   - Ethical Dilemmas   12
   - Ethical Issues in Criminal Justice   15
     - *Ethical Problems in the Use of Authority*   15
     - *Ethical Problems in the Relationship Between Personal and Professional Interests*   15
     - *Ethical Problems in Personal and Professional Commitments to Clients*   15
     - *Ethical Issues in Criminal Justice and Public Policy*   15
     - *Ethical Issues Resulting From Policing Policies*   16
     - *Ethical Problems in Information Sharing*   16
     - *Ethical Problems Dealing With Human Rights Issues in the Criminal Justice System*   16
     - *Ethical Issues in the Media Reporting of Crime*   16
   - Summary   16
   - Discussion Questions   17

2. Police Ethics: The Nature of Policing and Police Corruption — 18
   Ethics and Policing — 18
   The Nature of Policing — 19
   Police as an Institution — 20
   Police Culture — 20
     Changing Police Culture — 22
   Police Discretion — 24
     Limiting Police Discretion — 24
     Discretion and Accountability — 25
   Ethics and Codes of Ethics — 25
     What Is the Relationship Between Ethics and Codes of Ethics? — 26
     Police Compliance With Ethical Codes — 26
     Ethics Instruction — 26
   Policing and Stress — 29
     Nature of Police Occupational Stress — 29
     Stress and Crime Fighting — 30
     Coping With Stress — 31
     Angry Aggression — 31
   Police "Militarization" — 32
     Historical and Contemporary Context—Police and Military — 32
     The Militarization Thesis — 32
     Number and Deployment of SWAT Units — 33
     Causes of Militarization — 34
     The Consequences of Militarization — 35
     Critiques of the Militarization Thesis — 36
   Police Corruption — 39
     The Nature of Police Corruption — 40
     Accepting Gratuities — 41
     Explanations for Police Corruption — 42
     Personalistic Explanations — 43
     Institutional Explanations — 45
     Systemic Explanations — 46
     "Slippery Slope" Explanation — 47
     Noble Cause *Corruption* — 47
     Societal Stress as an Explanation for Corruption — 48
     Combating Corruption — 51
     Police Corruption in the United Kingdom — 51
     Reducing Corruption — 51
     Ensuring Police Accountability — 52
     "New Police Accountability" — 52
     Police Auditors — 52
     External Citizen Review of Police — 53
     Accountability in Other Countries — 53
   Whistle-Blowing — 55
     CASE STUDY 2.1 PUNISHED FOR WHISTLE-BLOWING? — 55
     When Is Whistle-Blowing Morally Justified? — 56
   Discrimination as a Corrupt Practice in Policing: Racial Bias, Racial Profiling, and Selective Law Enforcement — 56

Racism and Racial Bias	56
Racial Profiling	57
CASE STUDY 2.2 "LOOKING MEXICAN"	58
CASE STUDY 2.3 RACIAL PROFILING: WHEN COLOR SIGNALS DANGEROUSNESS	58
The Morality of Racial Profiling	59
"Driving While Black"	60
"Stop and Frisk"	61
Confidence in the Police	62
Selective Law Enforcement	62
Summary	62
Discussion Questions	63
Web Resources	63
3. Police Ethics: Use of Force, Investigations, Interrogations, and Lying	64
Police Use of Force	64
Police Use of Force: Arrest-Related Deaths	65
Deaths in Police Custody	65
Political Action on Police Use of Force, 2015	66
The Rise of the Citizen Journalist and Police Use of Force	66
The Continuum of Force	69
When to Use Force	69
Police Perspectives on Use of Force	70
Police and Citizen Interactions	71
CASE STUDY 3.1 COP GETS 15 YEARS IN TORTURE CASE	72
Police/Citizen Interactions and Procedural Justice	74
U.S. Supreme Court Decisions on Use of Force	75
Race and Use of Force	76
Policing and Implicit Racial Bias	76
Explaining Excessive Force	78
Assessing the Level of Force	79
Reducing the Level of Force	80
CASE STUDY 3.2 FIVE POLICE OFFICERS SENTENCED FOR SHOOTING UNARMED FAMILY	80
Excessive Force: Other Countries	81
Police Use of Force: Tasers	81
Excessive Use of Force: Dirty Harry/Dirty Hands and Jack Bauer in 24	85
Policing, Mental Illness, and Crisis Intervention Teams (CITs)	86
CASE STUDY 3.3 VIDEO SHOWS POLICE OFFICER USING BATON TO HIT MAN	86
Police Perceptions of Mentally Ill Persons	87
Crisis Intervention Teams	88
Ethical Issues in Investigation, Interrogation, and Custody	88
Rights of Suspects	88
Privacy	89
Entrapment	89
Deception	91
Informants	92
Confessions	93
Testimonial Deception	94
Police Lying	95
Electronic Recording of Interrogations	96

	Summary	96
	Discussion Question	97
4.	Racial Discrimination in the Criminal Justice System	98
	Ethical Background	98
	Historical Context	99
	Is There Racial Discrimination in the Criminal Justice System?	100
	Criminal Justice System: Discrimination and Decision-Making Points	101
	Discrimination in the Juvenile Justice System	102
	Police Encounters With Citizens and Police Arrest	103
	Prosecutorial Discretion	104
	Bail	105
	Jury Selection	105
	CASE STUDY 4.1 IN DALLAS, DISMISSAL OF BLACK JURORS LEADS TO APPEAL BY DEATH ROW INMATE	106
	Conviction and Sentencing	107
	Imprisonment Disparities	109
	Incarceration Rates	109
	Explaining Racial Disproportionality in Incarceration	110
	Death Penalty Disparities	110
	Hate Crimes	114
	Explanations for Racial Discrimination in the Criminal Justice System	118
	How Do We Explain the Existence of Racial Discrimination in the Criminal Justice System?	118
	Summary	125
	Discussion Questions	125
	Web Resources	125
5.	Judges, Lawyers, and Ethics	126
	Legal Ethics: Historical Context	126
	The Nature of Professional Ethics	127
	The Principle of Partisanship	128
	The Principle of Neutrality	128
	The Lawyer–Client Relationship	129
	Confidentiality	130
	Client Perjury	130
	Client Crime	131
	CASE STUDY 5.1 BURIED BODIES CASE	132
	Defense Lawyers	132
	The Prosecutor	136
	The Duty to Ensure Justice Is Done	136
	CASE STUDY 5.2 PROSECUTOR MISCONDUCT	137
	Discretion to Bring Charges	138
	Prosecution Disclosure of Evidence to the Defense	139
	Plea Bargaining	139
	Prosecutorial Misconduct	142
	CASE STUDY 5.3 WRONGFUL CONVICTION PAYMENT	144
	CASE STUDY 5.4 CONVICT'S DNA SWAYS LABS, NOT A DETERMINED PROSECUTOR	145
	CASE STUDY 5.5 PROSECUTOR WITHHOLDS EVIDENCE	146

CASE STUDY 5.6 RELEASE AFTER 14 YEARS 147

Judicial Ethics 147

    Ethical Rules Governing Judges 149

    Judicial Misfeasance 150

    CASE STUDY 5.7 PROSECUTOR SAYS TAPE SHOWS BROOKLYN JUDGE TOOK A BRIBE 150

    CASE STUDY 5.8 JUDGE RECEIVES 28-YEAR SENTENCE FOR TAKING BRIBES 150

    CASE STUDY 5.9 FEDERAL JUDGES AND FINANCIAL-INTEREST CONFLICTS 151

    CASE STUDY 5.10 APPEARANCE OF PARTIALITY 151

    CASE STUDY 5.11 JUDICIAL BRIBERY 151

    CASE STUDY 5.12 GROSS ABUSE OF POWER 152

    CASE STUDY 5.13 TEXAS JUDGE REPRIMANDED 152

Summary 152

Discussion Questions 153

6. The Purpose of Criminal Punishment 154

    What Is Punishment? 154

    Theoretical Approaches to Punishment 155

    Why Punish? The Philosophical Approach 156

      Deterrence 156

      CASE STUDY 6.1 THE NATURE OF THE PUNISHMENT: CORPORAL PUNISHMENT 157

      Retribution 160

      Just Deserts 164

      Reconciling Utilitarian and Retributive Theories 167

      Rehabilitation 168

      Incapacitation 170

    Restorative Justice 171

    Why Punish? The Sociological Approach 173

    Summary 176

    Discussion Questions 177

7. Ethics in Corrections: The Nature of Corrections 178

    The Prison Explosion 179

      Time Line of the Prison Explosion 183

    The Prison Explosion: Time Line of Events 184

      Prison Overcrowding 186

      Women's Incarceration 188

      New Forms of Incarceration 189

    Maximum Security 191

      Solitary Confinement 194

    Medium Security and Minimum Security 196

    Stateville Prison: The Changing State of Corrections 196

    Corrections Subculture 200

      Subculture and Socialization 200

      Kauffman's Guard Types 202

    Power and Authority in Prison: Controlling the Inmates 202

      The Battle for Compliance 204

      Rewards and Punishments 204

      Enforcing Rule Violations 205

      Informal Controls 206

	Prisoner "Power"	207
	Corruption of Authority	207
	Private Prisons	208
	CASE STUDY 7.1 PRIVATE PRISONS—A GOOD POLICY CHOICE?	212
	Disenfranchising Inmates	213
	Reforms	214
	Summary	215
	Discussion Questions	216
	Web Resources	216
8.	Ethics in Corrections: Guarding Ethically	217
	The Experience of Guarding	217
	Guarding Ethically	218
	Ethical Dimensions: Punishment, Prison Conditions	218
	Ethical Challenges	219
	Guarding With Discretion	220
	CASE STUDY 8.1 MALE PRISON RAPE AND "DELIBERATE INDIFFERENCE"	220
	Unethical Situations	223
	Use of Force	223
	Witnessing and Experiencing Violence in Prisons	223
	Using Force	224
	CASE STUDY 8.2 BRUTALITY AT RIKERS ISLAND, NEW YORK	225
	Officers' Perspectives on Use of Force	226
	Officer Violence as Informal Justice	226
	Justifications for Officer Violence	227
	Constraining Officer Violence	228
	Judicial Review of Use of Force	228
	Correctional Policy on the Use of Force	229
	Rape in Prison	229
	CASE STUDY 8.3 RAPE IN PRISON	232
	CASE STUDY 8.4 TRANSGENDER EXPERIENCES OF PRISON RAPE	232
	CASE STUDY 8.5 GUARD FORCES TRANSGENDER INMATE TO HAVE SEX WITH HIM	233
	Prison Rape Elimination Act	233
	Transgender Prisoners	234
	Corruption	235
	CASE STUDY 8.6 JAIL GUARDS CHARGED WITH SMUGGLING	237
	CASE STUDY 8.7 BALTIMORE JAIL INMATE BUILDS DRUG TRAFFICKING OPERATION WITH ACTIVE COOPERATION OF CORRECTIONS OFFICIALS	237
	Whistle-Blowing in Corrections	238
	CASE STUDY 8.8 EX-SC PRISON OFFICER SENTENCED	238
	Oversight of Prisons	239
	Ethical Issues in Probation and Parole	240
	Probation Officers and Law Enforcement	242
	Arming Probation Officers	242
	Treatment or Control?	243
	Privatizing Probation	243
	Parole	244

	Abolition of Parole for Life Imprisonment (LWOP)	245
	Parole Officers as Police	246
	Summary	246
	Discussion Questions	247
	Web Resources	247
9.	The Ethics of Criminal Justice Policy Making	248
	The Ethics of Policy Making	248
	Justifying Policy Choices	248
	Ethical Policy Making	249
	Moral Panics and Morality Policy Making	249
	Race and Crime Control Policies	251
	CASE STUDY 9.1 AN EXAMPLE OF UNETHICAL POLICY MAKING?	251
	Morality Policy	252
	Rationale for Morality Policy Making	252
	Penal Policies	253
	Ending Mass Imprisonment?	255
	Elderly Inmates	256
	Mass Incarceration as the New "Jim Crow"	256
	Public Opinion About Punishment	256
	Public Attitudes Toward Crime	258
	Public Participation in Sentencing Offenders	261
	Mandatory Minimum Sentencing	262
	The War on Drugs	264
	Crime Control Politics and the War on Drugs	265
	Fighting the War on Drugs: Prosecutions and Incentives	265
	Drugs and Incarceration	266
	Truth in Sentencing	268
	Predators and Superpredators	269
	Sexual Predators	269
	Juvenile Superpredators	273
	Capital Punishment	274
	Public Opinion on Capital Punishment	277
	Summary	283
	Discussion Questions	284
	Web Resources	284
10.	Ethics and the "War on Terrorism"	285
	Defining Terrorism	286
	Terrorism as a Moral Judgment	287
	Warfare or Crime Control?	288
	A Criminal Justice Approach to Terrorism	289
	Waging a War on Terrorism	291
	Risks of a Warlike Approach	292
	Justifications for Waging War	292
	Other Responses to Terrorism	293
	What Are the Morally Justifiable Constraints and Restrictions That a Government Should Be Permitted to Impose on Its Citizens in a War on Terrorism?	293
	Is Torture Morally Permissible as a Counterterrorist Strategy?	298
	The Morality of Targeted Killing	305

The United States and Targeted Killings 306
Armed Drones and Targeted Killings 307
"Post-Heroic" Warfare 308
Drones and Decisions to Use Force 308
Noncombatant Casualties 308
Proportionality 309
Legal and Moral Framework for Drone Strikes 309
The Disembodied Warrior 310
Arguments Against Targeted Killings 310
Summary 310
Discussion Questions 311

11. Media Ethics and Criminal Justice 312
Media Constructions of Crime 312
Crime, Media, and Ethics 313
Reporting the Truth 314
Crime and Media Stereotyping of Young Black Males 316
Media Stereotyping of Gender and Crime 318
Media Distortions of Crime and Victims of Crime 319
Media and Moral Panics 323
Media and Fear of Crime 328
Avoiding Bias 329
Newsworthiness: Shaping News 329
Media and Police 330
Avoiding Harm 330
Serving the Public 332
Crime and Infotainment 332
Maintaining Trust 334
Manipulation 335
Summary 336

PART II: THE APPLICATION OF ETHICAL THEORIES
TO THE CRIMINAL JUSTICE SYSTEM

12. Duty and Principle 341
Hypothetical and Categorical Imperatives 342
The Principle of Universality 342
Respect for All Persons 343
Kingdom of Ends 345
Conflicting Duties 345
Applying Deontological Theory 346
CASE STUDY 12.1 ROUGH JUSTICE IN A JUVENILE INSTITUTION ... 346
Summary 349
Discussion Questions 351

13. Considering the Consequences 352
Pleasure and Happiness 354
Act Consequentialism 354
Rule Consequentialism 355
Public Policy and Utilitarianism 355
Arguments Criticizing Utilitarianism 355

CASE STUDY 13.1 GOOD FRIENDS ARE HARD TO FIND		359
Applying Utilitarian Theory		360
Summary		362
Discussion Questions		364
14. The Importance of Character		365
Virtues		367
Aristotle and Happiness		368
The Golden Mean		369
Practical Wisdom		370
What's Wrong With Virtue		370
Applying Virtue Theory		374
CASE STUDY 14.1 PROFILING IN THE NEIGHBORHOOD		374
Summary		377
Discussion Questions		378
15. Egoism, Pleasure, and Indifference		379
Stoicism		379
Hedonism		381
Ethical Egoism		382
Psychological Egoism		382
Ethical Egoism		383
Applying the Theory of Ethical Egoism		384
CASE STUDY 15.1 GIVING YOUR OWN PUNISHMENT		384
Summary		387
Discussion Questions		388
16. A Sense of Justice		389
Application of the Principles		390
Justice as Fairness		391
Moral Development		392
Applying Rawlsian Theory		393
Summary		394
Discussion Questions		395
17. Caring for Others		396
Kohlberg and Gilligan		396
A Theory of Moral Development		397
"In a Different Voice": Carol Gilligan		397
Gender and the Ethic of Care		400
An Ethic of Care		400
Developing the Ethic of Care		401
The Ethic of Care and Justice		403
Peacemaking		404
Applying the Ethic of Care		406
CASE STUDY 17.1 TOUGH LOVE		406
Summary		409
Discussion Questions		411
References		412
Index		439

PREFACE

This is the fourth edition of this text that explores the articulation between criminal justice and ethics and presents ethical theories and applies them to elements of the criminal justice system. This edition maintains the critical perspective adopted in earlier editions, questioning and analyzing ethical issues as they apply within the criminal justice system and proposing modes of resolving such issues.

This new edition is the outcome of a thorough review of the third edition and includes much new material that assists in contextualizing and identifying ethical issues. It takes account of published scholarship and studies since the production of the third edition. This edition is thoroughly contemporary and continues to be an accessible but scholarly source of knowledge on ethics and criminal justice.

Following the positive responses to the third edition received from reviewers and colleagues, a number of changes have been made to the organization of the material, and I have tried to make the text more manageable and coherent by adding new chapters and new subheadings. As well, references have been added throughout to link different chapters where similar material is discussed—for example, the issues of mass imprisonment and racial bias in policing. Data and tables have been updated and new case studies added.

The changes in this edition also include the following:

- Substantive changes were made to the chapters in the previous edition that covered police ethics and ethics in corrections. As suggested by a number of reviewers, these topics are now divided into two chapters each to reflect the wealth of material. The new chapters are "Police Ethics: The Nature of Policing and Police Corruption" (Chapter 2), "Police Ethics: Use of Force, Investigations, Interrogation, and Lying" (Chapter 3), "Ethics in Corrections: The Nature of Corrections" (Chapter 7), and "Ethics in Corrections: Guarding Ethically" (Chapter 8).
- Chapter 3 on police ethics contains a greatly expanded discussion of police use of force, arrest-related deaths, and deaths in police custody; this topic is also linked to new discussions of police militarism, police use of Tasers, stress in policing, and police interactions with persons suffering mental illness. This chapter recognizes and takes account of contemporary debates concerning the issue of police discretion, especially in relation to use of force.
- Chapters 7 and 8 on ethics in corrections contain a revised and expanded discussion of the incarceration explosion, again reflecting current debates about the merits of a policy of incapacitation and the overall costs of that policy. In addition, the text highlights arguments about prison overcrowding and examines the ethics of solitary confinement. The topic of private prisons is now located in these chapters. New material has been added to discussions about rape in prison and transgender prisoners, and new topics include the privatization of probation services and the ethics of the sentence of life without parole.
- "The Ethics of Criminal Justice Policy Making" (Chapter 9) offers an expanded discussion of mass imprisonment polices and recent policy initiatives to reduce or end mass imprisonment. New material

addresses the issue of elderly inmates and mass incarceration as "the new Jim Crow." In the section on capital punishment, a new section has been added that reviews recent debates, litigation, and practice concerning the lethal injection procedure in capital cases.

- The chapter on terrorism (Chapter 10—"Ethics and the 'War on Terrorism'") now incorporates material discussing the ethics of using armed drones to make targeted killings, and the section on torture has been updated to take account of recent debates and publications.

- Chapter 11, "Media Ethics and Criminal Justice," contains a new section focusing on comic books as popular culture and a form of mass media. It explores how characters in comic books (as later transformed into screen characters) convey representations of crime, justice, and punishment. In addition, issues of alleged violence on college campuses and so called "binge-drinking," both framed by the media as threats to students and as moral panics, are critically examined.

ACKNOWLEDGMENTS

I'd like to thank James Baker for his research assistance and general support for this new edition and Jerry Westby, my editor at Sage, who has continued to encourage me in my endeavor to maintain this text as one of the leading textbooks on criminal justice ethics.

I also thank the reviewers of the third edition for their careful attention to reviews of the text and for proposing important changes that will continue to make this text relevant for students and faculty.

David A. Mackey
Plymouth State University

Shelly A. McGrath
University of Alabama at Birmingham

Benjamin Meade
James Madison University

Steven Ruffatto
Harrisburg Area Community College

Brandon L. Bang
Washington State University

Shannon Hankhouse
Tarleton State University

Vanessa H. Woodward
University of West Georgia

ABOUT THE AUTHOR

Cyndi Banks is a professor of criminology and criminal justice and Dean of University College at Northern Arizona University. She has more than 24 years' experience of research and project implementation in developing countries in the fields of juvenile justice, probation, justice policy, and child rights. She has worked as a criminologist in Papua New Guinea, Bangladesh, Iraq, Kurdistan, Timor Leste, Sudan, and Myanmar. She is the author of numerous articles and books, including *Criminal Justice Ethics*; *Youth, Crime and Justice*; *Developing Cultural Criminology: Theory and Practice in Papua New Guinea*; *Alaska Native Juveniles in Detention*; and most recently, *Comparative, International, and Global Justice: Perspectives From Criminology and Criminal Justice*.

PART I

THE INTERACTION BETWEEN ETHICS AND THE CRIMINAL JUSTICE SYSTEM

1

THE IMPORTANCE OF ETHICS IN CRIMINAL JUSTICE

To live ethically is to think about things beyond one's own interests. When I think ethically I become just one being, with needs and desires of my own, certainly, but living among others who also have needs and desires.

—Peter Singer 1995: 174

THE MEANING OF ETHICS

Ethics, also known as moral philosophy, is a branch of philosophy concerned with the study of questions of right and wrong and how we ought to live. Ethics involves making moral judgments about what is right or wrong, good or bad. Right and wrong are qualities or moral judgments we assign to actions and conduct. Within the study of ethics, there are three branches: *metaethics*, concerned with methods, language, logical structure, and the reasoning used in the interpretation of ethical terms, for example, what exactly the term *good* means; *normative ethics*, concerned with ways of behaving and standards of conduct; and *applied ethics*, concerned with solving practical moral problems as they arise, particularly in the professions, such as medicine and law.

Ethics provides us with a way to make moral choices when we are uncertain about what to do in a situation involving moral issues. In the process of everyday life, moral rules are desirable—not because they express absolute truth, but because they are generally reliable guides for normal circumstances (Singer 1995: 175). The focus of this book is on normative and applied ethics, particularly the exploration and analysis of ethical dilemmas and conflict situations that arise within the criminal justice system.

3

THE VALUE OF ETHICS

Do we need to study ethics? One view is that if we need to make a decision about a dilemma that confronts us, we can do so without any knowledge of ethics. From this perspective, ethics is too abstract and theoretical and is not related to the practical world. Another view is that we need a system of rules and principles to help guide us in making difficult decisions when moral issues arise. If we cannot draw on an ethical framework, we have to rely on emotion, instinct, and personal values, and these cannot supply an adequate answer to moral dilemmas. Among the reasons commonly given for studying ethics are the following:

- Ethical considerations are central to decisions involving discretion, force, and due process that require people to make enlightened moral judgments.
- Knowledge of ethics enables a person to question and analyze assumptions that are typically not questioned in areas of activity like business and politics. Questioning the criminal justice system should also be encouraged. This includes raising issues regarding such topics as the relationship between crime and justice, the role of law enforcement, the place of punishment, the limits of punishment, the authority of the state, the proper function of prisons, fairness in the workplace through creating a safe working environment, and equal opportunity.
- The study of ethics increases sensitivity to issues of right and wrong and the right way to conduct oneself, and aids in identifying acts that have a moral content.
- Only through studying ethics is it possible to define unethical behavior. A full understanding of ethical behavior demonstrates that it includes not only "bad" or "evil" acts but also inaction that allows "bad" or "evil" to occur.
- It is important to have the capacity to point to moral reasoning in justifying behavior, and the study of ethics develops that capacity.
- It is crucial that ethical decisions are made, and the study of ethics enables the development of tools that enhance ethical decision-making.
- Training in critical ethics helps to develop analytical skills and reasoning abilities needed to understand the practical as well as the theoretical aspects of the criminal justice system (Felkenes 1987).

- Understanding ethics enables an appreciation of the complexities of acts that involve ethical issues and dilemmas.
- Without knowledge of ethics, criminal justice professionals may be naïve about moral issues occurring within the criminal justice system.
- The study of ethics helps criminal justice professionals quickly recognize the ethical consequences of various actions and the moral principles involved.
- Within the criminal justice system, ethics is germane to most management and policy decisions relating to punishment and is the rationale used in making these decisions, such as whether to rehabilitate, deter, or impose just deserts. Examples of such management and policy issues include whether it is ethical to force someone to attend a treatment program against his or her will, and, given that the system of punishment is based on an assumption of rehabilitation, whether it is ethical to send an offender to jail and not offer treatment programs to help him or her change behavior to regain freedom (Felkenes 1987).
- The criminal justice system comprises professionals who exercise power and authority over others and who in some cases are authorized to use force and physical coercion against them. The law, or accepted standards of behavior, imposes ethical rules and responsibilities on these professionals. It follows that professionals in the criminal justice system must be aware of ethical standards in carrying out their functions. Ethics is crucial in decisions involving discretion, force, and due process because criminal justice professionals can be tempted to abuse their powers (Felkenes 1987).

In this book, the value of the study of ethics by criminal justice professionals will become apparent as the criminal justice system is analyzed to reveal how decision-makers sometimes fail to make the "right" choices or deliberately act unethically in carrying out their functions. It will become clear that studying and applying ethics is a prerequisite for any competent criminal justice professional. As an introduction to the kinds of ethical issues that can arise in criminal justice, two reports of criminal cases are presented in Case Studies 1.1 and 1.2.

It was not until 3 years after Archie was beaten to death that reports concluded that some officers had behaved brutally. Despite the extreme circumstances

Case Study 1.1 Police Brutality in New Orleans

In March 1990, Adolph Archie, an African American, was injured in an incident in which police claimed he shot and killed a white police officer during a downtown shootout. Archie later died under circumstances that are still far from clear. Transporting Archie to the hospital after the shooting took police 12 minutes, but the distance was only seven blocks. When he arrived, about 100 officers were present, having heard about the death of their fellow officer. While Archie was being taken to the hospital, police radios were used to utter death threats against him, and those accompanying him to the hospital believed there might be a lynching if he were taken there. According to their account, they decided not to take him to that hospital, and instead of taking him to a different hospital, they took him to the police station where the deceased officer had worked. Here, officers reported there was a scuffle involving Archie and he fell, causing bloodstains on the floor. However, the sergeant at the police station denied seeing either Archie or the officers and did not ask about the bloodstains, but simply ordered that they be cleaned up.

When Archie finally got medical treatment, it was clear that he had been severely beaten, but no officers were held responsible. At the hospital, X-rays of Archie's injuries disappeared, and staff members were unable to record details of Archie's name and background. He was injected with iodine, to which he was alleged to be allergic, for a medical test, and some concluded that this was the cause of his death. However, other accounts by pathologists reported that he had been beaten to death. Ultimately, his death was reported as a "homicide by police intervention" by the coroner. Within hours of his death, Police Superintendent Warren Woodfork cleared all officers involved in the incident of any violations of conduct. Reportedly, the rookie officer who arrested Archie was denounced by fellow officers for not killing Archie on the spot.

Subsequently, in May 1993 a report by the advisory committee on human relations found that some officers had brutalized Archie and that the department had failed to hold them accountable. The committee noted the existence of a police code of silence that was supported at the highest levels within the department.

SOURCE: Human Rights Watch 1998.

of this case, no police officers were prosecuted or sanctioned administratively, largely due to the police "code of silence," a part of the institutional culture of the police. However, it is significant that the officers transporting Archie did not enter the hospital but instead took him to the police station. Archie is supposed to have slipped and fallen at the police station, and by the time he did receive medical treatment, he had been severely beaten to such an extent that he died as a result of what was termed "a homicide by police intervention." Furthermore, Archie's family was compensated by the city in an out-of-court settlement. Ethical questions concerning police use of force, possible police perjury, and a police cover-up of illegal acts ultimately surfaced. These and other ethical issues in policing will be addressed in Chapter 3.

In the following report of a death row inmate released from prison after 19 years of incarceration, the state admitted there was a lack of evidence linking him to the crime for which he was convicted. His lawyers alleged prosecutorial misconduct, pointing out that the prosecution withheld critical eyewitness evidence from the defense that contradicted the main evidence used to convict him originally. This case illustrates the need for prosecutors to adhere to ethical standards of conduct, a subject that will be more fully explored in Chapter 5.

Case Study 1.2 Police Brutality During Katrina

On September 4, 2005, a week after Hurricane Katrina struck New Orleans, police shot six civilians who were crossing the Danziger Bridge, killing two and seriously wounding the others. It emerged that a cover-up of what happened there was organized by a high-ranking police officer. While police initially claimed that some of the civilians had been shooting at them, no guns were found at the scene, and the victims denied this version of events. A state grand jury charged seven officers with murder, but the case could not proceed for technical reasons. Then, in August 2011, Lt. Michael Lohman admitted to organizing a cover-up of the incident because he recognized it was a "bad shoot." On August 5, 2011, a federal jury convicted 5 former or current officers on charges resulting from the cover-up, and they were sentenced in 2012 to prison terms ranging from 6 to 65 years (Bureau and Kunzelman 2012).

In concealing the truth of the incident, retired Sgt. Arthur Kaufman and the four other officers planted a gun, fabricated witnesses' statements, and falsified reports after they had shot at unarmed, defenseless civilians who were simply trying to cross the bridge in search of food and help. One officer did not dispute having shot an unarmed man in the back.

The prosecution had contended that Kaufman took a gun from his home weeks after the shootings and turned it in as evidence, trying to pass it off as a gun belonging to Lance Madison, the brother of one of the deceased, Ronald Madison, a 40-year-old mentally disabled man. Police arrested Lance Madison on attempted murder charges, but a grand jury later cleared him.

SOURCE: "A Bad Shoot" 2010.

NORMATIVE ETHICS

Normative ethics is fundamental to ethical decision-making in the criminal justice system. A central notion in normative ethics is that one's conduct must take into account moral issues; that is, one should act morally, using reason to decide the proper way of conducting oneself. Effectively, ethics, in prescribing certain standards of conduct, gives us a way of making choices in situations where we are unsure how to act.

What are these standards of conduct and how do we decide what is right and wrong? Some argue that because standards of conduct and ways of doing things differ from society to society, there can never be one single standard for all people everywhere and that we must make ethical decisions based on each situation. This approach to setting standards of conduct is called *ethical relativism*. Others argue that one set of ethical standards applies across all societies, and people have an obligation to do what is "known to be right"; that is, they argue in favor of *ethical absolutism*.

ETHICAL RELATIVISM

Ethical relativists argue that what is morally right or wrong may vary in a fundamental way from person to person or from culture to culture. In other words, as Robert Arrington (1983) argues, we cannot simply say that a moral judgment is true for all purposes, persons, and cultures—we can assert only that it is true for a particular person or social group. Relativism does not mean that we cannot criticize people of other cultures on moral grounds, but it does mean that when we say that a person in another culture did wrong or acted immorally, we must judge that person by the standards of that culture and not by our own (Cook 1999: 35). In other words, there are objective moral standards as long as judgments about right and wrong are made relatively.

Robert Holmes (1998: 163–164) discusses three forms of ethical relativism: ethical relativism, cultural relativism, and extreme or individual relativism. *Ethical relativists* agree that there is moral right and wrong but contend that what is right for one person or culture may be wrong for another.

Case Study 1.3 Death Row Inmate Set Free

On February 28, 2005, an Ohio judge dismissed all charges against Derrick Jamison in relation to the death of a bartender in Cincinnati. Prosecutors had elected not to retry him in the case. He had been convicted and sentenced to death in 1985 based in part on the testimony of a codefendant, Charles Howell, whose own sentence had been reduced for testifying against Jamison.

The prosecution decision not to retry him followed a finding that the prosecutor had withheld statements that would have contradicted the testimony of Charles Howell, would have undermined the prosecution's theory about the victim's death, and would have suggested other possible suspects for the murder. Two federal courts ruled that the prosecution's actions had the effect of denying Jamison a fair trial. The victim, Gary Mitchell, was murdered on August 1, 1984, at the Central Bar in downtown Cincinnati. Customers found him almost dead, having received blunt-force trauma to the head. He died several days later. Several eyewitnesses gave different accounts of persons entering and leaving the bar, and a shoe print was found on top of the bar. Jamison was arrested 2 months later after robbing a restaurant. He was wearing the gym shoes that had produced the impression on top of the bar. A few months after Jamison's arrest, Charles Howell was also arrested as an accomplice in the murder, and he informed police that he and Jamison had robbed the bar and that Jamison had attacked the bartender.

Before trial, the prosecution indicated that it was unaware of any exculpatory evidence, but in fact such evidence had been excluded from the homicide book prepared by the Cincinnati police department. This is the book that is passed to the prosecutor for trial. Ultimately, Jamison argued that he did not receive 35 documents from the prosecution prior to trial and that the practice of the police department and the prosecutor's office had the effect of suppressing evidence material to his defense. Jamison's conviction rested principally on the testimony of Charles Howell, the shoe print found on the bar, and the testimony of a witness who positively identified Jamison as the perpetrator. She had identified him at the trial but in the police offense report had indicated that she could not make that identification. Obviously, the offense report could have been used to challenge her identification of Jamison at the trial.

SOURCE: Death Penalty Information Center 2007.

Cultural relativism is a form of relativism that claims that moral beliefs and practices vary from culture to culture. It is important to understand, however, that cultural relativists do not argue that certain acts or practices are right or wrong in a particular culture. They simply note the differences.

Extreme or *individual relativism* takes the position that moral beliefs and practices vary from person to person. In contrast to ethical absolutists (see the following section, Ethical Absolutism), ethical relativists draw attention to factors such as moral diversity among different cultures, the varying state of morals in a particular society at different historical periods, and the fact that at any given time there is a high degree of moral disagreement within a particular culture. One example is the moral disagreement in the United States concerning abortion (Bunting 1996: 73).

CULTURAL RELATIVISM

The proponents of *cultural relativism* argue that every society has a different moral code explaining what acts are permitted or not permitted. They argue that we cannot judge one moral code as being superior to another because there is no objective standard to apply to make such a judgment. In other words, the moral code that we in the United States subscribe to is not special. Accordingly, it is simply one moral code among many. If the moral code of a particular society determines that a certain act is right, then the act is right within that society. Accordingly, it is not for us to judge other people's conduct in other societies. We should be tolerant and avoid being judgmental.

At first, the notion of cultural relativism seems to reflect the way many of us see the world; for example, we believe in tolerance and understanding, and we recognize diversity in society. However, there are a number of objections to cultural relativism that show it cannot be viewed as a viable approach to ethical issues, including the following:

- There is the problem of identifying what constitutes a culture or society. For example, it is easy to imagine an isolated tribe in a far-off country as a separate culture with its own ethical standards and rules, but what of American culture? Although we may think of American culture as homogeneous, it is very diverse because many languages are spoken within it, and the various ethnic groups that make up American society may well maintain their own ethical standards of conduct, which differ from those of the dominant culture.
- If this difficulty in identifying a culture or society exists, then it is easy to see that we may end up in a position where our own individual values, family background, education, or religion can determine ethical standards. In other words, cultural relativism can become transformed into a matter of individual ethics (individual relativism), where each person can claim that his or her moral standards are those that should apply to society and others.
- Cultural relativists are not able to explain which ethical standards should apply when cultures overlap. Cultures are no longer totally isolated from each other, and it becomes increasingly difficult to avoid interacting with other cultures. This raises the problem of deciding whose ethical standards are to apply.
- In all societies, standards of conduct change over time, and the cultural relativist is faced with the problem of acknowledging these changes while arguing that morality is relative to a culture. However, which values in which historical period should apply? On the face of it, the values applying in all periods have equal validity. For the cultural relativist, therefore, there is no overall standard to apply.

- A major problem with cultural relativism is that it operates as moral isolationism. This means that arguing that everything is relative tends to suggest this must be the end of the issue and all debate must stop. It also suggests, in the view of Carol Gilligan (in Hinman 1998: 55), an attitude of "couldn't care less," because when we say that all things are relative, we are really saying we don't care about them. Therefore, cultural relativism fails to provide us with answers to issues and in fact tends to close off debate altogether.

Cultural relativism is closely associated with anthropology, and some even refer to it as an anthropological theory. Some philosophers argue that cultural relativism is in fact a methodology that requires that they adopt a nonjudgmental framework toward the culture they study, and therefore, as a methodological practice only, cultural relativism does not involve moral relativism (Cook 1999: Chap. 7; Ladd 1973: 2). However, other philosophers contend that cultural relativism contains elements of both methodology and a value system (Womack 1995: 48).

ETHICAL ABSOLUTISM

This view argues that there exists an eternal and unchanging moral law, the same for all people, at all times and places (Holmes 1998: 165). The absolutist believes that certain moral principles apply to all people everywhere and that people can recognize or discover these principles and be guided by them in deciding the nature of their own conduct and in judging the conduct of others. Also, the ethical absolutist, being already aware of these principles, believes himself or herself qualified to pass judgment on anyone (Cook 1999: 7). Absolutism is considered valid regardless of thought and feeling. This position is the opposite of relativism in that there can be no consideration of other perspectives because, it is argued, that there is only one "true" perspective.

An example of an absolutist position arises in arguments about capital punishment. As Jonathan Glover (1999: 245) points out, two absolutist views prevail on this question. One is emphatic that the murderer must be given the punishment he or she "deserves," which is death, and the other can see no justification for "judicial murder" under any circumstances. An absolutist would not change his or her view with respect to capital punishment, no matter what arguments were put forward by either side. Among the questions that arise from adopting an absolutist position include, "If there are universally accepted values, what are they?" and, "If universally accepted values exist, do they remain constant or do they change over time?"

If there is disagreement about moral issues between societies, then how should we act? On the one hand, the ethical relativist will say we should not judge and that there is no single truth that applies across societies and cultures. On the other hand, the moral absolutist will argue that one single truth must be applied across all societies and cultures regardless of beliefs and values. In favor of ethical relativism, it can be said that it is correct in warning us against assuming that our ethical standards represent some absolute standard because many, although not all, of our ethical standards apply only to our own society. Also, ethical relativism teaches us the value of an open mind, of tolerance, and of understanding. One way of resolving this disagreement about relative and absolute ethical standards is the notion of *ethical pluralism*.

ETHICAL PLURALISM

Ethical pluralism argues that in most situations there are many truths rather than one single truth. Lawrence Hinman (1998: 67–68) contends that ethical pluralism allows us to adopt four principles to resolve conflicts between differing ethical standards. These principles are the following:

The Principle of Understanding. This requires that we fully understand and appreciate the meaning of ethical standards found in another culture from the perspective of that culture. For example, before making any judgment about an issue such as female circumcision, we should possess a full understanding of the history and cultural context of this practice as it applies in the many societies in which it is performed. We should recognize that a Western response to an issue of this nature is shaped and constructed by our own cultural values.

The Principle of Tolerance. This means accepting the existence of differences as opposed to denying any diversity in ethical standards. This principle therefore rules out an approach based on ethical absolutism.

The Principle of Standing Up Against Evil. Hinman argues that understanding and tolerance ought not to lead us to a position where "anything goes," as the ethical relativists argue, but rather, we should be prepared to stand up against what he calls "egregious moral wrongdoing," especially when such conduct affects the powerless and the marginalized of the world. An example of this kind of moral wrongdoing would be the crime of genocide, which is internationally recognized as a crime against humanity.

The Principle of Fallibility. This principle argues in favor of our own fallibility. We should always be prepared to learn from other cultures and to have our own moral shortcomings exposed. Most countries have prohibited capital punishment for children (see Chapter 7). However, until recently[1] in the United States, the Supreme Court declared that states had the right to execute those as young as 16 years of age. The principle of fallibility would argue that the United States and its Court at that time did not choose the correct ethical position on the issue of capital punishment for juveniles and that it should be prepared to listen to the reasoning and experience of the rest of the world, which has outlawed capital punishment for juveniles.

Other philosophers seem to agree with an approach that emphasizes ethical pluralism, which Robert Kane (1996: 14–16) calls "openness." He stresses that a pluralistic point of view only suggests the possibility that other views are correct; it does not demonstrate that they are in fact correct. Pluralism challenges absolute values but does not rule out

---

1   In March 2005, in a 5–4 decision in *Roper v. Simmons*, the U.S. Supreme Court abolished juvenile executions, arguing that it is unconstitutional to sentence anyone to death for a crime he or she committed while younger than 18. The Court argued that teenagers are too immature to be held accountable for their crimes to the same extent as adults given the "national consensus" against executing juveniles and the medical and social science evidence demonstrating their immaturity.

their possibility. We can be open and tolerant to other points of view while still believing that some are better than others, even while we believe that only one is correct. Openness does not imply indifference; it only indicates recognition that we do not possess the truth and are willing to learn from others and to search for truths beyond our own limited point of view. Kane advocates an approach that assumes an attitude of openness to other points of view to allow others to prove themselves right or wrong.

John Cook (1999: 169) suggests an approach that sets aside an argument based on tolerance and that instead advocates taking cases one by one and examining them in light of the details of each particular case. He therefore suggests that the question of whether we ought to interfere with the practices of another culture is not a philosophical question but a practical, moral one. The examination of a particular case means understanding the nature of the problem, what considerations would be relevant to a solution, and what a "right solution" would be. This seems to parallel Hinman's point that there must be a full understanding of the cultural context of a particular case before any attempt is made to resolve conflicts among differing ethical standards.

RELIGION AND ETHICAL STANDARDS

As discussed earlier, when societies apply normative ethics, they are prescribing ethical standards for conduct. What is the origin of these standards? Many people believe that ethical standards and religion are connected, and that ethical standards are derived from religious principles and tenets. For example, many hospitals in the United States have ethics committees that typically include representatives of the clergy as members, and when ethical issues are discussed in the media, religious representatives are often invited to comment on them. People assume, therefore, that religious representatives who interpret religion are also able to define ethical standards of conduct. The *divine command theory* expresses this view and argues that what is morally right is what God directs, and conversely, what is morally wrong is what God prohibits.

In a famous discussion, the Greek philosopher Socrates took up the question of whether divine command theory was concerned with the power of the gods to command or the "rightness" of the gods' commands. He asked the question, "Is conduct right because the gods command it or do the gods command it because it is right?" The arguments about this question are considered in the following sections.

Conduct Is Right Because God Commands It

According to this perspective, the only issue is the simple matter of God requiring a particular kind of conduct. If God commands it, that is sufficient and the conduct is right regardless of what reason tells us. However, this raises the question of how we discover what constitutes God's will. If we argue that it is contained in religious texts, should we look to only one text—for example, the Bible; if not, how do we discover God's will from the multitude of religious texts that exist in the many religions on earth? It is also difficult to determine the exact nature of God's will. If we assume it is to be found from reading the Bible, what if we cannot find any statements there about a particular ethical issue, and what do we do if there are conflicting statements about God's will regarding a particular ethical issue? Also, if we argue that conduct is right because God commands it, this means we are giving God the power to issue whatever commands He wishes. This in turn means that God can give a different command from the one He has already given, so His commands can be considered arbitrary. However, the notion that God's commands are arbitrary is inconsistent with the belief that God is all-powerful and all-knowing. It is obvious that this argument raises a number of complex and difficult issues.

God Commands Right Conduct Because It Is Right

This is the second option offered by Socrates, and it means that God's commands are not arbitrary but emanate from the application of His wisdom in knowing what is best for us. However, there is a problem because in accepting the rightness of God's commands, we must also accept that there is some standard of right and wrong outside of God's will that must exist prior to and independent of God's command. In the final analysis, therefore, we must either accept that God's commands are arbitrary or recognize that His commands have reference to a standard of rightness and wrongness independent of His will. Those who take the position that ethical standards are set by God are therefore obliged to accept arguments that tend to conflict with their fundamental religious belief in God's goodness and omnipotence. The divine command theory raises so many complex and difficult issues that it leads to the conclusion that setting ethical standards by reference only to religion is highly problematic.

ETHICS AND NATURAL LAW

In looking at the origin of ethics, some ask whether natural law is the origin. The idea of natural law is that underneath the diversity of human cultures and beliefs about what is right and wrong, we can identify some factors that are common to our human nature. The notion of natural law was a favorite of ancient thinkers like Plato and Aristotle, who sought to identify universal traits of human nature with the aim of finding common goals or ends that would bring human fulfillment or happiness (Kane 1996: 46). This pattern of looking for natural laws continued into the medieval and later periods of Western culture, especially through the thinking of the 13th-century philosopher Thomas Aquinas (Haakonssen 2010: 76).

Natural laws are said to be laws that govern human behavior and define the right way to live. They are said to be "natural" because they are thought of as incorporating human nature and the goals that humans naturally seek. In effect, natural law represents a search for moral absolutes that define what is "normal" and "natural." For example, despite more progressive and inclusive modern attitudes toward homosexuality, some still argue that practicing homosexuality is "unnatural" because it is contrary to human nature. In modern ethics and law, natural law "refers to the more general idea that there is a 'higher' norm or law that is not the work of human action" (Haakonssen 2010: 76). In this sense, therefore, natural law is differentiated from positive law, such as the enactment of legislation.

Lloyd Steffen, in an argument grounded in elements of natural law, proposes to bridge the gap between ethical theory and lived experience. Arguing that it often seems that ethical theories are far removed from people's actual experiences, Steffen suggests an ethical framework that will assist those faced with ethical issues and dilemmas to resolve them by applying what philosophers term "practical reason"—a form of reasoning that we apply when faced with decisions about how to live and act. Steffen points to the difficulties of Kantian and consequentialist theories (see Chapters 12 and 13), especially in relation to Kant's conception of ethical absolutism where, for example, a person may be faced with a clash of duties such as protecting an innocent life or telling an untruth; the choice, according to ethical absolutism, must always be never to lie, whatever may be the consequences. As Steffen points out, this does not square well with general notions about lying that overlook so called "white lies" where no harm is caused by the act of lying.

Steffen argues that consequentialist ethical theory too has its problems because it concerns itself solely with calculating the maximum utility of an act (see Chapter 13 for a critique of consequentialism) and therefore does not condemn any lying that yields the greatest good for the greatest number (Steffen 2012: 8). In other words, while the Kantian will adhere to principles, the consequentialist operates in the belief that nothing is intrinsically wrong or immoral. Steen asks whether we should simply accept the shortcomings in these theories and apply them regardless or take a different approach that he terms a *hybrid*—"one that takes account of duty and principles yet steers clear of absolutism and that attends to consequences but avoids relativism."

Steffen's hybrid approach to ethical decision-making is based in natural law which, as noted previously, essentially claims that human beings as rational persons are naturally endowed with the capacity for reason and are therefore capable of identifying goodness. According to Steffen, the hybrid ethic is expressed most cogently in the structures and frameworks associated with "just war" thinking (see Chapter 10), itself a tradition found in natural law thinking. Essentially, the just war tradition argues that war, in certain circumstances, can promote the common good and serve the interests of justice. A war can therefore be said to be "just" if it satisfies certain criteria. Behind this just war framework, Steffens discerns an ethic that can guide action—namely that *"ordinarily force ought not to be used to settle conflicts"* (2012: 44). This ethic, he suggests, as a moral presumption or "common agreement" is applicable to war or to any use of force. It is, however, liable to be displaced by exceptions represented by the criteria that traditionally permit a just war, examples of which are acting in self-defense and protecting innocent civilians (p. 46). It is easy to see how this ethical approach can be applied to police use of force—that commonly, force ought not to be employed to settle conflicts and then only when necessary, applying exceptions using the graduated scale of responses such as those set out in Chapter 3.

Steffen (2012: 86) acknowledges that this hybrid ethic is not found in ethics textbooks and could be regarded as a more complex form of rule consequentialism (sometimes called rule utilitarianism; see Chapter 13). Other objections to Steffen's perspective center on its abandonment of ethical absolutism—for example, in the case of abortion where some take an absolutist approach and would argue no criteria could trump the moral argument against it, as well as to his reading of natural law. The same objections could be taken to his position on lying and cheating where he sees room for "just lying" and "just cheating" (pp. 101, 107). In spite of these challenges, Steffen's perspective for "doing ethics" resonates because it blends theory and practice and provides a clearly expressed and practical method of resolving ethical issues.

ETHICS AND LAW

Is law a source of ethical standards, and what is the relationship between law and ethics? It is important to understand that ethics and law are distinct categories. By *law*, we generally mean legislation, statutes, and regulations made by states and by the federal government on a host of subjects for the public good and public welfare. Laws do not, and are not intended to, incorporate ethical principles or values, but sometimes ethical standards will be reflected in laws. For example, both morality and the law prohibit the act of murdering another human being. Similarly, legislation regulating the legal profession or other professions may give legal

effect to certain professional codes of conduct. It is possible to argue, therefore, that codes of conduct regulating legal practice have the force of law. However, on a whole range of subjects from business practice to driving a vehicle, laws do not set ethical standards.

It is important to appreciate, therefore, that ethical standards are not necessarily written down in the form of laws or other rules, but represent the collective experience of a society as it regulates the behavior of those who make up that society. The fact that an ethical standard is not repeated or copied in a law does not affect the validity of that ethical standard. However, where ethical standards are incorporated into law—such as a law governing the right to choose an abortion—although people must obey the law, they are not necessarily required to hold the same ethical beliefs expounded by that law.

Sometimes laws can conflict with ethical standards. For example, laws promoting apartheid in South Africa and slavery in the United States were both clearly in violation of ethical standards relating to the dignity of the person but were nevertheless lawful and were expected to be obeyed when in force. From time to time, a mass movement develops against a particular law or set of laws, reflecting a section of public opinion that claims that the law is wrong and should be repealed. Where there is a deliberate disregard of the law by those protesting its wrongness, the result can be acts of civil disobedience. For example, in India during the British colonial period, Gandhi advocated and practiced civil disobedience to British laws because he and his followers wanted an end to the colonization of their country. Similarly, in the United States, civil rights workers and activists deliberately flouted laws that were racially discriminatory and were prepared to be arrested and jailed in pursuit of equal treatment for all citizens.

ETHICAL DILEMMAS

Ethical questions and issues arise for all people, not just for professionals in the criminal justice system or professors who teach ethics or members of the clergy. We may all have to make decisions involving ethical issues in our daily and professional lives because, as we have noted, ethical issues are concerned with questions of right and wrong and how we ought to act. For example, we might apply for a job, and to be considered for the position, we may have to decide whether to hide the fact that we were fired from a previous job for misconduct. In other words, we have to decide whether to lie to promote our own career interests or whether to reveal the truth. Another instance may arise as we walk down the street and see a person who is apparently homeless, panhandling from passersby. The ethical dilemma here is whether we should act to help the poor and needy or just pass by and give nothing.

We will have to make ethical decisions in our day-to-day lives, so it is helpful to recognize when an issue involves ethical considerations and then have the ability to apply a knowledge of ethics, including ethical terminology and concepts, in making our decision about what to do. A number of ethical approaches can be taken in making a decision about an ethical issue, and you will see in the following chapters that no ethical approach is the "correct" one; rather, different approaches are equally valid in ethical terms. The approach we adopt to an ethical issue will frame and give meaning to any decision we make and can be used to justify and validate our actions. Of course, it is always possible to abandon the responsibility for making an ethical decision. We might decide that we will simply follow the dictates of others rather than applying our own minds to a particular ethical issue. For example, during World War II, many war crimes were committed by members of the Nazi Party, who claimed they were simply following orders in committing those crimes. In effect, they abandoned their responsibility to make an ethical decision not to kill or murder and opted instead to obey unethical and inhumane directions.

Similar situations may arise in the criminal justice system. For example, a prosecutor may have to decide whether to seek the maximum penalty against an accused under three-strikes legislation. If he or she does decide to seek the maximum, the result may be that the accused will be incarcerated for the rest of his or her life. A prosecutor may decide to act ethically and fully weigh this issue in light of the facts of the case and the nature of the crime committed. Alternatively, he or she may choose not to follow that process and may simply

take the position that the law reflects public opinion and that he or she should always exercise discretion so as to impose the full penalty provided by the law.

When we decide to accept responsibility and make a decision involving ethical considerations, we are faced with a personal ethical dilemma. A personal ethical dilemma can be contrasted with an ethical issue. The latter is usually an issue of public policy involving ethical questions. Examples of such issues include the morality of capital punishment, whether to incarcerate more people or use alternative sanctions for convicted offenders, and other important social issues. A further distinction between ethical dilemmas and ethical issues is that an ethical dilemma is the responsibility of an individual and requires a decision to be made. Ethical issues, on the other hand, being broad issues of social policy, do not require individual decision-making beyond the decision of whether one is in favor of or opposed to a particular social issue. However, the fact that ethical issues do not require most individuals to decide the issue does not mean that an individual is helpless to influence the public debate on a social issue.

Ethical dilemmas are important in the criminal justice system because criminal justice professionals are often faced with having to make decisions that involve ethical issues. Much of the material in this book concerned with ethical practices in the criminal justice system will focus on ethical dilemmas faced by criminal justice professionals, and it will analyze options in light of ethical theories and any relevant rules and regulations.

How do we recognize when a dilemma is an ethical dilemma as opposed to merely a dilemma? An ethical dilemma arises only when a decision must be made that involves a conflict at the personal, interpersonal, institutional, or societal level or raises issues of rights or moral character.

What process is followed in resolving an ethical dilemma? Richard Hare (1987) argues that we initially use an *intuitive* level of moral thinking when we consider ethical dilemmas. This provides us with relatively simple principles derived from our upbringing and past experience of decision-making. *Critical thinking* is another process of thinking about moral decisions; in contrast to intuitive thinking, critical thinking applies principles established by philosophy and moral concepts, and it is therefore nonintuitive. In making moral judgments when faced with moral dilemmas, we may initially apply an intuitive form of thinking, relying on our intuition to identify possible courses of action to make the decision. However, we are likely to find that our intuitions do not adequately equip us to make moral decisions and that critical thinking is required. Consider the following scenario:

> A newly recruited correctional officer, Tom, overhears three other correctional officers, Fred, Bob, and Charlie, discussing arrangements to assault an inmate, Raymond, who has previously attacked another correctional officer, a close friend of the three officers.

Tom is faced with a dilemma: whether or not to prevent the attack on Raymond. His dilemma is an ethical dilemma because if he does act, this will involve a conflict between himself and Fred, Bob, and Charlie. It is also an ethical dilemma because it raises issues of rights and morality—that is, the right of Raymond to safety and security even in prison, and the morality of allowing a person to be assaulted other than in an act of self-defense. To resolve his ethical dilemma, Tom will need to pursue a process of analysis resulting in a decision. The following process is intended to provide Tom with a method for reaching his decision:

1. He will identify the fact that he is faced with an ethical dilemma and state the dilemma clearly.
2. In his mind, he will collect the facts and circumstances of what he overheard so that he is quite clear about what he heard, the identities of those involved, and all other relevant information.
3. He will collect all the facts and knowledge relevant to the decision, including his own values about the issue and the values of his workplace. He will consider his own position at the prison as a newly trained officer and the consequences of reporting the incident and of not reporting it.
4. This is an ethical dilemma, so he will call to mind his knowledge of ethical principles and theories with the aim of applying those ethical approaches to his possible courses of action.
5. Tom will now identify his available options for action. First, he could intervene in the situation by informing his supervisor of the conversation he overheard. This action will be based on his responsibility to ensure the safety and security of all inmates and to enforce the policies and rules of the institution. Second, he could choose to ignore the conversation because of his loyalty to his fellow officers and his need in the future to receive their assistance and support when carrying out his duties. Third, he could choose to intervene by talking to the officers involved in an attempt to prevent the misconduct with the aim of minimizing the harm for all involved parties. Tom must support each alternative action with reasoning derived from ethical principles to give credibility to his choice of action.
6. Tom will make his decision based on his analysis of the dilemma after applying the ethical approaches to each course of action. He will choose the option that for him is the most ethically appropriate. In other words, after considering the choices according to this process, he will decide, "This would be the right thing for me to do." He therefore resolves his ethical dilemma by making an ethical decision and acting on that decision.

Tom's process for making an ethical decision seems straightforward. However, making an ethical decision may involve factors such as personal values, personal priorities, or how a particular decision might affect friends or even strangers. Therefore, the most ethical choice is not always clear. To act ethically is not simply a matter of deciding what is right and wrong in advance and stubbornly sticking to that position. Since there are many gray areas where there are no specific rules, laws, or guidelines laid out in advance, it is not always easy to know which decision is the most ethical choice. In addition, if we are to act in an ethical way, we have to justify what we do, and the justification must be sufficient that it could in principle convince any reasonable human being. As James Rachels puts it,

> A moral judgment . . . must be supported by good reasons. If someone tells you that a certain action would be wrong, for example, you may ask why it would be wrong, and if there is no satisfactory answer, you may reject that advice as unfounded. In this way, moral judgments are different from mere expressions of personal preference . . . moral judgments require backing by reasons, and in the absence of such reasons, they are merely arbitrary. (1991: 438)

Hare (1987: 218) argues that moral judgments must be able to be applied universally. According to this principle, similar actions ought to be judged similarly, unless there are morally relevant differences between them. For example, if I judge it wrong for you to cheat in examinations, I must be prepared to say that it is wrong for me as well, unless I can explain how my situation is different from yours in a morally relevant way (Holmes 1998: 151). Thus, the principle does not say whether you should cheat, but it does require that whatever you do, you must be consistent. Singer (1995: 175) expands this notion somewhat by arguing that when thinking ethically, I ought to consider the interests of my enemies as well as my friends and of strangers as well as my family. If, after I have fully taken into account the concerns and preferences of all these people I still believe that a particular action is better than any alternative, then I can honestly say that I ought to do it.

What weight do we give to our *personal values* when making ethical decisions? By *values*, we mean what individuals care about and what they think is important. This can include such things as people's desires, such as social approval; what they enjoy, such as sports or music; their goals or purposes; their ideas of happiness or success; and their highest ideals. Each person develops a set of values that forms his or her value system. We often assume that our values are similar to others'; however, we may define values differently than others do. For example, we may have different definitions of what constitutes a "family," but we may all share "family" as a value. Even if we do have similar definitions of values, we often prioritize them differently. Thus, one person might give the value of "freedom" a higher priority than the value of "preservation of life." Another may prioritize the value of "loyalty" higher than "personal freedom." The fact that we may order our values differently explains why our thinking about ethical decisions differs from that of others and why we arrive at different conclusions.

ETHICAL ISSUES IN CRIMINAL JUSTICE

To illustrate the relevance of the study of ethics to the criminal justice system, a number of specific ethical problems and issues that might arise for professionals in the criminal justice system are sorted into the sections that follow. These problems and issues might be concerned, for example, with how to exercise authority, with how to deal with conflicts between the personal and the professional, or with ethical issues confined within one particular part of the system, such as juvenile justice.

Ethical Problems in the Use of Authority

- The use of authority to promote personal values
- The use of authority to avoid accountability for wrongdoing
- Police gratuities, free meals, discounts on purchases, and so on

Ethical Problems in the Relationship Between Personal and Professional Interests

- Using professional status to promote personal interests (religious, philosophical, financial, etc.)
- Using institutional time and materials for personal gain unrelated to legitimate work activity
- Engaging in or promoting professional activities that are contrary to personal values
- Engaging in public or private personal activity that is contrary to professional values (use of drugs, driving under the influence of alcohol, etc.)

Ethical Problems in Personal and Professional Commitments to Clients

- Behaving unethically in personal relationships with clients
- Using relationships with clients or the public for personal gain (acquiring goods more cheaply, having work done for personal benefit, accepting gifts, etc.)

Ethical Issues in Criminal Justice and Public Policy

- The war on drugs
- Government policies having implications for criminal justice professionals in issues such as youth confinement, fingerprinting of juveniles, and compulsory treatment such as mandatory participation in substance abuse programs or anger management
- Capital punishment
- The move away from rehabilitative juvenile justice policies toward more punitive policies
- Policies involving harsher penalties resulting in "prisoner warehousing"

- Government-imposed mandatory sentencing (three-strikes legislation, mandatory minimum sentences)
- Truth in sentencing policies
- Increased surveillance of citizens in society
- The policies implemented in the war on terrorism

Ethical Issues Resulting From Policing Policies

- Policing policy in domestic violence cases
- Racial profiling
- Use of force
- Use of police discretion

Ethical Problems in Information Sharing

- The ethics of withholding information—for example, from a client, the court, or the police
- Problems of confidentiality and privileged communication—for example, counselor–client relationships and participation in research

- Rules or practices relating to the retention or disposal of court records—for example, in the juvenile justice system where some states have considered making juvenile records and court hearings open to the public and the media

Ethical Problems Dealing With Human Rights Issues in the Criminal Justice System

- The administration of cruel and unusual punishment
- Human rights violations against prisoners (women, men, transgender individuals, juveniles)
- Capital punishment

Ethical Issues in the Media Reporting of Crime

- Crime and public opinion
- Crime as entertainment
- The politicization of crime
- Representation of particular groups of offenders and of women or girl offenders

SUMMARY

In this chapter, the role of ethics in shaping decisions has been explored. Ethics has been shown to be a central component in decisions involving ethical dilemmas, and the process of analyzing an ethical dilemma has been illustrated. Ethics is concerned with standards of conduct and with "how I ought to act," and standards of conduct may vary among different societies. Approaches to setting standards range from cultural relativism to moral absolutism; a perspective that emphasizes moral pluralism seems to offer the best hope for resolving problems of relativities. Investigating sources of ethical standards reveals that religion, natural law, and other forms of law have an influence in shaping ethical standards. An understanding of ethics is essential to competent decision-making by criminal justice professionals and to the proper working of the criminal justice system. In this chapter, case studies in the form of media reports of unethical conduct by police and prosecutors have been presented. In the next chapter, ethical issues in law enforcement will be explored in depth.

DISCUSSION CASE

In 2003, France legislated to ban the wearing of headscarves in public schools (CNN 2003). It was claimed that this action was necessary to protect the separation of church and state required by French law. There are an estimated 6 million Muslims living in France, many from former French colonies in North Africa, but very few wear headscarves. The French move seems to have spurred other European states to follow that lead, as a number are now advocating a ban on the burqa and niqab—the *burqa* covers a woman's body from head to toe and totally conceals her face, and the *niqab* is a headscarf that covers a woman's hair. In some German states and in Belgium, the niqab cannot be worn in schools.

In 2006, the right-of-center government of Holland committed itself to a prohibition on the wearing of the burqa and the niqab in public if it returned to office (Bell 2006; Clements 2006). Also in 2006, the British foreign minister was reported as having said that the niqab was a barrier to communication, and the then British prime minister, Tony Blair, commented that it was "a 'mark of separation' that makes people from other backgrounds feel uncomfortable" (Grice 2006). In May 2010, Belgium banned covering the face, and in June 2010, Spain approved a motion to ban the wearing of the burqa in public by a narrow majority, despite the fact that only about 2,000 women out of a Moslem population of 5 million in Spain wear the burqa (BBC 2010).

Advocates of the prohibition claim that wearing the veil challenges, or can be seen as a threat to, "progressive" Muslim women who refuse to wear it. However, women who chose to wear the veil say that the veil symbolizes modesty, humility, and devotion to their faith.

DISCUSSION QUESTIONS

1. How is *ethics* defined?

2. Why is it important for criminal justice professionals to study ethics? Explain how applying ethical approaches helps criminal justice professionals make appropriate and "correct" decisions.

3. What are the possible sources of ethical rules? Discuss the problems inherent in each source.

4. Discuss the advantages offered by ethical pluralism over ethical absolutism and ethical relativism.

5. Outline the steps involved in analyzing an ethical dilemma.

2

POLICE ETHICS: THE NATURE OF POLICING AND POLICE CORRUPTION

ETHICS AND POLICING

The study of ethics in policing has expanded considerably over the past few years as cases of police brutality and corruption have surfaced in the media and in the courtroom. Commentators agree that three issues have shaped the role of ethics in policing: *styles of policing, the police as an institution,* and *police culture.*

Generally, we think of the police as controllers of crime; however, the original English conception of the role of the police force emphasized the need for police to obtain the goodwill of citizens in performing their policing duties. The very first set of instructions to constables, published in England in 1829, reminded the new police officer,

> There is no qualification more indispensable to a Police Officer than a perfect command of temper, never suffering himself to be moved in the slightest degree, by any language or threats that may be used; if he does his duty in a quiet and determined manner, such conduct will probably induce well-disposed by-standers to assist him should he require it. (quoted in Skolnick and Fyfe 1993: 70)

When policing came to the United States, there was little concern among police officers about adhering to legal norms, despite their formal policing role as enforcers of the law (Haller 1996: 7). In fact, police received little training in law, and most of those arrested were tried before justices who also had little legal training. Police were part of the larger political system, seen as a resource at the command of local political organizations. In the early period, it was common for police and other public officials to earn rewards by operating rackets (p. 8). Patrolmen worked on the streets with little supervision, and the main expertise a detective offered was his knowledge of the underworld. Violence was an accepted norm because many policemen believed they were entitled to punish wrongdoers themselves, and on their patrols, they were expected to be able to physically dominate the streets without resorting to arrest. Police operated in neighborhoods as authority figures, sometimes whipping delinquent boys as a more effective sanction than arrest and incarceration. Police commonly used violence to persuade suspected persons to confess, and newspapers reported interrogations of this nature without unfavorable comment (p. 22). In addition, the police culture of the time supported the use of violence in upholding the dignity of the police officer. Over time and by the end of the 1930s, police organizations had become large bureaucratic structures organized along military lines (Walker 1996: 27).

During the 1930s era of reform, police began to narrow their functions to focus on crime control and the apprehension of criminals; consequently, police became enforcers of the law with the goal of controlling crime. Other activities that police formerly engaged in, such as solving problems in the community, became identified as "social work" and were ridiculed (Kelling and More 1996: 79). Notwithstanding the police attitude that constructs policing as crime fighting, many observers of police work regard the primary function of the police to be peacekeeping. In this view of policing, police occupy their time for the most part by attending to a range of problems that have little to do with law enforcement. In fact, they may spend as little as 10% to 15% of their time engaged in enforcing the law (Manning 1996: 225).

THE NATURE OF POLICING

Commentators on policing have struggled to adequately express and theorize the nature of policing in society, including its ethical base. Researchers have developed models of policing to assist in understanding the police function in society; these models are the crime fighter, the emergency operator, the social enforcer, and the social peacekeeper (Kleinig 1996: 24–29).

The *crime fighter* sees criminals as the enemy, and police and the community as the "good guys." In other words, police see their role in punitive terms—for example, treating suspects as though they were already guilty. Perceiving the policing role as crime fighting runs the risk of ends justifying means and dramatizes policing so as to condone invasions of privacy and abuse of power. This is especially the case when citizens have surrendered their right to use force to the police.

The influence of media representations of police, either through police dramas on television or in reality programming depicting police carrying out their duties, should not be underestimated. In constructing images of police as "fighters against evil" in drama and as "protectors of society against permissiveness" in police reality programs, the media reinforce the notion of the police officer as crime fighter. In terms of audience response to this entertainment, three notions emerge: that offenders are professional criminals who are clever and motivated by greed; that the interests of justice are not well served by liberal judges or lawyers who are preoccupied with defendants' legal rights; and that hardworking, dedicated cops are out there, on the streets, doing their best in the face of these constraints (Beckett and Sasson 2000: 118).

The *emergency operator* model sees the policing role as akin to that of other emergency personnel, such as ambulance operators and firefighters. Police offer emergency assistance, clearing the way for professionals such as social workers, who provide more substantive problem-solving services. This model emphasizes the policing mission as dealing with people rather than crime fighting; however, competence in crime control is still required in this model.

Viewing the police as *social enforcers* emphasizes coercion as the central feature of police work (Bittner 1967). This model sees the role of police as addressing many day-to-day problems whose solutions may require the use of force. The social enforcer model has been criticized for focusing excessively on coercion as a police function and for failing to recognize that other members of society may also use coercion, such as parents and schoolteachers.

In formulating the *social peacekeeper* model, Pollock-Byrne (1998) and John Kleinig (1996) argue for the need to adopt a broader definition of policing, with Pollock-Byrne advocating for policing as public service rather than crime fighting and Kleinig promoting policing as social peacekeeping. For Kleinig, this characterization offers the most satisfactory definition of the actual tasks that police perform, and he locates it historically in the Anglo-Saxon notion of the King's Peace, breaches of which were considered crimes. According to Kleinig, the peacekeeper model incorporates the crime fighter and social service models and reflects the range of acts that might occupy the police in a community (p. 28).

Jerome Skolnick (1966) noted the inherent tension between the police role of enforcing the law and at the same time protecting citizens, and he considered that tension irreconcilable. He argued that police could reconcile this conflict by giving priority to their duty to uphold the law. William K. Muir (1977) and Herman Goldstein (1977) saw a need for officers to be trained properly to exercise their considerable discretionary powers, while Muir noted that because officers are free to choose their style of policing, this enables them to act ethically or otherwise according to their desires. Edwin Delattre (1989) and Lawrence Sherman (1985) were concerned about issues of corruption in policing arising during the 1980s. Delattre argued that the best way to ensure ethical policing was to recruit officers with integrity. Sherman, however, saw the temptations open to police as an issue constituting a "slippery slope," where minor acts of corruption would lead to major acts, unless internal police controls and accountability sanctioned those minor acts.

Manning (2007: 63) identifies four "primary segments" found within policing: *patrol officers* who make up the bulk of a law enforcement unit and who often remain in this occupation throughout their police career; *middle managers* who rise through the ranks through seniority and examinations, supervise and handle paperwork, view themselves as "moderating and supervising the mistakes of others," and who generally remain at this level; *higher administrators* who are selected by local consultative political processes (including the mayor, city council, or a specific hiring committee), who rarely have contact with patrol officers, and whose duties involve political as well as policing considerations; and *detectives and investigators* who enjoy higher status than patrol officers and who are "information processors who investigate, define, clear and otherwise manage the tension between the 'case.'" To this analysis could be added the pervasive police paramilitary units known as SWAT teams described later in this chapter.

POLICE AS AN INSTITUTION

The institution of policing has been perceived either as a profession or as a bureaucracy. Kleinig (1996: 30–46) sees the police as possessing some of the aspects of a profession, such as discretionary authority and providing a public service, but not others, such as the possession of higher education and special expertise. The importance of the distinction between a profession and a bureaucracy for the study of police ethics is that professions emphasize ethical standards and a service ideal. Organizationally, police resemble any other large, bureaucratically organized occupation. Police commonly define themselves using the rhetoric of professionalism, sometimes to deflect criticism, arguing that outsiders are incapable of understanding police work and therefore should have no say in its performance (Walker 1996: 29).

POLICE CULTURE

Individuals within institutions carry out roles defined by the rules, regulations, and procedures of the institution, and these roles and their relationship to each other make up the structure of the institution. However, there is another dimension to the workings of an institution that commonly includes the attitudes, values, and norms of that institution, collectively described as the *institutional or organizational culture*. This culture largely determines the way in which institutional activity is performed, adding another layer to the official rules, regulations, and practices of the institution. Manning (1989: 360) explains police culture as the "accepted practices, rules and principles of conduct that are situationally applied, and generalized rationales and beliefs." The institutional culture should be differentiated from the *occupational culture*, which refers to the particular roles and experiences of the different occupational groups within the institution—for example, as between police middle management and patrolmen (Bacon 2014: 106). A number of commentators have attempted to analyze aspects of the police institutional culture. Peter Manning (1997: 4) argues that it is the occupational culture interacting with regulations, policies, law, and politics that constitutes the driving force of policing. For Manning, immorality, violence, and lies are routine in policing; teamwork is essential; and secrecy is endemic. Sherman (1982) identifies a set of values that new police officers acquire through their training process, through conversations with veteran officers, and in interactions with the public. These include the notion that enforcement of the law is not limited to the question of whether an offense has been committed but also includes the nature of the suspect. Accordingly, aspects of the individual—such as demeanor, the degree of cooperation with police, race, age, and social class—are all significant considerations in law enforcement decision-making. In a somewhat similar way, the institutional culture views any show of disrespect for police authority as a matter of great concern, and the perpetrator of such behavior is likely to be punished by arrest or use of force.

In terms of the use of force (see Chapter 3), police culture requires that police should never hesitate to use physical or deadly force against those who *deserve* it. Given that the role of police is to fight crime, police culture views due process as a practice that merely protects criminals and therefore as something that should be ignored when possible. From this perspective, rules concerning the protection of suspects and accused persons should be circumvented when possible because the function of such rules, so far as the police are concerned, is simply to handicap them in carrying out their true functions. Similarly, lying and deception are considered integral parts of the police function. Loyalty is a paramount duty, and the protection of one's colleagues, even when they perform acts of misconduct, is considered an overriding principle of police work. Finally, because the police engage in "danger work" in the protection of the public, it is considered appropriate for police to accept gifts from the public, such as free meals, coffee, and Christmas gifts. Sherman (1982) contends that police culture argues in favor of taking a reward that has no impact on what a police officer would do, such as eating a meal, but he argues that the culture rejects acceptance of money that would affect the policing task itself, such as accepting money for not giving traffic tickets.

Sherman contends that these values have weakened over time due to diversity within the police, the power of the police unions to defend individual officers, and the rise of investigative journalism, which has uncovered corruption in high places. Additionally, he points to the fact that police chiefs have taken significant steps to counter aspects of institutional culture.

In his explanation of police culture, John Crank (1998: iii) argues that existing literature oversimplifies the police, describing them in simplistic terms and minimizing the complexities of their employment. Crank presents various themes that he argues characterize police culture, ranging from "coercive territorial control" (the notion that the police view much of their work by reference to the use of force in controlling their assigned territory) to the vision of the police as "the new warriors" to guns as the ultimate expression of police authority. Crank extends his discussion to include the importance of suspicion in police work, the theme of "turbulence and edge control" (meaning triumph over unpredictable events), and cultural themes of solidarity. Other writers have identified suspicion as a characteristic of police work and the police personality, but Crank argues that it is a feature of police culture, a characteristic of the police worldview that provides a basis for all interaction between police and citizens. Importantly, in his discussion of the construction of police morality, Crank suggests that the police perceive themselves as "representatives of a higher morality embodied in a blend of American traditionalism, patriotism and religion" (p. 151).

Muir (1977) makes the case that police loyalty results in complicity. Once a police officer breaks or violates a rule or standard, he or she is bound to remain silent about other officers' violations, even if they are more serious.

Stuart Scheingold (1984) asserts that there are three dominant characteristics of police culture:

1. *Cynicism.* Police view all citizens with suspicion, and all citizens are seen as a "problem," especially if they can be categorized into a "type." Those who can be categorized are to be dealt with as though they have already committed a crime because they probably have. The very nature of police work leads police to the conclusion that all people are weak, corrupt, or dangerous.

2. *Force.* This is to be used in all situations where a threat is perceived. Threats can include perceived threats against the officer's authority rather than physical threats so that anyone with "an attitude" is thought to deserve a lesson in humility. Force, then, is both expressive and instrumental. It is a symbol of the officer's authority and dominance and is seen as the most effective method of control because it keeps all people in line.

3. *The Police Are Victims*. The idea that the police are themselves victims of public misunderstanding and scorn, recipients of low wages, and victims of vindictive administrators sets police officers apart from other people and legitimizes and rationalizes a different set of rules for them. Police perception is that the public does not mind when the civil rights of "criminal types" are violated; they are only upset when police misconduct targets "good people." A study of community policing in Seattle, observing interactions between police and the community, reveals how police see themselves as "members of a politically vulnerable group that deserves protection from ill-informed public meddling; they possess an authority to control situations to which the public should defer; they command a unique base of knowledge, and thus deserve an elevated professional status" (Herbert 2006: 86). Commentators, therefore, generally portray police culture as negative, defensive, and isolationist. In contrast to this portrayal, police often promulgate statements of values or of their policing mission that are positive in nature, as in the "Foster City Police Department Basic Values" Closer Look box.

Changing Police Culture

While some scholars of policing have suggested that police culture has changed with the advent of community policing, a greater focus on service to the public, enhancement of communication and interpersonal skills, and the impact of cultural, ethnic, and gender diversification of police organizations, Bethan Loftus (2010: 1) suggests that, in the United Kingdom at least, the "underlying world view" of police officers has not altered because the basic pressures associated with policing have remained constant. In an ethnographic study of police culture in the north of England, Loftus found that police officers still perceived themselves as crime fighters (despite the fact that arresting criminals took up very little of their time) and as constituting the line that separated order from chaos. Loftus observed that physical responses to incidents were highly valued and that police celebrated a confrontational approach to policing despite policies and programs that reconfigured the policing mission as servicing "customers" (p. 7). The tensions between the realities of police work—mundane, monotonous, and unexciting—and the expectations—an action-packed day of crime fighting—meant that police "developed a profoundly cynical and pessimistic view of their social world" (p. 8). Loftus concludes that

absent significant social change, police culture is unlikely to be impacted by radical change.

John Crank (1998: 119) argues that in relation to the United States over the past 25 years, police values have basically remained unchanged. One reason for this is that police recruits are selected from a pool of applicants who share police values, and persons attracted to law enforcement as a career are the same persons who have always been drawn to policing. Michael Caldero and Crank (2011: 66) suggest that officers are hired with a set of values already in place that are enhanced and fine-tuned through the academy and on-the-job training. They identify the formative influences as the academy, the police field-training officer, the police culture, the danger and isolation of policing, and other elements. Importantly, as they point out, officers are often recruited from police families, from small towns, and from the military. They are already imbued with the values that policing privileges, especially the focus on creating order in human interactions. In this sense, then, newly recruited officers are already committed to the noble cause—they are believers because the noble cause is an inherent part of their moral upbringing. (see definition of "noble cause" under the heading "'Noble Cause' Corruption" on page 47.)

Researchers have tended to describe police culture in monolithic terms and generalize its characteristics often by reference to the culture of the patrol officer level of policing (Punch 2007: 107). One approach to understanding police culture is to think of a set of core characteristics, as noted previously, which can be said to represent the dominant culture. While officers may carry their shared experiences—the dominant culture—into different occupational specialties within a police force, studies suggest that specialists[1] also develop a culture for their specific occupation, as for example in undercover policing (Bacon 2014: 113). In addition, policing today is staffed by white and minority officers, by women, and by gay officers who collectively bring a heterogeneity to policing that did not exist when many ethnographic studies of policing were being conducted in the 1960s and 70s

---

1   Manning (2007: 57) points out that within policing, prestige and status flow to officers working in "specialized units, investigative work, especially homicide, and positions most associated with crime control and crime suppression."

(Sklansky 2007: 35). The study of police ethics is especially important in light of the functions and duties of the police, as well as the wide powers of discretion that they enjoy. Police decisions can affect life, liberty, and property, and as guardians of the interests of the public, police must maintain high standards of integrity (Pollock-Byrne 1998: 3–4). In addition, police have assumed the right to use intrusive, covert, and deceptive methods of law enforcement and have a crucial role in protecting minority groups. They have also suffered a series of blows to their reputation for integrity through acts of corruption, incompetence, and racism (Neyroud and Beckley 2001: 38). All of these factors point to the centrality of fostering ethical standards in policing. Police discretion concerning how to act in a given situation can often lead to ethical misconduct.

A Closer Look

Foster City Police Department Basic Values

1. Integrity is basic to the accomplishment of the law enforcement mission. Both personal and organizational integrity are essential to the maintenance of the F.C.P.D. This means that we:

   - Ensure that accurate reporting occurs at all levels;
   - Promote and recognize ethical behavior and actions;
   - Value the reputation of our profession and agency, yet promote honesty over loyalty to the Department;
   - Openly discuss both ethical and operational issues that require change; and
   - Collectively act to prevent abuses of the law and violations of civil rights.

2. Due to the dynamic nature of our profession, the F.C.P.D. values innovation from all levels of the Agency. This means we:

   - Reward and recognize those who contribute to the development of more effective ways of providing policing service;
   - Strive to minimize conflict which negatively impacts our work product, yet we support the constructive airing and resolution of differences in the name of delivering quality police services;
   - Listen to and promote suggestions emanating from all levels of the Department; and
   - Wish to promote an atmosphere that encourages prudent risk taking, and that recognizes that growth and learning may be spawned by honest mistakes.

3. The law enforcement profession is recognized as somewhat close and fraternal in nature. The F.C.P.D. reflects this tradition, yet supports community involvement and ongoing critical self-appraisal by all its members. This means we:

   - Encourage employees to socialize with employees and community members alike to promote the reputation of the Agency;
   - Promote programs that improve the relationship between our members and the community at large;
   - Report and confront employees who violate laws and the basic values of the organization; and
   - Promote and discuss positive aspects of the Agency and its product throughout the county.

(Continued)

(Continued)

4. The provision of law enforcement services is a substantial expense to the taxpayer. The F.C.P.D. is obliged to provide the highest quality of police service for the resources expended. This means we:

   • Regularly assess the cost vs. benefits of the various programs of the Agency;

   • Require a standard of professional performance for all members of the Department;

   • Administer the Department funds in a prudent, cost-effective manner;

   • Publicly acknowledge and praise employees that excel at their jobs; and

   • Support and encourage employees in their pursuit of higher education.

5. Law enforcement, in the course of performing its primary mission, is required to deal with both dangerous and difficult situations. The F.C.P.D. accepts this responsibility and supports its members in the accomplishment of these tasks. This means we:

   • Review and react to an individual's performance during such an event based upon the totality of the circumstances surrounding their decision and actions;

   • Encourage all employees, as the situation permits, to think before they act;

   • Take all available steps and precautions to protect both the City's and employees' interests in incidents that provide either danger or civil exposure;

   • Keep our supervisor informed of any incident or pending action that jeopardizes either the reputation of the Agency or individual employee;

   • Attempt, conditions permitting, to reason with individuals in the enforcement setting prior to resorting to the use of force; and

   • Recognize that it is our duty to prevent, report, and investigate crimes, together with the apprehension and the pursuit of vigorous prosecution of lawbreakers. We also recognize that it is the domain of the court to punish individuals convicted of crimes.

SOURCE: From the Foster City Police Department, Foster City, California. Cited in More 1998: 48–49.

POLICE DISCRETION

By law, police are given the power to deprive citizens of their freedom by arresting them and the right to use force in the performance of their policing function, including lethal force in certain situations. The police are therefore given great authority under the law, and that authority is to be employed ideally in enforcing the law and protecting the public. Police authority and power is exercised within the discretionary sphere given them; any exercise of power or authority is an exercise of discretion. As well as authority conferred by law, police have another kind of authority derived from their role as police officers and represented by their physical, uniformed presence on the street. The public,

therefore, tend to treat police officers with circumspection in most cases, aware in a general sense that police have specific powers, such as to arrest, but they are unclear as to the total extent of police authority. Police culture insists on the public giving the police respect and cooperation; flouting or resisting police authority can result in arrest or other consequences that may sometimes amount to misconduct—for example, threatening a future arrest or even assaulting a person to punish him or her for an attitude considered disrespectful.

Limiting Police Discretion

In performing their policing duties, police officers are able to exercise a high degree of discretion.

This means that they have broad freedom to make decisions about how to act in a given situation. For example, a police officer may decide to investigate an occurrence, or he or she may decide that it is not worthy of his or her time and effort. Officers can also decide whether or not to make an arrest and may make decisions about the amount of force required during a confrontation. Caldero and Crank (2011: 79) argue that police discretion is not value-free and is shaped by a set of values, including the noble cause morality that is already in place when they begin patrol work. It is therefore possible to predict the probable police action in situations calling for the exercise of discretion.

Some commentators argue that police discretion should be limited so that, for example, the rules and regulations of the police department and ethical standards circumscribe that discretion. Jeffrey Reiman (1996) argues even more radically that "police discretion has no rightful place in a free society" (p. 80). Manning (1997) points out that policing guidelines themselves create uncertain circumstances and that the impact of guidelines is unclear because cases in which the guidelines were not adhered to are never reported to supervisors. From the police patrol officer's point of view, James Q. Wilson (1968) notes that patrol officers may legitimately complain that having no agreed-on standards for the exercise of discretion makes their task harder, especially if the existence of many procedural rules enables others to easily penalize them for acting in an allegedly improper manner. Manning summarizes the issue of guidelines by noting that the solutions offered for limiting the wide powers of police discretion include judicial rule making, legislative regulation, and developing internal codes and regulations (p. 295). Jerome Skolnick and James Fyfe (1993: 120) point out, however, that elaborate police rule books, although purporting to be definitive, actually provide limited guidance of any worth to police because hard and fast rules do not adequately assist police in dealing with the fluid and fast-changing situations they may be faced with.

Some police officers deliberately use their wide powers of discretion and their authority to perform acts of misconduct, as discussed in this section. Davis (in Cohen 1996: 97) argues that discretion ought to be confined so that it is used only when truly required. In other words, where a rule, law, or policy can be applied to a situation, it should be applied. If this is not done, he argues, justice may be seen to be arbitrary or subject to inequalities. James Fyfe (1996: 183) contends that police ought to enjoy some degree of discretion, but like discretion in any profession, it can be justified only to achieve a broadly agreed-on purpose; in the case of the police, this purpose is often hard to define. Like Manning (1997), he attributes this lack of clarity about police goals to those same police chiefs who complain that discretion in police organizations is broad at the base and much narrower at the top. However, most citizens, including most police officers, support police having *wide discretion* on the basis that their hands should not be tied in their role as guardians of the public.

Discretion and Accountability

Many argue that if police are permitted wide discretion, a high level of accountability should match it so that processes and machinery exist to investigate complaints of misconduct or abuse of discretion (see the section later in this chapter on Combating Corruption). Manning (1997: 146) notes that discretion creates uncertainty, and from the perspective of the police supervisor, it creates randomness in patrol practice that makes it difficult for administrators to enforce accountability.

Kleinig (1996: 4–5) outlines a distinction between decisions about scope and decisions about interpretation in exercising discretion. In the former, police must decide whether a given situation requires them to act, and in the latter, questions of definition arise, such as "Has an offense been committed?" and "Is this a situation in which I should act at all?" Police also must consider questions of priorities and make what Kleinig calls "tactical decisions" that bear on police attitudes, such as whether to react strongly to circumstances or to follow a more mediatory role.

ETHICS AND CODES OF ETHICS

Kleinig (1996: 234) traces the history of a police code of ethics, nothing that it was not until 1928 that such a code was formulated for police in the United States. Professions commonly have codes of ethics regulating standards for the protection of clients and the public, and the desire for professional status is a major rationale for the development of police codes of ethics (p. 234). Within the United States, individual police departments have codes or canons of ethics, and the International Association of Chiefs of Police (IACP), which is dominated by the United States, finalized its Law Enforcement Code of Ethics in 1991 (see the "Law Enforcement Code of Ethics" Closer Look box).

What Is the Relationship Between Ethics and Codes of Ethics?

Kleinig (1996: 239) suggests that statements of values and ethical standards generally are likely to be briefer and more general than codes, with the latter detailing what kinds of acts may or may not be performed. Most codes of ethics are directed toward an undefined client or public base, and it may be in the public interest to establish certain standards expected of a particular profession. In this external sense, codes may be seen to have a rhetorical function and can provide some assurance that police do follow standards or are being urged to follow them by the code. Kleinig says that it is increasingly common for codes to be used as internal documents so that even when they are phrased in generalities, they at least identify issues and provide criteria for decision-making.

Police academies apparently use codes of ethics as a teaching device; however, codes cannot be considered definitive and do not usually include enforcement procedures (Kleinig 1996: 248). Kleinig cautions that although police officers pledge themselves to their codes of ethics, this does not mean that they are required to sacrifice their reflexivity as individuals, and police may well find that their codes do not respond adequately to the situational demands placed on them. In one study, more than 75% of police officers surveyed responded that they depended mostly on their own personal ethics rather than the ethics of law enforcement to guide them in their professional activities (Felknes 1984: 217).

Police Compliance With Ethical Codes

The standards of conduct incorporated in codes of ethics are directed at each individual police officer, and therefore each officer must decide his or her own level of compliance. While some studies suggest that ethical standards held by officers during initial training diminish once they are "on the job" (Crank and Caldero 2000; Rokeach, Miller, and Snyder 1977; Zhao, Ni, and Lovrich 1998), Dennis Catlin and James R. Maupin (2004: 299) suggest that socialization within law enforcement has no effect on an officer's ethical orientation. Ultimately, compliance may become a question of character, and officers may be admonished to "do the right thing even when no one is watching." Part II of this book will explore various ethical theories, including virtue theory, which emphasizes the importance of character, and deontology, which argues that one must do the right thing even though others are not there to see simply because there is a duty to do the right thing. Clearly, this theory has considerable relevance for codes of ethics regulating standards of behavior in policing.

Ethics Instruction

Most would agree that ethics training and knowledge is essential for law enforcement in light of the complexities of policing and the legal liability issues that arise when police behave improperly and violate the public trust. Ethics training gained considerable traction in the 1990s when the IACP recommended providing ethics instruction for all ranks throughout an officer's career; incorporating decision-making models in instruction; discussing values and developing critical-thinking exercises; and using adult-learning models (Wyatt-Nichol and Franks 2009: 40). Pre-service training in ethics in police academies is usually mandated, but the time spent on the topic is typically only between 2 and 4 hours (p. 41). In a survey of 100 selected police departments, Heather Wyatt-Nichol and George Franks found that among departments that required ethics training in the academy as a pre-service requirement, most indicated that the instruction lasted half a day or less, and only a few departments required one full day of ethics training (p. 39). Nevertheless, some departments gave ethics greater prominence, with two departments reporting that 1 week of ethics training was required.

Only 14 departments required ethics training in service, while six reported that ethics was not mandated but was offered as an optional subject to fulfill in-service training requirements. Only 7% of departments required officers who have been disciplined for misconduct to complete ethics training. While most police chiefs took a positive view of ethics training, one chief gave his opinion:

By and large, people bring the moral and ethical values into the workplace and law enforcement is no different. Providing the training merely allows the agency to keep the subject of ethical behavior on the surface. The training will not, in my opinion, markedly change the behavior of attendees, either positively or negatively. (Wyatt-Nichol and Franks 2009: 47)

A Closer Look

Law Enforcement Code of Ethics* International Association of Chiefs of Police

All law enforcement officers must be fully aware of the ethical responsibilities of their position and must strive constantly to live up to the highest possible standards of professional policing.

The International Association of Chiefs of Police believes it is important that police officers have clear advice and counsel available to assist them in performing their duties consistent with these standards, and has adopted the following ethical mandates as guidelines to meet these ends.

Primary Responsibilities of a Police Officer

A police officer acts as an official representative of government who is required and trusted to work within the law. The officer's powers and duties are conferred by statute. The fundamental duties of a police officer include serving the community; safeguarding lives and property; protecting the innocent; keeping the peace; and ensuring the rights of all to liberty, equality and justice.

Performance of the Duties of a Police Officer

A police officer shall perform all duties impartially, without favor or affection or ill will and without regard to status, sex, race, religion, political belief or aspiration. All citizens will be treated equally with courtesy, consideration and dignity.

Officers will never allow personal feelings, animosities or friendships to influence official conduct. Laws will be enforced appropriately and courteously and, in carrying out their responsibilities, officers will strive to obtain maximum cooperation from the public. They will conduct themselves in appearance and deportment in such a manner as to inspire confidence and respect for the position of public trust they hold.

Discretion

A police officer will use responsibly the discretion vested in the position and exercise it within the law. The principle of reasonableness will guide the officer's determinations and the officer will consider all surrounding circumstances in determining whether any legal action shall be taken.

Consistent and wise use of discretion, based on professional policing competence, will do much to preserve good relationships and retain the confidence of the public. There can be difficulty in

(Continued)

(Continued)

choosing between conflicting courses of action. It is important to remember that a timely word of advice rather than arrest—which may be correct in appropriate circumstances—can be a more effective means of achieving a desired end.

Use of Force

A police officer will never employ unnecessary force or violence and will use only such force in the discharge of duty as is reasonable in all circumstances. Force should be used only with the greatest restraint and only after discussion, negotiation and persuasion have been found to be inappropriate or ineffective. While the use of force is occasionally unavoidable, every police officer will refrain from applying the unnecessary infliction of pain or suffering and will never engage in cruel, degrading or inhuman treatment of any person.

Confidentiality

Whatever a police officer sees, hears or learns of, which is of a confidential nature, will be kept secret unless the performance of duty or legal provision requires otherwise. Members of the public have a right to security and privacy, and information obtained about them must not be improperly divulged.

Integrity

A police officer will not engage in acts of corruption or bribery, nor will an officer condone such acts by other police officers. The public demands that the integrity of police officers be above reproach. Police officers must, therefore, avoid any conduct that might compromise integrity and thus undercut the public confidence in a law enforcement agency. Officers will refuse to accept any gifts, presents, subscriptions, favors, gratuities or promises that could be interpreted as seeking to cause the officer to refrain from performing official responsibilities honestly and within the law. Police officers must not receive private or special advantage from their official status. Respect from the public cannot be bought; it can only be earned and cultivated.

Cooperation With Other Officers and Agencies

Police officers will cooperate with all legally authorized agencies and their representatives in the pursuit of justice. An officer or agency may be one among many organizations that may provide law enforcement services to a jurisdiction. It is imperative that a police officer assist colleagues fully and completely with respect and consideration at all times.

Personal/Professional Capabilities

Police officers will be responsible for their own standard of professional performance and will take every reasonable opportunity to enhance and improve their level of knowledge and competence.

Through study and experience, a police officer can acquire the high level of knowledge and competence that is essential for the efficient and effective performance of duty. The acquisition of knowledge is a never-ending process of personal and professional development that should be pursued constantly.

Private Life

Police officers will behave in a manner that does not bring discredit to their agencies or themselves.

A police officer's character and conduct while off duty must always be exemplary, thus maintaining a position of respect in the community in which he or she lives and serves. The officer's personal behavior must be beyond reproach.

SOURCE: Center for the Study of Ethics in the Professions 2003. Copyright held by the International Association of Chiefs of Police, 515 North Washington Street, Alexandria, VA 22314, USA. Reprinted with permission. Further reproduction without express written permission from IACP is strictly prohibited.

*Adopted by the Executive Committee of the International Association of Chiefs of Police on October 17, 1989, during its 96th annual conference in Louisville, Kentucky, to replace the 1957 code of ethics adopted at the 64th annual IACP conference.

The IACP gratefully acknowledges the assistance of Sir John C. Hermon, former chief constable of the Royal Ulster Constabulary, who gave full license to the association to freely use the language and concepts presented in the RUC's "Professional Policing Ethics," Appendix 1 of the Chief Constable's Annual Report, 1988, presented to the Police Authority for Northern Ireland, for the preparation of this code.

POLICING AND STRESS

The notion that law enforcement is a stressful occupation is unsurprising given the nature of policing. For example, research studies have long focused on aspects of the policing mission and identified post-traumatic stress disorder (PTSD) as a condition likely to be experienced by police after shooting incidents. In such incidents, common reactions have been flashbacks, sleeping problems, time distortion, emotional reactions (including crying, anger, and elation), and fear of the legal repercussions of the shooting (Stratton, Parker, and Snibbe 1984: 127). Therefore, it has long been established that policing is a high stress and high strain occupation (Gershon, Barocas, Canton, Li, and Vlahov 2009: 276).

During the mid- to late-twentieth century, the study of stress began to focus on policing. While some police agencies conducted research into stress and established employee assistance programs, it was not until 2000 that the first confidential hotline for police and their families was established in New Jersey, following a series of police suicides, using retired officers with skills in crisis intervention techniques (Waters and Ussery 2007: 171).

As an at-risk group, police are exposed to more acute stressors than most occupations, as evidenced by officers beginning their careers in excellent physical health and retiring early or dying from stress-related causes. Suppressing emotions is often a precursor to forms of stress, and the task of policing generally inhibits free emotion, as does the police culture itself. The then-chief of the Cincinnati Police Department in the early 1970s spoke of police culture as leading "officers to believe that they are a special population that has superhuman abilities and no weaknesses." Nevertheless, police culture values the figure of the "tough cop" able to withstand any amount of pressure (quoted in Waters and Ussery 2007: 172). In fact, the contrary is true because officers become vulnerable to stress by having to be constantly vigilant. Exacerbating the stress problem is that departments tend to ignore it in favor of issues of training and equipment.

Nature of Police Occupational Stress

Manning (2007: 73) describes organizational tensions within policing as arising from officer perceptions that their organization is "capricious, unpredictable and punitive rather than democratic and fair" and because officers "feel at risk from the internal machinations of politics, supervision, policies and uncertain events or incidents."

Workplace problems are important stressors, and studies have identified the following factors:

- Unsatisfactory interactions with fellow officers
- Concerns about status and opportunities for advancement in the department
- Bias and harassment
- Over- and underestimates of physical capabilities (Morash, Haarr, and Dae-Hoon 2006: 27)

Some stress is the outcome of lack of support from networks both at work and at home. Shift work is also an issue in stress management because constant shift changes lead to serious health problems brought on by interrupted sleep patterns, digestive issues, and the general impact on physical and psychological well-being (Waters and Ussery 2007: 175). Excessive overtime, heavy workloads, and frequent interaction with the public all contribute to stress (Gershon et al. 2009: 276).

Organizational-based stress can seriously undermine law enforcement effectiveness through health issues, poor morale, and high staffing turnover rates (Gershon et al. 2009: 277). Studies have found that organizational stressors and not critical policing incidents are most closely associated with police stress (p. 284). Generally, police who experience high levels of stress report physical ailments and commonly have poor health, are often absent from work, experience burnout, experience job dissatisfaction, may not be truly committed to the policing mission, and may retire early (Morash et al. 2006: 26).

Stress and Crime Fighting

In terms of the policing mission, working in high-density–high-crime areas, working in metropolitan areas, and being employed in large departments differentiate the large municipal police departments from those that serve small cities and suburban and rural areas where different behaviors and attitudes are found. In large departments, stressors may be associated with high levels of

discipline and regulation and a more proactive, even militaristic approach to policing. In small departments, there may be less crime and more scope for community-type policing that diminishes the isolation of police from the local community (Morash et al. 2006: 29). However, in a survey of about 1,000 officers from 11 police departments, including one serving a population of more than 1.5 million and one of half a million, Morash and colleagues (p. 36) found that high crime rates and poverty did not have strong predictive value in explaining police stress. As well, it was found that the violent crime rate was not associated with high levels of stress. This result could be explained by the fact that even in a high-crime jurisdiction many police do not directly deal with violence most of the time or possibly a high crime rate is not a principal stressor.

Policing can mean that each call for police assistance has the potential for violence and injury or death: Domestic violence cases are especially dangerous as the protagonists may turn on the police. Police face three types of stress: *explosive events* (for example, crimes in progress); *daily tensions* that corrode confidence and resilience; and *implosive events* that challenge an officer's values and bring about internal conflicts (Waters and Ussery 2007: 175). Additionally, police continually swap "war stories" that illustrate the potential for danger and constantly view media images of danger in policing (Griffin and Bernard 2003: 12).

According to the *National Law Enforcement Officers Memorial Fund,* 111 officers died on duty in 2013, a decrease from the 120 deaths in 2012 and 169 in 2011. Traffic accidents were the leading cause of death with 46 killed, and firearms accounted for 33 fatalities. Job-related illness was the third highest cause of death, responsible for 18 deaths, including 14 officers who died of heart attacks associated with stressful events on duty. Policing also means adapting to change, which can itself be a stressor—for example, when a policy of community policing is introduced which might require significant role changes (Chan 2007: 134). Depression and heart disease are prevalent in police populations, and stress has been associated with problem drinking and hyperaggression, both on and off the job (Gershon et al. 2009: 276). The death of, or injury to, a fellow officer—an event that occurs only irregularly in other occupations—is known to be especially stressful.

Coping With Stress

It has been suggested that police culture itself develops in a way that helps police to cope with the pressures and tensions of police work; for example, officers may rely on the mutual assistance and solidarity that are core elements of police culture (Chan 2007: 130, 144). There are numerous types of treatment and prevention programs for police, ranging from psychological counseling and Alcoholics Anonymous to training about stress at police academies. An officer may decide to cope with stress through alcohol, even though alcohol abuse is associated with domestic violence and poor job performance. Nevertheless, as a coping mechanism, alcohol is generally condoned by police culture (Waters and Ussery 2007: 176). Studies have shown that police are reluctant to contact mental health professionals because police culture disapproves of such action, and officers tend to have little confidence in professionals who are not closely associated with policing. As well, an officer may fear loss of his or her job because consultations with mental health practitioners may be held against them in disciplinary proceedings or even in litigation if they abuse their authority by using excessive force (p. 177). Generally, individual coping strategies include the following:

- Access to a dependable support system
- Improved communication skills to better articulate individual concerns (an appropriate mechanism that allows feelings to be vented)
- A regular exercise program and a good diet
- Recreational activities that allow an individual to "turn off" from work
- Participation in self-help groups
- Regular vacations

Departments can assist officers to minimize or avoid stress through organizational practices and mechanisms that teach officers about stress and how to cope with it; by having open channels of communication to supervisors who are in turn supportive and understand how to recognize and respond to stressed officers; and by having debriefing sessions at the end of shifts (Waters and Ussery 2007: 184). Officers without a supportive family or friends may be especially vulnerable to stress (Gershon et al. 2009: 276).

Angry Aggression

Griffin and Bernard (2003: 3) have proposed that the use of extralegal (as opposed to excessive) force by police can be explained by "angry aggression theory." Extralegal force refers to the deliberate, knowing, and wrongful use of force by police, such that police are aware they are abusing their power. In other words, police have the intent to act extralegally (p. 5). The authors of this theory, which is composed of elements of sociology, psychology, and biology, argue that it better explains police extralegal force than theories that focus on individual psychological characteristics such as "authoritarianism" or on police culture.

The theory originated to explain violent responses to minor conflicts and insults by disadvantaged minorities in the inner cities. It claims that persons who experience chronic physiological arousal—the body's "fight or flight response"—tend to see threats and respond to them more aggressively than do others who do not have that experience. These responses become embedded in norms and values. The literature also supports the notion that police experience chronic arousal and therefore tend to see threats and respond with aggression to an extent that others do not. The theory makes the case that police transfer aggression to visible targets in their immediate environment—namely, members of the public with whom they interact. The stressful nature of policing (including citizen disrespect and challenges to police authority), its social isolation (police tend to socialize with other police), and the inability of police to actually relive the stress they experience (police are generally unable to relieve the stress of danger, citizen hostility, and organizational pressures) are all said to link angry aggression theory directly to use of extralegal force (Griffin and Bernard 2003: 12).

Clearly, research demonstrates that police experience numerous stressors on the job, and mechanisms for alleviating stress are crucial if stress is not to result in domestic violence in the home, alcohol abuse, angry aggression, or even suicide. Police use of force is an intrinsically complex issue impacted by training, experience on the job, police culture, occupational stressors, perceptions of illegitimacy by the public, and media representations of how and why it was used and to what degree (see Chapter 3 on police use of force).

POLICE "MILITARIZATION"

Since the late 1990s, scholars have been advancing a proposition that there has been a "militarization" of policing in the United States. This proposition, focused on one aspect of policing, drew little attention outside academia until the events in Ferguson, Missouri, a town of about 21,000 people, where in August 2014 a white police officer shot and killed an 18-year-old black male. The public response initially focused on questions of race and bias and resulted in protests in the streets, some of which turned to looting and violence. Local law enforcement handled the situation by sending in police equipped with military-type weapons and body armor and accompanied by armored vehicles. This was widely viewed as police overreaction to the protests and focused public attention on the style and tactics of the policing of the protests. Questions were raised, generally about the nature of policing in the United States and how it had become militarized and the consequences of this for the public (Kiker 2015: 282).

This section will examine the historical and contemporary context associated with the separation of police and the military, the theories and the narrative of militarization, and the nature of that militarization and how it has been said to have changed policing and the possible consequences.

Historical and Contemporary Context—Police and Military

Since 1776, the United States has sought to isolate the military from involvement in civilian affairs, citing the quartering of British troops in colonial Boston in the late 18th century as a show of power over a dissident population. However, the Reconstruction Act that followed the end of the Civil War divided the Confederate states into military districts and placed them under military control. Consequently, at that time, the military became the principal law enforcement agents. A rule prohibiting military involvement in domestic law enforcement was adopted in the *Posse Comitatus Act* (PCA) of 1878. The decisions of the courts have confirmed this isolation approach and have noted "a traditional and strong resistance of Americans to any military intrusion into civilian affairs" (*Laird v. Tatum* 1972).

In World War I, the PCA was suspended, enabling the military to be used in aiding the policing of domestic unrest, and the National Guard was deployed overseas (Hall and Coyne 2013: 491). In 1981, the PCA was substantially weakened when it was amended to allow the military to participate in the war on drugs (Kiker 2015: 294). Specifically, the *Military Cooperation With Law Enforcement Act* created exceptions to the PCA and allowed the Department of Defense (DOD) to share information, as well as the military to provide advice and assistance to local police agencies and to offer them military equipment for deployment in the war. As well as providing aerial surveillance to interdict drug shipments, National Guard troops (provided by federal funds) were used by many states in prohibiting drug activities (Hall and Coyne 2013: 494–495).

As noted earlier, events in the town of Ferguson, Missouri, raised the profile of militarized policing, and soon after, the U.S. Senate reacted to public concerns by debating and holding hearings about federal programs that allowed police departments to obtain military assets at no cost. The general approach of the Senate was that this kind of equipment and its deployment as part of police tactics brought about mistrust between police and the communities they were supposed to protect and serve.

The Militarization Thesis

The foremost proponents of the militarization thesis are Kraska and Kappeler, especially Peter Kraska, who alone or with other scholars has researched and drawn attention to the expansion in the creation of SWAT teams in U.S. law enforcement agencies (Kraska 2007c: 1). Kraska's argument is that there has been a "little noticed but nonetheless momentous historical change–the traditional distinctions between military/police, war/law enforcement, and internal/external security are rapidly blurring. . . . Two interrelated trends . . . embody this blur: the militarization of U.S. police and crime control, and the police-ization of the U.S. military." In support of this convergence argument, Kraska points to the following:

- The weakening of the law preventing military involvement in law enforcement
- The creation of cooperation between police and the military, including technology transfers, information sharing, an operational relationship on drugs control and terrorism, and cross-training on SWAT tactics and antiterrorism
- The growth and routine use of SWAT units modeled on military units
- A "growing tendency" for police to rely on the war/military model in designing crime, drug, and terrorism control and operations
- Constructing crime as "insurgency" and crime control as "low-intensity conflict," requiring the performance of counterinsurgency measures by police and the military (p. 2)

Kraska sees the notions of *militarization* and *militarism* as organizing concepts to better understand the changes that have occurred in policing since the 1960s, when the SWAT concept was first introduced. He offers this explanation of militarism:

[It is] an ideology focused on the best means to solve problems. It is a set of beliefs, values, and assumptions that stress the use of force and threat of violence as the most appropriate and efficacious means to solve problems. It emphasizes the exercise of military power, hardware, organization, operations and technology as the primary problem-solving tools. (2007c: 3)

Militarization is therefore the implementation of the ideology of militarism: It means "adopting and applying the central elements of the military model," and it is represented in policing by police drawing on and patterning themselves around "the tenets of militarism and the military model" (Kraska 2007c: 3).

Kraska recognizes that the police have always been militarized to some extent and suggests there is a continuum of militarization. He proposes a set of indicators from which the degree of militarization can be measured. The indicators relate to type of weapons, military style such as combat dress, the use of elite squads and command and control entities, and operational factors, including using SWAT teams

to execute "no-knock" drug warrants. Wherever SWAT units may be located on this continuum—Kraska does not offer an opinion on this—it remains unclear whether it is being argued that police have taken on the "primary war-fighting task of the standard military organization: to overwhelm and subdue" (Campbell and Campbell 2010: 338) or whether there role remains more limited than this. It is argued that even with a degree of militarization there is no convergence of police and military roles in terms of "cognitive demands" because while even a police patrolman may exercise significant discretion in carrying out missions, a rifleman is required to simply obey orders (p. 339).

Number and Deployment of SWAT Units

Based on survey research, Kraska argues that as of the late 1990s about 89% of police departments serving populations of 50,000 or more persons had an established paramilitary unit, representing a doubling of such forces that existed in the mid-1980s. In towns of fewer than 50,000, the growth in such units was even more marked, with about 80% having a paramilitary unit compared to only 20% in the mid-1980s. Also significant is the rate at which these units have been deployed. Kraska says there was a 1,400% increase in deployments between 1980 and 2000 and that there are now an estimated 45,000 deployments of SWAT teams annually among the departments he surveyed compared to an average of about 3,000 in the early 1980s. This trend began with the declaration of the war on drugs. The increase is not attributable to a growth in dangerous incidents for which SWAT units were originally conceived, such as hostage, terrorism, or "sniper" situations (Kraska 2007c: 6). In fact, regardless of the size of the town, more than 80% of deployments were for drug raids with "no-knock"[2] entries into property

---

2   Police are not required to "knock and announce" in order to execute a search warrant if they have reasonable suspicion that there is a threat of physical violence or that giving advance notice would result in the destruction of evidence. If they are satisfied that either of these situations exist, they can secure a "no-knock warrant," which allows forcible entry without prior announcement of police presence. The police have significant discretion in executing search warrants then, but even if a court finds police have violated the general rule that requires knock and announce, the Supreme Court has said that the evidence seized will not be excluded (ACLU 2014: 24).

searching for drugs (p. 7). Additionally, a high number of deployments were to undertake "routine patrol work in crime 'hot spots,'" indicating a normalization or routinization of SWAT units.

According to Kraska (2007a: 166), this represents a dramatic change in police tactics because, in his view, 20 years ago such tactics were almost unheard of and would have been considered an "extreme and unacceptable police tactic." This may be because there was perceived equivalent threat to the war on drugs at that time, but Kraska does not discuss this. Therefore, Kraska concludes that this represents "strong evidence that the U.S. police, and the 'war on crime' in general, have moved significantly down the militarization continuum" (Kraska 2007b: 793). An alternative view is that the frequent development of SWAT units was a reaction to the new demands placed on policing by the war on drugs—for example, in responding to well-armed and highly dangerous drug operations. This view therefore suggests that increased use of SWAT units is simply a response to needs and does not represent any real change in policing styles (Campbell and Campbell 2010: 329).

A 2014 study by the American Civil Liberties Union (ACLU) looked at 818 SWAT incidents involving more than 20 police agencies in 11 states covering the period from July 2010 to October 2013. In seven cases, civilian deaths occurred in the course of SWAT team deployments. The study found that 62% of SWAT callouts were for drug searches, and 79% involved raids on private houses. Only about 7% of callouts fell into the categories of action for which such units were conceived, namely "hostage, barricade and active shooter scenarios" (p. 2). The report describes SWAT raids as "undoubtedly violent events" involving 20 or more officers carrying assault rifles and grenades who break down the doors of premises and scream at those inside to get down on the floor. In the view of the ACLU, SWAT deployments often "unnecessarily entailed the use of violent tactics and equipment including Armored Personnel Carriers (APCs); and the training provided to such units encourages the development of a 'warrior' mentality" (p. 3).

The ACLU concluded in its assessment of deployments that the use of SWAT teams to serve search warrants was inappropriate because officer safety did not appear to be a genuine threat. Of the incidents where officers believed weapons would be present (usually a handgun, not an assault rifle), such were found in only 35% of cases. ACLU argues that SWAT units should not be deployed based solely on probable cause of the presence of drugs and that warrant service is only appropriate if it can be demonstrated that regular police cannot execute a warrant without facing "an imminent threat of serious bodily harm" (2014: 4). The ACLU notes that "reasonable standards for deploying SWAT teams appear to be virtually non-existent" (p. 4). In terms of targets for SWAT raids, the ACLU found that "the use of paramilitary weapons and tactics primarily impacted people of color" (p. 5). Specifically, in drug searches the targets were primarily people of color, but in hostage and barricade situations, whites were the targets. Overall, the ACLU study found that 42% of persons subjected to SWAT raids to execute warrants were black and 12% Latino; therefore, for all warrant deployments at least 54% of the suspects were minorities (p. 5).

Causes of Militarization

Kraska (2007b) and other commentators point to two government strategies as key in the growth of militarization—the war on drugs and the war on terror. These metaphorical wars are argued to have shaped policing through the use of militaristic rhetoric. It is not clear how this occurred, and there seem to be no empirical studies that actually map how and why police departments came to form SWAT units. There are, however, some demonstrable linkages between law enforcement and these wars in the form of military involvement in the war on drugs and the transfer of equipment to police agencies to support the two wars. It is also argued that a driver of the move to militarism was the perception among police that SWAT teams and the like are elite forces and associated with "real police work," similar to the high status that special forces enjoy within military culture (Campbell and Campbell 2010: 335).

The war on drugs is discussed in Chapter 7, but in summary, the "war" was declared by President Nixon in the 1970s and was conducted by the Drug Enforcement Administration (DEA) and local police agencies with military assistance and great publicity. By the end of the 1980s, mass arrests for drug offenses were taking place, fears about crack cocaine and drug abuse generally were being fostered, and popular support for the war increased so that by 1989 almost 40% of the public considered illegal drugs to be the "primary problem" facing the United States, and by 1993, 64% viewed drugs as a "critical" influence on crime. There was wide support for taking the war overseas to the drug-producing countries and for using the military to fight drug trafficking.

Some scholars have argued that while the effects of militarization in policing are clear and explicit in the growth and nature of SWAT type units, the causes remain contested; they also argue that the war on terror was not a cause of but rather an excuse for militarization and that policing has become militarized worldwide because of the amplification of threats to national security (Hill and Beger 2009: 29).

Applying a political economy perspective to militarization, Hall and Coyne (2013: 488) suggest that what they term "indirect militarization" occurs over time when police departments as bureaucracies engage in "mission creep" with the aim of expanding the range of their activities and increasing their spending. This tendency is argued to be "inherent" and exemplified by the increase in the military budget from $306 billion in 1988 to $698 billion in 2010. Similarly, police spending climbed, growing 445% between 1982 and 2007. Therefore, Hall and Coyne argue that police agencies expand their operations to secure additional staff and funds. Having secured more funds, tactical training, and weapons, they face an incentive to use them to justify the increase and seek yet more funding (p. 488).

Hall and Coyne (2013) also point out that actual or perceived crises as well as moral panics that are fear based and associated with forms of crime or terrorism give government the opportunity to expand its activities by formulating new programs. The war on drugs and the war on terror are instances of such crises, and both created the opportunity for expansion of policing services (p. 488). Improvements in military technology also play a role as they are transferred to police agencies in the form of drones, satellite monitoring, and facial recognition systems. This, they argue, facilitates the militarization of the police

(p. 490). Kraska (2007b) neglects to mention that many police agencies have regularly recruited military veterans as patrol officers since the end of the Civil War. Whether or not the presence of military veterans in line positions or in SWAT units affects police culture or tactical perspectives has not yet been studied (Crank, Kadleck, and Koski 2010: 408).

The Consequences of Militarization

Kiker (2015) has argued that the move toward militarizing police began in the 1960s in Los Angeles when then-police chief Darryl Gates, faced with riots and looting in the Watts district of the city, decided that traditional police tactics were inadequate to deal with the situation and created a tactical unit—the first Special Weapons and Tactics (SWAT) team. With assistance from a nearby U.S. Marine Corps unit, Gates deployed the SWAT unit for the first time against the headquarters of the Black Panthers. By 2007, about 80% of U.S. towns with a population of between 25,000 and 50,000 persons had an operational SWAT team (p. 288). In Maryland, a report was released, revealing that Maryland deployed a SWAT team an average of 4.5 times every day in 2014 and that more than 93% of those deployments were for the purpose of executing a search warrant, and about 60% were for nonviolent crimes (p. 288).

The deployment of SWAT teams has become a pervasive policing tactic. The following examples show how SWAT tactics have been employed inappropriately or recklessly, resulting in very adverse outcomes. Kiker (2015) argues that the existence of SWAT teams increasingly shapes aspects of policing that previously were conducted without militarized police units.

- In 2014, the U.S. Eleventh Circuit ruled in *Berry v. Leslie* that using SWAT tactics to conduct a regulatory raid on Orlando, Florida, barbershops was a violation of the Fourth Amendment.
- In St. Louis County, Missouri, the location of the town of Ferguson, police have determined that they will use SWAT teams to serve all felony warrants.
- In 2012, a police chief in Arkansas announced that he would bring in a policy that SWAT officers would patrol the streets of the small town he

policed and stop all pedestrians, requiring identification and an explanation of why they were walking the streets (pp. 289–290).

- In Detroit, a 7-year-old girl was shot in the head and killed by a SWAT team member who entered her home in search of a suspect who lived in another unit of the duplex owned by the girl's family. The team had been warned before the raid that there were children in the home (p. 290).
- In Cornelia, Georgia, a SWAT team that executed a no-knock warrant on a suspected drug dealer threw a flashbang grenade prior to entering his house. It landed in the crib of a small child, who was severely burned (p. 291).
- Today, police militarization has reached university police departments and schools: At least two university law enforcement units have obtained grenade launchers from federal sources, and the Ohio State University police unit has a mine-resistant ambush protected (MRAP) vehicle (specifically designed to withstand explosives attacks) to provide "presence" on football game days (ACLU 2014: 22).

Even while violent crime continues to decrease, the expansion of the tactical use of SWAT teams continues. Hill and Beger claim that militarization subverts democratic policing and encourages the perspective that inner cities are war zones with the urban underclass constituting the enemy (2009: 32). Thus, individual rights are in danger of being disregarded when the traditional police role of "protect and serve" is reconfigured to "overwhelm and defeat" (Campbell and Campbell 2010: 329). The degree to which this claimed erosion of rights is occurring is not explained by these scholars, but it is clear that even with an expanded jurisdiction SWAT units are not dominating policing, nor are they likely to do so. Any

claims that this is occurring would need to be supported by empirical research. As to the public reaction to SWAT units, Jefferis (2012: 71) argues that the public accepts their law enforcement officers behaving as and resembling soldiers because the rhetoric of fear associated with violent crime and terrorism warns that the "enemy" is always close by.

Some police agencies have, however, opted out of the drive to militarize. Police commanders have questioned the effectiveness of SWAT activities, such as patrolling in full tactical gear, noting that communities find these shows of force intimidating and offensive (Campbell and Campbell 2010: 335). Nevertheless, most departments have retained their equipment, and some scholars believe that as long as the wars on drugs and terror persist the militarization of policing will continue, promoted by the "drug-terror complex" (Hall and Coyne 2013: 500). It is not clear if this means policing operations will increasingly be handed over to SWAT units or whether the changes in policing said to have already taken place will be enhanced or even accelerated.

Critiques of the Militarization Thesis

Kraska (2007c) argues that SWAT teams engender fear and outrage within communities, but he has been criticized for the lack of evidence to support this assertion (Waddington 1999: 129). Waddington asserts that SWAT teams could not have expanded beyond the original Los Angeles model without political support and that the general public has at best remained apathetic about their expansion and the tactics they employ. He therefore disputes the notion that such units inspire public

A Closer Look

Military Equipment Transfers to Law Enforcement: The Federal 1033 Program and Homeland Security Grants

This federal program, begun in 1997 and administered by the Department of Defense (DOD), permitted the transfer of surplus military equipment to police departments at no cost. The initial purpose was to use the equipment in counterdrug activities, but this was later broadened to also assist in the global war against terrorism by securing the "homeland" against possible terrorist attacks (ACLU 2014: 16). Between 1995 and 1997 alone, the DOD gifted 1.2 million items of military hardware to police agencies, including M16 rifles, grenade launchers, and armored personnel carriers (Hill and Beger 2009: 30). The DOD-supported transfer program claimed that the considerable financial investment in various weapons was justified because these items possessed a "dual-use status" (Campbell and Campbell 2010: 335). The 1033 program required that agencies taking delivery of equipment put it to use within 1 year of receipt, thereby incentivizing agencies to deploy military equipment in law enforcement (ACLU 2014: 16). Of the equipment transferred under the program, 36% was brand new, and it was therefore possible for the DOD to purchase equipment and simply transfer it on to law enforcement agencies free of charge (ACLU 2014: 24).

The Associated Press (AP) reported on November 24, 2013, that the equipment transfers included 18-ton, armor-protected, military fighting vehicles called MRAPs with bulletproof glass and gun turrets that were used in Iraq to counter roadside bombs. At least 600 MRAPs have been given away (Peak 2015: 201). As one county sheriff in Albany, New York, stated, "It's armored. It's heavy. It's intimidating. And it's free." An AP investigation revealed that of the $4.2 billion worth of equipment distributed since 1990, a disproportionate share had been delivered to rural police and sheriffs with small police forces and little crime. The equipment transfers are justified on the basis that they are necessary in conducting the wars on drugs and terror and to generally enhance homeland security (p. 200). The equipment has been described by critics of these transfers as "representing symbolic statements of war" (p. 206).

Following the events of 9/11 and the formation of the vast Department of Homeland Security (DHS) with a 2013 budget of over $60 billion, the DHS began from 2003 to provide grants to law enforcement that could be used to acquire military equipment under the Homeland Security Grant Program, which states its objectives as including preventing future terrorist attacks. Significantly, the grant program does not authorize grants to be spent to "supplant inherent routine patrols and law enforcement operations or activities not directly related to providing enhanced coordination between local and Federal law enforcement services" (Peak 2015: 203).

There is now a network of private suppliers actively marketing weapons and tactical equipment to police agencies ensuring the persistence and growth of paramilitary units. As well, pressure and special interest groups comprising the "terror industry" made up of government agencies, technocrats, consultants, and private companies offer security and antiterrorist training and services and promote SWAT-type units as a means to counter the fear of terrorism (Hall and Coyne 2013: 489). In the war on drugs, police and prison officer unions lobbied for more funds, and police became increasingly dependent on federal funding for antidrug measures. The police wanted more stringent anti-drug laws, and the companies running private prisons saw the opportunity to expand their earnings by the increased incarceration of drug offenders (p. 496).

In an article in *The New York Times* of June 8, 2014, Matt Apuzzo describes the town of Neenah, Wisconsin, with a population of about 25,000, where police have taken delivery of a 30-ton armored truck. The town has not had a homicide in more than 5 years, but the police chief justified the truck on the basis that the "possibility of violence, however remote, required taking precautions." He is quoted as saying, "We're not going to go out there as Officer Friendly with no body armor and just a handgun and say 'Good enough.'" The police chief described a proactive police approach during a shooting or standoff; instead of setting up a perimeter and waiting out the suspect or negotiating, "police are trained to move in and save lives."

(Continued)

(Continued)

In another justification for armored vehicles, the Richland County Sheriff's Department in South Carolina has a website featuring its SWAT team flanking an armored vehicle resembling a tank with a mounted .50-caliber gun. The department spokesman said that the vehicle "allows the department to stay in step with the criminals who are arming themselves more heavily every day." Police take the truck to schools and community events where it is a "conversation starter." In the suburbs of Indianapolis, officers justified a mine-resistant vehicle to "protect against a possible attack by veterans returning from war."

At the same time that the president of the police federation was reported justifying the equipment to save the lives of hostages and ensure officer safety, the police chief of the town of Bloomingdale, Georgia, with a population of fewer than 2,800 persons, secured armored vehicles and grenade launchers through the 1033 program, even though he has not had to use deadly force against anyone in 20 years (Peak 2015: 202).

In 2014, President Obama ordered a review of the acquisition programs that dispatched military grade equipment to police forces, and in January 2015, he issued an executive order creating a working group that, among other tasks, was to examine the equipment issue (Kiker 2015: 295). On May 18, 2015, President Obama announced he would ban the transfer of some types of military-style equipment to police departments and restrict the availability of other equipment (Davis and Shear 2015).

On April 30, 2015, Montana passed legislation to ban the state from receiving categories of military equipment from the federal government under the 1033 program. The prohibition covers weaponized drones, combat aircraft, grenade launchers, silencers, and militarized armored vehicles (*Activist Post* 2015).

fear, drawing on international studies that show no correlation between public approval of the police and the weapons they carry and that have found police in armed jurisdictions to be no less popular than unarmed police.

The ACLU (2014: 23) points out that the Cary, North Carolina, SWAT team offers a training session called "Warrior Mindset/Chemical Munitions," but Waddington rejects the argument that SWAT teams constitute a "warrior culture" and are "warrior cops" who have adopted a military-style culture, enjoy action and combat, delight in possessing and using powerful weapons to fight crime, and maintain a strong *esprit de corps*. He contends that SWAT teams may well have their own culture, but it remains a police and not a warrior culture because SWAT team values are shared by most police (1999: 130). While Kraska argues that SWAT units see themselves as elite police involved in real crime fighting and in dangerous activities, it can be said that police culture (see earlier section on Police Culture) similarly perceives the policing mission as crime fighting. Therefore, there may be little

difference in role assumption between SWAT teams and patrolmen. Kraska (2007c) does not discuss the articulation between police culture and militarization.

Finally, Waddington points out that while the military is trained to use lethal force indiscriminately in order to defeat an enemy, police may only target specific individuals for good reasons, and while they have discretion to use force and violence, it is limited and circumscribed by rules and institutional practice (1999: 133). Therefore, he argues that it cannot be said that police have adopted a military culture or posture—their training and their missions are completely different. While it is true that SWAT units are heavily armed and protected by body armor, they must be discriminating in using their weapons compared to the military, who generally favor volume of fire as opposed to accuracy (p. 135). For example, if SWAT teams use flashbang grenades when entering a building, this contrasts with the military, whose practice is to throw a shrapnel grenade into a room and spray it with automatic fire. Nevertheless, while contending that Kraska overstates his case, Waddington agrees that "if the distinction between police and military disappears, then it threatens the very basis of democratic polity" (p. 137).

Den Heyer (2014: 347) reviews the militarization thesis, but like Waddington, he contends that police are not being militarized and that the establishment of SWAT type units is "a natural progression in the evolution and professionalization of one aspect of policing agencies." Den Heyer argues that contentions about the war on drugs, the war on terror, and the enticing culture of SWAT units "display a lack of understanding of policing, police institutions and of police officers" (p. 347). By this, he means that in his view, SWAT units both in the United States and in other countries were established in response to a specific incident or series of incidents or because police required a SWAT capability to respond to armed offenders. Thus, he denies the militarization thesis in favor of the proposition that police were merely responding to an actual or perceived need for specialist units. While agreeing there has been an increase in SWAT callouts, den Heyer argues that there is no data on the reasons for this increase or on the type of incident for which a unit was deployed. Conceding there has been a change in policing because SWAT units are now executing search warrants, especially in drug cases, den Heyer disagrees that this signifies the militarization of "mainstream policing." Instead, he argues it represents the "rational utilization of resources and the appropriate use of expensive and highly trained personnel" (p. 354). Relying on events in New Zealand when two officers were killed in making routine, drug-related inquiries, den Heyer suggests that the increased use of paramilitary units there relates to officer safety and notes that such units are subject to detailed regulation.

In the United States, officer safety appears to be the primary justification for the expansion in the deployment of SWAT units, but there are no studies that have analyzed the police rationale. Minimizing risk does, however, seem to be a central issue in the deployment of SWAT units. For example, Radley Balko describes how searching online police discussion boards often locates some version of the statement "Whatever I need to do to get home safe" (*The Wall Street Journal* July 19, 2013). Finally, den Heyer denies any convergence between police and the military and asserts that apart from some "cross-fertilization" in the adoption of policies and procedures there is a "clear vision" of the role separation (2014: 355).

Several levels of analysis can be applied to the issue of police militarization. One level situates the research and analysis of militarization within a wider discourse of increased state violence, fear of crime, and fear of terrorism. As Henry Giroux (2015) summarizes it,

> Militarism is one of the breeding grounds of violence in the United States and is visible in the ubiquitous gun culture, the modeling of schools after prisons, the exploding incarceration state, the paramilitarization of local police forces, the burgeoning military budget, and the ongoing attacks on protesters, dissidents, black and brown youth, and women. (para. 19)

Another level of analysis might regard SWAT teams as embodying one of the core elements of police culture—namely that the police are risk makers. As Manning puts it, "The police seek risks in high speed chases, arrests, raids and other interventions and act on behalf of society in taking on risks" (2007: 52).

POLICE CORRUPTION

Police corruption has been variously defined as the following:

- Accepting money or its equivalent for doing something that a public official is already required to do or not required to do or in consideration of exercising a discretion for improper reasons (McMullan in Kleinig 1996: 165)
- Accepting goods or services for performing or not performing duties that are part of one's employment. A gift becomes a gratuity according to the reason for which it is given, and it is the reason the gift is accepted that constitutes the corruption (Cohen and Feldberg in Kleinig 1996: 165)
- The misuse of authority by a police officer in a way intended to produce personal gain for the officer or others (Goldstein in Kleinig 1996: 165)
- Actions taken by a police officer that exploit police powers in exchange for considerations of "private-regarding benefit" (i.e., the range of awards acquired

by the officer and the officer's colleagues, family, and friends) that violate standards governing the officer's conduct (Johnston 1995: 287)

These definitions do not exhaust all forms of police misconduct. For example, improperly eliciting confessions and lying to secure a conviction are distinct forms of misconduct and is discussed in Chapter 3 (see Ethical Issues in Investigation, Interrogation, and Custody).

The Nature of Police Corruption

Kleinig (1996) offers the following definition of *corruption*: "Police officers act corruptly when, in exercising or failing to exercise their authority, they act with the primary intention of furthering private or departmental/divisional advantage" (p. 166). Kleinig admits that his definition covers many acts and practices that are never explicitly revealed as corrupt—for example, ignoring small jobs for the large, visible ones—but makes the point that such acts are not motivated by a spirit of corruption. The important point is that a police officer is motivated by a personal desire for gain, regardless of what acts he or she actually performs to secure that gain.

It may be helpful to characterize corruption in typologies because they explain, illustrate, and add specificity to the kinds of acts defined as corruption. The following represents a typography produced by Tom Barker (in Kleinig 1996: 168):

Kickbacks. These include goods, services, and money received for a multitude of services, such as referring business to various professionals (i.e., lawyers and bondsmen) with whom police regularly interact in their duties. Kickbacks have been condoned within police culture, as long as the rewards are modest and the businesses legitimate, the rationalization being that businesses providing kickbacks are simply demonstrating their enterprising nature.

Opportunistic Theft. This takes a number of forms, including stealing property from those arrested, those involved in traffic accidents, and other victims; stealing money or goods left behind by a burglar when investigating a burglary; removing items from unprotected property sites, such as building

materials; or stealing parts of confiscated evidence, such as drugs, drug money, or liquor.

Shakedowns. This is understood to include accepting payments for not making an arrest or issuing a summons that in the ordinary course of events would have been made or issued. Shakedowns may be protected by a police code of silence, but if revealed, they are usually strongly condemned by police supervisors.

Protection of Illegal Activities. There are many forms of protection that police may provide to those engaging in illegal enterprises so they may operate with the minimum of official harassment. Examples are payments to police by cab companies to park illegally and to operate cabs in breach of safety standards; payments by trucking firms to haul overloaded cargoes; and payments by construction companies to overlook violations of regulations. According to Julian Roebuck and Thomas Barker (1974: 430), some of these activities, where there are no complainants, are difficult to prosecute and have the effect of causing "resignation, ritualism, inaction, or corruption" in honest police officers. Kleinig (1996) proposes that selling confidential police information should also be included in this category.

The Traffic Fix. This involves taking money or other reward for disposing of traffic citations.

The Misdemeanor Fix. Here, a police officer quashes proceedings for a misdemeanor by, for example, not proceeding with a prosecution, tampering with evidence, or perjuring himself or herself in proceedings.

The Felony Fix. This is the same as the misdemeanor fix, except that felonies are involved.

Direct Criminal Activities. These occur when officers commit criminal acts for personal gain as if they were themselves criminals.

Internal Payoffs. There are various forms of internal corruption where police officers may buy, barter, or sell aspects of their employment, such as off days, holidays, and promotions. Officers who administer assignments may receive rewards for assigning officers to particular divisions or for providing transfers to or from specific or preferred assignments.

Corruption of Authority. This involves authorized and unearned benefits officers are given by virtue of their employment as police officers. Included are free meals, liquor, sex, entertainment, discounts on purchases, payments for property protection extending beyond normal police duties, secret payments by property owners to arrest robbers and burglars at their places of business, and payments by bondsmen to police for the arrest and notification of those who jumped bail where the bondsmen are acting as bounty hunters. It is common practice for restaurants to offer police free or half-price meals or free coffee. This raises the issue of the expectations of those businesses in giving these benefits. In one survey of 116 people in Reno, Nevada, about half reported that if they were to run a small business like a coffee shop or movie theater, they would offer police free coffee, meals, or movie tickets (Ivkovic 2005a: 39). Significantly, one third of those who would make such offers explicitly reported that they would expect special favors in exchange. An example of this kind is shown in the "No More Free Meals" Closer Look box.

Accepting Gratuities

Accepting gratuities such as free meals and coffee, free lunches, half-price dinners, and gifts from merchants during holiday seasons is a vexed and much discussed issue within policing. In 1988, Richard Kania (in Coleman 2004: 37; also see Kania 2004) argued that under certain circumstances, police ought to be encouraged to accept gratuities because most people offering them do not have the intention of corrupting police but are expressing a debt to police for their services, which they are attempting to repay through the offer of gratuities. Kania, a former police officer from Louisiana, suggested an analogy with tipping, where the recipient is being tipped for services rendered and where no future obligations are being created by the transaction. He argued that only in situations where the provider of the gratuity was seeking to establish

credit for future use were such transactions problematic and that if police did not vary the way in which they carried out their duty as a result of receiving gratuities, then receiving them was ethically appropriate.

Responding to Kania's arguments, Stephen Coleman (2004: 38) argues that police should refuse gratuities that could in the public mind be regarded as influencing their judgment in the conduct of their duties. He argues that the practice cannot be regarded as analogous to tipping because those who commonly receive tips come to expect them and perhaps even make a demand for them. Also, he argues that there may be a future orientation toward tipping, and he suggests that giving a generous tip may give rise to an expectation of above-average service in the future. Another objection is that police regard themselves as professionals, and most professionals do not receive tips. Further, accepting gratuities may well have an effect on how police conduct themselves, even if they fail to appreciate that fact. For example, if the police patronize establishments that offer gratuities, and this causes them to visit and spend time there more often to the detriment of other establishments, the result affects the distribution of police services in the community.

Jim Ruiz and Christine Bono (2004) also take issue with Kania, arguing that accepting gratuities is a harmful practice that should be actively discouraged. The authors are unable to accept that a police officer's acceptance of daily gratuities (amounting to thousands of dollars each year) will not give rise to expectations on the givers' part (p. 46). One of the authors, a former police officer, recounts that merchants who gave gratuities "were quick to remind him of their generosity when stopped for a traffic violation . . . at the very least they expected to be given special consideration when calling for service" (p. 46). Ruiz and Bono contend that the annual value of regular gratuities in the form of coffee, donuts, lunch, cigarettes, alcohol, laundry, and free movie tickets could be between $8,000 and $10,000 each year, and with an average national police gross salary of around $35,000, these gratuities comprise an increase in gross salary of more than 33% (pp. 50–51).

Michael Feldberg links gratuities with distributive justice, arguing that the effect of a gratuity is to induce a police officer to "distribute the benefit of his presence disproportionately to some taxpayers and not to others, a practice that undermines the democratic ethos of public service" (in del Pozo 2005: 28). Thus, if police eat lunch daily at one restaurant that offers a free or half-price lunch, they are providing their presence and therefore police protection and security to one restaurant during that period. In this view, their presence skews the distribution of police service in favor of a particular restaurant. One solution to this argument about distributive justice is to follow the approach tried in England in the 1970s where all police officers were required to eat their meals in a canteen located inside the police headquarters. However, Brandon del Pozo argues that this would "also have the effect of cutting off one's nose to spite one's face: were officers forced to take meals at the stationhouse, no location would benefit from their presence" (p. 33).

What policy should police departments follow concerning the issue of accepting gratuities? Many departments strictly prohibit their acceptance, but because police officers are often out of direct supervision, enforcing such a policy is very problematic. As well, those giving the gratuities have no incentive to report officers for violating their departmental policy (Withrow and Dailey 2004: 174). Some departments attempt to regulate gratuities by imposing a policy that limits the amount of gratuity on the basis that the value of the gratuity is related to the level of corruption (p. 175). Arguably the most important factor in the acceptance of gratuities is the rationale for offering the gratuity. Thus, a policy that merely seeks to limit the extent of the gratuity appears unrelated to the real likelihood of corruption.

An example of how those who give gratuities to police do so with an expectation of police assistance is given by Brian Withrow and Jeffrey Dailey, as shown in the "No More Free Meals" Closer Look box.

Explanations for Police Corruption

What justifications or explanations do police and others offer to explain the existence of police corruption? How can we explain or understand why police corruption occurs? This is an important issue because an analysis of the explanations for police corruption can contribute to possible solutions. Johnston (1995: 285) argues that explanations for police corruption may be *personalistic, institutional,* or *systemic*. Other scholars have identified a "slippery slope" that leads to corruption. "Noble cause" corruption is analogous to the slippery slope

A Closer Look

No More Free Meals

Withrow, while a headquarters staff officer in a state police agency, was conducting a routine inspection tour and was invited to lunch by local troopers. In the restaurant when the bills came, the troopers argued with the waitress about the full price stated on the bills. They were regulars at the restaurant, but the waitress told them that restaurant policy had changed, and now everyone had to pay the full price. One of the troopers responded very loudly, "We never pay full price, and we are not going to start now." In order to diffuse the situation, Withrow told the troopers to pay the full price plus a tip, and Withrow apologized to the waitress. He later discovered that the restaurant owner's son had recently been arrested for driving while intoxicated (DWI).

SOURCE: Withrow and Dailey 2004: 165.

A Closer Look

Detectives Receive Sex Services in Antiprostitution Campaign

Undercover police detectives from Spotsylvania County in northern Virginia involved in "rooting out prostitution" in the massage parlor business received sexual services from "masseuses." According to court papers, "Detectives allowed women to perform sexual acts on them on four occasions and once left a $350 tip."

The sheriff argued that this practice was "not new, and only unmarried detectives are assigned to such cases." The sheriff went on to defend his detectives. "Most prostitutes are careful not to say anything incriminating, so sexual contact is necessary. If I thought we could get a conviction without that, we wouldn't allow it. If you want to make them, this has to be done."

However, numerous police and experts told the reporter that they had no knowledge of any law enforcement agency in the Washington, D.C., area or in the nation that permitted sexual contact in prostitution investigations. As they put it, "Police should not break the law to enforce it."

It is normal practice for a verbal agreement to provide services plus an explicit act such as undressing or producing a condom to be considered sufficient evidence in charges of soliciting prostitution.

SOURCE: Jackman 2006.

and involves police justifying corruption or "bending the rules" as legitimate acts in the service of the noble cause of policing. These explanations are discussed in the sections that follow.

Whatever may be the explanation, one implication of corruption is that corrupters gain influence over the police, subverting police from their proper role and creating conditions that favor crime in the sense that there is an increase in public tolerance for some crimes. In the inner cities, corruption may permit crime to flourish. Most importantly, corruption undermines public trust in the police force and diminishes credibility in the integrity of individual police officers.

Personalistic Explanations

Three explanations emphasize the individual police officer as the ultimate cause of corruption: the *rotten apple,* the *recruitment perspective,* and the *police personality* explanation.

In the *rotten apple* explanation, corruption is described by police chiefs and others as merely the acts of a few rotten apples in an otherwise honest department. The aim of this explanation is to divert attention away from the possibility that corruption might be systemic. This argument may also function as an excuse for not instituting investigations that might uncover other corruption, as a way to limit investigations, or as a means to protect individuals. It implies that recruiting persons of the right character will eliminate corruption. Barker (1996: 39) asserts that police use the term *rotten apple* because they wish the public to believe that a publicly identified corrupt or racist cop is an aberration and not a departmental problem. He regards the labeling of individual police as rotten apples to be a management technique used to explain away corrupt behavior.

In the United Kingdom, investigations of corruption have revealed how close links between police and their criminal informants can result in passing

A Closer Look

Police Corruption in Australia

There have been two major investigations of police corruption in Australia: the Royal Commission into the New South Wales Police Service (1997) and the Fitzgerald Commission in Queensland (1989). Their findings of corruption in these two states are described as follows:

Royal Commission Into the New South Wales Police Service (1997) New South Wales, Australia	Fitzgerald Commission (1989) Queensland, Australia
A state of systemic and entrenched corruption, well organized	Corruption by prostitutes, gambling, drug dealers
A very serious state of corruption that is widespread and of long-standing origin	Thefts
Types: thefts of drugs and money; shake-downs of drug dealers; regular payments from drug dealers, gambling operations, clubs, and brothels; assaults	
"Process corruption" (noble cause corruption)	
Supervisors unaware or unwilling to respond	

SOURCE: Ivkovic 2005a: 52–53.

A Closer Look

The Rotten Apple

Local criminals regularly visit a gym that is also used by a police officer. The officer becomes friendly with some of the criminals and begins to socialize with them. As their relationship develops, they ask him to provide information from the police national computer and from the police intelligence system. In return for some favors, such as free meals or drinks, he passes this information on to them, and it is used by the criminals to build up a picture of the activities of the police.

SOURCE: Miller 2003: 10.

information that can be used for criminal activities. The "Corrupt Arrangements" Closer Look box shows an example of this kind of individual corruption.

In the *recruitment perspective,* it is argued that personal traits shared by officers recruited from similar social backgrounds make them particularly susceptible to corruption. It is true that in the early days of policing, officers tended to be recruited from certain groups. However, over the last decade, police forces have become more heterogeneous, and now it is common to see women, African Americans, Hispanics, and others in police departments. The argument is that whites with working-class, lower-status backgrounds and a lack of advanced education might harbor certain attitudes and values that could make them susceptible to corruption.

The *police personality* argument is analogous to one that asserts that the institutional police culture is responsible for creating an environment that encourages or fails to discourage police corruption. It contends that certain traits make up the police personality, including suspicion, authoritarianism, and loyalty. Caldero (in Crank and Caldero 2000: 58–60), in a 1997 survey of the values of police officers found that over the past 25 years, police values had remained constant, that these values are imported from particular groups in society, and that education has had little effect on these values. This contention concerning the influence of police values or police personality suggests that corruption therefore is linked to personality and values.

Institutional Explanations

The wide discretionary powers that police officers enjoy, as well as the difficulties in supervising that discretion, are aspects of policing as an institution, and it is argued that police discretion makes corruption more likely to occur. Police discretion can be used for illegitimate purposes, and while its existence does not make corruption inevitable, it does give a police officer scope to hide unethical decisions. The problems inherent in the task of supervising officers who have wide discretionary powers mean that corruption can be allowed to go unchecked and unrevealed. For example, in New York City in 1970 the Knapp Commission found that over half of all plainclothes officers in the New York Police Department

(NYPD) were engaged in profit-motivated corruption (Kane and White 2013: xv). The pattern of police corruption included plainclothes officers collecting regular payments from each gambling establishment within their operational area, with each officer receiving a monthly payment of $300 to $400 in midtown Manhattan, rising to $1,500 in Harlem. Supervisors involved received a share and a half. Investigation units within NYPD commonly conducted "shakedowns" of targets, and the largest narcotics payoff found by the commission was $80,000 (p. 45).

The commission divided corrupt police into two groups: "Meat Eaters" and "Grass Eaters." The former actively solicited opportunities for corrupt activities, and the latter comprised officers who accepted money for not reporting corruption but did not actually participate in the corruption themselves (Kane and White 2013: xvi). The NYPD has experienced cycles of corruption, with anticorruption commissions being established every 20 years since the mid-1800s (p. 19).[3]

Two factors that may bear on corruption from the institutional viewpoint are the *low public visibility* of police and the issue of *secrecy* within the institution. The public has little knowledge or sense of what police officers do, and much police activity is shielded from the public. This low visibility can provide opportunities for corruption. In terms of secrecy, it is argued that the person most likely to observe corruption firsthand is another police officer. Frequently, however, he or she will not reveal the corruption to anyone due to fear of retaliation, bonds of friendship, loyalty, or an institutional ideology that sets police against the public in an isolationist approach. It follows that information about corruption may be difficult to collect, and officers may refuse to testify against their colleagues. This so-called *wall of silence* is also found in other nations, as well as among U.S. police forces. For example, in the Netherlands, a survey conducted to ascertain the views of police on the seriousness of ethics violations and on their willingness to report

---

3   The NYPD is the largest police force in the United States. Its police composition has been as high as 41,000, with the addition of 14,500 civilian employees. This is more than three times the size of the Chicago Police Department, the second-largest U.S. police force (Kane and White 2013: 39).

such violations (either self-reporting or reporting others)—that is, to break the wall of silence—found that receiving free meals and discounts was seen as serious or very serious (Huberts, Lamboo, and Punch 2003: 226). Comparing these results to a similar survey in the United States, the researchers found that police in the Netherlands were significantly more ready to report receipt of such benefits than were U.S. police officers. A similar survey undertaken in Finland and Croatia revealed that while Croatian police regarded free meals and discounts as more serious than accepting occasional gifts, police in Finland took the opposite view, regarding receiving free merchandise as a serious wrongdoing (Ivkovic 2005b: 557). A similar survey conducted in the United Kingdom revealed that most officers surveyed believed that accepting free meals and gifts was contrary to police policy, but only 14% thought it was very serious behavior, and 11% considered it not serious at all (Westmarland 2005: 149). Similarly, accepting gifts during holiday periods such as Christmas was not regarded as very serious, but nevertheless, 36% of respondents said they knew that it was contrary to police policy (p. 149).

The wall of silence extends to civilians employed by police—in fact, a study in England found that police civilian staff were actually less likely to report misconduct by police than were police themselves. The traditional explanation for this is the shared group loyalty and solidarity between staff and officers (Wright 2010: 353); Kleinig (2000), in his ethical analysis of the code of silence, identifies this code as similar to the norms found in ideals of friendship and family. As Skolnick (2010: 37) points out, the code of silence can also operate to protect police who commit crimes and not simply acts of misconduct. Major investigations into police misconduct in the form of the Knapp (1972) and Mollen (1994) Commissions in New York and the Christopher Commission in Los Angeles (1991) have all highlighted the existence of the code of silence as an obstruction to investigations of corruption or excessive use of force. Outside the United States, the same was found to be true in Australia in the Fitzgerald inquiry in Queensland (1989) and the Wood Royal Commission in New South Wales (1997).

A final factor is *managerial secrecy,* suggesting that those in supervisory positions who were formerly patrol officers and who have risen through the ranks share police values and culture, including those values that ensure that corruption is hidden. This kind of secrecy extends to feelings of resentment about what is perceived to be interference by outsiders in police processes, including formal inquiries like the Knapp Commission's investigation into corruption. In essence, managerial secrecy will be strengthened by the values fostered by police culture.

Systemic Explanations

This type of explanation looks at pressures placed on the police by society that might provoke police corruption and suggests that police corruption is rooted within the police interaction with society, rather than within the individual police officer. For example, legislation dealing with social behavior such as alcohol consumption, gambling, and prostitution is often regarded by the public as an attempt to impose moral standards and is therefore often resisted. Thus, underage persons purchase alcohol, and citizens gamble and engage in prostitution. This ambivalence in society about personal morality tends to encourage police reluctance to enforce the law and can ultimately result in those engaged in crimes of vice offering bribes and incentives to police to look the other way. From the police point of view, violations of vice laws often constitute victimless crimes, providing further encouragement toward corruption.

In developing countries, low police salaries operate as a contributing factor to police corruption. For example, in Bosnia during the postwar period, police received low salaries and were not paid consistently, rendering them vulnerable to corruption (Ivkovic and Shelley 2005: 444). Examples of police corruption in Bosnia include taking bribes and looking the other way when cars are stolen and later handed back to their owners by the thieves in exchange for a kickback to the police officers concerned (p. 445). In Ghana, forms of police corruption include police deciding not to arrest, investigate, or prosecute offenders because they have family or friendship ties to police; accepting bribes from suspects for overlooking offenses or not making an arrest or making a weak presentation of a case in court; and erecting roadblocks to collect bribes from drivers who violate traffic laws (Tankebe 2010: 302). Noting that in a nationwide survey published in 2000 of 1,500 households in Ghana, more than two thirds of the respondents reported that they had paid bribes to police officers, Justice Tankebe suggests that in Ghana police corruption is systemic.

"Slippery Slope" Explanation

An important explanation for police corruption is termed the *slippery slope*. This notion was developed by Sherman (1985) and suggests that taking rewards and money begins on a small scale and is tacitly acknowledged by other police officers. Sherman suggests that officers who become accustomed to taking small rewards will eventually develop connections to other officers involved in corruption on a grander scale. In other words, officers become desensitized to the moral implications of their acts, and the acts themselves become addictive.

According to Sherman (1985), police officers find themselves on this slope as the result of social considerations that bind police together and because of the way in which police perceive their own behavior. He argues that young recruits learn early on that, as police officers, they are bound to one social group and are alienated from others. The pressures of the social group and the acceptance of minor perks alter the self-image of the young recruits to make them vulnerable to more substantial corruption. Sherman also suggests that the slide down the slippery slope is eased by the relatively small moral gap along the continuum of graft stages.

Sherman's solution to this problem is to decriminalize those activities that most easily tempt police into graft, and his solution finds anecdotal support from those corrupt police officers who have described their lapse into corruption. However, Feldberg (1985) disagrees, claiming that police officers can make a distinction between accepting minor perks and bribes intended to affect the performance of their duties. Fundamentally, the dispute between Feldberg and Sherman rests on a moral basis in that Sherman believes that to accept a free cup of coffee constitutes a moral compromise, whereas Feldberg does not. Kleinig (1996) offers the opinion that people commonly offer each other cups of coffee as a gesture, not with the intention of creating any obligation, and that police supervisors who see the acceptance of such small rewards as morally compromising are likely to be seen as over-reacting and risk losing the respect of their rank-and-file officers.

Noble Cause Corruption

Crank and Caldero (2000: 74) offer an alternative slippery slope model, describing a process of *noble cause corruption* rather than simply economic corruption. This slope begins with encouragement to accept free meals, not to test the willingness to accept graft but to establish whether an officer's loyalty to others in the squad can be relied on. This is followed by loyalty backup, where the officer is tested for his or her own willingness to back up other officers, which may involve giving false testimony or taking part in the shakedown of a suspect. The next stage is using physical violence against citizens, involving greater risks to the officer in terms of detection, risk of injury, or retaliation. Finally, "flaking" drugs is described as a much more serious form of noble cause corruption, in which police plant drugs to enhance the seriousness of the crime. In this model, therefore, police are able to justify their progress down the slippery slope by employing the justification of noble cause.

> [The noble cause] is a profound moral commitment to make the world a safer place to live. Put simply, it is getting bad guys off the street. Police believe that they're on the side of angels and their purpose in life is getting rid of bad guys ... it's something to which they are morally committed ... the noble cause is practical and immediate. It's about an officer's conduct in day to day police work. It motivates an officer's behavior with citizens and mobilizes a great deal of police solidarity. (p. 35)

In England, in a case involving alleged Irish Republican Army (IRA) terrorist suspects, it seems that the English police justified their actions in the noble cause of jailing IRA terrorists (Punch 2003: 185–189). Six suspects were imprisoned for up to 16 years on the basis of false confessions and doubtful evidence before they were released because of this police wrongdoing. In the early 1970s, the IRA commenced a bombing campaign in Britain, and in 1973 in Birmingham, two explosions occurred in pubs, resulting in 21 deaths. This caused a national outrage, putting pressure on the police to secure convictions. A number of the suspects arrested were assaulted by police, intimidated with threats of violence, and assaulted by fellow prisoners while on remand. Doubts arose about the convictions, which were upheld by the court of appeal in 1977. Ultimately, another group of alleged terrorists was arrested and admitted to the bombings for which the Birmingham Six were jailed. It emerged that the confessions were fabricated by the investigating officers, important evidence was withheld from the courts, and forensic evidence turned out to be highly questionable. According to Maurice Punch, the concept of noble cause corruption applied to this case, and the police involved believed that the ends justified the means, having already satisfied themselves about the prisoners' guilt (p. 187).

Crank and Caldero (2000) argue that the idea of the noble cause represents a value imported into police work from broader American life. In this sense, the police are no different than others, and they reflect a particular cultural value, incorporating a concern for victims and the notion that no one should stand above the law. Other commentators (Delattre 1989; Klockars 1980; Muir 1977) have recognized the existence of noble cause thinking in police work. In addition, Skolnick and Fyfe (1993: 89), in their discussion of police culture, argue that aspects of that culture, such as the police notion of suspicious persons, the Dirty Harry problem (see Chapter 3), the siege mentality (the idea that police emphasize crime control over all police work, this being the police concept of professionalism—a notion that tends to isolate the police from the community), and the code of silence within police departments, together with the police perception of themselves as soldiers engaged in a war on crime, shapes the worldview of the individual police officer on the street. This leads to the conclusion, for example, that "police brutality is inevitable" (p. 133). It is easy to see that such a worldview can be employed in justifying misconduct in pursuit of the noble cause.

Crank and Caldero (2000: 75) emphasize that when applying the justification of noble cause to corruption, police place personal morality above the law and act as if they are the law. In such an ethical environment, any efforts to control police behavior will be viewed as disloyal because, in their view, if

police are the law, what they do must be right. Consequently, accepting free dinners to look after a restaurant is considered acceptable practice because "society owes it to them," and mistreating suspects means suspects are "getting what they deserve" because police have already decided they are guilty. In contrast to the rotten apple explanation for corruption, when corruption is justified on grounds of noble cause, officers who carry out acts of misconduct themselves are not considered rotten apples, but are perceived to be dealing with crime efficiently and effectively. During the O. J. Simpson murder trial, the noble cause explanation came to light when it was revealed that Mark Fuhrman had once stated,

[If] you find a [needle] mark [on a drug suspect] that looks like three days old, pick the scab. Squeeze it. Looks like serum's coming out, as if it were hours old . . . that's not falsifying a report. That's putting a criminal in jail. That's being a policeman. (Dershowitz 1996: 55)

Societal Stress as an Explanation for Corruption

Another, more sympathetic explanation for police corruption is offered by Johnston (1995: 301), who suggests that corruption is produced by the pressures society has imposed on police. Citizens place the police in a position of tension, where they are expected to enforce the law but also to obey regulations about how they may obtain information and gather evidence. They are also expected to enforce personal morality while respecting constitutional rights to privacy and due process. Johnston argues that as long as we continue to place these pressures on police, we are fated to endure a certain degree of police corruption and that we should move on to consider the sorts of social behavior we have no choice but to accept and consider questions such as how much police corruption we can tolerate. In essence, therefore, this argument sanctions a level of police corruption and leaves open the question of the extent to that level.

Drugs and Corruption

Seamus Miller, John Blackler, and Andrew Alexandra (1997: 105–106) single out illegal drugs as a major contributing factor to police corruption, arguing that police operate in an environment where there is a widespread use of illegal drugs and a vast amount of drug money. They describe the circumstances of enforcing antidrug laws as follows:

- There exists a large amount of money and a willingness on the part of drug users and dealers to bribe police.
- There are no complainants because the "victims" are not likely to report that they have been the victim of a criminal act.
- In light of this victimless crime, bribes can be accepted and drugs or drug money stolen with relative impunity.
- Sections of the public see drug addiction as a medical condition rather than as a crime and therefore see corruption as less morally damning.
- Younger police officers may well share the attitudes of their peers who are not police officers and regard the use and sale of illegal drugs as a minor matter.
- Police officers working in drug investigations may, out of fear, turn a blind eye to drugs or even take drugs themselves, entering a spiral of corruption, moving from moral compromise to covert corrupt activities.

The contention that there is a relationship between drug dealing and police corruption finds support in a 1998 government report that cites examples of drug-related police corruption in a number of cities and reports that one half of all police officers convicted following FBI-led investigations into corruption cases between 1993 and 1997 were convicted for drug-related offenses. Particular forms of drug-related corruption identified in the report include stealing money or drugs from drug dealers, selling stolen drugs, and protecting drug operations (Government Accounting Office 1998). In New York City, the Mollen Commission (1990–1993) found that the most salient forms of police corruption included "groups of officers protecting and assisting drug traffickers for often sizeable profits—stealing drugs, guns and money—and often selling the stolen drugs and guns to or through criminal associates" (quoted in Kane and White 2013: 56).

The impact of such corruption can be seen in the "Officer Admits Planting Drugs" and "Officer Involved in Robbery Ring" Closer Look boxes.

A Closer Look

Officer Admits Planting Drugs

A former New Jersey police officer, Kevin Parry, admitted to planting drugs on suspects, conducting illegal searches, stealing the proceeds of drug sales, and threatening suspects who would not cooperate with him. As a result of Parry's actions, 185 drug cases have been dropped or convictions vacated because of the probability of tainted evidence.

SOURCE: Associated Press 2010.

A Closer Look

Officer Involved in Robbery Ring

Officer Emmanuel Tavarez, 30, was arrested on May 6, 2010, and charged with conspiracy to commit robbery, conspiracy to distribute drugs, and use of firearms in a crime. He pleaded not guilty.

(Continued)

(Continued)

According to the prosecution documents, on at least two occasions Tavarez provided his own police-issued firearm for use in a robbery, and he was also used as a lookout by the robbery crew. During one robbery, it was said he entered the house with other robbers, telling the occupants it was a police raid.

After a sting operation in March 2008, investigators found both real and fake law enforcement equipment, including a vehicle modified to look like a police patrol car. A 2-year federal investigation discovered that a robbery crew was posing as police officers and had been robbing drugs dealers since 2002. The crew included four of the officer's in-laws and is thought to have stolen more than $1 million in drug proceeds and a large quantity of cocaine over a period of more than 100 robberies.

On April 6, 2011, Tavarez pleaded guilty to three charges. His lawyer described the evidence against him as "overwhelming."

In a strikingly similar case, a former police officer, Jorge Arbaje-Diaz, pleaded guilty on May 13, 2010, to taking part in robberies of drug dealers set up to resemble police raids. There was no evidence suggesting a connection between the two cases or the two accused.

Arbaje-Diaz told the court that he frequently robbed drug dealers in Manhattan, Brooklyn, Queens, and the Bronx and later sold the drugs he seized. He admitted to sometimes committing the robberies while wearing his police uniform and badge, and sometimes he would show his off-duty revolver and use his NYPD handcuffs to restrain victims of his crimes.

SOURCE: Sulzberger 2010.

In the United Kingdom, a notorious example of the linkage between police corruption and drug dealing occurred in the early 1990s; it highlights the temptations of drug dealing as a source of corrupt benefits for police, as well as the dangers of consorting with informants without following police policies and procedures (see the "Corrupt Arrangements" Closer Look box).

A Closer Look

Corrupt Arrangements Within the Southeast Regional Crime Squad, South London, England

Members of a particular team within the Southeast Regional Crime Squad, who called themselves The Groovy Gang, engaged in corrupt activities that were organized around Detective Constable Bob Clark. Clark maintained a close relationship with Evelyn Fleckney, an informant who regularly socialized with the police team. She not only joined the team for evening social occasions but was romantically connected with Clark and took several holidays with him. Senior police officers failed to properly enforce policies regulating contacts between police and informants like Fleckney.

Fleckney was a drug dealer, and in return for police protection from investigation and prosecution, she passed on information about rival drug dealers to the team, who would then be able to claim successes in arresting and prosecuting Fleckney's drug-dealing competitors. Also, drugs seized in searches could be recycled back onto the streets by Fleckney, and team members stole cash discovered during drug raids.

SOURCE: Miller 2003: 12.

Combating Corruption

Some (e.g., Miller et al. 1997) suggest that corruption can be reduced through examining four basic aspects of policing–namely, recruitment, reducing the opportunities for corruption, detecting and deterring corruption, and reinforcing the motivation to act morally. With *recruitment,* it is clearly essential that only those with the highest moral character be recruited into policing (Delattre 1989), as well as those capable of becoming competent police officers because the incompetent might easily become disaffected and open to corruption. *Reducing opportunities for corruption,* for example, by regularly rotating officers employed in drug squads, may be effective, but the very nature of police work, especially the wide discretion given to police at the street level, makes opportunity reduction a daunting task. Ultimately, legislative and other policies that promote decriminalization will reduce opportunities for corruption. *Detection and deterrence* are achieved through accountability, internal and external, and through tools such as investigation, auditing, surveillance, and the use of informants.

Police Corruption in the United Kingdom

In the United Kingdom, a number of police forces have recently established professional standards units whose task is to "proactively cultivate and analyse information or 'intelligence' on unethical police activity from a range of sources, and mount formal investigations" (Miller 2003: 2). These units are divided into an intelligence cell and a number of operational teams, with the intelligence cell staffed by analysts tasked to manage a central database of information relevant to anticorruption efforts. The operational teams then conduct formal investigations into individuals. Examples of corrupt activities in the English police forces have included accepting protection money from criminals, stealing and recycling drugs to criminals, stealing cash from crime scenes, and fabricating evidence to secure convictions (p. 6). Contemporary corruption was found in scale to be smaller than that revealed by, for example, the Knapp Commission in 1972 and the Mollen Commission in 1994 in the United States or the Fitzgerald Commission in 1987 in Australia. According to the report, the level of staff identified as potentially corrupt amounted to between 0.5% and 1% of police staff, including both police and civilian staff (p. 6). The report suggests that corruption is for the most part committed by individuals, and the passing of sensitive information from police sources to those outside the force, including criminal informers, is a significant form of corruption in the United Kingdom (p. 10). Corruption was also found to arise from interactions between police and criminals in social networks outside of work involving, for example, friends or relatives of police staff or persons using the same gyms as police staff or the same pubs and clubs. Officers in the professional standards units believed that criminals involved in organized crime targeted police with the aim of gaining information to assist with their criminal activities (p. 21).

Reducing Corruption

Motivating police to do what is morally correct ought to reduce the temptations for corruption. Providing a just system of rewards and penalties within the police organization, rejecting systems of promotion that are unjust, and addressing police complaints about unfair workloads will assist in motivating police to resist inducements to illegality. The publication and dissemination of ethical standards and an emphasis on the ethical ends of policing can contribute to the development of proper motivation, especially if such statements of ethical standards are the subjects of ongoing discussion in training programs and supervision. Finally, an emphasis on the collective responsibility of police for controlling corruption will effectively assist in changing an attitude that only isolated individuals who heroically blow the whistle on others reveal corruption. Whistle-blowing is discussed in the next section.

Ensuring Police Accountability

The question of how to make police accountable is a complex one. Most police departments employ a wide array of mechanisms like police boards and other structures that involve the community to provide oversight and accountability. Arguments in favor of citizen review include the following:

- Involving citizens in oversight is likely to result in more objective and thorough investigations.
- Involving citizens is likely to deter police misconduct; citizen involvement leads to a greater rate of conviction because police are less able to conceal wrongdoing.
- Individual complainants and the public will have a higher level of confidence in the integrity of police practice (Alpert and Dunham 2004: 33).

Citizen oversight of the police began in the 1920s and has seen a steady growth despite consistent police resistance to the notion that outsiders should judge their conduct (Walker 2001). The heyday of citizen oversight and review was during the 1980s and 1990s, when police ceased to be the sole judges of whether their conduct toward citizens reached an acceptable standard (Bayley 1994: 91).

"New Police Accountability"

In his comprehensive exploration of the "new police accountability" in the United States, Samuel Walker (2005: 7) explains how police accountability refers both to holding law enforcement agencies accountable for services like crime control and also to the accountability of individual officers for the treatment they offer to the public in their use of force and discrimination. Ensuring police accountability involves setting up complex administrative arrangements, some of which have been introduced

under pressure as a result of court proceedings and settlements secured by the Department of Justice in its mandate to ensure police accountability (p. 11). According to Walker, there are two elements in the new police accountability: specific strategies intended to enhance accountability and a framework that brings strategies and tools together into a program of reform (p. 12). Best practices within policing have focused on a set of strategies relating to the following:

- Reporting the use of force and other critical incidents
- Maintaining an open and accessible citizen complaint procedure
- Establishing an early-intervention system that systematically collects and analyzes data on police performance for the early identification of issues needing correction
- External citizen oversight, which may take various forms, including the new concept of the police auditor (pp. 12–13)

The conceptual framework within which these strategies operate comprises the following:

- Moving police organizations away from an emphasis on the rotten apple theory and in the direction of actual organizational change that addresses organizational and management issues related to police misconduct
- Controlling street-level officer behavior through devices such as use-of-force reporting systems
- Systematic collection and analysis of data (a process essential to police reform) so as to develop a fact-based depiction of officer activity, including the program known as COMPSTAT that collects and analyzes data on crime patterns
- Convergence of internal and external accountability so that these are seen as interrelated and not as alternatives (Walker 2005: 14–16)

Police Auditors

As well as the typical civilian review board, a new form of oversight in the shape of the police auditor emerged in the 1990s. According to Walker (2005: 135), this office is likely to be more effective as a form of oversight than the civilian review board because of the auditor's focus on organizational change. Unlike civilian review boards, which are concerned with investigating individual complaints against police, the auditor scrutinizes organizational problems that generate such incidents. This opens up examination of systemic issues within the organization that affect training and policy making. For example, if the department provides insufficient training on a policy or procedure, this can lead to inadvertent violations. As of 2005, there were 12 police auditors within the United States, basically clustered in the western half of the country (p. 136). According to Walker (2005), they perform five basic functions:

1. Auditing the department's citizen complaint process, including the procedures and records relating to complaints.

2. Auditing police operations such as narcotics enforcement, personnel selection for particular policing activities, and specific training.

3. Conducting policy review as an outcome of auditing citizen complaints and police operations. Policy is crucial because recommendations for change in organizational structures and practices are designed to prevent future misconduct. Thus, the auditor will produce a set of policy recommendations for police chiefs and managers.

4. Community outreach, which includes the auditor meeting with community groups and providing information about the complaints procedure and related activities.

5. Creating transparency. The auditor exposes issues and concerns within the police department to the public gaze, rejecting the historically closed and secretive nature of American policing organizations (pp. 139–142).

External Citizen Review of Police

External citizen review takes a number of forms, and Samuel Walker and Betsy Wright Kreisel (1996) have analyzed 65 citizen review procedures and structures that existed in January 1995. Among the various structures, many lack full independence because police rather than citizens conduct the initial fact-finding investigations (p. 71). Some have no role in the investigation of individual complaints, while others are empowered to review police policies. A multimember board conducts the vast majority of review procedures, but a small percentage comprises administrative agencies headed by an executive director (p. 75). Boards may range in size from 3 to 24, with an average of 10 members, and some include police representatives. According to the authors, black and Hispanic communities are represented on almost all citizen review boards, reflecting the conception that the review body directly involves all elements of the community, especially minorities, in the review process (p. 77). The authors found that 27% of the 65 review boards include police officer members, and this membership raises questions about the degree of independence of the boards.

The procedures adopted by these citizen review bodies center on four processes: independent investigating power, the power to issue subpoenas, public hearings, and legal representation. Collectively, these elements produce a criminal trial model of complaint investigation. The alternative is an administrative investigation model that is closed to the public and closely resembles an organizational personnel procedure (Walker and Kreisel 1996: 78–79). The authors found that 34% of all citizen review bodies possess independent investigative power, 38% have subpoena power, about half conduct public hearings, and 32% allow legal representation. However, only about 10% possess all these four elements. There are questions about the appropriateness of the criminal trial model because in practice in the criminal field few cases actually go to trial (p. 80). As well, in only a handful of cases do the citizen review bodies have the power to impose discipline on police, and most may only make recommendations to the head of the police department. If the criminal trial model is considered inappropriate, other possibilities are the administrative process, which is more inquisitorial in nature, and forms of mediation that are provided by about 19% of review bodies (p. 80).

Accountability in Other Countries

From a comparative perspective, in many countries police accountability is lacking because the administrative response to police wrongdoing is deficient. For example, in Argentina, Ecuador, and Paraguay, police fabricate or destroy evidence for disciplinary proceedings (Mendes 1999: 16). In these countries, police forces tend to be militarized, and the police culture reflects an attitude of isolation and animosity toward citizens. Thus, a crime control approach based on the notion of combat has produced torture and extrajudicial violence (p. 17). Paul Chevigny (1999: 74) reports that in Brazil, where criminal prosecution may often be the only viable method of enforcing police accountability, police often resist the prosecution or interfere in investigations. For example, in Sao Paulo it is common for military police to remove forensic evidence by taking already deceased suspects whom they have murdered to a hospital "as though they are still alive" for the evidence removal. Similarly, police will plant a weapon in the hand of a victim they have killed in a shootout.

In Canada, a media focus on wrongdoing by provincial police departments has resulted in a number of public enquiries that have generated a demand for effective police accountability. Thus, in 1987 in Manitoba, in 1989 in British Columbia, and in 1990 in Quebec, provinces created structures of civilian oversight, and in 1986, the Royal Canadian Mounted Police Public Complaints Commission was established (Mendes 1999: 25). The Canadian model of civilian oversight leaves it to the police department concerned to make the initial investigation of a complaint and, where appropriate, to conduct any disciplinary proceedings. Civilian oversight arises only if there is a complaint concerning the internal police process (p. 26).

An Australian study on police accountability suggests a number of criteria that need to be satisfied to establish a viable civilian oversight of policing. These include the following:

- Capacity to conduct independent investigations
- Direct access to the legislature in the form of regular reporting
- An independent resource base so that government cannot thwart efforts to ensure accountability
- Political and moral support to the oversight body and links between government and the oversight body
- Decentralizing the operations of the civilian oversight body so that it has the capacity to capture all valid complaints rather than being isolated in one or two large cities (Goldsmith 1999: 54–61)

Police anticorruption measures in Australia have been classified in terms of three models: the minimalist, the intermediate, and the advanced (Prenzler and Ronken 2003: 149). Tim Prenzler and Carol Ronken suggest that the *minimalist* model gives primary responsibility to the internal police disciplinary mechanisms. Associated with this model is judicial scrutiny of police misconduct and political oversight through reports to the legislature. The authors judge this minimalist model to be inadequate in terms of preventing police misconduct. The *intermediate* model adopts the establishment of internal affairs departments as the key to a more aggressive anticorruption approach. This allows police to develop specialist anticorruption skills and provides a stronger focus for anticorruption efforts. This model emphasizes stricter processes of recruitment and increased stress on ethics in training. As well, this model includes the establishment of independent review bodies. The problem with this approach is that it remains essentially passive and relies substantially on recruitment, rejecting undesirable potential police officers and on compliance with codes of ethics and conduct. In the *advanced* model, there is recognition that police misconduct can take multiple forms. For example, different sections or units of a police department may experience different problems, and systems must be able to cope with a multiplicity of issues (p. 152). In this model, there is a much more proactive approach to corruption. Technology and covert methods of investigation are employed; integrated ethics training is considered essential. There may be random integrity testing, and there is a system of external review that is independent and may adjudicate alleged wrongdoing (p. 153). The authors found that within the eight Australian police departments (there are six state police departments, the Northern Territory Police, and the Australian Federal Police), none had adopted the advanced model, and many had hardly advanced beyond the minimalist model.

In Latin America, accountability for wrongdoing is said to be exceptionally deficient, with police accountability structures lacking resources and constrained by corruption (Eijkman 2006: 414). Members of the public are reluctant to complain about police because of fear of retribution and because the lack of political will to eradicate corruption tends to generate police impunity in the region. In Costa Rica, police regard accountability as an activity that interferes with the task of policing, and being held accountable is regarded as something hindering police work (p. 415). The majority of police are never involved in charges of misconduct; nevertheless, internal disciplinary mechanisms do impose accountability—for example, in 2002 eight police officers were dismissed for illegal use of force (p. 419).

WHISTLE-BLOWING

Two general types of whistle-blowers have been identified: *internal whistle-blowers,* who report misconduct to another person within the organization, who in turn may take corrective action, such as a supervisor or union representative; and *external whistle-blowers,* who expose abuse to outside agents such as police, lawyers, and the media (Miethe 1999: 15). Both external and internal whistle-blowers blow the whistle because they themselves lack the power to directly change organizational practices.

Kleinig (1996: 184) suggests that within police departments, whistle-blowing is often defined as involving any reporting outside of an immediate circle of officers. The term *whistle-blowing* is a substitute for derogatory terms such as *snitch, fink,* and *sneak* and was developed in response to the recognition that although citizens have become more

vulnerable to the acts of large organizations, many of those same organizations demand a loyalty of their employees that can conflict with the public trust they seek to foster.

Whistle-blowers may have to pay a heavy price for blowing the whistle, and some have been dismissed, demoted, ostracized, and even assaulted and their families threatened because they have violated organizational loyalty (see Case Study 2.1). Terance Miethe (1999: 227) reports that for many whistle-blowers, the experience of whistle-blowing is a transformation of their lives, and the process permanently scars many because the whistle-blowing event overpowers all other aspects of a person's life.

Kleinig (1996) argues that whistle-blowers should be offered protection and suggests anonymity and legislation to protect them against harassment or discrimination. According to Miethe, whistle-blowers are protected by the Constitution, by federal and state statutes, and by common law (1999: 212). However, protection focuses on the disclosure of particular information to particular sources, and so its extent in a particular case may be unclear. For example, under federal and state law, protection is often restricted to *particular* types of workers who disclose *particular* violations of conduct in a *particular* sequence to *particular* agents.

Case Study 2.1 Punished for Whistle-Blowing?

In December 2000, two police officers in Wilkinsburg, Pennsylvania, were punished after questioning their chief about his handling of drug money. The police chief, Gerald Brewer, resigned after an investigation resulting from the two officers' complaints.

The officers were punished through the demotion of Sgt. Robert Tuite to patrol officer and the removal of a police vehicle allocated to Lt. Thomas Kocon. A lawyer representing the two officers indicated that he would be filing a retaliation charge against the Borough of Wilkinsburg and would also be taking court action to reverse the officers' punishments. Mayor Wilbert Young, who imposed the punishments, denied they were connected to the whistle-blowing acts of the two officers. Their lawyer noted, however, that the action taken against them could have a chilling effect on police officers in that state.

SOURCE: The Pittsburgh Channel 2000.

When Is Whistle-Blowing Morally Justified?

Bowie (in Kleinig 1996: 185) suggests that moral justification exists if the following conditions have been satisfied:

1. It is done in good faith with the intention of exposing wrongdoing that violates human rights, causes harm to third parties, or violates the purpose of the organization. In other words, it should not be motivated by personal revenge, advancement, or other self-interested reasons.

2. Except in special circumstances, the whistle-blower has exhausted all other internal avenues before going public.

3. The whistle-blower has ensured that there is a proper evidential basis for his or her allegation of misconduct.

4. The whistle-blower has carefully analyzed the seriousness of the misconduct, its immediacy, and its definition.

5. The action of the whistle-blower is consistent with the general responsibility of a citizen to avoid or expose moral violations.

6. It has some chance of success because if it is unlikely to accomplish any significant change, the act of blowing the whistle lacks credibility.

According to Kleinig, these considerations apply equally to police officers who become aware of corruption; however, he warns that any act of whistle-blowing should be regarded as a last resort because it indicates that a department has failed to look after its own affairs. His view seems to apply primarily to Miethe's (1999) category of external whistle-blowing.

Thus far, corruption has been explained in terms of the receipt of goods and services and the performance of acts that generally involve some kind of financial or other benefit to a particular individual. However, there are other forms of corruption that have their source in discriminatory practices by police.

DISCRIMINATION AS A CORRUPT PRACTICE IN POLICING: RACIAL BIAS, RACIAL PROFILING, AND SELECTIVE LAW ENFORCEMENT

This discussion is concerned with two aspects of discrimination: racial discrimination in the form of police discrimination against minorities through racial bias and racial profiling and discrimination that the police may exercise in the enforcement of the law, either as individuals or as a result of department policy. In general terms, discrimination based on race is deeply embedded in U.S. society and culture, with blackness being associated with criminality. While overt and explicit racism has been replaced by a shift to color blindness and claims that racism is over, systemic structures, including law enforcement, continue to sustain it (Heitzeg 2015: 4). As Alexander (2010) expresses the issue in terms of criminal justice,

In the era of color-blindness, it is no longer socially permissible to use race, explicitly, as a justification for discrimination, exclusion, and social contempt. So we don't. Rather than rely on race we use our criminal justice system to label people of color "criminals" and then engage in all the practices we supposedly left behind. Today, it is perfectly legal to discriminate against criminals in nearly all the ways that it was once legal to discriminate against African Americans. (p. 11)

The media constantly disseminates and reinforces racial stereotypes (see Chapter 9); it frames white criminality as sickness and not badness and as calling for understanding rather than condemnation, while black criminality is framed as "black on black crime" or "violence among black youth" (Heitzeg 2015: 5).

Police racism and discrimination against minorities refer to the process through which police stigmatize, harass, criminalize, or otherwise discriminate against certain social groups on the basis of cultural markers or national origin (Chan 1997: 17). Police racism can arise in various situations, can take different forms and levels of intensity, and can reveal itself in the form of acts ranging from prejudicial attitudes and discriminatory law enforcement practices to the use of excessive violence against minority groups. Police, like other citizens, may show insensitivity to language and cultural diversity, and while this may not amount to racial discrimination as such, it may well have an influence on police attitudes toward certain minority groups.

Racism and Racial Bias

Studies have shown evidence of prejudicial attitudes and the regular use of racist language among police officers (Skolnick 1966). The Christopher Commission in Los Angeles, formed after the Rodney King incident, found abusive language by police officers to be prevalent and identified many computer messages between patrol officers that contained racially offensive language, such as, "I'm back here in the project, pissing off the natives," and, "Just got mexercise for the night." White, Cox, and Basehart (in Walker, Spohn, and DeLone 2000: 105) argue that the employment of general profanity by police serves the function of labeling, dominating, and controlling citizens.

In relation to prejudicial attitudes, a study comparing the attitudes of Denver police officers with those of the general public found that police officers were only slightly more prejudiced than the community as a whole. This may suggest that police are essentially ordinary citizens and not significantly different from the general population in their attitudes. However, police have a fundamental desire to be respected, and their inclination when they perceive a community as showing a lack of respect is to react by increasing police activity in that community. It is significant that officers assigned to racial or ethnic minority communities, high-crime areas, and poor neighborhoods in the Denver study believed they received less respect from the public than officers working in other areas.

In February 2015, the director of the FBI, James Comey, stated that police officers working in black neighborhoods where there is a high crime rate develop a cynicism that shades their attitudes about race. The director noted there was considerable research that showed that all persons have unconscious racial biases and that tensions between police and residents in black neighborhoods could be eased if police got to know those they were tasked to protect (Schmidt 2015).

Racial Profiling

Racial profiling uses racial characteristics as indicators of possible criminal activity. Skolnick (in Walker et al. 2000) argues that the tendency of police to stereotype people (racial profiling) is an intrinsic aspect of police work because officers are trained to be suspicious and to search for criminal activity. Consequently, they develop a "perceptual shorthand" that they believe allows them to pick out suspects among the general population. They identify suspects by relying on visual signs such as dress, demeanor, gender, and age (see Case Studies 2.2 and 2.3). Additionally, Robert Reiner (1985) found that young, low-income, ethnic males were more likely to be stopped and questioned by the police, and minorities were also more likely to be arrested, although there is some discussion that this might be due to factors such as perceived disrespect shown by suspects to police. The same study noted that while police used excessive force against white citizens twice as much as against blacks, the findings were reversed in cases of the use of deadly force.

Racial profiling has become a source of major concern to the African American community, particularly in light of the Rodney King incident and others, where police are alleged to have used excessive force and to have racially profiled African Americans. Studies show that in the 1960s and early 1970s, police fatally shot seven African Americans for every white person (Walker et al. 2000: 95), but following the Supreme Court's decision to declare unconstitutional the *fleeing felon rule* (allowing police to shoot to kill any fleeing suspected felon), the racial disparity between persons shot and killed has narrowed to about three to one (p. 96). The fact remains that while police continue to profile minority groups in law enforcement activities, there is a greater likelihood that disparity between whites and African Americans in shooting incidents will continue. Case Studies 2.2 and 2.3 provide examples of racial profiling.

Racial profiling is not confined to the police; other government agencies have also been accused of the same practice. For example, in 2000, the General Accounting Office revealed that even before the war on terror commenced in 2001, African American women traveling by air into the United States were being disproportionately targeted for custom searches (Newsome 2003: 32). The report found that these women were more likely than members of other groups to receive intrusive searches, including X-rays and strip searches.

Case Study 2.2 "Looking Mexican"

In July, 1997, the city of Chandler, a suburb of Phoenix, Arizona, with a population of 143,000, began Operation Restoration, which was intended to revitalize the town and construct a new civic center, including police headquarters, municipal court, and library. Since its founding in 1912, Chandler had become two cities: one affluent, the other the old impoverished downtown area.

Seeking a cause for the city center's decay, city officials fixed on illegal immigration and focused on alleged criminal activity by illegal immigrants. The city police and the border patrol collaborated on a plan linked to Operation Restoration, and on the first day of the operation, two dozen police officers and five border patrol agents moved through the downtown area, chasing suspected illegal immigrants from worksites and filling up buses with those they captured. In all, police eventually removed 432 illegal immigrants, all but three from Mexico.

However, the illegal immigrants in Chandler coexist with a large, well-established Mexican American community, with Latinos making up about 15% of the population. As police questioned those leaving markets favored by Latinos, they encountered U.S. citizens, from whom they also demanded identification and immigration papers. The police operations targeted legal residents and U.S. citizens who "looked Mexican."

Four months later, the Arizona attorney general revealed the results of his inquiry into this raid. These included that Chandler police had stopped residents, questioned them, and entered their homes without warrants, relying only on skin color, Mexican appearance, or use of Spanish language to identify them as suspected illegal immigrants. Moreover, the city officials had not requested formal permission from the U.S. attorney general to act against illegal immigrants, as is required by federal law.

The city manager officially reprimanded the police chief for the raid, and a group of Latinos launched a $35 million lawsuit against the city. Latinos commented that it would take 10 or 15 years for people to feel comfortable again in the town.

SOURCE: Tobar 1998.

Case Study 2.3 Racial Profiling: When Color Signals Dangerousness

Case 1. In Phoenix, Arizona, police questioned a man sitting in his car outside an apartment building. Why was he questioned? Police said he appeared nervous, he moved his car when a marked police car approached, and most of all, as one police officer reported, he was a Mexican male just sitting in his car in a mainly white neighborhood.

Case 2. At the Kansas City airport, a Drug Enforcement Agency agent stopped and questioned a young man. Why was he stopped and questioned? The agent reported that the man was young and not well dressed and had arrived on a direct flight from Los Angeles, known to be a source for drugs. He had no checked luggage, only two carry-on bags, and he walked rapidly to a taxi after his flight. He appeared also to be nervous. The fact that he was black was a factor in the agent's decision to stop him.

Case 3. In California, officers of the border patrol questioned the driver of a vehicle at the highway checkpoint some 30 miles north of the United States–Mexico border. They also searched his vehicle. Why was he questioned? They were prompted to do so because he was of Mexican ancestry.

Case 4. In Boston over a period of several weeks, police stopped, questioned, and searched young black men at random, following a report that a white man's pregnant wife had been shot and killed in that neighborhood by a black man.

Case 5. In New York City, police stopped and searched a young black man who alighted from a commuter train. He was clean-shaven, was carrying a briefcase, and was 6 feet 4 inches tall. Why was he stopped and searched? Police were investigating a report that a black man who regularly rode the train carried a gun. The report came in the form of an anonymous letter, and the man described in the letter was 5 feet 10 inches tall and had a mustache.

Case 6. After police received a tip that a white man with a bomb was inside an office building, they surrounded the building and entered. They examined white men more closely than nonwhite men.

SOURCE: Kennedy 1991.

Case 7. Complaints by Arab Americans against racial profiling by airlines have reportedly increased since 9/11, according to the American-Arab Anti-Discrimination Committee. The committee is aware of passengers with a Muslim or Middle Eastern appearance who have been removed from planes. For example, an Iranian-born U.S. citizen who was a software developer living in Dallas was on his way home from Seattle and, while reading his paper on an American Airlines plane, was approached by an airline employee holding a passenger manifest. He was told to leave the plane because the pilot did not feel comfortable with him aboard. Reportedly, the pilot did not like how he looked. He was questioned by three airport police about where he lived, his marital status, his religion, and where he worked, and he was treated as a suspect. He was allowed to board the next flight to Dallas, and when the plane landed, apologies were offered by an airline official.

SOURCE: CNN 2001.

The Morality of Racial Profiling

The question raised by racial profiling is whether it is morally right to use a person's race as an indication of increased likelihood of criminal conduct. Should police stop African Americans simply because there is official statistical evidence that young African American men are disproportionately involved in drug or gang activity? Randall Kennedy (in Walker et al. 2000: 104) argues that race should be used as the basis for a police action only in extraordinary circumstances. Prohibiting arrest by reference to racial profiling reduces the possibility of police harassment and the perception among minorities that police harbor racial attitudes toward them. Additionally, the hostility created by profiling tends to form barriers in those communities where police find it most difficult to operate, and profiling may also support segregation in the sense that African Americans become reluctant to venture into white neighborhoods for fear of police harassment. Most recently the U.S. Department of Justice (December 2014) issued new guidelines to federal law enforcement agencies on racial profiling that set standards covering routine or spontaneous decisions, such as traffic stops, and nonroutine activities. The fundamental principle stated is that "profiling by law enforcement based on a listed characteristic is morally wrong and inconsistent with our core values and principles of fairness and justice." (p. 3). The guidelines prohibit the use of pretexts to target minorities as often occurs under the practice known as "driving while black" (p. 5).

"Driving While Black"

The general public associates racial profiling with traffic stops, and some have argued that the police practice of stopping a disproportionate number of minority citizens for their driving infractions is so pervasive that it should be termed the crime of "driving while black." According to the Bureau of Justice Statistics (Smith and Durose 2006), in 2002 an estimated 8.7% of drivers aged 16 or older were stopped by police, and 11% of young male drivers were physically searched or their vehicle was searched. Among these, blacks (22%) and Hispanics (17%) were searched at higher rates than whites (8%). A number of studies suggest that targeting minority motorists does occur at least in some jurisdictions, and a number of police departments are now recording traffic stop information to establish whether they are racially biased (Warren, Tomaskovic-Devey, Smith, Zingraff, and Mason 2006: 710).

Racial profiling is less likely to be a factor in a routine speeding stop by a highway patrol officer because it is often difficult to identify the driver's race because of the speed of the vehicle, and also such stops are usually the result of speed detectors rather than sighting the race of the driver (Warren et al. 2006: 714). In one study conducted in 2000 in North Carolina that compared race disparities in highway patrol stops and in local police stops, researchers found only slight evidence of racial disparity in the highway patrol stops but stronger evidence in stops by local police (p. 709).

One analysis of police stops of drivers in Kansas City in 2003 and 2004, based on a survey of about 2,300 drivers and interviews with some, has shown how it is necessary to differentiate between *investigatory stops* and *traffic-safety stops*. Epp, Maynard-Moody, and Haider-Markel argue that there is an institutional police practice of making investigatory stops (the procedure to be followed is taught in police training courses and discussed in police educational material) and that such stops constitute the main source of racial disparities in police stops (2014: 7). The investigatory stop is "a police stop where the intent is not to sanction a driving violation but to look for evidence of more serious criminal wrongdoing" (p. 30). Thus, police identify traffic offenses, such as a broken tail light, as a pretext to stop drivers and make a search of the vehicle for drugs or unlicensed firearms. The investigatory stop is an instance of proactive policing—a shift from random to aggressive patrolling—thought by police to be a crime reduction measure (p. 31).

In 1996, the U.S. Supreme Court in *Whren v. United States* ruled that investigatory stops did not violate Fourth Amendment and other protections. In that case police pulled over the driver of a pickup in an African American neighborhood in Washington, D.C., for making a turn without signaling and after a search of the vehicle found illegal drugs. The Court held that stops are not a constitutional violation if the stop is based on an objective violation of the law, regardless of how minor. It also suggested that a stop would only be constitutionally discriminatory if the defendant was able to show that police had intentionally used race as the primary reason for selecting that person to stop.

In *Knowles v. Iowa* in 1998, the Court expanded police powers by authorizing police to conduct pat-down searches of the occupants of a vehicle as long as they were necessary to guard against a perceived risk of attack. Later in 2002, *United States v. Arvizu* authorized police to stop and search a vehicle if the "totality of the circumstances" supported reasonable suspicion of criminal activity even where no part of the circumstances amounted to probable cause. These cases offer police wide scope to conduct investigatory stops without any concerns about violation of rights (Epp et al. 2014: 35).

A study by Epp and others found that blacks were stopped for investigatory purposes at much higher rates than whites. Whites tended to experience normal traffic stops, such as for speeding, as do blacks, but whites are less likely to be subjected to investigatory stops (Epp et al. 2014: 8). In addition, blacks perceive such stops through a racial lens based on personal and shared experiences of their interactions with police. Police use investigatory stops to check on those they regard as suspicious, and Epp and others suggest that their study reveals that police racial biases are activated in these stops because officers target the stereotypical criminal, namely the young black male (p. 53).

In traffic stops, on the other hand, police are focused on violations of traffic laws and therefore target safety violators, black or white. Thus, while traffic safety stops tend to be brief and to the point for both blacks and whites, during investigatory stops officers ask questions, inspect the vehicle's interior, and if still suspicious ask to search the vehicle (Epp et al. 2014: 78). These stops are intrusive, tense, and sometimes result in conflict; they are viewed by blacks as less legitimate than traffic-safety stops and as treating them as second-class citizens (p. 129). Research now indicates that investigatory stops raise questions about police legitimacy, professionalism, and racial bias and arguably constitute a form of racial subordination (p. 135).

"Stop and Frisk"

Similar to investigatory stops of drivers discussed previously, police may act on their stereotypical images of suspicious conduct by stopping, questioning, and frisking people on the street, and this practice is a source of tension between police and the community. A study in San Diego found that nearly half of those stopped and questioned were African Americans, despite the fact that African Americans made up only 17.5% and 4.8%, respectively, of the populations of the two precincts covered by the study (Walker et al. 2000). Moreover, all those stopped and questioned were male, and about 60% were juveniles.

The legal basis for stop and frisk was provided by the U.S. Supreme Court in 1968 in the case of *Terry v. Ohio*; the case is so well-known to police that stop-and-frisk actions are referred to by police as "Terry stops" (Clemons 2014: 700). Before *Terry*, it was generally accepted that police could not stop and search a person unless they had a warrant or unless there existed probable cause to believe that a person was engaged in criminal actions. In *Terry*, the Court decided that if and when police observe unusual conduct by a person whom they believe to be dangerous and engaged in criminal activity, an officer may "for the protection of himself and others in the area" conduct a limited search "to discover weapons that might be used against the officer."

Therefore, a police officer need only have "reasonable articulable suspicion" of criminal activity and dangerousness in order to stop and frisk (Alexander 2010: 63). Since *Terry* was decided, federal courts have consistently accepted police explanations of what constitutes "reasonable suspicion" and thereby increased the possibility that a person will be stopped based on a police "hunch" or "gut feeling" that he or she is acting suspiciously. These kinds of police reactions are often based on implicit racial biases that stem from the stereotypical association between a black person and danger, violence, and criminality (Clemons 2014: 701).

The furor concerning racial profiling has spread to Canada, and in 2003, the police in Kingston, Ontario, conducted the first racial profiling survey, in which police officers were asked to record data on pedestrians and drivers they interrogated, suspected, questioned, searched, or detained (Closs and McKenna 2006: 144). The study found that black male residents of the city between the ages of 15 and 24 were 3 times more likely to be stopped and questioned by police than people from other racial backgrounds (p. 149). Police justify stopping and questioning on the street as an effective crime-fighting measure, intended to deter potential offenders through police scrutiny of them and to provide reassurance to the general public that patrol officers are protecting ordinary citizens.

In New York City in 2013, Shira Scheindlin, a federal judge, ruled that the city's "stop and frisk" law was unconstitutional because blacks and Hispanics had been disproportionately subjected to the practice over a 10-year period: 52% of those stopped were black and 31% Hispanic. The judge ruled that the NYPD had, over time, developed a policy of "indirect racial profiling," as it increased its number of stops in minority parts of the city. The judge said of the practice that stop and frisk was "a demeaning and humiliating experience" and that "no one should live in fear of being stopped whenever he leaves his home to go about the activities of daily life" (quoted in Stanford 2015: 71). Evidence demonstrates that the "reasonable suspicion" believed by police to warrant a stop and frisk is commonly justified by reference to a person's "furtive movements"—cited in 42% of stops from 2004 to 2009—and location in a "high-crime area"—cited in 55% of stops over the same period (Clemons 2014: 707).

Stop and frisk was justified as a crime control measure in New York City by Mayor Bloomberg. While violent crime declined by 29% in the city from 2001 to 2010, other large cities experienced similar declines without any stop-and frisk-policy in place. For example, there were declines of 59% in Los Angeles, 56% in New Orleans, and 49% in Dallas (New York Civil Liberties Union 2015). Stop and frisk was stopped in New York in 2015 by Mayor Bill de Blasio, who succeeded Mayor Bloomberg.

Confidence in the Police

From the point of view of the public, race and ethnicity play a major part in shaping public attitudes toward police. For example, in a 1998 survey, 61% of white Americans surveyed reported "a great deal" or "quite a lot" of confidence in the police, whereas only 10% had "very little" confidence. However, of the African Americans surveyed, only 34% fell into the first category, and 25% had "very little" confidence in the police (Walker et al. 2000: 91). Police tend to be negatively evaluated by residents in high-crime neighborhoods and by those who fear the incidence of crime in their neighborhoods (Schafer, Huebner, and Bynum 2003: 447), especially when they use aggressive policing techniques designed for zero-tolerance policing, which have resulted in disproportionate arrest rates for blacks (Eck and Maguire 2005: 228). In the case of Hispanics, attitudes fall somewhere between those of whites and African Americans. As already noted, age can be a factor in police profiling, and age also factors into the views of young people toward the police because young people, regardless of race, consistently have a more negative view of police than their elders. This can be explained by their more active presence on the street and their greater level of contact with police (Walker et al. 2000: 92).

Selective Law Enforcement

Police selectivity in enforcing laws may have the effect of discriminating against certain groups in society. For example, police treatment of domestic violence cases has historically involved a pattern of noninterference, based on the assumption that such violence was not a proper subject of crime control, unless it involved injury that could be defined as felony assault. Additionally, police gave priority to family solidarity and acted or failed to act in accordance with that goal (Fyfe in Kleinig 1996: 184). Thus, women who were battered by their partners received discriminatory treatment by police because whether or not action was taken against the batterer depended on whether the crime was considered a felony or a misdemeanor. Similarly, selective enforcement by the police can offer less protection to rape victims because most rape victims are victimized by known intimates, and police enforcement practice focuses on stranger rapists.

SUMMARY

In the past, effective policing in the United States depended on the police being able to physically dominate the streets. Police were seen as an arm of whichever political party was in power, and there was little or no conception that police needed to observe ethical standards and norms. Police corruption and police abuse of power are inextricably linked to the nature of policing and to police culture. The policing model may be that of the officer as the crime fighter, the emergency operator, or the social peacekeeper, and the type of model chosen by a police department influences relations between the police and community, police culture, and the overall ethical standards employed in policing. Police culture is enormously important in determining the level of police corruption or misconduct because if the culture adopts the characteristics of cynicism, the use of force in all situations, and the notion that police themselves are victims, ethical standards will take second place to the noble cause of fighting the war against crime.

The police have extensive discretionary powers that can be used for good or ill, and some argue that this discretion is too wide and should be curtailed by the law and by departmental rules and regulations. Others argue that placing limits on discretion is the only feasible option but acknowledge that enforcing these limits can be problematic. Public opinion seems to accept that police should have wide discretion to counter crime, but individual members of the public complain when that wide discretion is directed at them.

Codes of ethics may be one way of limiting police discretion, but there are problems with codes of ethics being rhetorical instruments directed toward a vaguely defined "public." In any event, the evidence seems to show that police mostly depend on their personal notion of ethics.

DISCUSSION QUESTIONS

1. Discuss the ways in which the noble cause argument explains and helps police rationalize police misconduct and involvement in corruption.

2. Are codes of ethics important in guiding police practices and minimizing police misconduct? Explain.

3. How does police culture influence police perceptions about their role and about the means they should use to carry out their duties?

4. Is there any relationship between the style of policing chosen by a department and the ethical practices it feels are legitimate for its officers to use in carrying out their duties?

5. Is it possible or desirable to limit police discretion, and would this step have the effect of minimizing ethical misconduct by police officers?

6. Why do some argue that it is correct to describe racial profiling as a form of police corruption? Explain the effects of this practice.

7. Compare systemic and individualistic explanations of police corruption.

WEB RESOURCES

Bureau of Justice Statistics, U.S. Department of Justice. http://www.bjs.gov/
International Association of Chiefs of Police (IACP). http://www.theiacp.org
Police Executive Research Forum. http://www.policeforum.org
Vera Institute of Justice. http://www.vera.org

3

POLICE ETHICS:
USE OF FORCE, INVESTIGATIONS,
INTERROGATIONS, AND LYING

POLICE USE OF FORCE

Police use of force is a dominant and contentious issue in policing because the capacity to use force or coercion goes to the very core of the police role. The police are the only authority empowered to use physical force, and it is to be used only as a last resort. Further, police are to use no more force than is necessary to subdue a suspect (Skolnick and Fyfe 1993: 13). While there is general acceptance of the fact that police are entitled to use force, there is an equal degree of uncertainty as to what constitutes excessive or unnecessary force. For example, in the well-known Rodney King incident, although the majority of the public considered the force used in subduing King to be excessive, a jury acquitted the police officers charged for the beating. Writing in 2000, Lt. Arthur Doyle, a retired police officer with 29 years of service in the New York Police Department, offers his description of the police attitude toward using force:

> A(n) . . . unwritten law covered chases as well. If an officer had to chase someone, by car or by foot, the person would invariably be beaten when captured. After a long chase, the officers would be pumped up, angry. They would want revenge for having put their lives in danger. That was the case in the Rodney King situation. It was taken to the extreme. (p. 174)

In general, *police use-of-force incidents* are rare occurrences when compared to the number of police and citizen interactions. In 1999, the national Police–Public Contact Survey (PPCS) conducted by the Bureau of Statistics found that about 1% of persons who had contact with police reported that officers used force or threatened to use force against them out of almost 44 million persons who reported face-to-face police contact. In 2002, the rate increased slightly to 1.5%, with 14% of those respondents claiming they suffered an injury in the encounter (Taylor, Alpert, Kubu, Woods, and Dunham 2011: 214). A 2008 survey of almost 60,000 respondents found that 16.9% aged 16 and over had face-to-face contact with police, and of these, 1.4% said force had been threatened or used against them during their most recent contact (Prenzler, Porter, and Alpert 2013: 344). In relation to injuries during police and citizen interactions, both officer surveys and reports from police agencies have found most injuries to be minor, typically comprising bruises, sprains, and abrasions (Taylor et al. 2011: 214).

State and local law enforcement agencies employing 100 or more sworn officers received more than 26,000 complaints about officer use of force during 2002 (Hickman 2006: 1). Of this number, about 8% were sustained in the sense that there was enough evidence to justify disciplinary action. About 34% were not sustained, and 25% were unfounded. About one fifth of large municipal police departments are accountable to a civilian complaints review board, and these departments received a higher rate of complaints than those without such boards (p. 1). Concerning the *use of excessive force,* there were more than 2,000 sustained citizen complaints in the United States in 2002 (p. 6).

This compares with a smaller number of complaints in *England and Wales* where, during the 12-month period ending March 2003, police received 6,154 complaints alleging assault by police officers. This reveals an overall rate of 4.6 complaints of assault per 100 officers compared to the U.S. rate of 6.6 complaints per 100 officers (Hickman 2006: 3). In 2003, 82% of large municipal police departments in the *United States* had an internal affairs or similar unit with full-time personnel, and 33% of such departments maintained an operational computer-based early intervention system for responding to officer conduct.

Police Use of Force: Arrest-Related Deaths

Approximately 300 persons are shot and killed by police in the United States every year (Parent 2006: 230). From 2003 to 2009, a total of 4,813 deaths were reported under the Department of Justice Arrest-Related Deaths Program. Of these deaths, about 6 in 10 (2,931) were classified as homicide by police, and 4 in 10 were attributed to other manners of death. The annual total of arrest-related deaths for each year from 2003 to 2009 ranged from a low of 355 to a high of 417. The southern states reported the highest annual totals of arrest-related deaths, with Florida and Texas reporting the highest in that region (Burch 2011: 10).

Over the same period, the FBI estimated there were nearly 98 million arrests in the United States (p. 1). Whites accounted for 42% of reported arrest-related deaths, while 32% were black deaths and 20% were Hispanic. Of the reported arrest-related deaths, 45% of those who died had allegedly engaged in assault either immediately before or during the arrest, and among such deaths attributed to homicide, 75% of those who died allegedly engaged in violent offenses (p. 2).

U.S. rates of police shooting and killing compare to a rate of about 10 per year in *Canada* and even lower rates in *Australia,* where 41 deaths occurred because of police shootings between 1990 and 1997, and *New Zealand,* where about 20 police shootings have occurred in the past 60 years. In the *United Kingdom,* seven incidents of police causing deaths by shooting occurred between 1991 and 1993. In the *Netherlands* between 1978 and 1999, 67 fatal police shootings were recorded, and during the same period, police wounded 288 persons (Burch 2011: 230).

According to a report by Amnesty International in June 2015, none of the U.S. states meet international standards for police use of force that require legislation to state that "lethal force may only be used as a last resort with non-violent means and less harmful means to be tried first." According to Amnesty, "The vast majority of laws do not require officers to give a warning of their intent to use firearms." In addition, nine states and the District of Columbia lack any laws on the appropriate use of deadly force, and laws in 13 states fail to provide the protection to citizens granted by decisions of the Supreme Court.

On average, about 70 police officers are murdered each year in the United States, and approximately 60 officers are accidentally killed through incidents involving motor vehicles and aircraft (Burch 2011: 235). Compared to Canada, where there are about two murders of police officers each year, the risk of a police officer being murdered is about 3 times greater in the United States.

Deaths in Police Custody

In the United States, the *Deaths in Custody Reporting Act 2000* was the first law to require states applying for certain grants to submit quarterly reports on the following:

- inmate deaths in state prisons and local jails,
- deaths in juvenile detention facilities and police lockups, and
- deaths occurring in transit and in the course of arrest.

In 2014, the *Deaths in Custody Reporting Act 2013* was signed into law and continued the previous reporting requirements under the law of 2000.

Deaths occurring when police attempt to apprehend or arrest a person are reportable under the act. Common examples of deaths occurring during apprehension include officer-involved shootings, death related to the use of force or police compliance weapons, vehicle accidents and collisions, other types of fatal accidental injuries sustained while persons attempt to elude police, and suicides committed during standoffs and barricade situations. Also reportable are deaths occurring during police interrogation, all deaths that occur before a physical arrest, and all deaths attributable to use of a weapon by state or local police (Planty et al. 2015: 3).

In its *Technical Report on Arrest-Related Deaths of March 2015*, the Bureau of Justice Statistics indicated a number of issues with collecting data on this topic. Different methodologies adopted by the reporting states (36 states have reported data every year since 2003) have produced the following results:

- Only 50% of the estimated law enforcement homicides were reported from 2003 to 2009 and in 2011.
- Even with improvements from 2003 to 2011 in data collection, from 31% to 41% of estimated homicides by law enforcement personnel were not captured in the 2011 data collection.
- Almost 40% of deaths occurring in the process of police arrest arise from causes other than officer-involved homicides of suspects.
- Deficiencies in data collection are due to a lack of standardized modes of data collection, definitions, scope, participation, and the availability of resources (Planty and Burch 2015: 1).

Inadequate data on deaths in police custody, or more generally relating to police encounters with citizens where force is applied, have constrained efforts to analyze the circumstances of such cases and formulate appropriate policy responses.

Political Action on Police Use of Force, 2015

In 2014 and 2015, deaths in police custody or associated with police interactions with citizens gained intense media attention and caused concern that police might be targeting certain groups within a community. Following the deaths of a number of unarmed black males by police shootings, President Obama established a task force on the issue of police shootings, which reported to him in March 2015. *The New York Times* reported that President Obama called for changes in police practice, including requiring independent investigations and independent prosecutors where police use of force results in injury or death. He recommended that police take steps to build trust with communities, collect more data on police shootings, address racial profiling and take a more relaxed approach to public demonstrations. In addition, it was recommended that law enforcement agencies be diversified to better reflect the demographic composition of communities. Concerning the issue of police wearing body cameras, the task force indicated the wholesale adoption of this technology would raise issues about privacy and costs (President Obama had already requested funding to buy 50,000 body cameras for police [Davis 2015]).

The Rise of the Citizen Journalist and Police Use of Force

Events involving police shootings and use of force are now being regularly captured on telephone cameras by bystanders and being published online and in the news media. This is especially the case where police and citizen interactions are associated with racial dynamics. The "rise of the citizen journalist" (Greer and McLaughlin 2010: 1041) brings with it an increased likelihood that police action will be captured visually by citizens and broadcast in the media, sometimes contradicting prior police accounts or at least casting doubt on public statements about justifications for police use of force, including lethal force.[1]

---

1   For a discussion of the law and policy concerning civilian recording of police activity, see Kies, Marianne F. 2011. "Policing the Police: Freedom of the Press, the Right to Privacy, and Civilian Recordings of Police Activity." *George Washington Law Review* 80: 274–302.

The confidence in and respect for police in some communities was affected by police shootings in 2014 and 2015, and generally the new visibility that citizens now possess has made them curious, skeptical, and better informed about police use of force (Brown 2015: 2). A poll conducted in August 2014 reported that 61% of Americans feel their police do a "poor" or "only a fair job" in using appropriate force (*USA Today* August 2014), and it has been noted that "the rise of the citizen journalist has been accompanied . . . by a decline in deference to authority and a deterioration of trust in official or elite institutions" (quoted in Greer and McLaughlin 2010: 1054). The police perspective, which was formerly privileged by the media in their published accounts of police violence, is now being questioned and contested as never before.

The capacity of citizens to make video recordings of police occurrences and to disseminate those recordings online was found in one study to have been "profoundly integrated into the consciousness of most rank-and-file officers" (Brown 2015: 1).

Brown surveyed 231 rank-and-file Canadian police in Toronto and Ottawa with 10 or more years of front-line urban policing experience concerning the capacity of citizens to record such events and found that these capacities had "influenced significant behavioral changes through the deterrence of certain practices, including moderations in police violence." The study found that half of the officers surveyed reported that citizen capacity to record events was "always present" in their consciousness, and 74% reported changes in behavior due to that capacity to video record (p. 11). One half of officers surveyed now employ less physical force than if video recording were not available, and slightly less than half now use force less often. Brown concludes that the new visibility associated with policing "can be characterized as a form of disciplinary power" (p. 11); that it operates to regulate police conduct; that it is likely to enhance police internal self-control; and that it will compel police to act in conformity with society-desired behaviors.

A Closer Look

Some Fatal Police Shootings, 2014–2015

August 2014: Ferguson, Missouri

A white police officer, Darren Wilson, fatally shot an unarmed black teenager, Michael Brown, 18, in a confrontation. His death sparked protests throughout the country and prompted a debate about police tactics and use of force. In November 2014, a St. Louis County Grand Jury decided not to bring charges against Wilson. An investigation by the Department of Justice cleared Wilson of any civil rights violations, found that the witnesses who corroborated Wilson's account of the event were credible, and that the evidence showed that Brown was shot by Wilson in self-defense.

November 22, 2014: Cleveland, Ohio

An officer shot and killed an unarmed 12-year-old boy who had been pointing a toy gun at people in a public park. A 911 caller reported the boy, Tamir Rice, who was black, to police but stated in his call that the gun was probably not real. It is likely that the police dispatcher did not pass on that information. A video released by Cleveland police showed a police car pulling to a stop a few feet from Tamir. Within seconds, the rookie officer in the passenger seat had fired and killed him. In December 2014, the death was ruled a homicide as opposed to an accident or suicide. Police claim that Tamir reached for a gun in his waistband and that an orange tip on the gun indicating it was a toy had been removed.

(Continued)

(Continued)

February 10, 2015: Pasco, Washington

Three officers fired 17 shots and killed a man who had thrown rocks at people. Police claimed the man hit some officers with rocks after they were called to the scene. It is not clear if Antonio Zambrano-Montes, a Hispanic, was mentally ill. A video by a witness shows him standing near the officers and throwing something at them or their car and then moving away. Two officers can be seen firing at him as he moved away, and then all three officers chased him. He turned to face them while lifting an object in his hand, and the three officers fired at him. In the video, a couple of shots can be heard after he fell to the ground. He was shot seven times, but police deny he was shot in the back.

February 23, 2015: Omaha, Nebraska

A police officer shot and killed an unarmed man suspected of having just robbed a store. He was shot twice in the back. Four officers had responded to the robbery call and confronted Daniel Elrod, 39, who was white. Police stated he had climbed onto a car, ignored commands to get on the ground, and reached repeatedly toward his waistband. Police and witnesses said he had dared police to shoot him. The deceased had an extensive criminal record, and there was evidence that he was distraught and suicidal.

March 1, 2015: Los Angeles, California

Police shot and killed an unarmed homeless man who police claimed had attempted to seize an officer's gun during a struggle. Multiple videos of the incident by bystanders show the man, Charly Leundeu Keunan, 43, who had a history of mental illness, fighting with a group of police. They show him being forced to the ground by four officers, and the clicking of a Taser can be heard, followed by at least five shots. Police have not said how many officers fired. Keunan was from Cameroon, Africa.

March 6, 2015: Madison, Wisconsin, and Aurora, Colorado

In Madison, a white police officer shot and killed an unarmed black man after he responded to a report that the man, Tony Robinson, 19, had assaulted two people, had been jumping in front of moving vehicles, and had attempted to strangle someone. The police claimed that Robinson fought with and injured the officer. In May 2015, the Dane County district attorney found that the shooting was justified self-defense and that Robinson had taken a number of drugs hours before the incident, which may have contributed to his behavior.

In Aurora, an unarmed man was shot and killed as officers tried to arrest him. The police stated that the deceased, Naeschylus Vinzant, 37, who was black, had a criminal history and was wanted for kidnapping and robbery and for removing an electronic parole monitor from his ankle. Police have not explained the reasons for firing at Vinzant.

March 9, 2015: Chamblee, Georgia

A white police officer shot and killed a naked, unarmed black man who was knocking on doors and running and crawling in an apartment complex; Anthony Hill was mentally ill. The police account was that Hill had refused the officer's command to stop, but it was unclear if he actually charged at the officer.

SOURCE: Adapted from "Fatal Police Shootings: Accounts Since Ferguson," by Richard Perez-Pena. *The New York Times,* April 8, 2015.

The Continuum of Force

What guidance is given to police by their employer departments concerning the permissible degree of force to be used in interactions with citizens? The common approach is for policing agencies to instruct officers through a written policy that they must adhere to a continuum of force, which may be expressed in linear, matrix, wheel, or other designs. These policies are not only used to instruct officers but are also applied after a use-of-force incident to assess whether an officer used the proper level of force. When courts become involved in such cases, judges may consider departmental policy in their decisions (Paoline and Terrill 2011: 180).

A typical linear continuum-of-force policy is described by Skolnick and Fyfe (1993: 38–39), showing an ascending scale of action that police can apply in handling street situations:

- *Presence.* Often, the mere presence of police will produce the desired outcome, and use of force is irrelevant.
- *Persuasive Verbalization.* Where the mere presence of officers has not been successful, police now speak persuasively in tones that are firm but not commanding.
- *Command Verbalization.* This is the next step up the scale from persuasive verbalization, which police call the "command voice." Here, police will use a stronger tone and tell the person with whom they are interacting what behavior they expect.
- *Firm Grips.* This is the next step beyond verbalization; it consists of police gripping parts of the body to warn the individual that he or she is to remain motionless or move in a certain direction. The objective is to guide and coax, not to cause pain.
- *Pain Compliance.* At this next level of forcible contact, officers try to gain the cooperation of a person by inflicting pain in a way that does not cause lasting physical injury. These contacts include holds such as finger grips and hammerlocks.
- *Impact Techniques.* These actions are designed to overcome resistance that is forcible but is not life threatening. Here, police may use batons or kicks or employ chemical sprays and the like. Over the past decade, conducted energy devices have been widely adopted by law enforcement in the United States. Especially well known is the Taser (discussed in the section Police Use of Force: Tasers). It should be noted that while police are obliged not to provoke confrontations, they are not obliged to use a lesser degree of force to counter the particular force used against them.
- *Deadly Force.* This is the most extreme use of force, often involving firearms and defined by law as "force capable of killing or likely to kill." Apart from firearms, some police are also trained in using neck holds intended to make a person unconscious. Under the law, police are permitted to use deadly force to apprehend fleeing persons who are shown to be dangerous, such as those who are armed or fleeing from a violent crime. Deadly force is not limited to the use of firearms; Kleinig (1996: 117) points out that each year police motor vehicle pursuits kill and maim more people, including innocent bystanders, than police firearms.

In a survey of police agencies in 2011, Terrill, Paoline, and Ingram (2011: ii) found that more than 80% of responding police agencies had a continuum-of-force policy in place and that 73% used a linear model. However, there was wide variation within agencies about force progression, with 123 different permutations. The greatest difficulty was properly placing the use of chemical sprays and Taser-type devices in the continuum. Thus, in one agency it might be acceptable to use a Taser device but not chemical spray on people pulling their arms away from police to avoid being handcuffed (defensive resistance), while in another agency chemical spray would be permitted in this situation but not the use of a Taser (Paoline and Terrill 2011: 178). About 30% of agencies placed chemical sprays within pain compliance techniques, 30% within hard-hand tactics, and over a third within impact weapons. In essence, there was no common approach to the issue of what modes of force should be used in relation to varying forms of suspect resistance (Terrill et al. 2011: iii).

When to Use Force

In what circumstances is it inappropriate for police to use force? In the early days of policing, police on the streets employed force as a matter of course to keep order and enforce their will. Skolnick and Fyfe (1993: 24) trace police brutality back to the lynching and vigilante acts invoked against African Americans, revealing how police violence links to racism and notions of white supremacy. Studies have shown that police routinely used excessive force in the riots and disturbances of the 1960s (Ericson 1992), and Crank (1998: 72) warns of the dangers of paramilitary-type police units, often used now to perform normal police functions, whose members often perceive themselves as "warriors" (see Chapter 2).

Police who are military veterans and who have experienced combat and found it stimulating may find it difficult to jettison this mind-set when they take up a career in law enforcement. Miller (2015) argues that those affected by the so-called "combat addiction syndrome" may seek to re-create situations in which they can re-experience the excitement of combat. In law enforcement, a preoccupation with weapons and fighting and experiencing police violence followed by lulls in stimulation may become a cycle and establish a pattern (p. 101).

The International Association of Chiefs of Police (IACP) Code of Conduct (1991) offers guidance on the use of force (see the "Use of Force" Closer Look box).

Research studies (Miller 2015: 107) have revealed that *deadly force* action is most likely to occur in the following circumstances in descending order of probability:

- Domestic violence and other disturbance calls
- Robbery in progress
- Burglary in progress
- Traffic offense
- Personal dispute and/or accident
- Stake-outs and drug busts

However, in any situation the line between correct and excessive use of force is not clear-cut, and much depends on the judgment of the officer, who should be guided in his or her decision-making by ethical standards and by use-of-force policies mandated by his or her agency. The FBI provides guidance to its agents by specifying four categories of threat to which it may be appropriate to *respond with deadly force:*

- A suspect is in possession of a weapon or is attempting to gain access to a weapon
- A suspect is armed and running to gain the advantage of cover
- A suspect who is capable of inflicting death or serious injury, with or without a weapon, demonstrates an intention to so
- A suspect is trying to escape a violent confrontation in which he or she has inflicted or attempted to inflict death or serious injury

It is important to note that agents are expected to react to a *threat* of violence and are not required to wait until a violent act has actually taken place (Miller 2015: 98).

Police Perspectives on Use of Force

Surveys have found that police are more likely to use excessive force if they believe that "real" police

A Closer Look

Use of Force

A police officer will never employ unnecessary force or violence and will use only such force in the discharge of duty as is reasonable in all circumstances.

Force should be used only with the greatest restraint and only after discussion, negotiation, and persuasion have been found to be inappropriate or ineffective. While the use of force is occasionally unavoidable, every police officer will refrain from applying the unnecessary infliction of pain or suffering and will never engage in cruel, degrading, or inhuman treatment of any person.

SOURCE: Center for the Study of Ethics in the Professions 2003. Copyright held by the International Association of Chiefs of Police, 515 North Washington Street, Alexandria, VA 22314, USA. Reprinted with permission. Further reproduction without express written permission from IACP is strictly prohibited.

work is action-oriented crime fighting and not solving problems (often referred to disparagingly as "social work"); it is also thought that when patrolling there are too many restrictions that constrain them in their battle with crime (Miller 2015: 100). Generally, police believe the only persons entitled to pass judgment on their use of force in tense situations on the streets are fellow officers and not administrators or civilians, and in general, citizens they encounter on their patrols will be hostile and disrespectful toward them and need to be taught to respect police (p. 100).

Research on police attitudes to the use of less than lethal force has revealed that 43% of officers responding to a survey reported that abiding by rules about use of force was not always congruent with getting the job done. However, two thirds of officers surveyed believed police were permitted to use sufficient force to make arrests, and about three quarters of officers agreed that it was unacceptable to use more force than was permitted to control a person who assaults an officer (Paoline and Terrill 2011: 180). Officers generally agreed that verbal control was the starting point of the force continuum, followed by low-level hands-on force (soft-hand tactics and pain compliance techniques), followed by chemical spray and Taser, followed by hard-hand tactics, then a baton and a projectile launcher (p. 183).

Officers were found to perceive verbal and passive resistance as similar; however, while about 44% of officers believed pain compliance techniques appropriate for verbal resistance, this increased to about 60% for passive resistance (Paoline and Terrill 2011: 184). Once a person becomes physically resistant, officers viewed chemical sprays, Taser, and hard-hand tactics as an appropriate response. While the survey revealed that the majority of officers believed there was no necessity to use high levels of force, a few officers favored hard-handed techniques and weapons for persons who did not resist physically—that is, they were compliant or resisted verbally or passively (p. 186).

In 2001, the Police Foundation surveyed police officers for their opinions on use of force, and after interviewing almost 1,000 officers from more than 100 agencies, the foundation reached the following conclusions:

- Most police officers disapproved of using excessive force.

- A substantial minority believed they should be permitted to use more force than the law allowed.
- A substantial minority believed that using more force than permitted by the law was sometimes acceptable.
- In the case of a physical assault on a police officer, almost 25% believed that using more force than was legally allowed in that situation was acceptable.
- More than 4 out of 10 police officers said that always following the rules was not compatible with doing police work.
- Only 7% of officers thought that police should be allowed to use physical force as a response to verbal abuse (Alpert and Dunham 2004: 38).

Generally, as noted earlier, the use of force in a given situation by police is nearly always ambiguous, so the boundary between excess and adequate force becomes difficult to establish. As an example of procedures that police must follow if force is used in an interaction with the public, the Miami-Dade Police Department requires that officers file a report in the following circumstances:

1. Force is applied that is likely to cause an injury or a complaint.

2. An injury results or may result from a struggle.

3. There is a complaint of an injury.

4. A chemical agent is discharged.

5. A baton is used.

6. The neck restraint is utilized.

7. There is an injury or complaint of an injury that results from guiding, holding, directing, or handcuffing a person who offers resistance (Alpert and Dunham 2004: 21).

Clearly, a report of this kind would be a vital document to any authority reviewing a particular instance of use of force.

Sometimes, there is a clear case of police brutality, such as that in New York involving the Haitian immigrant Abner Louima (see Case Study 3.1).

Police and Citizen Interactions

Studies concerning police encounters with citizens show that police should delay desires to immediately bring citizens into compliance with police orders and

---

Case Study 3.1 Cop Gets 15 Years in Torture Case

A former patrolman was sentenced to more than 15 years in prison for holding down Haitian immigrant Abner Louima as he was tortured in a police station bathroom. The sentencing came after former officer Charles Schwarz delivered a vitriolic speech declaring his innocence. U.S. District Court Judge Eugene Nickerson sentenced Schwartz to 15 years and 8 months, about half of the 30-year term given to fellow officer Justin Volpe, who pleaded guilty to carrying out the attack on Louima. He also ordered Schwarz to pay Louima $227,495 in restitution.

Schwartz, 34, was convicted in 1999 of violating Louima's civil rights by holding him down while Volpe viciously sodomized the skinny, handcuffed victim with a broken broomstick in August 1997. "But for Volpe's extraordinary brutality, it is unlikely Schwartz would now face a sentence for sexual assault carried out with such force," Nickerson said.

At a second trial in March 1999, a jury found Schwartz and two other former officers, Thomas Bruder and Thomas Wiese, guilty of federal obstruction of justice charges—a cover-up prosecutors said reflected a "blue wall of silence" code observed by some officers. Volpe—who is serving 30 years on his guilty plea—admitted wanting to punish Louima because he mistakenly thought the victim had punched him as police broke up a brawl outside a Brooklyn nightclub. But he claimed Schwartz was not the officer with him in the bathroom.

The attack by white officers on a black prisoner touched off protests alleging widespread police abuse of minorities. It triggered an ongoing Justice Department inquiry into whether the New York Police Department fosters brutality through lax discipline of wayward officers. Louima, who suffered internal injuries, sued the city, the police officers' union, and several individual officers for $155 million but later settled with the NYPD for $9 million (*Los Angeles Times* 2001). Louima insisted the second assailant—who put a foot in his mouth when he started to scream—was the same officer who drove him to the stationhouse. Records show the driver was Schwartz.

SOURCE: Based on "Cop Gets 15 Years in Torture Case," by Tom Hays. Associated Press, June 27, 2000.

---

should take into account that angry or emotionally charged persons are less likely to instantly comply with police orders (Lee and Vaughn 2010: 198). Some studies have found that suspects brandishing weapons were more likely to be subjected to police force, but others report mixed results. For example, a study found that female officers were no more or less likely to resort to verbal or physical force when the suspect had a weapon, but their male counterparts were more likely to use physical rather than verbal force. One study even found that possessing a weapon did not influence the likelihood of an officer resorting to force (Klahm and Tillyer 2010: 222).

The dynamic nature of police and citizen interactions is well accepted, rendering it important to capture behaviors that might precipitate the use of force. Studies suggest that where officers proactively initiate contact with a person they were more likely to apply force, but again, there are contrary findings. Empirical studies suggest that suspects who resist through passive, verbal, defensive, or active actions were more likely to experience police force, compared to compliant suspects (Klahm and Tillyer 2010: 222).

Alpert and Dunham (2004) coined the expression "authority maintenance ritual" to explain the nature of ongoing interactions during which police attempt to assert authority and control over persons through coercive means. The officers desire to control an encounter, and the citizen's responses to that exercise of police power are significant dimensions of such encounters and their possible outcomes.

The level of police coercion will ordinarily increase relative to the perceived threat posed by the citizen until a "tipping point" is reached (Miller 2015: 102). It follows that passive resistance is likely to evoke a verbal rebuke, and weapons are likely to be used where there is physical resistance. In 1975, Sykes argued that because of the power they possess police expect deferential behavior, and if they receive it, there is unlikely to be any escalation in the police response. However, if deference is not forthcoming and the citizen is judged to be guilty of "contempt of cop" (Miller 2015: 102), this will be read as a challenge to the officer's power and authority, with the outcome that the encounter may involve physical resistance and use of force. Consequently, when expectations are confounded, disrespect on both sides is the likely outcome (Rojek, Alpert, and Smith 2012: 305).

In a study on the use of force in the Miami-Dade Police Department based on written reports from 1996 to 1998 (Alpert and Dunham 2004: 66), researchers reported that almost all cases involving police use of force concerned acts of resistance by the suspect (97%). Resisting arrest (39%) and attempting to escape or fleeing the scene (26%) rated highest. In 21% of cases, the police officer was assaulted, and the most common type of force was striking or hitting an officer (36%). In terms of force used by officers to subdue suspects, the primary method was using hands and fists (55%), but officers also used dogs, batons, other weapons, and firearms in 23% of cases (p. 68).

Drawing on interviews of deputies of Richland County (South Carolina) Sheriff's Department who were involved in use-of-force incidents during the first half of 2007 and their use-of-force written reports, Rojek and colleagues (2012: 309) found that the accounts of officers and witnesses differed. All the officers described their actions in the encounters as reasonable and necessary behavior, but every citizen claimed improper or excessive force. Suspicion that drugs or alcohol were present elevated the threat level in the minds of officers because as one officer explained, "When on narcotics, they [suspects] get stronger and have a higher pain tolerance." Another responded, "In past experiences, I have seen where people under the influence of drugs and alcohol were not affected by pressure points or a Taser" (p. 312). In such situations, officers were more likely to regard suspects as posing a serious threat to them and the public. The threat of losing a weapon was similarly associated with an immediate and high-level application of force to avoid serious injury to the officer or the public.

Citizen accounts in the Rojek and colleagues study (2012) stressed overzealous actions by police in that levels of force were regarded as excessive. In one case, after leading police in a high-speed pursuit the driver complained that he was taken from the car and thrown on the ground.

> Fifteen officers jumped on me, kicked and punched me, kicked me in the head. Threw me in the car and booked me. . . . I didn't hit one of them, I didn't hit no citizen. It wasn't a violent crime or anything. (p. 314)

These encounters reveal citizens' lack of knowledge of likely police reactions to their conduct and show that each account, whether by police or citizens, is essentially self-serving, as it seeks to justify actions as proper and reasonable. Public ignorance about police use of force extends to assuming that when a suspect does not possess the same weapons as police or match the police physically he or she cannot be regarded as a menace; therefore, applying deadly force would violate some kind of "fair play" rule. However, this perspective fails to take account of the unpredictability of encounters in which, for example, any nearby object can function as a sometimes-deadly weapon (Miller 2015: 101).

Another issue that causes public confusion is the number of shots police fire when using deadly force. Multiple shots at a subject may simply reflect the fact that police are generally poor shots and that the average police officer misses the target at least as often as he or she hits it, even after extensive firearms training. Police training stresses that once a decision has been made to use deadly force, that force must be applied quickly and must be deadly (Miller 2015: 102).

In relation to police *arrests,* empirical research has consistently found police more likely to use force when making an arrest, but this may be a product of policies that require use of levels of force to handcuff suspects, including verbal commands (Klahm and Tillyer 2010: 223).

When a number of officers are involved in an incident, studies are mixed as to whether this increases the likelihood of use of force. However, in the case of *bystanders* the recent evidence suggests that the number of bystanders has no influence, but there are also conflicting studies that found the opposite to be the case (Klahm and Tillyer 2010: 223).

Officer age has been found unrelated to the propensity to use force in one study, but another found that older officers were less likely to resort to force, and when they did, it was less severe than that used by younger officers (Klahm and Tillyer 2010: 226). Concerning an officer's *years of experience,* some evidence suggests that officers with greater experience were less likely to use force and held less favorable attitudes to the use of force than did their counterparts with fewer years of experience, but there are studies that found that greater experience was not an influencing factor. Research has shown that the *level of education* of an officer impacts the outcome. For example, the research reveals that officers with a college degree are less likely to use verbal and physical force compared to their counterparts with only a high school degree. Other studies of this aspect have produced mixed results (p. 227).

Police/Citizen Interactions and Procedural Justice

Most recently, studies about police and citizen interaction have focused on procedural justice and police legitimacy. For example, Jackson and colleagues (2012: 1053) argue that if police ensure procedural justice when they interact with citizens this will increase the legitimacy, or public favorability, of the police because police will be regarded as "rightful holders of authority; that they have the right to dictate appropriate behavior and are entitled to be obeyed; and that laws should be obeyed simply because *that is the right thing to do*" (p. 1053). Procedural justice describes how police can exercise their powers in a way that is fair and just through the quality of treatment they give citizens and through the quality of their decision-making (Mazerolle, Bennett, Davis, Sargeant, and Manning 2013: 245). This has been termed *process-based policing*. When police treat citizens unfairly, they can be regarded as communicating the message that *you are not valued by society* (Jackson et al. 2012: 1053). As well, some studies have

shown that people are more concerned about being treated fairly by police than they are about the outcome of their experience (Tyler 2011: 258).

An example of a police strategy that may call into question police legitimacy and fairness is the strategy known as *hot spots policing*, which is based on geographic location and involves a concentrated police presence in an area that has a greater-than-average number of criminal incidents (Kochel 2011: 350). Typically, hot spots policing will comprise aggressive-order maintenance and zero-tolerance policing. Conceived in the time of high crime rates, hot spots policing has been well received in law enforcement, but there has been a lack of investigation into how it affects perceptions of police legitimacy among residents in targeted areas. Hot spots policing requiring police saturation of the selected area does not easily coexist with community policing because it involves sweeps, crackdowns, and multiple arrests. Research in Chicago in 1998 found that residents living in highly disadvantaged communities with high crime rates (likely by definition to be designated hot spots) are less likely to regard police as legitimate, less likely to be satisfied with police, and more likely to tolerate deviance (p. 350).

Generally, four components make up procedural justice:

- Dialogue exists that encourages citizen participation before a decision is made by an officer—the existence of a dialogue has been found to be important in establishing legitimacy.
- Neutrality in decision-making is demonstrated by conducting a dialogue with citizens.
- Respect for citizens is demonstrated throughout the interaction.
- Trustworthiness is present, evidenced by adherence to the preceding components.

Research has shown that when these principles are applied in police and citizen interactions citizens are more satisfied with the interaction itself and the outcome. When even one of these elements is applied in an encounter, there is likely to be increased citizen cooperation and compliance (Mazerolle et al. 2013: 265). One study by Dai, Frank, and Sun (2011: 159) looked at whether procedural justice specifically influenced two types of behavior toward police: citizen disrespect to police and citizen noncompliance with police requests.

It found that only police demeanor and their reception of citizen voices were significant factors in reducing citizen disrespect and noncompliance.

When citizens are dealt with fairly by applying procedural justice, they are less likely to believe they have been racially profiled and more likely to accept the decision. When an encounter lacks procedural justice, citizens are more likely to disobey and resist police commands (Mazerolle et al. 2013: 247). This approach to police and citizen encounters has found support in studies in the United Kingdom, Australia, and Israel, but it may not produce similar results in countries where consent and cooperation are regularly obtained by force, such as in Ghana, which experiences high crime rates and significant police abuse of powers (p. 248).

Research reveals that when police treat people with courtesy and respect police legitimacy is enhanced, and this treatment promotes compliance with police commands. As Tyler (2011: 260) points out, changing police procedures to incorporate procedural justice means

- allowing citizens to offer explanations before making decisions;
- explaining to citizens how and why decisions are being made;
- providing citizens with a means to complain; and
- always treating citizens with respect.

Why should police implement process policing? Police might claim that policing is dangerous and they are therefore safer if they project dominance, but studies have shown that using coercion in the form of handcuffing, commanding, or arresting has minimal impact on compliance (Tyler 2011: 260). Some evidence exists that procedural justice extends beyond police and citizen interactions. For example, one study showed that persons who had observed police acting violently were more likely to distrust police compared to those who had not seen police acting in that way. Similarly, it is possible that media reports of police violence may undermine confidence in the police (Jackson et al. 2012).

U.S. Supreme Court Decisions on Use of Force

Two U.S. Supreme Court decisions are relevant in assessing use of force. In the case of *Tennessee v. Garner* (1985), late one evening in October 1974 two Memphis police officers investigated a complaint about a prowler, going to the rear of the house on arrival at the homeowner's address. They observed someone running away across the backyard, and as the suspect stopped at a chain link fence, one of the officers saw that he was 17 or 18 years old and unarmed. The officer called out, "Police—halt!" However, when the suspect began to climb the fence, the officer, thinking he would escape, shot him in the head and killed him. According to Tennessee law at the time, police were permitted to use all necessary means to effect an arrest once they gave notice of their intention to arrest, consequent to the suspect fleeing or forcibly resisting. In considering the case, the Supreme Court determined that whether or not deadly force was justifiable in a particular case depended on whether or not it was "objectively reasonable." An officer might only use *deadly force* "if he has probable cause to believe that the suspect poses a threat of death or serious physical injury either to the officer or to others."

In *Graham v. Connor* (1989), the Court applied the test of the reasonableness of the force used to all claims of the use of *excessive but nondeadly force*, noting that there is no precise definition of reasonableness but that four factors are relevant:

- The severity of the suspected crime
- Whether or not the suspect threatens the safety of the arresting officers
- Whether or not the suspect actively resists arrest
- Whether or not the suspect is attempting to evade arrest by fleeing from the scene

The Court also determined that "reasonableness" concerning the use of force must be judged after taking the perspective of a reasonable officer at the scene and must take account of the fact that police sometimes have to make split-second decisions concerning the use of force. Studies have revealed that this split-second syndrome is often the result of functioning in low-lit areas, pursuing suspects who try to hide from police or officers, speculating about dangerousness, and inaccurate shooting by police (Lee and Vaughn 2010: 197). Therefore, following the two previous cases, "objective reasonableness" is now established as the standard for excessive force, and each case of alleged excessive force must be judged and assessed on its merits (p. 194).

In cases that followed, such as *Scott v. Harris* (2007), the Court validated police use of deadly force during a high-speed vehicle pursuit when the suspect endangered the lives of police and innocent strangers because a speeding vehicle attempting to evade police is itself an instrument of deadly force. Additionally, in *Canton v. Harris* (1989), the Court held that municipalities are liable civilly for failure to train police officers when "failure to train amounts to deliberate indifference to the rights of persons with whom the police come into contact." This case prompted more police training and policy formulation on police use of force.

Race and Use of Force

Research on the association between race and police use of force is inconclusive. While several studies document that race did not influence a decision to use force, other studies report contrary results, some finding that black suspects were more likely to be subjected to force than their white counterparts and others finding that race produced mixed results, depending on the circumstances of the encounter. Thus, one study found that black suspects were more likely to have force used against them in situations where police expected compliance with orders, but race was not considered a factor in encounters that involved suspect resistance (Klahm and Tillyer 2010: 218). A series of studies has shown that the race of an officer is not related to the likelihood or appropriateness of officer use of force (p. 224).

In 2006 and 2008 in a series of interviews with urban youth, frequent complaints of excessive force were reported, especially among black males. Respondents claimed police had bad attitudes toward them, used force that was usually unprovoked, and frequently coerced from them information about criminal activity. In addition, the respondents complained that officers tended to use force against them if it appeared they were showing insufficient respect or deference to police (Rojek et al. 2012: 304). Unfortunately, these studies did not include the police perspective.

Policing and Implicit Racial Bias

Explicit racial bias, in the sense of conscious expressions of racism, is rare these days. Recent research studies have, however, shown how implicit racial bias can affect any form of decision-making in the criminal justice system and elsewhere. *Implicit bias* refers to implicit associations that our minds draw upon subconsciously: These associations help us to order the categories into which we place persons, places, and things we encounter in order to make sense of our daily life. As we make these associations, over time they become "hardwired" into our minds, and we unconsciously call upon them when needed. Implicit association is a useful tool because it frees our conscious mind from having to consider basic functions, but it also sustains biases. Psychologists test for implicit bias through the Implicit Association Test (IAT), which measures differences in reaction times as persons sort words on a subject into different categories. A short reaction time indicates a subconscious association is being made and therefore an implicit association, and a longer reaction time indicates a conscious and not implicit-based reaction (Clemons 2014: 693).

Implicit associations about race become translated into implicit racial bias because of the negative racial stereotypes to which we are all exposed. That implicit bias will then shape the reaction to an event. According to Clemons (2014), the majority of Americans harbor negative implicit associations about black Americans. This has been demonstrated by a sample of about 760,000 persons who between 2000 and 2006 took either a "race-attitude" or "child-race attitude" IAT at an online project site. Of those tested, 68% showed significantly faster response times when black/dark skin was paired with "bad" and when white/light skin was paired with "good." Only 14% showed the reverse (p. 694). Researchers have found implicit associations that link blackness with danger, violence, aggression, and criminality and in reverse, criminality with blackness.

Most empirical research on implicit racial bias has been conducted with law enforcement officers, who are often required to make difficult decisions very quickly within their wide discretion. When police speak of their "gut reaction" and of "hunches" about persons who may be suspicious, subconscious associations between race and criminality may be influencing them. This helps to explain why police stop black citizens at disproportionate rates (Clemons 2014: 694). Research has also demonstrated the presence of implicit bias in police decisions concerning the use of deadly force.

Police use of force tends to be more frequent in higher crime areas that are often associated with minorities, and it has been argued that neighborhood factors such as minority disadvantage may engender psychological factors in officers that make recourse to excessive force probable (Prenzler et al. 2013: 344). Police profiling of young black males as suspicious or dangerous may also be a factor (Miller 2015: 106), and racial bias has been shown in shoot/don't-shoot decisions. For example, in one study a simplified video game presented black and white males as targets, with each holding a gun or threatening object. Participants were told to shoot only armed targets but were required to decide shoot/don't shoot immediately after seeing each target.

The results indicate racial bias, given that participants fired more quickly on an armed target when he was black than when he was white, and they decided not to shoot more quickly when the unarmed target was white than when he was black. This study found there was no difference in shooter bias between black and white participants (Lawson 2015: 340–341).

Police profiling of young black males as dangerous may reflect a stereotypical fear of black males among police. A 2004 study tried to assess if officers perceived black males as violent and criminal; it asked 182 police officers to view black and white faces and to indicate if they thought a face "looked criminal." The outcome was that black faces looked more criminal to police, and in fact, the darker the skin color, the more an officer tended to believe him criminal (Lawson 2015: 341).

A Closer Look

U.S. Department of Justice: Investigation of the Ferguson Police Department

On September 4, 2014, the Civil Rights Division of the Department of Justice opened an investigation of the Ferguson (Missouri) Police Department under the Violent Crime Control and Law Enforcement Act of 1994. The investigation followed the shooting of an unarmed black teenager, Michael Brown, in August 2014 by a white Ferguson police officer, which provoked unrest, protests, demonstrations, and some looting by residents who believed the shooting was not justified and may have exhibited racial bias. The investigation into the Ferguson police force, comprising 54 sworn officers, uncovered a policing culture that included the following elements:

- Officers expected and demanded compliance with their commands, even when they lacked any legal authority. They made enforcement decisions based on how persons spoke to them or what they said to police, and police reacted quickly to challenges and verbal slights. Officers believed that arrest was the appropriate response to "contempt of cop," and such arrests were commonly associated with charges of failure to comply, disorderly conduct, interference with officer, or resisting arrest.

- There was a pattern of stops without reasonable suspicion and arrests without probable cause and with use of excessive force. African American citizens accounted for 85% of vehicle stops, 90% of citations, and 93% of arrests by officers from 2012 to 2014, despite the fact they constituted only 67% of the town population. These disparities were the outcome of "unlawful bias against and stereotypes about African Americans."

- Police engaged in a *pattern of excessive force*. Officers quickly escalated encounters with persons they perceived to be disobeying commands or resisting arrest; they came to rely on Tasers when less or no force would have sufficed; they released canines on unarmed persons

(Continued)

(Continued)

unreasonably and before attempting to use force less likely to cause injury; and almost 90% of the force used was applied to African Americans. Instances of excessive use of force included an incident in August 2010 when a lieutenant used a Taser in stun mode against a black woman in the city jail who refused to remove her bracelets, even though five officers were present and the woman presented no physical threat. This action violated the department's own use-of-force policy, which required that force not be used until all reasonable alternatives had been exhausted or would be ineffective. A policy direction describes the Taser as "designed to overcome active aggression or overt actions of assault."

- Police used force to punish behavior that was annoying or distasteful but did not pose any threat. In January 2013, a patrol sergeant stopped an African American male and detained him without any explanation. When the man declined to answer questions or to submit to a search, the officer grabbed him by the belt and drew his Taser, ordering the man to comply. The man crossed his arms and stated he had done nothing wrong. Video from the Taser showed no aggression toward the officer. The officer fired the Taser, causing the man to fall to the ground, and then applied the Taser again, claiming later that the man had tried to stand. The video showed he had not moved from the ground. The man was charged with failure to comply and resisting arrest but with no substantive criminal charge.

- The system of oversight for use of force was ineffective because force use was often not reported; when it was, there was seldom any meaningful review of it. Policies on use of force were routinely ignored, and supervisors almost never investigated use-of-force incidents, even though policy required they do so. Supervisors almost never interviewed nonpolice witnesses, and there was a presumption that the officer's account of the incident was correct. Supervisors readily accepted "boilerplate" justifications for use of force, such as that the person took "a fighting stance."

SOURCE: U.S. Department of Justice: Investigation of the Ferguson Police Department, March 4, 2015.

Explaining Excessive Force

There are three theoretical approaches to the causes of police use of excessive force. The first comprises psychological theories that focus on individual officers and apply the "rotten apple" argument that contends there is no systemic issue and the incident is merely an aberration; the second comprises sociological theories that regard police culture as a determining factor because police are seen as isolated from citizens; and the third comprises organizational theories that focus on the systems in place in police agencies for managing officers. Generally, the issue of police use of excessive force is complex, and none of these theoretical approaches can claim to be an adequate explanation of why some police use excessive force and others do not (Lersch and Mieczkowski 2005: 552).

The "Rotten Apple" Explanation

While there may not be a "police personality" type as such, research suggests there are personality types among police who appear to be associated with high rates of use of force, including deadly force. Some officers may suffer from personality disorders or other dysfunctions and have typically been found to have personality traits that may be antisocial, narcissistic, borderline, and paranoid. Dysfunctional personalities may manifest egocentricity, impulsivity, immaturity, inflexibility, and lack of empathy, which can predispose to abusive behavior—especially when they perceive threats to their authority from citizens.

Such officers are unlikely to learn from mistakes or change their style of policing and tend to be the subject of a disproportionate number of citizen complaints (Miller 2015: 100).

Proposals for responding to the rotten apple view include establishing early warning systems to target officers who show indicators of poor conduct, such as multiple citizen complaints.

Sociological and Organizational Theories

Sociological approaches recommend community policing and civilian review boards as mechanisms for lessening the distance between police and the public, and organizational approaches argue that designing better policies for internal control—such as setting explicit rules instead of allowing broad discretion and thoroughly assessing use-of-force reports—will be effective strategies.

When faced with complaints of excessive force, police often adopt the strategy of characterizing the excess as an aberration by a particular officer, but many argue that police brutality is systemic (Lawrence 2000). Given that incidences of police abuse now often attract media attention, researchers have investigated the relationship between the media and police. Results have revealed that police are on intimate terms with the media in their role as providers of news and have developed a high level of competence in public relations. In fact, one researcher has suggested that the police employ a media-centered framework in their work because they believe that the public obtains its notions of acceptable police standards and conduct from television and the movies (Perlmutter 2000). Media coverage of claims of excessive police violence may therefore rely significantly on police narratives of an incident, but as noted previously, media privileging of police accounts is now being challenged by the activity of citizen journalists.

Assessing the Level of Force

Fundamentally, whether or not force is excessive must depend on the context, and even witnesses often cannot resolve the issue. Kleinig (1996: 99–102) identifies a number of factors that he considers relevant to assessing the use of force in ethical terms:

- *Intentions.* Police may use force wrongfully as a means of punishment rather than to contain a suspect. For example, tightening handcuffs may be employed to punish an arrested person, or police may use rough handling or an overnight stay in the lockup as punishment. In *Graham v. Sauk Prairie Police Commission* (1990, in Lee and Vaughn 2010: 196), a suspect was shot twice in the head and killed after being handcuffed behind his back, despite that fact that at the time he was not fleeing from police and not behaving threateningly. Kleinig argues that measures of this kind are clearly unethical and outside the scope of the police function.

- *Seemliness.* Force not only must be employed in good faith but also must be seemly. When police methods shock the conscience or offend even hardened sensibilities, they are not considered seemly. In one case, for example, a suspect's stomach was pumped to recover apparently swallowed evidence of drug possession, and the court judged this as unseemly (*Rochin v. California* 1952).

- *Proportionality.* The force used to achieve legitimate police aims ought to be proportionate to the seriousness of the offense alleged or threatened. Thus, shooting a person suspected of committing a misdemeanor would be an example of employing disproportionate force.

- *Minimization.* This requires that police use the least means to secure their aims and is known as *the principle of the least restrictive alternative.* For example, if handcuffs will do the job, they should be used rather than some more draconian method of immobilization, and deadly force should not be employed if a person can be arrested without it.

- *Practicability.* Since there is a presumption against using force, it must be shown that its use will achieve the purpose for which it is deployed. In other words, police need to appreciate those situations in which a forceful presence is required as opposed to those in which a softer strategy is called for. This relates to the need for police to exercise their discretion according to the demands of a particular situation rather than applying one rule, such as to intimidate or punish, in all cases.

According to Regina Lawrence (2000), ambiguity about the use of force has the effect of reducing or limiting media coverage of police abuse because ultimately journalists ask for proof of abuse, and this can almost never be demonstrated. She argues that as long as much of the public is willing to give police the discretion they seek, incidents such as the one involving Rodney King can always be rationalized by police as "collateral damage" in the "war against crime." In the examples of police violence in Case Study 3.2, the first case was explained as an "unintentional outcome" and the second as violence used as punishment.

Reducing the Level of Force

What has been the impact of interventions designed to reduce police use of force? Several case studies of such interventions are described by Prenzler and colleagues (2013: 345). Examples of these programs include the following:

- In 1969, the Oakland Police Department created a Violence Reduction Unit following criticism of its strategy for crime fighting that depended on making maximum arrests. This strategy led to high rates of police and citizen conflict and the alienation of the black community. A reforming police chief, Charles Gain, established the Violence Reduction Unit and staffed it with officers to study the issue of police violence and develop interventions to address the problem. One strategy was to establish a peer review panel that was tasked

to assess officers referred by supervisors for having been involved in an above-average number of violent conflicts with citizens. The program was not adequately evaluated and was phased out in the 1970s.

- The Metro-Dade Police Citizen Violence Reduction Project began as a partnership in 1985 between the Metro-Dade Police Department and a research and policy institute, The Police Foundation. The project aimed at enhancing patrol officers' skills in diffusing conflicts. Four areas of policing were identified as mostly closely associated with police violence and public complaints: routine traffic stops, high-risk vehicle stops involving offenses other than traffic violations or DUIs, reported or suspected crimes in progress, and disputes. A 3-day training program was developed using role play, pre-intervention data was collected, and a thorough analysis of incidents performed. These interventions were generally positive, largely because of enhanced dispute settlement procedures.

- The New York Police Department began a project in 1969 aimed at assessing and reducing the incidence of police shootings. The success of the program can be measured by the fact that from 2008 to 2010 the total number of shots fired by police showed an 80% reduction over figures in 1995. The number of persons shot by police showed a decline of 91.8% from a peak of 221 in

---

Case Study 3.2 Five Police Officers Sentenced for Shooting Unarmed Family

On April 4, 2012, five officers from the New Orleans Police Department were sentenced to terms of imprisonment of 38 to 65 years for events arising out of the devastation caused to New Orleans by Hurricane Katrina in August 2005.

The trial revealed that a group of police opened fire with assault rifles and a shotgun on an unarmed family walking on the east side of the Danziger Bridge in New Orleans on September 4, 2005. Police had received a call from an officer at the bridge reporting gunfire, and the five police officers arrived at the scene in a rental truck. The family had been walking to a grocery store and took shelter behind a concrete barrier when the gunfire began.

Police claimed initially they had been fired on, but it was shown that this story had been fabricated and a cover-up had been arranged. Police inflicted multiple wounds on the family, and two died. Five other officers pleaded guilty before trial and testified at the trial that the shooting was unjustified and a massive police cover up had taken place. The cover up included one officer bringing a gun from his home and planting it on the bridge and later claiming he had found it there the day following the shooting. The existence of two eyewitnesses and their alleged statements of what occurred were also fabricated.

SOURCE: Federal Bureau of Investigation, New Orleans, April 4, 2012.

1971 to an average of 18 in the period 2008 to 2010. The NYPD attributes the decline to the operation of the "SOP 9" process that involves analysis of the elements and sequence of each shooting and then feeds the results into training and improved procedures. For example, a policy of "shoot to stop" and not "shoot to kill" was introduced. Despite these significant improvements, police shootings in the city continue to attract controversy.

- In Portland, Oregon, in the 1990s, there was considerable public concern over police shootings and alleged use of excessive force. Responding to the concern, the city developed two projects: one focused on officer-involved shootings and the other on broader issues relating to police use of force. The Police Assessment Resource Center (PARC) was engaged to assess shooting incidents, and it recommended the mandatory use of use-of-force reports as well as improvements to policy and police tactics. A new use-of-force review board examined all shootings. In 2006, a task force that included a citizen review committee worked with police to analyze use-of-force data to improve the management of force and made a series of recommendations, which included the following:
  o Officers report their justification for use of force
  o Give more attention to reducing officer provocations
  o All force complaints require a debriefing, which lowers the threshold for use-of-force intervention
  o Conduct a review of street policing strategies in the precincts with the highest use-of-force ratios

Generally, all the recommendations were implemented, with a consequent reduction in complaints about use of force, a 35% decline in force incidents from 2007 to 2009, and a fall in citizen and officer injuries.

Excessive Force: Other Countries

Internationally, excessive force is said to be prevalent in all *Asian* countries. Basil Fernando (2003) comments that in these countries police officers "are expected to use coercion, including torture, in criminal investigations" (p. 30). This is justified by reference to the need to maintain order because the maintenance of public order has a higher priority than law enforcement in Asian countries. In *Nigeria*, Etannibi E. O. Alemika (2003) suggests that the maintenance of

the colonial policing model has resulted in police–citizen interactions being largely involuntary and "characterized by police brutality, corruption and hostility to citizens" (p. 72). Alemika explains that the police are primarily used to maintain order, but citizens see police as oppressor and repressor, and police employ various methods of torture, including

> whipping with electrical cables; hanging or suspending suspects from ceiling fan hooks; chaining suspects to the ground in a squatting position or against the wall in a standing position; shock batons and chairs; insertion of sharp objects into male genitals and blunt objects (such as bottles) into female organs; forceful removal of fingernails; deprivation of sleep, food and medical care; and solitary confinement and denial of access to relations, friends and attorneys. (p. 78)

In *Argentina*, a crime survey conducted in 1998 revealed that 18.5% of those reporting believed that retired police and military personnel most frequently committed crimes, and about 7% believed that active police officers committed crimes (Smulovitz 2003: 132). In *Brazil*, according to Paulo Mesquita Neto and Adrianna Loche (2003), government and police responses to crime control have been "undermined by the persistence of police brutality and the low level of respect for and cooperation with the police and the criminal justice system on the part of the community" (p. 191). Police killings of civilians in Brazil are not recorded as homicides. Rather, Martha K. Huggins (2010) reports, they are registered as police having used "legitimate force" against a "criminal's threatening actions" (p. 73). She notes that regular police in Brazil are accustomed to supplementing their low police incomes by moonlighting as private security for upper-class, white, gated communities (p. 74). Within a framework of violence in one of the most violent countries in the world, police are responsible for a high proportion of all homicides. Huggins concludes that police violence is systemic, and death squads (that include police officers) undertake killing for profit (p. 81).

Police Use of Force: Tasers

The Taser was originally developed during the mid-1970s as a nonlethal replacement for the firearm and was one of a collection of devices with that objective that included chemical sprays. Tasers and other devices were therefore portrayed as having the capacity to humanely control persons. Despite these claims, Tasers have always remained controversial because of instances where persons are said to have died after being subjected to "Tasering" (Wolf and De Angelis 2011: 659).

One of the most common forms of Taser is the X26 made by Taser International. It is a handheld weapon that delivers a high voltage electrical charge using two delivery systems: As a "stun gun," it can be used for compliance enforcement and deliver a high voltage shock by pressing two probes against the body; in "probe mode," two modified fishhook barbs can be fired at a person up to a distance of several dozen feet. When the two probes attach to the skin or clothing of the target, they create a circuit, and a rapid, pulsed electrical charge is delivered that impacts the nervous system, causing severe pain, intense muscle contractions, and a loss of control over voluntary muscles. Consequently, Tasers deliver an exceedingly painful electrical shock, bring about almost instant paralysis, and bring the target to the ground. Taser discharges can be recorded and downloaded, and recent models incorporate a video system (Wolf and De Angelis 2011: 659, 667).

Over the past decade, Tasers and similar electroshock devices have become standard equipment in numerous U.S. police forces. In 2005, the Government Accounting Office estimated that almost half of law enforcement agencies had adopted the device, and by 2008, according to the National Institute of Justice, more than 11,500 law enforcement agencies had acquired Tasers (Wolf and De Angelis 2011: 659). There are no common standards for the use of Tasers among police forces, but in a 2008 survey of 40 law enforcement agencies, Amnesty International found that most agencies had policies stating that Tasers may be used when officers face "active resistance" to a lawful attempt at controlling a person. The Department of Justice gave guidance in 2011 that the Taser was a "less-lethal" and not a "non-lethal" weapon (U.S. Department of Justice and Police Executive Research Forum 2011).

Many policing agencies place Tasers on the same level in the use-of-force continuum as pepper spray and other less-than-lethal weapons. The U.S. Court of Appeals for the Ninth Circuit held in 2009 that Tasers constitute an "intermediate, significant level of force that must be justified by a strong government interest that *compels* the employment of such force" (emphasis in the court decision; *Bryan v. McPherson* 2009). Other court decisions on Taser use state the following:

- An officer uses excessive force when he or she deploys a Taser against a person whose crime is minor and who is not actively resisting, attempting to flee, or posing any imminent danger to others (*Brown v. City of Golden Valley* 2011).
- Minimal defensive resistance, including stiffening the body to impede being pulled from a car and raising an arm in defense, does not make use of a Taser reasonable.
- Use of a Taser is not objectively reasonable when the suspect pulls away from an officer but does not actively resist arrest, attempt to flee, or pose an immediate threat (*Casey v. City of Fed. Heights* 2007).

Ethical Constraints on Taser Use

In police and citizen encounters involving police use of force, a balance has to be struck between the risks faced by police officers and efforts to curtail injury to those whom police seek to bring under control. These encounters are not for the purpose of inflicting punishment but rather for control purposes only. A number of devices provide police with the capacity to inflict severe pain, and in ethical terms, police may be tempted to employ a device whose use would be inappropriate in a situation that calls for a lesser level of force (Kleinig 2007: 284). A key issue is assessing the level of risk to the officer.

It therefore becomes critical for police departments to develop rules and procedures for correct Taser use in order to avoid misuse so that Tasering does not become an automatic police response to every risk situation. Incorporating these instructions in training courses on Taser use helps to ensure that procedures are applied by all officers armed with these devices; this in turn will add public legitimacy to instances where Tasering is justified (Kleinig 2007: 288). Such procedures ought also to consider groups for whom Taser use would be inappropriate, even where there was an active level of resistance. Examples would be with young children, pregnant women, the elderly, the disabled, and persons already placed in handcuffs (p. 291).

Police forces that authorize the use of a Taser where an officer is faced with only passive resistance may be criticized for applying too much force because the threat to an officer is negligible. In one incident that occurred on the campus of the University of California, police Tasered a student who failed to provide adequate identification to enter a library and then refused to leave (Kleinig 2007: 290). At all times, his resistance was passive, and he posed no danger to police or to others. This clearly seems to have been a police overreaction to a person resisting their orders and authority.

While there is scant research on the effectiveness of use-of-force policies in controlling officer actions, one recent study of Dallas, Texas (with a population of about 1.2 million and a police force of about 3,500), examined this issue when a policy change on police Taser use was put into operation at the end of 2005. Originally, all patrol officers who had completed a 4-hour training program could check out a Taser, though they were instructed to use it only when met with what the police department termed "defensive resistance," meaning any form of physical noncompliance to a police order, such as refusing to stand when seated if ordered to do so (Bishopp, Klinger, and Morris 2014: 5). This permissive policy lasted only 1 year, and by the end of 2005, officers were no longer permitted to use Tasers against those who failed to comply with verbal orders. Under the new policy, Taser use was limited to situations referred to by the department as "active aggression," meaning that some sort of physical action was being directed at an officer, such as punching, grabbing, or kicking. Thus, the Taser was relocated to a higher level on the use-of-force continuum. Researchers compared use-of-force reports before and after the policy change and found that the change had affected the frequency of Taser use: Officers used Tasers more than 60% fewer times during the study period of 2007 than in the 8-month period in 2005 before the policy change.

Analysis of Taser Use

Research into police use of Tasers includes an analysis by Crow and Adrion (2011: 366) of the use-of-force data for a medium-sized municipal police department (144 officers for a population of about 54,000) over the period 2004 to 2010. Following a use-of-force incident, officers were required to complete a report, and the study examined aggregate reports over the period. Previous studies had revealed that the level of resistance offered by a person is a significant determinant of the level and type of force used by an officer and that the resistance level is an important indicator of the dangerousness of the person. Thus, dangerousness is assessed according to the level of resistance. In the police department studied, subject resistance followed an ascending continuum from Presence, Verbal, Flight, Physical, and Weapons stages. The analysis revealed the following (p. 376):

- The Taser was used in more than half of all use-of-force incidents over the study period—a similar rate of use to that found in a previous study.
- Cases involving Taser use were associated with more minority and male subjects compared to other incidents where force was used.
- The incidents in which the Taser was used tended to involve relatively lower levels of resistance compared to instances in other studies.
- The Taser was less likely to be employed when the level of resistance was only Presence, Physical or involved a Weapon; therefore, officers were most likely to use Tasers in Verbal and Flight situations.
- Nonwhite subjects were almost twice as likely as white subjects to be Tasered.
- Older officers and female officers were more likely to use the Taser.

In addition to the level of resistance shown by a subject, psychological factors also play a role in determining Taser use. The effects of stress on police officers are discussed in detail in Chapter 2, but generally, policing has been described as an especially stressful occupation because it can involve dangerous incidents, disturbing crime scenes, and bureaucratic rules that exacerbate stress. Consequently, an association has been found between policing and burnout, poor health, and alcohol abuse. It has also been suggested that police tend to see threats to their safety more frequently and to respond to such threats more aggressively than would nonpolice (Stinson, Reyns, and Liederbach 2012: 6).

Improper Use of Tasers

In a study of the criminal misuse of Tasers, Stinson and colleagues (2012: 1) examined data on 24 cases involving officers arrested for crimes involving inappropriate use of Tasers between 2005 and 2010. In the cases examined, there was little or no situational risk to the officer concerned, and criminal misuse of a Taser was found to be associated with suspects already in handcuffs or against persons who were not criminals. In the 24 cases, the majority of the officers were charged with assault-related offenses—half with misdemeanors and half with felonies, with aggravated assault being the most common felony. In eight cases, the officers were convicted. The victims were commonly handcuffed criminal suspects, and many cases involved victims with apparently close relationships to the officers, including their wives and girlfriends.

In six cases, the victim was female, including one case where an off-duty officer shot his 15-year-old stepdaughter in the eye with a Taser during a family dispute while he was driving a police cruiser. All the off-duty cases involved some form of domestic violence, and one third of those cases involved an intoxicated off-duty officer armed with a Taser. In two cases, off-duty police Tasered their spouse or girlfriend, having found them *in flagrante delicto* with another man (Stinson et al. 2012: 12). In one case, an officer fired a Taser at a homeless man standing in a church parking lot until it ran out of power, then hit him with a baton so hard that it crushed his face bones. In another, the officer shocked a black suspect nine times, and he died of a heart attack. None of the cases examined involved much situational risk to the officer involved, and as described earlier, in a number of cases the objective seems to have been to teach the victim a lesson.

Associated with questions about police use of force is the notion that within police culture there is a perspective that the ends always justify the means.

A Closer Look

Excessive Force in the Cleveland Police Department

In May 2015, the Department of Justice announced that after an almost 2-year investigation of the Cleveland Police Department it had found a pattern of "unreasonable and unnecessary use of force" by police officers. The Justice Department reported that the excessive use of force by Cleveland police involved Tasers, chemical sprays, and fists, which were used for retaliation. Police had also used force against the mentally ill. The instances of excessive force included police using Tasers and assaulting and pepper-spraying persons who were already under restraint. In one case in 2014, police fired two shots at a man who was fleeing from two armed assailants. In 2011, a man who was restrained on the ground with spread arms and legs was kicked by police and treated for a broken facial bone.

The city of Cleveland agreed to enter into a consent decree that would tighten policies and practices concerning the use of force and make police subject to oversight by an independent monitor. While the city is 53% black and 37% white, its 1,513-person police department is 25% black and 65% white. Eleven years ago, the city entered into a similar settlement with the Justice Department following a federal investigation of reported police abuses.

The settlement mandates new rules that include new firearms rules that prohibit warning shots and neck holds; enforce better data collection on use-of-force incidents; state that Tasers must not target head, neck, or genitals; and provide improved use-of-force training to ensure that force is constitutional and lawful.

SOURCES: Taken from New York Times, May 12, 2015 and The Guardian May 26, 2015: *Cleveland Announces Historic Second Settlement Over Chronic Police Abuse.*

This perspective is termed *Dirty Harry/dirty hands*, but in more contemporary terms, it can also be referenced to the character Jack Bauer from the television series *24*.

Excessive Use of Force: Dirty Harry/Dirty Hands and Jack Bauer in *24*

The use of "dirty hands" or dirty means by police to secure their goals (Kleinig 1996) has been characterized as the "Dirty Harry problem" (Klockars 1980). Drawing on the 1971 film *Dirty Harry*, which shows Inspector Harry Callahan using torture to establish the whereabouts of a kidnapped girl, Carl Klockars raises the issue of the morality of using force to extract information from suspects. Dirty means are not limited to actual torture, but they can include beating confessions out of suspects, making false arrests, stopping and searching without proper cause, and using threats and coercion to obtain evidence.

Modern-day popular culture has conspicuously featured torture—not by police, but by the counterterrorist agent Jack Bauer in the very popular television show *24*. Bauer often uses torture in "ticking-bomb scenarios" and also in the normal course of his antiterrorist activities: A television watchdog group counted 67 scenes of torture during the first five seasons of the show (Keslowitz 2009: 1126). Critics have complained that the show glorifies torture, but in the seventh season, characters are shown to be struggling with the morality and legality of torture, and Bauer stands trial for his acts of torture, which he justifies as necessary to protect the innocent (p. 1129). (See Chapter 10 for a full discussion of the ethics of torture).

An analysis of the components of the Dirty Harry situation reveals four conditions faced by the police officer (Miller, Blackler, and Alexandra 1997: 119):

1. The police officer has an opportunity to achieve a morally good end or outcome and intends to do so. (In the *Dirty Harry* movie, Callahan used torture to discover the location of the girl.)

2. The means used to achieve this good end are normally considered morally wrong (dirty). (In *Dirty Harry*, the torture included standing on the suspect's mangled and wounded leg to obtain the location of the girl.)

3. The use of these means is perceived by the police officer to be the best or only practicable means of ensuring that the good end is met.

4. The good likely to be achieved far outweighs the bad consequences of using dirty means, a perspective held by utilitarianism (see Chapter 13).

The crux of the problem raised by *Dirty Harry* and *24* is whether means that are illegal and morally questionable may be used to achieve ends that may themselves be considered moral. In policing, employing dirty means to achieve moral ends is known as *noble cause corruption* (see Chapter 2). Using dirty hands is, of course, morally problematic because it involves the use of unlawful methods. Some argue that public life necessarily involves dirtying one's hands (Walzer in Kleinig 1996: 55), whereas others, such as Kleinig (p. 56), are not convinced that the scenarios usually presented justify the use of dirty hands. Others suggest that such situations should be avoided as much as possible because the person using dirty hands will often feel moral qualms about what he or she has done, and frequent use of dirty means may induce a moral callousness in an individual (Miller et al. 1997: 123).

Klockars (1980) concludes that police officers who use dirty means should be punished because they will grasp the wrong moral choice they have made only if this happens. Importantly, Klockars implies that as far as the public is concerned, if it fails to condemn the use of dirty means, it becomes complicit in noble cause corruption. Conversely, if the public insists on punishing police officers who use dirty means, the ironic effect is to increase our fear of crime since criminals may go unpunished.

In Europe, the Committee for the Prevention of Torture and Inhuman or Degrading Punishment or Treatment, a body established by the European Convention on Human Rights which prohibits torture or inhuman or degrading treatment or punishment, can investigate the improper use of force by the police (Jobard 2003). Members of the committee may visit places in which people are held against their will, including police stations, at any time. By the year 2000, the committee had visited France five times, and in 1999, the European Court of Human Rights found that France had tortured a person held in custody by its Criminal Investigation Service (p. 424). During its visits to France, the committee also heard accusations of behavior against the police that included punches and slaps, the deprivation of prisoners' food and medication, and psychological pressures (p. 424).

Case Study 3.3 Video Shows Police Officer Using Baton to Hit Man

On June 18, 2010, jurors in Manhattan watched a video showing a police officer, charged with assault, hitting a suspect with a baton over and over as he lay handcuffed on the floor of a housing project on West 93rd Street, Manhattan. Nevertheless, as the police officer's lawyer also pointed out, the video footage (shot from five different angles from lobby cameras) also shows the suspect, Walter Harvin, struggling with the officer David London, resisting his directions, and shoving him with his hands before the officer hit him.

Officer London has been charged with second-degree assault, filing false reports, falsifying business records, and making a false written statement; if convicted, he could face up to 7 years in prison.

The video shows Officer London in uniform, closing the door of the building and then opening it as he saw Mr. Harvin approaching. The prosecution claimed Mr. Harvin did not have his key, but when the officer asked him whether he lived there, Mr. Harvin ignored his questions. They exchanged words, and then Mr. Harvin pushed the officer's hand away and entered the building. The video then shows Mr. Harvin turning and pushing the officer with both hands as he followed him in and tried to stop him. Officer London's partner came into the building, and then as Mr. Harvin stepped into the elevator, Officer London grabbed him and tried to spin him around. Mr. Harvin drew himself up, but Officer London took out his baton and struck Mr. Harvin near the face, causing him to fall to the ground. There, the officer began hitting him repeatedly with more than a dozen blows from his baton.

Mr. Harvin tried to avoid the blows until he was handcuffed by the two officers, and even after that, Officer London struck him again with the baton a few times. Officer London's lawyer claimed that Mr. Harvin had threatened to kill Officer London, but the prosecution said that even though Mr. Harvin should have cooperated with him, the fact that he did not was no justification for the beating he suffered and that Officer London used excessive force.

On June 28, 2010, Officer London was acquitted of the charges. Mr. Harvin, an Iraq war veteran, did not give evidence at the trial because he could not be located. Prosecutors indicated he had suffered some mental problems after returning to the United States from Iraq.

SOURCE: Eligon 2010.

POLICING, MENTAL ILLNESS, AND CRISIS INTERVENTION TEAMS (CITs)

One of the challenges faced by police is interacting with persons suffering from mental illness who may become confrontational or even violent during such interactions. It has been estimated that police are involved with persons suffering from mental illnesses between 7% and 10% of their time (Morabito 2007: 1582; Franz and Borum 2011: 265). How are police to handle such cases?

Police have generally been considered to be major contributors to the involvement of persons with mental illness in the criminal justice system. They have been criticized for actively arresting such persons for minor offenses as a means of handling difficult behavior, as an act of compassion, or based on police beliefs that persons with mental challenges are more violent than others without such challenges (Morabito 2007: 1582).

In 2006, the U.S. Bureau of Justice Statistics found that at midyear 2005 more than half of all prison and jail inmates had a mental health problem explained as a recent history or symptoms of a mental health problem that occurred in the 12 months prior to the survey interview (James and

Glaze 2006: 1). Female inmates had higher rates of such problems than males: in state prisons 73% of females as compared to 55% of males and in local jails 75% of females compared to 63% of males.

During the 1970s and 1980s, a "criminalization hypothesis" emerged to explain the increasing number of persons with mental illness entering the justice system. It was contended that following deinstitutionalization and the release of persons from state mental institutions, along with stricter rules about commitment for mental illness but no corresponding increase in community mental health facilities, the issue of controlling the sometimes-deviant behavior of people with mental illness was displaced on to the criminal justice system. Behavior that was previously constructed as a psychiatric problem was now reconstructed as an issue of public order and safety and as quasi-criminal (Morabito 2007: 1583; Johnson 2011: 128). This hypothesis has since been called into question, including for its lack of attention to police decision-making and behavior. Studies also found that when other factors were controlled for, police were, in fact, less likely to arrest persons with mental illness compared with other persons (Morabito 2007: 1583). Nevertheless, when such persons show resistance to police commands or are substance abusers, as is often the case, police will make a decision to arrest. Overall, however, studies have shown that police are more lenient toward the mentally ill, but they are disproportionately represented in arrests because they disproportionately commit serious crimes and resist police (Johnson 2011: 127, 129).

Police Perceptions of Mentally Ill Persons

Do police expect mentally disordered persons they encounter to display hostility and violence?

While research suggests that persons who are mentally ill are no more hostile or violent than the general population there are some exceptions:

- Studies in 1992 and 1996 found that those with psychotic symptoms were more likely to self-report having engaged in illegal and violent behavior.
- When treatment and medication regimes are not followed, mentally ill persons' self-control is diminished: One study in 1998 found that in

delusional and psychotic persons medication noncompliance almost tripled the likelihood of violent acts.
- Use of alcohol or illegal drugs aggravates the symptoms of mental disorder and negates the effect of medications, again lowering self-control levels: In 2005, about 74% of state prisoners and 76% of local jail inmates met the criteria for substance dependence or abuse (James and Glaze 2006: 1). A recent study that analyzed use of force reports from the police in Portland, Oregon, over the period 2008 to 2011 noted there was tendency to conflate mental illness and alcohol and drug abuse (Morabito and Socia 2015: 6), but the study showed that perceived mental illness in itself did not significantly affect the likelihood of injury to police or a suspect when it was not combined with substance abuse. Substance abuse alone did increase the likelihood of injury to the suspect and to a lesser extent, the officer. In encounters where there was a perception of mental illness and substance abuse combined, the likelihood of injury to both parties was increased (p. 16).
- When mentally disordered persons experience stressful events such as homelessness or conflicts with others; their emotional reaction is likely to be more intense and to express itself in negative ways.

Consequently, overall a population exists of violent, mentally disordered persons, comprised mainly of those having personality disorders with psychotic or delusional features (Johnson 2011: 133).

Do police commonly use force against those perceived to be mentally ill?

Officers are concerned about interactions with mentally ill persons because of their perceived unpredictability. These encounters can also be time-consuming, with officers waiting hours to have a person admitted to hospital (Morabito et al. 2012: 59). Using self-report data from two municipal police forces, Johnson (2011: 140) found that generally physical force was used less often against those perceived by police to be mentally ill than against mentally stable persons. All suspects, whether mentally stable or unstable, who physically resisted, possessed a weapon, or displayed hostility were significantly more likely to receive force compared to others without these characteristics. Finally, it was found that mentally unstable suspects were significantly more likely to physically resist or assault officers and possess a weapon than persons not perceived to be unstable.

Crisis Intervention Teams

The issues associated with mental illness and policing have led to the development of specific police strategies, such as crisis intervention teams (CITs), intended to improve police response to this population. Police lack the training to handle mental health crises and, as noted earlier, may resort to arrest because they lack alternative options.

Beginning with a pioneer scheme in the Memphis Police Department, law enforcement agencies have developed teams of trained officers who are often paired with mental health professionals in the community to respond to calls involving mentally unstable persons. The specialist officers, trained in de-escalation techniques, are able to relieve patrol officers of the duty of responding to such calls. This initiative was intended to reduce the arrest and incarceration of the mentally ill through "jail diversion," which can occur before or after a person is booked or arrested and has become accepted as a best-practice model or prebooking diversion (Franz and Borum 2011: 266). Officers who participate in CITs have received 40 hours of specialist mental health training to provide on-scene intervention and are able to act as liaisons to the formal mental health system in a state. CIT officers conduct regular patrol duties, but when a mental disturbance call is received, the CIT officer can be called to the scene where he or she acts as the principal officer present (p. 66). Studies have shown that the existence of operational CITs has prevented arrest so that in many regions the arrest rate is only 3%, compared to one study finding that 19% of calls would probably have resulted in arrest before the CIT program was implemented (p. 269; Compton et al. 2014: 523).

CIT training is not intended to eliminate the use of force, and police may still find it necessary to apply an appropriate level of force to bring a person under control. Findings from a survey of CIT and non-CIT officers in two Chicago districts indicated that a CIT-trained officer was likely to respond with less force for an increasingly resistant demeanor in comparison to a non-CIT officer because a CIT officer may be able to identify resistant behavior as a symptom of mental illness and utilize de-escalation techniques (Morabito et al. 2012: 71). To the contrary, a study by Compton and colleagues (2014: 523) found that there was no difference in the force level between CIT and non-CIT officers, probably because encounters involving force are driven by the risk of violence and the person's resistance, but the highest level of force tended to be used by non-CIT officers.

ETHICAL ISSUES IN INVESTIGATION, INTERROGATION, AND CUSTODY

Ethical issues may arise when police are investigating incidents that suggest a crime has been committed and where persons are suspected of criminal conduct. In investigating crime, police must have regard for the rights of suspects, be sensitive to issues of privacy, and be aware of the moralities associated with attempting to entrap individuals.

Rights of Suspects

A suspect—that is, a person who is only *suspected* of having committed a crime—has certain moral rights, as well as specifically defined legal rights. These include a right to life, a right not to suffer ill treatment, and a right to privacy. *Suspects* who become accused persons are entitled to a fair trial, and a trial can be considered fair only if it is based on evidence. It follows that suspects are morally entitled to be convicted based only on evidence that is real and not fabricated and on evidence given by truthful witnesses. Fabricating evidence or committing perjury violates the moral rights of suspects, affects the fairness of trials, and ultimately undermines the administration of justice.

Police also have a duty to the *victim* of a crime that extends to the victim's family if there is a need to protect persons who have been terrorized by the crime, although not its direct target. Fundamentally, police are under an obligation to employ the greatest possible effort to apprehend a suspect and to provide evidence for a successful prosecution. In doing this, they satisfy their ethical obligation toward the victim (Miller et al. 1997).

Privacy

This is a constitutional right and a moral right that a person possesses in relation to others, particularly with regard to information possessed by others or in relation to the observation of others. A violation of privacy takes place through acts such as observation and body searches. Similarly, a person's intimate personal relations with others must be regarded as a privacy issue, as is information relating to the ownership of objects or assets where there is a presumption that the person need not disclose assets except in defined circumstances, such as tax collection. Also regarded as private are facts concerned with a person's public roles, such as voting decisions and business plans. Finally, the law grants privacy in respect of certain data collected relating to an individual that may be released only under defined conditions.

The right to privacy is clearly not absolute, and a balance has to be achieved between rights to privacy and confidentiality and rights to protection from crime. In achieving this balance, Miller and colleagues (1997: 204–205) advocate applying the following principles:

1. Accessing and interception are prima facie an infringement of privacy and are presumed a violation that ought not to be overridden except in exceptional circumstances.

2. The benefits of violating privacy must be greater than the likely costs, especially the cost of reducing public trust in those who seek to violate privacy.

3. Accessing and interception ought to relate to a serious crime; there ought to be probable cause that the person whose privacy is to be violated has committed the crime and that the resulting information is likely to further the investigation of that crime.

4. There must be no practicable alternative method of gathering the information.

5. Law enforcement officials must be accountable for the violation in terms of obtaining any necessary warrant.

6. Persons whose privacy has been violated should be informed of the violation at the earliest possible moment consistent with not compromising the investigation.

Miller and colleagues suggest this framework of principles should regulate police action that might violate the right to privacy.

Entrapment

Miller and colleagues (1997: 206–207) suggest that the practice of entrapment includes operations—such as surveillance, undercover investigations, and entrapment itself—which are of a covert nature and involve deception of one kind or another. Deception seems to be an inevitable part of law enforcement and may not necessarily infringe on moral rights. Entrapment, however, is regarded as morally problematic because of the belief that the offender involved in a case of entrapment has not attained the required degree of criminality to be arrested and must therefore be entrapped. Entrapment may be random or targeted at a particular person or persons, and random entrapment is considered particularly morally problematic. In the case of targeted entrapment, moral objections may cease to apply if certain conditions are met. These are the following:

1. There is sufficient evidence to believe that the target is likely to commit a crime.

2. The person would have committed the crime or a similar crime whether he or she was a victim of the entrapment or not.

3. The entrapment succeeds as a technique of detection where other methods, such as complaints investigation, have failed.

The second condition is the most morally problematic because it assumes facts that cannot really be clearly ascertained and relies on evidence such as the suspect's disposition to commit crimes, which is a matter of subjective interpretation. It also relies on evidence of opportunity, and this, together with disposition, would lead to the formation of an intention to commit the crime.

In the United States, entrapment is considered a legal limit on the government's use of deception in investigation, and it occurs when a government agent, usually a police officer, initiates action that induces an otherwise innocent person to commit a crime so that he or she may be prosecuted. Entrapment operates as a defense, which, if established, will result in an acquittal. The courts apply a *subjective test* in determining whether the defense of entrapment has been proven. This involves the court looking at the mental predisposition of the offender to commit the crime rather than the objective methods of the police (Marx 1985; Skolnick 1982; Stitt and James 1985). In 1958, a minority of the U.S. Supreme Court in *Sherman v. United States* proposed an *objective test,* focusing on the nature of the police conduct, as opposed to the predisposition of the offender. Under this test, the Court would look at the character of the state's involvement in the commission of the offense; in other words, it would make an assessment of whether the police acted in such a way as would be likely to instigate or create a criminal offense.

Kleinig (1996: 158) suggests an alternative approach based on the nature of the government's involvement in the entrapment, arguing that sometimes this involvement figures so large that it suggests a lack of confidence that the individual would have committed the particular offense. He suggests that if this degree of involvement can be determined, the defense of entrapment should be available (see the "A Successful Entrapment Defense" Closer Look box). He focuses on the power of the government to draw into the entrapment those who might not otherwise engage in that kind of conduct. Tom Barker and David Carter (1995) offer the example of the Broward County (Florida) Sheriff's Department, which began to manufacture $20,000 worth of crack cocaine when it did not have enough crack to provide to undercover officers, to illustrate a situation where the government's involvement could easily be objectively assessed as entrapment. The "An Unsuccessful Entrapment Defense" Closer Look box shows an example of an unsuccessful entrapment defense.

A Closer Look

A Successful Entrapment Defense

On July 31, 2000, Indianapolis police officer Genae Gehring was working an undercover vice detail as a prostitute on the east side of the city along with about 10 other officers with the objective of arresting those soliciting for prostitution. At about 4 p.m. on that day, James Ferge was driving his truck and was stopped at a two-way stop sign. Officer Gehring was walking and made eye contact with Ferge in his stationary truck. She walked over to his vehicle and they spoke. He asked if she needed a ride and invited her to get in. She asked him if he was "looking for a little more," and he replied in the affirmative. She then asked if he was "looking for a little head," and again he replied in the affirmative, and she then suggested a price of $20, to which he agreed.

She told him to meet her in an alley behind a building close to the intersection and walked over to that location. Instead of proceeding to the alley, Ferge drove in another direction for about seven blocks until he was stopped by the police and arrested.

On August 1, 2001, Ferge was charged with patronizing a prostitute, which is a Class A misdemeanor, and at his trial, he claimed that he offered the officer a ride because it was raining, that he could not understand everything she said because of the noise of the diesel engine, that he was surprised when she asked him some questions about sex, and that as far as he was concerned, he would give her a ride if she wanted, but if she did not, that was the end of it. He was found guilty, sentenced to serve a year, and given credit for 4 days. The remaining 361 days were suspended, and he was placed on probation for 180 days.

Ferge appealed, arguing that the state had failed to produce enough evidence to negate his defense of entrapment. Under Indiana Code, entrapment is a defense if the conduct charged was the result of a law enforcement officer using persuasion likely to cause the person to engage in the conduct and if the person charged was not predisposed to commit the offense. The court, on appeal, said that the defense of entrapment turns on the defendant's state of mind, and, in this case, the state had to prove beyond reasonable doubt that Ferge had a predisposition to commit the crime.

The court said that the evidence at trial showed that the police officer initiated the conversation about sex and that the defendant did not meet the officer in the alley but instead drove away until stopped by the police. According to the court, the suggestion of criminal activity—that is, sexual activity—was made by the police officer after Ferge offered her a ride, and his action in driving away from the alley where he had been told to meet her showed that he did not intend to make a deal with her and was therefore evidence that he was not predisposed to commit the crime. Accordingly, the state had not presented enough evidence to prove the crime, and Ferge had successfully established the defense of entrapment.

SOURCE: Ferge v. State 2002.

A Closer Look

An Unsuccessful Entrapment Defense

On January 8, 2007, Shahawar Matin Siraj, a Pakistani, was sentenced to 30 years in prison for planning to blow up the Herald Square subway station on 34th Street in New York City. Siraj claimed that he was entrapped by a paid police informant who showed him photographs of inmates being abused at Abu Ghraib prison in Iraq and who recorded on tape his responses in the form of threats against the United States. He was convicted of conspiracy, based partly on testimony of police informant Osama Eldawoody, an Egyptian American who was recruited by New York police to monitor radical Muslims following 9/11. Siraj admitted taking preliminary steps to attack the subway station but claimed he had only done so at Eldawoody's prompting. His entrapment defense seemed to have convinced at least half the members of the jury early in the trial, but they later dismissed it. His defense was aided by the fact that the police paid Eldawoody a total of $100,000 for his work as an informer. The defense claimed it was this salary that kept Eldawoody interested in interacting with Siraj and in encouraging Siraj in his plotting.

SOURCE: Hays 2007.

Deception

To what extent, if any, are police entitled to rely on deception to promote law enforcement? There are many forms of verbal and nonverbal deception, and police deception may take forms such as withholding and manipulating information, lying, using ruses, using informants, enacting sting operations, installing wiretaps and bugging devices, creating false friendships, manufacturing evidence, and using the good cop/bad cop routine in interrogations (Kleinig 1996: 124). Many of these forms of deception involve lying in one form or another.

Skolnick (1982), in considering police deception, focuses on three stages of deception: investigative deception, interrogatory deception, and testimonial deception. He makes the point that the acceptability of deception varies according to the stage reached in the criminal process. Deception is most acceptable to police and the courts at the investigation stage, less acceptable during interrogation, and least acceptable in the courtroom. The reason for this is that each stage implies a greater number of constraints in the criminal justice process. For example, testimony in court is given under oath, but in the process of interrogation, it is not. Deceptive practices can include acts associated with the fabrication of evidence, such as the following:

- Telling a suspect that he or she has been identified by an accomplice when this is not true
- Showing a suspect faked evidence, such as fingerprints, to confirm his or her guilt
- Telling a suspect that he or she has been identified by an eyewitness[2]
- Holding a lineup in which a supposed witness identifies the suspect
- Getting a suspect to agree to a lie-detector test and telling him or her that it has proved their guilt (Skolnick and Fyfe 1993: 61)

Informants

What ethical issues are associated with police use of informants? Harfield (2012: 73) indicates the use of informants is ethically problematic on several levels. He describes informers as "individuals who supply information about other persons covertly to the authorities, usually in expectation of some form of reward and usually at the instigation of the authorities." Commonly, the informant's information cannot be acquired by any other means, and the informant has gained that information through a relationship with the subject of the information. Harfield (2012) argues that using informers who inform against a third person, unknown to that person, is itself unethical. In terms of policing, it can only be justified morally if

- it facilitates the purpose of policing;
- reasonable suspicion exists that the person informed against is intending to commit a crime;

- the crime is sufficiently serious in nature to justify recourse to an informant in order to obtain knowledge of it;
- no other less morally harmful means of obtaining the information exists;
- the information itself is central to an investigation in the sense that the investigation or a prosecution could not proceed without it; and
- the information is not simply desirable, but essential (p. 76).

Investigative Deception

The line between deception and entrapment—and the fact that police justify lying in the investigative stage as the means justifying the end (noble cause corruption)—has already been discussed. Skolnick (1982) suggests that the courts impose fewer constraints on lying during this stage and that judicial acceptance of deception in the investigation process tends to have the effect of making deception in the other stages of the process more acceptable morally and, therefore, more likely to occur. In other words, deception in one context is likely to increase its probability in others. For example, Kleinig (1996: 135) points out that both the courts and society accept the limited use of investigative techniques, such as the use of informants, wiretapping and bugging, unmarked patrol cars, and concealed radar traps. Gary Marx (2001: 262) contends that there are minimal ethical objections in using decoys as potential victims to combat a pattern of sexual assault and harassment. He gives the example of a policewoman used as a decoy after a series of rapes in a public park. Acceptability here is judged by the fact that crimes have already been committed, that there has been coercion by an offender, and that the policewoman acting as decoy is a relatively passive response.

Interrogatory Deception

In the 1966 case of *Miranda v. Arizona*, which dealt with the interrogation of a suspect in the custody of the police, the court held that arrested persons must be informed of their rights to remain silent, that any statement they make may be used as evidence, that they have the right to the presence of an attorney, and that an attorney will be provided if they cannot afford one. In addition, the court

---

2   Since the 1970s, studies have been conducted on the accuracy of eyewitness evidence, and now more than 2,000 studies in various disciplines have shown that eyewitness accounts are subject to a variety of influences that can affect their reliability (Lassiter and Ratcliff 2004: 1).

determined that the state is under a heavy burden in attempting to prove that any waiver of these rights occurred voluntarily, knowingly, and intelligently. Under *Miranda*, police are not required to give a suspect his or her rights unless they have taken the suspect into custody or "otherwise deprived [him] of his freedom . . . in any significant way" (quoted in Ross 2008: 452). Therefore, police are able to avoid the *Miranda* requirements by delaying an arrest until after they have finished questioning a suspect.

The *Miranda* decision evolved out of the admission in courts of confessions that were obtained with the use of torture, in the early period, and later, with the use of the third degree,[3] and then that used techniques of deception and psychological pressure. Over time, police have devised strategies that minimize the effect of *Miranda*. For example, police may question suspects in apparently noncustodial settings, or they may read suspects their rights but then proceed to question them as if the rights did not really exist. Police also try to persuade suspects to waive their rights, suggesting this would be in their own best interests. In any event, studies have shown that suspects routinely waive their rights— up to 80% of the time—often because they fail to understand their nature, effect, and purpose (Kassin et al. 2007: 383) and that persons with no prior felony record are far more likely to waive their rights than those with a criminal history (Meissner and Kassin 2004: 97).

As Kleinig (1996: 138) notes, sometimes interrogations are characterized as "interviews," where the language used is more respectful and the investigating officer constructs himself as a "seeker of truth" rather than "an accuser." Police interviews do not require the police to Mirandize the suspect. However, every custodial situation is inherently coercive and, depending on the circumstances, bears on the issue of whether what a person says can be said to be voluntary. It is clear that in a custodial interrogation, police are able to control the physical conditions of the encounter, the length of the interrogation,

the time given to the suspect to respond to questioning, and, generally, the terms under which it takes place. The outcome of the coercive nature of the interrogation, when combined with the police control of it, is that an innocent person or a person easily intimidated may react in ways that imply guilt. Further, a guilty person may be persuaded to confess to a more serious offense than the one he or she has committed. Questions of the mental capacity of the person being interrogated may also arise.

Leo (2008: 20) argues that police ought to be fact finders and not identify with the role of the prosecution. However, in practice, police have become partisan and committed to the aim of incriminating a suspect so as to help the state conduct a successful prosecution. Leo notes that police demonstrate this partisanship through their values and culture, through the goals of the process of interrogation, in the psychological methods they employ to secure confessions, and in the impression management they perform for suspects, judges, and juries. He suggests that while police techniques are not illegal, they do raise normative concerns about the process and quality of American criminal justice (p. 36) in the sense that fraud and deception in the interrogation process corrupt the integrity of the criminal justice process. Police interrogation remains one of the most secretive and morally questionable of all police activities because it involves behaviors that in other contexts would be ethically unacceptable (p. 187).

Confessions

Studies have revealed that for jurors confession evidence is a potent indicator of guilt, possibly exceeding eyewitness evidence (Meissner and Kassin 2004: 86). However, in its investigations, the Innocence Project has uncovered many cases in which confessions have been shown to be false, and some of these were given in response to police threats that, absent a confession, the accused person would face the death penalty. In the first DNA exonerations, 37 out of 123 exonerations involved homicides, and in two thirds of those cases, false confessions or incriminating statements figured in the convictions (Lassister and Ratcliff 2004: 3).

Research into the personal and situational influences that lead both guilty and innocent persons to confess shows that interrogation tactics such as

---

3   The term *third degree* connotes extreme forms of interrogation. The Wickersham Commission (in Leo 2008: 46) explains the term as "the employment of methods which inflict suffering, physical or mental, upon a person in order to obtain information about a crime." It was common practice in the 1930s for police to kick and beat suspects with nightsticks, leather saps, pistol butts, and baseball bats (p. 47).

minimizing a crime by suggesting to a suspect that he or she was morally justified in committing it makes suspects believe that that they will be dealt with leniently after confessing. As well, presenting false evidence can lead innocent persons to confess to acts they did not commit (Meissner and Kassin 2004: 86).

The *polygraph* or *lie detector* has been made a familiar police tool through television and movies and is essentially a means of intimidating a suspect into making a confession. It was invented to overcome the issues associated with the third degree and remains a powerful interrogation tool. The device measures changes in a person's physiology that occur in response to questions, based on the theory that the act of lying causes fear and anxiety, bringing about internal tensions that can be measured on a chart. It is said that truth telling is signified by a suspect who is "composed and very direct while answering questions," "light-hearted," "talkative," and "cooperative and sincere" (Leo 2004: 61). As Leo expresses it, this device is "a testament to the triumph of scientific ideology in American police work" (p. 60), and its effectiveness is associated with its appearance as an instrument of science and its supposed infallibility (p. 62).

Confessions are elicited through the polygraph by the polygraph examiner, who plays on the fears of exposure of the suspect that arise before, during, and after the test and particularly when the suspect is informed that he or she has "failed" the test. The suspect will be told that the polygraph has found him or her to be "deceptive" and that since it never makes mistakes the suspect might as well confess (Leo 2004: 62).

Police interrogation manuals teach officers that they too can recognize when a suspect is lying by using "behavioral analysis." Since 1986 when this method was developed, police have claimed to be able to detect lying by conducting an interview (prior to an actual interrogation) in which a set of questions designed to evoke particular behavioral responses is put to the suspect. There are 15 suggested questions to which, according to the manual writers, suspects who are lying will react defensively and evasively. Guilt can also be inferred, it is said, by analyzing the behavior of the suspect during the questioning: abrupt body movements, grooming and cosmetic actions like stroking the back of the hair or head, shuffling the feet, biting fingernails, and supportive gestures such as placing the hand over the mouth while speaking or crossing the legs are all claimed to signal guilt (Leo 2004: 65). Behavioral analysis therefore functions like the lie detector with the interrogator being a kind of human polygraph because it too examines stress reactions and deviations from the normal that indicate deception and therefore guilt.

Leo explains that since no unique physiological or psychology response that can be explained as signifying lying or deception has ever been discovered, the theory behind the polygraph and this kind of behavioral analysis, which finds no support in research studies, remains "implausible" (2004: 67).

Testimonial Deception

Kleinig (1996) points out that a good deal of police testimonial deception is said to be directed at securing *worthy ends*—that is, the control of crime and the conviction of those responsible (noble cause corruption). However, the police often take the view not only that deception in testifying is done with the aim of furthering the noble cause, but also they are forced to practice deception to correct deficiencies in the criminal justice system. Police might argue that the standards of proof required of the state, the constitutional restraints under which police operate that protect the rights of suspects, and the abilities of cunning defense lawyers and unsympathetic judges mean that the odds are stacked against them, and evidence, therefore, ought not to be excluded by technicalities or a case lost because of a clever lawyer. This ignores the fact that *the task of the police is to arrest and apprehend and not convict* and that police ought to be satisfied at having fulfilled their role within the criminal justice system.

However, like others, police experience dissatisfaction if their work does not produce the desired end. Proposals for reducing police perjury, such as sensitizing police to the dangers of perjury, having laypersons accompany police when executing a search warrant, subjecting police witnesses to lie detection, and requiring that all police action be videotaped, are discussed by Christopher Slobogin (1996).

Police Lying

Barker and Carter (1995) propose a typography of police lying, comprised by accepted lying, tolerated lying, and deviant lying.

Accepted Lying

In discussing accepted lying, they note that certain forms of lying are an accepted part of police work, the justification being that they fulfill the objective of controlling crime and arresting the guilty—that is, the noble cause of policing. While lying may be acceptable to the police themselves, this does not answer the question of whether their lies are ethically acceptable. Many deceptive practices involve lying in the broad sense, especially in undercover operations, and in such cases, police must be aware of the possible defense of entrapment. According to Barker and Carter, police believe that it is proper to lie to the media or the public when necessary to protect the innocent, to protect the image of the department, or to bring calm in a crisis. As far as the police are concerned, a lie is acceptable if the following are true:

- The lie is made in pursuit of a legitimate organizational goal.
- There is a clear relationship between deceiving and achieving that organizational goal.
- The lying is such that police and management within the police believe that lying will better serve the public interest than providing the truth.
- The ethical and legal aspect of lying is not considered a concern.

Tolerated Lying

In tolerated lying, lies are tolerated as necessary evils, and police will admit a lie when confronted. Again, from the police perspective, such lies are seen as necessary to the policing mission. An example is using lies and deception to handle what police regard as "nuisance work" as opposed to "real police work." Given that police are called out to deal with a wide variety of problems, most of which do not involve criminal activity, they sometimes promise to investigate a matter or threaten to take action when they have no intention of doing so—for example, in domestic violence cases, where the

officer may have no warrant to arrest but feels that something needs to be done and may threaten to take action. Similarly, sometimes police lie in a situation where they have no legal authority—for example, telling people on the street to move along when they have no legal basis for giving such a direction.

In the important area of police interrogation, lies are tolerated, and police are even trained to lie. Standard police texts on interrogation techniques advocate and instruct in deceptive and lying practices employed in interrogation. For instance, it is recommended that the officer conducting an interrogation seem sincere to such an extent that he may appear tearful or that an interrogator present a fabricated evidence file to a suspect. A familiar interrogation technique is to separate two suspected offenders and play off one against the other, and here, the interrogation texts suggest that the interrogator may actually inform one suspect that the other has confessed. There is also no legal rule that prevents police from pretending that a suspect's fingerprints were found on the murder weapon (Ross 2008: 447).

The leading text on police interrogation, Fred Inbau and John E. Reid's (1962) *Criminal Interrogation and Confessions*, is now in its fourth edition, and Reid suggests that a trained investigator can achieve 85% accuracy in differentiating truthful and untruthful statements. Research indicates that police are confident in their skills and believe they possess a "sixth sense" in truth seeking (Kassin et al. 2007: 382). As Leo notes (2008: 21), influenced by their values and the police culture, police assume that suspects will lie to them unhesitatingly. They also believe that they can assess guilt or innocence in advance of an interrogation (Meissner and Kassin 2004: 88). Several studies have provided evidence of an investigator bias—that is, a tendency for police to perceive those they interview as guilty, despite the fact that research has revealed that people generally do not perform above the level of chance in determining whether there is deception and that police and professional interrogators perform "only slightly better than chance, if at all" (p. 89).

The courts have held that police may employ deceit to obtain confessions as long as their actions do not "shock the conscience" or constitute actions that would induce an innocent person to confess (Alpert and Noble 2009: 242). Again, the justification for these techniques is said to be the noble cause of enforcing the law. Nevertheless, an attitude suggesting that using lies in interrogation is an acceptable practice because it serves the end of the noble cause can constitute the beginning of another slippery slope toward what Barker and Carter (1995) call deviant lying.

Deviant Lying

In *deviant lying*, police use lies that violate police regulations as well as the law. The major example here is police perjuring themselves in giving evidence in court, and at least one well-known defense attorney believes that almost all police lie in court (see Dershowitz 1983). Some police have even developed their own term for police perjury called *testilying* (Commission to Investigate Allegations of Corruption and Anti-Corruption Procedures of the Police Department, City of New York 1994). Barker (1996) has asserted that the public has lost confidence in the police as a result of high-profile cases like the O. J. Simpson trial, and he argues that the effect of this is to create an expectation that police will engage in testilying.

Electronic Recording of Interrogations

Electronic recording of interrogations is gaining favor in the states. For example, in 1985, the Alaska Supreme Court required that the police record all custodial interrogations; if not, they would be inadmissible at trial. In 2003, Illinois legislated to require all custodial interrogations in homicide cases be recorded (p. 292). However, the FBI maintains its refusal to record, as do several other major urban police departments. In 1984, England and Wales enacted the Police and Criminal Evidence Act (PACE) that requires all police interrogations to be recorded. The act has changed police interrogation practice in that country from an adversarial model to an investigative model designed to obtain information and not to secure confessions. There has been no falloff in the confession rate; in fact, it has increased (p. 326).

Kleinig (1996: 126) discusses the consequences of police lying and identifies three deleterious consequences:

- *Others Are Harmed.* This occurs in the sense that persons are led to do what they have not chosen to do. They may also be deprived of their possessions or placed at physical risk.
- *Social Trust Is Destroyed.* The argument here is that a person who is lied to and who discovers the lie suffers the consequence of cynicism, and this may in turn affect his or her interactions with others because suspicion erodes trust.
- *The Liar Is Harmed.* This may occur through the liar becoming more evasive for fear of being found out, developing a suspicion of others, and perhaps developing a reduced ability to resist other forms of corruption.

Summarizing the objections raised by scholars to police lying in interrogation, Leo (2008: 191) notes the following: It is not required to solve most crimes; it breaches social trust and infringes the suspect's dignity; it taints the integrity of the fact-finding process and may therefore reduce public confidence in the criminal justice system; it tends to expand into other areas of policing, such as police lying in evidence at trials; and it produces false confessions.

SUMMARY

Police misuse of force is a major area in which ethical considerations come up against the practicalities of police work. Although there are rules that stipulate the degree of force to be used in given situations, ultimately the police themselves decide in their discretion what degree of force it is necessary to employ. Their decisions will be influenced by police culture and by the historical fact that force was employed as a matter of course. Often, incidents of excessive force will be characterized as aberrations by particular officers rather than as a systemic issue. Questions about appropriate levels of force will continue to be raised, especially where egregious instances of brutality and violence occur.

Police practices in apprehension, investigation, and interrogation may be ethically questionable because they may violate the rights of suspects, entrap them, and invade their privacy. Methods of deception, especially lying, are an accepted part of police work. Again, these techniques are often justified as the means of supporting the "noble cause," although some argue that it is necessary to accept a degree of police corruption as the price we pay for keeping communities safe.

DISCUSSION QUESTION

1. Is it entrapment if the police attempt to catch child molesters on the Internet by pretending to be juveniles?

RACIAL DISCRIMINATION IN THE CRIMINAL JUSTICE SYSTEM

ETHICAL BACKGROUND

It is generally agreed that discrimination based on racial or ethnic origin is morally wrong and a violation of the principle of equality. The equality principle requires that those who are equal be treated equally based on similarities and that race not be a relevant consideration in that assessment (May and Sharratt 1994: 317). In other words, it is only possible to justify treating people differently if there exists some factual difference between them that justifies such difference in treatment (Rachels 1999: 94). *Equality* is a nonspecific term that means nothing until applied to a particular context. Thus, in a political context, equality means equal access to public office and equal treatment under the law, and equal treatment extends to equality in terms of job hiring, promotion, and pay.

Race refers to groups of persons who are relatively alike in their biological inheritance and are distinct from other groups (American Anthropological Association 1997: 2). *Ethnicity* is a cultural phenomenon referring to a person's identification with a particular cultural group (Hinman 1998: 403). However, race is socially constructed, and the notion that persons "belong" to a particular race was developed in the last century, based on the belief that there was a biological basis for categorizing groups of people. Biologically, however, the term *race* has no meaning, yet society continues to give the notion meaning by using it as a social category. The notion of race gradually took hold in U.S. society when the institution of slavery reinforced the idea that one race could be inferior to another (Banks and Eberhardt 1998: 58). In the United States, the law has had the effect of distributing benefits and burdens based on race, and the assignment of a person to a racial category has often, in the past, determined his or her rights and obligations (e.g., in the "Jim Crow" laws passed at the end of the Civil War).

Racism in its most general sense can be defined as "social practices which (explicitly or implicitly) attribute merits or allocate values to members of racially categorized groups solely because of their 'race'" (Zatz and Mann 1998: 3). There are at least three aspects to racism: personal prejudice; ideological racism, where culture and biology are used to rationalize and justify the superior position of a dominant culture; and institutional racism, where the policies and practices of institutions operate to produce systematic and continuing differences between racial groups (p. 4).

One aspect of institutionalized racism has been termed *petit apartheid*. This concept includes daily informal or hidden interactions between police and minorities, such as stop-and-question and stop-and-search law enforcement practices, which may or may not result in an arrest and consequent entry into the criminal justice system (Zatz and Mann 1998: 4). The notion of petit apartheid has been explored both theoretically and in terms of those activities that might fall within its definitional scope (Milovanovic and Russell 2001). The focus of petit apartheid appears to be attitudinal factors that influence policing and other decisions within the system—that is, "culturally biased beliefs and actions" extending, in the view of Daniel Georges-Abeyie (2001: x), to insults, rough treatment, and lack of civility faced by black suspects, the quality and objectivity of judicial instructions to a jury when an African American is on trial, and other discretionary acts within the system.

Petit apartheid contrasts with grand apartheid. The latter encompasses overt racism. Studies on racism within the criminal justice system have been critiqued for giving undue emphasis to overt racism and ignoring petit apartheid (Georges-Abeyie 2001: x). This chapter aims to explore *overt racism* within the criminal justice system. Issues such as racial profiling and racial slurs, which appear to constitute an aspect of petit apartheid as well as being discriminatory practices, have already been discussed in Chapter 2.

HISTORICAL CONTEXT

African Americans have suffered discrimination on grounds of race, initially through the system of slavery, and then through a pattern of exclusion and segregation, both informal and formal, in the shape of legislation and court decisions that have historically endorsed overt racial discrimination. From the time of the inception of slavery in the early 17th century until 1865, slaves were considered the property of their masters, based on a view that they were naturally unequal and inferior people. They were subjected to slave codes, which prohibited the possession of any rights or freedoms enjoyed by whites;

experienced brutal and inhumane treatment of an extralegal nature; and were exploited for their labor. Following the Civil War, amendments to the Bill of Rights prohibited slavery and granted all persons, regardless of race, a right to equal protection. However, despite these legal statements of freedom, patterns of discrimination persisted after the war because many states passed Jim Crow laws, which had the effect of maintaining forms of discrimination in legal, social, and economic forums. For example, African Americans were denied the right to vote or to enter into contracts, and the doctrine of *separate but equal* was applied to keep the races separate.

In terms of black incarceration, while the 1890 census revealed the disproportionate number of blacks in prison, whites perceived this only as proving the criminality of blacks and did not recognize any pattern of racial disparity. The census was used to justify discriminatory laws regarded by whites as necessary until blacks were able to overcome the legacy of slavery through their own efforts—"black criminality was considered blacks' problem" (Gottschalk 2015: 141). Later when blacks began to debate the place of white racism in explaining black criminality, this served only to reinforce the importance of crime in defining the black experience (p. 142). When black reformers turned to the federal government to intervene in law enforcement at the state level so that blacks could be better protected in the exercise of their civil rights, one outcome was a strengthening of the supposed link between criminality and blackness (p. 144). The association between blackness and criminality framed the debate on civil rights laws because southern Democrats portrayed segregation as the maintenance of law and order (while integration signified more crime) and argued for more resources to curb what they saw as increased black lawlessness (p. 145). It was not until 2008 that black civil rights leaders under the leadership of the NAACP asserted that the mass incarceration of blacks was the paramount civil rights issue of the 21st century. At its 2010 convention, the NAACP called for the repeal of laws that imposed life sentences without parole. In 2011, it published a report on the growth of correctional budgets as compared to budgets for education, and at its 2011 convention called for an end to the war against drugs (p. 160).

The courts continued to enforce *Jim Crow laws* until the mid-1900s, and African Americans were also subjected to extralegal treatment in the form of physical assaults and practices such as lynching, where police were often present. About 3,000 African Americans were lynched between the mid-1800s and the early 1900s (B. Smith 2000: 75), and those performing the lynchings were seldom prosecuted.

During the 20th century, legal rights were accorded to African Americans and have been protected by the courts. In the landmark case of *Brown v. Board of Education* in 1954, the U.S. Supreme Court struck down the "separate but equal" doctrine, and the civil rights acts passed in the mid-20th century attempted to restate and reinforce a policy against segregation.

Today, the black community in the United States is diverse, comprising, for example, Jamaicans, Nigerians, Ethiopians, Somalis, and other African and West Indies nationalities, each with its own culture distinguishable from that of African Americans. Nevertheless, despite this heterogeneity, racist attitudes continue to be manifested based on skin color.

The history of *Latinos* in the United States has been one of contention with the Anglo American culture. Spanish colonies were established in the United States in the late 16th century, predating the Anglo American presence; however, in 1847, Mexico lost approximately half of its territory to the United States. In recent times, it has been common to associate Latinos with the issue of immigration, and Mexicans in particular are constructed as an illegal immigrant group (De Uriarte in Alvarez 2000: 88). Racist stereotyping of Latinos depicts them as sneaky, lazy, and thieving (Levin in Alvarez 2000: 88), and law enforcement practices and the criminal justice system have been shown to collaborate in discrimination against Latinos in the form of police harassment of Mexican Americans (Turner in Alvarez 2000: 88).

It is important to appreciate the heterogeneity of the Latino population in the United States because issues affecting Mexican Americans may differ from those impacting Puerto Ricans, Cubans, or immigrants from Central America. For example, Puerto Ricans are the most economically disadvantaged group (Myers et al. in Alvarez 2000: 89), whereas Cuban immigrants to the United States have tended to come from the middle class, be well educated, and possess significant economic resources. Nevertheless, like African Americans and other black groups, the heterogeneous Latino population tends to be viewed as homogeneous.

American Indians, Alaska Natives, and *Native Hawaiians* are the only indigenous groups in the United States. The history of contact between American Indians and Anglo Americans is replete with acts of violence against American Indians and with the dispossession of their lands. Alaska Natives, as a colonized and marginalized people, have experienced and continue to experience severe trauma generated by social change, with high rates of suicide, alcohol abuse, and a disproportionate representation in the criminal justice system (see, e.g., Banks 2002; Brod 1975; Fienup-Riordan 1994; Kraus and Buffler 1979; Travis in Phillips and Inui 1986; Schafer, Curtis, and Atwell 1997). Similarly, American Indians continue to be disproportionately represented in arrest and incarceration data in those states where they are primarily located (see, e.g., Greenfeld and Smith 1999; Grobsmith 1994; Perry 2004; Ross 2000). Both groups suffer economic, educational, and social stereotyping, which is revealed in their treatment by the criminal justice system.

Is There Racial Discrimination in the Criminal Justice System?

One report suggests that racial discrimination does occur at some points in the criminal justice system. Following the Rodney King incident, the 1991 report of the Independent Commission on the Los Angeles Police Department (also called the *Christopher Commission*) found that there was excessive use of force by LAPD officers and that this was compounded by racism and bias. One quarter of the 960 LAPD officers surveyed by the commission agreed that officers held a racial bias toward minorities, and more than one quarter agreed that this racial bias could lead to the use of excessive force. The commission also reviewed radio transmissions within the LAPD, which revealed disturbing and recurrent racial remarks, often made in the context of discussing vehicle pursuits or beating suspects. Testimony from witnesses depicted the

LAPD as an organization whose practices and procedures tolerated discriminatory treatment, and witnesses repeatedly testified about LAPD officers who verbally harassed minorities, detained African American and Latino men who fit generalized descriptions of subjects, and employed invasive and humiliating tactics against minorities in minority neighborhoods. As well as racism in relations with the public, racial bias was also reflected in conduct directed at fellow officers who were members of racial or ethnic minority groups. These officers were subjected to racial slurs and comments in radio messages and to discriminatory treatment within the department.

In another report, that of the *New York State Judicial Commission on Minorities* (1991), a panel of judges, attorneys, and law professors found that "there are two justice systems at work in the courts of New York State; one for whites, and a very different one for minorities and the poor" (p. 1). The panel found inequality, disparate treatment, and injustice based on race. It reported that many minorities received "basement justice" in that court facilities were infested with rats and cockroaches, family members of minorities were often treated with disrespect and lack of courtesy by court officers, and racist graffiti appeared on the walls of court facilities. The panel also concluded that minority cases often take only 4 or 5 minutes in court, suggesting a form of assembly line justice, and that black defendants outside of New York City frequently have their cases heard by an all-white jury.

Criminal Justice System: Discrimination and Decision-Making Points

One method of determining whether racial discrimination exists within the U.S criminal justice system is to examine the major decision points within state and federal criminal justice systems. This approach draws a distinction between systemic discrimination and acts of discrimination that occur at decision points, such as the grant of bail and the decision to prosecute. Most researchers agree with William Wilbanks (1987) and Joan Petersilia (1983) that although there is racial discrimination within the criminal justice system, the system itself is not characterized by racial discrimination; that is, discrimination is not systematic

(Blumstein 1993; DiIulio 1996; Russell-Brown 1998; Tonry 1995). There are, however, individual cases occurring within the system that appear to demonstrate racial discrimination at certain decision-making points (Wilbanks 1987). According to Petersilia (1983), racial disparities have come about because procedures were adopted within the criminal justice system prior to any real assessment about the effect of those procedures on minorities. For example, she wrote that

> although the case processing system generally treated offenders similarly . . . we found racial differences at two key points: Minority suspects were more likely than whites to be released after arrest; however, after a felony conviction, minority offenders were more likely than whites to be given longer sentences and to be put in prison instead of jail. (p. vi)

Petersilia also suggested that "racial differences in plea bargaining and jury trials may explain some of the difference in length and type of sentence" (1983: ix).

While as noted earlier the majority of researchers do not believe there is systematic racial bias in the criminal justice system, some believe it exists (Russell-Brown 1998: 28). These scholars argue that prior studies have assessed discrimination at a single stage in the system and have therefore been ineffective in detecting discrimination that might exist at other stages. For example, the finding that there is no racial disparity in sentencing within a system does not exclude the possibility of discrimination in other parts of the system.

As already discussed, Georges-Abeyie (in Russell-Brown 1998: 32) has drawn attention to how research on racial discrimination in the system focuses on formal, easily observed decision-making points and fails to take account of more informal law enforcement action. He argues that this informal decision-making determines who will be arrested and who will enter the system and that these encounters should be included in any assessment of whether the system operates in a discriminatory manner. If such informal action were to be included, he suggests that a system of petit apartheid would be revealed that would demonstrate that African Americans are consistently treated in a discriminatory manner compared to whites.

Another criticism is that official statistics on race and crime do not provide a proper basis for research on discrimination in the justice system because the data collection procedures make these statistics unreliable and distort any analysis derived from them (Knepper 2000: 16). This argument points out that the primary classification scheme employed in crime statistics designates four official races—white, black, American Indian/Alaska Native, and Asian and Pacific Islander—as well as two official ethnic groups, "Hispanic origin" and "not of Hispanic origin." In contrast, the 1990 census includes 43 racial categories and subcategories. If race is made the focus of inquiry, there is an assumption that races constitute discrete groups, but in fact, the races in America are not monolithic. For example, the designation "black" fails to capture the most significant aspects of what it means to be black in the United States because the designation "black" includes persons of Caribbean, African, and Central and South American origin, and within each of these groups are populations distinguished by culture, language, and shades of color (p. 19). Paul Knepper argues that no objective statements can be made based on these race categories, which are essentially political rather than social definitions of races, derived from a legal ideology of separate races grounded in the institution of slavery (p. 23).

As noted earlier, in considering racial discrimination within the criminal justice system, researchers have isolated and examined various decision-making points, including arrest, bail, jury selection, conviction, and sentencing. These decision-making points will be considered in the following sections. Scholars have, however, critiqued this approach of focusing on decision points because it fails to take account of the broad social context in which patterns of racial discrimination are located. Specifically, it is argued that sources of crime are grounded in structural differences between communities, cities, and states in the organization of families and the local economies, and therefore, disparities in criminal justice also ought to reflect broader inequalities in society (Peterson 2012: 308). This approach brings into account patterns of disadvantage—for example, showing that rates of violent crime increase across levels of disadvantage, whether the disadvantage is of blacks or whites (p. 310). Murakawa and Beckett (2010: 712)

similarly critique this approach for not taking account of "the totality of conditions that perpetuate inequality." Nevertheless, the majority of research adopts the points of the decision-making approach and relies heavily on complex statistical measures in analyzing racial disparities.

Discrimination in the Juvenile Justice System

In relation to the juvenile justice system, it has been argued that any discrimination within that system should be considered separately from the adult system for two basic reasons (Pope and Feyerherm 1990). Firstly, a high level of discretion is permitted in the juvenile justice system, and this may tend to produce more discrimination. Secondly, because most adult offenders begin their contact with the adult system through the juvenile justice system, characteristics acquired in the juvenile system, such as a prior record, may influence their treatment in the adult system.

As to whether racial discrimination exists within the juvenile justice system, after a review of the literature, Carl Pope and William Feyerherm (1990) conclude that two thirds of the studies reviewed suggested evidence of direct or indirect discrimination against minorities, or a mixed pattern of bias, especially in the processing of juveniles through the system. Their survey also suggests there is evidence that race differences in outcome may seem to be minor at a certain decision-making stage in the system but that these differences have more serious implications, as earlier decisions in the system move toward a final disposition. Pope and Feyerherm state that although the relationship between race and juvenile justice decision-making is complex, their analysis suggests that various factors do interact to produce racial differences in juvenile justice dispositions. Certainly, race seems to continue as a factor in responses to juvenile crime. Information collected by the organization Building Blocks for Youth (2000) revealed that African Americans represent 15% of the population nationwide, 26% of juvenile arrests, 44% of youth who are detained, 46% of youth who are judicially waived to criminal court, and 58% of youth admitted to state prisons.

Race is a relevant factor in the juvenile justice system not only for blacks but also for Latino and American Indian youth. Rodriguez (2010: 391) found after analyzing a random sample of about 23,000 youth processed through the juvenile justice system in Arizona during the year 2000 that black, Latino, and American Indian youth were treated more severely in the juvenile court in terms of the outcomes of proceedings than were white youth. Similarly, race and ethnicity have been found to affect sentencing outcomes of juveniles dealt with in the adult court system (Jordan and Freiburger 2010: 185).

What explains the overrepresentation of minorities in the juvenile justice system? Bishop, Leiber, and Johnson (2010: 213) have theorized it as an outcome of the combination of the organizational concept of "loose coupling" and the "focal concerns" approach. The focal concerns perspective argues that judges' sentencing decisions are affected by three major focal concerns: a desire to protect the community from dangerous offenders; a desire to impose a sentence that can be regarded as just in light of the blameworthiness of the offender; and a desire to avoid negative social consequences. According to this framework, due to time constraints, judges employ a "perceptual shorthand" in decision-making that relies not only on relevant legal issues but also brings into account stereotypes associated with offenders, including race. Therefore, minorities may receive more severe sentences than whites due to stereotypical beliefs that minorities can cope with incarceration more easily than whites, that incarceration will not disrupt black families as much as it would white families, and that giving lenient sentences to blacks will give a perception that a judge is not "tough on crime" (pp. 214–215).

The organizational notion of "loose coupling" is relevant to the issue of racial disparities because each juvenile justice system comprises multiple actors and agencies with decision-making powers. These actors collectively constitute a set of bureaucracies, each applying separate spheres of knowledge to a case. Because of their differing knowledge and approaches, agencies are therefore likely to find it problematic to reach a consensus when they work together (Bishop et al. 2010: 216). The focal concerns approach and the loose coupling perspective allow decision-making and the application of stereotypes to be applied as a framework for analyzing racial disparities.

Police Encounters With Citizens and Police Arrest

Racial origin may sometimes influence police decisions about making an arrest. In the case of suspected *juvenile offenses*, research has shown that for minor offenses police officers may take into account the demeanor of a juvenile in deciding whether to make an arrest (Black and Reiss 1970; Piliavin and Briar 1964). If the police perceive the suspected offender as showing them disrespect, this may increase the likelihood of an arrest. Along with racial origin, Douglas Smith (1986) found that the context of a particular neighborhood also influenced police decisions about arrest or use of force because police were more likely to arrest, threaten, or use force against suspects in racially mixed or minority neighborhoods.

Police Powers and Minorities

Research into how police use their powers against minorities, whatever may be the race of the officer, has been an important issue in policing research, and the approach has been to explore whether white officers treat black citizens differently than nonblack citizens (Brown and Frank 2006: 104). In one study of police employed by the Cincinnati Police Division between 1997 and 1998, where about 65% of the population was white and 35% black, researchers examined 614 police–suspect encounters during which 104 citizens were arrested. They discovered that about 18% of the white officer–suspect encounters ended in arrest, compared to 15% of the black officer–suspect interactions. Further, male and juvenile suspects were significantly more likely to be arrested than females or adults, and police were significantly more likely to arrest black suspects than white suspects (p. 118). They also found that citizens who show disrespect to the police increase their likelihood of arrest. Interactions involving black officers and black suspects were significantly more likely to result in arrest than interactions involving black officers and white suspects (p. 119). Thus, the authors suggest that black officers are more likely to use coercion with black citizens than white citizens. The authors are unable to offer any explanation for this differential arresting behavior other than that race seems to make a difference and that more research is required (pp. 120–121).

In considering the proportion of blacks involved in police shootings of criminal suspects, James Fyfe (1982) demonstrated that in New York City, blacks were more likely than whites to be shot by police because they were disproportionately involved in armed incidents that involved shooting. In contrast, research in Memphis showed that blacks were no more likely than whites to be involved in armed incidents, but nevertheless, police shot disproportionately more blacks when they were fleeing. Fyfe concludes that police use of deadly force in Memphis is influenced by the race of a suspect.

In Seattle, a study of race and drug-delivery arrests revealed that most drugs, including powder cocaine and heroin, are delivered by whites and that blacks are the majority delivering only one drug—namely, crack cocaine (Beckett, Nyrop, and Pfingst 2006: 129). However, 64% of those arrested for delivering drugs other than crack cocaine are black. The explanation suggested for this disparity is the law enforcement focus on crack cocaine and also the fact that the white drug markets in Seattle receive less attention from law enforcement than the more racially diverse markets in the city (p. 129). Thus, the researchers conclude, "Race shapes perceptions of who and what constitute Seattle's drug problem" (p. 105).

Drug Enforcement

Why have police in many states prioritized drug enforcement as a police function and engaged in repeated traffic stops to conduct drug searches? Some commentators have argued that the Comprehensive Crime Act of 1984 has been the cause of this high ranking enjoyed by drug enforcement. The reason is that this act permitted local police agencies to retain the proceeds from assets seized in drug-enforcement activity where federal and local police cooperated in the investigation (Mast, Benson, and Rasmussen 2000: 287). As Brent Mast, Bruce Benson, and David Rasmussen put it, "Entrepreneurial local police shift[ed] production efforts into drug control in order to expand their revenues" (p. 287). In fact, the Department of Justice went further than the act's provisions because it decided that local police could arrange for federal authorities to "adopt" local police forces' drug seizures, even when federal agents were not involved in the investigation. Interestingly, drug arrests per 100,000 population in states with limits on the assets that local police could retain averaged 363 during 1989, while the arrest rate in such cases where police were able to keep seized assets averaged 606 per 100,000 (p. 289). Mast and his colleagues, after conducting an empirical study, found that where legislation permits police to keep assets seized in drug investigations raises the drug arrest rate as a proportion of total arrests by about 20% and drug arrest rates themselves by about 18% (p. 285).

Prosecutorial Discretion

The question of whether the exercise of prosecutorial discretion produces discrimination has also been investigated. Where sentences are fixed, charging and plea bargaining become crucial, and attempts have been made to uncover the full dimensions of prosecutorial discretion. Looking at the prosecutor's decision to charge, one analysis of more than 30,000 cases from Los Angeles County showed that cases against blacks and Hispanics were significantly more likely to be prosecuted than cases against whites (Spohn, Gruhl, and Welch 1987). This contrasts with a Supreme Court ruling that the decision to prosecute shall not be "deliberately based upon an unjustifiable standard such as race, religion, or other arbitrary classifications" (Walker, Spohn, and DeLone 2000: 140).

A number of studies have concluded that white defendants are offered plea bargains more frequently and obtain better deals than minorities (Walker et al. 2000: 146), although other studies have found that race has an insignificant effect on plea negotiations (Albonetti 1990; Miethe and Moore 1986). It is unclear whether implicit racial bias may influence the exercise of a prosecutor's discretion, but prosecutors are guided by the same factors as police in making the decision to prosecute and for what charge. It follows that considerations of dangerousness will play a part in decision-making and time constraints may encourage prosecutors to make speedy judgments that are affected by implicit bias.

A study of more than 77,000 federal criminal cases from 1991 to 1994 has shown that when federal prosecutors request a sentence lower than the stipulated minimum for defendants who are "salvageable" and "sympathetic" they were significantly less likely to request lower sentences for black and Hispanic male defendants than for white males, and even where prosecutors did request lower sentences for nonwhite defendants, the reductions in sentence were on average 6 months less than those received by white defendants (Clemons 2014: 697).

Bail

For most offenses charged, prosecutors and judges have a wide discretion about whether defendants should be released on bail, and the courts may use factors such as dangerousness to the community and the possibility of flight in making bail decisions. Generally, the court looks at the employment, marital status, and length of residence in an area of the accused as an illustration of community ties, which may allow the court to conclude that the accused is unlikely to flee (Albonetti, Hauser, Hagan, and Nagel 1989).

Studies tend to show that race is not a factor in bail applications once an accused's dangerousness to the community and prior history of appearance at trial are controlled for. However, race does relate to the decision to grant bail in other ways. For example, in a study of more than 5,000 male defendants, Albonetti and colleagues (1989) reveal that defendants with lower levels of education and income were less likely to get bail and more likely to receive onerous bail terms. They also found that white defendants with the same education, background, and income as black defendants were more likely to be granted bail and that in considering bail applications, a prior criminal record counted against blacks more than whites. However, in assessing the criteria for bail, dangerousness and seriousness of the offense were of greater weight for whites than for blacks. Overall, the study shows that under certain conditions whites are treated more severely on bail applications but that, generally, white defendants receive better treatment. Samuel Walker, Cassia Spohn, and Miriam DeLone (2000: 135) note that it is impossible to guarantee that judges will

refrain from taking race into account in determining applications for bail and that the simple stereotyping of minorities as less reliable and more prone to violence than whites will likely result in a higher rate of bail denial regardless of any other assessed factors.

Jury Selection

Is there any evidence of racial discrimination in the jury selection process?

Historically, laws have tried to entrench racial discrimination into the process of jury selection. In *Strauder v. West Virginia* (1880), the Court struck down a statute that limited jury service to white men on the grounds that it violated the Fourteenth Amendment to the Constitution. However, this ruling did not prevent some states from attempting to preserve the lawfulness of an all-white jury by other means. For example, in Delaware, jury selection was drawn from lists of taxpayers, and jury members were required to be "sober and judicious." Although African Americans were eligible for selection under this rule, they were seldom if ever selected because the state authorities argued that few African Americans in the state were intelligent, experienced, or moral enough to serve as jurors (Walker et al. 2000: 156). The Supreme Court subsequently ruled this practice in Delaware as unconstitutional.

Since the mid-1930s, the Supreme Court has ruled on jury selection issues in a way that has made it difficult for court systems to practice racial discrimination in jury selection. For example, the Court has ruled it unconstitutional to put the names of white potential jurors on white cards and the names of African American potential jurors on yellow cards and then to supposedly make a random draw of cards to determine who would be summoned for jury duty (Walker et al. 2000: 157). Walker and colleagues argue that many states still practice discriminatory procedures in selecting jury pools. For example, obtaining the names of potential jurors from registered voters, the Department of Motor Vehicles, or property tax rolls seems to be an objective process, but in some jurisdictions, racial minorities are less likely to be registered voters, own automobiles, or own taxable property (p. 157). The effect, therefore, is to stack the jury pool with middle-class white persons and to marginalize minorities.

Prosecutors and defense lawyers are able to use peremptory challenges to excuse potential jurors without identifying any cause or explanation and without any accountability to the court, so it is therefore possible to employ peremptory challenges in the practice of racial discrimination in jury selection. According to Samuel R. Sommers and Michael I. Norton, such is the force of stereotypes concerning jurors of different races, especially in relation to judgments that are made on the basis of limited knowledge, under "cognitive load," and under pressure of time (all factors present in a voir dire), that "the discretionary nature of the peremptory challenge renders it precisely the type of judgment most likely to be biased by race" (2008: 527). Initially, the Supreme Court was unwilling to restrict a prosecutor's right to use peremptory challenges to excuse potential jurors on racial grounds, preferring to rely on the presumption that the prosecutor was always acting in good faith in making such challenges. However, the Court determined that it would intervene if a defendant could establish a case of deliberate discrimination by showing that eliminating African Americans from a particular jury was part of a pattern of discrimination in a jurisdiction. Not surprisingly, this stringent test has proved difficult to satisfy because few defense lawyers possess information proving a pattern of discrimination. In 1986, the Supreme Court rejected this test, ruling that it was not necessary to establish a pattern to show discrimination and that a defendant need only bring evidence showing the prosecutor had exercised his or her peremptory challenges on racial grounds. Once a prima facie case of discrimination has been made out, the state must explain why an African American has been excluded from the jury pool. Even so, Walker and colleagues (2000: 160) contend that judges have given the benefit of the doubt to prosecutors and have shown themselves willing to accept the prosecutor's explanations rather than make a finding of deliberate discrimination. Case Study 4.1, derived from a report from *The New York Times*, illustrates an alleged case of racial discrimination in jury selection.

Case Study 4.1 In Dallas, Dismissal of Black Jurors Leads to Appeal by Death Row Inmate

Thomas Miller-El is an African American charged with shooting two white hotel clerks during a robbery in 1985. One of the hotel clerks died, and Miller-El, age 50, was due to be executed by the State of Texas in 2002. The 2005 Supreme Court case decided in Miller-El's favor (Death Penalty Information Center 2015). In 2002, he had asked the Texas Board of Pardons to commute his sentence and appealed his case to the U.S. Supreme Court on the ground that the jury that convicted him was chosen using racial discriminatory standards that have been applied by the Dallas County district attorney's office in many cases. The district attorney's office opposed the appeal, arguing that there is no evidence of any racial discrimination.

The jury in the original trial comprised nine whites, one Filipino, one Hispanic, and one African American. Three other African Americans were excluded from the jury by prosecutors, as were seven of eight other African Americans interviewed as prospective jurors.

Racial discrimination in jury selection is prohibited by the Constitution, and until 1986, to establish race discrimination, an accused had to meet a heavy burden of proof because he or she had to show a pattern of discrimination. In 1986 in *Batson v. Kentucky*, the U.S. Supreme Court lowered the standard, determining that if the accused was able to show that the prosecution appeared to be using its peremptory challenges to jurors to exclude minorities, the trial judge could call for an explanation.

Miller-El was convicted and sentenced 1 month before the Batson ruling, but the decision applies to his case retroactively. To date, both state and federal courts have upheld his death sentence, determining that no racial discrimination occurred during jury selection. Miller-El's argument is that the courts considered only the number of challenges to jurors (10 out of 11 prospective African American jurors) and failed to consider other evidence showing that prosecutors in Dallas County had for years excluded blacks from juries as a matter of routine practice. This argument is supported by four former prosecutors whose terms of office cover the period from 1977 to 1989 and who confirmed that the Dallas County office did apply a policy of excluding blacks from juries. Further supporting this argument is a 1986 article in a local newspaper citing a 1963 internal memo in the district attorney's office advising prosecutors not to include "Jews, negroes, Dagos, Mexicans or a member of any minority race" as a jury member. Further, in the early 1970s, the prosecutor's office employed a training manual that contained advice on jury selection to the effect that a prosecutor should not include any member of a minority group because "they almost always empathize with the accused."

The *Dallas Morning News* has examined 15 capital murder trials from 1980 through 1986 and has revealed that prosecutors excluded 90% of African Americans qualified for jury selection. Nevertheless, the assistant district attorney in the Miller-El case disclaimed any notion that he had challenged the 10 African American jurors on grounds of race. He claimed that he was trying to assemble the best possible jury and that his office had no policy of racial discrimination. Despite these claims, at least three of the potential African American jurors challenged in the Miller-El case supported capital punishment and wanted to be on the jury.

SOURCE: Rimer 2002.

Conviction and Sentencing

Conviction

In the aggregate, blacks tend to be convicted less than whites (Petersilia 1983; Wilbanks 1987), and according to Robert Sampson and Janet Lauritsen (1997), no consistent evidence exists of racial discrimination at the point of criminal conviction. Data on trials for the period of 1990 through 2004 indicates that there is no significant difference between the likelihood of a judge or a jury convicting black or white defendants, but for blacks, a bench trial is more likely to bring a verdict of not guilty than a jury trial. There are negligible differences between whites and blacks across offense categories: While blacks are more likely than whites to be convicted of violent crimes and drug offenses, whites are more likely than blacks to be convicted of property and public order crimes. It is at the point of sentencing, not conviction, that racial disparities appear (Moore 2015: 20–21).

Sentencing

Research on sentencing has generated the most interest among those studying racial disparity. A review of a large number of studies conducted for the National Academy of Sciences (Hagan and Bumiller 1983) concluded that it was the prior criminal record rather than race that affected the sentencing disposition and that, once this was controlled for, the direct effect of race was basically eliminated. Racial disparities in sentencing arose from the disproportionate representation of minorities in officially processed criminal conduct, and this in turn was reflected in longer or more serious prior criminal records. Some concerns were raised that race might have a cumulative effect on sentencing by operating indirectly through other factors that disadvantage minorities and that race might interact with other factors, such as initial arrest, to influence decision-making.

Blacks disproportionately commit crimes that carry long prison sentences, and the time served for those offenses has greatly increased since the 1970s. As well, data for 2008 relating to sentences in state prisons shows that for all offenses for which parole could be granted blacks served a greater percentage of the maximum sentence than did whites. For example, in convictions for drug trafficking, blacks served 42% of the sentence imposed compared to 28% for whites; and for property offenses, blacks served 46% of the sentence compared to whites, who served 38% (Moore 2015: 29). In studies conducted in the 1970s and 1980s, researchers investigated racial bias by considering the victim's status rather than that of the offender, explored historical changes in sentencing, and included in their research crimes not previously covered, such as drug processing. In drug prosecutions, Ruth Peterson and John Hagan (1984) found that low-level black drug dealers in New York were treated more leniently than white drug dealers, but major black dealers were treated more harshly than their white counterparts because they were perceived as inflicting still more harm on the already victimized nonwhite population. Overall, the research conducted during this period seemed to suggest that there was some discrimination, sometimes, in some places.

Research has focused on determinate sentencing, including three-strikes legislation. In one analysis of over 11,000 such cases in California, researchers found some racial disparities in sentencing, but once the results were controlled for prior record and other variables, it was concluded that racial disparity in sentencing was not the result of racial discrimination (Klein, Petersilia, and Turner 1990).

The most recent research on race and sentencing indicates that while race does not in general directly affect the likelihood of imprisonment it does have an effect due to the factors of pretrial detention, prior imprisonment, and quality of legal representation. As Spohn puts it (2015: 3), "Blacks . . . are more likely than Whites to be imprisoned after conviction because they were more likely to be detained pretrial, more likely to have a prior prison sentence, and less likely to be represented by a private attorney." However, as Spohn notes (p. 4), it may be incorrect to conclude that sentencing based on prior imprisonment is a racially neutral factor when police aggressively target certain types of crime, such as drug dealing, in neighborhoods that are predominantly black. Where this occurs, blacks are more likely to accumulate a record of imprisonment than are whites. In relation to pretrial detention, blacks are less likely than whites to be able to post bond and are therefore more likely to be detained pretrial and less likely to be able to engage a private lawyer. These indirect factors suggest that racial disproportionality and racial bias will not be eliminated without substantial policy reforms in criminal justice.

Economic and Social Factors

Researchers have begun to pay attention to macrosocial and macroeconomic contexts, attempting to frame research that could identify the role of poverty, urbanization, and related factors in sentencing. Walker and colleagues (2000: 62) point out that a large economic gap exists between white Americans and minorities and that over the past 20 years there has been considerable growth in the number of the very poor. The first official definition of poverty was developed by the federal government in 1964, and it reflects the minimum income needed for an adequate standard of living. In 1995, the poverty line was $7,763 for a single person and $15,569 for a family of four; in that year, 13.8% of all Americans were below the poverty line (p. 65). In 2005, about 10.6% of all whites were below the poverty line compared with 24.9% of blacks and 21.8% of Hispanics (DeNava-Walt, Proctor, and Lee 2006). Although the African American middle class has grown significantly, the percentage of African Americans among the very poor has also increased. In terms of wealth—that is, the measure of all accumulated assets such as a house, a car, or savings—the 2005 median of white families was $48,554, compared with only $30,858 for African Americans and $35,967 for Hispanics. In 2013, the median household wealth was $81,400, dropping from $135,700 since the great recession of 2007. The median net worth of black households was $11,000 (falling from $19,200 in 2007), Hispanic $13,700 (down from $23,600 in 2007), and whites $141,900 (down from $192,500 in 2007; Pew Research Center 2014).

Economic and social factors also come into play through postrelease penalties imposed federally and by the states that can have the effect of amplifying racial disparities already experienced by minority felons. For example, released drug felons are not permitted to live in federally funded public housing and both federal and state laws permit private housing to be denied to drug felons. Former prisoners are barred from obtaining federal student loans for a fixed period, and access to public benefits for the needy are denied to those with drug-related convictions. When almost one in four black prisoners has served time for a drug offense, the impact of these penalties on poor, former black prisoners can be very significant (Moore 2015: 36–37).

As well as investigating decision-making points within the criminal justice system for racial discrimination, the racial disproportion in prison populations and the place of race in seeking and imposing the death penalty have been the subject of research attention.

IMPRISONMENT DISPARITIES

Incarceration Rates

Table 4.1 shows rates of incarceration for different ethnic/racial groups. At the end of 2014, there were an estimated 1,561,500 state and federal prisoners (down 1% from 2013), and the total state and federal incarceration rate was 612 per 100,000 population (Carson 2015: 1). At midyear 2014, the total estimated jail population was 744,600, with a jail incarceration rate of 234 per 100,000 population; 47% of all jail inmates were white, while 35% were black and 15% Hispanic (Minton and Zheng 2015: 1).

Black inmates with sentences of more than 1 year in state or federal institutions were incarcerated at a rate of 2,805 per 100,000 population in 2013, decreasing to 2, 724 in 2014, compared with a rate of 466 for white non-Hispanic males down to 465 in 2014, while Hispanic males were incarcerated at a rate of 1,134 per 100,000 in 2013 and down to 1,090 in 2014 (Carson 2014, 2015).

A study of almost 34,000 cases between 2000 and 2001, compiled by the U.S. Sentencing Commission, covering sentences in the federal courts found that male Hispanics and blacks receive harsher sentences than whites and that young Hispanic males have the highest odds of being incarcerated. Young black males receive the longest sentences (42% longer than young white males). Harsh punishments are disproportionately focused on the youngest Hispanic and black males, and sentencing outcomes are dependent on a defendant's relative social-structural position in society. Age was therefore found to have a significant effect on sentence, and the authors suggest that racial and age stereotypes may be influential (Doerner and Demuth 2009: 1). Data from 2014 reveals that the imprisonment rate declined from 621 per 100,000 in 2013 to 612 per 100,000 in 2014. Half of imprisoned males (50%) and more than half (59%) of imprisoned females in federal prison were serving time for drug offenses on September 30, 2014 (Carson 2015: 1). Women in prison sentenced to more than 1 year increased by 2% in 2014 from the previous year, while the federal population declined by 2.5% from 2013 (p. 1).

Table 4.1 Racial and Ethnic Rates of Incarceration Under Federal and State Jurisdiction, December 31, 2013, and December 31, 2014

Racial/Ethnic Group	2013 Rate per 100,000 Males	2014 Rate per 100,000 Males	2013 Rate per 100,000 Females	2014 Rate per 100,000 Females
White	466	465	51	53
Black	2,805	2,724	113	109
Hispanic	1,134	1,090	66	64

SOURCES: Carson 2014, 2015.

Explaining Racial Disproportionality in Incarceration

How can the racial disproportionality that exists in the U.S. prison population be accounted for? At one level of analysis, a study conducted by Alfred Blumstein (1993) concluded that between 1979 and 1991 there was an enormous growth in the rate of imprisonment and that the incarceration rate had tripled between 1975 and 1990. While the total number of drug offenders had increased nearly 10 times, there was little change between 1979 and 1991 in the level of racial disproportionality in incarceration rates. Importantly, the war on drugs had focused on offenses involving high levels of discretion, opening up the possibility of charges of discrimination. In light of the increase in the proportion of those incarcerated that were drug offenders—from 5.7% in 1979 to 21.5% in 1991—Blumstein (1993) suggested that an adequate investigation of racial disproportionality in incarceration should specifically examine the issue of disparity by crime type. In particular, having considered the growth in the number of drug offenders, he concluded that the war on drugs had contributed to racial disproportionality to a major degree, despite what he saw as the futility of that strategy.

In 2013 in federal prisons, out of a total inmate population of 193,775, those serving time for drug offenses made up 98,200 of that total (Carson 2014: 17). The war on drugs continues to impact African Americans and Hispanics disproportionately; as of December 3, 2012, black and white inmates both made up 4% of all offenders convicted of drug offenses serving time in state prisons, and Hispanics made up 4.2% (p. 15).

Table 4.2 shows the number of inmates in state and federal prisons and local jails under the jurisdiction of state or federal correctional authorities; Table 4.3 illustrates federal and state prisoners by race, gender, ethnicity, and age; and Table 4.4 shows the rate of incarceration per 100,000 population through these same categories.

Death Penalty Disparities

Historically, race and the death penalty have been closely associated. Extralegal lynching of blacks by white mobs and cases where blacks were sentenced to death by all-white juries are prominent instances of this connection. In the South, crimes that carried the death penalty were defined differently for blacks and whites: The death penalty was applied against whites mainly in cases of homicide, but for blacks, death was the sentence for a range of crimes, including homicide, rape, robbery, assault with a deadly weapon, and kidnapping a white female (Girgenti 2015: 2).

In 1987, research compiled by David Baldus and others, known as the "Baldus Study," revealed racial disparities in capital punishment cases in Georgia. Baldus analyzed the association between race and sentencing outcomes in about 2,400 homicide cases charged and sentenced in Georgia between 1973 and 1979 and found a pattern of discrimination by race of victim and a weaker pattern of discrimination by race of defendant (Girgenti 2015: 3). Even after taking into account nonracial variables, the study found defendants charged with killing white victims were 4.3 times more likely to receive the death sentence than those killing black victims.

In the landmark 1987 U.S. Supreme Court case of *McCleskey v. Kemp*, the Baldus research was rejected by the Court, which held that it was necessary to prove "purposeful discrimination" that had a "discriminatory effect" on the defendant (Moore 2015: 71). The Court did not dispute the validity of the Baldus Study and conceded that blacks were "singled out for different treatment in the Georgia capital sentencing system" (p. 72). However, the Court stated that accepting McCleskey's claim would raise serious questions about the criminal justice system, and the Court might be forced to evaluate all laws based on claims of alleged bias. The Court said that this process would challenge "the fundamental role of discretion in our criminal justice system" (quoted in Clemons 2014: 705).

As noted earlier, research has shown that when type of homicide is controlled for, race is a factor in the prosecutor's decision to seek the death penalty and in its imposition (Aguirre and Baker 1990; Baldus, Woodward, and Pulaski 1990; Paternoster et al. 2003). It appears that the race of the victim, together with the race of the offender, has a significant influence on the prosecutor's willingness to seek the death penalty and on the willingness of judges and jurors to impose it (see Table 4.4). Black offenders convicted of murdering white victims are at the highest risk for receiving the sentence of capital punishment, and offenders, whether black or white, convicted of murdering black victims are least likely to receive the death penalty. Evidence of discrimination in relation to black offenders is paralleled by similar discrimination in cases involving Hispanic victims, according to research that examined all death eligible homicides in one county in California from 1977 to 1986 (Lee 2006: 17). Girgenti (2015: 1) has shown that there is a significant "black victim effect" because cases involving black victims are the least likely to be regarded by jurors as involving brutality, heinousness, and victim suffering.

There is a substantial difference between white and black views about the death penalty. In the 2002 General Social Survey, 69.8% of whites favored the death penalty as compared with only 42.1% of blacks (Barkan and Cohn 2005: 40). Some argue that racial prejudice plays a significant role in white support for the death penalty, and several studies have found such racial prejudice combined with a punitive approach among whites (see, e.g., Soss, Langbein,

Table 4.2   Sentenced Prisoners Under the Jurisdiction of State or Federal Correctional Authorities, December 31, 2004–2014

Year	Total	Federal[a]	State	Male	Female
2004	1,433,728	159,137	1,274,591	1,337,730	95,998
2005	1,462,866	166,173	1,296,693	1,364,178	98,688
2006	1,504,598	173,533	1,331,065	1,401,261	103,337
2007	1,532,851	179,204	1,353,647	1,427,088	105,763
2008	1,547,742	182,333	1,365,409	1,441,384	106,358
2009	1,553,574	187,886	1,365,688	1,448,239	105,335
2010	1,552,669	190,641	1,362,028	1,447,766	104,903
2011	1,538,847	197,050	1,341,797	1,435,141	103,706
2012	1,512,430	196,574	1,315,856	1,411,076	101,354
2013[b]	1,520,403	195,098	1,325,305	1,416,102	104,301
2014[c]	1,508,636	191,374	1,317,262	1,402,404	106,232
Percent change					
Average annual, 2004-2013	0.6%	2.0%	0.4%	0.6%	0.8%
2013–2014	−0.8	−1.9	−0.6	−1.0	1.9

Note: Jurisdiction refers to the legal authority of state of federal correctional officials over a prisoner, regardless of where the prisoner is held. Counts are based on prisoners with sentences of more than 1 year under the jurisdiction of state or federal correctional officials.

[a]Includes inmates held in nonsecure privately operated community corrections facilities and juveniles held in contract facilities.

[b]Nevada did not submit 2013 National Prisoner Statistics (NPS) data, and Alaska did not submit sex-specific jurisdiction counts to NPS in 2013, so data for these states were imputed. See *Methodology* for imputation strategy.

[c]Total and state estimates include imputed counts for Alaska, which did not submit 2014 NPS data. See *Methodology* for imputation strategy,

SOURCE: Carson 2014: 5.

Table 4.3 Sentenced Prisoners Under the Jurisdiction of State or Federal Correctional Authorities by Age, Sex, Race, and Hispanic Origin, December 31, 2014

Age group	Total[a]	Male					Female				
		All male[a]	White[b]	Black[b]	Hispanic	Other[b]	All female[a]	White[b]	Black[b]	Hispanic	Other[b]
Total[c]	471	890	465	2,724	1,091	968	65	53	109	64	93
18–19	169	317	102	1,072	349	542	14	8	32	17	12
20–24	746	1,365	584	3,868	1,521	1,755	96	72	152	94	109
25–29	1,055	1,912	958	5,434	2,245	2,022	170	150	244	165	208
30–34	1,161	2,129	1,111	6,412	2,457	2,193	185	163	264	174	225
35–39	1,067	1,982	1,029	6,122	2,272	1,878	155	138	229	137	189
40–44	904	1,689	942	5,105	1,933	1,619	132	119	213	107	174
45–49	758	1,417	815	4,352	1,602	1,444	111	90	203	94	161
50–54	567	1,081	633	3,331	1,320	1,112	72	57	128	67	124
55–59	358	698	400	2,178	978	832	37	27	72	42	63
60–64	212	422	252	1,265	680	483	20	15	37	25	37
65 or older	72	158	109	418	299	208	5	4	8	7	12
Number of sentenced prisoners[d]	1,508,636	1,402,404	453,500	516,900	308,700	123,300	106,232	53,100	22,600	17,800	12,800

Note: Counts based on prisoners with sentences of more than 1 year under the jurisdiction of state or federal correctional authorities. Imprisonment rate is the number of prisoners under state or federal jurisdiction with a sentence of more than 1 year per 100,000 U.S. residents of corresponding sex, age, and race or Hispanic origin. Resident population estimates are from the U.S. Census Bureau for January 1, 2015. Alaska did not submit 2014 data to the National Prisoner Statistics (NPS), so totals include imputed counts for this state. See *Methodology*.

[a]Includes American Indians and Alaska Natives; Asians; Native Hawaiians and other Pacific Islanders; and persons of two or more races.
[b]Excludes of Hispanic or Latino origin.
[c]Includes persons age 17 or younger.
[d]Race totals are rounded to the nearest 100 to accommodate differences in data collection techniques between jurisdictions.

SOURCE: Carson 2015: 15.

Table 4.4 Imprisonment Rate of Sentenced Prisoners Under the Jurisdiction of State or Federal Correctional Authorities, December 31, 2004–2014

Year	Per 100,000 U.S. residents of all ages					Per 100,000 adult U.S. residents		
	Total[a]	Federal[a,b]	State[a]	Male[a]	Female[a]	Total[c]	Male[c]	Female[c]
2004	487	54	433	923	64	649	1,248	84
2005	492	56	436	932	65	655	1,257	86
2006	501	58	443	948	68	666	1,275	89
2007	506	59	447	955	69	670	1,282	90
2008	506	60	447	956	69	669	1,279	90
2009	504	61	443	952	67	665	1,271	88
2010	500	61	439	948	66	656	1,260	86
2011	492	63	429	932	65	644	1,236	84
2012	480	62	417	909	63	626	1,201	82
2013[d]	477	61	416	903	65	621	1,189	83
2014[e]	471	60	412	890	65	612	1,169	84
Percent change								
Aaverage annual, 2004–2013	−0.2%	1.3%	−0.4%	−0.2%	0.1%	−0.4%	−0.5%	−0.2%
2013–2014	−1.3	−2.6	−1.1	−1.5	1.3	−1.5	−1.7	1.1

Note: Jurisdiction refers to the legal authority of state or federal correctional officials over a prisoner, regardless of where the prisoner is held. Counts are based on prisoners with sentences of more than 1 year under the jurisdiction of state or federal correctional officials.

[a]Imprisonment rate per 100,000 U.S. residents of all ages.

[b]Includes inmates held in nonsecure privately operated community corrections facilities and juveniles held in contract facilities.

[c]Imprisonment rate per 100,000 U.S. residents age 18 or older.

[d]Nevada did not submit 2013 National Prisoner Statistics (NPS) data, and Alaska did not sumbit sex-specific jurisdiction counts to NPS in 2013, so data for these states were imputed. See *Methodology*.

[e]Total and state estimates include imputed counts for Alaska, which did not submit 2014 NPS data. See *Methodology*.

SOURCE: Carson 2015: 7.

Table 4.5   Inmates Under Sentence of Death, by Race and Hispanic Origin, 2010, 2013

Race/Hispanic Origin	Total Under Sentence of Death: Males 2010	Total Under Sentence of Death: Males 2013	Total Under Sentence of Death: Females 2010	Total Under Sentence of Death: Females 2013	Prisoners Executed 2010	Prisoners Executed 2013	Mean Time Elapsed Since Sentenced to Execution 2010
Total	3,483	2,979	66	56	52	39	152 mo. (male) 118 mo. (female)
							All 169 mo.
White	1,738	1,663	42	38	24	23	155 mo.
Hispanic Origin/	346	389	4			3	
Non-Hispanic; Number		2,312					
unknown		278					
Black	1,302	1,248	15	14	21	13	155 mo.
All other races	73	68	3		0	0	

SOURCE: Snell 2010, 2014.

and Metelko 2003: 416). Research based on the 1992 American National Election Study (ANES) concluded that "for white people living in an all white county, racial prejudice emerges as the strongest predictor of white death penalty support. . . . In more racially integrated counties this effect is more than doubled" (Barken and Cohn 2005: 41). The results of this study have been confirmed in similar research based on the 1992 ANES and data from the 1990 U.S. Census (Soss et al. 2003). The researchers also found that whites with higher family incomes were more likely to support the death penalty than whites from lower-income-earning groups (p. 407).

Tracy Snell (2010: 1) notes that the 3,483 inmates held under a death sentence at year-end 2009 represent the ninth decline over the same number of years; 98% of those on death row were male, while 2% were female. Executions declined from 85 in 2000 to 46 in 2010 (Death Penalty Information Center 2010). Public opinion also seems to be changing. When asked in a national poll what the penalty for murder should be, 33% said the death

penalty, 39% said life without parole plus restitution, 13% said life without parole, and 9% said life with parole, giving a total of 61% choosing an alternative sentence to death. The Death Penalty Information Center describes the drop in death sentences as representing near historic lows. Snell (2010) attributes this trend to

ongoing controversy over lethal injections, the high cost of capital punishment, and increasing public sentiment in favor of alternative sentences. Executions dropped by 12% compared with 2009, and by more than 50% since 1999. The number of new death sentences was about the same as in 2009, the lowest in 34 years. (p. 1)

HATE CRIMES

An act of racial discrimination may take the form of a hate crime. Hate crime statutes fall into two types (Russell-Brown 1998: 86), some treating

Table 4.6 Incidents Per Victim Type by Bias Motivation, 2013

Bias motivation	Total incidents	Victim type					
		Individual	Business/ financial instititution	Government	Religious organization	Society/ public[1]	Other/ unknown/ multiple
Total	**5,928**	**4,696**	**298**	**177**	**171**	**64**	**522**
Single-Bias Incidents	**5,922**	**4,690**	**298**	**177**	**171**	**64**	**522**
Race	2,871	2,402	145	107	10	43	164
Religion	1,031	450	87	44	158	5	287
Sexual Orientation	1,233	1,154	25	12	1	4	37
Ethnicity	655	572	35	13	2	5	28
Disability	83	69	4	1	0	6	3
Gender	18	15	1	0	0	1	1
Gender dentity	31	28	1	0	0	0	2
Multiple-bias Incidents[2]	**6**	**6**	**0**	**0**	**0**	**0**	**0**

[1]The victim type *society/public* is collected only in the National Incident-Based Reporting System. See Methodology.
[2]A *multiple-bias incident* is an incident in which one or more offense types are motivated by two or more biases.

SOURCE: Federal Bureau of Investigation 2014.

Table 4.7   Incidents, Offenses, Victims, and Known Offenders by Bias Motivation, 2013

Bias motivation	Incidents	Offenses	Victims[1]	Known offenders[2]
Total	**5,928**	**6,933**	**7,242**	**5,814**
Single-Bias Incidents	**5,922**	**6,921**	**7,230**	**5,808**
Race:	**2,871**	**3,407**	**3,563**	**2,733**
Anti-White	653	728	754	680
Anti-Black or African American	1,856	2,263	2,371	1,747
Anti-American Indican or Alaska Native	129	146	159	108
Anti-Asian	135	158	164	130
Anti-Native Hawaiian or Other Pacific Islander	3	3	3	7
Anti-Multiple Races, Group	95	109	112	61
Religion:	**1,031**	**1,163**	**1,223**	**682**
Anti-Jewish	625	689	737	393
Anti-Catholic	70	74	75	72
Anti-Protestant	35	42	47	17
Anti-Islamic (Muslim)	135	165	167	127
Anti-Other Religion	117	135	137	44
Anti-Multiple Religions, Group	42	51	53	25
Anti-Atheism/Agnosticism/etc.	7	7	7	4
Sexual Orientation:	**1,233**	**1,402**	**1,461**	**1,514**
Anti-Gay (Male)	750	849	890	975
Anti-Lesbian	160	185	191	174
Anti-Lesbian, Gat, Bisexual, or Transgender (Mixed Group)	277	317	329	324
Anti-Heterosexual	21	24	24	20
Anti-Bisexual	25	27	27	21
Ethnicity:	**655**	**794**	**821**	**743**
Anti-Hispanic or Latino	331	418	432	418
Anti-Not Hispanic or Latino[3]	324	376	389	325
Disability:	**83**	**92**	**99**	**77**
Anti-Physical	22	23	24	23
Anti-Mental	61	69	75	54

Gender:	18	30	30	20
Anti-Male	5	5	5	7
Anti-Female	13	25	25	13
Gender Identity:	31	33	33	39
Anti-Transgender	23	25	25	30
Anti-Gender Non-Conforming	8	8	8	9
Multiple-Bias Incidents[4]	6	12	12	6

[1]The term *victim* may refer to a person, business, institution, or society as a whole.

[2]The term *known offender* does not imply that the identity of the suspect is known, but only that an attribute of the suspect has been identified, which distinguishes him/her from an unknown offender.

[3]The term *anti-not Hispanic or Lantino* does not imply the victim was targeted because he/she was not of Hispanic origin, but it refers to other or unspecified ethnic biases that the not Hispanic or Latino.

[4]The *multiple-bias incident* is an incident in which one or more offense types are motivated by two or more biases.

SOURCE: Federal Bureau of Investigation 2014.

hate crimes as independent offenses and others providing enhanced penalties for crimes that are motivated by bias. Additional penalties may be imposed by the court where it finds that an offense has been committed and was motivated by bias based on race. To successfully convict a person of a hate crime, the prosecution must establish the motive of the accused, which is extremely difficult to do. Sometimes the nature of the crime provides a motive, such as painting a swastika on the side of a house owned by a Jewish family, which common sense would interpret as a hate crime because the family is Jewish. The language used by an offender during the offense may be particularly important, especially if racial slurs are used. Prosecutors also pay attention to the severity of the attack, the absence of any provocation by the victim, any prior history of contact between the victim and suspect, and any history of similar incidents in the same area (Byers and Spillane 2000: 265). The definition of *bias-motivated* or *hate crimes* was defined by the 1990 Hate Crime Statistics Act as "crimes that manifest evidence of prejudice based on race, religion, sexual orientation, or ethnicity" (Langton and Planty 2011: 1). This definition was amended in 1994 to include "crimes motivated by bias against persons with disabilities" and again in 2009 to include "crimes of prejudice based on gender or gender identity" (p. 1).

Data published by the FBI in 2014 in its annual *Hate Crime Statistics* report revealed there were 5,928 hate crime incidents involving 6,933 offenses reported to the FBI by law enforcement agencies in 2013. The number of such crimes was down compared to 2012 when 6,573 crimes were reported. A breakdown of the single bias hate crimes shows that 48.5% of hate crime incidents were motivated by race, 11.1% by ethnicity, 20.8% by sexual orientation, and 17.4% by religion. According to the National Crime Victimization Survey, in 2012, an estimated 293,800 nonfatal violent and property hate crime victimizations occurred in the United States, an estimate not statistically different from 2004 (281,700). About 90% of all hate crimes in 2011 and 2012 were violent victimizations, an increase from 78% in 2004. In 2012, about 27% of hate crimes were classified as serious violent crimes—rape or sexual assault, robbery, and aggravated assault—while the majority of hate crimes (63%) were simple assaults.

EXPLANATIONS FOR RACIAL DISCRIMINATION IN THE CRIMINAL JUSTICE SYSTEM

How Do We Explain the Existence of Racial Discrimination in the Criminal Justice System?

As discussed earlier, racial disparities within the criminal justice system have been exhaustively researched by scholars over many years and have been clearly identified, but nevertheless persist. Sustained disproportionate treatment within the justice system raises questions about the morality of policies that produce such outcomes and about the level of commitment of policy makers to eradicating racial inequalities (Moore 2015: 41).

Most research on racial discrimination draws on consensus and conflict theories to explain discrimination. According to *consensus theory*, individuals share their values with the state, which is organized to protect the interests of society and employs criminal law as an instrument of protection. Punishment is based on rational factors such as the seriousness of the offense and prior convictions. On the other hand, *conflict theorists* perceive society as comprising groups with conflicting values, with the state organized to represent the interests of the powerful ruling class. Criminal law is viewed as an instrument of protection for the powerful and elite, and punishment is based on nonrational factors, including race and social class. Conflict theorists argue that groups that threaten the power of the rulers are more likely to be the subjects of social control; that is, these groups are more criminalized and suffer greater rates of incarceration. They argue that minorities, the unemployed, and the poor represent these threatening groups (Brown and Warner 1995; Chambliss and Seidman 1971).

Conflict Theory

Laws concerning vagrancy help to illustrate conflict theory. Being a vagrant is defined as simply occupying public space without resources and with no clear purpose for being there. It is argued that only the poor engage in vagrancy, and making vagrancy a criminal act and enforcing laws against it are attempts by the powerful to control the poor (Walker et al. 2000: 18). The era of segregation in the South from the 1890s to the 1960s also demonstrates conflict theory in action. During this period, the criminal justice system enforced laws providing for white supremacy and declared the subordinate status of blacks. Nowadays, street crime is a primary target of law enforcement, and this kind of crime is for the most part committed by the poor and by racial and ethnic minorities. This targeting of street crime contrasts with the relatively sparse enforcement of white-collar crime committed primarily by middle- and upper-class whites. Accordingly, conflict theorists argue that street crime is another demonstration of conflict theory. In general terms, as far as race is concerned, conflict theory argues that the larger the size of the minority population, especially African Americans, the greater the perceived threat of crime and therefore the more punitive must be the effort to discourage this possibility (Moore 2015: 266).

In reviewing the applicability of conflict theory to instances of police brutality involving minorities (see Chapter 3 for police use of force), Malcolm D. Holmes and Brad W. Smith (2008: 11) argue that police and minorities should be viewed as distinct groups that are dynamically and intractably opposed and that police brutality is an outcome and a symptom of that relationship. While policing accords with conflict theory in that the police represent dominant interests, police are far more concerned for their personal safety in entering and policing impoverished minority neighborhoods than with that representation. For minorities, police represent oppression and an ever-present threat in their daily lives. Each group stereotypes the other—the police see minorities as criminal threats, and minorities regard police as racist and authoritarian (p. 13).

Emotional responses, including fear and anger, are significant factors in the intergroup dynamics. The role of emotions in policing is under-researched, especially the place of fear in interactions with the public, but studies show that police regard danger as a defining element of their work and, in terms of minorities, perceive young black males in impoverished neighborhoods as "dangerous until proven otherwise" (Holmes and Smith 2008: 90). Police rely heavily on stereotypes to shape their actions and responses with minorities at street level, reducing complex interactions to manageable situations. Police arrive at the training academy with mental stereotypes that associate race with crime, and when they work the streets, they employ the same typifications to structure their interactions, save time, and resolve uncertainties (p. 71). The stress of working in such neighborhoods is likely to call up stereotypical and emotional responses that are aggressive and authoritarian in the face of what police regard as imminent threats to their safety (p. 92). Thus, minorities and police are conditioned to distrust and fear each other. Where police use brutality against minorities despite the likely adverse career consequences, the authors suggest this has little to do with cognitive, rational decision-making but rather is an outcome of emotional responses and prior stereotyping (p. 122). It is therefore a normal by-product of intergroup relations. There are few easy solutions in light of police cultural norms that condone violence and value concealing discipline violations, but psychological screening and increased professionalism and education may go some way toward minimizing the incidence of police brutality toward minorities.

A further theoretical explanation for racial discrimination argues that *the symbolic aspect of social conflict drives crime control.* For example, perceptions of threats, rather than actual threats, are influential in the design of crime control policies (Tittle and Curran in Sampson and Lauritsen 1997). Some studies support this position. For example, one study in Washington State found that non-whites were sentenced to imprisonment at higher rates in counties with large minority populations, and interviews with justice officials and leaders in the community showed a consistent public concern with "dangerousness" and the "threat from minorities." Accordingly, crime was perceived as a minority problem, and race was used as a code for certain lifestyles and forms of dress thought to signal criminality. According to this view, it follows that the poor and the underclass are seen not as a threat to rulers and elites, but to the middle and working classes who make up the dominant majority of American society.

Sampson and Lauritsen (1997: 362), after reviewing most of the studies on discrimination in the criminal justice system, conclude that discrimination appears on occasion at some stages in the criminal justice system, in some locations. However, there is little evidence of any systematic or overt bias on the part of criminal justice decision-makers. They contend that there is a perception of racial discrimination in the administration of justice that is fueled by the regular moral panics and political responses to those panics such as the war on crime, the war against drugs, and the concern with sexual predators. These are targeted at particular lifestyles or locations associated with minorities and have the effect of subjecting the behavior of minorities to increased levels of social control (Chambliss 1995; Tonry 1995).

Explaining African American Incarceration: The War on Drugs

Scholars have argued that sentencing policies and moral panics have long targeted minorities. For example, in discussing the history of marijuana policy, Mauer (2006) points out that when this drug was first used in the 1900s, it was perceived to be a drug used only by blacks and Mexican Americans. Its use was penalized in the 1950s with a sentence of 2 to 5 years' imprisonment for first-time possession. Yet in the 1960s, when marijuana came to be widely used by the white middle class, public attitudes began to change, and marijuana began to be perceived as a relatively harmless drug, nonaddictive, and not likely to lead to other criminal activity. By the 1970s, legislation had separated marijuana from other narcotics and had lowered the penalties, and some jurisdictions even effectively decriminalized its possession in small quantities (pp. 148–149).

Mauer contends that since the 1980s no policy has impacted black incarceration more than the war on drugs (2006: 158). He identifies two factors from which to map the impact of this war: firstly, the enormous increase in the number of drug arrests, and secondly, the fact that blacks have accounted for an increasing proportion of those arrests (p. 159). Between 1980 and 1990, drug arrests almost doubled, but this did not reflect an increased rate of drug use because data reveals a decline in drug use since 1979, when 14.1% of the population reported using drugs in the past month. This percentage had reduced to 6.7% by 1990 and further declined to 6.3% by 2000. It would be expected that with fewer drug users, arrests would decline, but this did not occur. Instead, yet more police resources were allocated to drug enforcement, and police increasingly began to target inner-city black communities (p. 160). Mauer notes that in 1980 blacks accounted for 21% of drug possession arrests; this rose to 36% by 1991 and then declined to 32% in 2000. Given that blacks constitute only 13% of the U.S. population, the data clearly shows disproportionality in arrests for drug offenses (p. 160).

Is this disparity explained by arguing that blacks use drugs more heavily than whites? According to data compiled by the Substance Abuse and Mental Health Administration, which conducts an annual household survey of drug use over the previous month and other periods, blacks were no more likely than whites to have used drugs during the previous month (both groups indicate 6.4%), but the much greater number of whites in the population means that whites constitute the vast majority of drug users. According to the survey data for the year 2000, whites made up 75%, blacks 12%, and Hispanics 9% of drug users. It follows that greater drug use by blacks does not explain the disproportionality in 2000 between 12% use and 32% of arrests for drug possession.

Michael Tonry (1998) argues that the targeting of black drug offenders was far from unconscious and that those who launched the drug war knew that "the enemy troops would mostly be young minority males" and that making mass arrests would disproportionately incarcerate those males (p. 52). He believes that those promoting these policies were well aware that the laws distinguishing powder from crack cocaine would disproportionately affect blacks. Thus, the drug war exemplifies the effect produced by a deliberate policy choice to focus on the enforcement of drug offenses.

Tonry later points to the reality of ghetto life that entices young black males into selling drugs and to police targeting drugs sold by blacks and the places where they are sold (2011: 54). It is relatively easy for drug agents to infiltrate the disorganized black urban drug markets: Ethnographic research has shown that drug sales are conducted openly in the inner cities and often to strangers in the streets. In white communities, however, the pattern differs because there drugs are sold by word of mouth, and

there are no fixed locations for selling: Whites obtain drugs through the party lifestyle, through contacts at their place of work, and in bars and at sporting events. These practices are therefore far harder to detect than open sales in the inner cities (p. 68). Lynch and Sabol (in Mauer 2006: 164) conclude that the war on drugs has resulted in increased targeting of black working- and middle-class areas for drug enforcement. While the processes that produce this outcome may not have been racially motivated, they have produced racially disparate outcomes.

Mandatory imprisonment laws have also played a role in that this policy approach has been applied most commonly to drug offenses. For example, the chance of receiving a prison term after being arrested for a drug offense increased by 447% between 1980 and 1992 (Mauer 2006: 167). As well, between 1985 and 1995 the number of drug offenders in prison increased by 478%, compared to a rise of 119% for all offenses; a substantial part of this increase is attributable to black Americans (p. 167).

The most discussed disparity in drug sentencing in recent years has been the issue of sentencing for possession of crack cocaine (Mauer 2006: 170). The mandatory sentencing laws passed by Congress provided a far harsher punishment for possession of crack cocaine than for powder cocaine in that the sale of 500 grams of powder resulted in a mandatory 5-year prison term, whereas possession of only 5 grams of crack cocaine triggered the same mandatory penalty. Significantly, crack cocaine is used primarily by urban blacks, and powder cocaine is used by middle- and upper-class whites. These mandatory sentencing laws have significantly impacted blacks because the vast majority of persons charged with crack trafficking in the federal system have been black (p. 171). As a result of the disparity in these offenses, the average prison sentence served by black federal prisoners for possession of crack cocaine is 40% longer than the average sentence for whites convicted of possession of powder cocaine (McDonald and Carlson 1993).

Congress finally voted to change the 25-year law that mandated a sentence for possession of crack cocaine–equivalent to the prison term for trafficking 100 times the amount of powder cocaine—and reduced the ratio to 18: 1 from 100: 1. The legislation also eliminated the mandatory 5-year prison sentence for first-time offenders (Associated Press 2010). In July 2011, Ohio became the 38th state to address the sentencing disparity required under the old law, and the U.S. Sentencing Commission made the new guidelines retroactive (Fields 2011). A significant motivating factor for states to reform crack laws derives from the high costs of imprisonment that states have borne since 1986 when the law was first passed. As one policy maker noted in Fields (2011),

> It's only been in the last three or four years that you have seen a very unusual alliance between fiscal conservatives and social progressives emerge around prisons. . . . Prisons are really expensive. Then you add in the state budget crisis that every state is grappling with right now. . . . So we've had this rethinking of priorities in the criminal justice system which I think really opens the doors for what had been advocated for already to emerge. (para. 14–15)

Alexander (2010: 100), responding to the issue of how to explain racial disparities, rules out "old-fashioned racism" because today few espouse explicitly racial policies or practices. Defenders of mass incarceration claim the justice system is nondiscriminatory and identify black violent crime rates as the explanation for the mass imprisonment of black citizens. However, this is problematic because while violent crime rates have fluctuated over time they bear little relationship to incarceration rates; today, violent crime rates are at their lowest, but mass incarceration rates remain largely unchanged (p. 101). Alexander points to racial indifference, which she defines as "a lack of compassion and caring about race," as the foundation of the control of blacks (p. 203). She believes the war against drugs (which she argues is the major cause of the mass incarceration of blacks) was designed to guarantee that blacks would comprise the new undercaste and explains how the war achieves this aim (p. 102). She identifies a two stage process:

- In the first stage, law enforcement was granted extremely wide discretion to stop and frisk and make vehicle stops for suspected drug offenses through proactive policing, thereby ensuring that such decisions would be influenced by stereotypes of black male criminality and that blacks and black neighborhoods would be targeted;
- In the second stage, the courts required that challenges of discrimination or profiling in conducting proactive policing offer proof of intentional discrimination. This high bar would ensure that challenges would almost never succeed (p. 103).

Murakawa and Beckett (2010: 702) join with Alexander in seeing the intent standard in proving racial discrimination as "a significant barrier to efforts to challenge criminal justice practices and policies that produce racially disparate outcomes" and, like Alexander, regard the expansion of wide police discretion as a major constraint to proving discrimination (see previous discussion for Supreme Court decisions on stop and frisk and on vehicle stops that support Alexander's argument).

Alexander characterizes the war on drugs as "a political ploy to capitalize on white resentment against African Americans" and as a tool, through the emergence of the panic about crack cocaine and its associated violence, "to build a racialized public consensus in support of an all-out war" (2010: 205). She argues that it should have been "glaringly obvious" that there existed a high risk of racial bias in the drug war and that this should have concerned the Supreme Court. Instead, the Court made rulings that would enable maximal discrimination by giving police wide discretion to stop and search persons and vehicles for drugs (p. 108). In Alexander's view, the decision in McCleskey was driven by a desire to protect the entire criminal justice system from challenges of racial bias and discrimination because the Court said that accepting McCleskey's claims of racial bias would mean opening the door to similar challenges to the exercise of discretionary powers in the system—for example, challenging prosecutors for decisions to prosecute (p. 111). Today, Alexander (2010) asserts that mass incarceration has been "normalized" and

all of the racial stereotypes and assumptions that gave rise to the system are embraced (or at least internalized) by people of all colors. . . . It is simply taken for granted that, in cities like Baltimore and Chicago, the vast majority of young black men are currently under the control of the criminal justice system or branded criminals for life. This extraordinary circumstance—unheard of in the rest of the world—is treated here in America as a basic fact of life, as normal as separate water fountains were just half a century ago. (p. 181)

The policy decision to conduct a war on drugs and the current debate about the high costs of imprisonment are further discussed in Chapter 9.

Racial Disparities: Social and Political Explanations

In an exposition of the social, psychological, and political causes of racial disparities in the criminal justice system, Michael Tonry (2010: 273) points to police practices and legislative and executive policies that systematically treat black criminality differently and more severely than white criminality. Asking why this has occurred, he suggests that the answers may range from "deliberate antiblack racism to innocent inadvertence" (p. 274). Tonry discounts both blatant racism and inadvertence—the former because racism is no longer explicitly expressed, and the latter because policy makers must have foreseen the adverse consequences of their policy choices for blacks. He concludes that one possible explanation is that "officials knew that blacks would disproportionately suffer but did not care. For reasons of political self-interest, ideology, or partisanship, they enacted disparity-causing policies anyway" (p. 275). As an example of this perspective, he cites the persistent refusal of policy makers to make changes to the law to remove the punishment disparity between crack cocaine and powder cocaine (see Chapter 9).

Tonry (2010: 276) argues that the foundations for disparity-causing policy choices lie in the cultural and social forces that combined historically to shape U.S. society, namely the following: a *psychology of race relations* that embraces stereotypes of blacks, prefers whiteness to blackness and consequently expresses little empathy for black criminality; a 300-year-old practice of white subordination of blacks in all fields; and the Republican

"Southern Strategy"[1] that appealed to racial concerns and anxieties and replaced explicit racial terminology by code words that, while seemingly neutral, in fact reflected continued white subordination of blacks.

According to Tonry (2010: 294) then, long-standing white self-interest has meant unconscious support for programs and policies that sustain white dominance, such as anti-immigration policies, where the real agenda is not the violation of laws by illegal immigrants but white concerns about "jobs, fear of social change, and worry that their own well-being will suffer." Beside these concerns, rational arguments hold no sway. Similarly, drug and crime control policies ensure that black communities remain destabilized and reinforce persistent white dominance of economic, social, and political forces. White privilege holds that all members of society deserve their status, and therefore stereotypes of black criminality and of the poor operate to rationalize racial inequities and disparities (p. 300).

Tonry cites work by sociologist Loic Wacquant (2008) who has identified patterns of racial dominance within U.S. history and argues that when one mechanism for maintaining white dominance ended it was replaced by another. Slavery was the mechanism that fulfilled this function until the Civil War, then the Jim Crow laws restored the status quo ante, then the ghettoization of the northern cities ensured discrimination as blacks were excluded from white suburbs, then as the ghetto became less secure, the prison system took over the housing of a black population viewed as dangerous and deviant. As Tonry notes, this has been the *effect* of criminal justice policies, not necessarily their

---

1 Tonry (2010: 277–280) explains that the Southern Strategy was a deliberate decision by Republican strategists in the 1960s to deploy stereotypes of black criminals and promote "tough on crime" and other policies that would be proxies for race, such as crime, welfare fraud, "forced" busing, states' rights, and affirmative action programs. These policies would resonate with white working-class southern voters. The strategy took advantage of the loss of support to the Democrats in the South consequent to the advance of the civil rights program. Strategists concluded that manipulating racial perspectives and biases would enable Republicans to dominate the South and capture white working-class voters who had traditionally voted Democratic, a group later to be known as the "Reagan Democrats."

conscious *intent*, and he points to the influence of deeply embedded social forces that operate to serve the interests of white Americans (2010: 295, 297).

Moore (2015) presents an array of evidence to support her belief that "the race problem in the American criminal justice system endures because the public and policymakers enable it" (p. xiii). Arguing that racial concerns and disparities have been consistently ignored, Moore explores the political context of crime control policy and puts forward two basic conclusions:

1. There are two distinct modes of law enforcement in the United States—one white and one black. The treatment accorded blacks by the criminal justice system, whether by police, prosecutors, or the courts, so differs to that accorded whites that it exists as a separate and distinct track based on race—it amounts to a form of racial tracking.
2. Racial tracking is the outcome of the actions and views of the American public and of policy makers who give tacit consent to its operation and continuance (p. xvi). Moore asserts that regardless of the factors that create and sustain racial disparities, those factors could be corrected by policy reform, but this has not occurred.

Why have policy makers failed to act? In her review of the institutions that have failed to act and could have influenced or altered the dynamics of racial tracking, Moore suggests that the *U.S. Supreme Court* has perpetuated racial disparities in its decision-making by consistently applying "colorblind jurisprudence" and that the Court has "consistently sidestepped, ignored, or dismissed the constitutional significance of racial influences in the criminal process" (2015: 55). She supports this argument with a detailed review of Court decisions between 1932 and 2005 (pp. 63–99).

In regard to the *Congress,* while concerns about racial tracking, especially racial profiling by police, have been raised by legislators, it has generally proved impossible to achieve reform. For example, between 2004 and 2009, 11 major sentencing reform bills were introduced, including bills to eliminate mandatory minimum sentences and mandatory drug sentences (Moore 2015: 110). Of the 45 reform measures examined, Moore finds that only two were enacted. The single major achievement was the Fair Sentencing Act of 2010 (pp. 56, 118).

After analyzing the seven omnibus crime bills[2] that constitute the corpus of laws reflecting federal crime control policy (p. 57), Moore concludes that Congress was the chief architect of the current punitive penal policies and showed minimal concern with the black experience of criminal justice in fashioning these anticrime laws and policies (see Chapter 9 for a discussion of these laws relating to minimum penalties, the war on drugs, and truth in sentencing). Instead of addressing concerns about racial disparities, Congress opted to follow a "crime-fighting approach" that gave far less weight to the racial tracking agenda than to the law and order agenda. In the fight against crime, racial disparities amounted to only "collateral damage" (p. 135).

In fact, research has consistently shown that in the case of drug use, for example, there is no difference in rates of selling and abusing illegal drugs, yet the drug arrest rate for blacks doubled from 1980 to 2000 while the white arrest rate remained basically unchanged. As for crimes of violence, while the rate of violent crime is higher for blacks than whites, this can be explained by socioeconomic factors that disproportionately affect blacks. Disadvantaged neighborhoods, both black and white, experience higher rates of crime than those that are not so disadvantaged (Clemons 2014: 691).

Race and the Politics of Crime

While the early positions of the two parties on race and crime acknowledged a connection between race and crime with the enactment of laws such as the Civil Rights Act 1964, the Voting Rights Act 1965, and the Federal Equal Housing Act 1968, Moore argues that after the 1960s, controlling crime was reconfigured to be a problem that concerned all Americans and not one that disproportionately affected minorities. From the 1960s, blacks were sidelined as the victims of a racialized justice system in favor of a new class of victims: women, children, and the elderly (Moore 2015: 184). Thus, Moore notes, "Racial justice concerns were relegated to the sidelines of the politics of criminal

---

2 The seven laws examined are Omnibus Crime Control and Safe Streets Act 1968, Comprehensive Drug Abuse Prevention and Control Act 1970, Sentencing Reform Act 1984, Anti-Drug Abuse Acts 1986 and 1988, Crime Control Act 1990, and Violent Crime Control and Law Enforcement Act 1994.

justice, where they remain" (p. 59). The politics of crime control focused largely on incarceration, particularly of drug offenders, and the federal government, through enforcement grant programs, promoted and encouraged more criminalization and more incarceration. For example, the 1994 Violent Crime Control and Law Enforcement Act required that offenders serve not less than 85% of their sentence for the state to qualify for "Truth in Sentencing Incentive Grants," which would finance prison expansion (pp. 152, 163; see Chapter 9 for Truth in Sentencing). Moore asserts that "at no point did the Republican or the Democratic party vigorously decry the foreseeable damage a heavy-handed law enforcement approach to drugs would likely yield in racial terms" (p. 205).

Racial Disparities and Public Opinion

Public opinion gave "tacit consent and endorsement" to the previously discussed institutional and political approaches because there exists "a public mindset that is generally supportive of a crime policy approach that is devoid of racial progressivism" (Moore 2015: 60). Americans do not regard racial disparities within the criminal justice system as a priority, even though they acknowledge they exist and disapprove of them. For example, up to 80% of citizens understand that race figures in the mass incarceration of blacks, with 51% considering it a major factor and about 28% minor. Only 18% believe race has no effect at all (p. 221). Nevertheless, according to Moore these acknowledgments about race do not lead citizens to conclude that the system as a whole should be condemned (p. 224). A majority believe that blacks are largely to blame for their high arrest and incarceration rates and therefore attribute racial disparities to black criminality rather than to the criminal justice system (p. 225).

While communities generally deny racial bias in law enforcement in their neighborhoods and individuals do not fear being a victim of violent crime, citizens do have fears about potential threats based on their perception of what is occurring beyond their neighborhood. There is a feeling that steps must be taken to forestall this happening, hence the public support for continually strengthening the criminal justice system and the disregard of racial disparities (Moore 2015: 248). Voters therefore want legislators to continue with the "get tough" policies that have

disproportionately impacted blacks. This perspective illustrates how race shapes crime control policies.

The public viewpoints on crime are largely derived from the media from which Americans receive most of their information (Moore 2015: 291). While academic opinion is united in seeing racial disparities as a structural and not an individual problem, the media persistently presents crime as an individual pathology and perpetuates negative stereotypes of black males. Attuned by society to an individualistic ideology, the public absorbs the media perspective and rejects structural explanations (see Chapter 11 on media ethics and criminal justice for a full discussion of media representations of crime). As Murakawa and Beckett (2010: 696) express it, "In . . . the conventional wisdom of many whites, racism is waning, aberrant, and located in the bad intentions of individual actors." Scholarly and expert opinion is discounted or ignored by the public because it provides a depth and context not favored by the media and is generally not disseminated by the media to the public. The end result is that, broadly, the public has only a superficial awareness of the relationship between crime and race (Moore 2015: 296).

Negative stereotypes about blacks are reflected in one survey of public opinion taken from 2000 to 2010 which found that while 50% of blacks believed blacks were committed to strong families only 32% of whites held that belief; and while only 19% of blacks believed blacks were lazy, 33% of whites held that belief about blacks (Moore 2015: 227). More specifically, a 2009 survey asked, "Which do you find more convincing to explain the reason why blacks have higher arrest and imprisonment rates? Blacks commit more crimes or blacks receive unfair treatment by the criminal justice system?" In response, 21% of blacks believed blacks committed more crime, but 62% of nonblacks believed they did. Fully 79% of blacks believed they received unfair treatment from the criminal justice system compared to 38% of nonblacks who believed this (p. 232). Moore explains the overall majority public opinion about race and blacks in the following terms:

> Americans seem to have reached a point of fatigue in regard to continued advocacy on behalf of blacks in any sphere of American life. . . . Indeed, there is growing frustration over what some see as a misguided and incessantly persistent emphasis on race. (2015: 242)

In responding to the question of how we explain racial disparities in the criminal justice system, Moore argues for the explanatory power of the several factors discussed earlier—namely, the American belief in individual responsibility for one's actions, daily reminders from the news media and infotainment generally of black criminality, and the media perpetuation of racial stereotypes of black males, together with a public perspective that maintains a "tough on crime" approach and subordinates all other considerations to that perspective, including a racialized justice system.

SUMMARY

The debate about racial discrimination in the criminal justice system remains unresolved. While most research suggests an absence of systematic racial discrimination, there is agreement among researchers that acts of discrimination occur at specific decision-making points, and some argue that informal and hidden forms of discrimination occur both within and outside the system. It follows that the majority opinion supports arguments that acts of discrimination occur and that they may perhaps be deeply rooted in cultural and social attitudes toward other races. These may express themselves in complex and nuanced ways that are difficult to capture within research strategies. Associated with acts of discrimination is the issue of the public perception of the workings of the criminal justice system. Regardless of the conclusions of research studies, there is a widespread belief among minorities that the system discriminates against them and is therefore unjust. To counter this perception, those exercising decision-making powers within the system must act ethically and strive to eradicate any suggestion of racial bias and discrimination from their decisions.

DISCUSSION QUESTIONS

1. Explain why the term *race* is an inadequate category of analysis.

2. What historical events and circumstances influence the possibility of the existence of racial discrimination within the criminal justice system?

3. What are the difficulties involved in focusing on decision-making points in the criminal justice system to determine whether racial discrimination occurs?

4. Explain the concept of petit apartheid and how its existence might generate acts of discrimination in the criminal justice system.

5. How can the study of drug policy and the prosecution of drug offenders assist in establishing the existence of racial discrimination in the criminal system?

6. What theoretical explanations are offered for racial discrimination in the criminal justice system? Explain with examples.

WEB RESOURCES

Brennan Center for Justice at New York University School of Law. http://www.brennancenter.org/
Bureau of Justice Statistics—Hate Crimes. https://www.fbi.gov/about-us/cjis/ucr/hate-crime/2013/resource-pages/about-hate-crime
Stop the Drug War. http://stopthedrugwar.org/
Drug Watch International. http://www.drugwatch.org
Families Against Mandatory Sentencing. http://www.famm.org/
Marijuana Policy Project. http://www.mpp.org
The Sentencing Project. http://www.sentencingproject.org
Drug War Chronicle. http://stopthedrugwar.org/chronicle

5

Judges, Lawyers, and Ethics

Legal Ethics: Historical Context

In the early days of colonization in the United States, lawyers working in the colonies were few in number, poorly trained, and not recognized as members of a profession. Although detailed histories of the early legal profession in the United States have yet to be written, researchers such as David Papke (1986) have identified some aspects of the early practice of law in Virginia and Massachusetts.

In Virginia, the planter class conceived the law as functioning to support the existing social structure. The landed gentry supplied judges and legislators. To the Virginia elite, an independent legal profession was problematic; in fact, in 1645, an early piece of legislation ordered all lawyers practicing for a fee to be expelled from office. The leaders in that state felt that lawyers encouraged legal suits and showed more interest in fees than in the good of the community. Well into the 18th century, Virginia sought to limit the practice of law to "gentlemen," and the prescribed form of legal education was study at the English Inns of Court.

In the early days of the colony of Massachusetts, natural law applied in the form of scriptures as well as imported law (Chapter 1 discusses natural law). This contributed to the idea that legal education was unnecessary, as well as to public skepticism about the usefulness of lawyers at all. By the end of the 17th century, however, the colony, in effect, had accepted the legitimacy of the legal profession, but the courts determined who might take the oath to become a lawyer, what lawyers could charge, and what forms of practice they could engage in. In one case in the late 17th century, the court ordered a lawyer to be whipped for charging excessive fees.

It was not until the mid-18th century in the colonies that the legal profession began to gain general acceptance, but its size remained small; even in cities, lawyers engaged in clerical work, copying, and bookkeeping services, as well as providing legal advice. With greater acceptance and security, lawyers began to develop a professional identity and to become a self-conscious professional group. This, in turn, led the profession to address matters such as professional conduct and ethics, and county bar associations that were generally voluntary in nature began to create ethical rules. The prominence of lawyers such as John Adams, Patrick Henry, and Thomas Jefferson during the Revolutionary War period confirmed the strong growth of the legal profession. In fact, of the 56 delegates who signed the Declaration of Independence, 25 were lawyers.

Between the American Revolution and the Civil War, the practice of law grew rapidly, consistent with the growth of cities and the economy (Papke 1986). During the early 19th century, the public appeared hostile toward lawyers, an attitude fueled partly by their role as postwar debt collectors. During this period, legislators and courts continued to decide issues of legal training and admission to the bar, entrance examinations were often perfunctory, and apprenticeship periods were very short. Legislated codes of professional conduct existed but were short and vague. The legal profession grew from 22,000 lawyers in 1850 to 60,000 in 1880 and to 114,000 by 1900.

The work lawyers performed in the period from 1865 to 1915 varied according to location, but criminal work remained a staple along with debt collection. In rural areas, lawyers began to speculate on land. In the cities, many sole practitioners worked for low rates, and legal specialization existed in the form of tne early Wall Street corporate lawyers and criminal law specialists. In 1870, the Bar Association of New York City was founded, and in 1878, the American Bar Association (ABA) was established. With these institutions came comprehensive bar associations that attempted to control the practice of law. During the last decade of the 19th century, some 20 bar associations adopted codes of professional responsibility. In 1908, the ABA accepted a draft of Canons of Professional Ethics, inspired by *An Essay on Professional Ethics* written by George Shars Wood in 1854 (Papke 1986). Wood insisted that lawyers' primary responsibility was to their clients and argued that social utility was not a factor that should concern lawyers in any cause they argued. He advocated prudence, restraint, and a taste for fine literature as the best qualities for lawyers. His proposals concerning contingency fees provoked some argument; however, many lawyers agreed with him that such fees corrupted and degraded the profession. Nevertheless, with urbanization and industrialization, work- and transport-related accidents had made such fees common, and the Supreme Court ruled them valid in 1877.

By 1914, three quarters of all state bar associations had adopted the Canons, and in most states,

complaints about lawyer misconduct were heard by bar association committees, followed by a possible appeal to the court. By this time, the profession was virtually self-directed in ethical matters. With the 20th century came bureaucratization, as private law firms, sometimes with hundreds of lawyers, spread throughout the cities, and nearly every corporation had in-house legal staff. In the public arena, the number of prosecutors and defense lawyers expanded, raising questions about the relevance of the Canons as well as issues relating to admission standards.

After World War II, law school enrollments grew rapidly, and in the 1960s, with the civil rights movement and professional self-criticism, some lawyers began to argue in favor of public interest law and against too great a concern with making money. In 1969, the ABA replaced the Canons with a new Code of Professional Responsibility specifying ethical considerations for all lawyers. Since that time there has been a continuing debate about legal professional ethics, and the dialogue has centered on the ABA's Commission on Evaluation of Professional Standards, which was formed in 1977. In 1980, the commission provided the ABA with new draft Model Rules of Professional Conduct that were approved in a revised version in 1983. The Model Rules also proved controversial, and the American Trial Lawyers Association offered an alternative code.

The ABA has been active in reviewing law school courses on legal ethics and professional responsibility with the aim of strengthening ethical standards. Despite this, a high percentage of law students in an ABA survey of seven law schools indicated that they were "not very" or "not at all" concerned with the subject of professional responsibility or ethics (Papke 1986: 45).

THE NATURE OF PROFESSIONAL ETHICS

Professional ethics is an expression that has a multitude of possible meanings, and it is frequently used to signify rules governing professionals and professions. The standards of conduct for professions are organized around the way in which a profession carries out its work. The development of canons and codes of ethics within professions has given professional ethics the status of law within those professions. Setting ethical standards is one way in which professions seek to persuade the public to entrust their affairs and confidence to members of the profession. *Trust* is an aspect of professionalism, and the encouragement of trust has become a fundamental characteristic in professional relationships because clients depend on the superior knowledge of the professional. In the legal profession, trust is a core value because trust between a lawyer and client is crucial if the lawyer is to gain full knowledge of the client's concerns. From the client's viewpoint, trust is an expression of faith or confidence in an expectation of honesty, competence, and diligence on the part of the lawyer. Breaching a client's trust undermines faith in the legal profession.

Discussions about the role of the lawyer often stress the lawyer's commitment to the pursuit of justice as a central purpose. Lawyers tend to see their role in securing justice as an important contribution toward establishing an efficient legal system, as supporting law as an institution, and as promoting procedural justice. These objectives are derived from the *adversarial system* that equates justice with the protection of rights. In the adversarial system, the decision-maker or judge adopts a passive role, listening to the arguments from both sides and making a decision based on the evidence and arguments presented. This contrasts with the *inquisitorial system* in which the judge takes an active role and controls the progress of the case. The adversarial system gives lawyers a great deal of control over the court process, and an underlying assumption of the system is that if lawyers do their job well, the court will reach a wise decision.

The Principle of Partisanship

The adversarial system reflects an individualistic ethic, and this emphasis on the individual in society means that in some cases lawyers will do things for clients about which they may have moral qualms, such as misleading others or engaging in bullying tactics. In other words, lawyers may exercise virtue in their relationships with clients but in pursuing their clients' interests may engage in practices that could be considered unfair, uncooperative, or selfish, acts that would not be considered virtuous. Once it is accepted that lawyers see justice in terms of defending the rights of individuals, the lawyer's

role in society becomes one of giving citizens access to vigorous representation, and this commitment is embodied in codes of conduct and ethics. In terms of ethics, therefore, the Anglo-American criminal adversarial system has the effect of putting the interests of the client above all other considerations, including the general social good. The ethical standards of conduct promulgated in codes and canons reflect this emphasis.

The Principle of Neutrality

The principle of neutrality requires that lawyers adopt a neutral stance in relation to their clients or their causes and that they defend causes that they may personally find morally repugnant. The lawyer, therefore, must put aside questions of personal morality when deciding to represent a client and determining how best to represent that client. The exercise of this principle enables the lawyer to abdicate responsibility for assisting a client in achieving a purpose that the lawyer might otherwise consider morally questionable.

The principles of neutrality and partisanship are seen as supporting the notion of equality before the law, which is itself considered a social good. Arguably, the effect of these two principles is to narrow the number of moral choices that lawyers may face because lawyers will make moral choices based on the duty owed to their clients and on their need to maintain neutrality in relation to clients' causes.

Richard Wasserstrom (1986: 122) argues that the lawyer's concentration on the interests of the client above all other considerations, including moral considerations, is especially justified in the case of the criminal defense lawyer. Specifically, he argues that factors such as the potential deprivation of liberty, the vast prosecutorial resources of the state, and a concern about punishment and its nature and extent justify what might be considered the "amoral" behavior of a defense lawyer.

In contrast to this argument that lawyers are entitled to disregard any issues of morality in the interests of their clients, William Simon (1994) has suggested that such a position is an affront to the dignity of the legal profession and the legal system because it turns lawyers into mere instruments of their clients and the trial into an irrational battle. He argues that the purpose of judicial proceedings is to produce wise and informed decision-making and that within this context the lawyer's task is to assist the decision-maker in achieving such decisions. Therefore, according to Simon, the lawyer's obligation to protect and advance his client's interests ought to be subordinated to the process of truth seeking, and the lawyer ought not to mislead the decision-maker by discrediting accurate testimony. The lawyer's basic job is, therefore, to introduce accurate evidence, and any attempt by lawyers to influence decision-makers based on their own judgment of the evidence would usurp the function of the decision-maker. Simon contends that lawyers have a "professional duty of reflective judgment" and should therefore assess the client's instructions to establish if they are "likely to promote justice" (p. 196). In other words, he suggests that lawyers should not assist clients who wish to employ procedural rules or technicalities to defeat, rather than promote, the interests of justice. This, he argues, applies even in an adversarial context.

Charles Fried (1994) attempts to resolve the issue of lawyers' morality or amorality by equating the lawyer and client relationship with one of friendship. He argues that friends typically do things for each other that they would not do for a stranger and that this behavior is widely accepted in society. However, this argument has been subjected to considerable criticism because it appears to license a pure form of legal advocacy, such as would justify a lawyer remaining silent when a client lies under oath or lawyers attempting to influence the evidence of potential witnesses.

Stephen Pepper (1994) reasons that the autonomy of the client gives moral justification to the lawyer's role, contending that law in itself is a public good, and through the courts and legislature, society has created the means enabling individuals to achieve goals and resolve conflicts. The system of freedom under the law is founded on individual autonomy as a social and moral good, so all persons should be entitled to make their own choices, and our legal system accommodates such individual autonomy and choice. The exercise of autonomy may require access to the law, and this is usually available only through a lawyer. Pepper suggests that it would be wrong for lawyers to impose their moral judgment in such a way as to interfere with the exercise of their clients' autonomy and that to do so would put the lawyer's morality above client autonomy. According to this argument, therefore, the lawyer should not merely participate in a client's immoral objective but is *obliged* to do so. However, Pepper does recognize that there may be circumstances that are so offensive to the lawyer's sense of morality that the lawyer may decline to represent the client; he calls this *conscientious objection.*

The Lawyer–Client Relationship

The most fundamental expression of legal ethics is that the client's interests should take precedence over those of the lawyer. Clients are dependent on lawyers to accomplish the particular tasks they assign their lawyers but are unable to assess the adequacy of the work that lawyers carry out. Thus, the lawyer's relationship with the client is such that incompetence or wrongdoing on the lawyer's part is considered a betrayal of the client's trust. The lawyer–client relationship requires that the lawyer hear a client's individual story before deciding what is to be done. This is part of a continual dialogue between lawyer and client. The progress of the lawyer's work should be evaluated at regular intervals in the context of the lawyer's aims and interests, and the relationship should be client centered, involving shared decision-making responsibility and the mutual participation of both lawyer and client. Neither the lawyer nor the client should dominate the relationship. In effect, the client controls decision-making while the lawyer takes the role of a technical advisor and counselor.

This modern view of the lawyer–client relationship can be contrasted with the older paternalistic view that held that once engaged by the client and broadly instructed about the client's objectives, the lawyer was left to make decisions in the best interests of the client. The paternalistic view contends that lawyers have superior knowledge, skills, and experience and therefore must know what is best—the issues being considered too complex for clients to understand and hence the need for a lawyer in the first place. The code of the American Bar

Association does not mention the best interest of the client, but it does stress that the role of the lawyer is to do whatever the client requires, even if this is unwise. Thus, lawyers must "abide by a client's decisions concerning the objectives of the representation" (American Bar Association and Center for Professional Responsibility 1998: Model Rule 1.2). As David Luban (1984: 262) concludes, "The American model is loyalty to the client's wishes and not his interests."

Is a lawyer required to accept any client who approaches him for assistance? In the United States, there is an obligation to accept particular types of clients based on the ABA Model Rule 1.2, which requires that legal representation should not be denied to those who are unable to afford legal services, whose cause is controversial, or who are the subject of popular disapproval. However, the comment to Model Rule 6.2 adopts a flexible approach by stating that a lawyer is not ordinarily obliged to accept a client whose character or cause the lawyer regards as repugnant. However, a lawyer has pro bono responsibilities under Model Rule 6.1 that can be met by accepting a fair share of unpopular matters or indigent or unpopular clients.

When does the lawyer–client relationship end? ABA Model Rule 1.16 allows lawyers to withdraw their representation if "a client insists upon pursuing an objective that the lawyer considers repugnant or imprudent." Sometimes it may be difficult to determine when the lawyer–client relationship has ended, and in some situations, duties toward clients, such as confidentiality and avoiding conflicts of interest, will continue even when there is no active relationship.

Can a defendant be required to accept a lawyer in a criminal case? The Supreme Court in *Faretta v. California* (1975) held that even in a serious criminal case, a defendant cannot be forced to be represented by counsel. The Court argued that the right to defend is personal, and the defendant will bear the personal consequences of a conviction; the lawyer or the state will not. The minority opinion in that case thought that the integrity of the system and public confidence in the system are undermined when the defendant's waiver of counsel results in an easy conviction.

Confidentiality

Keeping the affairs of the client confidential is a fundamental ethical duty imposed on lawyers. Confidentiality represents a respect for privacy, and in practical terms, clients will be reluctant to consult lawyers who are known to gossip about their affairs. Further, breaching the duty of confidentiality would run afoul of other principles, such as acting in the client's best interests and not personally profiting from information given by the client. It is important to note that this confidentiality belongs to the client and not to the lawyer, and thus only the client can waive it. Where the client is accused of a crime, confidentiality is particularly important because without confidentiality the client is likely to be less than frank, which will affect the lawyer's ability to represent a client and give a zealous defense. The concept of confidentiality between lawyer and client has been doubted by some who argue that ethical rules relating to the practice of law should not protect the guilty client over an innocent third party (Simon 1988; Wasserstrom 1975). For example, as long ago as 1827, Jeremy Bentham strongly attacked the notion of confidentiality that protected a lawyer from testifying when a client had admitted guilt (in Kipnis 1986: 75). Similarly, Goldman (in Kipnis 1986: 75) argues that there ought to be limits to confidentiality and disclaimers warning clients of those limits. However, as Kenneth Kipnis (1986: 75) points out, the arguments favoring limiting confidentiality necessarily lead to the conclusion that clients will not disclose information for fear of it being revealed, and this might prevent a zealous defense.

The general duty of confidentiality to the client should not be confused with lawyer–client privilege. The latter is a principle of evidence relating to revealing information during trial, and it provides that client confidences that are revealed by an attorney may not be used as evidence (Luban 1988: 187). The duty of confidentiality is broader because it requires the lawyer to keep the client's confidences generally, whereas the privilege relates only to confidences being used as evidence.

Client Perjury

What should a lawyer do when a client commits perjury or makes it clear that he or she intends to commit perjury? Monroe Freedman (1966) argues that the first duty of the lawyer is to try to persuade the client not to commit perjury, but if the lawyer cannot persuade the client, the lawyer should present the testimony as if it were true. He contends that imposing a duty on the lawyer to divulge perjury would involve the lawyer in a situation of inconsistent obligations. Thus, the lawyer must find out all the facts of the case to offer the best defense and must keep the client's confidences but must also divulge that the client's testimony is false, a fact that has been learned through the client's confidences. It is clear that if any two of these are to be honored, the third cannot be honored. Attempting to withdraw from the case is not a solution because doing so would merely provide defendants with an excuse for a delay or a mistrial, and in any event, the next lawyer would be faced with the same situation as the withdrawing lawyer.

Until the mid-1980s, the law on this ethical issue was unclear, but courts generally held that in a civil case, a lawyer who is aware that a client has committed perjury must disclose it to the court if the client refuses to do so. However, in criminal cases, there is an added constitutional dimension that produces more complexity, the argument being that informing on one's own client is such a grave violation of the confidentiality rule as to be unconstitutional. Model Rule 3.3 now requires that lawyers "take reasonable remedial measures" when they come to know that evidence is false, and this duty applies even if it involves the disclosure of confidential information (Luban 1988: 198–199).

Client Crime

Lawyer–client confidentiality is completely negated if the client consults the lawyer in furtherance of a crime or fraud. This applies even if the lawyer was unaware of the true nature of the client's purpose. Where this exception applies, information that would otherwise have been privileged must be disclosed when a proper demand is made (Hazard and Hodes 2002: 9–34). In addition, Model Rule 1.6 (b)(1) allows a lawyer, in certain narrowly defined circumstances, to disclose confidential client information to prevent future harm. For example, disclosure is permitted to the extent necessary to prevent a client from committing a criminal act that the lawyer reasonably believes is likely to result in imminent death or substantial bodily harm. It is important to note that this exception applies to crimes that have *yet to be committed,* and it should be contrasted with completed *past* crimes for which disclosing client information is *not permitted.* A good example of the completed crimes rule is the "Buried Bodies" case discussed in Case Study 5.1.

If, in Case Study 5.1, the lawyers had taken physical possession of the bodies or had in some other way impeded the police discovery of that evidence, the confidentiality situation would be different because despite the existence of lawyer–client confidentiality, courts commonly require lawyers to make voluntary disclosure of the benefits and means of their client's crimes. Court decisions concerning this duty begin with the principle that a lawyer may not actively participate in hiding an item or take possession of it in such a way as to impede its discovery by the authorities (Hazard and Hodes 2002: 9–103). For example, in one case, a lawyer removed a sawed-off shotgun and the proceeds of a robbery from a client's safety deposit box and put them in his own box in the same bank. The court held the lawyer's conduct to be improper. The court cases also indicate that lawyers must comply with statutes that prohibit destroying, altering, or concealing evidence or that require lawyers to voluntarily turn over physical evidence that has come into their possession. For example, the Alaska Supreme Court has ruled that a lawyer had a duty to turn over a client's written kidnap plan to prosecutors, even without having been asked for it, and in a California case, after the defendant was arrested on charges of strangling his girlfriend, his family found incriminating writings in his room, which they gave to the defendant's lawyer, who passed them to the judge, who in turn gave them to the prosecutor (*Morrell v. State* 1978). The court held that the defendant's lawyer was fulfilling his legal obligation when delivering the documents to the judge (Hansen 2005: 3).

Case Study 5.1 Buried Bodies Case

Lawyers represented a defendant charged with murder, and during the period before trial, the defendant told his lawyers about two other murders he had committed and described where the bodies were buried. The lawyers located the bodies, which were those of two young women who had been missing for some time. It happened that the authorities came to suspect the defendant of murdering the missing women, and the father of one of the victims asked one of the lawyers if he knew anything about her fate. The lawyers did not disclose the location of the bodies to the authorities or the father but attempted to use their knowledge to the advantage of their client in plea bargaining. It was only when those negotiations failed and the case went to trial that the location of the bodies was revealed, together with the lawyers' knowledge of that fact. The lawyers had information about a completed crime given to them in confidence by a defendant in a criminal case and acted properly within the bounds of the ABA Code of Ethics in withholding that information.

In moral terms, it can be argued that even without a rule of nondisclosure, nondisclosure would not have been morally required because the victims were already dead and could not be helped. Of course, the victim's father suffered, and withholding the truth increased his period of uncertainty, but if such suffering were to outweigh confidentiality, a client's disclosure of a past crime would never be protected. If, in this case, the lawyers had discovered the two victims wounded but still alive, then they would have been faced with a scenario falling under the rule concerned with preventing future harm. Morally, however, it is hard to imagine any lawyer leaving the victims to die, and in practice, rules of ethics would play little part in such a scenario.

SOURCE: Hazard and Hodes 2002: 9–79.

DEFENSE LAWYERS

The two main systems under which lawyers represent clients in the West are adversarial and inquisitorial. In *adversarial* systems of law, the parties and their lawyers play the principal role of gathering evidence and examining witnesses in court, and the court plays a less active role. In the *inquisitorial* system, the court plays the main role in gathering evidence and questioning witnesses. It is sometimes argued that the judge in the inquisitorial system is more concerned with discovering "the truth," whereas in the adversarial system, lawyers dominate, and judges, acting as referees, are mainly concerned about due process and procedures being followed and not so much the search for the truth. Marvin Frankel (1975) contends that the legal profession in the United States is held in low regard because establishing truth has a low priority as an overall objective of the process. This raises the issue of the adversarial system privileging procedural fairness over truth, and Frankel suggests that too much emphasis is placed on the advancement of the client's interests and not enough on public interest in discovering the truth. Freedman (1975a) refutes Frankel's position by arguing that the notion of truth has been an elusive concept throughout history and that those who devised the adversarial system took account of the complexities of determining truth.

Luban (1988: 67–93) outlines six reasons commonly argued in favor of the adversarial system:

1. It is the best system for discovering the truth.
2. It is the best way of defending the rights of clients.
3. The nature of the lawyer–client relationship is intrinsically good.
4. It prevents abuse through checks and balances.
5. It honors human dignity.
6. It is so embedded in the social fabric that adopting another system would be too disruptive.

After examining each justification, Luban (1990) concludes that only the last has any validity because in his view the adversarial system has merit in the sense that it is not shown to be worse than any other system. In terms of criminal defense, Luban suggests that adversarial advocacy is crucial for protecting the rights of individuals "against a powerful and potentially dangerous bureaucratic institution" (p. 1019).

The defense lawyer carries out the function of representing an accused within an adversarial system that emphasizes *due process*. According to Model Rule 1.3, a lawyer is to act with reasonable diligence and promptness in representing a client. The comment to this Model Rule makes it clear that the lawyer is expected to use *zeal, commitment, and dedication* and that zeal is an appropriate method in litigation. Lawyers operate as agents of their clients and must serve their clients' interests loyally and effectively. There is no absolute standard against which a lawyer's performance may be measured, and every case in which an issue of diligence or promptness arises is dependent on its own context (Hazard and Hodes 2002: 4–8).

It has been suggested that criminal defense lawyers may run into conflict with the commitment that a lawyer must use the utmost zeal and dedication in representing clients. In particular, because criminal defense lawyers may have aims and motivations that extend beyond the interest of their client, they can be regarded as "cause lawyers" (Etienne 2005: 1200)—that is, "activist lawyers who use the law as a means of creating social change" (p. 1196), including public interest and poverty lawyers. Thus, for the cause lawyer, the client's defense is not necessarily an end in itself because the cause lawyer has a broader set of objectives, such as using the law as a vehicle to build a better society. An example of a potential conflict comes from the field of so-called *impact litigation* where lawyers select certain cases to raise certain issues. In this sense, the criminal defendant and the case are a means for effecting social change; this departs somewhat from a client-centered approach to the conduct of the law (p. 1251). An impact litigation lawyer might forego an argument in one case that could possibly benefit the client to employ that argument in another case where there is a greater chance of its success. Ethically, this is a questionable practice in view of the lawyer's duty to devote herself to the client's interest with the utmost zeal.

The ethical questions that commonly arise in the minds of nonlawyers about the role of a defense lawyer include the following three questions:

1. Is it ethically proper to represent a client accused of a criminal offense when the lawyer knows the client is guilty?

Some commentators have stated that lawyers will seldom be in a position to conclude from the available facts that their client is definitely guilty. However, there will still be times when lawyers will be quite confident of their client's guilt. When lawyers know their client is guilty, can they still conduct a defense leading to their acquittal? Model Rules 3.1, 3.3, and 6.2 set the ethical standard in such situations. Under these rules, a lawyer is not permitted to defend a proceeding unless there is a basis for doing so that is not considered frivolous. Further, a defendant's lawyer in criminal proceedings may defend the proceedings to require that every element of the case be established.

The comment to these rules requires that if a defendant has admitted to defense counsel the facts that establish guilt, and defense counsel's independent investigation has also established that the defendant's admissions are true, yet the defendant insists on standing trial, defense counsel must strongly discourage the defendant from perjury in testifying. Further, if in advance of the trial the defendant insists that he or she will take the stand and perjure himself or herself when testifying, the lawyer may withdraw from the case and seek leave of the court to do so if necessary, but the court must not be advised of the lawyer's reason for seeking to withdraw.

The problem with lawyers determining that their client is guilty is that a lawyer will not really know that the client is factually guilty unless the client admits all the facts that constitute the offense. This is the case even in circumstances when the client may be lying or mentally ill or mistaken. Also, a client who confesses to his or her lawyer may not understand the existence of certain legal defenses, such as provocation or self-defense, and admitting guilt might result in the lawyer failing to explore these possibilities. In addition, the prosecution is required to prove to a jury that the client is guilty beyond a reasonable doubt, and it is argued, therefore, that a client cannot be legally guilty so far as the lawyer is concerned without undergoing the full scrutiny of a trial.

There are significant differences between a client who may be *factually guilty* and a client who is *legally guilty* (Pool 1979). Usually, the standard required for a lawyer to be satisfied that a client is guilty is that the lawyer has proof of the client's guilt through credible evidence that meets the standard of "beyond reasonable doubt." However, some commentators go further, arguing that lawyers need to be certain, not merely of guilt, but that a conviction will be obtained (Subin 1987). One lawyer suggested that the fleeting and temporary nature of the truth was rationale enough for this argument when he expressed his view of this issue in the following statement: "Truth cannot be known. Facts are indeterminate, contingent, and in criminal cases, often evanescent" (Babcock 1983: 177).

Lawyers offer a number of reasons for defending those who are "guilty." They might argue that by providing defendants with competent counsel, whether or not they have committed a serious offense or are innocent, they uphold the human dignity of that person. Freedman (1975a) endorses this view, arguing that the right to counsel is a significant demonstration of our regard for the dignity of the individual. Further, he makes the case that lawyers have an obligation to protect their clients and not to sit in judgment over them because the determination of a client's guilt or innocence is not a lawyer's function.

Another reason put forward for lawyers not to decide their clients' guilt is that it is their function to ensure that those operating the criminal justice system do so in a proper manner. In this context, criminal defense lawyers not only induce prosecutors to prove their case but also ensure that they do so ethically and legally. The adversarial system requires lawyers to present a fearless defense of their clients, and lawyers may therefore argue that they are simply fulfilling the aims of that system. From this perspective, the lawyer is a functionary in the system.

Others justify the representation of the "guilty" by reasoning that lawyers have an obligation as agents in the legal system to provide their services to those in need. Thomas Shaffer (1981), for example, contends that by serving the guilty, lawyers

fulfill their Christian role to those in need. Thus, defending criminals is considered by Shaffer as an act of Christian charity by helping and not judging one's neighbors. Finally, some defense lawyers argue that by providing a defense, they may prevent people who are guilty, but who do not deserve to be put in prison, from going to prison. As John Mitchell (1980: 334) states,

> Those guilty of serious crime merit the wrath of our society. But almost no one deserves the hellholes we call jails and prisons. There is almost no case I would not defend if that meant keeping a human, as condemnable as he or she may be, from suffering the total, brutal inhumanity of our jails and prisons.

2. Is it ethically proper to cross-examine a witness with the aim of discrediting the witness's credibility or reliability when the lawyer knows the witness is telling the truth?

Assume a lawyer represents a criminal defendant charged with robbery who admits to his lawyer that he committed the crime but does not testify at his trial. The lawyer then attempts to attack the credibility of a truthful prosecution witness who observed the crime. The lawyer does this by establishing, through cross-examining the witness, that she had been drinking heavily before the crime, had a violent argument with the defendant immediately before the crime, and had convictions for shoplifting. Essentially, the lawyer intends to mislead the jury and challenge the credibility of this truthful witness.

It might be argued here that the lawyer's conduct, even though legally permissible, is immoral because it is an effort to obscure the truth and frustrate justice and because it inflicts harm on the innocent witness. There seems to be no social good in this case because the only purpose of the deception is to obtain an undeserved acquittal for the client (Haskell 1998: 66). However, Freedman (1966) argues that in light of the importance of the lawyer's adversarial role as protection against the power of the state, a lawyer is obliged to act zealously, and it therefore follows that the lawyer in this example is entitled, and in fact obliged, to do everything he or she can on the client's behalf to discredit a witness known to be telling the truth.

John Noonan (1966) protests that Freedman (1975a), in conceiving trials as battles in which lawyers are bound do everything in zealous defense of their clients, misrepresents the nature of the justice system. He contends that a lawyer's duty is to assist the judge in making an impartial, wise, and informed decision in seeking to establish the truth. In other words, a lawyer's level of zeal should be defined by the promotion of a wise and informed decision in the case. Fundamentally, therefore, the argument is that unrestrained zeal undermines the system of justice. In addition to the zeal argument, it can also be said that the lawyer may have no absolute knowledge of the witness's truthfulness. How does the lawyer know the witness is truthful? From this point of view, the level of honesty may often be discovered only through a rigorous cross-examination that tests the witness's credibility.

Additional arguments against Freedman's view include the nature of the lawyer's duty to the court, particularly in not misleading the court, given that it can be argued that lawyers ought not to attack the credibility of a truthful witness when they have no basis to do so (Noonan 1966). Such an attack conflicts with a lawyer's duty to the court and with his or her overriding obligation to promote justice. Ultimately, the resolution of this difficult question seeks to define the limits of a zealous defense and calls into question conflicts between the lawyers' duty to clients and duty to the court, to the administration of justice, and to the promotion of truth seeking in criminal proceedings. It should be noted that Freedman does not advocate the lawyer's unlimited zealousness in noncriminal proceedings. However, in the final analysis, many would argue that in criminal proceedings, the lawyer's duty to protect the client against the state justifies the lawyer's conduct.

3. Is it ethically proper to have a witness give testimony when the lawyer knows that the witness will commit perjury?

Freedman (1966) proposes that the most common method of avoiding this problem is for the lawyer to withdraw from the case in circumstances where the witness is the accused. However, he suggests that the accused would simply find another lawyer and withhold the facts of his or her guilt from that new lawyer. Accordingly, on ethical grounds, the first lawyer ought not to withdraw because perjured testimony will ultimately be presented. Freedman concludes that the obligation of confidentiality in the context of the adversarial system gives the lawyer no alternative but to put the perjuring witness on the stand without disclosing his or her knowledge of the perjury to the court or jury. Noonan (1966) disagrees, arguing again that the presentation of such evidence must be unethical because it will lead to injustice. Two cases contradict Freedman's position. In one, the court decided that the lawyer was entitled to withdraw from a case in which the client admitted perjury and would be subject to disciplinary action only if he continued the case without reporting the matter to the court (*McKissick v. United States* 1967). In the other case, the conduct of a lawyer who advised several persons, including the client, to perjure themselves was considered bad enough to warrant disbarment (*Dodd v. Florida Bar* 1960). In other countries, Freedman's position is considered untenable because lawyers may not knowingly lend themselves to any false story being put before the court and, if asked to do so, must immediately cease to act for the client.

Will disclosure of future perjury violate the Sixth Amendment to the Constitution? In *Nix v. Whiteside* (1986), the U.S. Supreme Court held that a criminal defendant has no right to the assistance of counsel in giving false testimony and that lawyers who refused to give such assistance or who threatened to disclose the future perjury of the client have not denied the client effective legal assistance under the Sixth Amendment to the Constitution. The ABA has endorsed the view put forward in this case but also points out that the case may not overcome the constitutional provisions of some states that may still prohibit the lawyer's disclosure of the client's perjury. It should be noted that under Model Rule 3.3 lawyers may not assist a client in committing perjury. Lawyers have attempted to avoid a violation of this rule by adopting what is called a "narrative approach" in which they do not question the client but simply allow the narration of evidence without asking questions. However, this narrative approach can also be criticized because when the lawyer does not question the client and does not refer to the narrative in closing arguments, it may seem obvious to the jury that the defendant has given flawed testimony.

THE PROSECUTOR

Freedman (1975b: 79) explains that ethical difficulties and their solutions differ between prosecution and defense lawyers because of the significantly different roles and functions they each play. In essence, the contest between prosecution and defense counterbalances the rights of the individual to the power of the state. The prosecutor has extraordinary discretion in directing investigations, deciding on the crime to be charged, and influencing the punishment to be imposed. In contrast, the defense lawyer has particular responsibilities that link with the adversarial system and to issues of lawyer–client confidentiality, as well as the assertion of constitutional rights to due process and to freedom from self-incrimination.

In their role as protectors of the state and the public, prosecutors act in an adversarial capacity, which requires zealous advocacy. Prosecutors are supposed to represent the public interest, but they may also see themselves as accountable to the police and to victims. Unlike other lawyers, prosecutors, in their representation of the public, in effect make their decisions without the assistance of a client. Prosecutors ought to place themselves in the shoes of the public, who is the client, before deciding on the best course of action. It follows that, in practice, prosecutors have an important role in the creation of public policy within criminal proceedings.

Many district attorneys are required to maintain a high conviction rate and to win big, public cases that arouse strong passions. Failure to do so might lead to the loss of their office in the next election (Fisher 1988). Thus, prosecutors are subject to a number of stresses and tensions, including their public constituency; their need to adhere to professional codes and standards; and pressure from academics, the judiciary, and the media to act fairly. As Bennett Gershman (2001) notes in reference to Rule 6.2, a prosecutor who is under a duty to keep the public informed about pending cases has a corresponding duty not to make statements out of court that might prejudice the right to a fair trial,

and prosecutors must also not use the media in a way intended to benefit themselves personally.

Gershman (2001) argues that many prosecutors have violated these duties and that experienced news reporters are able to draw improper statements out of prosecutors by using trickery and persuasion. With respect to statements to the media, Gershman explains that prosecutors have come under criticism for calling press conferences to celebrate indictments and for using such occasions to "improperly characterize charges, disparage defendants, disclose evidence, and otherwise employ inflammatory rhetoric that often presumes guilt" (Rule 6.4). Among the prohibitions on prosecutorial conduct, Gershman lists the release of grand jury material, making references to a defendant's bad character, commenting on the nature of the crime with which a defendant is charged, and revealing a defendant's confession to the media.

The Duty to Ensure Justice Is Done

At least since 1935 when the Supreme Court decided *Berger v. United States,* it has been the law that for prosecutors, winning is not everything. According to the Supreme Court, the primary duty of a prosecutor is to see that justice is done. In other words, the prosecutor must "seek justice, not merely to convict" (American Bar Association 1993: Standard 3–1.2 [c]):

> While (a prosecutor) may strike hard blows, he is not at liberty to strike foul ones. It is as much his duty to refrain from improper methods calculated to produce a wrongful conviction as it is to use every legitimate means to bring about a just one. (*Berger v. United States* 1935)

In performing the function of achieving justice, the prosecutor must assist the court in arriving at the truth fairly. Thus, if an accused has incompetent counsel who neglects to present all the material facts that might assist the defendant, the prosecutor has an ethical duty to make sure these facts are presented consistent with the responsibility to achieve a just result (Fisher 1988). Gershman (2001) specifies that prosecutors have a duty to the truth based on a number of sources, such as their role as a "minister of justice," their constitutional obligation not to use false evidence or suppress evidence favorable to the defendant, the ethical rules that apply to the prosecutor, their domination of the criminal justice system, and their role as a representative of the state. Gershman sets out instances in which prosecutors may violate their duty to the truth. These include situations in which the prosecutor engages in misleading conduct by confusing the jury's view of the evidence; inflammatory conduct, such as appeals to racial or class biases, in the practice of attacking the defendant's character; and subverting and suppressing the truth. Stanley Fisher (1988: 218) seeks to further define the prosecutor's quest for justice and concludes that its definition is problematic. He argues that the prosecutor's role in seeking justice suggests that "justice" has some independent meaning of special relevance to prosecutors. However, he suggests that its meaning may shift according to the context. Thus, where effective adversarial system safeguards exist, the role most consistent with justice is to be a zealous advocate; however, where those safeguards are lacking, the prosecutor's

quasi-judicial function should be emphasized (p. 226). Further, he suggests that where safeguards do function properly, the prosecutor's primary duty is to promote crime control values (p. 254).

Case Study 5.2 is an example of a prosecutor focusing on winning the case rather than on pursuing justice.

Model Rule 3.8 sets out the general duties for a prosecutor in a criminal case, which are designed to ensure that an accused receives a fair trial. Specifically, a prosecutor

- must not prosecute a charge unless it is supported by probable cause;
- must make reasonable efforts to ensure that an accused has been advised of the right to obtain counsel and has been given a reasonable opportunity to do so;
- must not seek to secure from an unrepresented defendant any waiver of important pretrial rights such as the right to a preliminary hearing;
- must make timely disclosure to the defense of all evidence or information that the prosecutor is

---

Case Study 5.2 Prosecutor Misconduct

After 16 years in prison, Jabbar Collins was freed when Brooklyn prosecutors vacated his murder conviction. He was arrested in March 1994 on charges that he murdered a landlord during an attempted robbery. The prosecution relied on three witnesses who, Mr. Collins claims, were forced by threats from the prosecutors to testify falsely against him.

After being released from prison in 2010, in August 2011 he filed a suit for $150 million against the Brooklyn district attorney's office, accusing the prosecutors in that office of a range of unethical and illegal practices and claiming that Charles J. Hynes, the district attorney, directly fostered that behavior. The case was settled with the city for $10 million, and Collins was released after spending 15 years in prison (Marzulli 2014).

The suit claimed that improperly using court orders to detain witnesses, physically threatening witnesses, and forcing them to provide false testimony to support the prosecution case were standard practices of the district attorney staff. It is alleged that while the purpose of a subpoena is to compel a witness to attend court, the district attorney's office regularly uses them to direct witnesses to attend their office, where they try to convince witnesses to cooperate with the prosecution. As well, it is claimed that the district attorney staff regularly brought witnesses picked up on warrants to their office to be interrogated, rather than talking them directly to court. A material witness warrant is issued by a judge, requiring the arrest of a witness who has ignored a subpoena to testify in court. But the order requires the witness to appear in court, where they are given legal representation and can secure bail.

SOURCE: Eligon 2011 and Marzulli 2014.

aware of that tends to negate the guilt of the accused or that mitigates the offense; and

- with respect to sentencing, must disclose to the defense and to the court all mitigating information known to the prosecutor, unless the court directs otherwise.

In terms of the administration of criminal justice, ABA standards state that prosecutors are administrators of justice and advocates and officers of the court and must exercise sound discretion in the performance of their functions. Prosecutors are subject to the same standards of professional conduct as other lawyers. However, additionally, the prosecutor has a general obligation to improve the administration of criminal justice and to seek remedial action if defects are discovered in the system.

Discretion to Bring Charges

The prosecutor has broad discretion over bringing charges; this charging decision is protected by almost absolute immunity. It is arguable that the probable cause standard adopted in Rule 3.8 is an insufficient deterrent against prosecutorial abuse because a violation of that rule can generally be found only in instances in which prosecutors must have known that they lacked probable cause (Hazard and Hodes 2002: 34–36). Geoffrey Hazard and William Hodes argue that rather than knowledge, a better basis is "reasonable belief" in the presence of probable cause—that is, whether prosecutors can show that they carefully considered the issue and formed a reasonable belief that a conviction would be secured. Freedman (1975b) argues that merely being charged with a crime results in a damaged reputation, regardless of a failure to convict. The anguish, anxiety, and emotional strain of a criminal trial as well as the financial burden are all set in motion when an indictment is sought. In view of the grave consequence of an indictment, Freedman (p. 85) suggests that this test (that charges be supported by probable cause) is inadequate because probable cause may be based on hearsay and satisfied by less than a substantial likelihood of guilt.

Michael Gottfredson and Don Gottfredson (1988: 114) point out that the breadth of the discretion granted to the prosecutor in making the decision to charge is not accompanied by any controls over its exercise and that the decision of whether or not to charge is "the single most unreviewed exercise of the power of the criminal law available to an individual in the American system of justice." They argue that there is no guidance available about the exercise of this discretion in statutes and that charging decisions are not judicially supervised. For example, in a study of felony processing in Washington, D.C., in half of the felony arrests referred by police, the prosecutor decided not to charge, but the decision not to prosecute was not justified publicly or reviewed by any authority (p. 115).

Sometimes prosecutors elect not to enforce a particular statute and follow a policy of nonprosecution. Abrams (in Gottfredson and Gottfredson 1988: 118) suggests some criteria that might influence a prosecutor to adopt such a policy, including community opposition, difficulties in legally enforcing a statute, the existence of an alternative, and the ability to prosecute for another offense. The ABA (in Gottfredson and Gottfredson 1988: 119) suggests that in deciding whether to bring charges, the criteria to be considered should include

- the prosecutor's assessment of guilt;
- the harm caused by the offense;
- the disproportion of the punishment to the offense;
- the possibility of improper motives for a complaint;
- any extended nonenforcement of a statute where the community accepts that nonenforcement;
- the reluctance of the victim to testify;
- the cooperation of the accused in the arrest or conviction of others; and
- the possibility of prosecution by another jurisdiction.

Although welcoming any criteria that would circumscribe the prosecutorial discretion, Gottfredson and Gottfredson note that criteria of this kind do not go far enough and that the criteria need to be ranked in priority and given weighting and better definition. Fisher (1988: 232) has suggested that in deciding to bring charges,

the prosecutor's usual orientation should be one of special alertness to the existence of facts supporting guilt and a corresponding eagerness to seek them out. In "borderline" cases she should rely on rebuttable presumptions of guilt to resolve factual conflicts and certainties against the defendant.

Forst (in Gottfredson and Gottfredson 1988: 132) summarizes the results of an empirical study of prosecution decisions, noting that for many, if not most cases, the decision to prosecute is virtually automatic, regardless of whether the evidence is weak or strong or the offense serious or minor. Most recently, a study in Maryland has found that prosecutors there are far more likely to seek the death penalty for accused African Americans charged with killing white victims (Levine and Montgomery 2003). The research suggests that offenders who kill white victims are significantly more likely to be charged with a capital crime and that the probability of such a charge is twice as high as when an African American kills another African American. As well, geography has proved a significant factor in prosecutorial decision-making in capital cases. The study found, for example, that in Baltimore County a death sentence was 26 times more likely than in the city of Baltimore and 14 times more likely than in Montgomery County.

Prosecution Disclosure of Evidence to the Defense

Rule 3.8, requiring disclosure of evidence to the defense, is broader than the Brady rule on which it is based (Hazard and Hodes 2002: 34–38). The ABA Standing Committee on Ethics and Professional Responsibility, in a formal opinion on Rule 3.8, has noted, "Courts as well as commentators have recognized that the ethical obligation is more demanding than the constitutional obligation." The prosecutor's constitutional duty to make voluntary disclosure of evidence to the defense is set out in *Brady v. Maryland* (1963) and subsequent cases. In considering this constitutional duty, the courts determined that a conviction can be overturned based on the prosecutor's failure to provide evidence. However, this constitutional rule takes account of other factors such as the significance of the evidence and whether the defense made a proper request for it. When a prosecutor fails to disclose evidence to the defense and suppresses that evidence, the Supreme Court in *United States v. Agurs* (1976) held that exculpatory evidence not made available to the accused could result in denial of the constitutional right to a fair trial, with the outcome that a new trial will be ordered. This duty to disclose exculpatory evidence applies even if it has not been requested by the defense.

In a number of ways, the pretrial disclosure standard remains imprecise. For example, the exculpatory evidence that was not disclosed must be "material" and prosecutors and defense lawyers can disagree on this. As well, there are issues about the timing of disclosure: While many courts require disclosure well in advance of trial, others do not enforce this rule until immediately before the trial. As noted, the ABA standard is higher than that imposed by the Constitution, and the ABA has stated that the rule requires disclosure before the entry of a guilty plea (Yaroshefsky and Green 2012: 274). Some prosecutors follow a practice of "open file discovery," under which virtually the entire prosecution file is disclosed, while others take a less liberal approach and produce very little or nothing at all. Sometimes prosecutors will adopt a restrictive approach because they fear that liberal disclosure will adversely affect their conviction rates (p. 275).

When a prosecutor violates Rule 3.8, he or she is liable to be disbarred, as occurred following a prosecution involving rape charges filed against members of the men's lacrosse team at Duke University by Michael Nifong, the district attorney for Durham County, North Carolina. After filing charges, Nifong failed to disclose to the defendants that their DNA samples did not match any of the DNA from unidentified males found on the alleged victim's body and clothing. Nifong's failure to disclose not only resulted in the dismissal of all charges against them but also in disciplinary proceedings against him by the North Carolina State Bar that led to his disbarment in 2007 (Libby 2009).

The Innocence Project reported in 2011 that prosecutorial misconduct, including failure to disclose evidence to the defense, had contributed to the convictions in 45% of the first 100 cases of exoneration revealed by the Project. There have been calls for the systematic review of prosecutors' disclosure practices (Yaroshefsky and Green 2012: 270).

Plea Bargaining

After charging but before trial, the prosecutor may begin negotiating with the defense to arrive at a plea bargain. The aim is to achieve a compromise by reducing the charges against the defendant or securing a reduced sentence in exchange for a guilty plea (McDonough, McDonough, and Keenan 2000: 58). Plea bargaining is not supported by the public, even though it disposes of 95% of all criminal cases (Bureau of Justice Statistics 2002: 416, tbl. 5.17). For example, in a survey of public attitudes in Washington State, while most expressed positive views toward courts, 82% of respondents rejected plea bargaining as a means of processing criminal cases (Herzog 2004: 590–591). Similarly, in a survey in Chicago, 64% rejected the practice. Some have suggested that this negative public attitude reflects its punitive views on criminality and that the secretiveness of plea negotiating practices increases public suspicion (p. 591). Thus, the more lenient the sentence handed down, the less support for plea bargaining.

In relation to plea discussions, ABA Standard 3–4.1 states that it is "unprofessional conduct for a prosecutor knowingly to make false statements or representations in the course of plea discussions." The ABA Standards Relating to Administration of Criminal Justice were adopted in 1971 and have strong moral force (Hazard and Hodes 2002: 34–35). In spite of the moral force of these standards, a prosecutor may deliberately overcharge a defendant as a plea-bargaining tactic. Hazard and Hodes (pp. 34–36) give the example of a prosecutor charging an accused with three offenses arising out of the same incident, intending to accept a guilty plea to the least serious charge in exchange for dismissal of the others, assuming that such a plea bargain is advised by the defense. In such a situation, the prosecutor is aware that he or she lacks probable cause for the first and most serious of the charges and has deliberately included it, purely as a bargaining chip. The second charge could be sustained, but the prosecutor doubts whether he or she could gain a conviction and in any event is not inclined to put in the effort required to prove it. In this sense, therefore, this second charge is also a bargaining chip. The inclusion of the first charge is clearly improper and a violation of Rule 3.8, and the prosecutor must not present it. Presenting the second charge is not considered improper and is normal procedure in plea bargaining. The second charge is proper because it could legitimately be prosecuted

to a conclusion, and if the prosecutor gives up this charge in a plea bargaining, he gives up something of legal significance.

Freedman (1975b: 88) points to the device of overcharging as a means of obtaining a sufficient number of plea bargains, arguing that cases are commonly drawn up as felonies with prosecutors ready to accept a plea for a misdemeanor and thereby coercing defendants into foregoing their right to trial by jury. He argues that the justification for this practice, seen to be the need to transact a great volume of business through the criminal justice system, is insufficient to justify the infringement of a constitutional right by "duress and trickery." He refers also to instances in which prosecutors have failed to advise the court of ineffective assistance provided to an accused by counsel and to situations in which prosecutors have placed their prosecution of a case in a forum where the defense lawyer is likely to overlook defects in the prosecution's case.

Chris McDonough, Diana McDonough, and Raymond Keenan (2000) point out that although some may see a plea bargain as beneficial to the defendant, in fact, a plea bargain benefits the prosecutor because a guilty plea saves many hours of the prosecutor's time and, in eliminating the expense and time of a trial, prevents the criminal justice system from becoming overloaded. They note that plea bargains may also assist the prosecutor if an essential element of the prosecution case is weak (p. 59). For example, Hal Pepinsky (2000: 67) reports that in his home county in Indiana, prosecutors bring only 25 to 30 criminal cases a year to jury trial and that these together compose less than 1% of all prosecuted cases. He points out that this number is all that can be accommodated on the local court calendar each year. In 1974 in New York City, 80% of all felony cases were settled as misdemeanors through plea bargains, and only 2% of all felony arrests resulted in a trial (Kipnis 2001: 362). As long ago as the 1920s and 1930s, crime surveys documented the dependence of the criminal justice system on plea bargaining. Researchers found that plea bargaining had largely displaced trial by jury so that, for example, in Chicago 85% of all felony convictions resulted from guilty pleas. Similar rates applied in Detroit (78%) and Los Angeles (81%) (Remington 1993: 80).

In discussing the negotiated plea, Kipnis (2001: 362) points out that both sides have bargaining power. The prosecutor may be burdened with conducting many cases, and perhaps in some there is insufficient evidence to secure a conviction. At the same time, the prosecutor is under administrative and political pressure to complete cases and secure convictions. On the defense side, a number of factors may influence a defendant to plead guilty. These include feelings of guilt, which may or may not be relevant to the crime charged; the stresses of being locked up before trial; the costs of going to trial; and the delays that always occur in awaiting trial (p. 363). Kipnis points out that the practice of negotiating pleas has never been discussed by any deliberative body or legislature; rather, it has evolved within the criminal justice system in an unregulated, ad hoc manner (p. 364).

Plea bargains are required to be voluntary; however, the question of whether duress has been applied can be problematic. The Federal Rules of Criminal Procedure require the court to be satisfied that a plea of guilty is voluntary through "addressing the defendant personally in open court, determining that the plea is voluntary and not the result of force or promises apart from a plea agreement" (in Kipnis 2001: 365). Kipnis notes two cases in which defendants agreed to plead guilty to avoid probable death sentences and where the court decided that the pleas were voluntary, even though in one case the defendant testified at the time of the entry of his plea that he was innocent of the crime charged and had pleaded guilty because he said he had been told that if he did not "they would gas me for it" (p. 365). The essence of plea bargaining in such situations is that a defendant must make a hard choice between something certain and something uncertain, and even when the defendant is innocent and the prosecution's case weak, the defendant may accept the plea bargain for its certainty rather than take the chance on what may happen at trial.

Kipnis (2001) points out that hard choices of this kind contain an element of duress where "the state forces a choice between adverse consequences that it imposes" (p. 367). He concludes that plea bargaining "falls short of the justice we expect of our legal system" (p. 371). He identifies plea bargaining's adverse effects in its coercion of criminal defendants, its acceptance of a measure of punishment less than that consistent with a guilty plea, and its relaxation of the standards for conviction.

Rudolph Gerber (1999: 31) agrees that the issue of duress harms innocent defendants and that "the accused enjoy few truly realistic strategic choices." He suggests that innocent defendants may plead guilty because of their lack of expertise in plea bargaining and their inability to demonstrate their innocence (p. 32). Gottfredson and Gottfredson (1988: 130) summarize the criticisms of plea bargaining as follows

- Some innocent persons may be induced to plead guilty by promises of leniency.
- Plea bargaining results in excessive leniency.
- It is impossible to control.
- It shifts sentencing policy from the judge and legislature to the prosecutor and in so doing blurs the distinction between guilt and proper punishment.

What would be the effects of a ban on plea bargaining? White (in Gottfredson and Gottfredson 1988: 130) studied the effects of a ban on plea bargaining in Alaska and concluded that the court processes did not become overloaded, that defendants seemed to plead guilty at the same rate, and that there was little change in conviction rates.

Giving a judicial view of plea bargaining, Gerber, a judge of the Arizona Court of Appeals, maintains that the complexity of the criminal trial is a major cause of plea bargaining because detailed trial procedures have meant that the trial has "ceased to be an efficient routine disposition of a criminal charge" (Gerber 1999: 25). He argues that the strongest justification for plea bargaining is expediency and that there are no principled arguments to justify the practice. In his view, the practice is unfair because it determines a defendant's guilt without investigation, evidence, or fact finding by an impartial body and may adversely affect the poor and unsophisticated (p. 26). Gerber suggests that lawyers' caseloads are a major reason for the practice and that neither prosecutors nor defense lawyers want to try criminal cases. The prosecutors' aversion arises because they cannot progress with their cases without guilty pleas, and the defense lawyers entertain plea bargains because they are less able to secure new clients if they are tied up with a multitude of trials. Gerber stresses that victims often find plea bargaining to be an offensive practice because they believe that the sentence imposed in a plea is more lenient than would have been imposed for the original charge. He agrees with other commentators that prosecutors often overcharge to gain a negotiating advantage (p. 28).

Gerber (1999) explains the political aspect of plea bargaining by suggesting that an elected district attorney is concerned with securing a high conviction rate, maintaining his or her good relationships with private lawyers of influence in the community, and avoiding the loss of high-profile trials. Ensuring a conviction through plea negotiation keeps the conviction rate high and supports the likelihood of reelection at the end of the prosecutor's term (p. 29).

One consequence of plea bargaining is the absence of a public trial that shows accountability and condemnation. Gerber (1999: 35) suggests that a criminal justice system that displaces guilt out of the public space of the courtroom and avoids the public display of due process, guilt, and punishment abandons the public role of criminal law.

Prosecutorial Misconduct

Freedman (1975b: 79) argues that the ABA ethical standards are inadequate in ensuring the ethical duty of a prosecutor. Specifically, he suggests that the prosecutor's decision about whether to investigate a suspected crime is not the subject of any code of professional responsibility, even though the prosecution's motive in conducting an investigation might be open to question. He reasons that selective prosecution based on improper motives is an abuse of official power and a violation of fundamental rights, and as such, it constitutes unethical conduct.

There have been a number of reported cases of prosecutorial misconduct, some of which result from overzealousness in seeking a conviction, but most of which involve issues such as conflict of interest, failure to enforce the law, and filing charges vindictively (Wolfram 1986: 764). Gershman

(1986: 132) provides examples of what he terms "outrageous conduct," such as *Miller v. Pate* (1967), where the prosecutor in a murder case concealed from the jury a crucial piece of evidence—namely, the fact that a pair of undershorts with red stains were stained not by blood, but by paint. Another example was in the case of *United States v. Perry* (1981), where the prosecutor in his summation said that the "defendants and their counsel are completely unable to explain away their guilt." The Center for Public Integrity in Texas identified almost 600 appeals in Texas between 1970 and 2003 in which defendants raised allegations of prosecutorial misconduct. In 152 of those cases, a court held that the prosecutor's conduct prejudiced the defendant and that 118 of those cases involved improper trial behavior, including making improper statements during arguments, improperly cross-examining witnesses, discrimination in jury selection, withholding evidence from the defense, and failing to correct false testimony (Gier 2006: 193). Prosecutorial misconduct was a factor in 45% of recent cases overturned because of DNA evidence and in 24% of recently overturned death penalty cases (Scheck, Neufeld, and Dwyer 2000). In considering the issue of why misconduct occurs, Gershman (1986: 133) suggests that the reason lies in its success, pointing out that if prosecutors are prepared to take ethical risks in argument, they do so because they believe that approach to be effective. The opening statement by the prosecutor is crucial in the process, according to Gershman, because juries are most affected by the first strong presentation they observe and hear. In addition to presenting an action-packed opening statement, a prosecutor who uses the same strategy for the closing argument is more likely to be effective.

Gershman (1986: 136) concludes that when prosecutors are faced with a difficult case, they might be tempted to influence the jury to decide in favor of a conviction by referring to a matter that might be highly prejudicial. Referring to inadmissible and stricken testimony, Gershman (2001) argues that such testimony does have an impact on the individual juror, and that the prosecutor, who is aware of jury psychology, knows this. He suggests that prosecutors have a general duty to the truth, which includes refraining from misleading conduct that distorts the search for truth. Although he argues that the prosecutor has the capacity to mislead at many stages during the trial process, he identifies the prosecutor's relationship with the jury as one area where misleading conduct occurs. Arguing that the jury is likely to place great confidence and trust in the prosecutor, he notes that familiar types of misleading conduct include

- attempts to place in the jurors' minds innuendo that is damaging and prejudicial to the defendant;
- allusions to expert testimony casting doubt on a defense witness's credibility;
- attempts to enhance a witness's credibility by referring to the witness's willingness to take a polygraph test; and
- comments and questions that suggest that a defendant's reliance on constitutional rights establishes evidence of guilt.

For example, a defendant who offers an innocent explanation for his conduct at trial may have that explanation impeached by the prosecutor, who insinuates that the defendant's failure to give an account of his conduct following a Miranda warning suggests that his account is fabricated. Similarly, Gershman (1986) asserts that it is misleading for a prosecutor to ask a jury to conclude that the defendant's failure to testify is evidence of guilt. Distortion of the process can occur when prosecutors appeal to a jury's fears and prejudices, and Gershman also points out that presenting gruesome physical evidence and engaging in impassioned oratory can have the effect of manipulating the jury's prejudices. Another form of prosecutorial misconduct involves the prosecution attempting to intimidate or improperly influence key witnesses. For example, in a ruling in the 2009 case of *United States v. Ruehle,* District Court Judge Carney found gross prosecutorial misconduct where prosecutors contacted the employer of a witness who refused to cooperate and caused her to be terminated from that employment. They also subjected her to 26 "grueling interrogation" sessions, during which they attempted to shape her testimony to benefit the prosecution case. Another witness was forced to submit to 30 interrogation sessions and was ultimately forced to agree to an "unconscionable plea

agreement" under which he would "plead guilty to a crime he did not commit and pay a ridiculous sum of $12 million" (Chalmers 2010). Prosecutors also threatened to issue a grand jury subpoena to the 13-year-old son of one defendant and to force the boy to testify against his father (Chalmers 2010).

Gershman (1986: 141) suggests that prosecutorial misconduct continues to exist because of the absence or inadequacy of penalties imposed on the prosecutor for such misconduct. Even when an appellate court does sanction a prosecutor by cautioning him or her or by reversing the case, this may not be enough to dissuade prosecutors from further impropriety. Fisher (1988: 213) argues that for prosecutors the endorsement of "conviction affirmed" in appellate opinions is more important than any condemnation of prosecutorial misconduct. He notes that such opinions often refrain from identifying the prosecutors whose conduct has been condemned and that the courts rarely make references to disciplinary bodies in such incidents. Furthermore, prosecutors are not personally liable for their misconduct and enjoy absolute immunity, so during the course of a trial, the prosecutor is free from any civil liability arising from any misconduct, even if it was performed with malice (Gershman 1986: 142).

Explanations for prosecutorial misconduct include the notion that prosecutors aim to secure justice and, believing most defendants to be guilty, feel compelled to avoid problems that might render a not-guilty verdict. Such conduct would include allowing a witness to lie in the interest of serving the prosecutor's "truth" (Schoenfeld 2005: 252). Thus, it is the prosecutor's firm belief in the defendant's guilt that allows him or her to use means that justify the end. In this sense, prosecutorial misconduct appears to mirror the police noble cause corruption discussed in Chapter 2. Other explanations blame misconduct on the mentality that compels prosecutors to win at all costs (p. 252). A district attorney, for example, may be under some pressure to secure convictions to ensure reelection because voters commonly look at conviction records to assess the competence of a prosecutor.

Case Study 5.3 Wrongful Conviction Payment

New York City has agreed to pay $3.5 million to a man from Queens wrongfully imprisoned for 12 years after being convicted of attempted murder. The man, Shih-Wei Su, was convicted in 1992 on what turned out to be false testimony from a star witness. The prosecution was aware that the evidence was false, and the district attorney's office was condemned by the U.S Court of Appeals when overturning the conviction. Mr. Su's lawyer said that he was aware that about 80 convictions in Queens had been overturned because of wrongdoing by prosecutors, but no disciplinary or other action had ever been taken against them.

It was alleged at trial that Mr. Su had ordered fellow members of a youth gang to shoot a member of a rival gang at a pool hall in 1991. He was convicted after a key witness was offered leniency by prosecutors. Mr. Su received a sentence of 16 to 50 years and was released in 2003. The federal appeals court found that the prosecutor, Linda Rosero, had secured false testimony and misled members of the jury.

Mr. Su was 17 years old when he went to prison. After his release, he filed a complaint against prosecutor Linda Rosero with the Grievance Committee of the 2nd and 11th Judicial Circuits. The committee accepted Ms. Rosero's argument that the misconduct was not hers but that the responsibility lay elsewhere within the district attorney's office. The committee considered her conduct to have been "naïve, inexperienced and, possibly, stupid" and issued her a written admonition.

SOURCE: Kilgannon 2008.

Some commentators also suggest that the Supreme Court has been reluctant to control prosecutorial misconduct (Fisher 1988). For example, Gershman (1987: 218) contends that the Court has refused to specify ethical standards for prosecutors and has encouraged "prosecutorial overreaching." In one case, the Illinois Supreme Court said that a prosecutor had acted improperly but refused to discipline him because he was motivated by "a sincere, if misguided, desire to bring corrupt attorneys to justice" (*In re Friedman* 1979). Generally, in cases of prosecutorial misbehavior, the courts excuse misbehavior by applying arguments of fundamental fairness and harmless error. Francis Allen (1985: 335) has concluded that the problem of controlling prosecutorial excess "is one of . . . [the] great unsolved problems in criminal law administration." Allen (p. 334) cites the position taken by a court in Texas on an apparently deliberate attempt by a prosecutor to mislead a jury when the court decided that even though there had been a deliberate attempt to mislead, it would only consider the effect of the prosecutor's comment and not the intent of the speaker. In that case, the court found that the error had been ameliorated by the court's instruction to the jury.

State bar associations and disciplinary bodies are empowered to sanction prosecutorial misconduct but do so infrequently. For example, a 1999 investigation by the *Chicago Tribune* found that not one single prosecutor was sanctioned by a professional body in relation to 381 convictions reversed on appeal because of misconduct (Schoenfeld 2005: 261). In February 2006, the *San Jose Mercury News* reported that after reviewing 1,464 lawyer discipline cases published in the *California Bar Journal* between 2001 and 2005, they were able to find only one case where disciplinary action was taken against a prosecutor for misconduct (Ridolfi 2007: 11). The possibility of criminal prosecution for misconduct is equally remote, and according to Heather Schoenfeld (2005), "Criminal sanctions for misconduct are practically nonexistent" (p. 261). She gives one example, however, of a prosecutor who fabricated and withheld evidence and knowingly introduced perjured testimony who received a $500 fine and an official censure from the court.

Model Rule 3.6 forbids prosecutors from making specific kinds of statements out of court that might prejudice a criminal trial. However, the rule includes an exception for necessary statements directed toward public information and for legitimate law enforcement purposes. Hazard and Hodes (2002) give the example of an accused escaping from prison after murdering a prison officer and the prosecutor being permitted to issue a warning that the accused was armed and dangerous as a legitimate exception.

The practice of deferred sentencing, in which the prosecutor delays the sentencing of a witness who has pleaded guilty but will not be sentenced until after giving testimony against another defendant in a way satisfactory to the prosecution, is also condemned (Freedman 1975b: 89). Freedman points to another common form of witness coercion involving the use of prior convictions to impeach a defendant or defense witness as an instance where the prejudicial effect on the jury outweighs the attempt to cast doubt on credibility. He suggests that a prosecutor's actual motive in using prior convictions should be considered, noting that in one case the prosecutor argued before the jury that it should consider the "kind of person the defendant was" in view of the criminal records of the defense witnesses with whom the defendant had associated. Freedman (p. 91) also notes that prosecutors must maintain strong relationships with the police, and this may influence the prosecutor's conduct because it could lead to covering up police abuses such as brutality, perjury, and unlawful interrogation.

Case Study 5.4 is an example of a determined prosecutor who resisted DNA evidence that would have exonerated a convicted rapist who asserted that he had given a false confession because of threats from the police who interrogated him.

Case Studies 5.5 and 5.6 reveal prosecutors who withheld information in the interests of securing a conviction.

A Closer Look

Justice Department Acts on Prosecutor Misconduct

On August 9, 2011, the Department of Justice announced the establishment of a new unit to assess disciplinary action for career officials who commit prosecutorial misconduct. That action could include referral to a state bar association for punishment.

The unit, called the "Professional Misconduct Review Unit," will be tasked to review cases in which the department's ethics watchdog—the Office of Professional Responsibility—finds that an official intentionally or recklessly violated the rules under which they operate—for example, the obligation to reveal mitigating evidence to the defense.

SOURCE: Savage 2011.

Case Study 5.4 Convict's DNA Sways Labs, Not a Determined Prosecutor

In May 1987, Bruce Godschalk, 26, was convicted of raping two women who lived in the same housing complex in a suburb of Philadelphia. He was sentenced to 10 to 20 years in prison, and his conviction was based largely on a confession that he retracted long before his trial. Following his conviction, tests by two laboratories engaged by the prosecution and the defense produced the same outcome—namely, that both rapes were committed by the same man, but that Mr. Godschalk was not the perpetrator.

(Continued)

(Continued)

The Montgomery County District Attorney, Bruce L. Castor Jr., has rejected cause to release Mr. Godschalk, claiming that the DNA testing is flawed and that he has confidence in the tape-recorded confession. Mr. Castor wanted more time to review the DNA testing results in Godschalk's case, orders for which Godschalk obtained after 7 years of battling with prosecutors. Over the last decade, DNA testing has freed more than 100 wrongfully convicted persons, with about 20% of those convictions resulting from false confessions. Mr. Godschalk's only previous arrests were for possession of marijuana and driving while impaired.

During the investigation, Mr. Godschalk's picture was shown to one of the rape victims by police 6 months after the rape incident, and after considering his and other photographs for more than an hour, the victim identified Godschalk as the rapist. Godschalk was then interrogated by a police detective and admitted the crime, but the detective did not record the hours of interrogation leading up to the confession. According to Mr. Godschalk, his confession was false as a result of threats made by the detective, but his motion to suppress the confession was denied during the trial. Mr. Castor refused to let Mr. Godschalk out of prison and stated, after being asked what scientific basis he had for deciding the testing was flawed, "I have no scientific basis. I know because I trust my prosecutors and my tape-recorded confession. Therefore the results must be flawed until someone proves to me otherwise."

At the request of *The New York Times*, the DNA test results from the prosecution and the defense were reviewed by a third expert, who concluded that Mr. Godschalk was not the rapist.

SOURCE: Rimer 2002.

Case Study 5.5 Prosecutor Withholds Evidence

In 2004, Ernest Ray Willis was released from death row after spending 17 years there for a crime he did not commit. He was convicted in 1987 of setting a house on fire and killing two women. During his trial, the prosecutor referred to him as a "rat," "an animal," "a mean vicious dog," and "a satanic demon." Jurors had to decide during the sentencing procedure whether Willis posed a future danger to society, and they answered in the affirmative and sentenced him to death.

It was discovered during a postconviction investigation that a state psychologist had examined Willis before trial and reported that he would not present much of a future danger to society, but this information, which could have helped him avoid a death sentence, was never given to his lawyer. However, the prosecutor did know of this report because a FedEx record showed that it had been delivered to his office; additionally, the psychologist remembered personally meeting with the prosecutor and advising him that Willis would not make a convincing death penalty case. The prosecutor has denied lying about the psychologist or the report.

A federal judge ordered the state to retry Willis or set him free, determining that suppressing the report plus other factors violated his rights. Following the investigation, the new district attorney requested Willis's immediate release from jail. The original prosecutor maintains that Willis was guilty and has no second thoughts about his prosecution of the case.

SOURCE: Gier 2006: 192.

Case Study 5.6 Release After 14 Years

On December 28, 2000, Michael Ray Graham Jr., 37, was freed from death row at Louisiana State Penitentiary at Angola after 14 years of incarceration. The state had dismissed all charges against him because it did not have any credible evidence linking him to the crime for which he had been incarcerated. As compensation, he received only a check for $10 from the prison to cover his transportation out of Angola.

In another trial, Albert Ronnie Burrell, 45, had been convicted of the same crime as Mr. Graham—the murder of an elderly couple in Louisiana—and he, too, had spent almost 14 years at Angola on death row. He, too, had all charges against him dismissed by the state. Mr. Burrell, who is mentally challenged and illiterate, came very close to being executed, missing it by only 17 days.

The release of the men brought to eight the number of wrongfully imprisoned death row inmates exonerated in the year 2000; altogether, over 100 such inmates on death row have been cleared of all crimes and released since the reintroduction of the death penalty in 1973.

According to their lawyers, prosecutorial misconduct was the cause of the incarceration of these two men. No physical evidence linked them to the crime, and their convictions rested largely on the evidence of a jailhouse snitch, who, according to law enforcement officials, was known to them as a habitual liar. The snitch claimed that both men had confessed to the murders while in jail, but he admitted at his own trial that he had spent time in several mental hospitals and had written countless bad checks. The fact that the prosecution had made a plea agreement with the snitch had not been revealed at Mr. Graham's trial, nor had the fact that the snitch had previously been found to be mentally incompetent. As well, demonstrating the weak case against Mr. Graham and Mr. Burrell, even the prosecutor had admitted to the court that the case should never have been taken to the grand jury.

SOURCE: "Texas Judge Reprimanded in Death Row Case." 2010. *New York Times*, July 17; "92nd Death Row Inmate Freed Since '73." *New York Times*, January 5, 2001.

JUDICIAL ETHICS

The judicial function is a core part of our society. Judges must be competent and ethical, and their actions must always promote respect for their decisions. Judges have considerable power and authority over individuals, and they exercise substantial discretion when acting judicially. They are expected to conduct themselves according to high standards of professional conduct and are held to higher standards of law than lawyers or other persons not invested with the public trust. A judge's duty extends beyond the limits of his or her court and into the judge's personal life, where standards of propriety are far higher than those set for others (Shaman, Lubet, and Alfini 2000: 1). These strictures concerning judges and judicial conduct are reflected in the Code of Judicial Conduct of the American Bar Association (ABA Standing Committee on Ethics and Professional Responsibility 1999).

A Model Code of Judicial Conduct was adopted by the ABA in 1990 and establishes standards for ethical conduct by judges. The ABA warns that the code is not intended as an exhaustive guide for the conduct of judges but is intended to state basic standards governing judicial conduct and provide guidance to assist judges in maintaining high standards of personal and judicial behavior. Some of the most important canons of the code relate to impartiality and bias. Under Canon 3, judges are to perform their duties without bias or prejudice and are not to exhibit bias or prejudice, including that based on race, sex, religion, national origin, disability, age, sexual orientation, or socioeconomic status. Further, judges are not to allow staff and court officials to show bias or prejudice.

Judges must also be faithful to the law; must not be swayed by partisan interests, public clamor, or fear of criticism; and must be patient, dignified, and courteous to those with whom they deal. Judges are not to make public comments about proceedings that are pending in court that might reasonably be expected to affect the outcome of such proceedings, impair their fairness, or substantially interfere with a fair trial. However, judges are allowed to make public statements explaining the procedures of the court for public information.

One significant aspect of the U.S. judicial system is the election of judges, sometimes through partisan elections. This raises questions about the influences that elected judges may be subject to in performing their judicial duties. In many states, judges are elected through partisan or nonpartisan elections. When an election is nonpartisan, the candidate's political party affiliations do not appear on the ballot (Comisky, Patterson, and Taylor 1987: 9). In states that use partisan elections, judicial candidates are usually nominated in primaries or conventions or through nominating petitions. The proponents of partisan elections for judges argue that judges are policy makers and should therefore be directly chosen by, and be accountable to, the people who are affected by those policies; that a partisan election is an open method of selection; and that identifying a potential judge's political affiliation gives voters an indication of his or her political ideology (p. 8).

Would-be judges who conduct campaigns to get elected usually have to raise money to fund their election, but in 29 of the 38 states that require judges to be elected, there are bans on them directly soliciting funds. As reported in *The New York Times* (Editorial 2015), such a ban was challenged by a candidate for a county court seat in Florida who sent out a letter to local voters soliciting funds, contrary to a Florida rule that bans such conduct. She claimed that the ban was a violation of the First Amendment, but the U.S. Supreme Court ruled that judges are not politicians even when they have to go through an election process, and their authority depends on the public's confidence in their integrity. The ruling of the Court has limited effect in practice because judges may still raise money through campaign committees, and it does not prevent them from learning the identity of their donors.

The former chief justice of Alabama, Sue Bell Cobb, has stated that she needed $2.6 million to win the election for chief justice there and that her opponent raised nearly $5 million. Judges are permitted to directly solicit funds in Alabama, and Judge Cobb made calls to friends, family, and also to lawyers "who have appeared before us, lawyers who are likely to appear before us, officials with companies who may very well have interests before the court" (*Politico* March/April 2015). Judge Cobb considers that public trust is eroded when candidates for judicial office have to seek funds from donors and claims to have seen cases where "fellow justices consistently ruled a certain way because business community backing alone had brought them to the court."

Those who argue against partisan judicial elections contend that

- voters generally have no knowledge of the candidates' qualifications and in any event are not competent to assess qualifications;
- that nominees are selected by political leaders based on political grounds rather than merit;
- that successful candidates are likely to feel obligated to the political leaders who selected them and to those who contributed to their campaign funds;
- that many otherwise qualified candidates are deterred from seeking office because they are required to conduct political campaigns;
- that voters have a tendency to be influenced by nonjudicial qualifications such as political affiliation; and
- that having to periodically seek reelection discourages many potentially worthwhile candidates (Comisky et al. 1987: 8).

To what extent do judges take ideological approaches in their judging? Even though judges in Arizona are no longer elected but are appointed, Susan Philips (1998: 22) found that the judges with whom she worked generally agreed that the judicial selection process remains a political one. In one study of judges in a superior court in Arizona, Philips (p. 14) found that judges presented themselves as mere implementers of law, divorced from their political and social backgrounds, despite the fact that they were required to be significantly involved in local political processes to become judges. Her research indicates that judges who take a

A Closer Look

Election of Judges Proposed for Maricopa County, Mesa, Arizona

In Maricopa County, judges have not been elected since 1974, when a system was installed under which judges are chosen by a panel of legal experts and the state governor. However, in a recent move to change the system, Rep. Russell Pearce (R-Mesa) wants to change the law and have judges elected, as they are in other states. Critics of the move say that the proposal will result in the election of judges who will make decisions based on political popularity.

Chief Justice Ruth McGregor of the Arizona Supreme Court is firmly against the proposal, pointing out that the present system has meant that judges have not had to campaign to secure office and that they have been able to remain independent of political influence in their decision-making. The chief justice believes that changing the system to a ballot of judges will conflict courtrooms because of the influence of lawyers and lobbyists who provide campaign funds. Also, she points out that judges are not representative officials and are responsible for upholding the laws and the constitution.

Chief Justice McGregor argued that if passed the measure would vastly increase the number of Republican judges, disturbing the existing balance in which the courts have an even number of Democrats and Republicans. McGregor favors every judge in Arizona to be appointed and said she would oppose the proposal, which appeared on the November ballot, where voters would decide whether Maricopa County judges should again be elected. The proposal was defeated, and again in 2012.

SOURCE: "Judges Might Go on Ballot in Maricopa County." 2008. *East Valley Tribune*, March 24.

procedure-oriented stance on due process represented a politically liberal approach to the role of the state in relation to the individual. By contrast, judges who take a record-oriented stance followed a politically conservative notion of the role of the state in relation to the individual (p. 79).

Philips's (1998) study revealed that the conservative view sees the state as attempting to minimize interference in the lives of individuals, whereas the liberal view considers the state as the protector of human liberties (p. 79). In looking at judicial approaches to guilty pleas, she observed that record-oriented judges did not regard it as their responsibility to ensure that a defendant knowingly and voluntarily pleads guilty. These judges often referred to their assumption that defendants are aware of what they are doing and that they are capable of comprehending judicial instructions. In the case of procedure-oriented judges, however, the responsibility for protecting the defendant's due

process rights is taken on by the judge, who also recognizes that some persons need more help than others in comprehending court procedures. Philips's study, along with the systems of political appointment and partisan election of judges, raises the issue of the linkages between political ideology and judicial performance, especially in relation to the ethical duty of a judge to make nonpolitical, unbiased decisions (see the "Election of Judges Proposed for Maricopa County, Mesa, Arizona" Closer Look box).

Ethical Rules Governing Judges

As well as acting without prejudice or bias, judges are expected to disqualify themselves in any proceeding in which their impartiality might be questioned. This includes instances in which a judge has a personal bias or prejudice concerning a party or lawyer, has personal knowledge of disputed evidence, or has previously served as a lawyer in the matter in dispute.

In terms of a judge's personal life, under Canon 4 personal activities are categorized as "extra-judicial activities," and judges are required to minimize the risk of conflict between those activities and their obligations as judges. Accordingly, judges are not to act in extrajudicial activities in a way that will cast doubt on their impartiality, demean the judicial office, or interfere with the proper performance of judicial duties. The commentary to this canon gives as examples of expressions of extrajudicial bias or prejudice racial slurs and jokes that may cast doubt on the judge's capacity to act impartially.

In financial activities, judges are not to engage in financial and business dealings that may be seen as exploiting their positions as judges or to become involved in transactions or business relationships with lawyers or other persons likely to come before the court. Judges are not to accept, and are to urge members of their families not to accept, gifts, loans, or favors—except those permitted as listed in the code. Permitted activities include accepting public testimonials or gifts, ordinary social hospitality, scholarships and fellowships, and loans, provided they are not from lawyers or their firms if they have come or are likely to come before the judge.

Canon 3 prohibits judges from commending or criticizing jurors for their verdict. In Utah, which has a code of judicial conduct almost identical to the ABA Code, a judge was criticized for violating this prohibition. He reportedly told the jury, "This was a pretty clear case . . . I don't know how you came out with this result, and this is one of the very few times I've criticized the jury" (Averett 2004: 698).

In a discussion of the application of virtue ethics to judges (see Chapter 14 for a discussion of virtue ethics), Farrelly and Solum (2007: 1) identify the following virtues as being relevant to the social role of a judge: incorruptibility, sobriety, courage, good temper, impartiality, diligence, and carefulness. They argue that these virtues, which they refer to as "uncontested judicial virtues" are widely expected assumptions about what constitutes "good judging" and ought to be applied when federal judges are selected instead of focusing on their views on social issues. Case Studies 5.7 through 5.13 show examples of breaches of judicial ethics.

Judicial Misfeasance

The following case studies provide examples of judicial misfeasance.

Case Study 5.7 Prosecutor Says Tape Shows Brooklyn Judge Took a Bribe

On February 8, 2002, *The New York Times* reported that a Brooklyn judge had been arraigned on a charge of accepting a bribe. Prosecutors had obtained a covert tape recording showing the judge laughing as he persuaded a lawyer to give him what both men seemed to understand was a payoff in a civil case that would net the lawyer a $1.6 million fee. The lawyer had been wired by the prosecutors and had delivered $18,000 to the judge's robing room at the state supreme court in Brooklyn. Prosecutors claim the judge wanted the payment in exchange for his approval for the settlement of a civil case. Justice Barron was charged with one count of bribe receiving and could face a prison term of 15 years. The prosecutor explained that his investigators were expanding their inquiry into judicial wrongdoing in Brooklyn, including examining hundreds of Justice Barron's cases.

SOURCE: Associated Press 2011.

Case Study 5.8 Judge Receives 28-Year Sentence for Taking Bribes

In Pennsylvania, former Luzerne County Judge Mark Ciavarella received a jail sentence of 28 years in federal prison for taking $1 million in bribes from the builder of two juvenile detention centers.

Because of the actions of the judge, the state supreme court had to vacate about 4,000 convictions entered by former Judge Ciavarella between 2003 and 2008 because of violations of the rights of the juveniles involved to legal counsel and to enter an informed plea.

Prosecutors said that Ciavarella and another judge, Michael Conahan, had accepted more than $2 million in bribes and had extorted hundreds of thousands of dollars from the co-owner of the juvenile facilities. Ciavarella made sure that the two juveniles facilities were kept full of juveniles, many of whom were first-time offenders convicted of minor offenses. Former Judge Conahan pleaded guilty and was later sentenced to 17½ years. Ciavarella was sentenced to 28 years.

SOURCE: Associated Press 2011.

Case Study 5.9 Federal Judges and Financial-Interest Conflicts

Responding to criticism from Congress about lapses in judicial ethics, the chief justice decided in 2006 that all federal judges would be required to install software on their computers to avoid unknowingly participating in cases in which they have a financial interest. Also, judges were prohibited from being reimbursed for attending a private seminar, unless the seminar sponsor filed a public disclosure statement on the program content and financing sources. About 700 complaints a year are received about federal judges.

SOURCE: Greenhouse 2006.

Case Study 5.10 Appearance of Partiality

In October 2006, a panel of the Washington Supreme Court reprimanded a judge of the court who visited a facility holding sexually violent predators who had completed their sentences but had been determined by the court to be likely to engage in predatory acts of sexual violence. The judge was sanctioned with admonishment, the mildest punishment, for creating an appearance of partiality when he questioned inmates and accepted documents from them at the facility. The complaint was made by prosecutors, and the judge was invited by several inmates.

SOURCE: Liptak 2006.

Case Study 5.11 Judicial Bribery

In August 2004, it was reported that surveillance tapes recorded in a Brooklyn matrimonial judge's office showed the judge offering a lawyer detailed instructions on how to argue a case before him and informing the lawyer that he would award his client the rights to a house in a divorce case. The judge has been charged with accepting cash, cigars, and dozens of meals from the lawyer in exchange for giving him an advantage in divorce cases and referring clients to him. The tapes also show the judge accepting $1,000 cash and a $250 box of cigars from the lawyer.

SOURCE: Newman 2004: 1.

Case Study 5.12 Gross Abuse of Power

In December 2004, it was reported that an upstate New York judge had been censured for sending people to jail for minor misbehavior at his courthouse. In one case, a college student at Skidmore College was told by the judge that he was "an obnoxious young man," to which the student responded that the judge was "an obnoxious old man." In retaliation, the judge ruled the student in contempt and sent him to jail, where he was held in solitary confinement for 4 days. In a second case, the judge ordered the parents of a young man to attend before him after their son had pleaded guilty on some traffic tickets. Reportedly, the judge told the parents he had overheard them exchange curse words in the parking lot before the court case began. The judge ordered the father to be handcuffed and taken to a jail cell and, despite her objections, told the wife that she needed an order of protection from her husband. The state's Commission on Judicial Conduct censured the judge, calling the two acts a gross abuse of power.

SOURCE: Baker 2004: 5.

Case Study 5.13 Texas Judge Reprimanded

A Texas judge who refused to keep the courthouse open for a last minute appeal from a death row inmate was reprimanded by a judicial panel on August 12, 2011. It was on September 25, 2007, that lawyers for Michael W. Richard requested the court to stay open to receive an appeal, but the judge reportedly told the clerk that the court closes at 5 p.m. That same night, Mr. Richard was put to death.

The judge, Sharon Keller, is the state's highest ranking criminal judge and was warned publicly by the State Judicial Commission on Judicial Conduct for "willful or persistent misconduct" that "casts public discredit on the judiciary."

SOURCE: "Texas Judge Reprimanded" 2010.

SUMMARY

Like members of most professions, lawyers enjoy the benefit of detailed rules concerning ethical conduct, and judges are in a similar position. Ethical dilemmas for lawyers can usually be resolved by applying the relevant ethical standard. This mechanism has the effect of simplifying moral issues that arise in legal practice. There are notable tensions within the criminal justice system affecting lawyers, and the adversarial system itself underpins and promotes these tensions. Questions about a defense lawyer's proper role are answered by ethical standards, but the morality of keeping silent about a client's criminal conduct continues to provoke debate among the general public. However, once an understanding is gained about the connection between the protection of individual rights in the criminal process and the task of the defense lawyer in ensuring those protections are enforced, these moral issues can be seen within context, particularly within the framework of the adversarial system.

Prosecutors are in a special position because of the tensions and conflicts to which they may be subjected. To a great extent, these arise as a result of the existence of wide prosecutorial discretion. Whether the primary concern is for the victim, the community, reelection, or discovering the truth, prosecutors must make choices and decide their constituency, either generally or in a particular case.

Generally, there exists considerable potential for judges and prosecutors to become corrupted because they enjoy such wide discretions and powers. Although judges perform in public and are subject to a high level of accountability, prosecutors' positions are much more problematic due to the lack of transparency surrounding their prosecutorial decision-making.

DISCUSSION QUESTIONS

1. Explain the importance of lawyer–client confidentiality, and discuss any exceptions to the confidentiality rule.

2. The existence of the adversarial system and the need for lawyers to act zealously explains why lawyers are not troubled by what some see as their "immoral" actions in defending those they know to be guilty. Discuss.

3. In what circumstances must lawyers disclose crimes committed by their clients?

4. What are lawyers' responsibilities if their clients insist on perjuring themselves in testimony to the court?

5. Consider the advantages and disadvantages of plea bargaining from the prosecutor's point of view.

6. Prosecutors have too much discretion and are accountable to no one for the exercise of their discretion. Discuss.

7. If accused individuals have incompetent counsel who neglect to present all the material facts that might assist them, prosecutors have an ethical duty to make sure these facts are presented consistent with their responsibility to achieve just results. Discuss.

8. Explain how public opinion about crime might influence the decisions of prosecutors and judges in light of the fact that both are often elected officials.

9. Discuss the ethical requirement for prosecutors to "seek justice, not merely to convict" and how this expectation might be enhanced in the justice system.

10. The practice of overcharging as a means of obtaining a sufficient number of plea bargains, in which cases are commonly drawn up as felonies with the prosecutor ready to accept a plea for a misdemeanor, coerces the defendant into foregoing the right to trial by jury. Discuss and explain the consequences.

11. The exercise of discretion granted to the prosecutor in making the decision to charge is not accompanied by any controls, and the decision of whether or not to charge is "the single most unreviewed exercise of the power of the criminal law available to an individual in the American system of justice" (Gottfredson and Gottfredson 1988: 114). The ABA has made recommendations for criteria that a prosecutor should consider when deciding to charge, including the disproportion of the punishment to the offense. Discuss the prosecutor's decision to overcharge in drug offenses in light of the mass incarceration outcome of the war on drugs, mandatory sentencing, three-strikes-and-you're-out legislation (see Chapters 4 and 9), and the conspiracy laws that punish small drug users and dealers the same as kingpins.

6

THE PURPOSE
OF CRIMINAL PUNISHMENT

Does society have the right to punish? Is the infliction of punishment morally justifiable? These complex questions will be addressed in the following discussion of the rationale, justification, and nature of punishment. Rules about punishment, such as how much punishment can be inflicted and for what kinds of behavior, are of course contained in laws and regulations, so in this sense, law justifies punishment. However, the moral justification for punishment is a separate issue from the legal justification because although the law may provide for the infliction of punishment, society's moral justification for punishment still has to be established. Indeed, some philosophers argue that it is morally impermissible for the state to punish people for breaking the law despite general acceptance of the notion that if the state prohibits some forms of conduct it should have the right to punish those who perform it (Boonin 2008: 1).

To better understand the nature of punishment, it is first necessary to examine its conceptual basis and then to consider the various theories that have been developed to morally justify society's infliction of punishment. These theories are deterrence, retribution, just deserts, rehabilitation, incapacitation, and, more recently, restorative justice. As well, it is important to appreciate that there are three perspectives about the issue of punishment: the philosophical, the sociological, and the criminological. Each perspective represents a different and distinct way of looking at the issue of punishment, and each will be addressed in this chapter.

WHAT IS PUNISHMENT?

We use the word *punishment* to describe anything we think is painful; for example, we refer to a "punishing work schedule" or a "punishing exercise program." We also talk of punishment in the context of parents or teachers disciplining children. However, in this discussion we will consider punishment in a particular sense. Flew (in Bean 1981: 5) argues that punishment, in the sense of a sanction imposed for a criminal offense, consists of five elements:

1. It must involve an unpleasantness to the victim.
2. It must be for an offense, actual or supposed.

3. It must be of an offender, actual or supposed.
4. It must be the work of personal agencies; in other words, it must not be the natural consequence of an action.
5. It must be imposed by an authority or an institution against whose rules the offense has been committed. If this is not the case, then the act is not one of punishment but is simply a hostile act. Similarly, direct action by a person who has no special authority is not properly called *punishment* and is more likely to be revenge or an act of hostility.

In addition to these five elements, Benn and Peters (in Bean 1981: 6) add that the unpleasantness should be an essential part of punishment, and Feinberg (1965: 400) indicates that punishment should also reflect "attitudes of resentment and indignation, and . . . judgments of disapproval and reprobation, on the part of the punishing authority himself or of those 'in whose name' the punishment is inflicted." As will be discussed later in considering punishment as retribution, these attitudes are termed the *censure* and *hard treatment* elements of punishment.

Questions about the "unpleasantness" of a punishment and what constitutes a punishment can raise interesting issues. For example, a masochist who is whipped but is not harmed by that punishment does not suffer any punishment, and some argue that mandatory community service willingly entered into by an offender is a genuine form of punishment but cannot be said to be unpleasant for the offender (Boonin 2008: 11). In the case of convicted sex offenders, the U.S. Supreme Court has ruled that posting their photograph and information about them on the Internet after their release from prison is not an additional punishment: While it may harm them, it does not punish them (p. 15).

The value of this definition of punishment resides in its presentation of punishment in terms of a system of rules and in its differentiation of punishment from other kinds of unpleasantness. Another definition of punishment, proposed by David Garland (1990), is "the legal process whereby violators of criminal law are condemned and sanctioned in accordance with specified legal categories and procedures" (p. 17). This chapter will not be concerned with punishment that takes place in schools, within families, or in other institutions, but instead will discuss forms of punishment that take place as the result of legal processes defined earlier. It will examine the major arguments relating to punishment, illustrate the ways in which those arguments relate to justice and the justice system, and examine how that system would be affected should one argument prevail over another.

THEORETICAL APPROACHES TO PUNISHMENT

Thinking about the issue of punishment gives rise to a number of questions, the most fundamental of which is why should offenders be punished? This question might produce the following responses:

- They deserve to be punished.
- Punishment will stop them from committing further crimes.
- Punishment tells victims that society disapproves of the harm that they have suffered.
- Punishment discourages others from doing the same thing.
- Punishment protects society from dangerous or dishonest people.
- Punishment allows offenders to make amends for the harm they have caused.
- Punishment ensures that people understand that laws are there to be obeyed.

Some of the possible answers to the question of why offenders should be punished may conflict with each other. This is because some answers are based on reasons having to do with preventing crime, whereas others are concerned with punishment being deserved by an offender (Hudson 1996: 3). When a court imposes a punishment on an offender, it often tries to balance the sorts of reasons for punishment noted earlier, but sometimes certain purposes of punishment dominate other purposes (p. 4). Over time, there have been shifts in penal theory, and therefore in the purpose of punishment, due to a complex set of reasons, including politics, public policy, and social movements. Consequently, in a cyclical process, an early focus on deterrence as the rationale for punishment gave way to a focus on reform and rehabilitation. This, in turn, has led to a return to punishment based on the notion of retribution and just deserts.

The concept of punishment has been theorized by moral philosophers, social theorists, and criminologists, and these various approaches will be considered in this chapter to provide a better basis for understanding the place of punishment within the criminal justice system and society in general. As Garland (1990) argues, punishment is a complex concept, and an approach to punishment that is limited to a reading of moral philosophy fails to represent the full dimension and complexity of the subject. For moral philosophers, the "ought" of punishment is of great importance and leads to a set of questions, including the following:

- What should be the goals of punishment?
- What should be the values contained in and promoted by the criminal law?
- What is the purpose of punishment?

In contrast to the philosophical view of punishment, the sociological perspective is concerned with the "is" of punishment—that is, what punishment is actually intended for—and the nature of penal systems (see Hudson 1996: 10). Criminologists and policy makers, who focus on penalties for offenses and policy concerns relevant to the punishment of offenders, offer the third perspective on punishment. Some critics, such as Philip Bean (1981: 9), argue that criminology has tended to ignore the moral and sociological implications of punishment in favor of the social and personal characteristics of offenders as well as the nature of penal institutions and methods of social control. In the same vein, Nigel Walker (1991) points out that the practical ends of penal action, particularly with the aims of sentencing and the administration of prisons and probation, are concerns that pay little attention to the philosophy or sociology of punishment. The criminological perspective will be discussed in Chapter 7 in the context of corrections; this chapter will explore the philosophical and sociological perspectives.

WHY PUNISH? THE PHILOSOPHICAL APPROACH

In the philosophical debate about punishment, two main types of theories of punishment dominate:

utilitarian theory and retributive theory (utilitarian theory is discussed more fully in Chapter 13). These philosophical theories have in turn generated further theoretical discussions about punishment concerned with deterrence, retribution, incapacitation, rehabilitation, and, more recently, restorative justice.

Theories that set the goal of punishment as the prevention of future crime (deterrence) are usually referred to as *utilitarian* because they are derived from utilitarian philosophy. Past-oriented theories (theories that focus on the past actions of the offender) are referred to as *retributivist* because they seek retribution from offenders for their crimes. The retributivist conception of punishment includes the notion that the purpose of punishment is to allocate moral blame to offenders for the crimes and that their future conduct is not a proper concern for deciding punishment (Hudson 1996: 3). Theories of deterrence, retribution, just deserts, rehabilitation, and incapacitation, as well as the idea of restorative justice will be considered in this chapter. Each of these theories tries to establish a basis for punishment as a response to the question "Why punish?"

The "Punishment and History" Closer Look box gives a short history of the concept of punishment in Western cultures, while Case Study 6.1 provides a contemporary example of corporal punishment.

Deterrence

People are deterred from actions when they refrain from carrying them out because they experience an aversion to the possible consequences of those actions. Walker (1991: 15) suggests that although penologists believe that penalties do, in fact, deter, it is hard to determine whether the kind of penalty or its severity has any effect on whether a particular penalty is successful. Some question whether deterrence is morally acceptable. They argue that it is unacceptable because it is impossible to achieve, and if deterrent sentences are not successful, inflicting suffering in the name of deterrence is morally wrong (p. 13).

To utilitarian philosophers such as Bentham, punishment can be justified only if the harm that it prevents is greater than the harm inflicted on the offender through punishing him or her (Hudson 1996: 18). In this view, therefore, unless punishment

A Closer Look

Punishment and History

Before the installation of constitutional governments in most of western Europe in the 18th and 19th centuries, penalties were arbitrary, dependent on the whims of monarchs or the local nobles to whom they delegated authority to punish. There was very little proportionate graduation of penalties, with capital punishment available for everything from murder and high treason to fairly minor theft—as reflected in the old saying "One might just as well be hanged for a sheep as a lamb" (Hudson 1996: 19).

Draconian Punishments

The notion of "draconian punishments" derives from the laws promulgated for Athens in 621 BCE by Draco (e.g., see Carawan 1998). It appears from later accounts of the Draco code that the punishment of death was prescribed for even the most trivial offenses. Draconian punishments are essentially deterrent in nature, being so severe as to dissuade most people from committing crimes. Draconian-type notions of punishment are often advocated by those in the "get tough on crime" lobby.

Case Study 6.1 The Nature of the Punishment: Corporal Punishment

On May 4, 1994, Michael Fay, a U.S. teenager who had pleaded guilty to several acts of vandalism in Singapore, was caned by Singapore's authorities (in Nygaard 2000: 1). He was stripped, bent at the hip over a padded trestle, tied down at his ankles and wrists, and his buttocks were lashed by a martial arts specialist four times with a 4-foot long, half-inch wide stick of rattan soaked in antiseptic. Fay, 18, had lived in Singapore since 1992. He was sentenced to 4 months in prison, a fine of $2,230, and the caning after his guilty plea.

The sentence of corporal punishment secured great media attention in the United States, with many people expressing their views. President Clinton, in a personal letter to the Singapore president, urged him to spare the rod and revoke the punishment, which Clinton described as "extreme." Also, 24 U.S. senators appealed to the president of Singapore that clemency would be "an enlightened decision." However, U.S. public opinion expressed support for the punishment, some even writing to the Singapore embassy in Washington expressing their approval. In Dayton, Ohio, where Fay's father lived, citizens supported the punishment by a 2-to-1 margin.

The Singaporean courts and government rejected the various appeals for clemency, except for reducing the number of lashes. A Home Affairs Ministry official stated that Singapore was able to keep its society orderly and crime free because of its tough laws against antisocial crimes and that Singapore did not have a situation like that in New York, where acts of vandalism were commonplace and where even police cars were vandalized.

deters further crime, it simply adds to the totality of human suffering. In other words, utilitarians justify punishment by referring to its beneficial effects or consequences. In this sense, utilitarian theory is a consequentialist theory that considers only the good and bad consequences produced by an act as morally significant (Ten 1987: 3). Therefore, deterrence is a forward-looking punishment theory because it looks to future criminality (Brooks 2012: 35). Jeremy Bentham is considered the main proponent of punishment as deterrence, and in Bean (1981: 30), he expressed his early conception of the notion as follows:

> Pain and pleasure are the great springs of human action. When a man perceives or supposes pain to be the consequence of an act he is acted on in such manner as tends with a certain force to withdraw him as it were from the commission of that act. If the apparent magnitude be greater than the magnitude of the pleasure expected he will be absolutely prevented from performing it.

Cesare Becarria took a position similar to Bentham's, arguing that "the aim of punishment can only be to prevent the criminal committing new crimes against his countrymen and to keep others from doing likewise" (in Bean 1981: 30). Utilitarians understand punishment only as a means to an end and not as an end in itself. They perceive punishment in terms of its ability to reduce crime and do not focus on the punishment that "ought" to be imposed on offenders. To utilitarians, a "right" punishment (or one with the greatest utility) is one that is beneficial to the general welfare of all those affected by the criminal act. Critics of utilitarianism argue that because utilitarians see the aim of punishment as promoting public welfare and maximizing the happiness of all, this means that utilitarians are willing to punish the innocent to achieve that objective (p. 4).

Utilitarian theories of punishment suffer from the "punishing the innocent" objection. This states that if punishing a person is morally justified because it results in more utility than any alternative, then in some circumstances punishing the innocent is also morally permissible because it produces more overall utility than any available alternative. An example might be a state that decides to deliberately punish an innocent person, widely believed to be guilty, in order to prevent a riot taking place if he or she were to be acquitted. While the interests of the innocent person would be taken into account, these would have to be balanced against the interests of all others. So for the utilitarian, the right action to take would be that which produced the highest utility, and it would therefore be morally acceptable to punish an innocent person in this situation (Boonin 2008: 42). This outcome is itself morally unacceptable and contrary to moral intuition unless a utilitarian proponent is prepared to accept the notion that it is sometimes permissible to punish innocent persons.

The mirror image of this situation also presents problems for utilitarian theory. Just as the most utility can be produced by punishing the innocent person as discussed earlier, there are cases where the most utility is produced by *not* punishing the guilty person. For example, the offender might be so widely believed to be innocent that the pain caused to all those who would hate to see him or her suffer would outweigh the benefit to be gained by punishing the offender. In such a situation, would a utilitarian be ready to see the offender remain unpunished (Boonin 2008: 53)? Those supporting the theory of punishment as deterrence distinguish between individual deterrence and general deterrence. *Individual deterrence* involves deterring someone who has already offended from reoffending; *general deterrence* involves dissuading potential offenders from offending at all by way of the punishment administered for a particular offense (Hudson 1996). Individual deterrence relies on offenders receiving a taste of the punishment they will receive if they reoffend, and it can be seen operationally in "short, sharp, shock punishments," such as boot camps, which are used as an alternative to imprisonment and are clearly aimed at subjecting offenders to a regime that will shock them out of any further criminal conduct. General deterrence takes the form of legislation imposing penalties for specific offenses in the belief that those penalties will deter or prevent persons from committing those offenses. An example of an attempt at general deterrence would be significantly increasing the penalties for driving under the influence (DUI) in an effort to deter citizens from drunk driving.

Does Deterrence Work?

Beyleveld (in Hudson 1996: 23), after carrying out a comprehensive review of studies that have considered the deterrent effects of punishment, concluded that

> there exists no scientific basis for expecting that a general deterrence policy, which does not involve an unacceptable interference with human rights, will do anything to control the crime rate. The sort of information needed to base a morally acceptable general policy is lacking. There is some convincing evidence in some areas that some legal sanctions have exerted deterrent effects. These findings are not, however, generalizable beyond the conditions that were investigated. Given the present state of knowledge, implementing an official deterrence policy can be no more than a shot in the dark, or a political decision to pacify "public sentiment."

The empirical evidence suggests that, generally, punishment has no individual deterrent effect (Ten 1987: 9; Brooks 2012: 42). Walker (1991: 16) argues that evidence from research studies has established that capital punishment has no greater effect than life imprisonment. Daniel Nagin (in Ten 1987: 9) comments on the difficulty in distinguishing between individual deterrence and rehabilitation. In another overview of research on deterrence, Nagin (1998: 345) identifies three sets of studies, which he refers to as interrupted time-series studies, ecological studies, and perceptual studies.

The first set, time-series studies, explores the effect of specific policy initiatives, such as police crackdowns on open-air drug markets. Nagin finds that such policy targeting has only a temporary effect and is therefore not a successful deterrent.

Ecological studies look for a negative association between crime rates and punishment levels that can be interpreted as having a deterrent effect. Nagin points out that a number of such studies have been able to isolate a deterrent effect.

In perceptual studies, the data come from surveys. Such surveys have found that self-reported criminality is lower among those who see sanctions, risks, and costs as higher. Nagin therefore concludes that, collectively, the operations of the criminal justice system exert a substantial deterrent effect.

In discussing whether the threat of punishment has a deterrent effect, Johannes Andenaes (1972: 345) explains that two positions are usually debated. Bentham's position is that man is a rational being who chooses between courses of action, having first calculated the risks of pain and pleasure. If, therefore, we regard the risk of punishment as sufficient to outweigh a likely gain, a potential criminal applying a rational approach will choose not to break the law. The alternative position considers this model unrealistic, arguing that people remain law-abiding not because they fear the criminal law, but as a result of moral inhibitions and norms of conduct. Criminals, they argue, do not make rational choices but act out of emotional instability, through lack of self-control, or as a result of having acquired the values of a criminal subculture (p. 345). Andenaes points out the dangers of generalization; that is, he suggests it is necessary to distinguish between various offenses such as murder and drunk driving. Offenses vary immensely in terms of an offender's motivation, and any realistic discussion of general deterrence ought to take into account the particular norms and circumstances of each particular type of offense.

He also notes that the threat of punishment, although directed to all persons, affects individuals in different ways (Andenaes 1972: 346). For example, in his view, the law-abiding citizen does not need the threat of the law to remain law-abiding. On the other hand, the criminal group may well fear the law but still break it, and the potential criminal might have broken the law if it had not been for the threat of punishment. It follows that the threat of punishment seems relevant only to the potential criminal. In some cases, however, there is evidence that punishment has a deterrent effect on individuals. Andenaes refers to a study of department store shoplifting, where amateur shoplifters were treated as thieves by the store management and reacted by changing their attitudes and experiencing great emotional disturbance (p. 343). This contrasts with the professional shoplifter, who does not register any shock at getting caught and accepts jail as a normal hazard of the trade.

Gordon Tullock (1974: 109), after surveying the economic and sociological models of deterrence, concludes that multiple regression studies show empirically that increasing the frequency or severity of punishment does reduce the likelihood of a given crime being committed. However, Alfred Blumstein, Jaqueline Cohen, and Daniel Nagin (1978: 66) contend that although the evidence does establish a negative association between crime rates and sanctions, this does not necessarily establish the general deterrent effect of sanctions. This is because, in their view, the negative association can be explained by lower sanctions being the effect and not the cause of higher crime rates. Overall, there seems to be little agreement among researchers that punishment has a general deterrent effect.

How Much Punishment Must Be Imposed to Deter?

For the utilitarian who regards punishment as bad in itself, a particular punishment will be justified only if the suffering it inflicts is less than the harm caused by the criminal act that would have taken place had there been no punishment. If various forms of punishment would achieve the same result, a utilitarian will opt for the most lenient punishment that minimizes the potential suffering. It follows that if a sentence of capital punishment and the lesser punishment of a term of imprisonment are both equally effective in deterring murder, the utilitarian will choose the lesser punishment and regard capital punishment as unjustified. However, utilitarian approaches can result in the infliction of excessive punishment. C. L. Ten (1987: 143) gives the example of petty thefts being widespread in society, with hundreds of cases occurring, frequently perpetrated by efficient thieves who are difficult to catch. The harm caused by each individual theft is minor, but the total harm, according to utilitarian approaches, is great and therefore may be greater than the harm caused by severely punishing one minor criminal. If a newly enacted law were to impose a punishment of 10 years' imprisonment on a petty thief and no less a penalty would have a deterrent effect, it is arguable that a utilitarian would have to accept what would be considered an excessive sentence for the one petty thief unlucky enough to be arrested and convicted (pp. 143–144).

Retribution

Retribution is the theory that punishment is justified because it is deserved. Retribution does not concern itself with public goods or with the safety or security of society or the moral improvement of the criminal. Rather, retributivism justifies punishment on the basis that a person who knowingly breaks the law deserves to be punished. Systems of retribution for crime have long existed, with the best known being the *lex talionis* of biblical times, calling for "an eye for an eye, a tooth for a tooth, and a life for a life" (Hudson 1996: 38). Retributionists claim a moral link between punishment and guilt and see punishment as a question of responsibility or accountability (Bean 1981: 14–15). Once society has decided on a set of legal rules, the retributivist sees those rules as representing and reflecting the moral order. Society's acceptance of legal rules means that the retributivist accepts the rules, whatever they may be; accepts that the rule makers are justified in their rule making; and claims that those who make the rules provide the moral climate under which others must live. Accordingly, retributivists cannot question the legitimacy of rules. They argue that retribution operates on a consensus model of society where the community, acting through a legal system of rules, acts "rightly," and the criminal acts "wrongly" (p. 17). It follows that the retributivist position makes no allowance for social change or social conditions, looking instead only to crime. Raising the issue of the social causes of crime and questioning the effectiveness of punishment are irrelevant considerations to a retributivist.

Retributivism looks backward because it punishes persons for wrongful acts they have performed. Thus, retributivists are not concerned about the consequences of a wrongful act or about what might happen in the future (Brooks 2012: 16).

"An Eye for an Eye"

Ernest van den Haag (1975) and John Kleinig (1973) have suggested that in historical terms the lex talionis did not operate as a demand for retribution. Instead, it set a limit on the nature of that retribution and therefore prevented the imposition of excessive penalties in the course of acts of vengeance. Capital punishment may be the only form of punishment still supported by appeals to the lex talionis. The basic principle of lex talionis is that punishment should inflict the same on offenders as offenders have inflicted on their victims. It, therefore, can be seen as a crude formula because there are many crimes to which it cannot be applied. For instance, what punishment ought to be inflicted on a rapist under lex talionis? Should the state arrange for the rape of the offender as his due punishment? In addition, the lex talionis can be objected to because its formula to determine the correct punishment considers solely the harm caused by the crime and makes no allowance for the mental state of the offender or for any mitigating or aggravating circumstances associated with the crime. Thus, even though a person's death may have been brought about accidentally or negligently, the lex talionis, strictly applied, would still call for the imposition of the death penalty (Ten 1987: 152). However, Kramer (2011: 77) argues that the lex talionis is qualitative rather than quantitative in nature and therefore does not call for a punishment of matching severity to the crime but for "a punitive response that partakes of cognate features."

A further objection is found in the view that in a civilized society certain forms of punishment are considered too cruel to be defended as valid and appropriate. For example, a sadistic murderer may horribly torture his or her victim, but society would condemn the imposition of that same form of punishment on the offender. It can also be said that although the death penalty may constitute a just punishment according to the rule of lex talionis, it should nevertheless be abolished as part of "the civilizing mission of modern states" (Reiman 1985: 115).

Retributivists believe that wrongdoers deserve to be punished and that the punishment imposed should be in proportion to the wrongdoing the offender committed. In contrast to utilitarians, retributivists focus their line of reasoning on the offender's just desert (a proportionate punishment) and not on the beneficial consequences of punishment. Retributivists ask questions such as "Why do offenders deserve to be punished?" and "How are their just deserts to be calculated and translated into actual sentences?"

Justifying Retribution

A number of explanations have been suggested to justify retribution, including the notion that retribution is a payment of what is owed—that is, offenders who are punished are "paying their debt to society" (Walker 1991: 73). Walker notes that this seems to confuse "the victim" with "society" because we generally do not perceive offenders as liable to pay compensation or make restitution to their victims; furthermore, if society is compensated for anything at all, it is for a breach of its peace.

Censure is also an important component in retributivist thinking. For example, Andrew von Hirsch (in Walker 1991), the leading theorist on just deserts sentencing, writes,

> Desert and punishment can rest on a much simpler idea, used in everyday discourse: the idea of censure. . . . Punishment connotes censure. Penalties should comport with the seriousness of crimes so that the reprobation on the offender through his penalty fairly reflects the blameworthiness of his conduct. (p. 78)

For von Hirsch (1994: 120–121), censure is simply holding individuals accountable for their conduct and involves conveying the message to perpetrators that they have willfully injured someone and must face the disapproval of society for that reason. On the part of the offender, an expression of concern or remorse is expected. As well, the censure expressed through criminal law has the role of providing third parties with reasons for not committing acts defined as criminal. In other words, censure can have a deterrent effect. It may also express retributive and even rehabilitative goals (Brooks 2012: 101). Some theorists of desert argue that notions of censure cannot be adequately expressed verbally or symbolically and that hard treatment is needed to properly express societal disapproval.

Some retributivists argue that punishment is morally justified because it gives satisfaction. James Fitzjames Stephen, an English Victorian judge, is often cited as an advocate of this theory. He expressed his view of punishment as follows (in Bean 1981):

> I think it highly desirable that criminals should be hated, and that punishments inflicted upon them should be so contrived as to give expression to that hatred, and to justify it so far as the public provisions of means for expressing and gratifying a healthy, natural sentiment can justify and encourage it. (p. 21)

This conception of the purpose of punishment became known as **denunciation theory.** Another English Judge of more recent times, Lord Denning, echoed Stephen saying that "the ultimate justification of any punishment is not that it is a deterrent but that it is the emphatic denunciation by the community of a crime" (quoted in Wood 2010a: 473). While those who adopted denunciation theory did little to analyze its elements, expression theorists have focused on the values and emotion expressed through punishment with the aim of identifying retributive responses and showing that such responses were not simply expressions of vengeance (p. 474). The notion of the expressive or communicative character of punishment is closely associated with the idea of "punishment as censure." This conception recognizes punishment as comprising not merely harsh treatment but also elements of condemnation, denunciation, and censure. Thus, for example, punishment in the form of a fine is quite different from the payment of a tax, although both involve payment to the state. In the same vein, imprisonment contrasts with other forms of detention such as quarantine or detention for psychiatric disorders (Duff and Garland 1994: 13–14). Imprisonment, it is argued, carries with it an expressive function of censure, whereas detention for reasons of quarantine or for mental disorder does not. Joel Feinberg (1994: 74) explains the expressive function of punishment in the following terms:

> Punishment is a conventional device for the expression of attitudes of resentment and indignation, and of judgments of disapproval and reprobation, on the part either of the punishing authority himself or of those "in whose name" the punishment is inflicted. Punishment, in short, has a symbolic significance largely missing from other kinds of penalties.

Feinberg (1994: 76) further argues that punishment expresses more than disapproval; it amounts to a symbolic method of hitting back at the criminal and of expressing "vindictive resentment." In similar fashion, Herbert Morris (1994: 92) contends that punishment serves to teach offenders a moral lesson so that in the process of being punished and being made aware that a crime violated communal values, they will come to see what is good and choose it in the future. According to this account, the aim of punishment is to persuade and not to manipulate or coerce. However, as Morris himself points out, this approach does not account for the punishment of those who are already repentant, nor is it able to cope with those who understand the values of society but are indifferent or opposed to them (p. 106). Philosophers such as Duff (in Walker 1991: 79) see the main benefit of punishment as the effect on the offender. They argue that punishment has the effect of restoring the offender to the community in the same way that penance restores a penitent to the communion of the church. Robert Nozick sees retributive punishment as a message from those whose values are assumed to be correct and normative to someone whose act or omission has displayed incorrect and non-normative values (in Walker 1991: 81). For Nozick then, the purpose of punishment is reconnecting the offender with the correct values (Konigs 2013: 1042).

Walker (1991: 81) explains that "man is a rulemaking animal" and that rules and notions of rules are acquired during childhood. Rules, in the form of transactions involving promises, establish codes of normative conduct, including "penalizing rules" that specify action to be taken against those who infringe the rules (Garfinkel in Walker 1991: 84–85). It follows that failing to penalize an offender for infringing the rules would itself be an infringement of those rules; thus, an unpunished infringement would create two infringements. A similar argument is proposed by Hoskins (2011: 53), who sees compliance with rules that institute punishment as a response to crimes as a fair-play obligation arising from reciprocal obligations shared by members of a community.

Jean Hampton contends that when they disregard moral norms offenders are asserting moral superiority over their victims and thereby denying that all persons have equal moral worth. Retribution corrects this by nullifying the alleged inferiority of the victim (Konigs 2013: 1043).

Denouncing criminality, as described earlier, can clearly include conduct by the community that Bennett (2002: 149) refers to as "alienation"—that is, withdrawing from wrongdoers, "cutting them off, no longer treating them as people with whom we share a community." While Bennett claims that this does not mean that an offender has been "cast out" of the community, an alternative view is that in modern times some offenders are perceived by some members of a community not only as cast out but also as less than human and as irredeemably evil.

Dehumanization theory describes this extreme form of denunciation as "animalistic dehumanization," referring to "the denial of attributes that are uniquely human" (Vasiljevic and Viki 2013: 129). Studies have shown that dehumanization depicts offenders as less than human and that in the case of sex offenders, for example, some members of the community are willing to exclude such offenders from a community and support forms of violence against them, including castration and murder (p. 137). This mode of denunciation may be expressive of a desire that a wrongdoer should suffer disproportionate punishment, a stance that is generally morally impermissible (Holroyd 2010: 343) and that perhaps approaches a form of vengeance (p. 345). However, it has also been contended that "retributive hatred" can be morally permissible in the service of defending "certain values of the self," especially self-respect when a person has been victimized by criminal conduct (p. 346).

Punishment as a Communicative Practice

This notion of communicative practice asserts that punishment communicates to the criminal a response appropriate to the crime committed (Duff 1999: 48). The element of communication requires that the person to whom the communication is directed must be an active participant in the process and must receive and respond publicly to the communication. Additionally, the communication should appeal to the person's rational understanding. The communication must be focused primarily on the offender being punished as a response to him or her and must be justified by his or her offenses (p. 50). The message communicated by punishment must focus on and be justified by the offender's past offense and must be appropriate to that offense. R. A. Duff argues that the message communicated should be the degree of censure or condemnation the crime deserves and that communicative punishment aims at reforming offenders (Brooks 2012: 104).

In the context of criminal law, punishment might be communicated in a formal conviction of guilt or through a system of harsh punishments such as imprisonment, fines, or community service. Prison is seen as offering an opportunity for reflection and reformation (Brooks 2012: 104). Duff argues that the aim of hard treatment is ideally to cause offenders to understand and repent crimes committed (1999: 51). It should attempt to direct their attention to the crime and give them an understanding of crime as a "wrong." It must be painful or a burden to the offender and should take some time to accomplish. Offenders should also accept that punishment is deserved, and penance—not merely an apology—is expected of the offender. By undergoing hard punishment, offenders can become reconciled with the community and restored back into the community from which the offense caused them to be excluded. Thus, "time served is a concrete act communicating apologies through repentance" (Brooks 2012: 105).

One problem with communicative theory is the unrepentant offender. If repentance is a goal, does this mean that an unrepentant criminal should remain incarcerated until he or she shows true and actual repentance? Duff contends that the attempt to bring about repentance by the end of the sentence is not pointless, even where there is no repentance, because while we are justified in punishing the offender, it is the offender who must decide whether or not to repent, and she has "gone through the motions" and shown that she was willing to do what was expected (Brooks 2012: 120).

Unfair Advantage

Another theory that attempts to justify punishment as a retributive act is that an offender should be viewed as a person who has taken an unfair advantage of others in society by committing a crime and that imposing punishment restores fairness (Ten 1987: 5). Philosophers such as Herbert Morris, John Finnis, and Jeffrie Murphy subscribe to the **unfair advantage theory**. For example, Morris argues that the effect of criminal law is to confer benefits on society because others are not permitted to interfere with areas of an individual's life, given that certain acts are proscribed and prohibited. To gain the benefits of noninterference, individuals must exercise self-restraint and not engage in acts that infringe the protected areas of the lives of others (in Ten 1987: 53). It follows that when people violate the law but continue to enjoy its benefits they take an unfair advantage of others who follow the law—they are free riders. Punishment, it is argued, is therefore justified because it removes this unfair advantage and restores the balance of benefits and burdens disturbed by the criminal activity. Morris has been criticized for failing to acknowledge that we feel offenders ought to be punished because their wrongdoing is inherently wrong, regardless of any unfair advantage (Konigs 2013: 1043). In other words, free riding fails to capture the wrongs suffered by the victim. As Boonin (2008: 123) notes, most people do not wish to molest a child, for example, and there is therefore no cost to them in refraining from doing that. Because they bear no burden by refraining, the offender who molests does not in fact enjoy any unfair advantage over them. Thus, people have no burden in not doing acts prohibited by law that they lack the capacity to perform—for example, hacking into a government computer. The end result is that the unfair advantage theory of retribution does not justify punishment, even when the law is broken.

The unfair advantage argument has also been challenged by those who argue that it distorts the nature of crime itself. For example, the wrongfulness of rape does not merely consist of taking an unfair advantage of those who obey the law. Also, it is difficult to show that offenders have in any real sense "willed" their own punishment (Murphy 1994: 44). Additionally, although unfair advantage might constitute an ideal theory for the justification of punishment, the question arises about whether it can be applied to an actual society. In other words, do those who commit criminal acts actually take an unfair advantage for themselves?

Finally, relating the previous discussion to the harshest form of treatment, it should be noted that in 1972 and 1976 the U.S. Supreme Court stated that it considered retribution "a legitimate justification for capital punishment" (*Furman v. Georgia* 1972; *Gregg v. Georgia* 1976).

Is Retribution, in Fact, Revenge?

Retributive theories of punishment argue that punishment should be imposed for past crimes and that it should be appropriate to the nature of the crime committed; that is, the severity of the punishment should be commensurate with the seriousness of the crime. Sometimes, retributive punishment is confused with notions of revenge. Critics of retributionist theories of punishment argue that retribution is basically nothing more than vengeance. However, Nozick (1981) argues that there is a clear distinction between the two because "retribution is done for a wrong, while revenge may be done for an injury or harm or slight and need not be a wrong" (p. 366). He also points out that whereas retribution sets a limit for the amount of punishment according to the seriousness of the wrong, no limit need be set for revenge. In this sense, therefore, revenge is personal, whereas the person dispensing retributive punishment may well have no personal tie to the victim. As Nozick points out, "Revenge involves a particular emotional tone, pleasure in the suffering of another" (p. 367). A further distinction between the two is that retribution in the form of punishment is inflicted only on the offender, but revenge may be carried out on an innocent person, perhaps a relative of the perpetrator.

Just Deserts

Up until about 1970, criminologists generally thought of retribution as vengeance. During the 1970s, criminologists reconsidered the idea of retribution and advanced new formulations. By the 1980s, the new *retributionist theory of just deserts* had become influential (Hudson 1996: 39). Fundamentally, the concept of desert conveys the idea that punishment for violating the law is morally permissible because offenders deserve to be punished. This reflects the general feeling that criminals deserve to be punished. Importantly, the new thinking indicated that although there should continue to be treatment programs a defendant would not ordinarily be incarcerated to receive treatment (Morris 1974). Influential writings such as *Struggle for Justice* (American Friends Service Committee 1971) and *Doing Justice* (von Hirsch and Committee for the Study of Incarceration 1976), the latter written in the aftermath of the riot at Attica Prison in 1971, elaborated on the new retributivism in philosophical and civil libertarian terms.

This theory gained support as a reaction against the perceived unfairness of systems that favored treatment, which had developed over the first half of the 20th century, especially the use of the indeterminate sentence. This form of sentence vested the power of determining the date of release to a parole board and signifies the practice of individualized sentencing. The intent was to sentence according to the treatment needs of the offender rather than the seriousness of the offense (Duff and Garland 1994: 12). One of the criticisms of indeterminate sentencing was the fact that the sentencing courts had a wide discretion in choosing a sentence, and although they tended to adopt tariffs for classes of crime, individual judges could depart from them without providing reasons. Along with the just deserts movement, many states and federal sentencing authorities repealed indeterminate sentencing laws, with the aim of reducing judicial discretion in sentencing and promoting consistency and certainty, as well as a set of standards that would help in the process of deciding the sentence.

Among the retributivists, Immanuel Kant argued that the aim of penalties must be to inflict desert and that this was a "categorical imperative" (Kant's categorical imperative is discussed as an aspect of deontology in Chapter 12). By this, he meant that inflicting what was deserved rendered all other considerations irrelevant (Walker 1991: 53). Kant wrote that "whatever undeserved evil you inflict upon another within the people, you inflict upon yourself . . . if you kill him, you kill yourself" (quoted in Brooks 2012: 27). Thus, Kant argued in favor of strict equality between the wrongdoing and the punishment. One problem with strict equality is that it sanctions very harsh punishments despite differences in character between a crime and what can constitute a punishment for that crime. For example, rape is a crime but not a punishment, and no one argues that prisoners should be raped (p. 27). Moreover, strict equality is inconsistent with the criminal justice practice of plea bargaining in which an accused admits guilt to a lesser offense and receives a more lenient punishment than would otherwise be "deserved" (p. 28).

Just deserts proponents emphasize the notion that **punishment should be proportionate**; that is, there should be a scale of punishments with the most serious being reserved for the most serious offenses, and penalties should be assessed according to the seriousness of the offense (Hudson 1996: 40).

This is often called *tariff sentencing*. In this method of punishing, the offender's potential to commit future offenses does not come into consideration, but his or her previous convictions are taken into account because most proponents of just deserts support reductions in sentences for first offenders. Desert theorists contend that punishment should convey blame for wrongdoing and that blame is attached to offenders because they have done wrong. Consequently, the blameworthiness of the offender is reflected in the punishment imposed.

Thus, advocates of desert focus on two dimensions only—the harm involved in the offense and the offender's culpability. Von Hirsch (1998: 669) enlarges on these two main elements, stating that, in looking at the degree of harm, a broad notion of the quality of life is useful because "invasions of different interests can be compared according to the extent to which they typically affect a person's standard of living" (p. 670). As to culpability, he suggests that the substantive criminal law, which already distinguishes intentional from reckless or negligent conduct, would be useful in sentencing law.

Von Hirsch (1998: 667) argues that a focus on the censuring aspect of punishment has coincided with a change in criminological thinking. Criminologists had previously regarded the blaming aspects of punishment as a stigmatizing label that might create obstacles to the reintegration of the offender into the community and might also cause offenders to reinforce their own deviance, making them more likely to continue offending. Desert theorists now emphasize that responding to criminal acts with a process of blaming encourages the individual to recognize the wrongfulness of the action, to feel remorse, and to make efforts to refrain from such conduct in the future. In contrast, a deterrent punishment requires the individual to simply comply or face the consequences. The difference between the two approaches is that a moral judgment is required from the offender under just deserts that is not required under a purely deterrent punishment.

Issues associated with the concept of desert include the situation of a person who breaks the law but does not deserve to be punished. Boonin (2008: 99) gives the example of a husband who makes himself fully familiar with laws concerning spousal abuse and does all that he can to injure his spouse but without acting in violation of the law—for example, he screams at her, cheats on her, and in any legal way degrades, insults, and embarrasses her. He remains legally innocent, but our intuition tells us he should suffer. It is argued that desert-based retributivism would make it morally permissible for him to be punished even though he has broken no laws. Another example might be a racist who does everything legally possible to insult black people, such as playing racist songs and celebrating publicly when many black people suffer death in a natural disaster. Again, the racist remains innocent, and again, our intuition says he should be punished for his acts. As well, just as there are law breakers who do not deserve punishment, there are people who do not break the law but nevertheless do deserve to suffer punishment. Boonin (p. 101) offers the example of a woman who tells Nazi authorities that they have overlooked a Jew who is hiding from them. We would likely think that she should suffer punishment for her act, but she has broken no law.

During the 1980s, many states, as well as the Federal Sentencing Commission, introduced desert-based sentencing schemes (Hudson 1996: 43).

Ranking Crimes for Seriousness

In considering questions of proportionality and seriousness, the issue arises as to how offenses are to be ranked in terms of their seriousness. Who is to determine the degrees of seriousness? In some jurisdictions, the judge's views determine the issue; other approaches include the use of sentencing commissions and legislating sentencing schedules. In California, the Determinant Sentencing Laws allow politicians and others to raise the tariffs for offenses in response to public or media pressure to give effect to "get tough on crime" policies (Zimring 1976, 1994).

Some critics argue that just deserts theory leads to harsher penalties, but von Hirsch (1998: 672) contends that the theory itself does not call for harsher penalties and that sentencing schemes relying specifically on just deserts theory tend not to be severe. He draws attention to sentencing guidelines in Minnesota and Oregon that provide for modest penalties by U.S. standards. The Minnesota

sentencing guidelines provide a grid with a horizontal axis showing previous convictions and a vertical axis showing offense type (Hudson 1996: 44). The sentencing judge is required to locate the appropriate cell on the grid for the offender being sentenced, where the severity of the offense and the number of previous convictions intersect. Each cell stipulates a presumptive prison term that represents the normal period of incarceration for a standard case of that offense. In addition to the presumptive sentence, there is a band indicating the range that should apply in the actual case. For example, in the case of an aggravated burglary, when the offender has three previous convictions, there is a presumptive term of 49 months and a range of 45 to 53 months. The actual sentence depends on aggravating and mitigating factors. According to Barbara Hudson (p. 45), sentencing guidelines have had the effect of reinforcing relatively lenient punishments in states with that tradition, although states with a history of imposing severe punishments, such as New Mexico and Indiana, have produced severe schedules and guidelines.

Criticisms of Desert

The fundamental difficulty with deserts theory is that it lacks any principle that determines a properly commensurate sentence (Hudson 1996: 46). Deserts are determined by a scale of punishment that fixes the most severe penalty. This might be imprisonment or death. It then determines ordinally proportionate penalties for lesser offenses. It follows that if imprisonment is the most severe penalty, then proportionality will provide shorter terms of imprisonment and noncustodial penalties for lesser offenses. If the term of imprisonment for severe offenses is moderate, then short sentences and penalties such as probation will soon be reached when considering proportionate sentencing options on the scale of seriousness. If the penalty for the most serious offenses is death, it follows that long terms of imprisonment will be considered proportionate penalties for less serious offenses. This is the situation that prevails in many states.

Many argue that retribution based on just deserts fails to account for the problem of just deserts in an unjust world. Just deserts theory ignores social factors such as poverty, disadvantage, and discrimination and presumes equal opportunity for all. Michael Tonry (1994: 153) notes that most sentencing commissions in the United States will not allow judges to bring personal circumstances into account in their sentencing decisions, despite the fact that the average offender has a background that is likely to be either deeply disadvantaged or deprived. Franklin Zimring (1994: 165) suggests that desert sentencing fails to take account of the fact that there are multiple discretions involved in the sentencing power. He points to the legislature that sets the range of sentences, the prosecutor who has the legal authority to select a charge, the judge as the sentencing authority, and the correctional authority, which is able to modify sentences after incarceration, as constituting a multiplicity of decisions and discretions that make the task of achieving just and proportionate sentences extremely problematic. Given that prosecutors and legislators act under political influence and attempt to implement policies that reflect public opinion, the sentencing process is not the monopoly of the trial judge but is all too often an expression of varying perspectives based on periodic concerns about whether current philosophies reflect notions of being "tough on crime."

Reconciling Utilitarian and Retributive Theories

Is it possible to reconcile utilitarian and retributive theories of punishment? For utilitarians, desert is not seen as necessary to justify punishment or as a reason for punishment because desert does not look to the consequences of punishment—it simply punishes. For the utilitarian, the only good reasons for punishment relate to the consequences of that punishment. The contrast between the two theories lies in the fact that for utilitarians, the aim of punishment is to control future action, whereas the retributivists see the aim in terms of desert (Bean 1981: 32). The strength of the utilitarian argument is that rules can be changed according to changes in society but that no such change is built into theories of retribution.

Can a retributivist ever be forgiving or merciful? During the sentencing process, offenders often say they are remorseful for their actions, and in this sense, remorse represents regret and self-blame.

Those charged with the task of determining the sentence are urged to accept statements of remorse as mitigating factors. The issue, therefore, is whether genuine remorse should lead a sentencer toward leniency. If the sentencer is a utilitarian, he or she will be concerned only about whether a remorseful offender will be less likely to reoffend. However, for the retributivist, the question is whether remorse should mitigate culpability (Walker 1991: 112). According to Walker, forgiveness has no degrees but may take the form of "interested" or "disinterested" forgiveness, with the victim being interested and the sentencing authority disinterested. He suggests that the sentencing authority, whether working from a utilitarian or retributivist viewpoint, must choose the sentence that is most appropriate and that a retributivist may take extenuating circumstances into account. He considers, however, that forgiveness, being an act of absolution, should not be considered an extenuating circumstance (p. 113). Thus, according to Bean (1981), "Forgiveness is a moral sentiment where ill-will is no longer retained. It may occur before or after punishment but does not affect it" (p. 99). Murphy (2012: xiv) argues that emotions are "easy to fake" and that permitting reduced sentences for expressions of remorse simply provides an incentive to fake.

Mercy must be distinguished from forgiveness because granting mercy is an act, but forgiveness is an attitude of mind (Walker 1991: 115). Mercy is also less "personal" than forgiveness since the grantor of mercy, such as a judge, may well not be a victim of wrongdoing (Murphy 2012: 54). Mercy may be prompted by expressions of remorse or by a statement that the victim has forgiven the offender. Walker argues that mercy is not equivalent to "reasoned leniency" and that mercy, in effect, suggests other considerations such as proportionality, any suffering experienced by the offender, and mitigation generally (p. 116). Fundamentally, therefore, mercy is a synonym for various kinds of leniency and has no force or effect of its own.

Nowadays, because there are major objections to both utilitarian and retributive theories of punishment on both moral and empirical grounds, many philosophers opt for hybrid solutions to the problem of punishment (Boonin 2008: 207). One example is that of mixed retributivism, which argues for punishment as an *institution* to be justified on utilitarian grounds whereas its actual *implementation* is to be justified on retributive grounds (Nadelhoffer 2013: xvii).

Another approach is proposed by Steffen (2012: 165), who argues for what he terms an ethically-based framework for *just punishment*. Steffen draws on the work of Michael Tonry, who has written extensively about punishment and proposes a set of criteria that would, if satisfied, constitute just punishment and just sentencing (p. 165). He highlights the need for punishment to restore harmony and for its purpose to be not the infliction of pain, but to meet a demand for justice for those who have "misused freedom" (p. 164). The criteria are as follows:

- The punishment and sentence must be properly authorized.
- The offense must be sufficiently grave that society is aggrieved and the well-being of the community affected adversely.
- The motivation for punishment must be justice, not vengeance.
- Punishments must not be associated with discrimination based on gender, race, religion, or class.
- Punishment must express cherished values and be aimed at restoring peace and harmony and even restitution for injured parties.
- Punishments should not be cruel and should be the least harsh sentence and aim to restore offenders to their rightful place within the moral community.
- Punishment should be a last resort after every effort has been made to restore relations between the offender and the victim through restitution; restorative justice and alternative punishments to incarceration should be considered rather than a focus solely on imprisonment.
- Punishment should restore a "value equilibrium" distorted and disturbed by the wrongdoing.
- Punishment policies should observe the principle of proportionality in a social justice sense and should recognize that not all persons in a society enjoy equal opportunities. The punishment should therefore be capable of mitigation based on social injustice and an offender's personal circumstances.

While acknowledging that the present U.S. criminal justice system does not reflect all these criteria and that the criteria do not give effect to mainstream thinking about punishment, Steffen argues that his proposal is concerned with the morality of the present system, not with its politics, and that public discourse about punishment "is notoriously shallow" and expresses notions about being "tough on crime" that are promoted by candidates for public office (2012: 171) and result in closing off discussion about morality and alternative policies. In other words, Steffen calls for a punishment system that "conforms to a moral vision where thought is reconciled with experience" (p. 172).

Rehabilitation

Retribution and deterrence involve a process of thinking that proceeds from the crime to the punishment. As Brooks explains (2012: 52), "A rehabilitation theory of punishment holds that punishment should aim at the reformation of offenders and assist their transition from criminal to law abiding citizen. Rehabilitation is successful where criminals come to reject crime out of choice." Rehabilitation is a complex notion involving an examination of the offense and the criminal and a concern for the criminal's social background and punishment. Further, those in favor of rehabilitation theories acknowledge the possibility of additional problems developing during the offender's sentence or treatment that may be unconnected with the offense and that may require an offender to spend additional periods in treatment or confinement (Bean 1981: 54).

Utilitarian theory argues that punishment should have reformative or rehabilitative effects on the offender (Ten 1987: 7–8). The offender is considered reformed because the result of punishment is a change in the offender's values so that he or she will refrain from committing further offenses, now believing such conduct to be wrong. Thus, consequentialists argue that if rehabilitation works then we will all be better off. Reforming a person can be distinguished from simply abstaining from criminal acts due to the fear of being caught and punished again; this amounts to deterrence, not reformation or rehabilitation by punishment. The difference between deterrence and rehabilitation is that "deterrence attempts to convince us to avoid crime out of fear of punishment," whereas "rehabilitation attempts to convince us to avoid crime because we should not perform crime" (Brooks 2012: 59).

Deontological theory (see Chapter 12) argues that we should rehabilitate criminals not because we wish to save costs or reduce crime, but because it is just to do so and because each person possesses moral worth (Brooks 2012: 52).

Proponents of rehabilitation in punishment argue that punishment should be tailored to fit the offender and his or her needs, rather than fitting the offense. Underpinning this notion is the view that offenders ought to be rehabilitated or reformed so they will not reoffend and that society ought to provide treatment to an offender. Rehabilitation theory regards crime as the symptom of a social disease and sees the aim of rehabilitation as curing that disease through treatment (Bean 1981: 54). In essence, the rehabilitative philosophy denies any connection between guilt and punishment (p. 58).

Bean (1981: 64) outlines the strengths of the rehabilitation position as being its emphasis on the personal lives of offenders, its treatment of people as individuals, and its capacity to produce new thinking in an otherwise rigid penal system. He suggests its weaknesses include an unwarranted assumption that crime is related to disease and that social experts can diagnose that condition; that treatment programs are open-ended and do not relate to the offense or to other defined criteria; and the fact that the offender, not being seen as fully responsible for his or her actions, is capable of manipulating the treatment to serve his or her own interests. In addition, rehabilitation theory tends to see crime as predetermined by social circumstances rather than as a matter of choice by the offender. This, it is said, denies the agency of the offender and arguably treats an offender in a patronizing, infantilizing way (Hudson 1996: 29).

Indeterminate sentences gave effect to the rehabilitative perspective because terms of imprisonment were not fixed at trial, but rather the release decision was given to institutions and persons operating within the criminal justice system, including parole boards, probation officers, and social workers. The notion of rehabilitation enjoyed considerable political and public support in the first half of the 20th century, but modern rehabilitationists now argue that fixed rather than determinant sentences should be the context for rehabilitation (Hudson 1996: 64). They argue that with indeterminate sentences offenders become preoccupied with their likely release date, and this leads to their pretending to have made more progress in treatment than is really the case.

The demise of rehabilitation as a theory of punishment began in the 1970s and was the result of a complex set of factors, one of which was a much quoted article by Robert Martinson (1974), who was perceived to have argued that "nothing works"—that is, that no treatment program works very successfully in preventing reoffending and that no program works better than any other. Martinson later attempted to rectify this pessimistic view of rehabilitation and treatment by acknowledging that some programs work, sometimes, for some types of offenders. Nevertheless, from that point on, policy makers and legislators abandoned rehabilitation as an objective of punishment. On the issue of indeterminate sentencing, the publication of *Criminal Sentences: Law Without Order* by Marvin Frankel (1972), then a federal judge, which argued that judges exercised "almost wholly unchecked and sweeping authority" in sentencing (p. 5), provided substantial support to the proponents of determinate sentencing. By the 1980s, the retributionist theory of just deserts had become the most influential theory of punishment.

Effective Rehabilitation

The effectiveness of rehabilitation is assessed almost entirely by reference to officially recorded offenses. Thus, "rehabilitative treatments are considered effective when they decrease the proportion of offenders who are rearrested or reconvicted relative to control groups not receiving the treatment" (Lipsey, Landenberger, and Chapman 2004: 214). In a review of themes and outcomes that characterize effective programs of rehabilitation, Lipsey and others (p. 219–220) identify four themes for effectiveness as follows:

1. Programs that target criminal conduct directly or specific causes of criminality, such as cognitive-behavioral programs, as opposed to fear-based or punitive approaches such as boot camps and intensive supervision.
2. Programs that incorporate structure such as training as a primary component. Thus, skill-building and behavioral programs are more successful at reducing recidivism than less structured programs such as those involving counselling, mentoring and restorative processes.

3. Programs that use multiple treatment strategies are more successful than those employing a single mode of addressing criminality.
4. Treatment needs to be extensive enough to be effective. Programs that extend over more than 25 weeks with 5 to 10 contact hours of treatment each week delivered in multiple sessions have been shown the most effective.

Some contend that rehabilitation programs ought to include "the inculcation of moral principles" so that offenders become aware that their crime was a moral as well as a criminal wrongdoing. It is believed that moral education will impart the message that punishment is not so much focused on paying a debt to society as on the need to avoid criminality because it is morally wrong (Brooks 2012: 56). A difficulty with this perspective is that not all crimes are immoral and not all immorality constitutes criminality. One question therefore is how to educate a criminal about the moral wrongfulness of an immoral crime (p. 57).

Day (2011: 353) argues that many rehabilitation programs fail for reasons of incompetency and lack of staff commitment to their principles. He notes that such programs commonly omit "any formal consideration of the ethical underpinnings of antisocial and criminal behavior" and calls for the design of ethical frameworks that would instruct in, for example, the elements of virtue ethics (see Chapter 14). He points also to the lack of empirical assessment of the value of religious programs for offenders despite their widespread use in prison systems throughout the United States (p. 355).

Any program that includes morals education would have to grapple with the difficulty of assessing whether the person has in fact been rehabilitated. The nature and content of the applicable standard of morals in such an assessment would be problematic (Wood 2010b: 462).

Justifications for Rehabilitation

Nowadays, rehabilitationists contend that their rationale for punishment is the only one that combines crime reduction with respect for an offender's rights. According to this view, although capital punishment and long terms of imprisonment may deter and will certainly incapacitate, rehabilitation can be accomplished only if criminals reenter society; consequently, extreme punishments should be ruled out. Edgardo Rotman (1994), for example, argues in favor of a "rights oriented rehabilitation," which accepts the offender's liability to receive punishment but claims a corresponding right on his or her part to "return to society with a better chance of being a useful citizen and staying out of prison" (p. 286). This perspective is often termed **state-obligated rehabilitation** and contends that if the state assumes the right to punish, it should ensure that no more harm is inflicted than was intended when the sentence was pronounced. That is, the intent of the prison sentence is deprivation of liberty and not loss of family ties or employability (Gallo and Ruggiero 1991).

Rotman, for one, argues that a failure to provide rehabilitation amounts to cruel and unusual punishment. Pat Carlen (1994) and Roger Matthews (1989) argue that states are entitled to punish offenders because offenders act out of choice. However, they suggest that the offenders' choices are often limited because of circumstances and social conditions such as poverty and inequality, which might lead people into crime. Therefore, Hudson (1996: 66) claims, the state should recognize that it plays a part in causing crime and should recognize its role in crime prevention by providing rehabilitation to assist offenders in not committing further crime. Offenders, on their part, have a corresponding obligation to take part in rehabilitation programs offered by the state. Nevertheless, even for those offenders who are unwilling to enter rehabilitation programs, rehabilitation may be coerced or pressured in the sense that their decision about whether or not to undertake the program will be influenced by the existence of adverse consequences for nonparticipation—for example, the denial of parole if the program is not completed (Day, Tucker, and Howells 2004: 259). In this view, rehabilitation may be seen as an alternative to punishment rather than as something to be achieved through the means of punishment. As Carlen (1994: 329) contends, a purely punitive approach to sentencing does little to decrease crime and serves only to increase the prison population.

Incapacitation

Penal practice has always tried to estimate the risk that individual offenders might commit crimes in the future and has tried to shape penal controls to prevent such crimes from happening. Through the incapacitative approach, offenders are placed in custody, usually for long periods of time, to protect the public from the chance of future offending (Morris 1994: 238). In utilitarian theory, incapacitation is seen as a good consequence of punishment because when serving their sentences offenders are removed from society and are therefore unable to commit further offenses. This applies regardless of whether offenders are deterred, reformed, or rehabilitated through the punishment they are given. Incapacity may also be present in other forms of punishment, such as parole, in the sense that although offenders are free from incarceration they are placed under supervision, which may restrict their opportunity to commit crime (Ten 1987: 8).

Some criminologists claim that certain offenders commit crimes at very high rates and that applying a policy of selective incapacitation aimed at these "career criminals" will assist with the aims of crime prevention. There are two basic objections to following a policy of incapacitation based on selecting offenders for this kind of punishment. The first is that predicting criminal dangerousness is problematic and will inevitably mean that a number of persons will suffer incapacitation who would not have committed further crimes if left free because, given the inaccuracies of prediction, it is necessary to lock up or incapacitate large numbers of non-dangerous offenders so we can ensure we incapacitate dangerous offenders. In fact, if our goal is to deter as much crime as possible, then the more people we imprison the more crime we deter. Thus, we can deter all crime if we were to imprison just about everyone (Brooks 2012: 37). Second, there is the moral objection that it is wrong in principle to punish offenders based on a prediction of their future conduct; that is, they ought to be punished for what they have done and not for what they *might* do in the future. Herbert Morris (1994: 241) argues that sentences intended to incapacitate an offender ought to be permitted only when there exists reliable information showing a high probability of future offending. Morris suggests that taking account of dangerousness in the future should be considered as statements about an offender's present condition and not as a prediction of future conduct.

Some of the problems inherent in incapacitative sentencing include that it works only if

- we lock up those who would have committed further offenses if they had been left free;
- those we lock up are not immediately replaced by new recruits; or
- the crimes committed after release are not so frequent or serious so as to negate the effects of the crimes prevented through incapacitative sentencing.

Ethical questions that arise from the sentencing rationale of incapacitation include the following (also see Travis 2002):

- Is it ethical to punish persons for crimes not yet committed?
- Is it ethical to base punishment on inaccurate predictions?
- Is it ethical to punish repeat offenders for past crimes they committed and have already been punished for?

The notion of incapacitation is reflected in such punishment policies as three-strikes legislation, mandatory minimum sentences, and truth in sentencing. These polices will be discussed as penal policies in Chapter 9.

RESTORATIVE JUSTICE

John Braithwaite (1998) argues that restorative justice has been "the dominant model of criminal justice throughout most of human history for all the world's peoples" (p. 323) and that it is grounded in traditions from ancient Greek, Arab, and Roman civilizations and in Hindu, Buddhist, and Confucian traditions. Braithwaite emphasizes that restorative justice means restoring victims as well as offenders and the community. In addition to restoring lost property or personal injury, restoration means bringing back a sense of security. He points to the shame and disempowerment suffered by victims of crime. He observes that Western legal systems generally fail to incorporate victims' voices because the justice system often excludes their participation. Restoring harmony based on an acceptance that justice has been done is, in his view, inadequate. Essentially, restorative justice proponents emphasize the need to support both victims and offenders and see social relationships as a rehabilitative vehicle aimed at providing formal and informal social support and control for offenders (Bazemore and Dooley 2001: 117). Rather than separating out the offender as a subject for rehabilitation, restorative justice sees social support and social control of offenders as the means to rehabilitation.

The origins of restorative justice in the United States lie in part in court orders for reparation taking the form of restitution and community service. Since the 1970s, restitution and community service have been employed as sentencing tools in criminal and juvenile courts, and during the 1980s, an expansion occurred in victim–offender mediation programs resulting partly from interest in restitution and community service programs (Bazemore and Schiff 2001: 25). Along with the increased interest in these alternative sanctions, attention to the interests of victims increased during the 1990s, focusing on repair and healing influenced by the "faith community" and feminists (p. 26). Today, numerous programs can be brought under the rubric of restorative justice, but they often remain small-scale experiments and tend to be associated with community approaches to crime control.

In considering the nature of a restorative justice approach to offenders, it is useful to note the three core principles suggested by Dan Van Ness and Karen Heetderks Strong (1997: 8–9):

1. Justice requires the healing of victims, offenders, and communities injured by crime.
2. Victims, offenders, and communities should be permitted to actively involve themselves in the justice process in a timely and substantial manner.
3. Roles and responsibilities of the government should be rethought, and in its promotion of justice, government should be responsible for preserving a just order, and the community should be responsible for establishing peace.

Restorative justice may be considered unique in its emphasis on not just one component of the criminal justice system such as punishment, but as incorporating victims, offenders, and the community in its strategies and designs. It is considered important that all three parties actively participate

in the restorative justice process so that relations among them can be restored. Programs that do not include all three parties are not considered true restorative justice programs because at least one important component of the triangle is absent. Thus, mediation programs that focus on achieving a resolution only between the offender and victim and leave out the community are normally not considered true restorative processes. Probation is a sentence of the formal system and, although a sentence carried out in the community, involves the official system through the supervision of the offender by the probation officer, but does not involve the community in resolving the harm caused by the offense. It leaves out victims in terms of their participation in the process. Even though some probation sentences include an order to pay the victim restitution or compensation for the offense committed, the participation of victims is passive in that their role is only to receive that payment.

In relation to offenders, Gordon Bazemore and M. Dooley (2001: 108) state that there is a normative focus on harm and repair. Repair, in the context of restorative justice, implies a particular form of rehabilitation. However, Bazemore and Dooley concede that there is an absence of theory to explain how the operation of restorative justice is supposed to bring about a change in the offender. Some restorative justice proponents argue that repair in relation to offenders involves a focus on *restoring, strengthening, and building relationships between offenders, victims, and communities* (p. 111), and therefore intervention intended to prevent future crime must focus not only on the offender's obligation to repair harm done to victims and the community but also on the need to repair broken relationships between the offender and the community, the victim and the community, and the victim and the offender.

Critics of restorative justice point to its too-ready assumption that it will be possible to secure agreement between offenders, victims, and communities. Garland (in Hudson 1996: 150) notes that one of the functions of punishment is to relieve the feelings of victims and communities where crimes are committed and that restorative justice avoids the ceremonies and rituals of criminal law that recognize these emotions. In addition, it can be argued that a greater reliance on restorative justice and a consequent restriction on the operation and expression of criminal law might lead to a situation in which those victims processed through restorative justice might come to believe or feel that the harm they have suffered is of less importance than "real crime." Feminists, who have argued for severe sentencing for domestic violence as well as for sexual offenses, have adopted this argument (Daly and Stubbs 2007). Criminalization and punishment show the limits of tolerance, and depenalizing through restorative justice processes tends to suggest that society has a different attitude toward certain kinds of behavior (pp. 158–159; Hudson 1996: 151). Von Hirsch (1998: 674–675), in his investigation into the basis for restorative justice, contends that no clear principles have been formulated for restoring the harm done by offenders to community standards, and unlike victim restitution, which involves a task of mediation between the victim and the offender, there are no disputed claims involved in crime because, for example, a robber appropriates something that is clearly the property of the victim. Maria R. Volpe (1991) has warned of the propensity of restorative justice to widen the net of social control.

If the rationale of restorative justice is to repair relations between victim, offender, and the community, the question arises, should restorative justice be seen as "alternative punishment" or "alternatives to punishment"? R. A. Duff (1992) argues that restorative justice should be perceived as an alternative punishment and advocates developing alternative modes of punishment. In practice, restorative justice responses to crime incorporate forms of punishment; for example, the process of acknowledging the harm done to the victim and performing measures of reparation is intended to cause pain and be a burden to the offender. Thus, it can be argued that retribution is an element of the restorative justice process (Lokanan 2009: 299). However, restorative justice proponents generally reject the punishment paradigm, arguing that retribution is oppressive and divisive. Public acceptance of restorative justice processes may well depend on a perception that it contains retributive elements, and some commentators have suggested this be made more explicit by incorporating a custodial regime called *restorative detention* (p. 302). They envisage that an offender would undergo therapy, counseling, or training during the time in custody in a restorative prison, which provides a therapeutic regime that permits all stakeholders to be involved in the punishment process.

WHY PUNISH? THE SOCIOLOGICAL APPROACH

In sociological terms, punishment raises questions such as why particular punishments were used and why they are no longer used, why a punishment like capital punishment has been abandoned to a great extent in the West, and why imprisonment has become the major form of punishment for criminal activity.

In social terms, research has concluded that punishments depend less on philosophical arguments and more on the currents and movements in social thinking and in climates of tolerance and intolerance. A focus on history and changes in social conditions has illuminated the relationship between punishment and society, which in turn has broadened the investigation of the notion of punishment into questions concerned with how order and authority are maintained in society. Garland summarizes social theory about punishment as "that body of thought which explores the relations between punishment and society, its purpose being to understand punishment as a social phenomenon and thus trace its role in social life" (1990: 10).

Garland (1990) has argued that punishment is the product of social structure and cultural values. Thus, whom we choose to punish, how we punish, and when we punish are determined by the role we give to punishment in society. If we construe criminal punishment as a wrong for a wrong, then we must conclude that society is, in a sense, wronging the offender. We must therefore ask, "Can the infliction of pain or a wrong upon an offender be justified ethically?" To answer this question, one must first look at the purpose of criminal punishment and question the various rationales put forward for punishment, such as deterrence, incapacitation, rehabilitation, just deserts, retribution, and restorative justice.

Sociological perspectives on punishment include the thinking of Émile Durkheim, Max Weber, the Marxist tradition, and post-Marxist sociologies of punishment, particularly that propounded by

Michel Foucault. Sociologists expand the notion of punishment to penalty, which they explore in various societies at various times. Hudson (1996) defines *penality* as

> the complex of ideas (about proper punishment, about effective punishment), institutions (laws, policies and practices, agencies and buildings) and relationships (who has the power to say who is punished, whose ideas count, what is the relationship of those who punish and are punished to the rest of society) involved in the punishment of offenders. (p. 6)

Only a broad outline of the various perspectives on penality will be provided here.

According to Durkheim, society has an objective reality apart from the individuals who compose it, and he argues that people behave according to social rules that, together with customs and traditions, form a culture for a particular society (in Hudson 1996: 81–86). Durkheim took a functionalist approach; that is, he examined aspects of social life in terms of the functions they performed in society. He applied this approach to punishment by looking at the functions that punishment fulfills in maintaining social order. Durkheim identified beliefs and sentiments held by members of society, which he called the "conscience collective," and argued that crimes are those acts that violate that conscience collective and produce a punitive reaction (in Garland 1990: 29).

He developed two laws of penal evolution. The first is that punishment is more intense the less developed a society is and the more the central power within that society is of an absolute nature. Thus, in industrial societies, collective sentiments are embodied in law rather than in religion, so crimes are seen as wrongs against individuals. He tried to demonstrate that penalties changed from ancient societies to his time, from aggravated penalties such as death with torture and mutilation to reduced forms of punishment. In his second law, he developed the notion of punishments having lesser intensity, arguing that imprisonment will become the main punishment replacing death and torture.

Overall, Durkheim saw the function of punishment as promoting social solidarity through the affirmation of values, and he argued that punishment's importance lies in its expression of outrage on the commission of an offense. He believed punishment to be a "passionate reaction" to crime, and this expressive view of punishment can be seen in modern-day notions of censure in retributivism. His focus was not, therefore, on whether punishment was effective in controlling crime but in its function as a means of maintaining social solidarity through expressions of outrage and through the affirmation of societal values. Among critics of Durkheim, Garland (1990) suggests that Durkheim's analysis of punishment is focused too strongly on punishment's expressive function, causing all other explanations to be discarded. Nevertheless, Garland points out that Durkheim's insight into the role of punishment—as one of expressing community outrage against criminal acts—does single out one aspect of punishment that seems to resonate in the context of today's debates about "getting tough on crime" (p. 252). In similar fashion, George Herbert Mead, in *The Psychology of Punitive Justice*, contends that the indignation that members of society feel toward the criminal amounts to a cultural sublimation of the instincts and hostilities that the individual has tamed in the interest of social cooperation with others (in Garland 1990: 64).

Weber's ideas on punishment are implied rather than made explicit in his notions about authority and power in modern society. Having identified three types of authority, the traditional, the charismatic, and the legal, Weber promoted legal authority—the process of making rules by those given the right to rule—as being the most appropriate form of rule for modern societies. For Weber, legal authority carries with it a duty to obey laws. He argued that systems of laws might be rational or irrational; in a rational system of criminal law, crimes would be defined and rules put forward for adjudicating those crimes. He favored formal rationality, which he termed *bureaucratic rationality*, and saw this as an essential feature of a modern state. His notion of bureaucratic rationality appears in certain features of modern society, such as our processes for making judgments according to rules and the way in which officeholders exercise authority. Developments such as a professional police force and a judiciary as well as due process can be traced to the bureaucratization of society.

Marxist perspectives on punishment evolve out of Marx's concern for the place of capitalism and the relations between production and society. In his view, institutions such as law are shaped to parallel the relations of production and the maintenance of the capitalist system. Marxist penologists have argued that punishment regulates the supply of labor; this view was put forward in 1939 by Georg Rusche and Otto Kirchheimer in *Punishment and Social Structure* (in Howe 1994: 12). In discussing the history of punishment in Europe from the 13th century until the development of capitalism, the authors perceive the severity of punishment as being tied directly to the value of labor. Thus, the severity of punishment, they argue, is relatively lenient when labor is scarce and its value high, whereas when labor is abundant, punishments become more intense.

Another key aspect of their view is the principle of *less eligibility* (Howe 1994: 12). The argument is that the conditions offenders will experience in prison must be worse than anything they are likely to endure outside the prison to restrain the "reserve army of labor" from crime—that is, to serve as a deterrent to the lowest social classes. The idea of less eligibility encompasses matters such as discipline, diet, accommodation, and general living conditions in prisons. Rusche argued that this principle limited penal reform because punishments and prison conditions could not be improved beyond a point that would bring the offender into line with the standard of life of the least advantaged nonoffender (p. 20). This analysis has been criticized for its economic reductionism (it offers only an economic argument to explain changes in punishment). Nevertheless, it has led to a series of studies that have tested the basic framework and found some correlation between punishment and the labor market in the United States over time. The important point is that the authors, together with other Marxists, have provided the insight that all punishment cannot be understood simply as a response to crime. In other words, when changes in the use of imprisonment and other punishments are examined in historical contexts, other factors appear to have influenced their development.

Other Marxist theorists like Dario Melossi and Evgeny Pashukanis have asked why imprisonment persists as opposed to other forms of punishment. One answer from Pashukanis is that there is a correspondence between the development of wage labor, which puts a price on time, and paying for crime by "doing time." In this sense, Marxist theory concerning the relations of production is found mirrored in the punishment of imprisonment, and Marxists therefore argue that a crucial principle in society is the exchange of equivalence. Punishment, therefore, becomes an exchange transaction in which the offender pays his debt, an expression commonly used today both in that form and in the notion of "paying a debt to society" (Garland 1990: 113). Feminists have heavily criticized Marxist analysis of society generally for ignoring gender and for outmoded interpretative frameworks (Howe 1994: 41).

In 1977, Foucault published *Discipline and Punish: The Birth of the Prison*, revolutionizing the study of penality and punishment by presenting the notion of penality and highlighting *discipline* as the key element in modern forms of punishment. In his complex exploration of penality, Foucault follows an approach that examines the issue from the ground up through a detailed examination of penal practices. His central focus is the *exercise of power* in modern society and its linkages with knowledge to exercise power of and over the body. Describing first the effect and content of the public execution, Foucault shows how the infliction of pain on the body gave way to an exercise of power through the new practice of disciplining the individual through institutions such as the factory and the modern prison and how this led to the development of a class of "delinquents." Foucault claims that disciplinary regulation is the fundamental principle of social control in modern society and is most fully realized in the form of the prison.

Foucault (1977) emphasizes the role of punishment in producing the "right-thinking citizen"— that is, the trained and disciplined individual (Hudson 1996: 7). He draws on both Weber (in his emphasis on bureaucratization) and Durkheim (in his description of punishment as an expressive force) in his account of penality. However, he adopts a much broader analytic framework that links punishment and penality and connects them directly to changes in society and to the exercise of power over the individual. Foucault's ideas have inspired many followers, including Garland who, in *Punishment and Modern Society* (1990), argues that a full understanding of punishment and penality should incorporate the theoretical insights of all the writers discussed in this section, together with those of Norbert Elias and his notion that the West has undergone a "civilizing process" that has sensitized society against harsh punishment. Importantly, Garland has drawn attention to the need to consider punishment not simply as the consequence of a criminal act, but as a "complex social institution" requiring us to think beyond simply crime control. Punishment, he argues, should be viewed as a social institution, and its social role and significance can be properly understood only through developing the insights of social theorists.

SUMMARY

The morality of punishment rests on theories of deterrence, retribution, just deserts, rehabilitation, incapacitation, and most recently, restorative justice. These theories attempt to justify society's imposition of punishment on offenders and try to provide an adequate ethical rationale for inflicting harm.

Deterrence maintains that people are deterred from crime because they are concerned about the possible consequences of their actions. Utilitarian philosophers first put forward this justification for punishment. A number of studies have considered the effectiveness of deterrence as a theory, but there is no clear conclusion about whether deterrence works.

Retribution theorists argue that punishment is justified because it is deserved, and punishment therefore becomes a question of responsibility and accountability for acts that harm society. In retribution theory, the punishment imposed should be proportionate to the wrongdoing. Retribution is justified in a number of ways, including the notion that offenders are paying their debt to society, that they are being censured by society, and that punishment has an expressive character that ought to be communicated to an offender.

The emergence of just deserts theory in the 1980s put an end to indeterminate sentencing and introduced sentencing guidelines and sentencing commissions as attempts were made to fix proportionate sentences. Just deserts theory lacks any principle that determines how to constitute a properly commensurate sentence, and it ignores social factors as well as the multiple decisions and discretions that go into the sentencing decision.

Rehabilitation shows a concern for an offender's social background and regards crime as the outcome of a social disease that should be cured through treatment. In the past, indeterminate sentences supported rehabilitation programs because the release decision was given over to boards and not determined by the court. The idea that "nothing works" brought about the demise of rehabilitation, which had been the dominant rationale for punishment until the 1970s. It has now been displaced by just deserts and incapacitation.

According to incapacitation theorists, placing offenders in custody for lengthy periods of time protects the public from the chance of future offending, but this means that offenders are being punished based on a prediction of what they might do in the future. It raises the question of whether it is ethical to punish persons for crimes they have yet to commit.

Restorative justice is a newcomer to the field of penal theory, and some suggest that it lacks theoretical support. However, its emphasis on the victim and on community involvement in solutions to crime have attracted a body of support, at least at the local level, where it has been employed to deal with delinquency and relatively minor offenses.

The philosophical approach to punishment is concerned with the "ought" of punishment, whereas the sociological approach raises questions about the use and severity of particular punishments and the relationship among punishment, society, and social change. The criminological approach focuses on the fact of imprisonment and on penal policy making and crime control. Some suggest that no single approach adequately provides justification and rationale for punishment and that a full explanation can be gained only by combining these various perspectives.

DISCUSSION QUESTIONS

1. Offenders are punished because we hold them accountable and responsible for their actions. Explain by reference to the various theories of punishment.

2. Does deterrence work? Explain with examples.

3. How can just deserts theory be criticized, and why has just deserts become the predominant view in penal policy?

4. Contrast rehabilitation and incapacitation as theories of punishment, explaining their justification, their operation, and the criticisms that have been made of them.

5. What advantage would society gain if restorative justice were the only method of punishment? In your answer, consider all the advantages and disadvantages offered by a restorative justice approach to punishment.

6. Contrast the philosophical and sociological perspectives on punishment.

7. What is the lex talionis, and what are its drawbacks as a form of punishment?

7

ETHICS IN CORRECTIONS:
THE NATURE OF CORRECTIONS

The preceding chapter explored philosophies of punishment and the rationales for punishment generally and sets the context for the discussion in this chapter concerning ethics in corrections. Here, we are concerned with the prison system, inmates, and prison officers[1] and with ethical dilemmas that may arise within the prison system. A further concern is the treatment afforded to those who are incarcerated. For example, is it ethically correct to impose severe restrictions on amenities and comforts for prisoners? Is an offender sent to prison *for* punishment or *as* punishment for an offense? Should offenders, in effect, be warehoused in prison and left to languish under strict supervision, or should they be provided with treatment programs, psychological services, and educational opportunities? First, however, it is necessary to set the context by looking at the state of the prison system in this country.

---

1. I have consciously decided not to use the terms *guard* and *correctional officer* and replace them with the term *prison officer* in this chapter and in Chapter 8. The terms *keepers, guards* (as in "guarding ethically"), and *correctional officers* are all used in the field. Much of the classical ethical literature refers to guarding. The literature goes back and forth, and my discussion of some of the earlier studies and the ethical case studies usually reflects how such workers are referred to in the original source. The prison system has been a place of change over time, depending on the societal philosophy toward punishment and the role of deprivation of freedom in that philosophy. *Correctional officer* was a term that was created when rehabilitation was a much stronger force in prison systems and philosophy, and the title was changed in the hope that the approach would follow (which was not usually the outcome). Thus, the terms *corrections* and *correctional officers* might be seen as a leftover of a historical penal strategy. Very few prisoners in the United States are currently involved in any type of rehabilitation programs of any kind. Prison officers rarely are provided the training or skills that might result in "correction," or "rehabilitation," regardless of how broadly the term is defined. The terms *corrections* and *correctional officer* now seem in contradiction with the current philosophy of punishment given that over the last 30 years more punitive approaches have taken hold and have influenced societal views about what is considered appropriate prison conditions. Another term is *prison worker*, which can mean a much broader range of roles—anything from psychologists, medical workers, therapists, and COs to food service employees. All are workers, and therefore it seems somewhat deceiving. Most of the ethical issues come out of the relationship between what has been referred to as the "keepers and the kept" or the role encompassing those responsible for security and safety and those being imprisoned. There are, of course, other ethical issues involving other roles, but those mainly concern policy and philosophy that address the larger structures and approaches to punishment and imprisonment more broadly—the control being exercised through drugs (medicalization) in women's prisons and in juvenile institutions as examples.

THE PRISON EXPLOSION

Since about 1982, there has been an explosion in incarceration and criminal justice supervision in the United States that has resulted in the United States having the highest rate of imprisonment in the world. This explosion did not occur by accident nor through misadventure. It was the outcome of a specific set of social forces and policies that have variously been termed "penal populism," "mass incarceration," and "get tough on crime." The policies and rationale that led to the prison explosion are discussed in Chapter 9, "The Ethics of Criminal Justice Policy Making," and in Chapter 4, "Racial Discrimination in the Criminal Justice System." As will be seen, race shapes or is implicated in almost every aspect of crime control and punishment policy in the country. While the focus of this chapter is on ethical issues in corrections, knowledge of the prison explosion and its consequences provides part of the context for that discussion.

Figure 7.1   Estimated Number and Rate of Persons Supervised by Adult Correctional Systems, 2000–2013

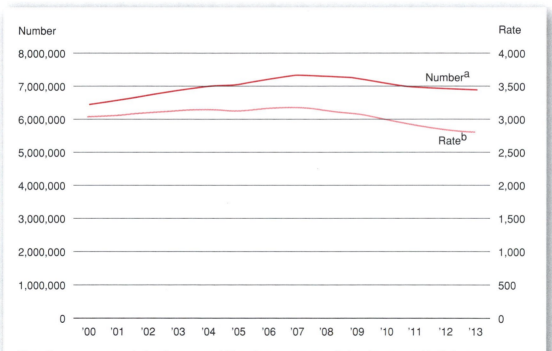

Note: Counts were rounded to the nearest 100 and rates were rounded to the nearest 10. Estimates may not be comparable to privisously published BJS reports due to updated information or rounding. Counts include estimates for nonresponding jurisdictions. See *Methodology*.
[a]Total was adjusted to account for offenders with multiple correctional statuses. See *Methodology*. [b]Rates were computed using the U.S. adult resident population estimates from the U.S. Cessus Bureasu for January 1 of the following year.

SOURCE: Glaze and Kaeble 2014: 3.

Table 7.1 Estimated Number of Persons Supervised by Adult Correctional Systems, by Correctional Status, 2000, 2005, and 2010–2013

Year	Total correctional population[a]	Community supervision			Incarcerated[b]		
		Total[a,c]	Probation	Parole	Total[a]	Local Jail	Prison
2000	6,467,900	4,565,100	3,839,500	725,500	1,945,400	621,100	1,394,200
2005	7,055,800	4,946,800	4,162,500	784,400	2,200,400	747,500	1,525,900
2010	7,088,500	4,887,900	4,055,500	840,700	2,279,100	748,700	1,613,800
2011	6,990,400	4,814,200	3,971,300	853,900	2,252,500	735,600	1,599,000
2012	6,940,500	4,781,300	3,942,800	851,200	2,231,400	744,500	1,570,400
2013	6,899,000	4,751,400	3,910,600	853,200	2,220,300	731,200	1,574,700
Aaverage annual percent change, 2000–2012	0.6%	0.4%	0.2%	1.3%	1.1%	1.5%	1.0%
Percent change, 2012–2013	−0.6%	−0.6%	−0.8%	−0.2%	−0.5%	−1.8%	0.3%

Note: Estimates were rounded to the nearest 100 and may not be comparable to previously published BJS reports due to updated information or rounding. Counts include estimates for nonresponding jurisdictions. All probation, parole, and prison counts are for December 31; jail counts are for the last weekday in June. Detail may not sum to total due to rounding and adjustments made to account for offenders with multiple correctional statuses. See *Methodology*.
[a]Total was adjusted to account for offenders with multiple correctional statuses. See *Methodology*.
[b]Includes inmates held in local jails or under the jurisdiction of state or federal prisons.
[c]Includes some offenders held in a perison of jail but who remained under the jurisdiction of a probation or parole agency.

SOURCE: Glaze and Kaeble 2014: 2.

The number of state and federal prison inmates on December 31, 2014, totaled 1,561,500, an imprisonment rate per 100,000 U.S. residents age 18 or older of 612 (Carson 2015: 1). This custodial population is supplemented by a jail population that at midyear 2014 stood at an estimated 744,600 (Minton and Zheng 2015: 1). Convicted persons on probation and parole in 2013 totaled 3,910,600 and 853,200, respectively. Collectively, therefore, about 6.8 million persons were under the supervision of adult correctional systems at year-end 2013, representing a rate of 2,830 per 100,000 U.S. adult residents (Glaze and Kaeble 2014: 1, 4).

By way of comparison, in 1982 about 200,000 persons were imprisoned, but this number tripled between 1982 and 1999 as the U.S. prison explosion took hold. In the same period from 1982 to 1999,

- over 600 state and at least 51 federal correctional facilities were opened;
- the number of jail inmates tripled from approximately 200,000 to 600,000;
- the number of adults on probation increased from more than 1.3 million to almost 3.8 million; and
- the number of correctional staff more than doubled from nearly 300,000 to over 700,000 (Gifford 2002).

At the federal level, between 1980 and 2013 the imprisonment rate increased by 518%, from 11 inmates per 100,000 to 68 per 100,000, and annual spending on the federal prison system increased

Figure 7.2   Prison Spending Growth Was Twice Other Justice Departments, 1980–2013

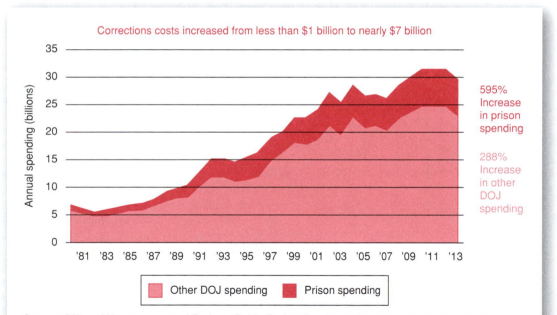

Source: Office of Management and Budget, "Public Budget Database: Outlays," http://www.whitehouse.gov/omb/budget/Supplemental © 2015 The Pew Charitable Trusts

Notes: All spending figures are adjusted to 2013 dollars. Those for the prison system do not include federal grants to states or funding for Federal Prison Industries Inc., a wholly owned corporation of the U.S. goverment that employs and provides job training to inmates. Justics Department spending figures do not include one-time expenditures for the September 11th Victim Compensation Fund.

SOURCE: Pew Research Center 2014.

Table 7.2   Prison Expansion by the Numbers, 1980–2013

Sharp increase in number of inmates and facilities fueled spending growth		
	1980	**2013**
Prison population	24,363	215,866
Imprisonment rate per 100,000 U.S. residents	11	68
Number of prisons	43	119
Annual prison spending (adjusted for inflation)	$0.97 billion	$6.7 billion
Share of Justice Department funds spent on prisons	14%	23%
Estimated number of federal crimes in statute	3,000	5,000
Drug offenders as share of total sentenced prison population	25%	51%
Average time served in prison (in months)	15.9	40.1

Note: The federal prison pupulation peaked at 217, 815 inmates in 2012. The federal imprisonment rate peaked at 69 inmates per 100,000 U.S. residents, also in 2012. The proportion of drug offenders as a share of the total sentenced prison population peaked at 61 percent in 1994. Prison system expenditure figures do not include federal grants to states of funding for Federal Prison Industries Inc., a wholly owned corporation of the U.S. government that employs and provides job training to inmates. Justice Department spending figures do not include one-time expenditures for the September 11th Victim Compensation Fund. The number of federal crimes in statute is an approximation that does not include regulatory offenses, such as environmental infractions.

SOURCE: Pew Research Center 2014.

Table 7.3   Prison Population Rate Per 100,000 Population

Country	Prison Population Total	Prison Population Rate (Per 100,000 Population)
Seychelles	735	799
United States	2,217,000	698
St. Kitts and Nevis	344	607
Turkmenistan	30,568	583
Virgin Islands (USA)	577	542
Cuba	57,337	510
Rwanda	55,618	492
El Salvador	31,433	489
Guam (USA)	797	469

Country	Prison Population Total	Prison Population Rate (Per 100,000 Population)
Thailand	313,303	466
Belize	1,545	449
Russian Federation	644,696	446
Grenada	456	430
Virgin Islands (United Kingdom)	119	425
Panama	15,508	392
American Samoa (USA)	212	382
South Africa	159,241	292
Iran	225,624	290
Colombia	121,257	244
New Zealand	8,641	190
Saudi Arabia	47,000	161
Australia	35,804	151
United Kingdom (England & Wales)	85,892	148
United Kingdom (Scotland)	7,716	144
Spain	64,271	139
Iraq	45,634	133
China	1,657, 812	119
Canada	37,864	106
France	66,864	100
Germany	63,628	78
Egypt	62,000	76
Japan	61,794	49
India	411,992	33

SOURCE: Institute for Criminal Policy Research (ICPR) 2015.

595%, from $970 million to more than $6.7 billion in inflation-adjusted dollars. While the federal prison rate has recorded dramatic increases in incarceration and costs over the past 30 years, between 2007 and 2013 a number of states changed penal policies with the aim of containing prison growth and reducing costs (Pew Research Center 2014).

Time Line of the Prison Explosion

What events and actions contributed to this prison explosion? While researchers have not been able to identify every incident or factor or policy that played a role in the prison explosion, it is possible from the "The Prison Explosion" time line to gain a general sense of what events, actions, and policies contributed to it. This time line draws heavily on the 2006 book *Race to Incarcerate: The Sentencing Project* by Mark Mauer.

As noted by Mauer, since about 2007 a new dialogue on crime control and punishment has turned attention to the incarceration explosion. This is the outcome of a series of factors that include

- the overall decline in crime that has resulted in a reduced focus on crime politically;
- the fiscal crisis that has affected the states and resulted in plans to reduce prison costs and prison populations; and
- the failure of the war on drugs (see Chapter 9), which has shown how supply side policy approaches to drug abuse have failed to reduce the use of illicit drugs.

While since 2007 there has been a refocusing on whether the punishment policies of the last 30 years were prudent, it is important to be aware of how they came about, as this may avoid history repeating itself in the future. The following time line informs how a series of political initiatives and policy changes resulted in mass incarceration.

THE PRISON EXPLOSION: TIME LINE OF EVENTS

1940s–Early 1970: The prison population was largely stable at around 200,000 per year, leading some to argue for a "theory of the stability of punishment," suggesting that society reaches a level of punishment with which it is comfortable and then adjusts policies to maintain it. The public supported rehabilitation, and the system of indeterminate sentencing was designed to allow an inmate to be rehabilitated. Indeterminate sentencing was applied throughout the country as it had been for almost 100 years, judges applied a minimum and maximum term of imprisonment, and inmates were eligible for parole, with the parole authority having discretion to determine when the sentence would be ended. However, this system was criticized by liberals for its potential for abuse of discretion, including wide variations in practice and bias in terms of race and gender. The conservative approach was to challenge indeterminate sentencing as allowing early release of offenders who ought to serve a longer sentence. Conservatives also questioned the value of rehabilitation.

1960s: Crime rates began to rise for reasons which remain unclear; however, one factor might have been the coming of age of the baby boom generation, bringing an unprecedented number of young males into society's mainstream. There was an epidemic of heroin addiction in urban areas. This was a time of social unrest centered on the Vietnam War and the civil rights movement. Urban unrest and public protests and demonstrations became treated as forms of criminality, and public fears about disorder mounted. The feminist movement focused on protection and safety, adding to the concern about crime and unrest and giving more focus to incarceration.

1964: In his presidential campaign, Barry Goldwater made crime a signature issue in politics for the first time.

1967: The Safe Streets Act enlarged the federal role in crime control and made funding available to the states to purchase hardware and to upgrade technology. This resulted in higher rates of crime reporting.

1972: Federal and state prison populations totaled 196,000, with another 130,000 held in jails. This gave an overall incarceration rate of about 160 per 100,000.

1973: The prison population began to increase. New York passed the so-called Rockefeller drug laws, the harshest in the country, that imposed mandatory prison terms for drug offenses and set the stage for later tough anti-drug laws.

1974: The publication of the essay "Nothing Works" by Robert Martinson and his colleagues following their review of juvenile and adult rehabilitation programs gave wide publicity to the notion that rehabilitation did not work. (Martinson's finding was challenged at the time and he later renounced it). The effect of this and other factors was that liberals and conservatives both now favored a determinate sentencing system with decreased rehabilitation, although for different reasons. However, liberals favored short determinate sentences and conservatives, long sentences.

Late 1970s: Cocaine became a widely used illicit drug. States began to pass laws that set mandatory terms of incarceration. Utah adopted sentencing guidelines to curtail judicial discretion in sentencing.

1980s: Crack cocaine, much cheaper to buy than cocaine, became widely used. In 1980, Minnesota adopted sentencing guidelines.

1980: The election of Ronald Reagan as president reinforced the movement to be "tough on crime." An individual pathology approach to crime was adopted and no regard given to structural social and economic factors in crime causation. Desiring to enlarge the federal role in crime control, the Reagan administration decided to enhance the already existing war against drugs by federalizing it.

1982: Congress authorized $125 million to create 12 new regional drug task forces, staffed by more than 1,000 federal law enforcement personnel from the FBI, DEA, and federal prosecutors.

1984: The Sentencing Reform Act established a Federal Sentencing Commission. In 1987, the Commission's guidelines took effect. They stipulated a heavy presumption of imprisonment and little regard for mitigating factors. The guidelines were considered mandatory until 2005 when the Supreme Court ruled they were advisory only. Nevertheless, in the period from 1987 to 2005 many states adopted the federal guidelines, ensuring long sentences would be imposed.

1986: The war on drugs began to severely impact the criminal justice system as prosecutions increased. Following media frenzy around the growth in the use of crack cocaine, more "get tough" measures were proposed and introduced.

1988: The Anti-Drug Abuse Act is passed, prescribing even more mandatory sentences and declaring its objective to be a "Drug-Free America by 1995." George H. Bush's election campaign for president used the Willy Horton incident to give a focus to getting tough on crime.

1988: Following the election of George H. Bush as president, the Department of Justice continued its policy of playing a leading role in campaigning for more punitive crime control policies.

1992: The publication of *Combating Violent Crime: 24 Recommendations to Strengthen Criminal Justice* by the attorney general recommended more mandatory minimum penalties and building more prisons. The election of Bill Clinton as president brought more get-tough measures. Clinton's campaign strategy included a stance of never being less tough on crime than Republicans. At this point, the crime rate and violent crime began a steady decline.

1993: Under the Reagan and Bush administrations between 1980 and 1993, corrections spending increased by 521%. By 1993, some practitioners and

government officials were showing concern at the growth of the prison population and were beginning to debate alternatives to incarceration; this brought attention to racial disparities in criminal justice. However, this trend abruptly reversed due to the efforts of the media, the law-and-order lobby, and through political appropriations of the crime control issue. In Washington State, the first "three strikes and you're out" law was passed, requiring life without parole for three violent felonies.

1994: The Clinton administration passed its crime bill, the Violent Crime Control and Law Enforcement Act 1994, which included a federal "three strikes" provision and a $30 billion funding package for more prisons and law enforcement. Almost $8 billion was appropriated for prison construction, and states were required to adopt tougher laws to qualify for funding. "Truth in sentencing" provisions required that inmates serve at least 85% of their sentences before release. Only at the end of his second term did President Clinton call for a reexamination of mandatory minimum penalties for nonviolent offenders and removal of the sentencing disparity between crack cocaine and cocaine powder. By the late 1990s, the public had begun to recognize that crime rates were declining, and crime no longer figured as a central issue in most political dialogue.

2000: The election of George W. Bush as president on a platform that included "compassionate conservatism" did not bring about radical change. Despite statements about crack cocaine and lengthy drug sentences that suggested changes might be forthcoming to slow prison growth, this did not occur, and plans for prisoner reentry programs, for example, received little of the promised funding. The overall approach to crime continued to be punitive.

2001–2005: Attorney General John Ashcroft overruled prosecutors who recommended noncapital prosecutions. The U.S. Sentencing Commission was ordered to ensure that lesser sentences than those required by the sentencing guidelines ("downward departures") were substantially reduced, and federal prosecutors were directed not to agree to downward departures generally unless a case was exceptional and to report nonsanctioned departures to the attorney general. These measures exacerbated an already punitive punishment system. Overall, the prison explosion was consolidated, and no substantive moves were made to ameliorate its nature and effects.

2007: Under fiscal pressure, some states reviewed their prison costs and looked for ways to reduce them. However, there was no radical reconfiguration in the existing punishment policies at state or federal levels, despite a continuously decreasing crime rate.

2010: Congress finally changed the 25-year law mandating a sentence for possession of crack cocaine that was equivalent to the prison term for trafficking 100 times the amount of powder cocaine and reduced the ratio to 18:1 rather than 100:1. The legislation also eliminated the mandatory 5-year prison sentence for first-time offenders. The largest decline in the prison population—2.1%—was recorded. However, in 2013 the decline was only 0.6%.

2013: About 1 in 35 adults in the United States was under some form of correctional supervision, and 1 in 51 adults on probation or parole. The U.S. federal prison population decreased for the first time since 1980 (down 1,900). Since 2010, the female prison population has been the fastest growing category of inmates, increasing by an average of 3.4% each year.

2015: In June, three states presented to Congress recent sentencing and corrections reforms; since 2007, more than half the states have carried out reforms that have assisted in stabilizing the incarceration rate. Reforms include prioritizing prison space for serious and repeat felons and promoting alternatives to incarceration for nonviolent offenders. South Dakota has canceled construction of two new prisons, and Utah has strengthened probation and parole and invested in re-entry programs designed to reduce recidivism for released offenders (Pew Charitable Trusts 2015).

Prison Overcrowding

One outcome of mass incarceration policies has been prison overcrowding. It is difficult to get an accurate view of this issue, but there are numerous documented adverse effects of prisons being occupied far beyond their capacity level. These include mental and physical health issues, including a higher risk of suicide. Overcrowding

Figure 7.3   U.S. Incarceration Rate, 1880–2000

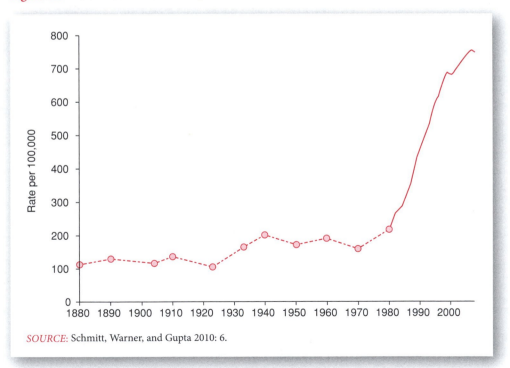

SOURCE: Schmitt, Warner, and Gupta 2010: 6.

results in the imposition of additional behavioral controls, including lockdowns and solitary confinement, a decrease in treatment programs, and a consequent increase in recidivism as inmates receive no preparation for their re-entry into society (Simon 2014: 6).

As of late 2011, half of the states were operating their prisons above the designed capacity, with California and Alabama operating at nearly double capacity. Similarly, overcrowding in federal prisons has increased: In 2012, the system was operating on average of 38% to 52% above capacity (Gottschalk 2015: 41–42). Simon (2014: 6) points out that states expected an increase in the rate of incarceration because prisons were designed with plumbing and electrical connections for up to double the specified capacity.

California provides a case study of how prison overcrowding can constitute a violation of constitutional rights. In the late 1970s, California shifted to a punishment policy that Simon (2014: 18)

terms "total incapacitation" and resulted in gross overcrowding in its prisons. There was an assumption that criminals were incapable of change and would remain intractably criminal. This caused incapacitation as a policy to be seen as the most appropriate response, and the policy went largely unchallenged (pp. 39, 43). Between 1980 and 2000, 22 prisons were constructed in the state, but even that high rate of construction could not keep pace with the rate of imprisonment, and by the end of 1990, prisons were operating at almost 200% of capacity (p. 20).

Litigation was launched against the state, and in 2011, confirming the decision of a three-judge court in 2009 in *Coleman v. Plata*, the U.S. Supreme Court ruled by a 5-to-4 majority in *Brown v. Plata* that overcrowding in California's prisons violated the constitutional prohibition against cruel and unusual punishment. The Court ordered that the prison population be reduced to 137.5% of design capacity within 2 years—a

Figure 7.4   U.S. Prison and Jail Population, 1980–2008

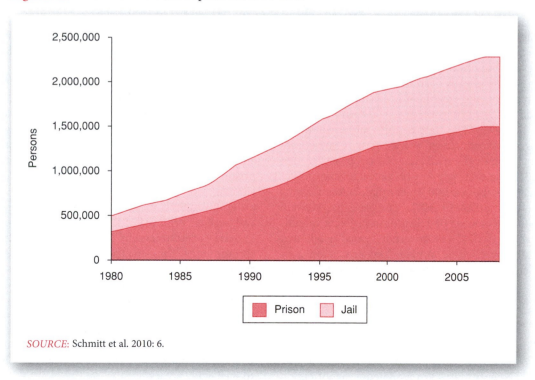

SOURCE: Schmitt et al. 2010: 6.

reduction of about 40,000 prisoners (Simon 2014: 7). Justice Kennedy, for the majority, expressed the need to recognize the human dignity of inmates, stating, "Prisoners retain the essence of human dignity. . . . A prison that deprives prisoners of basic sustenance, including adequate medical care, is incompatible with the concept of human dignity and has no place in civilized society" (p. 133).

A week before the decision the governor of California had signed into law the Public Safety Realignment Act. The objective of this law was to conduct a "realignment" of the prison system by transferring or diverting prisoners from state prisons and parole systems to county jails and local community sanctions. Block grants were to be given with little or no state oversight and no evaluation of the outcomes. In response, many counties began investing in jail expansion but have not utilized the funding for community sanctions, such as mental health programs and substance abuse treatment. By July 2012, 21 counties had decided to build more than 10,000 new jail beds for $1.2 billion. In addition, the state planned to spend an additional $500 million for the construction of new jails.

Clearly, this strategy does not represent decarceration but is a displacement of the state prison system overcrowding on to county jails. However, in many cases jails are already overcrowded and lack the security, medical, and treatment needs required to meet the demands of housing not short-term, but long-term prisoners. The state has also said it will house thousands of inmates in private prisons, sometimes out of state. In the final analysis, it is projected that by 2017 the total jail and prison population might actually be about 5,000 higher than before realignment took effect in 2011. The state has resisted reducing sentences or releasing nonviolent offenders, and in 2013, the governor vetoed a bill that would have charged simple drug possession as a misdemeanor rather than a felony (Gottschalk 2015: 269–270).

Women's Incarceration

The Central California Women's Facility (CCWF) is the largest women's prison in the world. New inmates are assigned a classification signifying their level of security risk derived from the offense for which they were imprisoned and their history of prior commitments (Owen 1998: 64). Over 75% of the inmates are classified as low risk. The prison is divided into four separate units, including administrative segregation (AD SEG), security housing, and a death row. Women are received into the prison in the receiving and release building, which is located within A-Facility, the most closely controlled section of the prison. Women may not walk around unescorted in A-Yard, which contains the most secure housing unit, unless they wear state-issued clothing. The inmates occupy two-person cells. The daily schedule begins at 6:30 a.m. when the inmates are required to get up, clean their rooms, and make their beds by 7 a.m. Morning and afternoon activities take the form of job or school assignments, and the women return to their housing units after dinner to socialize before returning to their cells for the evening (p. 88).

The administrative segregation unit functions like a jail, and women are moved to this facility if they are under investigation for rule infractions or for other offenses, and following such investigations, they may be housed in this facility for short periods of time as punishment for minor offenses. Typically, inmates are confined to AD SEG for fighting, drug-related offenses, and assaults on staff. It is common for terms of less than 1 month to be served in AD SEG. The security housing unit (SHU) houses the small number of women whose behavior constitutes a danger to themselves or others in the institution, and it is best conceived of as a prison within the prison (Owen 1998: 113). The SHU is used for women found guilty of a serious offense, and programs in SHU may last for more than 6 months and perhaps even years. The length of term served in SHU is determined by the nature of the offense committed within the prison; offenses include assaults on staff or inmates, weapons possession, and serious drug misconduct. The daily life within these units takes the form of a lock-down, and women can only conduct loud conversations with their "vent-partners" or shout across the unit in a group discussion (p. 115). In death row, the few women sentenced to death are confined within a six-cell-wide area.

A Closer Look

Women in Prison

- The female prison population has more than doubled since 1990, with an annual growth rate since that year of 7.6%, higher than the 5.9% average increase in the number of male inmates.

- Between 1990 and 2001, the total number of male prisoners increased 77%, but the number of female prisoners increased 108% (Gifford 2002).

- By the end of 2007, the incarceration rate for females between the ages of 35 and 39 was 1 in 355 for white women, 1 in 297 for Hispanic women, 1 in 100 for black women, and 1 in 265 for all women ages 35–39 (Pew Center on the States 2008: 6).

- Between 1995 and 2005, the number of male prisoners grew 34% and the number of females 57% (Harrison and Beck 2006: 4). During the same period, the annual rate of increase for female prisoners averaged 4.6%, compared to 3.0% for male prisoners (p. 4). In 2005, females made up 7.0% of all prisoners, up from 5.7% in 1990 and 6.1% in 1995.

- Between 2012 and 2013, the number of female prisoners increased by 2.3% in state prisons and 0.9% in federal prisons. This compares to an increase of only 0.1% for males in state prisons and a reduction of 1% for males in federal prisons (Carson 2014: 3).

- As of December 31, 2012, women in state prisons were serving sentences for three major categories of offenses: violent crimes (37.1%), property offenses (28.2%), and drug offenses (24.6%). For males, drug offenses made up only 15.4% of all offenses (Carson 2014: 15).

New Forms of Incarceration

In light of the costs of maintaining large prison populations, criminal justice systems have sought ways to recoup some of those costs. The result, ironically, has been the creation of a new class of prisoner: those essentially in prison for debt. One pathway to incarceration has been through civil contempt proceedings against court debtors. Beckett and Murakawa (2012: 227) report that states have authorized a range of legal financial obligations (LFOs), including fees, fines, and orders for restitution that may be imposed by courts and agencies on persons convicted of crimes. In most states, defendants may now be required to pay the adjudication costs, the costs of court-ordered tests, and the costs of their imprisonment and supervision. When the fees and fines are not paid, they are commonly subject to increases of interest charges and surcharges.

By 2004, courts had required more than two thirds of incarcerated prisoners and more than 80%

of other felons and persons convicted of misdemeanors to pay fees and fines. Fees and fines are not assessed according to a means test, and the outcome is that indigent persons are being required to pay substantial sums. For example, by 2008 defendants sentenced in 2004 had been charged an average of $11,471 by the courts over their lifetime (Beckett and Murakawa 2012: 228).

LFOs have resulted in a new class of actors with authority to impose and collect fees and to impose sanctions on those who default. For example, in Washington State, county clerks may impose additional fees, garnish wages of debtors, and seize bank assets and tax refunds. They are also empowered to apply to a judge to issue an arrest warrant for the arrest of legal debtors, who are often subsequently incarcerated. In order to circumvent laws that prohibit the imprisonment of debtors, civil contempt charges have been used so that debtors are arrested and incarcerated not for nonpayment, but for contempt of court—that is, for failing to

Table 7.4 Imprisonment Rate of Sentenced State and Federal Prisoners per 100,000 U.S. Residents, by Demographic Characteristics, December 31, 2014

Age group	Total[a]	Male					Female				
		All male[a]	White[b]	Black[b]	Hispanic	Other[b]	All female[a]	White[b]	Black[b]	Hispanic	Other[b]
Total[c]	471	890	465	2,724	1,091	968	65	53	109	64	93
18–19	169	317	102	1,072	349	542	14	8	32	17	12
20–24	746	1,365	584	3,868	1,521	1,755	96	72	152	94	109
25–29	1,055	1,912	958	5,434	2,245	2,022	170	150	244	165	208
30–34	1,161	2,129	1,111	6,412	2,457	2,193	185	163	264	174	225
35–39	1,067	1,982	1,029	6,122	2,272	1,878	155	138	229	137	189
40–44	904	1,689	942	5,105	1,933	1,619	132	119	213	107	174
45–49	758	1,417	815	4,352	1,602	1,444	111	90	203	94	161
50–54	567	1,081	633	3,331	1,320	1,112	72	57	128	67	124
55–59	358	698	400	2,178	978	832	37	27	72	42	63
60–64	212	422	252	1,265	680	483	20	15	37	25	37
65 or older	72	158	109	418	299	208	5	4	8	7	12
Number of sentenced prisoners[d]	1,508,636	1,402,404	453,500	516,900	308,700	123,300	106,232	53,100	22,600	17,800	12,800

Note: Counts based on prisoners with sentences of more than 1 year under the jurisdiction of state or federal correctional authorities. Imprisonment rate is the number of prisoners under state or federal jurisdiction with a sentence of more than 1 year per 100,000 U.S. residents of corresponding sex, age, and race or Hispanic origin. Resident population estimates are from the U.S. Census Bureau for January 1, 2015 Alaska did not submit 2014 data to the National Prisoner Statistics (NPS), so totals include imputed counts for this state. See *Methodology*.

[a]Includes American Indians and Alaska Natives: Asians, Native Hawaiians, and other Pacific Islanders; and persons of two or more races.

[b]Includes persons age 17 or younger.

[c]Includes persons age 17 or younger.

[d]Race totals are rounded to the nearest 100 to accommodate differences in data collection techniques between jurisdictions.

SOURCE: Carson 2015: 15.

A Closer Look

Sexual Assault at Women's Prison in Alabama

In May 2015, the U.S. Department of Justice announced it had reached an agreement with the state of Alabama to compel the state to carry out reforms at the maximum-security Julia Tutwiler Prison for Women at Wetumpka, Alabama, where inmates had for many years been subjected to sexual assaults, including rape, sodomy, forced oral sex, and fondling at the hands of prison staff. The Tutwiler Prison opened in 1942 and was named after Julia Tutwiler, a prison reformer and advocate for improved conditions in women's prisons.

In January 2014, the Justice Department issued a letter with its findings that the prison had subjected female prisoners to a "pattern or practice" of sexual abuse in violation of the Eighth Amendment's prohibition on cruel and unusual punishment.

Justice Department investigators found that prison staff helped organize a "strip show" for prisoners, that male staff openly watched women shower and use toilet facilities, that women who reported abuse were commonly placed in segregation with limited or no access to a telephone or visitors, and that complaints of abuse often resulted in punishment and threats of physical abuse by staff. It was found that prison staff treated women who reported sexual abuse "with the presumption that they were lying, subjecting them to polygraph examinations as a prerequisite to investigating the allegation."

SOURCE: "Justice Department Acts to End Sexual Assault at a Women's Prison in Alabama," Sari Horwitz, *The Washington Post*, May 28, 2015.

comply with a court order to pay a fine or fee (Beckett and Murakawa 2012: 229).

MAXIMUM SECURITY

To better understand the ethical issues that may arise in correctional practice, it is helpful to have a general knowledge of prison regimes and conditions. Knowledge of the daily routine within types of prisons and the nature of the restrictions that both prisoners and staff experience in their daily interactions help reveal how the management and administration of a captive population generate ethical issues and dilemmas. In particular, contextualizing ethical issues in this way highlights questions of control and coercive power and reveals how a rationally organized bureaucracy (see discussion of Max Weber in previous chapter) administers a "total institution" (Goffman 1959, 1961), as well as how it formulates and operates policies and

procedures within a professional and ethical framework. The daily experience of imprisonment under maximum security is discussed in the following sections, and general descriptions of medium- and minimum-security prisons are provided.

Today, the number of inmates in supermax prisons in the United States is unknown, as is the number of confinement units in such prisons, but it is estimated at between 25,000 and 80,000 inmates in 44 states (Guenther 2013: 131). In his classic work on a maximum-security prison, Gresham Sykes (1958/1999) singles out as central to maximum security the fact that "the maximum-security prison represents a social system in which an attempt is made to create and maintain total or almost total social control" (p. xiv).

In his exploration of conditions at the New Jersey State Maximum Security Prison in 1958, Sykes noted that the prison did not inflict acute "physical discomforts" or impose hard living conditions. Instead, for Sykes (1958/1999), it appeared to possess "a grinding dullness, an existence lacking the amenities of life we take for granted, but an existence which is still tolerable" (p. 8). Sykes identified the task of keeping persons in custody as the main task of the custodians at New Jersey State Prison, with the maintenance of internal order as the next priority. Rules and regulations were designed both for custody purposes and for maintaining order. The inmates viewed the regulation of their conduct to the minutest degree as a form of punishment, whereas administrators justified prison codes of conduct in the name of custody and internal order.

Conditions in maximum-security prisons have changed since Sykes conducted his research in 1958. For example, the conditions at Wisconsin's Supermax Correctional Institution are depicted by the district court in the class action *Jones 'El and Others v. Berge and Litscher* (2001) as follows:

- This supermax prison has 500 beds and is designed to incarcerate the worst of the worst offenders.
- There are a number of levels of achievement within the prison as part of an incentive program, with Level 1 being the lowest level with the most restrictive conditions of confinement.
- New prisoners are assigned to Level 1 on arrival and remain there until they have been evaluated in terms of behavior and medical and program needs. They are housed in single-person cells and have little face-to-face contact with staff. The cell doors are constructed of solid metal and are boxcar doors, which are constantly slammed as inmates move in and out of their cells. Light accesses the cell through a five-inch strip of opaque glass running along the top edge of one wall, and if he stands on his bed and cranes his neck, an inmate may see the sky through a small sealed skylight. Inmates are not permitted to wear watches or have clocks.
- Cells are illuminated 24 hours a day. Lighting cannot be turned off, but it can be adjusted from high to low. At night, inmates must sleep in a way that allows prison officers to see their faces, and they will be awakened if they have covered their faces.
- Inmates are not able to regulate cell temperature, there is no air conditioning, and the solid cell doors and lack of windows inhibits air circulation. A report that monitored the temperature and humidity showed an inside cell temperature of

91 degrees when the outdoor temperature was also 91 degrees, producing a heat index in excess of 100 degrees.
- Although cells contain showers that might provide relief from the heat, inmates may only shower three times a week.
- Inmates are allowed 4 hours of exercise a week in an exercise cell, which is a slightly larger version of a regular one-person cell with no windows and no exercise equipment. The room will permit only pacing or stationary exercises; inmates are transported to the exercise cell wearing restraints and are pat-searched before entering the cell and after leaving it. There is no regular exercise schedule, and exercise is permitted at the discretion of prison officers.
- There is a small law library set up in a cell, but inmates using the library must be shackled and cuffed with their cuffs attached to a belly chain while out of their cells. Inmates are not allowed face-to-face visits except with their lawyers and must rely on video visitation, where inmates remain in their cell block and see their visitors on small video screens with poor audio quality. During video visits, inmates remain handcuffed, shackled, and belly chained.
- Level 1 inmates are permitted one 6-minute telephone call each month. They are not allowed library books in their cells, but they may keep a Bible, Qur'an, or equivalent and up to 25 letters.
- Inmates who start at Level 1 spend a minimum of 30 days in that level and, if they advance to a higher level, may be demoted back to Level 1 if staff determine they have behaved improperly.
- Confinement in a supermax security prison is known to cause severe psychiatric morbidity, disability, suffering, and mortality.
- The isolating conditions in supermax confinement mean that many prisoners are unable to maintain their sanity, and a high number attempt suicide.

The class action also alleges that prisoners are obsessed with suicidal thinking, smear feces, swallow metal objects, cut their flesh, and attempt to hang themselves and that excessive use of force is a daily occurrence at the prison. Self-harm occurs because prisoners have no contact with others, and therefore, their main outlet for expressing anger and aggression is toward themselves.

Another example of maximum security is Pelican Bay, a supermax prison in California located in a very remote area. The prison is entirely automated and is constructed so that inmates have almost no face-to-face contact with officers or other inmates (Austin and Irwin 2001: 127–128). Inmates are confined in their windowless cells constructed of concrete and stainless steel for 22.5 hours a day. They are not permitted to work in prison industries, have no access to recreation or to other inmates, and are not permitted cigarettes. All meals are eaten in their cells, which they leave only for brief showers and the daily 90-minute exercise, which is taken in miniature yards enclosed by 20-foot-high walls. The doors of their cells contain slots for food trays, and meal delivery is almost the only time officers approach cells because unlike the usual prison arrangement, officers do not walk tiers but are locked away in glass-enclosed booths, communicating with the inmates through a speaker system. The majority of Pelican Bay's inmate population comes from the Los Angeles area, located 900 miles away with no access by air, making family visits extremely difficult.

The justification for the creation of the costly supermax prison is by no means clear. Generally, they are said to have been constructed to house "the worst of the worst" (King, Steiner, and Breach 2008: 144). In 1978, the Marion prison was designated as the highest security federal prison, but in October 1983, prisoners in Marion went on a rampage, stabbed two prison officers to death, and injured four others. A regime of 24-hour lockdown was imposed, and prisoners were locked in their cells 24 hours a day. The lockdown at Marion is regarded as marking the birth of the supermax regime (Shalev 2009: 21). A research group in a 1997 report to the National Institute of Corrections explained the rationale for the supermax prison as follows:

> For the management and secure control of inmates who have been officially designated as exhibiting violent or serious and disruptive behavior while incarcerated. Such inmates have been determined to be a threat to safety and security in traditional high security facilities, and their behavior can be controlled only by separation, restricted movement, and limited direct access to staff and other inmates. (in King et al. 2008: 145)

Despite these claims, there is an absence of validating empirical evidence, and the rationale for the supermax prison continues to be questioned on theoretical, empirical, and moral grounds (Sundt, Castellano, and Briggs 2008: 95). Basically, the assumption is that a small number of disruptive and violent inmates cause disorder within the general inmate population and thus need to be removed to a separate facility that houses them in appropriate conditions. In this sense, the need for the supermax prison is perceived to be self-evident. There is scant research on supermax prisons because of the difficulty of gaining access, and their rationale is not questioned within prison management spheres. As Shalev (2009) puts it, "Managerial objectives (maintaining prison order and discipline) are predominant in official discourses about the roles of supermax confinement" (p. 57). There is no pretense that inmates will be rehabilitated, and the principal function of the supermax prison is to punish (p. 127). While it is claimed that inmates can work their way out of supermax prison or units, some cannot, according to one administrator, "because this is where they belong and this is where they'll stay until they are released from the agency" (p. 57).

Hoskins (2013: 1) terms supermax confinement "contemptuous" punishment because it "fails to respect offenders as moral persons, who as such are always capable of moral reform." As noted earlier, supermax prisons are not concerned with inmate rehabilitation or moral reform but are designed only to incapacitate or "warehouse" inmates. Hoskins argues, following Kant who contended that contempt was the opposite of respect, that maximum-security punishment is impersonal, shows no concern for the inmate, and is therefore contemptuous and morally wrong because it constitutes a denial of a person's dignity (p. 6). Hoskins is especially disturbed that contemptuous treatment is imposed by institutions: He argues that it is one thing for a person to treat another with contempt but quite another for government institutions to do so when they are supposedly acting on behalf of the entire community. Hoskins sees a shift from censure of the inmate for his or her criminal acts by the community to contempt for what he or she is as a person. This personalization of punishment is reflected in the institutional rejection of any pretense that a prisoner might be morally reformed.

For Hoskins, sentences and treatment should not undermine the prospect of inmate reform and should not hold inmates in conditions that have that same effect (2013: 9). In response to the argument that some inmates are incapable of reform, Hoskins points out that labeling persons as "monsters" or "irredeemable" raises the issue of how this is to be judged. Other philosophers have argued similarly that an inmate's potential for moral reform should always be taken into account on the basis that every person has the capacity to choose to be moral (p. 13).

In the United Kingdom, maximum-security prisons are quite different than U.S. supermax facilities. They were first established in the late 1960s and had significant issues with order maintenance during the following 20 years. In England, the prison conditions in maximum security allow prisoners to interact, be employed in a range of educational and vocational programs, and associate with staff. The original thinking was that long-term imprisonment was in itself a harsh punishment, and providing inmates with a reasonably liberal regime was appropriate (Drake 2011: 4).

What explains the growth of the supermax prison in the United States? In her study of solitary confinement and supermax prisons, Shalev (2009: 40) identifies a range of factors:

- An economic crisis that affected rural areas from the 1980s and encouraged rural communities to support the construction of supermax prisons in their area
- The privatization of prisons and the growth of a robust market for goods and services for both private and public prisons that was satisfied by new prison supply industries
- Fear of crime and punitive public attitudes toward criminals
- The political and lobbying capabilities of the prison officer unions, especially that of the largest union in California, which strongly promoted safer working conditions for prison officers

As Shalev elaborates (2009: 51), supermax prisons and solitary confinement exist as management tools to manage prisoners labeled as "disruptive" or as gang members or as inmates who are judged difficult to control. "Dangerousness" is a key element in the calculation of risk, and the use of this concept has given rise to a new type of offender—"uncontrollable, unpredictable, highly dangerous and crucially, beyond redemption." Despite the implication that dangerousness is related to the criminal acts of an inmate against society, supermax prisons commonly hold prisoners who have violated prison rules (p. 54).

How should the success of supermax prisons be evaluated? Has there been a decrease in prison violence by removing inmate troublemakers from the general population and placing them in isolation? In California, not only has there been no reduction in prison violence, but it has actually increased (Shalev 2009: 209). Studies in Arizona, Illinois, and Minnesota also found no reduction in prison violence. Has the supermax prison contributed to resolving the problem of prison gangs? In California, studies have found that gangs simply regrouped and found new leaders. It is also claimed that supermax confinement means that prisons programs will be able to operate more effectively in the general prison population because inmates who commonly disrupt those programs have been removed to a supermax prison. There is little evidence that in California there has been any effect on programming, but removing inmates to isolation has meant they are largely deprived of any programs.

A major argument in favor of the supermax model is that staff safety has increased. In fact, in California this has not proved to be true, but correctional staff certainly feel safer because the possibility of an assault on a staff person is unlikely, given the supermax environment and conditions of extreme control.

Solitary Confinement

As discussed earlier, the defining characteristic of supermax prisons is the isolation of prisoners in solitary confinement. In this sense, these prisons represent a return to the penal conditions that prevailed in the golden age of the penitentiary. Solitary confinement can be traced back in time to the establishment of the Cherry Hill Prison (Eastern State Penitentiary) in Philadelphia in 1823 where inmates were kept isolated at all times. By the 1830s, reports were being made about a sharp increase in mental disorders among inmates undergoing solitary confinement, including hallucinations and "dementia." Over time, the symptoms of inmate isolation manifested in "anxiety, fatigue, confusion, paranoia, depression, hallucinations, headaches and uncontrollable trembling" (Guenther 2013: xi). These continue to be the effects of solitary confinement today. By the late 19th century, the penitentiary system of isolation had been dismantled (Shalev 2009: 17).

In her account of the evolution and practice of solitary confinement, Guenther (2013) maps three waves:

- Firstly, beginning in the 1850s, it was championed by moral and religious reformers who believed that prolonged periods of solitude in a penitentiary led to transformation from criminality.
- Secondly, in the 1960s and 1970s, it was led by behavioral scientists who believed in the power of psychology to resocialize and rehabilitate criminals using the techniques of behavior modification.
- Thirdly, commencing in the 1980s, prison administrators promoted and implemented notions of carceral control that would reduce risks to prison staff from possible inmate violence and would support policy makers in designing regimes of total control within the experience of incarceration. This third wave reflects the current view that inmates selected for solitary confinement "have become risks to be managed, resistances to be eliminated, and organisms to be fed, maintained and even prevented from taking their own lives" (p. xvi).

As Shalev (2009: 2) explains, there are three main forms of segregation—*punitive segregation* for punishing prisoner misconduct and usually imposed for a fixed period following a disciplinary adjudication; *protective segregation*, used to hold vulnerable prisoners apart from the general population for their own protection (e.g., sex offenders and convicted former police officers); and *administrative segregation*, used to isolate prisoners that fall into certain categories such as escape risks, gang members, predators, high risk, and terrorists. The decision to place an inmate in solitary is almost always made by the prison administration and very rarely by a court.

Are there any legal restrictions concerning the punishment of solitary confinement? The Eighth Amendment prohibits cruel and unusual punishment, and solitary confinement has been challenged as a violation of this prohibition in the courts. In 1890, the U.S. Supreme Court in *In Re Medley* rejected prison administration claims that prisoners were kept in "close confinement" and not solitary confinement; it categorized solitary confinement as problematic because it did not reform inmates and caused serious mental problems (Shalev 2011: 159). Since then, the courts have generally been ready to intervene in cases where physical conditions were deficient but have otherwise given deference to prison administrations. Judicial decisions concerning physical conditions have found isolation and deprivation of hot water, soap, and clothing to be constitutionally intolerable but permitting inmates in isolation to shower once every 5 days is acceptable practice, and without additional deprivations, solitary confinement does not in itself amount to a violation of the constitution (p. 159).

In 1995 in *Madrid v. Gomez*, a U.S. district court provided a detailed analysis of the conditions prevailing at Pelican Bay. The court noted that the meaning of the Eighth Amendment varies according to a test of "evolving standards of decency" and that prisoners are not wholly divested of constitutional rights when incarcerated, although rights may be diminished by the nature of the prison environment. To demonstrate a violation of the Eighth Amendment, it would have to be shown that the punishment either "inflicts unnecessary or wanton pain" or is "grossly disproportionate to the severity of the crime warranting punishment," and to meet this test, prison officials must have acted with "deliberate indifference" (Shalev 2011: 161). The court found that conditions at Pelican Bay did not violate the Eighth Amendment except in relation to certain categories of inmates, including those "already mentally ill . . . , persons with borderline personality disorders, brain damage or mental retardation, impulse-ridden personalities, or a history of prior psychiatric problems of chronic depression" (p. 164).

The courts have, however, been reluctant to hold that access to human social contact is protected or that supermax confinement may cause mental illness in persons with no prior history of that illness (Shalev 2011: 167). Philosopher Kimberley Brownlee (2013: 199) argues that such a right exists, which she terms "the right against social deprivation" and explains as "a persisting lack of minimally adequate opportunities for decent or supportive human contact." She identifies the holding of inmates in long-term solitary confinement as a violation of this right and bases her argument on the duty to respect persons and the inherent worth of social inclusion (p. 212).

MEDIUM SECURITY AND MINIMUM SECURITY

Approximately one third of all inmates are incarcerated in medium-security prisons, which generally secure inmates with double fences topped with barbed wire. Most medium-security prisons have been built since 1925. Although the term *medium security* suggests a diminished focus on security, in fact, medium-security prisons adopt many of the practices found in maximum security, such as head counts and a high level of supervision and guarding. One difference between maximum- and medium-security prisons is that inmates work without constant supervision in medium-security facilities.

Minimum-security prisons hold only about 10% of all prisoners; most were constructed after 1950. The emphasis in this form of incarceration is on vocational training and treatment. Minimum-security inmates are generally nonviolent, first-time offenders and white-collar criminals who are not considered dangerous. Generally, minimum-security prisons emphasize a more normal lifestyle, the gates are open, and inmates even have a degree of privacy. These prisons provide a range of programs, and some supply family-visiting facilities where prisoners are able to stay with their families for up to 3 days at a time.

These partial descriptions of prison and prison life provide some sense of the order and regimentation of incarcerated male and female inmates. Later discussion will explore relations between prisoners and prison officers, especially in terms of the power and authority that officers exercise over inmates and the corresponding "power" of inmates. The nature and employment of this coercive correctional power has been a focus of correctional studies because it often generates ethical issues and ethical dilemmas for staff.

This chapter does not provide an exhaustive history of the development of the penitentiary or of incarceration generally in the United States. The emphasis in this discussion is on ethical conduct within the prison environment. Instead, the following discussion explores the history of Stateville Prison in Illinois, as explained by James Jacobs (1977) in his classic study. The aim is to show through Jacobs's study how prison administration moved from being ad hoc to being bureaucratized and professionalized and how ethical standards and norms within the prison changed over time to parallel social change. This examination also reveals how changes in the bureaucratic structure reflected changes in the agency as correctional administrators introduced new policies and practices.

STATEVILLE PRISON: THE CHANGING STATE OF CORRECTIONS

In his study of Stateville Prison in Illinois, Jacobs (1977) showed how patterns of authority in prison changed over time. In the early days of the Stateville penitentiary, rules about conduct were made on an ad hoc basis, and discipline was exercised in an arbitrary and capricious way. Subsequently, as the prison administration became bureaucratized, the early authoritarian regime was replaced with one that depended on rules and regulations and emphasized a professional approach to corrections. Jacobs (p. 9) traces the introduction of the rule of law into Stateville to the judicial activism of the 1960s and to legislation concerned with civil rights, the poor, and the criminal defendant.

Stateville opened in 1925, and during its first decade of operations, it was free from any form of outside oversight. Early wardens were political appointees, usually former sheriffs, and political patronage even decided the appointment of officers, who lost their jobs with each change in the governorship of the state (Jacobs 1977: 21). In the 1930s, prison officers worked up to 16 hours a day and regularly worked 12-hour shifts. They were untrained, underpaid, and physically unfit. Disciplinary measures included locking up an inmate in solitary confinement and "stringing up," a process in which the inmate stood handcuffed to the bars of his cell 8 hours a day for up to 15 days, and perhaps longer (p. 22). Violence between staff and inmates was common, the prison was overcrowded, and most inmates were left idle.

During the period from 1936 to 1961, Stateville was "ruled" by Warden Joe Ragen, who sought to make Stateville the world's most orderly prison. He exercised control over every detail and established an authoritarian regime that transformed Stateville into a venue internationally known among penologists. Ragen demanded absolute loyalty from his officers; in exchange, he often ignored their physical assaults on inmates (Jacobs 1977: 30). Prison officers exercised intense supervision over inmates and applied countless rules covering every aspect of prison life. In place of the earlier system where the untrained and politically appointed officers relied on inmate bosses and gang leaders to maintain order, Ragen established a patriarchy rule based on what Jacobs calls "charismatic authority" (p. 31). The warden distrusted all outsiders and declined to share authority with any subordinates. The backbone of the Ragen administration was its informers, who contributed to an atmosphere of insecurity and distrust that was exemplified in Ragen's concern with the behavior of his officers on and off the job (p. 38).

As for the inmates, although he stressed their entitlement to good food, clothing, and housing, Ragen maintained that they had no other entitlements beyond this and that all other benefits were considered privileges. Order was maintained within the institution through a system of internal security that ensured complete enforcement of a set of comprehensive rules and regulations. For example, an inmate's failure to button a shirt or salute a captain was reason enough for disciplinary action. Although Ragen reformed the practice of "stringing up," inmates in isolation were nevertheless required to stand at attention in silence inside their cells for 8 hours a day (Jacobs 1977: 42). In spite of the severity of the disciplinary regime, exceptions had to be made to the code of discipline if the organization were to function, and this resulted in a reciprocal relationship in which officers overlooked infractions in exchange for inmate compliance, especially in supplying information.

In the Ragen era, rewards were a much more effective tool of prison management than is the case today because of the great disparities in the living conditions of inmates, who, in the 1940s and 1950s, faced very long prison terms. Whereas the average prisoner was confined with two other men in a tiny cell from 3 p.m. to 7 a.m., inmates who held administrative positions could work at night and remain in their offices, as well as enjoy mobility within the prison. The warden offered top jobs to inmate leaders and tough prisoners as a form of reward. In 1955, the disciplinary system was described as "absolute," with a silent system enforced in the dining room and while marching in lines. Even when the ideology of rehabilitation came into vogue in the 1950s, Ragen was able to cast himself as a humanitarian, claiming to place the underprivileged and those from the slums on the path of morality (Jacobs 1977: 44–45). The movement for prison reform resulted in Ragen increasing the size of his academic and vocational schools, but the vocational school reportedly was devoted to performing personal services for staff by repairing cars and electrical equipment—staff would bring in run-down cars and appliances, pay for the parts and supplies, and have the labor provided free by the inmates.

The relationship between prison officers and inmates during Ragen's regime was one of great social distance. The rule was that fraternization was to occur no more than was necessary and that relations between officers and inmates were to remain impersonal (Jacobs 1977: 49). Those who attempted to challenge the warden's authority by complaining to outsiders, by trying to escape, or by defying an officer could expect to be beaten by the officers or their selected inmate helpers (p. 50). When Ragen left Stateville in 1961, the institution underwent a transition from a charismatic to a traditional system of authority and then emerged as a professional bureaucratic institution in the style that is now prevalent in all correctional systems.

In the 1960s, under a traditional authority administration, the system of informers died out, and relationships between prison officers and inmates became more complex and problematic, with a greater number of African American prison officers. Privileges for inmates became less valued, and the civil rights movement contributed to inmate politicization when black Muslims made demands for the recognition of their religion and linked the prison to racism and repression (Jacobs 1977: 59).

As Crouch (1980: 12) explains, during the 1960s the courts reoriented their view of inmate petitions and claims, defining four general categories of prisoners' rights:

1. Prisoner access to the court to challenge convictions and treatment during confinement
2. The Eighth Amendment prohibition on cruel and unusual punishment, extending it to include conditions such as overcrowding and isolation
3. Procedural protections applying to decisions on issues like discipline, transfer, and eligibility for parole
4. The First Amendment freedoms of religion, assembly, and speech, as well as the prohibition on discrimination on grounds of race

As a result of judicial activism and the social activism of the late 1960s, many inmates, especially minorities, were provided with a political rhetoric and ideology that radicalized prisons (Crouch 1980: 22).

During the period from 1960 to 1980, there was a marked change in the inmate population because prisons increasingly housed African Americans and young men who had access to radical ideas. Traditional solidarity among inmates gave way to sectional arrangements based on race, and the fundamentals of the old inmate code, like doing your own time and avoiding confrontations with staff, were displaced in the face of new attitudes by young, tough, and often gang-affiliated inmates (Crouch 1980: 23). As Crouch notes, such inmates did not adhere to the familiar pattern of interactions between officers and inmates, resulting in a much greater level of uncertainty for the officers in these interactions. In the case of women inmates, Owen (1998: 176) similarly noted in her research in a California women's prison that the old convict codes had changed now that gangs had entered the prisons, with the older inmates stressing the rude, disrespectful, and inconsiderate attitudes of the new, young gangbangers.

At Stateville Prison, professional administration emerged during the period from 1970 to 1975, based on what Jacobs calls a rational-legal bureaucracy comprising the state Department of Corrections, an educated elite occupying the highest administrative positions, and civilians filling specialized treatment roles in the prison. The state Department of Corrections now took a much greater role in governing Stateville, and a new code of corrections introduced a more legalistic relationship between prison officers and prisoners, with a complex of administrative regulations covering matters that had previously been within the authority and discretion of prison officers. However, the gap between rules and working

procedures was evident because rules were simply not followed (Jacobs 1977: 79).

The new administration viewed the inmates as men who were redeemable, in contrast to the view under Ragen that the inmates were a separate species who needed to be kept away from society (Jacobs 1977: 82). The principal reason for ignoring rules was disorganization among the staff because job responsibilities were not clearly defined, and staff operated according to tradition and not procedure. The introduction of counselors for the inmates complicated the officers' task because this change had the effect of taking away the officers' role as the "givers of favors" for inmates, leaving them only with the "dirty work." Consequently, the officers' ability to offer rewards in exchange for adherence to the rules was much diminished (p. 97).

Finally, concluding his historical account of Stateville in 1975, Jacobs (1977) explains how the new relationship between prison officers and inmates became formalistic and bureaucratic. This is best exemplified by a grievance procedure under which inmates might lodge complaints about any aspect of prison life and have those complaints investigated and answered in writing within 10 days. Holding the staff accountable in this way had the effect of setting norms against which the legitimacy of decisions could be measured. This clearly affected the authority and power of the officers and created a new level of uncertainty. Nevertheless, Stateville could no longer cope with the demands of prisoners, interest groups, and the courts and still maintain control without the governance of a rational, legal bureaucracy (p. 103).

What does the history of Stateville Prison tell us about ethics and ethical norms in the prison environment? Insofar as the history of Stateville can be considered a representative history of correctional change, it shows how the discretion given to prison officers over their captives changed over time, as an authoritarian regime relying on inmate informers and favors, such as awarding administrative jobs to selected inmates, and a regime of intense supervision and an extreme level of discipline was replaced with an administration accountable to the courts and an environment where radicalized prisoners practiced social activism, political rhetoric, and ideology. As the nature of the prison population changed, so did interactions between officers and inmates, and in

A Closer Look

American Correctional Association Code of Ethics Preamble

The American Correctional Association expects of its members unfailing honesty, respect for the dignity and individuality of human beings, and a commitment to professional and compassionate service. To this end, we subscribe to the following principles.

Members shall respect and protect the civil and legal rights of all individuals.

Members shall treat every professional situation with concern for the welfare of the individuals involved and with no intent to personal gain.

Members shall maintain relationships with colleagues to promote mutual respect within the profession and improve the quality of service.

Members shall make public criticism of their colleagues or their agencies only when warranted, verifiable, and constructive.

Members shall respect the importance of all disciplines within the criminal justice system and work to improve cooperation with each segment.

Members shall honor the public's right to information and share information with the public to the extent permitted by law subject to an individual's right to privacy.

Members shall respect and protect the right of the public to be safeguarded from criminal activity.

Members shall refrain from using their positions to secure personal privileges or advantages.

Members shall refrain from allowing personal interest to impair objectivity in the performance of duty while acting in an official capacity.

Members shall refrain from entering into any formal or informal activity or agreement which presents a conflict of interest or is inconsistent with the conscientious performance of duties.

Members shall refrain from accepting any gifts, service, or favor that is or appears to be improper or implies an obligation inconsistent with the free and objective exercise of professional duties.

Members shall clearly differentiate between personal views/statements and views/statements/positions made on behalf of the agency or Association.

Members shall report to appropriate authorities any corrupt or unethical behaviors in which there is sufficient evidence to justify review.

Members shall refrain from discriminating against any individual because of race, gender, creed, national origin, religious affiliation, age, disability, or any other type of prohibited discrimination.

Members shall preserve the integrity of private information; they shall refrain from seeking information on individuals beyond that which is necessary to implement responsibilities and perform their duties; members shall refrain from revealing nonpublic information unless expressly authorized to do so.

(Continued)

(Continued)

Members shall make all appointments, promotions, and dismissals in accordance with established civil service rules, applicable contract agreements, and individual merit, rather than furtherance of personal interests.

Members shall respect, promote, and contribute to a work place that is safe, healthy, and free of harassment in any form.

SOURCE: Reprinted with permission of the American Correctional Association, Alexandria, VA.

terms of ethical standards, a level of uncertainty in relations between officers and prisoners was generated as traditional prison attitudes were radicalized. With the coming of professional administration after 1970, a new managerial approach introduced different levels of governance and a much more legalistic relationship between prison officers and prisoners. Now, administrative regulations replaced prison officer discretion, but rules were nevertheless broken because of an absence of clearly defined job responsibilities. Over time, officers became subject to oversight through grievance procedures, and an atmosphere in which ethical conduct could be monitored by prison administrators and by the prisoners themselves replaced the certainties and absolutism of the early period.

CORRECTIONS SUBCULTURE

The notion that an inmate subculture exists in prison was first proposed by Donald Clemmer (1940) in *The Prison Community,* where he argued that inmates take on the customs and culture of the penitentiary. Later studies, however, have proposed that features of the inmate subculture are imported into institutions by the inmates themselves and are not derived from the culture developed through prisonization.[2] *Is there a guard*

subculture that parallels that of the inmates? If so, is it imported, or is it generated by prison work itself? How does the guard culture impact ethical practice and standards?

In light of the popular image of prisons and "guards," suggesting that "guards" are brutal and uncaring and that inmates and prison officers maintain relations that are hostile and even violent, it is easy to argue that men and women become prison officers because the occupation of guarding captives appeals most to those who are sadistic and who enjoy exercising arbitrary power over the powerless. Kauffman (1988: 166), drawing on her experience as a prison officer and as a researcher in prisons, contends, however, that the importation model is inappropriate, and that the prison subculture as it relates to prison officers is fostered and maintained by the prison work itself. She explains that initially she entered the prison with sympathetic attitudes toward inmates and skeptical attitudes toward prison officers, but within a short period, her sympathies had reversed. She observed that other new officers also appeared to be substantially influenced by their prison experience and underwent a similar transformation. Her own study of the issue suggests that neither importation nor prisonization by itself shapes officer recruits and the guard culture (see Chapter 8) but that the culture appears to be the product "of a complex interaction of importation, socialization, deportation, and cultural evolution" (p. 167).

Subculture and Socialization

Prison officer recruits are socialized to the guard subculture during their training, and their individual

---

2. The term *prisonization* was coined and defined by Donald Clemmer (in Wheeler 1961: 697) as "the taking on in greater or lesser degree, of the folkways, mores, customs and general culture of the penitentiary." The outcome, according to Clemmer, was that inmates internalized a "criminal outlook" that made them impervious to conventional values systems (p. 697).

motivation for joining corrections may contribute to their socialization. Looking at the motivation of prison officer recruits, Kauffman (1988: 170) found that the guard occupation appealed to those who were unemployed or were from communities in which any state job was considered a significant benefit. More than half of the 40 recruits in her study gave financial considerations as their only or primary reason for becoming prison officers, and recruits were typically drawn from locations with high unemployment rates where any state job was welcomed not only by the individual but also by his or her family members. Some recruits gave social work motivations for seeking employment as an officer, seeing the prison officer career as a stepping-stone to other careers in criminal justice. Some 20% of those interviewed gave their main motivation as a desire to become law enforcement officers, and this group would seem to be the one most attracted by the power and authority enjoyed by prison officers (p. 175). This group exemplified the stereotype of the prison guard (the "frustrated cop") for whom corrections is a second choice but at least gives them the opportunity to sanction criminals in the prison if not on the street. This group focused mainly on family tradition and their wish to achieve status within the community. In terms of tradition, a number of groups were the sons or relatives of police or prison officers, and others saw themselves as having grown up with the law.

When the recruits as a whole were asked to respond to hypothetical dilemmas involving inmates, most approved of an officer acting in a sympathetic manner toward inmates. For example, 95% responded that an officer who broke up a fight between inmates should investigate the cause but do nothing if the fight was not serious, instead of giving the inmates an automatic disciplinary charge (Kaufmann 1988: 179). In terms of ethical standards of conduct, 45% approved of an officer not intervening if he or she observed fellow officers assaulting an inmate (p. 180). This question evoked the least sympathetic response toward inmates.

In discussing the socialization of prison officers, Kauffman (1988: 186) found that officers tended to appropriate the values of the prison over their own established behavioral norms. There was a considerable dichotomy between the formal training program the officers had undergone and their on-the-job training at Walpole because the new recruits were left on their own to handle difficult and dangerous positions within the institution without, as they perceived it, receiving any substantial support from the administration. To add to their burden, new officers received little or no support from their fellow officers, who tended to show indifference to their plight, even ignoring them altogether beyond the minimum communications necessary to change shifts. Conover (2001) reports a similar experience at Sing Sing (see Chapter 8).

Kauffman (1988) discusses how the new recruits found themselves in a state of depression about the institution and the inmates, seeing themselves faced with the reality of violence and the pervasive atmosphere of fear. Therefore, in contrast to typical prison officers, recruits entered the prison tasked, as a result of their training, with the aim of being sympathetic to inmates. Once there, they were thrown into a hazardous and difficult job, suffering isolation from colleagues and feeling the same degree of alienation from the administration and inmates. To survive, prison officers had to give up old values and norms of behavior and adopt those of the officer subculture (p. 198). Kauffman explains that some recruits were unable to vary their behavior toward inmates, and as a result of making their sympathy toward inmates widely known became casualties and were expelled by their fellow officers, who would respond angrily and with resentment to their liberal views about inmates (p. 206). These recruits suffered complete isolation (one was assigned to the guard towers on the midnight shift), and many officers refused to talk to these recruits. Finally, as one recruit put it, "You're either going to have to fit in and be like these people or you're going to get hurt" (p. 207).

Accordingly, those recruits who were unable to adapt to prison values and complete the process of socialization were subjected to ostracism, harassment, or assignment to the outermost bounds of the prison as forms of expulsion from the prison culture. In some cases, where expulsion was neither practical nor desirable, but where socialization had also failed, the prison culture was obliged to accommodate differing values. This was particularly true during the early 1970s, when prison riots occurred at Attica and in New Mexico, and values had to change. In this respect, Kauffman (1988: 209) reports that Walpole was quite a different institution in the late 1970s than it had been at the beginning of that decade.

Kauffman's Guard Types

Noting that guards varied in their attitudes toward inmates and other guards, Kauffman (1988: 250–251) identified five types of guards: Pollyannas, white hats, hard asses, functionaries, and burnouts. *Pollyannas* were guards who cared about their colleagues but were critical of the manner in which they dealt with inmates. These guards adopted a helping strategy as a means of coping with the prison environment, and they expressed their sympathy for inmates, helped them if they had needs, talked to them, and found rewards in doing these things. *White hats* were guards holding positive attitudes toward inmates but negative attitudes toward their fellow guards. They were invested in working with people, showed compassion and understanding for inmates, and pointed out the absence of such compassion in their fellow guards. *Hard asses* were the antithesis of white hats, showing hostility toward inmates but identifying closely with fellow guards. This group was typically young and inexperienced, regarded Walpole as an adventure, and found its violence stimulating. They tended to see the prison world as guards in conflict with inmates—a conflict of good against evil. Nevertheless, Kauffman found hard asses few in number at Walpole, mainly because the attitudes displayed by the hard asses were likely to provoke payback from inmates. *Burnouts* displayed negative attitudes toward both their fellow guards and inmates and were able to cope with the prison experience only barely, if at all. For these guards, prison had become such a dominating factor in their lives that they were unable to cope with the outside world. For example, one burnout always kept his back to the wall, another would jump if a door slammed, and another was unable to cope with the crowds in the city or in stores. *Functionaries* coped with prison by closing their minds to it, including both inmates and guards. They saw prison work as a dead end, as nonproductive, and as "maintaining that human warehouse" (p. 257). They expressed no enjoyment in their work, but simply needed the job and found no reward in it.

Crouch and Marquart (1980) argue that the guard subculture is crucial to the process of socializing the newly recruited guard because for all intents and purposes, recruits imitate the more experienced prison officers and learn from them how to perceive inmates, how to manage them, and how to anticipate trouble. According to their study, new recruits are taught to perceive inmates as lazy, averse to work, and having "turned to crime" as the easy way out. New recruits are continuously reminded to dominate inmates, to keep a social distance from them, and to keep the upper hand in dealing with inmates through using profanity freely and routinely.

Some researchers argue that there is no guard subculture. For example, John Klofas (1984: 174) makes the case that while prison work has unique aspects, there is no set of norms adverse to inmates, something that underpins popular conceptions of a prison guard subculture. He suggests that existing studies indicate that the notion of a guard subculture serves only to reinforce guard stereotypes. In his view, a more accurate account of the practice of guarding reveals important processes in the guard group that merely provide the illusion that certain guard norms favor harsh attitudes toward inmates.

POWER AND AUTHORITY IN PRISON: CONTROLLING THE INMATES

The most obvious fact about the prison environment is that prison officers are vested with power and authority over the prisoners and exercise that power to control them in accordance with prison rules and regulations. A number of studies have attempted to explain the basis and nature of this coercive power and authority. It is the exercise of this power that creates ethical issues and dilemmas.

In his conceptualization of power in prisons, Hepburn (1985: 146) catalogs five forms of power: legitimate power, coercive power, reward power, expert power, and referent power. With *legitimate power*, officers are invested with authority to command as a result of their position as a guard of prisoners. It is the position of prison officer itself within the institutional structure that confers the right to give instructions and to be obeyed. In other words, an officer's orders are obeyed because they are the orders of a prison officer, and prisoners comply by virtue of their status as prisoners. In a 1981 survey of prison officers at New York's Auburn Prison, Lombardo (in Hepburn 1985: 46) found that nearly half of the 50 officers surveyed believed the source of their power over prisoners derived from their position as enforcers of prison rules.

Coercive power is based on inmate perceptions that prison officers have the capacity to punish prisoner disobedience. As was discussed earlier, Sykes (1958/1999) notes that officers who rely on this kind of power run the risk of prisoner retaliation as well as the risk that their superiors will question their ability to exercise control over inmates.

Reward power describes situations where prisoners perceive that prison officers are able to issue rewards—for example, through making recommendations to committees dealing with matters such as work assignments, participation in programs, and release on furlough. The fact that officers may confer rewards is itself a basis of power. However, as a result of bureaucratic and judicial action, prison officers nowadays are less able to influence internal decisions than they have been in the past. Nevertheless, although the ability to make these formal rewards may have lapsed, a system of informal rewards has been sustained under which officers will compromise with prisoners on the basis of reciprocity. This form of reward making encompasses such things as the toleration of minor rule violations, petty stealing, and making concessions to inmate leaders.

Expert power derives from the prisoners' perception that prison officers have some special skill or expertise. Such power is especially likely to arise in prisons where treatment is emphasized and where officers are seen as part of the overall therapeutic environment. This power may be undermined by the unwillingness of prisoners to acknowledge the competence of prison officers as well as through bureaucratic administrative procedures that reduce guard autonomy and consequently provide them with fewer opportunities to demonstrate expertise.

Finally, *referent power* is the power a guard exercises as a result of gaining the respect and admiration of prisoners. Here, the officer's personal qualities, including in particular leadership skills and success in the art of persuasion, give some officers what Lombardo calls "personal authority" (1989: 149). Prison officers with this power are considered fair in their relations with prisoners, as showing a degree of respect for them, and as not acting out of malice or in an arbitrary manner.

In his survey of how these kinds of power operated in one prison, Hepburn (1985: 155) discovered that prison officers thought that their powers of control derived largely from their position as officers—that is,

from their legitimate authority—and from their reputation for competence and good judgment (i.e., Lombardo's "personal authority"). Of the five bases of power, prison officers considered legitimate and expert power to be instrumental in ensuring prisoner compliance, followed by referent power, coercive, and finally, reward power. Also, the greater the guard's experience, the greater the importance he or she attached to expert power and the less importance was placed on coercive and legitimate power (p. 160).

Lombardo (1989: 93) developed a typography of prison officer authority comprising *personal authority* and *legalistic authority*. In his survey of guard attitudes toward inmates, over 60% of the officers perceived that their authority derived from their personal style of presentation—that is, from the way they handled and dealt with inmates—and from their interactions with inmates. These officers did not feel that rules or the fact that they were wearing a uniform endowed them with authority, and they thought it was necessary to develop and, in effect, *earn* the necessary authority, the key to which was the ability of the guard to get an inmate to recognize the legitimacy of his authority. Most agreed that consistency was key in gaining legitimacy. However, earning legitimacy was seen to be a long-term process, and some officers suggested that a period of 5 to 10 years was required. These officers saw reliance on rules as unnecessary once a guard had developed a realistic appreciation of his own abilities and of inmates' expectations. At this point, rules no longer constituted a major source of authority and were deemed necessary only in extreme cases. The more experienced officers thought that the younger officers, who were unsure of themselves, would experience more difficulty in gaining compliance from inmates. They considered that interactions with inmates about rules could erupt into major confrontations, principally because the younger officers would be anxious not to "lose face" and have what they considered their weak authority diminished further (p. 94).

In the case of legalistic authority, a group of prison officers thought their authority derived from legal foundations, and they saw no need to earn the right to it. They saw themselves as a part of the criminal justice system, having lawful authority over those who had broken the law. Some thought this legally based view of authority derived from their job description as a prison officer, whereas others considered its origin to be the rules and regulations of the institution, backed up with support from the prison administration (Lombardo 1989: 97).

Those professing a belief in personal authority as well as those favoring legalistic authority agreed that full enforcement of institutional regulations would effectively cause the institution to cease operating because all inmates would be forever locked down for rule violations. As a whole in Lombardo's study, prison officers were always cognizant of the actual or potential impact of any inmate's conduct on the officers themselves, on other inmates, and on the overall climate within the institution. As well, most agreed that it was not the rules per se that created problems but inconsistencies in rule enforcement, a matter of great concern to the inmates (Lombardo 1989: 99).

The Battle for Compliance

According to Sykes's 1958 study, prison officials saw themselves engaged with the prisoners in a "battle for compliance" that superseded any task of reform or rehabilitation (1958/1999: 38). To support this observation, he points to the existence of violence, sexual violence, and theft as commonplace events within prisons. One might think that the prison bureaucracy would be able to impose its will on the inmates in an unchallenged fashion and would be able to act in an arbitrary or capricious manner if it thought fit. However, Sykes insightfully observed that the prison officers were in fact "engaged in a continuous struggle to maintain order" and that their dominant position did not reflect the prison reality (p. 42). He concluded that the reason the officers needed to negotiate their power rather than simply enforce their authority arose in part from constraints imposed on officers' use of force by the prison society. Physical coercion, while it might seem an obvious way of enforcing an authoritarian rule, was simply ineffective, and prison officers had to fall back on a system of awards and punishments in negotiating order with the inmates. Physical violence was always affected by the low guard/inmate ratio and by the danger that using violence might touch off further violence.

The close, intimate relationship and association between prison officers and prisoners in the New Jersey State Maximum Security Prison in Sykes's (1958/1999) study gave rise to a relationship of reciprocity because officers could not remain distant from inmates or completely withdraw from them. Prison officers were evaluated by their supervisors on their ability to control inmates; they would therefore want to demonstrate that they were able to perform their tours of duty with the minimum amount of trouble; and they would always be aware that riots and hostage taking are possible causes of ruptures in the negotiation of power. This view of evaluating an officer's capability to handle inmates is supported by Eric Poole and Robert Regoli (1980: 221), who found in a survey of prison officers that a high rate of disciplinary action was perceived by superiors as evidence of poor work performance and of an inability to handle inmates. This is an inevitable consequence of evaluating officers in terms of the inmates they control. Similarly, in a study in three California prisons, Daniel Glaser and Lincoln Fry (1987: 34) found that a clear majority of staff at all three institutions agreed with the statement that officers reporting all rule violations coming to their notice would be seen by supervisors as individuals who could not control the inmates on their units.

Rewards and Punishments

Sykes (1958/1999: 50) does not think that the use of rewards and punishments offers an adequate basis for prison officers to enforce control. He considers that punishments are insufficiently different to the regular routine of prison life to count for anything and notes that rewards are already offered at the start of a prison term, principally in the form of "good time."[3] Thus, privileges and rewards are

---

3. The term *good time* refers to the proportion of the inmate's sentence that is deducted for "good behavior." In indeterminate sentences, this time is automatically deducted from the sentence imposed by the court, unless the inmate commits a new offense while in prison or violates disciplinary rules that result in a reduction of the reduced period of the sentence. Although the deducted period in indeterminate sentences is automatically applied if there are no violations within the prison environment, it is considered "earned" on the basis of the inmate's good behavior. Indeterminate sentences were developed under the rehabilitative model of punishment. However, the fact that good time is automatic except when violations of prison rules occur can reduce its value as an incentive. In cases where the court sentence specifies a determinate sentence, the possibility of good time does not apply. Determinate sentences without good time are the result of "truth in sentencing" policies.

not specifically tied to everyday conduct and compliance but are already granted, and this means there is an absence of any ongoing positive incentives for either "guards" or inmates (p. 52). Sykes argues that ultimately the authority of the guards is corrupted by their having to continually compromise with their captives so that, paradoxically, their dominant position can only be enforced through accommodations with inmates (p. 58).

In her study of the prison system in Massachusetts, with a central focus on Walpole, the maximum-security prison, Kauffman (1988: 54) discusses inducements and rewards and finds that at Walpole, in particular, systematic rewards for inmates were essential to ensure their sustained cooperation. For example, inmate workers in the institution were allowed to obtain food from the kitchen, and even small tasks performed by inmates prompted award giving. According to Kauffman (pp. 54–55), although rewards might be limited to a packet of cigarettes or buying an inmate a soda, guards might offer more significant rewards in the form of contraband (especially drugs), information, and refraining from prosecuting inmate offenses. Nevertheless, award giving was not without its dangers, including these possibilities:

- Inmates might try to corrupt guards and make allegations about officer corruption (such allegations were regularly made).
- Rewards might be used by inmates to blackmail guards to ensure the continuation of those rewards.
- The rewards themselves might cause disputes or even violence among inmates unless they were evenly distributed.
- Valuable rewards such as drugs would engender more conflict.
- Officers engaging in the reward process ran the risk of endangering their own fellow guards—for example, through bringing drugs into the prison.
- Rewards might not be adequate to induce compliance.

Enforcing Rule Violations

Based on his study, Lombardo (1989: 105) maintains that the process of corruption is far more complex than Sykes describes it and that although inmate cooperation with prison officers is a factor, the relationship between officers and inmates with respect to rules also plays a part in handling minor rule violations. The inmates viewed prison officers who write violation reports for minor offenses as lacking the ability to handle things on a man-to-man basis and as having a strategy designed to avoid losing the cooperation of the inmates by creating tensions over minor rule violations. Minor violations included failing to shave or have a haircut and violating rules concerned with cell neatness, a common occurrence (p. 106). The officers' focus was very much on the use of rule violations within an ongoing testing process with the inmates. Informing the inmate of a rule violation rather than writing a citation for it was not considered an exercise of leniency. Instead, it was regarded as an act of strength because the guard was asserting his control over the situation, and by not writing a citation, the guard was demanding the inmate's acknowledgment of the guard's control (p. 109). Like police officers dealing with the public, the inmate's attitude or perceived attitude becomes crucial in determining a guard's response to a minor rule violation; many officers in the Lombardo study perceived inmate attitude as more important than actual conduct. Clearly, prison officers are alert for challenges to their authority and person and are prepared to interpret conduct as a personal challenge, sometimes pursuing questions of attitude and ignoring the behavior that prompted the interaction with the inmate. One guard summed up his view of inmates' behavior as follows:

> Seventy to seventy-five percent there's no problem with. Tell them to do things and they do it. They look at the CO as doing a job. But fifteen to thirty percent you have problems with regardless. They hate the world and the CO's because they deal with the CO's most frequently and the CO's represent the state. Those guys give you lots of problems with drugs, extortion and verbal abuse. They're constantly into something. (in Lombardo 1989: 115)

Prison officers pointed out that inmates are better educated and more organized than before and move in groups that are involved in drugs and extortion (Lombardo 1989). They stressed that control within the prison is now in the hands of younger inmates and gangs rather than with the "old timers," as was previously the case.

Noting the changes at Auburn Prison between 1976 and 1986, officers affirmed that violence and drugs were now factors that were not present in 1976, that individual discretion had been replaced during that period by formal procedures requiring staff to give explanations to inmates, and that this change had rendered them more accountable (Lombardo 1989: 121). One outcome of this reduced discretion is that officers no longer perceive themselves as participants in the functioning of the institution and that they sense a lack of support from administrators. These perceptions have created a greater sense of isolation because officers feel alienated both from the workplace and from the administration.

Informal Controls

In addition to formal controls over inmates through the formal disciplinary process, it is common within the prison environment to find that prison officers exercise various informal controls. Again, the operation of these controls can produce ethical issues and dilemmas.

An example of these informal controls operated within the Massachusetts state prison system. Writing disciplinary reports was not seen as an appropriate means of maintaining control because writing reports for rule breaches resulted in inmate threats of reprisals, derision from fellow prison officers, and a general loss of respect for the ticket writer (Kauffman 1988: 62). Kauffman found that most officers rarely wrote disciplinary reports, except for major infractions. The actual disciplinary sanctions that might be imposed were limited and did not substantially affect a prisoner's status because they were restricted to loss of "good time," being placed in isolation, or being relocated to a more secure block within the prison. The limited sanctions meant that officers considered writing disciplinary tickets a waste of their time, and they therefore resorted to informal punishments. As one officer put it, "If you give them your own type of punishment they'll think more" (p. 64). At Walpole, a guard might resort to locking inmates in their cells instead of issuing a disciplinary report for an infraction such as an inmate refusing to get back into line. This informal punishment would be implemented when the guard simply refrained from unlocking that inmate's cell during the daily prison routine.

This practice of locking down the guilty inmate would be especially effective on Friday nights because the inmate usually had to wait in his cell until Monday morning before he could see the deputy superintendent.

Similarly, Lombardo (1989) found that at Auburn guards sometimes resorted to unofficial action if they believed that established procedures would be ineffective. For example, an officer might submit a violation report on Friday, knowing that no action would be taken on that violation until Monday. However, issuing the violation would have the effect of placing the inmate in "keep lock" for 2 days, whereas the actual penalty would probably have been less severe.

Other informal methods of control included guards flushing toilets back into particular cells, shutting off the electricity for an entire tier of cells, turning off the hot water, withholding toilet paper or matches, or even keeping back food (Kauffman 1988: 65). Sometimes, more indirect and secretive methods were employed, such as making inmates wait substantial periods of time before allowing them to make phone calls, denying access to writing paper, destroying an inmate's plants that he had carefully cultivated in his cell, or scratching a piece of furniture manufactured by an inmate in the prison factory. As one officer explained, "There's so many ways you can get these guys" (p. 66). These methods would often be employed as an alternative to physical reprisals that might provoke administrative action against the guards themselves.

Lombardo (1989) also noted forms of informal control at Auburn. For example, one device included locking a man out of his cell for some time while others were locked in, isolating the inmate and causing a sense of anxiety. Guards also resorted to disconnecting an inmate's water supply or electricity supply and leaving a "keep lock" tag on a cell door, which would result in an inmate being locked up for a number of days until it was discovered that the tag was an error. Methods of getting back at inmates in an unofficial way included not informing an inmate of a scheduled appointment. In these extralegal approaches, it is important that the inmate is aware of the deliberate nature of the guard's action and appreciates that a message is being given that the guard can make the inmate's life uncomfortable (p. 101).

Prisoner "Power"

The notion that prisoners have any "power" within a prison seems to contradict the very nature of the prison environment. However, some activities on the part of inmates can be viewed as attempts to gain power or to resist guard power; these actions include using the court process to enforce rights, manufacturing weapons, employing unprovoked violence against prison officers, and coercing other inmates.

Kauffman (1988: 71) points to the upsurge in prison litigation during the 1960s and 1970s as instances of inmate power that counterbalanced administration power over inmates. During this period, jailhouse lawyers began to gain status within the prison as sources of authority who could contest prisoners' rights with prison officers and with the administration. Similarly, some inmates attempted to influence the course of events within the prison through their positions as trustees. For example, in some prisons, trustees unofficially break in new officers and provide them with assistance in maintaining control. Most important, some inmates seek to control prison officers through coercion, either through direct violence or threats. A more nuanced approach to gaining power takes the form of inmates competing with officers for control over the inmate population, such as through the formation of gangs or through persuasion, inducement, and manipulation. This kind of control can include victimizing other inmates, itself a major problem in U.S. prisons (p. 73). For example, at Walpole, inmate coercion of other inmates included stabbings over card games or a carton of cigarettes, rapes, robbery, and murder (p. 74).

In the contest between inmates and prison officers, inmates may manufacture weapons. In contrast, officers do not carry guns, which are consigned to the prison perimeter and never brought inside. Officers are limited to the use of batons or, in larger scale conflicts, tear gas and perhaps dogs. The exercise of guard power also relies on the flow of information, and in this respect, Kauffman (1988: 79) reports that in Massachusetts prisons, officers were often ill informed about occurrences amongst inmates. Prison officers were few in number, were socially distant from their captives, and were present in the prison only while on duty, as compared to inmates, who occupied the prisons continuously. Generally, while the use of coercion and force might have some attraction in offering an immediate solution to a power struggle, its use may cost officers dearly over time by decreasing their authority and undermining their legitimacy.

Kauffman (1988: 125–126) distinguishes spontaneous and unprovoked violence against prison officers from spontaneous provoked violence. Spontaneous and unprovoked violence was feared the most by the officers, and they considered drugs to be the main cause of such unprovoked acts. In the case of provoked violence, officers would sometimes precipitate spontaneous violence against themselves through miscalculation or ineptness by forcing inmates into situations where they felt compelled to resist with violence. The most common occasion for such provoked violence was within an inmate's cell block at a time when he was about to be removed to segregation. In such situations, some inmates would resist; however, they were usually handled. Others would fight after provocation or because of their belief that they would receive a beating no matter what they did. Sometimes inmate violence would be calculated as an act of retaliation for the officer's conduct. An officer who wrote too many tickets or beat too many heads would eventually set himself up for payback, usually within a year or even 2 years. In one study of incident reports in New York state prisons, S. C. Light (1991) looked at the motivating factors underlying inmate assaults on prison officers and found that the majority of assaults were random acts of violence (26%). The second-most frequent reason for an assault (13%) was as a response to a direct order from an officer, such as to leave an area. A further 11% of assaults were classified as protests where inmates believed they had been treated unfairly. Drugs and alcohol and emotional instability accounted for the lowest number of assaults.

Corruption of Authority

The notion that a prison officer's authority over inmates can become corrupted is well established in correctional studies and is frequently referred to as a category of ethical misconduct. In essence, *corruption of authority* refers to a practice by prison officers of deliberately refraining from enforcing prison rules and regulations.

Contrasting police and prison officers' use of discretion, Lombardo (1989: 201) notes that when a policeman decides whether and how to enforce the law, this decision is considered an exercise of his or her discretion; however, when a guard decides when and how to enforce rules, his or her decision is constructed as an exercise in corruption of authority. This is because deciding not to enforce the rules is perceived by prison officers as necessary to gain inmate cooperation and is a reflection of the officers' relative powerlessness. Both decisions are exercised with discretion, but the police action is cast in positive terms and the guard's decision in negative terms, thus reflecting the general perception that prison officer work is distasteful, unrewarding, and of low, nonprofessional status.

Sykes (1958/1999) describes the corruption of authority, and Crouch and Marquart (1980: 77–78) summarize two other forms of potential corruption. The first is the loss of authority that may arise when officers become too friendly with inmates and fail to maintain the required social distance. This may be particularly prevalent with new recruits when the new officer feels herself or himself to be closer to the inmates than to superiors. The second form of potential corruption involves handing over officer tasks to inmates. When inmates carry out duties like mail delivery and housekeeping, the officers may become dependent on their labor, and to that extent, their authority may be undermined or dissipated. Webb and Morris (1980: 150), in their interviews with prison officers, found that although the officers frequently commented on the need for discipline and thought that strict discipline was good for inmates, they were also quick to point out the need not to go strictly by the book, that rules were made to be broken, that rules were not absolutes, and that a commonsense approach had to be taken in applying discipline.

James Hepburn (1985: 191) discusses how prison officers operate as agents of social control and draws attention to the "role ambiguity" that officers experience as a result of having to perform both treatment and custodial roles. The *treatment* role requires that officers demonstrate helping behaviors, enforce the rules with discretion, and establish a degree of personal relations with inmates. In contrast, the *custody* role calls for impersonal relationships, a controlling demeanor, and complete enforcement of prison rules. As well, role ambiguity is created when vague or contradictory instructions determine how the role is to be exercised. While prison officers are expected to show flexibility and discretion, they are still liable to be disciplined themselves if they violate or allow inmates to violate prison rules. Officers are also dependent on prisoners for their own physical safety, and they depend on inmates for the successful fulfillment of their own duties (p. 193). For example, inmates may resist officer control through work slowdowns or an increase in disciplinary problems, and this tends to focus the prison administration on an officer's inability to maintain control. Officers, therefore, may have to depend on prisoner cooperation to demonstrate their ability to manage prisoners and to obtain recognition and promotion. At the same time, officers may not be provided with adequate or clear rules for managing a potentially hostile inmate population.

PRIVATE PRISONS

For many years, certain institutions concerned with offenders have been de facto privatized because juvenile institutional facilities and adult community facilities were contracted out early on to the private sector. For example, in Massachusetts, juvenile institutions changed from being a network of state-run institutions in 1969 to a series of community-based programs and facilities by 1974. The Massachusetts Division of Youth Services operates all community-based facilities through private contractors (Logan 1990: 15).

Charles Logan (1990) defines private prisons as "those that are privately owned, operated, or managed, under contract to government" (p. 13), and Shichor (1995) regards them as "prisons or other institutions of confinement (jails, immigration and nationalization service facilities, detention centers, and secured juvenile justice facilities) operated and managed by private corporations for profit" (p. 2). Adult community facilities managed and operated by private contractors include shelters and halfway houses, while institutional facilities include detention and diagnostic centers and training schools (p. 14).

In addition, the Immigration and Naturalization Service has for many years contracted facilities to detain illegal aliens awaiting deportation. The most recent form of privatization has been the contracting of adult confinement facilities. By mid-1989, about a dozen private companies were running almost two dozen adult confinement institutions in about one dozen states (p. 20).

According to Aviram (2015: 99), the biggest private prison provider is the Corrections Corporation of America, which by 2012 was operating 67 correctional facilities and owned 49 located in 20 states and the District of Columbia. Most recently, there has been strong growth in the provision of privatized detention centers to house undocumented immigrants under threat of deportation. Prison privatization has spread to other countries, including the United Kingdom, Australia, and Canada, and is being actively promoted in South Africa.

There is a wide variation by state in the use of private prisons, with about half of the states having no inmates or just a few inmates housed privately and about one third having 10% or more housed in private prisons. Private prisons are concentrated in certain parts of the country: In the South and Southwest, 7% to 9% of inmates are accommodated in private prisons, compared to 2% to 3% in the Northeast and Midwest (Gottschalk 2015: 67). The states with the highest private rate are New Mexico (43%) and Montana (40%). In the federal system, about 16% of all inmates are in private prisons, and the federal government is the largest customer of the Corrections Corporation of America, providing 40% of its business in recent times (p. 68).

Studies have revealed that using private prisons saves little in costs—a 2001 report from the Department of Justice found that savings averaged only about 1%, mainly attributable to lower labor costs (Gottschalk 2015: 70). Private prisons tend to be more dangerous places, partly because prison officers are paid significantly less than those working in public facilities, provide less training, and have higher inmate-to-staff ratios. Consequently, staff turnover is higher (p. 70).

The proponents of prison privatization tend to justify their support by advancing pragmatic, rational arguments that emphasize the supposed economic benefit of contracting. Those against privatization stress the ethical and moral implications. This discussion will confine itself to the ethical implications, which fall broadly into four categories of questions:

1. Is it appropriate for imprisonment to be administered by anyone other than the state and its employees?
2. Is the profit motive compatible with the task of imprisoning offenders?
3. Does the existence of private prisons, in effect, create a demand for imprisonment that needs to be satisfied by greater levels of imprisonment than would otherwise be the case?
4. How do private prisons cope with the issue of use of deadly force?

These questions will now be considered.

1. Is it appropriate for imprisonment to be administered by anyone other than the state and its employees?

A core issue in the ethical debate about private prisons is the role of the state in administering punishment. As Richard Lippke (1997) puts it,

> Punishment has been seen as a state function in order to limit if not eliminate the influence of private interests over the detection, trial, and sanctioning of law breakers—in short, to ensure that all individuals are treated equally before the law. (p. 26)

As already explained in Chapter 6 a legal punishment is defined as that which is imposed and administered by an authority established by the legal system against which the offense has been committed. Punishment involves the state because the legal rules that constitute offenses are created by a legislature that operates in the name of the state. Theories concerning the relationship between the individual and the state involve the notion of the social contract. Thomas Hobbes argued that individuals freely transfer their rights to a powerful authority, the head of the state, who is thereby enabled to ensure that those individuals keep their promises and contracts. In exchange for this surrender of rights, the head of the state provides security and protection for citizens. John Locke argued along somewhat similar lines that individuals give up their political power to secure order, but he maintained that this power remains with those individuals who collectively constitute society. The task of the state is to protect individuals, but if the state fails in this task, individuals have the right to dissolve the state. In other words, Locke argued that the transfer of powers to the state operates conditionally on the state maintaining the life and liberty of its citizens (Shichor 1995: 47).

Classical liberal thinking argues that in spite of this social contract political power remains with the individuals who have delegated their powers to the state and that therefore ultimate power remains in the hands of the people. Consistent with this approach is the ideal of the "minimal state," which sees the state using a restricted, coercive power. Robert Nozick (1974: ix) argues that this coercive power is limited, for example, for the purpose of citizens giving aid to others or for the purpose of prohibiting activities for the good or protection of people. The notion of privatization stresses the role of the state as minimal and in fact questions the very principle of a state monopoly on crime control and punishment.

Opposed to classical liberal philosophy is the view that the state has the sole right to use legal coercive power (Weber 1964). Max Weber argues that offenders violate laws, and those laws are created by representatives of the state and in fact in themselves constitute the state. Therefore, it is the state that possesses sole authority to use coercive force for punishment because its sovereignty, based on the supremacy of the rule of law, has been violated by the criminal act (Reisig and Pratt 2000: 214). John Rawls supports this view, arguing that in a liberal society, coercive agencies must be under the control of the state because rational individuals would not endorse a political system that allows coercive force to be used privately. However, he sees the state as having the right to delegate lower-level functions of the state to private contractors if it serves the interests of society (p. 214).

Related to this debate is the constitutional question of whether, and to what extent, the state may delegate to private entities the power of punishing lawbreakers. On this issue, in 1986 the ABA criticized private prisons, expressing the view that "incarceration is an inherent function of the government and that the government should not abdicate this responsibility by turning over prison operation to private industry" (in Shichor 1995: 52). The ABA therefore takes the position that there is a principle that prevents the state from delegating the administration and control of punishment to private contractors and that the scale of delegation of state authority is irrelevant.

Those who argue in favor of privatization point to the fact that the state has the power to delegate its functions and has done so for many years in the field of punishment through juvenile programs and institutions and adult correctional programs. However, it can also be argued that the prison, as a total institution with almost complete control over inmates' lives, is in a special position in the field of punishment. In other words, the high level of coercion exercised by the state militates against any extensive delegation of its power to punish.

Associated with this issue of state delegation is the specific issue of the quasi-judicial functions exercised by prison administrations. There are a number of stages and issues in the process of imprisonment that give rise to quasi-judicial duties. For example, the term of imprisonment may depend on parole decisions, and the computation of good time and of release dates relies on administration reports about the conduct of inmates. Also, disciplinary action may have to be taken against inmates, and generally reports about inmate behavior are significant in the decision-making process. Those who favor privatization argue that proper government oversight and monitoring can ensure that these substantive and due process issues can be properly addressed. However, this tends to ignore the fact that the administration and staff of private prisons owe a duty to the company that employs them and may give loyalty and allegiance to the company rather than to a set of rules imposed by the state responsible for a particular private prison.

Opponents of privatization raise the issue of the symbolism surrounding punishment in the form of the uniform and insignia of correctional staff and the judiciary that express the public nature of punishment. Supporters of privatization argue, on the other hand, that symbolism is less important than substance and that those working in corrections are not elected by the people or politically appointed and are seen as symbols of the state's role in punishment only by virtue of their jobs (Shichor 1995: 55).

2. Is the profit motive compatible with the task of imprisoning offenders?

Those against the privatization of prisons find it a cause of concern that private corporations are attempting to make a profit on the punishment of people by running prisons. Shichor (1995: 259) argues that the government ought not to create such opportunities for private profit, but DiIulio (1990) does not think the profit motive amounts to a moral issue in the debate. The American Civil Liberties Union has argued that "the profit motive is incompatible with doing justice" (in Logan 1990: 72). This position essentially questions whether a private corporation is likely to put its own interests and welfare ahead of the interests of justice when it views the profit motive as crucial and therefore argues its incompatibility with the interests of justice. Historically, the prison system, however, has profited from the use of prison labor employed by private contractors and, particularly in the southern states, leasing out prisoners to corporations was a standard feature of the prison system. In this sense, therefore, profit and incarceration have a long tradition of association, and it makes little sense to suggest that the entire task of managing prisoners is somehow more morally objectionable than profiteering from the labor of inmates.

3. Does the existence of private prisons in effect create a demand for imprisonment that needs to be satisfied by greater levels of imprisonment than would otherwise be the case?

The argument here is that the corporations running private prisons may seek to influence policy makers and administrators through lobbying and associated activities to ensure that private prisons continue to be built and that they continue to profit from a high rate of incarceration. Originally, privatization was seen as a solution to the immense overcrowding caused by a deliberate policy of incapacitation and was intended to be a supplement to the existing prison system. The argument against privatization is that expanding the state's resources to punish will increase state control and that large numbers of people who would otherwise not be incarcerated will come under state control. In other words, an expansion of the prison system will be self-perpetuating; if prisons are built, they will be filled (Shichor 1995: 61).

Some now see corporate involvement in crime control—that is, the involvement of private industry in crime control generally, and in particular, the continuation of high incarceration rates—as part of an evolving criminal justice industrial complex. In states like New York, where prisons have been constructed in rural areas, they provide in some cases almost the only form of local employment and have replaced dying local industries (Christie 2000: 137). There is a powerful political and economic argument (often made by correctional unions) that these prisons must be supported as a source of employment and local economic activity. While unions may make this argument, it is easy to see how private corporations running prisons can ally themselves with such views and advocate them themselves. As Nils Christie (pp. 140–141) points out, the prison industry absorbs a large part of the workforce, and he estimates that the crime control industry employed 4% of the entire labor force in 1999.

Robert J. Lilly and Paul Knepper (1992: 175) have analyzed the characteristics of this criminal justice industrial complex and have shown that participants in the field of corrections have a close working relationship; that there is an overlap between the interests of corporations, unions, and agencies—for example, in terms of influence and the transfer of personnel (many employed in private prisons as prison officers and administrators were formerly public employees in the same field); that this complex operates with little public scrutiny; and that the participants define themselves as acting in the public interest by referring to their role in the punishment of law breakers.

4. How do private prisons cope with the issue of use of deadly force?

Chapter 8 discusses the legal position on the use of force by prison officers, pointing out that there are severe restrictions on its use. Those opposed to private prisons argue that, as a sensitive and complex issue, the use of force by employees of private companies against inmates raises questions about the legitimacy of any exercise of force by those employees. Some believe that private companies will try to cut costs through inadequate staffing and training of private prison staff and that this will result in a greater willingness to use force to maintain order (Shichor 1995: 102). It is unrealistic to argue that private prison staff should be prohibited from using any force because this might endanger their own safety and is not a realistic option. If it were to be prohibited, this would presumably mean that state employees would have to be located in the prison and called on for the use of force when needed. This, however, would defeat the purpose of privatization and add significantly to the organizational problems within the prison. Another suggestion is that private staff should be able to use nondeadly force

under a set of rules reserving the use of deadly force for government employees. Again, however, common sense suggests that this would be unworkable in practice.

This issue has only recently become significant because private companies have only lately become involved in managing maximum-security prisons and housing offenders considered violent (Harding 1998: 635). The private sector was able to compete for the management of a maximum-security prison for the first time in 1990 when bids were requested for a federal detention center in Kansas, and as of 2012, "137,200 (almost 9%) of the total U.S. prison population were housed in private facilities" (Carson 2015: 13; see Case Study 7.1).

Case Study 7.1 Private Prisons—A Good Policy Choice?

Report to the Attorney General: Inspection and Review of the Northeast Ohio Correctional Center

On November 25, 1998, the Department of Justice concluded a report to the U.S. Attorney General reviewing the management and operations of the Northeast Ohio Correctional Center in Youngstown, Ohio, owned and operated by the Corrections Corporation of America (CCA).

The report cited "fundamental breakdowns attributable to the institution and corporate management in meeting their most basic security missions" (p. 19). Among the major events that occurred at Youngstown prison were the following:

- The escape of six inmates
- Two homicides, including one that took place between known enemies in the high-security unit
- The stabbing of approximately 17 inmates as well as many other serious assaults on staff and inmates
- The discovery of numerous homemade weapons—30 were discovered in the first 2 months of operation
- The facility being forced to operate under full or partial lockdown to prevent further incidents

Among the particular issues of concern noted in the report was the absence of experienced midlevel managers and uniformed supervisors. Many persons placed in supervisory and senior positions lacked the experience and training required. For example, among the 30 sergeants, 16 had no prior correctional experience, and among the nine lieutenants, two had no prior correctional experience.

The practical arrangements for monitoring CCA performance at Youngstown involved the Department of Corrections hiring a consultant firm to monitor the contract to CCA on a less-than-full-time basis. No contract monitors were placed on site. However, finally, an experienced deputy warden was placed at the facility for monitoring purposes.

The report indicates that within 2 weeks of the arrival of the first inmates at the facility serious disturbances occurred, due in some cases to missing personal property of inmates, causing inmates to make threats to staff. One incident involved a supervisor ordering three canisters of gas to be dropped in each housing unit, causing the inmates to pour water on them, place garbage cans over them, and throw them into the showers. Inmates began making weapons, and two inmates were stabbed within a month.

In 2012, an audit report by the Ohio Department of Rehabilitation and Correction cited the Youngstown facility for 47 violations of state prison standards and found that the CCA was in compliance with only 66% of the state's standards (Aviram 2015: 106).

SOURCE: U.S. Department of Justice 1998.

DISENFRANCHISING INMATES

According to The Sentencing Project (2008: 1), by 2008 all states other than Maine and Vermont prohibited inmates from casting a vote while incarcerated for a felony. The Sentencing Project estimates that "5.3 million Americans, or 1 in 41 adults, have currently or permanently lost their voting rights as a result of a felony conviction." The organization points out that 13% or 1.4 million African American men are disenfranchised at a rate 7 times the national average and that 676,730 women are ineligible to vote based on a felony conviction. Two million white Americans (Hispanic and non-Hispanic) are disenfranchised, and 1 in 4 African American men are permanently disenfranchised in five states that deny the vote to ex-offenders. Felons on parole may not vote in 33 states, and in 29 of these, felony probationers are also excluded. Seven states disenfranchise categories of ex-offenders or disqualify them for specified periods of time, after which they may seek restoration of their right, and six states permanently disqualify ex-offenders (Kleinig and Murtagh 2005: 217–218).

It is estimated that on the basis of present incarceration rates, some 40% of African American males will come to be permanently disenfranchised in the states that exercise that option. Significantly, in the 2000 presidential elections, Florida contained an estimated 600,000 ex-offenders who could not vote. Disenfranchisement has an ancient history and in modern times reflects the Common Law notion of attainder, under which offenders could lose all their civil rights (Kleinig and Murtagh 2005: 218). Under the U.S. Constitution, the Fourteenth Amendment provided for disenfranchisement for "participation in rebellion, or other crime" (p. 219). The Supreme Court in 1974 interpreted the reference to other crime to allow disenfranchisement for any crime.

What justifies the notion of disenfranchising felons? For example, although many would consider the right to vote a crucial activity in a democracy, only 51.3% of those eligible to vote actually voted in the 2000 presidential elections (Kleinig and Murtagh 2005: 219). Arguments that are used to support disenfranchisement include these:

- *The social contract argument.* The idea here is that the felon rejects established authority and has rejected the constraints of the social contract. Given that attitude, such a person ought not to be allowed to participate in the electoral process (p. 220). Even if this argument is accepted, it does not necessarily justify a perpetual prohibition extending beyond imprisonment.
- *So-called electoral purity.* The Alabama Supreme Court in a case in 1884 cited the importance of the "purity of the ballot box" (p. 222). The idea here is that only worthy persons are fit to cast a vote, that allowing convicted felons or ex-felons to participate would undermine the electoral process, and that adverse consequences could flow from allowing felons to participate. For example, it might call into question the legitimacy of the outcome (p. 224).

John Kleinig and Kevin Murtagh (2005: 227) argue that there may be some offenses that justify disenfranchisement, such as electoral offenses and offenses representing a rejection of the state's authority—that is, offenses committed by those on death row or sentenced to life imprisonment. They suggest, however, that there should be no automatic presumption of forfeiture during a period of imprisonment. They offer three arguments in favor of prisoners having the right to vote:

- Voting would encourage prisoners to take a more active role in society as they reintegrate back into it.
- Ethically, it can be argued that those affected by decisions ought to have some say in the making of those decisions. For example, the concerns of prisoners and their interest in events affecting the prison system are not currently considered.
- If prisoners were able to vote, politicians would need to take account of their concerns, and they might reveal the serious deficiencies that exist in penal policy and practice. (pp. 229–230)

Several questions are raised by this issue. For example, is disenfranchisement part of the punishment for the crime, or is it a civil sanction that is a consequence of the crime? Is it morally justifiable as a policy and practice, especially when the contemporary effect is to disenfranchise significant numbers of African Americans? Conversely, can we really argue that the franchise is such a crucial attribute of democracy when only slightly more than half of those eligible to vote actually voted in the year 2000? Can there be any justification for disenfranchising anyone permanently and if so under what circumstances?

Reforms

Recently, policy changes in a number of states have introduced reforms so that during the period 1997 through 2010 an estimated 800,000 persons have regained the right to vote. Public opinion surveys now show that 8 in 10 Americans support voting rights for those who have completed their sentence, and almost two thirds support voting rights for those on parole or probation (Porter 2010: 3–4). Some states have simply repealed the lifetime disenfranchisement laws, for example, Iowa (2005) and Maryland (2002, 2007), while others have opted to restore rights to those on probation, for example, Connecticut (2001) and Rhode Island (2006). Many have introduced streamlined restoration processes.

The "Cutting Prison Time for Organ Donors" Closer Look box gives an example of an additional ethical consideration for the treatment of prisoners.

A Closer Look

Cutting Prison Time for Organ Donors: Is This Ethical?

South Carolina legislators are considering a law that would allow prisoners to donate organs or bone marrow in exchange for a reduced sentence. Questions about the ethics of this proposal include a comment from the executive director of Donate Life South Carolina, who is reported to have said, "It really muddies the water about motive. We want to keep it a truly altruistic act." Given the coercive environment of the prison and the reward for donating organs, is this not akin to selling body parts?

SOURCE: Adcox 2007.

SUMMARY

Crime control policies over the last 2 decades have produced an explosion in the prison population, and it is in the context of a policy of mass imprisonment and the consequent concerns about security and safety that ethical concerns in the prison environment now arise. When considering ethical issues, it is crucial to have an understanding of how prisons operate, their disciplinary regimes, and the experience of being both a prisoner and a guard. Contextualizing the prison environment and the experience of imprisonment provides a basis for analyzing and assessing ethical issues and dilemmas. This chapter has therefore provided this contextualization.

The organizational framework of guarding inmates has changed over time as early ad hoc individualistic approaches gave way to managerial and bureaucratic regimes that formulated detailed standards and rules about prisoner conduct. The composition of both the prison and the guard population has also changed over time, as prisoners have become radicalized and have claimed their rights through the courts.

What should be the basis for an ethical system of guarding prisoners? Some researchers emphasize the issue of punishment, pointing out that it is deprivation of liberty that is sanctioned by the courts and not additional penalties such as controlling visits, strip searching, or depriving prisoners of normal amenities. An ethical standard, therefore, that recognizes the essential humanity of prisoners would reflect the purpose of incarceration and protect prisoners from additional abuse. The role of prison officers and their interactions with coworkers and administrators are factors that should play a part in a correctional ethic. Strong power differences exist between officers and inmates, and decisions are constantly being made in uncertain situations. This creates a need to incorporate an ethical dimension into guard work. One extreme position, however, suggests that such is the nature of imprisonment that establishing any moral basis for the role of a guard is problematic. The brutality and degradation engendered by incarceration, it is argued, make it almost impossible for ethical and professional standards of conduct to be applied.

The detailed contextualization of prison work provided in this chapter shows how prison officers choose correctional employment, how they consider danger and mental tension as the core of their work, and how security and control are fundamental in their interactions with inmates. From this framework comes a guard's sense of suspicion about events that are different or which interrupt prison routines. A number of studies have shown how prison officers have no absolute power over inmates but are required to negotiate their dominance and how this can lead to what is called *corruption of authority*. Tensions within the role of guard include those between their treatment role and custodial role, each calling for different skills and perspectives. Ultimately, officers are dependent on the prisoners for their own safety and at the same time have to show to their superiors an ability to manage prisoners competently. This means that rule books are often ignored in the interests of flexibility and negotiation.

Studies have examined the nature of power in prisons, how guard authority is made up of a guard's personal authority and his or her legalistic authority, and how informal controls are employed to get back at inmates and to convey messages that reinforce guard authority. As with law enforcement, discretion is an important part of correctional work, even though the correctional discretion is considerably constrained by written rules and regulations that determine conduct for both prison officers and inmates. Closely linked to the issue of discretion is the prison guard subculture, which has been extensively studied, revealing how new guard recruits are socialized to follow the prison guard code, especially those aspects that promote solidarity between officers against all outside groups, including inmates. Typographies of "guards" have been produced that show types ranging from those who adopt a helping strategy to others who display negative attitudes toward both prison officers and inmates and are barely able to cope with the prison environment.

DISCUSSION QUESTIONS

1. There have been dramatic increases in the number of persons imprisoned in the United States over the last 20 years and a trend toward constructing supermax prisons. Discuss at least three ethical concerns that these two developments have given rise to in relation to inmates.

2. Explain the relationship between the different styles of prison management and how ethical issues might differ under each style of management.

3. In an ethical correctional system, all prisoners would be treated with humanity. Explain how prisoner humanity would be respected in the use of force and in the conditions of confinement.

4. What are some of the issues faced by prison officers in their interactions with inmates, and how do they cope with these issues?

5. What models explain prison officer power? How can officer authority be corrupted?

6. We know that prison officers often overlook minor rule violations because they need inmate cooperation. Is this ethical?

7. Does the prison officer subculture provide answers to ethical issues and dilemmas? If so, evaluate those solutions in terms of ethical standards.

8. Why is it considered unethical by some for the state to abdicate its responsibility for the administration of prisons to private companies?

9. Comment on the ethics of prisoner disenfranchisement in light of the fact, for example, that if such disenfranchisement is permanent, more than 40% of the African American male population will have no say in the policies and laws that have a significant effect on them

WEB RESOURCES

American Civil Liberties Union National Prison Project. https://www.aclu.org/issues/prisoners-rights
Amnesty International Women's Human Rights. http://www.amnestyusa.org
Correctional Association of New York. http://www.correctionalassociation.org/
The Corrections Connection. http://www.corrections.com
Mass Incarceration. Southern Poverty Law Center. https://www.splcenter.org/issues/mass-incarceration
National Institute of Corrections (NIC). http://www.nicic.org
Penal Reform International. http://www.penalreform.org
Vera Justice Institute. http://www.vera.org

8

ETHICS IN CORRECTIONS: GUARDING ETHICALLY

THE EXPERIENCE OF GUARDING

To understand how ethical issues arise in the practice of corrections, it is necessary to contextualize the experience of guarding. This contextualization can expose the anxieties and pressures faced by prison officers within the prison environment. A number of authors (Conover 2001; Crouch 1980b; Lombardo 1989) have pointed to common characteristics in those choosing a career in corrections. In particular, they note that people do not typically aspire to become prison officers; rather, seeking this work is often a reaction to the need for employment or is a result of an unexpected job change. For most seeking positions as prison officers, job security and a regular salary are paramount. In many rural areas, working in the prison system represents the only form of employment, and the prison offers the opportunity to remain in the local environment rather than having to travel to the city for work.

Lucien Lombardo (1989: 140) explains that about one third of the officers he interviewed at Auburn Prison considered danger and mental tension as the most dissatisfying parts of their job. From their point of view, *danger* referred not to the likelihood of violent events, but to the unpredictability of a violent occurrence. Conover (2001: 82) reports one incident in Sing Sing involving an inmate porter who had been sweeping the flats outside the cells with a push broom. When another inmate appeared, the porter attacked him, broke the broom handle over his head, and then tried to spear his face with the splintered ends. Most officers consider prison violence a constant possibility that might result from seemingly arbitrary events, and they believe in their ability to sense the likelihood of violence through their awareness of behavior patterns within the prison.

Prison officers frequently experience personal challenges from inmates. It follows that security and control are fundamental tenets of guard work because inmate misconduct not only threatens the prison order but also may impact the officers' personal safety (Crouch and Marquart 1980: 89). This concern for security and order tends to cause officers to view suspiciously any events that interrupt prison routines. For instance, the entry of "free world" treatment personnel into the prison is a particular cause of concern for most prison officers, who believe that outsiders know very little about inmates and fail to appreciate the need for constant security. Nonetheless, as was explained to Edgar May (1980: 111) by one prison commissioner, prison officer attacks on inmates have been greatly reduced because prisons are now far more open to outsiders. However, according to the same prison commissioner, when there is a physical conflict between an officer and an inmate and force is used to bring the inmate under control, inmates commonly claim that the officer "gets in a few extra licks" (p. 128). According to Ben Crouch and J. Marquart (1980), additional tenets of guard work taught to new recruits include the need to maintain social distance from the inmates and the dictum that guards must be "tough, knowledgeable, and able to handle inmates" (p. 90). *Knowledgeability* relates to the need for prison officers to understand the informal rules and processes that shape daily prison interactions and how to avoid being manipulated by inmates.

Prison officers are concerned about the lack of inmate understanding of their situation, especially in view of the fact that the inmates want the officers to understand their position. Some officers pointed to the sarcasm and perpetual insults they receive from inmates on a daily basis, which they say creates a hostile environment for them (Lombardo 1989: 143). Similarly, officers felt that they lacked the support of their supervisors and administrators, saw themselves as working against everyone, and felt isolated from both inmates and supervisors. G. L. Webb and D. Morris (1980: 150) found that officers perceived prison administrators as outsiders with political connections whose main focus was "looking good" and who did not possess the prison officers' knowledge of the institution and the inmate population.

The prison officers in Lombardo's study showed a particular concern for what they regarded as benefits conferred on inmates by the state department of corrections (1989: 155). For these officers, programs like work release, education release, and the ability for an inmate to receive a college education were considered improper benefits for inmates because, in their view, inmates were obtaining work while law-abiding citizens were unemployed.

GUARDING ETHICALLY

The modern era of corrections brought with it a set of written ethical standards for correctional officers and management. The code of ethics shown in the "Probation and Parole Officer's Code of Ethics" Closer Look box balances the welfare and legal rights of prisoners with obligations toward colleagues and the public. There are specific rules prohibiting corruption in the form of gifts, personal privileges, and conflicts of interest. There is also an obligation for staff to report corrupt or unethical behaviors, as well as a declaration of commitment to professional and compassionate service.

Commentators and correctional administrators have offered their own views about correctional ethics. The former commissioner of corrections in Massachusetts, George A. Vose Jr., articulated a philosophy of corrections around the concept of "good citizenship" (in Carroll 1998). He saw offenders mainly as individuals who had failed in their obligations as citizens after having received fewer benefits from that citizenship than others. He argued that if offenders are to become responsible citizens, it is essential that they are treated in a civil manner by correctional authorities, whose task is to model good citizenship by protecting certain fundamental rights. According to Vose, prisoner rights include "the right to safety, adequate care, personal dignity, meaningful activity, [and] ample opportunity for self improvement and hope for the future" (p. 262). Inmates on whom these rights are conferred must in turn act responsibly and respect the rights of others, and those inmates who do not act accordingly should be called to account through the firm, consistent, and lawful enforcement of correctional rules and regulations.

Ethical Dimensions: Punishment, Prison Conditions

In his discussion of ethics in corrections, John Kleinig (2001: 7) singles out the issue of punishment as central. He emphasizes that it is incarceration itself that is the punishment and that the purpose of incarceration is not to administer additional punishment over and above the inmate's deprivation of liberty. It is true that confinement and deprivation of liberty carry with them other deprivations, but he argues that these need to be related to the deprivation of liberty and must not be constructed so as to impose additional penalties. For example, control over visits may be justified as part of prison security but ought not to invalidate other practices concerning visitation and conjugal relations. Similarly, searching prisoners can also be justified on grounds of security, but the predominant practice of strip searching[1] may be considered as carrying an element of humiliation outside the bounds of proper security considerations. As Kleinig specifies, inmates "do not forfeit their essential humanity" (p. 7). Treatment that is intended to degrade or dehumanize inmates is not authorized by the sanctions society has imposed on them. Ultimately, most inmates will reenter society, hopefully having learned during incarceration more about their social responsibilities.

Agreeing with Kleinig, Richard Lippke (2007: 2), in suggesting the need for a normative theory of imprisonment, argues that many countries imprison offenders under conditions that cannot be morally justified. As he puts it, "Harsh and restrictive prison conditions, combined with disrespectful or abusive treatment of inmates, sends the message that offenders are contemptible, little more than dangerous wild animals to be severely chastised and restrained" (p. 3). In relation to conditions of confinement, Lippke makes a case for "minimally restrictive and reasonably humane prison conditions" in contrast to "extreme conditions of confinement" (p. 104). The latter category equates to supermaximum-security prisons, and Lippke argues that as a matter of morality we ought to prefer minimum conditions that are more consistent with the aims of punishment. Lippke's view is that basic prisoner welfare demands that prisoners receive adequate food and nutrition, are protected from violence, are not exploited or preyed on by others, receive physical and mental health care, live in clean and properly ventilated accommodation with adequate heat or air conditioning, wear appropriate clothing, and are provided with the means to maintain personal hygiene and enjoy some degree of privacy (p. 112).

Kleinig (2001: 9) suggests that a correctional ethic should also take account of the roles played by prison officers, especially of how they interact with their coworkers, the way in which their work is coordinated with others employed in the prison system, and the connections they make with the correctional administrative structure. There will also be ethical considerations in relation to the larger society and to institutions like legislatures. Relations where strong power differences exist, where conflicts of interest are likely, or where decisions are made in uncertain situations are all areas where particular attention to ethics is needed. As Kleinig (p. 10) notes, Kauffman's description of the prison system in Massachusetts portrays a culture where prison officers are corrupted and inmates are denied their humanity; these concerns are repeated in Ted Conover's (2001) work, where he portrays the correctional training process as a course in "emotional detachment" and "degrading treatment." It is significant that, as Conover reveals, there was no ethical content in his correctional training, and, as Kleinig points out, "An academy training that fails to focus explicitly and pervasively on the ethical dimensions of correctional work undermines any claim it may have to professionalism" (p. 11).

Margaret Leland Smith (2001) argues that the "intractable brutalities that inhere in the practice of imprisonment" (p. 30) make it extremely difficult to establish any moral basis for the role of a prison officer. She calls attention to the failures that have occurred within the prison system as a whole, causing the federal courts in the 1970s and 1980s to impose oversight on prison practices to ensure compliance with constitutional norms of conduct.

Ethical Challenges

Human rights activists have shown how brutalizing and degrading practices continue to exist in the prison system. Similarly, Derek Brookes (2001) claims that "anything posing as a correctional ethics is a nonsense" (p. 40). Z. W. Henriques (2001: 194) agrees that the operation of a humane correctional system is rendered almost impossible because correctional practice has retribution as its dominant ideology, and in institutions where inmate rights are easily violated, it is easy to ignore ethical and professional standards of conduct. Ben Crouch (1980) argues that the quality of prison life for inmates has been affected by the increase in

---

1   As Margaret Leland Smith (2001: 34) notes, the process of a strip search involves a presentation of nakedness and an inspection of body openings, during which mouths and ears are pulled open and the inmate is required to bend over and pull open the vagina or anus using the fingers and to cough energetically.

political and racial awareness and by judicial activism to the extent that inmates now have the ability to look outside the prison for the norms of prison life. As Crouch puts it, inmates have become

> increasingly able to compete with their keepers in the daily process of defining prison situations. That is, what was once an unambiguous case of rule violation may now be interpreted by inmates as a case of racial disrespect or legal deprivation. (pp. 33–34)

In the case shown in Case Study 8.1, the U.S. Supreme Court decided that the officer's failure to respond to the threat of violence against an inmate amounted to "deliberate indifference."

GUARDING WITH DISCRETION

As already noted, although prison officers' discretionary powers have been curtailed over time, they nevertheless continue to exercise significant discretion in carrying out their day-to-day tasks. Discretionary power can easily involve questions of ethical conduct, and some argue that it is preferable to limit discretion even more by expanding the written rules and regulations of the prison. Michael Gilbert (1999: 275) argues that administrators ought to allow correctional officers to exercise discretion whenever there is an absence of policy or where that policy is vague or inconsistent, on the basis that full enforcement of prison rules, policies, and procedures is an impossibility. The discretionary power of prison officers is shaped less by formal rules than by "an explicit understanding of the shared operational values and ethical principles that govern correctional practice" (Pollock in Gilbert 1999: 275).

Gilbert calls for formal training to develop an ethical framework within which officers may exercise their discretion. He sees a need for managers to assist prison officers to understand the limits of their discretion but also to recognize that guards will make exceptions to rules that are "ethically

---

Case Study 8.1 Male Prison Rape and "Deliberate Indifference"

Dee Farmer, a young African American man, was brutally raped while serving a 20-year prison sentence (Wyatt 2006: 585). As a preoperative transsexual, Farmer "projected female characteristics" when he entered the prison and was consequently viewed as a problem case for the Federal Bureau of Prisons. Despite his protests, prison staff classified Farmer as male and placed him in general population with other male prisoners, which left him a target for sexual assault (Vaughn 1996: 141). Farmer was sometimes housed in general population but more often in protective custody and was therefore kept away from other prisoners. After being transferred to a federal penitentiary for disciplinary reasons, he was placed in general population with more "troublesome prisoners" and again found himself the victim of physical and sexual assault.

In a lawsuit against the prison administration, Farmer claimed that prison officials were "deliberately indifferent to his constitutional rights to be free from inmate-against-inmate assault" (Vaughn 1996: 141). In its decision in *Farmer v. Brennan* (1994), the U.S. Supreme Court held that "deliberate indifference resides on a continuum between mere negligence … [and] something less than acts or omissions for the very purpose of causing harm or with knowledge that harm will result" (p. 141). The Court also held that prison officials violate the Eighth Amendment when they "deliberately disregard the occurrence of male rape" (Wyatt 2006: 585) and noted the following:

> [P]rison officials have a duty under the Eighth Amendment to provide humane conditions of confinement. They must ensure that inmates receive adequate food, clothing, shelter, and medical care, and must protect prisoners from violence at the hands of other prisoners…. A constitutional violation occurs only where the deprivation alleged is …"sufficiently serious" … and the official has acted with "deliberate indifference" to inmate health and safety. (*Farmer v. Brennan* 194)

defensible." He argues that if officer decisions are reasonable and in line with legal and ethical parameters, they should not be disciplined for making reasonable exceptions to rules when they face complex situations. In situations when following the rules would make little sense or would constitute a danger to security, this approach, he suggests, should be supported even more. Conover (2001) also recognizes the discretionary powers of prison officers:

> After five months at Sing Sing, I understood. Experience mattered. More precisely, it took time (and confrontations) to decide (or to discover) what kind of person was going to be wearing your uniform. A hardass or a softy? Inmates' friend or inmates' enemy? Straight or crooked? A user of force or a writer of tickets? A strict overseer or a lender of hands? The job was full of discretionary power and the decisions about how to use it were often moral. (p. 249)

A major component of prison life for both prison officers and inmates is the prison guard subculture described in Chapter 7, which plays as important a role in the prison environment as it does in law enforcement (see Chapter 2). One element of that subculture is the informal code of ethics—the prison guard code—that according to Kauffman (1988) expresses the obligations that prison officers owe to each other and how they should exercise their discretion in defined circumstances. Kauffman (1988) argues that prison officers possess a distinct subculture, setting them apart from other professions. The central norms of this subculture inform

Figure 8.1   The Prison Guard Code

Norm	Comment
Always go to the aid of an officer in distress.	This is the foundation for guard solidarity, applying to any officer in distress. It permits conduct that might otherwise violate bureaucratic norms. The norm applies whatever may be the standing of a particular guard, regardless of race or the guard's own record in responding to calls of distress. This norm is fundamental. Ignoring this norm is likely to result in a guard being ostracized by his or her coworkers.
Don't lug drugs.	This again is regarded as fundamental because of its potential for causing danger to coworkers, such as the possibility of violence by inmates acting under the influence of drugs or alcohol. Sanctions for breach of this norm include removal from the job and physical reprisal. Many guards are prepared to rat on an officer who violates this norm, and such ratting is supported by coworkers.
Don't rat.	This takes the form of not "ratting" on an officer to an inmate and never cooperating with authorities in an investigation or, worse, testifying against a fellow guard about a guard's treatment of inmates. Betraying a fellow officer to inmates is regarded as a great sin likely to jeopardize the other guard's safety and is associated with the taboo against giving inmates information about the identity and background of guards. As for testifying against other guards, Kauffman found that the norm was not absolute. When an inmate was killed, at least some guards would take into account the circumstances of the death and the identity of those involved and would consider testifying against the responsible guard(s). Guards who opposed violence but felt the need to show loyalty to their coworkers found this norm very troubling, and those who violated it would never work again at that prison.
Never make a fellow officer look bad in front of inmates.	Violations of this norm are perceived to undercut guard solidarity and enhance the vulnerability of guards as a group. This injunction extends to an unwillingness to stop fellow guards taking part in a beating, at least while it is in progress.

(Continued)

Figure 8.1   (Continued)

Norm	Comment
Always support an officer in a dispute with an inmate.	This is the counterpart of the previous norm and reflects the belief that a guard ought to supply unquestioning support to his or her coworkers, especially in the face of inmate resistance and unreliable support from prison administrators. Unlike behavioral norms, the sanction for the violation of this norm is less severe. For example, a guard might refuse to sign a disciplinary report for a violation that he or she had not personally observed but would not be sanctioned because someone else would be found to sign that report.
Always support officer sanctions against inmates.	This goes beyond general support for coworkers and extends into active participation in applying informal sanctions such as physical force and coercion in response to inmate violence. Among the guards, Kauffman found some differing perceptions about the adherence to this norm. For example, whereas many new guards felt they had to participate in a situation involving beating up an inmate or be judged an outcast, others consistently refused to take part or would deal with situations without using violence. In such instances, fellow guards might frown on not becoming the aggressor. Kauffman found that a few guards, well regarded by their coworkers, sometimes intervened to stop beatings and did not incur any sanctions for doing so other than a short period of rejection by their coworkers.
Don't be a white hat.	This prohibits any conduct indicating sympathy or identification with inmates, and this is the norm most easily and regularly violated. Breach of this norm is perceived as likely to jeopardize fellow guards who did not themselves show leniency or sympathy to inmates. Although it is considered appropriate to be respectful of inmates and engage in small talk, deep conversations with inmates are disapproved, and guards who cross that line are likely to be termed *Joe Nice-Guy*. Nevertheless, senior guards who do not violate any other norms concerning guard/inmate relations enjoy considerable discretion in adhering to this norm.
Maintain officer solidarity against all outside groups.	This relates to outsiders, such as the administration, the media, and even a guard's own family. It reflects the general feeling found by prison researchers among guards that the prison administration does not care for them, neglects them, and has no confidence in their abilities. Relations between guards and those outside the prison, as regulated by this norm, require that guards never talk about the institution to outsiders, especially the news media because journalists are seen as allied with inmates and not capable of adopting the guard perspective. Speaking to journalists is considered so serious that a violation would invoke a sanction similar to that applied to those testifying against their coworkers in court. Although many guards refrain from talking about their work to their families to avoid creating concern and worry about the dangers of their job, others adopt the view that no one could possibly understand the job, and this includes members of a guard's family.
Show positive concern for fellow guards.	Although this covers a range of conduct, Kauffman identifies two situations: Never leave another guard a problem, and help your fellow guard with problems outside the institution. Leaving problems for other guards to address can include causing problems in a fellow guard's block or leaving at the end of a shift with an outstanding problem that must be faced by the incoming guard. Kauffman notes that in practice, this norm is widely violated, largely because there are few sanctions that can be imposed from one shift to another. In relation to problems outside the institution, the ideal guard helps out fellow guards by offering assistance to the family if a guard is injured or by taking up collections to meet debts.

SOURCE: Kauffman 1988: 86–117.

their daily performance of duty. She distinguishes the norms shown in Figure 8.1, which she says amount to a code for prison officers.

Kauffman's (1988) prison guard code highlights a number of situations where prison officers, in supporting a particular norm, would likely be acting unethically. For example, helping other officers beat an inmate would usually be regarded as unethical conduct but from the officer's point of view would conform to the norm that an officer must always support another officer against inmates. Clearly, there is considerable scope for conflicts to occur between ethical standards and the norms of the prison subculture.

Unethical Situations

Prison researchers have examined the nature of imprisonment, its changing structure over time, the exercise of power by prison officers and inmates, the officer subculture, and the use of force within prisons. Other specific forms of unethical conduct are illustrated in the following sections, including violent attacks through acts of rape on inmates, the importation of contraband into prisons, and other forms of corruption that occur in prisons. Finally, transgender persons present special problems because correctional facilities are highly gendered.

Use of Force

Many situations in the prison environment might provoke the use of force by prison officers to control inmates. Each instance of the use of force may give rise to an ethical question about whether the force ought to have been used at all, whether excessive force was used, or whether the force was justified, perhaps for the purpose of self-defense against inmate attack. The American Correctional Association Code of Ethics (ACA 1990) stipulates that members of the ACA must respect the "dignity and individuality of human beings" and must be committed to "professional and compassionate service." The ACA subscribes to a number of principles in its code of ethics, including respect and protection of the civil and legal rights of all individuals,

and it requires that members report any corrupt or unethical behavior "where there is sufficient cause to initiate a review."

Witnessing and Experiencing Violence in Prisons

Kauffman's (1988: 222) research found that most prison officers were horrified at the extent and nature of violence within prison. Officers tended to characterize the issues they faced within the prison as "moral dilemmas" involving a clash between their own personal ethical standards and the expectations of them as prison officers. In coping with these dilemmas, many attempted to avoid actions that would injure inmates by refusing, explicitly or implicitly, to carry out certain duties. However, as they spent more time within the prison and absorbed its culture, as well as the guard subculture, their ability to abstain from morally questionable acts weakened, and they began to construct the prison as a separate moral realm and to perceive their dealings with prisoners as outside common ethical norms.

Alternatively, some would shut their minds to the implications of the actions of others as well as to their own actions. Kauffman (1988: 223) makes a case that officer recruits who come to prison work with no prior exposure to violence are initially shocked at the events they witness, including the stabbings and murders. Veterans, however, had seen such violence before and seemed unaffected by it.

Over a period, the less experienced prison officers gradually became inured to the violence, got used to it, and said they were no longer bothered by it. As this process of socialization continued, many officers became dismayed by the changes they saw in themselves, especially in relation to their acceptance of the use of violence. Some rationalized their changes by stressing the difference between prison and the outside world: "This is a prison and it's not society. When you step in here, you step into a different world. . . . It's brutality anyway you look at it. . . . But you got no other choice" (in Kauffman 1988: 229).

As Kauffman (1988) points out, constructing a separate moral world within the prison and living in that world as well as in the "normal world" can provoke behavioral conflicts. For instance, one officer acknowledged that signing disciplinary reports about events that he had not witnessed was morally wrong outside the prison context. Another officer, heavily involved in violence, judged his conduct to be wrong and then spoke of coworkers who behaved in a similar way as being persons he would not wish to associate with out on the streets. As already mentioned, it was possible for some prison officers to rationalize morally suspect behavior by judging inmates as beyond morality and as having relinquished their claims to morally correct treatment when they committed their crimes. As one officer put it, "They're just programmed. These guys have nothing in their brains or nothing in their lives other than violence and danger. . . . Those aren't really like people. Most of them are animals" (in Kauffman 1988: 230). Overall, such rationalizations operated to lower barriers to violence.

Using Force

In reviewing his training experience in New York State, Conover (2001: 32) explains the position on use of force under various directives, laws, and employee manuals in that state. He reports that in New York it is permissible to "lay hands on or strike an inmate for self-defense, to prevent injury to a person or to property, to quell a disturbance, to enforce compliance with a lawful direction, or to prevent an escape." Deadly physical force can be used in three situations: to prevent an escape, in self-defense, or to prevent arson. Conover remarks that although the trainees spent significant time learning about firearms, including the range of different types of buckshot as well as actually firing weapons, there was no discussion about "what shooting someone meant, in an ethical sense—how officers might be not only legally but morally justified in doing it" (p. 43).

Generally, officers' use of force in prison takes place within the formal structure and framework of prison rules and regulations designed to control prisoner conduct. However, sometimes force may be used informally—that is, outside the boundaries circumscribed by rules. For example, in a study of a Texas penitentiary, Marquart (1986) investigated the unofficial use of physical force and concluded that the exercise of force outside the terms prescribed was a strategy for the control of prisoners and that this strategy ran parallel to the formal

control process and was entrenched within guard subculture. He himself was employed as a prison officer at the prison and was able to observe officer violence first hand. The guard culture at this prison defined "good officers" as those who were able not only to perform routine prison actions like counts but also to break up fights and maintain discipline without citing inmates for disciplinary infractions. Marquart found that a willingness and initiative to break up fights, a readiness to engage in confrontations with inmates, and an inclination to fight inmates were essential attributes for promotion.

While most prisoners were controlled through the structure of sanctions and privileges embodied in the prison rules, there were some inmates who were controlled through verbal intimidation and the use of punitive physical force (see the "Forms of Coercion" Closer Look box). Verbal assaults were intended to bring about an inmate's humiliation and to destroy his standing in the eyes of other prisoners. Such assaults commonly included name calling, the use of racial terms of abuse, and threats. For example, one officer was recorded as saying to an inmate, "You stupid nigger, if you ever lie to me or any other officer about what you're doing, I'll knock your teeth in" (in Marquart 1986: 351). Sometimes the threats included a promise of physical injury or even death, and those who failed to vary their conduct after verbal assaults "were roughed up as a matter of course" (p. 351).

Kauffman (1988: 59), based on her study of the Massachusetts prison system, observes that the use of force varies from prison to prison according to the level of security applied. She points out that the use of force is itself limited in that it cannot be relied on to ensure that routine tasks are accomplished. Nor can it be employed in daily tasks such as moving inmates through the prison. She notes that serious inmate offenses are supposedly within the jurisdiction of prosecutors and the courts but that prosecutions for such offenses committed inside prisons are rare, and internal systems of punishment are usually relied on.

As for prison officer violence against inmates at Walpole, while a few officers claimed never to have witnessed or participated in such events, the majority confirmed their participation or the fact that they had witnessed violence and their assumption that such events were common knowledge within the prison (Kauffman 1988: 130). However, the term *inmate assault* itself was questioned in terms of its definition, and some officers framed their discussions about prison officer violence by concentrating on the "deserved" nature of a beating. This nuanced approach toward violence extended to the distinction made between force used in restraining a violent inmate and force that went beyond what was necessary to restrain. The latter category included beatings inflicted by groups of prison officers on a single inmate in situations, for example, where inmates were moved to segregation (p. 132). One officer recalled a beating in which he was involved:

> There was a black guy who threw some urine in [the supervisor's] face. . . . Here there were nine beating the shit out of one guy. Then they'd back off and they'd taunt him and say, "Had enough, had enough?" And the guy would stand there and start swinging. . . . That particular guy didn't deserve

what he got. But there are guys who deserve what they get. (in Kauffman 1988: 132)

In another incident, described in Case Study 8.2, corrections officers at New York's Rikers Island jail complex systematically abused and beat alleged offenders and inmates. The U.S. Attorney reported that a culture of violence that had developed at Rikers.

Marquart (1986: 355) concludes that these instances of violence were illegal in both civil and criminal terms and certainly violated prison rules and policy. However, he points out that the use of this kind of unofficial coercion was so common in the institution in which he worked that it had become a norm for the prison officers, and it was not employed in an arbitrary fashion but in a structured and systematic process intended to maintain control, enforce inmate deference behaviors to officers, and build officer solidarity. Prison officers who used this informal system were regarded as good promotion prospects.

Case Study 8.2 Brutality at Rikers Island, New York

In August 2014, the U.S. Attorney of the Southern District of New York issued a damning report about violence and abuse occurring at New York's Rikers Island, a complex of 10 jails with an average daily population of 14,000. The U.S. Attorney reported to the mayor of New York that the New York City Department of Corrections had violated the rights of adolescent inmates and that investigators had found the following:

- Force is used against adolescents at an alarming rate and violent inmate-on-inmate fights and assaults are commonplace, resulting in a striking number of serious injuries.

- Prison officers resort to "headshots," or blows to an inmate's head or facial area, too frequently.

- Force is used as punishment or retribution.

- Force is used in response to inmates' verbal altercations with officers.

- Use of force by specialized response teams within the jails is particularly brutal.

- Prison officers attempt to justify use of force by yelling "Stop resisting," even when the adolescent has been completely subdued or was never resisting in the first place.

- Use of force is particularly common in areas without video surveillance cameras.

In partial response to the report, city officials agreed in January 2015 to a plan that would halt the placement of inmates age 21 and under in solitary confinement; however, the plan will not go into effect until January 2016 and is contingent on funding additional staff.

SOURCE: *The New York Times*, January 13, 2015. CRIPA Investigation of the New York City Department of Correction Jails on Rikers Island, U.A. Attorney, Southern District of New York, August 4, 2014.

A Closer Look

Forms of Coercion

Marquart (1986) identified a number of forms of coercion. He referred to the first type as *counseling* or *a tune-up*. This kind of force was used for minor offenses, such as refusing to obey an order, and incidents rarely involving serious physical injury, being limited to verbal abuse, kicks, and slaps to the head and body. He documents an instance in which a prison officer was experiencing difficulties with an inmate who had pushed his way into the food line. The inmate was ordered to get to the back of the line, and the officer reported him to his supervisor. The inmate resisted by yelling at the guard, and as a result, he was taken to the major's office (the location for the enactment of discipline) by the officer and his supervisor. There, he was slapped across the face and tackled by the officer and supervisor. A third officer joined the original two in punching and kicking the inmate, and one officer threatened to cut his head off with a knife.

The second form of physical force was termed *ass whippings* and was employed in more serious rule breaches, such as threatening an officer or fighting back during a tune-up. For ass whippings, weapons such as blackjacks and riot batons were used by the prison officers, although the amount of force applied was limited to avoid hospitalization. In one case, an officer stood on an inmate's head, while another hit him on the buttocks and thighs with a riot baton and several others kicked him.

The third form of coercion involved *severe beatings* and was reserved for inmates who violated rules considered sacred, such as those concerned with escaping or attacking the prison officers. In this coercive form, the intent was to cause physical injury, even to the extent of requiring hospitalization. Marquart observed one situation in which an inmate who had earlier struck an officer was dragged from the hall into the major's office, beaten, and then beaten again while confined in a solitary cell. Sometimes beatings were staged in public to set an example, but most took place out of sight of witnesses.

SOURCE: Marquart 1986: 352–353.

Officers' Perspectives on Use of Force

In the context of the officer subculture, fighting an inmate was seen as an expression of masculinity and machismo. As one officer put it, "You have to make a convict fear you or respect you or you won't make it here" (in Marquart 1986: 359). Further, because the unofficial use of force had become a parallel system for social control within the prison, it built a culture of secrecy in which prison officers at the higher levels refrained from talking about coercive displays of force with lower-ranking officers. Although lower-ranking officers often asked their superiors about instances of use of force, their questions were never met with a substantive response but with a simple denial of any knowledge of an incident

(p. 361). Despite the fact that the prison was managed as a large bureaucracy, Marquart found that its informal structure seemed to be the predominant method used for managing the prison. Unlike other researchers, he found that this prison, like others in Texas, had a high degree of autonomy from the central administration, which rarely interfered in prison administration. As a result, prison officers had wide discretion, which was exercised in the form of the extensive use of physical force, and this became the underpinning of the officer subculture there.

Officer Violence as Informal Justice

Fundamentally, the exercise of violence by prison officers was not intended as a symbol of their power, but was rather a reflection of their sense of vulnerability. Officers were often dissatisfied about official punishments and therefore sought their own form of justice (Kauffman 1988: 145). In particular, although inmates involved in violent acts against officers would be sanctioned when it came to furloughs or parole, there was little by way of sanctions in the short term that would protect and reinforce the officer's position of having to be present in the prison every day.

As expressed in the following officer norms, regardless of their personal views, officers at Walpole experienced considerable pressure not only to acquiesce to violent means of handling the prisoners but also to engage in violence consistent with norms requiring them to support their colleagues in disputes with inmates and to support officer sanctions against inmates. These pressures to conform (Kauffman 1988: 153) were reinforced by the officers' genuine fear for their survival. Prison officers seemed to take the attitude that while they might not personally participate in violence, they would not object if it occurred, and they would gradually acquire the belief that this was the way things happened in a prison environment. However, some officers reported that their coworkers enjoyed the violence, thrived on it, seemed to get "high" on it, and even instigated it to cause excitement and a break in the monotonous prison routine (p. 153). Comments ranged from "I like having action" to "It really peps up my day." Some officers, however, believed that coworkers who initiated violence had a need to prove themselves, to show that they were not scared, and that their persistent acts of violence were attempts to constantly prove themselves.

Some prison officers saw no need for explicit justification, seeing violence as natural, as a way of life, and even as a game and part of the prison culture. These officers perceived violence as a routine method of resolving differences and effectively screened out any other courses of action. In one situation, inmates confronted one officer after he had beaten another inmate, and he rationalized the beating as a response to the inmate, calling his mother a "punk." The officer saw no need to justify his actions, reporting that anyone would respond in the same way (Kauffman 1988: 158).

Justifications for Officer Violence

In ethical terms, many prison officers at Walpole honestly believed that the use of violence was an appropriate course of action, especially in cases when an inmate had assaulted an officer. These officers had an honest belief in the correctness of their approach and were convinced that the institutional environment demanded such violent reprisals. Officers who accepted this view suggested that those outside the prison, including local and political leaders, had no interest in events inside prisons, accepted no responsibility, and demonstrated no real concern for what occurred inside prison walls (Kauffman 1988: 163). Nevertheless, some prison officers categorically rejected the use of violence, considering it counterproductive given their assumption that violence begets more violence. Some opposed it on humanitarian grounds and were appalled at the severe beatings they had witnessed or even participated in. One officer expressed the view that beating an inmate into submission was the worst thing he could do "because it's not the right thing to do" (p. 164).

When discussing their justifications for using violence, officers focused on the inmate himself, on relationships among guards, and on the individual officer who engaged in the violence (Kauffman 1988: 141). Prison officer violence was commonly justified as a means of controlling inmates, and many officers felt unable to maintain control without at least referring to violence. Another justification offered was the belief that officer violence deterred inmate violence against officers. The systematic use of violent reprisals was seen as a means of preventing future assaults as well as punishing past ones. Officers defined self-defense very broadly so as to *anticipate the need to defend themselves,* and many officers and inmates believed they needed to establish and uphold a reputation for meeting aggression with aggression. If an inmate assaulted an officer, reprisals were considered not only appropriate but also essential. As one officer put it, an inmate who assaulted a guard

> should be beaten until he can't stand up anymore. And if he does stand up, beat him some more. Beat him until it gets through his head what will happen

and then he'll think twice about what he is doing. (in Kauffman 1988: 142)

Kauffman (1988: 67) remarks that during the 1970s the Massachusetts prison system relied on brutality and physical coercion, despite the fact that its use had declined considerably within the United States as a whole over the first half of the 20th century. During that period, prison officers routinely used violence to enforce control. In discussing the advantages and disadvantages of extralegal force, Kauffman points out that many of the inmates in maximum-security institutions have committed violent crimes and may be serving multiple life sentences. In effect, they have nothing more to lose, and some officers consequently conclude that they need to meet violence with violence. Other prison officers attributed inmate violence to the fact that many inmates have spent their entire lives in situations where force has determined the course of events, and accordingly, they will only respond to like treatment when officers attempt to establish control. For that reason, some guards took the position that maintaining order often required the "cracking of a few heads," at least initially, to establish control (p. 68).

Constraining Officer Violence

Kauffman (1988) concludes that the use of physical coercion failed at Walpole and other Massachusetts prisons because staff were unable and generally unwilling to use the extreme measures that were perceived as necessary to ensure absolute control. She contrasts Walpole with the Texas penal system, which she believes has its roots more in southern slavery than in the emergence of the prison system (p. 69). In addition, she argues that the use of coercion as a technique was a failure because it could not be applied to the inmates generally but had to be enforced inmate by inmate, and also because coercion tended to fuel inmates' anger and hatred rather than suppressing their resistance and rebellion.

Another difficulty was that the use of coercion required staff to constantly increase the severity of sanctions if they were to be useful over the long term. Ultimately, in her view, coercion failed because it was unable to resolve the inherent conflict between inmates and prison officers. At some point, inmates would take the position that only so much could be taken away from them; with this conclusion, they would have effectively won the battle even if beaten time and time again (Kauffman 1988: 71).

Judicial Review of Use of Force

Walker (1996: 144) examines the attitude of the courts toward correctional use of force, noting that over the past few decades, the courts have limited such force but that correctional officers are still given more latitude than police officers in the use of deadly force. In *U.S. v. Nix* (1974), the U.S. Supreme Court articulated its rationale for the use of deadly force against escaping prisoners, arguing that a determined escapee may kidnap a hostage or kill an officer or commit other unlawful acts to ease his escape. This aspect of dangerousness was sufficient to convince the Court in favor of the use of deadly force against escaping prisoners. In *Whitley v. Albers* (1986), a prison officer shot an inmate during a disturbance, and the Supreme Court ruled that cases of excessive force in corrections are governed by the Eighth Amendment, which prohibits cruel and unusual punishment. The legal standard for brutality is whether the force is "applied in a good faith effort to maintain or restore discipline, or whether it was applied maliciously and sadistically for the very purpose of causing harm" (*Hudson v. McMillian* 1992; *Whitley v. Albers* 1986).

Following the case of *Clark v. Evans* (1988), in which a prison officer shot and killed an inmate trying to escape, arguments were made concerning whether the officer could have used a different means to prevent the escape or whether he should have only used force sufficient to disable the escaping inmate rather than using deadly force. The Court decided in favor of the officer on both issues, holding that there was no duty to use disabling force rather than lethal force.

There have been some decisions that have gone against prison officers, such as *McCullough v. Cady* (1986), in which an officer shot a prisoner during a disturbance while attempting to break up a fight among the prisoners. He initially fired a warning shot and then shot a prisoner who, it was later determined, was not involved in the fight. Here, the Court found that even though the officer shot with the intention of wounding the inmate, the use of force was not a decision of last resort made after all other means of restoring order had failed, and therefore, the officer's actions amounted to deliberate infliction of pain on the prisoner.

In *Kenny v. Indiana Youth Center* (1991), an officer shot an 18-year-old inmate in the process of escaping from a juvenile institution. Before shooting, the officer gave a verbal warning that she intended to shoot. The Court noted that it was relevant to look at various factors in deciding whether the officer had inflicted unnecessary and wanton pain and suffering. Such factors included whether force needed to be used, the relationship between that need and the amount of force used, the actual injury inflicted, the nature of the threat to the safety of staff and inmates, and any efforts made to adopt a less severe course of action. The Court concluded again that "dangerousness" was the predominant consideration and repeated its view from the *Nix* case that any inmate who is attempting to escape is dangerous enough to justify using deadly force, provided the force is applied in good faith to maintain or restore discipline. Taken together, these rulings illustrate that prison officers are basically free to use deadly force to prevent escapes.

Correctional Policy on the Use of Force

Walker (1996: 149) presents an analysis of the policies in four states on the acceptable use of deadly force. All policies explicitly authorize the use of deadly force to prevent escapes, and in two states, the policies suggest that disciplinary action will be taken against prison officers if they fail to use deadly force. The ACA suggests that a policy on deadly force should be more specifically related to the institution the inmate is escaping from, and ACA guidelines propose, for example, that a halfway house denotes offenders in its custody who do not represent a threat to public safety and in respect of whom deadly force might be prohibited.

The Federal Bureau of Prisons explicitly limits deadly force by prohibiting the use of firearms in minimum-security institutions in ordinary circumstances. It does permit deadly force to prevent an escape but only when authorized by the warden or when based on a prison officer's judgment that the use of firearms is necessary to prevent the loss of life or grievous bodily harm. There is, however, a specific prohibition on using firearms if a guard sees that the potential escapee is a juvenile. A similar prohibition applies in ACA policy statements and in the state of Nebraska, but the Nebraska Department of Corrections explicitly declares that all persons housed in its correctional system are deemed to be adults.

Each of the states' policy statements deals with the use of warning shots, but policies vary widely. Nevertheless, a common feature is that warning shots should not be fired if it is likely that innocent persons might be injured. One state absolutely prohibits the use of warning shots, and another confines warning shots to within the grounds of a facility unless there is an immediate threat to life. These policies reflect the possibility that warning shots will harm innocent bystanders, and it is significant that almost all police departments in the United States prohibit the use of warning shots.

RAPE IN PRISON

Prisoner rape has been defined by the organization Stop Prisoner Rape (2007) as "all forms of sexual violence inflicted on anyone in custody, including someone awaiting trial in a county jail" (p. 4). The first study measuring rates of sexual assault among male inmates was conducted in 1966 in Philadelphia, and the researcher found that 4.7% of inmates reported sexual assaults while incarcerated or being transported to and from court (Hensley, Koscheski, and Tewksbury 2003: 18). A 1980 study of New York State male prisons revealed that 28% of inmates reported being targets of sexual aggression, but only one inmate reported being raped. In 1977, a study of 400 male inmates in six North Carolina state prisons showed an average report rate of sexual assaults of 2.4% (p. 18). Other studies have similarly shown a wide variation in sexual assaults and coercion. For example, a 1982 study in a California prison produced a rate of 14%, and a study of 17 federal prisons in 1984 revealed a 2% rate of "sexual targets" and a 0.3% rape rate (p. 19).

The highest rate of sexual victimization was found in a study conducted in 1994 in the Nebraska prison system, where 22% of male inmates reported being pressured or forced to have sex against their will (Hensley et al. 2003: 19). In a study conducted in 2003 in three Oklahoma prisons, about 14% reported being sexual targets, and 1.1% victims of completed sexual assaults. A study of sexual coercion in a female southern prison found about 4.5% had been victims of attempted or completed rapes (p. 20). It appears that prisons with higher numbers of inmates are more likely to have official reports of sexual attacks or threats of attacks filed, while this is less likely at minimum-security prisons (p. 23). Thus, reducing the size of the inmate population may result in a reduction of sexual assaults (Stop Prisoner Rape 2006: 11).

Bureau of Justice Statistics for 2011 to 2012 reveal that an estimated 4% of state or federal prisoners and 3.2% of those in jails reported experiencing at least one incident of sexual abuse by another inmate or facility staff within the past 12 months (Beck, Berzofsky, and Krebs 2013: 6). Of juveniles

between the ages of 16 and 17 who were held in prisons and jails, 1.8% reported being victimized by another inmate, and 3.2% of juveniles of the same age held in prisons and jails reported being the victim of sexual misconduct (p. 6).

A 2001 study by Human Rights Watch on male rape in U.S. prisons argues that acts of rape are far more pervasive than is acknowledged by prison authorities (see Case Studies 8.3 and 8.4). In another 2001 study of 378 state male prisons in the United States, wardens were asked about their knowledge of forced and consensual sex in their institutions. Generally speaking, the wardens indicated that sexual activity was "relatively rare" in their institutions (Hensley and Tewksbury 2005: 186). There is a wide disparity between reported rapes as noted by prison

Table 8.1 Prevalence of Sexual Victimization, by Type of Incident and Inmate Characteristics, National Inmate Survey, 2011–2012

Characteristic	Prison inmates reporting sexual victimization[a]			Jail inmates reporting sexual victimization[a]		
	Number of inmates[b]	Inmate-on-inmate	Staff sexual misconduct	Number of inmates[b]	Inmate-on-inmate	Staff sexual misconduct
Sex						
Male*	1,345,200	1.7%	2.4%	628,600	1.4%	1.9%
Female	96,600	6.9**	2.3	91,600	3.6**	1.4**
Race/Hispanic origin						
White[c]	430,000	2.9%**	1.6%**	240,500	2.0%**	1.4%**
Black[c]*	507,900	1.3	2.6	239,200	1.1	2.1
Hispanic	339,800	1.6	2.2	159,300	1.5	1.5**
Other[cd]	38,200	1.7	2.6	18,900	12	1.8
Two or more races[c]	108,300	4.0**	3.9**	54,300	3.0**	3.2**

*Comparison group.

**Difference with comparison group is significant at the 95% confidence level.

[a]Percent of inmates reporting one or more incidents of sexual victimization involving another inmate or facility staff in the past 12 months or since admission to the facility, if less than 12 months.

[b]Estimated number of inmates at midyear 2011 and yearend 2011 in prisons and jails represented by NIS-3, excluding inmates under age 18. Estimates have been rounded to the nearest 100.

[c]Excludes persons of Hispanic or Latino origin.

[d]Includes American Indian, Alaska Native, Asian, Native Hawaiian, and other Pacific Islander.

[e]Includes persons with an associate degree.

SOURCE: Beck et al. 2013: 17.

Table 8.2   Prevalence of Sexual Victimization Across Inmate Surveys, by Type of Incident, National Inmate Survey, 2007, 2008–2009 and 2011–2012

	Percent of prison inmates			Percent of jail inmates		
Type of incident	NIS-1 2007	NIS-2 2008-09	NIS-3 2011-12*	NIS-1 2007	NIS-2 2008-09	NIS-3 2011-12*
Total	4.5%	4.4%	4.0%	3.2%	3.1%	3.2%
Inmate-on-inmate	2.1%	2.1%	2.0%	1.6%	1.5%	1.6%
Nonconsensual sexual acts	1.3	1.0	1.1	0.7	0.8	0.7
Abusive sexual contacts only	0.8	1.0	1.0	0.9	0.7**	0.9
Staff sexual misconduct	2.9%	2.8%	2.4%	2.0%	2.0%	1.8%
Unwilling activity	1.7	1.7	1.5	1.3	1.5	1.4
Excluding touching	1.3	1.3	1.1	1.1	1.1	1.0
Touching only	0.4	0.4	0.4	0.3	0.4	0.3
Willing activity	1.7	1.8**	1.4	1.1**	1.1**	0.9
Excluding touching	1.5**	1.5**	1.2	0.9**	0.9**	0.7
Touching only	0.2	0.3	0.2	0.2	0.2	0.1

Note: Detail may not sum to total because inmates may report more than one type of victimization. They may also report victimization by both other inmates and staff.

*Comparison group.

**Difference with comparison group is significant at the 95% confidence level.

SOURCE: Beck et al. 2013: 10.

authorities and as shown by inmate victimization surveys. The latter show far higher rates than the official statistics. This underreporting is exemplified in a 1996 Nebraska study, which found that only 29% of victimized inmates reported abuses (Human Rights Watch 2001: 132), and a 1968 study of prisons in Philadelphia, which found an estimated 2,000 rapes, only 96 of which had been officially reported.

Human Rights Watch (2001) suggests that prisoner failure to report rapes is a response to prison administrators' indifference toward such reports. If, it is argued, prisoners could be certain of protection, they would be more likely to report rapes (p. 132). The study contends that many inmates point out that prison officers fail to take protective measures on their behalf when they seek help and instead advise them to fight their attacker. In this sense, the prison system condones forced rape as,

for example, was found in Florida, where physical sexual attacks were revealed as commonplace in Florida prisons (p. 142). The response of correctional authorities to rape is often the imposition of minor disciplinary sanctions, such as 30 days in segregation or moving rapists to another facility. In contrast, the victims of the rape may have to be located in protective custody with all the restrictions that such confinement imposes (p. 143).

According to Human Rights Watch (2001: 153), the response of guards to complaints of rape is often inadequate and even callous, and gay inmates in particular, unless able to show clear physical injury, tend to have their complaints ignored because prison officials tend to assume consent in sexual acts involving gay inmates. Many guards respond to such charges and complaints with the advice that the inmate should defend himself against attack. This is

Case Study 8.3 Rape in Prison

In 1993, Eddie Dillard was serving time in a California prison. He was a young first timer, a slight man, and was transferred to share a cell with Wayne Robertson, a huge muscular man, nearly twice the weight of Dillard, serving a life sentence for murder. Robertson was known by all as "The Booty Bandit," having earned this nickname through his practice of violently raping prisoners. Before the end of the first day in the cell they shared, the inevitable had occurred: Robertson had beaten Dillard and sodomized him, and he continued to do this for the next 2 days until finally Dillard ran out of the cell, refusing to return. A correctional officer working on the unit informed the *Los Angeles Times,* "Everyone knew about Robertson. He had raped inmates before and he's raped inmates since." Documentation submitted to a California legislative hearing supported this report, showing Robertson had committed more than a dozen rapes inside that and other prisons.

SOURCE: Human Rights Watch 2001: 148–149.

Case Study 8.4 Transgender Experiences of Prison Rape

Jackie Tates told Stop Prisoner Rape (2007) that when she was incarcerated in Sacramento "the deputies were letting inmates into my cell to have sex with me against my will. The first time it happened, I tried to tell the inmate no. He showed me some autopsy photos. He said, 'This is what happens to people who fuck with me.' I ended up submitting. I did what he told me to do. I orally copulated him, and he sodomized me. Thirty or 40 minutes later, the deputy came onto the speaker and asked him if he was done. He said, 'I'm done.' The door clicked and let him out.

"They must have let 12 to 14 inmates into my cell to have sex. One day, I said to a deputy, 'If you're going to make me do this, could I at least have some condoms so I don't get AIDS?' He told me to shut the fuck up. The next day, he came in and threw 15 condoms at me.

"Where I am now, it's just as bad. They have me in general population. I've asked over and over to be put on the unit with the gay and transgender inmates, but I always get denied.

"In September 2004, it was so crowded here that they had us sleeping on pads on the floor of the day room. The inmate on the next pad over told me to come to the shower with him, or he was going to slice me. I was afraid, so I went with him. He was fucking me in the shower when a deputy walked by. He just started laughing.

"Later, they moved me to a cell, and I was so happy because I thought I had escaped this inmate. Then they moved him into the cell with me. When I finally got out of there, I had two black eyes that were completely closed up. I didn't deserve this.

"In September 2005, I was put into a 'protective custody' tank with five or six other inmates. Two of them jumped me right away. They both made me suck them off. The deputy walked by and saw me fighting and struggling with them, but he didn't do anything.

"The next day, the deputy made jokes about it. He asked me how much I charge for that.

"Gay people, transgender people in this jail—they put us in compromising positions. They chain us to 12 inmates and throw us in the back of a van with no supervision. People get dragged into bathrooms. One of my friends got dragged into a bathroom—she walks with a walker now.

"The deputies call me names—they call me 'it,' and 'he/she,' and 'punk,' and 'faggot.' They whistle at me in the shower. They come to my cell door asking to see my breasts.

"Sometimes I want to die. I'm scared to close my eyes at night."

SOURCE: Stop Prisoner Rape 2007: 11. Reprinted by permission of Jackie Tates and Stop Prisoner Rape.

Case Study 8.5 Guard Forces Transgender Inmate to Have Sex With Him

On August 11, 2011, a New York City prison officer was charged with forcing a transgender inmate to have sex with him in a Manhattan jail in September 2009. The victim was a 23-year-old transgender woman housed in a male unit at the Manhattan Detention Complex, where she was being held for a parole violation. She had not had gender reassignment surgery but had undergone hormone therapy.

The woman filed a civil suit against the city, claiming that prison officer Roberto Morales, 40, had sexually harassed her over the course of a month. She alleged that she had complained about Morales's conduct in a formal complaint to the corrections department. The alleged sexual assault occurred when Morales was escorting her from a clinic. He pushed her into a stairwell and assaulted her, and according to her lawyer, a rape kit found DNA that implicated Morales.

Morales has been employed in corrections for 13 years but now faces up to 4 years' imprisonment if he is convicted of the charge of committing a criminal sexual act.

In her suit against the city, the woman claimed to have previously been assaulted as an inmate at Rikers Island when she was taken to a prison hospital ward for treatment. She alleged that a nurse forced her to perform oral sex with him there; the nurse later pleaded guilty to committing a criminal sexual act. The suit also objected to the city's lack of policy for housing transgender inmates.

SOURCE: O'Connor 2010.

tantamount to guards abdicating their responsibility to protect prisoners from violence and amounts to guards urging inmates to commit disciplinary infractions because the use of force by inmates, even in self-defense, is usually a punishable act.

Prison Rape Elimination Act

In September 2003, President George Bush signed the Prison Rape Elimination Act (PREA), the first U.S. law addressing the issue of male prison rape. The purposes of the act include the following:

- Setting a zero-tolerance standard for prison rape
- Prioritizing the prevention of rape in each prison system

- Devising and implementing national standards to detect, prevent, reduce, and punish rape
- Collecting data and information on the incidence of rape
- Increasing prison staff's accountability for failing to detect, prevent, reduce, or punish rape (Mair, Frattaroli, and Teret 2003: 602; also see National Institute of Justice 2006)

The law establishes a review panel on prison rape within the Department of Justice; the panel is required to hold public hearings each year on operations in the country's three prisons with the highest and the two prisons with the lowest incidents of rape. The attorney general is required to submit annual reports to Congress on the review panel's activities. The law also establishes a National Prison Rape Reduction Commission, made up of nine members with expertise on the subject. This body is principally a research commission with a comprehensive mandate, including examining the extent to which prison rape contributes to the transmission of HIV (Mair et al. 2003: 604).

In 2014, the Bureau of Justice Statistics of the U.S. Justice Department reported that PREA data collection activities had found the following:

- In 2011, corrections administrators reported 8,763 allegations of sexual victimization, an increase over the 8,404 incidents reported in 2010 and 7,855 in 2009.
- In 2011, 902 allegations of sexual victimization (10%) were determined to have occurred following an investigation into the allegations, and about 48% of substantiated allegations involved prison staff with inmates. Females committed more than half of all substantiated incidents of staff misconduct and one quarter of all incidents of sexual harassment.

Transgender Prisoners

U.S. prisons may adopt one of two categories for the accommodation of transgender prisoners: genitalia-based placement or identity-based placement. Those who have not undergone genital reconstructive surgery are generally categorized according to their assigned sex at birth. Less frequently, a transgender prisoner may be housed according to the gender with which he or she self-identifies, but prisoners born as male yet who self-identify as female are liable to suffer sexual abuse and violence in the correctional environment. For example, a study of assaults in the California prison system found that 59% of transgender inmates reported having been sexually abused, compared with 4% of the general inmate population (Nader 2010: 83).

In January 2010, media reports indicated that Italy planned to open a prison solely for transgender prisoners (BBC News 2010), but this solution was rejected in Canada, largely because of the small number of inmates involved. For example, in 2000 Canadian federal prisons housed only 10 preoperative transgender inmates out of 12,500 (Mann 2006: 110). Often, a prison will simply segregate a transgender inmate as a convenient means of resolving the placement issue, leaving him or her excluded from social contact and prison facilities.

As in the United States, the placement of transgender inmates is an issue in Australia, and two approaches are followed. The first is a "social-based" perspective that emphasizes the social aspects of identity and how a person self-identifies. The second is a "surgery-based" approach, which considers whether the individual has undergone sex reassignment surgery (Mann 2006: 117). Australia also makes use of protective custody, but inmates are allowed to wear gender-appropriate clothing. According to studies, transgender prisoners are likely to be perceived as homosexual males participating in acts of consensual sex and are therefore unlikely to receive consideration if assaulted. They are also subject to victimization by prison staff conducting "gender-check" strip searches; mocking of genitals; verbal, physical, and sexual assault; and rape (Tarzwell 2006: 180).

In the United Kingdom, the Gender Recognition Act has resulted in the Ministry of Justice (2011) issuing guidelines that mandate, "An establishment must permit prisoners who consider themselves transsexual and wish to begin gender reassignment to live permanently in their acquired gender." This means that self-identified transgender inmates must be permitted to wear their own clothes and be given access to devices that disguise their physical sex.

In the United States, transgender inmates are often held in solitary confinement based on PREA laws for "their own protection" (Shah 2010). Even in segregation, the inmate still faces the possibility of attack, harassment, or sexual assault by prison officers. Transgender inmates have litigated the issue of whether they are entitled to hormone therapy while in prison based on the Eight Amendment prohibiting cruel and unusual punishment and the claim that such a denial constitutes "deliberate indifference" to an inmate's serious medical needs (National Center for Lesbian Rights 2006). In one case in Georgia, the U.S. Justice Department supported a claim by a prison inmate alleging that the state illegally cut off hormone treatment that she had been taking for 17 years. The Justice Department indicated that it regarded policies that prohibited new hormone treatment for transgender inmates to be in violation of the Constitution because the Constitution requires prison officials to make treatment decisions based on health assessments that are made independently of the prison. Prison records showed that mental health professionals had diagnosed the inmate with having gender dysphoria, a condition formerly termed *gender identity disorder* and used by the American Psychiatric Association. The Department of Justice argued that gender dysphoria has to be treated in the same way as any other medical condition.

In 2005, Wisconsin legislated a ban on hormone treatment for transgender inmates, regardless of whether the treatment was underway when an inmate was arrested. This law was challenged on constitutional grounds and overturned by a federal court in 2011. So-called "freeze frame" policies apply in many state prisons that allow inmates to continue any treatment they were receiving before their arrest but ban expanding or commencing new treatments. This policy applied at the federal level until 2011 when the policy was changed: Now treatment plans are regularly reviewed, and hormone treatment may be permitted, regardless of whether it was ongoing at the time of arrest (Apuzzo 2015).

The Justice Department reported in June 2015 that for the first time it was able to provide accurate estimates of rates of sexual victimization among transgender inmates. It found the following:

- An estimated 35% of transgender inmates in prisons and 34% in jails reported experiencing one or more incidents of sexual victimization by another inmate or by a staff person in the past 12 months, or since admission when less than 12 months.
- About one quarter of transgender inmates in prisons and jails reported an incident involving another inmate, and almost three quarters said the incidents involved nonconsensual sex acts.
- Transgender inmates reported levels of sexual misconduct by staff in prisons and jails as 17% in prisons and 23% in jails. Staff pressured 66% of transgender inmates to engage in sexual acts; among those victimized by staff, more than 40% reported physical injury by the staff member involved (U.S. Department of Justice 2015: 2).

CORRUPTION

In examining the official records of an internal affairs unit of a state department of corrections, McCarthy (1995) distinguished patterns of corruption and the level of staff involved in that corruption, as shown in Figure 8.2. Defining *corruption* as "the intentional violation of organizational norms (i.e., rules and regulations) by public employees for personal material gain" (p. 281), McCarthy examined 122 cases of alleged corrupt practices in the department, which revealed four major offense categories and a miscellaneous category comprising theft, embezzlement, trafficking, and misuse of authority. Theft made up one quarter of all cases.

Petty theft was alleged by inmates in complaints of loss of both personal valuables and contraband claimed to have been stolen during cell searches or after handing it over to staff for safekeeping. Complaints were also made by visitors that their possessions had been stolen during searches in the visiting room. Also, goods and materials were alleged to have been stolen from the state, including articles such as a walkie-talkie, tools, and a calculator. Generally, acts of theft appeared to be opportunistic individualistic acts with an absence of evidence indicating any conspiracy.

Trafficking with inmates relates to *smuggling contraband* (see Case Studies 8.6 and 8.7) into prisons for money, drugs, or services, usually of a sexual nature. McCarthy identified a number of contraband items, including drugs, alcohol, money, and weapons, as well as items such as food and reading materials. He found that the more individuals involved in smuggling contraband, the more organized was the operation, with a greater scope of items being made available. Sophisticated smuggling rings had inmates as ring leaders. These operations ranged from a guard bringing in alcohol for a single inmate to large-scale conspiracies involving drug smuggling. Generally, those involved in smuggling were guards, but sometimes counselors and job placement officers were implicated. Prison officer involvement varied from simply collecting drugs from prearranged locations and transporting them into the prison to actually controlling smuggling operations by directly selling items to inmates and by using inmates as pushers and salesmen within the prisons.

Worley, Marquart, and Mullings (2003: 185) point out that trafficking with inmates also involves inmates who exploit relationships with prison officers in order to make illicit profits in the underground prison economy. Reported cases include a male inmate who befriended a female staff member

Figure 8.2   Pattern of Corruption by Type of Decision

Corrupt Acts by Type of Decision	Officials Involved
Misfeasance	
Provide preferential treatment and special privileges	Line staff
Selective application of rewards and punishments	Line staff
Forms of legitimate release	Administrators
Misappropriation of resources	Administrators
Malfeasance	
Trafficking	Line staff
Extortion/exploitation	Line staff
Protection rackets	Line staff
Embezzlement/theft	Line staff and administration
Criminal conspiracies	Line staff
Nonfeasance	
Failure to enforce regulations	Line staff
Cover-ups	Line staff and administration

SOURCE: Adapted from "Keeping an Eye on the Keepers: Prison Corruption and its Control," by Bernard McCarthy in The Prison Journal, 64(2): 113–125. Reprinted by permission of Sage Publications, Inc.

and persuaded her to bring in contraband cigarettes by the carton; a female prisoner who deliberately developed a relationship with a male officer, to the extent that he began bringing into the prison eyeliner, perfume, and cigarettes, which the female sold in the prison economy; and inmates who entrap guards by offering them a candy bar or soda to establish an inappropriate continuing relationship (pp. 186–187). In Texas, where it is difficult to hire sufficient staff to run the many correctional facilities, guards' salaries are low, and according to one inmate account, prison staff earn extra money to the extent of $1,000 a week by bringing in cocaine (p. 188).

Conover (2001: 104) explains how *contraband* comprising weapons, drugs, and alcohol entered Sing Sing Correctional Facility. All these items could easily be obtained inside the prison. According to Conover, some drugs came in during prison visits, but he noted that most drugs entered the prisons through officers who were paid off to allow their entry.

Embezzlement relates to the conversion of state property or goods to one's own use. Acts involved

guards, shopkeepers, and clerks embezzling money from administrative units within the prison system, such as canteens, commissaries, and prison warehouses. Staff audits commonly reveal that these acts involve both staff and inmates working alone or together—for example, colluding with each other through working together in commissaries.

The *misuse of authority* concerns a willful misuse of one's discretion for personal material gain; this conduct accounted for almost one half of complaints received by the internal affairs unit (see Case Studies 8.6 and 8.7). The kinds of discretion involved were transfers, assignment to jobs and housing blocks, and overlooking minor infractions or rules. McCarthy (1995) distinguished a number of forms of misuse of authority, including accepting gratuities for favorable consideration of inmate requests. For example, an officer in charge of a work release program was alleged to have solicited a $20 fee from an inmate for finding him a job. Other examples of misuse of authority included accepting gratuities to protect illicit activities, such as allowing gambling, drugs, or prostitution in a facility or protecting illicit activities from discovery or competition from other inmates; extortion through mistreatment or harassment involving shaking down inmates and personally sanctioning inmates for refusal to obey instructions; mismanagement, including allegations concerning the operation of prison industries for personal gain; and a miscellaneous group, including suspicious deaths of employees, concealment of prior criminal backgrounds by prospective employees, and charges of sexual coercion against a supervisor by a female employee.

Case Study 8.6 Jail Guards Charged With Smuggling

In 1994, 10 prison officers at Westchester County Jail were charged with smuggling contraband to prisoners in the form of food, vodka, cash, and cocaine. In exchange for bringing in the contraband, the guards were paid bribes of up to $1,000 and given trips to Atlantic City. The officers even facilitated escape attempts; in one case, it was alleged that an officer had provided a prisoner with a key to unlock his shackles and handcuffs. The acts of the staff came to light through a sting operation involving federal agents who posed as the relatives of some cooperating inmates. These inmates provided officers with contact numbers for their relatives. When the officers met with the relatives, they discussed various deals to bring in contraband. One officer reportedly bragged to the federal agents that he had been engaged in this kind of conduct for the last 15 years.

SOURCE: Berger 1994.

Case Study 8.7 Baltimore Jail Inmate Builds Drug Trafficking Operation With Active Cooperation of Corrections Officials

The Baltimore City Detention Center is a collection of seven buildings, housing more than 2,000 prisoners awaiting trial for a range of offenses. In places, the buildings are more than 150 years old. Prisoners experience extreme temperatures, and cells are infested with rodents. Court documents filed by the FBI containing transcripts of wiretaps show that Tavon White, 36, who was in the jail for 3 years, took advantage of the jail's poor security and its female officers to build what prosecutors described as a lucrative drug trafficking and money laundering operation. Some of the staff who are alleged to have conspired with White stated they did it for the cash they earned: The base salary of a prison officer is $35,000 to $45,000 a year, plus overtime. Thirteen women officers have been charged.

White is alleged to have used a smuggled cell phone to arrange exchanges between drug dealers outside the jail and corrections officers who brought the smuggled drugs to him to be sold in the jail—a one-gram bag of marijuana sold for $50 and one tablet of Percocet for $30. White boasted in one taped conversation that he made $15,800 in 1 month, but that was less than normal. Investigators were told that White, who had gang connections, and other gang leaders in the jail agreed with jail staff that they would reduce violence inside the jail in exchange for staff turning a blind eye to smuggling contraband into the jail.

Reportedly, four of the female correctional officers have had children by White. One had his name tattooed on her neck and drives two Mercedes-Benz vehicles, allegedly financed by White and his jail operations. She had two children by White.

SOURCE: Vargas, Marimow, and Shin 2013.

During his first 5 years as director of corrections in Massachusetts, George Vose Jr. fired or permitted to resign between 80 and 100 staff as a result of forms of misconduct (Carroll 1998: 282). In one case, an affair between an officer and an inmate was discovered when the inmate was found using the officer's phone card to call her while she was on vacation. In another case, an officer assaulted a coworker on duty over a gambling debt, and it transpired that the officer who was subjected to the assault was a bookie employed by a major organized crime figure. In the first 2 months of 1996, two officers were arrested for smuggling heroin into the prison, another was arrested for bookmaking and possession of a needle and syringe, and another for possession of marijuana (p. 283).

In the case of *Dreyer v. Jalet* (1972), inmates testified that *building tenders* (the term used to describe inmate guards who were used to supplement the power of employed prison officers) were given access to pipes, bats, and clubs to administer discipline on behalf of the regular guards. In one case involving building tenders, 10 of these inmates, armed with axe handles, clubs, and iron pipes, assaulted a group of prisoners while accompanied by an assistant warden and several officers.

WHISTLE-BLOWING IN CORRECTIONS

Mark Hamm (1995: 202) provides several case studies of whistle-blowing that had a positive effect on a correctional organization (see Case Study 8.8). In one case, a warden used institutional funds to purchase equipment he later used to operate a section of his cattle ranch. Further, the warden insisted that guards supervise inmate labor at his ranch while they operated this equipment. Two officers complained, claiming that the warden had abused his authority, and their complaint was upheld by the state personnel board, which ruled that the prison officers had been required to act in ways that were undefined and not relevant to their job descriptions.

In 1997, the television news program *60 Minutes* reported cases of whistle-blowing by two prison officers at a California prison concerning what they considered unethical conduct by their fellow officers. They claimed that inmates from different

---

Case Study 8.8 Ex-SC Prison Officer Sentenced

A former prison officer was sentenced to 3 months in jail for having sex in prison with Susan Smith, who is serving a life sentence for drowning her two sons in a lake in 1994. South Carolina Circuit Court Judge Lee Casey Manning also sentenced Houston Cagle to 5 years of probation and 250 hours of community service.

Cagle pleaded guilty to having sex with Smith and another inmate at the Women's Correctional Institution in Columbia. Investigators found out about the relationship between Cagle and Smith the previous summer when they were looking into a tabloid report alleging that Smith had been beaten in prison.

While reviewing medical records, officers found Smith had been treated for a venereal disease. She then admitted she had sex with Cagle. He was fired shortly after his arrest.

The revelations led to a broad investigation into prison misconduct. More than a dozen corrections department officers and employees were charged with having sex with inmates or smuggling drugs since a state investigation began the previous year.

Two prison officers, including Cagle, and three other corrections workers pleaded guilty to having sex with inmates.

SOURCE: "Ex-S.C. Correctional Officer Sentenced" 2001.

ethnic groups in the prison had been set up to fight each other in a small prison exercise yard and that it was not unusual for officers to place bets on the outcome of such fights. They further claimed that when the fights got out of control, officers would sometimes shoot at the inmates and that since the prison had opened in 1988, eight inmates had been shot dead by officers and many others wounded in this way. On the program, video footage was shown of two inmates of the same ethnic origin fighting two other inmates of a different ethnic origin. One of the inmates, not considered the aggressor, was shot and killed during the fight, and the claim was made that officers had told this inmate after he had assaulted an officer that he would never leave the prison alive (Jones and Carlson 2001: 76).

In the mid-1980s, a female officer at a medium-security prison reported her fellow officers for sleeping on the night shift, claiming she had approached them and advised them that she felt unsafe and vulnerable while they slept. She warned them that if their conduct did not change she would have to report them to the superintendent. They continued to sleep, she reported them, and the consequences were severe for her in that she was later the subject of graffiti on the prison walls, received abusive phone calls and letters, and had her car deliberately damaged in the parking lot (Jones and Carlson 2001: 77).

Oversight of Prisons

Whistle-blowing operates as a form of oversight of prisons, but in the United States, there is little systematic oversight of prison conditions and operations. Instead, the judiciary has been the primary oversight mechanism, but the extensive prisoner litigation of the 1970s met a backlash in the 1980s and the courts have been greatly restricting prisoners' access to the courts. The federal Prison Litigation Reform Act (PLRA) 1995 gave state and local governments the right to end judicial oversight of their correctional facilities (Gottschalk 2015: 44).

In 2006, the Katzenbach Commission drew attention to the lack of oversight and public monitoring of the prison systems. The U.S. situation stands in stark contrast to systems in Europe and Canada, where independent oversight is the standard. In 2008, the American Bar Association called on all levels of government to establish instrumentalities tasked to monitor and report publicly on correctional conditions, but this has not been taken up by the states (Gottschalk 2015: 44). Private prisons are subject to even less oversight than public prisons and are not subject to state freedom of information acts or to the federal Administrative Procedures Act (p. 72).

A Closer Look

A Probation and Parole Officer's Code of Ethics

- I will render professional service to the justice system and the community at large in effecting the social adjustment of the offender.

- I will uphold the law with dignity, displaying an awareness of my responsibility to offenders while recognizing the right of the public to be safeguarded from criminal activity.

- I will strive to be objective in the performance of my duties, recognizing the inalienable right of all persons, appreciating the inherent worth of the individual, and respecting those confidences which can be reposed in me.

- I will conduct my personal life with decorum, neither accepting nor granting favors in connection with my office.

(Continued)

(Continued)

- I will cooperate with my co-workers and related agencies and will continually strive to improve my professional competence through the seeking and sharing of knowledge and understanding.

- I will distinguish clearly, in public, between my statements and actions as an individual and as a representative of my profession.

- I will encourage policy, procedures and personnel practices, which will enable others to conduct themselves in accordance with the values, goals and objectives of the American Probation and Parole Association.

- I recognize my office as a symbol of public faith and I accept it as a public trust to be held as long as I am true to the ethics of the American Probation and Parole Association.

- I will constantly strive to achieve these objectives and ideals, dedicating myself to my chosen profession.

SOURCE: American Probation and Parole Association, n.d. Reprinted with permission of the American Probation and Parole Association.

ETHICAL ISSUES IN PROBATION AND PAROLE

Probation remains a widely employed sanction within the United States. In 2013, about 3.9 million persons were on probation. The probation population did not vary to any great extent between 2000 and 2013, averaging 3.9 to 4.0 million a year during this period (Glaze and Kaeble 2014: 2). In 1990, however, there were about 2.6 million adults on probation. Over time, the workload of probation and parole officers has dramatically increased with the rise in intensive probation supervision. Probation and parole functions are commonly considered a component of corrections because both functions are concerned with the management and control of former inmates.

Like prison officers, probation and parole officers must concern themselves with ethical issues, and their association has developed a code of ethics (see the "Probation and Parole Officer's Code of Ethics" Closer Look box).

Ethical issues in probation and parole tend to center on tensions between the role of parole or probation as treatment or as punishment, the supposed ineffectiveness of probation and parole as a form of punishment, and concerns relating to the duty of these officers toward their clients. Traditionally, probation and parole have involved supervising offenders in the community, and this supervision suggests there will be regular contact between the officer and those who make up his or her caseload. Yet, these contacts vary from full counseling sessions to brief, perfunctory contacts once a month.

The supervisory role brings to the fore the conflict between treatment and control functions or, as some describe it, between surveillance and service (Studt 1973). Studt argues that parole is more surveillance- than service-oriented because, for example, officers are instructed to make surprise visits to parolees. Some argue that this tension can be eliminated by giving the surveillance function to the police, leaving probation officers to provide services (Conrad 1973, 1982), whereas John Rosecrance (1986) holds that probation officers provide neither service nor surveillance but in effect function primarily as report writers for the courts. Howard Abadinsky (1982) has proposed a typography of probation officer styles of probation work comprising the *law enforcement model*, the *therapeutic model*, and the *synthetic model*. The law enforcement model involves a primary role of public protection, the therapeutic model sees rehabilitation and aiding the

Table 8.3   U.S. Adult Residents on Community Supervision, Probation, and Parole, 2000–2013

Year	Community supervision population	Probation	Parole
2000	4,565,100	3,839,500	725,500
2001	4,665,900	3,934,700	731,100
2002	4,748,300	3,995,200	753,100
2003	4,847,500	4,074,000	773,500
2004	4,916,500	4,140,600	775,900
2005	4,946,800	4,162,500	784,400
2006	5,035,200	4,237,000	798,200
2007	5,119,300	4,293,200	826,100
2008	5,095,200	4,271,000	828,200
2009	5,017,900	4,198,200	824,100
2010	4,887,900	4,055,500	840,700
2011	4,814,200	3,971,300	853,900
2012	4,781,300	3,942,00	851,200
2013	4,751,400	3,910,600	853,200
Average annual percent change, 2000–2012	0.4%	0.2%	1.3%
Percent change, 2012–2013	−0.6	−0.8	0.2

Note: Counts rounded to the nearest 100. Detail may not sum to total due to rounding. Counts based on most recent data and may differ from previously published statistics. Reporting methods for some probation agencies changed over time. See *Methodology*.

SOURCE: Herberman 2014: 2.

offender as central, and the synthetic model is a blend of both law enforcement and rehabilitation.

There has been a trend over the past decade toward making probation tougher, emphasizing risk control, and stressing the enforcement of sanctions for breaches of probation. Parole has always had a greater law enforcement emphasis than probation, even though it has come to be regarded as the agency responsible for "letting inmates out of prison early" (Petersilia 1999: 480).

Like prison officers, probation and parole officers are faced with decisions about whether to emphasize the protection of society or to aid the offender, and they are also accountable to demands from administrators and politicians about how their duties should be carried out. Domurad (2000: 43) suggests that as administrators try to organize the implementation of new concepts and programs, such as restorative and community justice, this has the effect of placing additional roles and responsibilities onto line officers and creates more confusion for them about the purpose of their work.

In many states, probation agencies are located in the executive branch of government, where they operate as rational bureaucratic agencies far removed from the probation officer in the field. This separation has the potential to create conflicts for the officers. For example, conflict can occur in cases where state-level policy makers make demands about how probation officers should interact with their clients, while at the same time the local community may have different requirements and demands of these interactions (Silverman 1993: 89).

When probation is located within the judicial branch of government, there is less likely to be administrative pressure on probation work because the supervision and treatment functions may be considered subordinate to sentencing and punishment. Nevertheless, it is possible that a probation officer may have to make decisions about treatment that can conflict with the intentions of the adjudicated punishment. This becomes even more complicated due to the fact that local-level judicial officers are often subject to local pressures in their punishment decisions (Silverman 1993: 90).

Probation Officers and Law Enforcement

Today in most states, the role of the probation officer has gained a new law enforcement emphasis, and the probation officer is identified more closely with law enforcement agencies. It is now common for probation officers to be proactive in enforcing probation conditions through measures such as monitoring, surveillance, search and seizure, drug testing, and even by accompanying police on enforcement actions (Small and Torres 2001: 24). It is now a regular practice for such officers to take part in vehicle surveillance, the execution of search and arrest warrants, gang task forces, and even sting operations (p. 26). Legally, a probation or parole officer may ask law enforcement personnel for assistance in searching probationers, but the primary purpose of that search must be related to probation or parole and must not be a cover for other police purposes (del Carmon, Barnhill, Bonham, Hignite, and Jermstad 2001: 115). If police attempt to induce a probation officer to exercise his or her powers to search and if the officer agrees to the search, he or she must be satisfied that it is necessary for the proper functioning of the probation system.

A common condition of probation is that a probationer agrees to waive Fourth Amendment rights and allow searches to be conducted on his or her person, residence, and automobile. The California Supreme Court has held that as a general rule, probationers have "a reduced expectation of privacy," and this leaves them open to intrusions by governmental authorities, which "are necessitated by legitimate governmental demands" (del Carmon et al. 2001: 116). In one case, police searched a juvenile, who was associating with suspected gang members, at a football game and discovered marijuana on his person. Police did not know that the juvenile was on probation, a condition of which allowed a search of his person, and no probation officer was present when the search was conducted. In this case, the California Supreme Court ruled that the probation condition allowing searches was sufficient to authorize the police search of the juvenile (*In re Tyrell* 1998). This decision was later overruled in *In re Jaime P* (2006).

Today, police rely on probation officers for information about probationers, including their place of residence, living situation, and behavior, and in return, probation looks to law enforcement for protection when brought into contact with high-risk offenders (Small and Torres 2001: 26). Increasingly, probation officers supervise offenders convicted of violent crimes because probation is being granted to those with serious criminal backgrounds and substantial drug abuse histories, especially in metropolitan areas.

Arming Probation Officers

A major ethical debate within the probation field concerns the issue of arming probation officers. (Parole officers carry weapons in two thirds of the states.) Some argue that probation officers cannot carry out the traditional role of a probation officer effectively while armed because bearing arms contributes to an atmosphere of distrust between the officer and the client. On the other hand, officers who are more enforcement-oriented typically view carrying firearms as a means of protection from risk, especially as they have come to associate with more violent or high-risk offenders. Some contend that officers should not be required to carry firearms if they are personally opposed to carrying weapons, but rather, they should be given the option to carry them on certain assignments where risks would warrant such protection (Small and Torres 2001: 27).

One possible result of increased arming, however, is that probation officers will be regarded more as police officers than probation officers, and this will further diminish any treatment role they may still have. This debate has now entered the juvenile justice arena, and in some states—for example, in most jurisdictions in Arizona—juvenile probation officers now carry firearms (Banks, Rector, and Jackson 2005).

The ACA's view on this issue is that there should be a demonstrated need for firearms, and once this need is clear, adequate and ongoing training in their use must be provided. In many ways, the issue of carrying arms strikes directly at the difference between probation and police work, and it is significant that those entering the profession of probation do not receive the training and awareness in the use of firearms that is provided to law enforcement personnel. Psychologically, probation officers have not traditionally been sensitized to the use of weapons, and probation officers have not been recruited with a role involving weapons in mind.

In the federal justice system, the majority of judicial districts permit federal probation officers to carry arms, and in California, out of 58 probation departments surveyed in 2008, 46 were armed to some extent. A midway position between arming and not arming has been to carry arms on home visits only (Teague 2011: 327).

Treatment or Control?

As already noted, the traditional tensions between treatment and control have been affected by an increased focus on dangerousness, risk, and criminality. As a result, treatment is de-emphasized, and security tends to be stressed. Nevertheless, the notion that probation is granted for the purpose of treatment persists, and a goal of probation remains one of matching the probationer with treatment and rehabilitation services in the community. The increased numbers of probationers have put an end to the commonly accepted notion that individual officers' caseloads should be set at between 30 and 50 cases (Champion 1996: 437). Consequently, probation officers are challenged ethically in terms of having to choose who among their clients will

receive adequate treatment services, especially as the caseloads continue to rise (Silverman 1993: 91).

Associated with the problems in supervising large caseloads and the decisions about treatment responsibilities are the increased demands for, and time constraints in, the preparation of presentence reports. With very large caseloads, officers may well lack the time to prepare detailed presentence reports or may have to trade off one offender against another in the interests of performance (Silverman 1993: 91).

Privatizing Probation

Most recently, one ethical issue affecting probation has been the granting of contracts to private companies to supervise persons ordered to pay low-level fines and persons placed on probation. Much like prison privatization, therefore, in some states the service of probation has been contracted out to private enterprise as a cost-saving measure. In Georgia, legislation in the 1990s permitted the use of private probation service companies for community supervision. CSRA Probation Services, Inc., a private company providing probation and other services, states that it is "uniquely qualified to provide a wide array of community supervision options to local courts, counties, and cities" (quoted in Teague 2011: 324). The company now serves over 60 courts. In Florida, Washington, and Tennessee, the Providence Service Corporation founded in 1997 had by 2006 secured more than 100 contracts for community supervision services. The services it provides include "the collection and disbursement of court-ordered fines, fees and restitution" (p. 325).

In Alabama, the city of Clanton contracted probation out to Judicial Correction Services, the largest private probation company in Alabama. In June 2015, the city agreed to terminate its relationship with the company following lawsuits claiming the company had violated federal laws by threatening to jail indigent persons if they failed to pay fees and fines due to the company and to the Clanton municipal court. In Clanton, the company charged a "supervision fee" to probationers of $40 a month. It has been claimed that the private probation industry marks a return to the debtor's prisons of times past when it was permissible to imprison persons for nonpayment of debts (Seville 2015).

The trend toward privatization of probation services is also found in the United Kingdom, where, in 2014, 70% of probation services were outsourced to the private sector. Probation staffs in the U.K. National Probation Service have expressed strong opposition to the introduction of a profit motive to the management of offenders (Deering and Feilzer 2015).

Parole

In 2014, the Department of Justice reported that at year-end 2013 about 853,200 persons were on parole. The reincarceration rate for parole violations remained stable at about 9% of parolees (Herberman and Bonczar 2014: 1). Where parole is still available under state and federal laws, it is increasingly difficult to secure, especially for life sentences. For example, in California, although almost 4,000 prisoners serving life sentences apply for release on parole every year, the Board of Parole Hearings recommends parole only 2% to 5% of the time, and those grants are often revoked by the governor because parole decisions have become politicized (Henry 2012: 69). Since 2008, under Marsy's Law the interval between successive parole applications following a rejected application has been fixed at between 3 and 15 years, as determined by the Board of Parole, with an average waiting time of 5 years (Dolovich 2012: 113).

Treatment programs for parolees are scarce, and parole officers focus their efforts on surveillance rather than on rehabilitation. Safety and security are now major issues in parole services (Petersilia 1999: 482), and in large, urban areas, parole agents are commonly occupied in drug testing, electronic monitoring, and verifying curfews. Greater numbers of parolees are not completing their parole supervision and are being returned to prison, which contributes to the explosion in the prison population (p. 483). For example, in 2005 parolees were 11% of the correctional population and accounted for a 9.1% increase in correctional population growth (Glaze 2006).

In some states, there are significant numbers of persons on probation and parole. For example, in 2013 parolees and probationers numbered 381,600 in California and 508,000 in Texas (Glaze and Kaeble 2014: 11). Partly due to zero-tolerance policies, a greater number of parole violations are being detected, and revocation to prison is becoming a

Figure 8.3   Adults on Parole at Year-End, 2000–2013

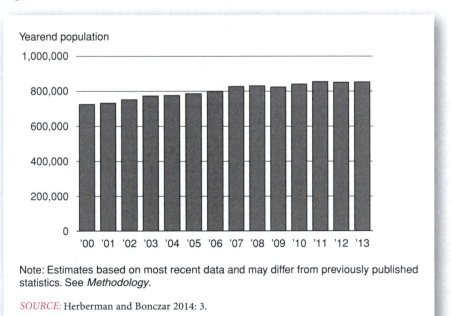

Note: Estimates based on most recent data and may differ from previously published statistics. See *Methodology*.

SOURCE: Herberman and Bonczar 2014: 3.

Figure 8.4   Estimated Percentage of the At-Risk Parole Population Returned to Incarceration, 2000–2013

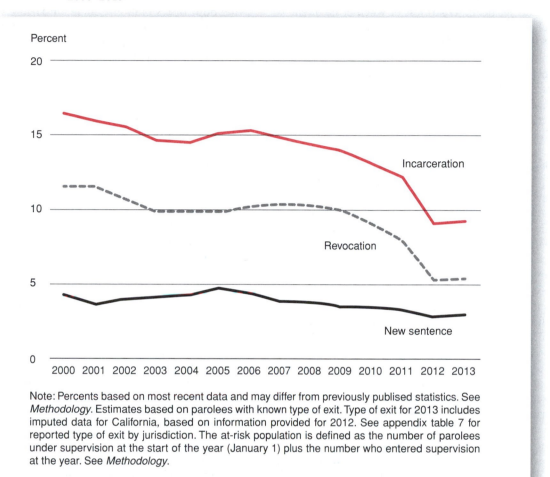

Note: Percents based on most recent data and may differ from previously publised statistics. See *Methodology*. Estimates based on parolees with known type of exit. Type of exit for 2013 includes imputed data for California, based on information provided for 2012. See appendix table 7 for reported type of exit by jurisdiction. The at-risk population is defined as the number of parolees under supervision at the start of the year (January 1) plus the number who entered supervision at the year. See *Methodology*.

SOURCE: Herberman and Bonczar 2014: 9.

routine affair because the process of being sent to prison, later released on parole, and then sent back again to prison sets up a revolving door for parolees.

Abolition of Parole for Life Imprisonment (LWOP)

Many U.S. states have laws that allow for the sentence of life imprisonment without parole (LWOP) to be imposed. This constitutes a lifetime sentence, and an inmate sentenced to LWOP will spend the rest of his or her life in prison. Many are now arguing that LWOP, as a sentence, raises questions about human dignity. This sentence is currently being served by more than 41,000 inmates, an increase of 28,500 since 1992 (Dolovich 2012: 110). As well, more than 140,000 persons are serving life sentences with the possibility of securing parole after having served a minimum period of years (Henry 2012: 66), but in those states that have abolished parole—Florida, Illinois, Iowa, Louisiana, Maine, Pennsylvania, South Dakota, and the federal system—a life sentence is the functional equivalent of LWOP (p. 68).

As noted, subject to the remote possibility of a pardon, the inmate will likely remain in prison until his or her death, regardless of whether he or she is rehabilitated. Therefore, it is argued that such sentences constitute "uniquely severe and degrading punishments because of the nature of the punishment itself, because they deny human dignity, and because they are *de facto* irrevocable" (Henry 2012: 72). In fact, whole-of-life sentences are often regarded as worse than death sentences because they allow for extended periods of suffering, fail to respect the worth and dignity of the individual, and deny all redemptive possibilities.

It is instructive to compare the U.S. LWOP sentence with international practice. The Council of Europe has declared that imprisoning a person for life without hope of release is inhuman and incompatible with the idea of reintegrating prisoners into society. While other countries have retained life imprisonment as a sentence, sentences must be reviewed after a minimum period of years has been served—for example, after 10 years in Belgium, after 15 years in Germany, Austria, and Switzerland, and after 30 years in France (Henry 2012: 78).

While the U.S. Supreme Court has generally supported life sentences, in 2010 in *Graham v. Florida,* the Court for the first time held that a noncapital sentence was a violation of the prohibition against cruel and unusual punishment. The Court struck down the use of LWOP for juvenile offenders convicted of offenses other than homicide—in that case, a 16-year-old boy had committed an armed robbery and received probation, which he violated. For that violation, he received a life sentence, and because Florida had abolished parole, he would never be released from prison. The Court noted that LWOP was the second-most severe penalty

under the law and said that it deprived the convicted person of "the most basic liberties, without giving hope of restoration" (quoted in Henry 2012: 80). It should be noted that despite the severity of the LWOP sentence, unlike the death penalty, it receives no special judicial scrutiny.

Parole Officers as Police

Over the past several years, at least for parole officers, the tensions between treatment and control roles appear to have been resolved in favor of control; consequently, ethical considerations in relation to this issue would seem to be much less of a concern than for probation officers. Nowadays, the parole officer's task is, to all intents and purposes, a policing role because parole officers have legal authority to carry and use firearms, to search without Fourth Amendment constraints, to order arrests without probable cause, and to confine without bail (Rudovsky, Bronstein, Koren, and Cade 1988). Some argue that these powers make the parole officer a "walking court system."

According to Petersilia (1999: 505), over 80% of parolees are supervised on caseloads that average 69 parolees, and parolees are seen face to face less than twice a month. Parole officers complain about lack of time and resources, increased paperwork, and higher caseloads. Moreover, newly recruited parole officers now tend to adopt the surveillance rather than the rehabilitation model of parole and perform a "quasi-policing role" in some areas (p. 508). For the future, in light of the convergence of the roles of parole officer and police officer, parole officers are likely to find themselves having to respond to ethical issues similar to those that confront police officers.

SUMMARY

Prison officer use of force is a major ethical issue in the prison environment, and it is clear that in the early period, officer violence was endemic. Despite detailed rules and regulations about the use of force, including deadly force, it is clear that some prison systems allow extralegal physical force to be used against inmates and that this represents a part of the

prison officer subculture because fighting an inmate is regarded as an expression of prison officer masculinity and machismo. Justifications for using violence include the prison officer perspective of being unable to maintain control without violence or the threat of violence and the belief that violence deters inmate violence against officers. *Self-defense* tends to be defined very broadly, and reprisals for inmate assaults are considered not only appropriate but also essential. Ultimately, however, unrestricted violence against inmates can only threaten the security of officers themselves because it tends to fuel inmates' anger and hatred rather than repress their resistance. As well as rule books regulating the use of violence, the courts and state and federal governments have issued their own standards and directives, especially in relation to the use of deadly force.

Studies have identified a number of other forms of unethical conduct, including how prison officers react to rapes in prison and how corruption can be maintained through smuggling, drug trafficking, embezzlement, and theft. Sometimes whistle-blowing reveals acts of corruption, but at other times, whistle-blowers themselves are penalized for revealing misconduct.

Probation and parole raise some similar ethical concerns to those in corrections, especially in relation to the tension between treatment and punishment. Increasingly, probation is less directed toward treatment and more focused on enforcement and punishment, and probation officers appear to have moved closer to a policing role, which includes carrying weapons and collaborating with law enforcement officers in various activities. Parole officers have always been regarded as enforcement agents, and they have become even more law enforcement-oriented, resulting in a situation where the ethical issues that affect parole may in fact be similar to those relevant to the policing function.

DISCUSSION QUESTIONS

1. How do prison officers justify the use of force against inmates? Are there any ethical implications in their justifications?

2. Explain why prison officers are ethically responsible for protecting the safety of prisoners. What situations might arise where this responsibility should be exercised?

3. What ethical issues do probation and parole officers face in carrying out their duties? Given the recent emphasis on law enforcement in probation and parole practice as well as on policies of zero tolerance, explain how this change from treatment to enforcement affects ethical issues and standards for the professions.

WEB RESOURCES

Family and Corrections Network. https://www.prisonactivist.org/resources/family-and-corrections-network
International Center for Prison Studies. http://www.kcl.ac.uk/depsta/rel/icps
National Institute of Corrections (NIC). http://www.nicic.org
National Prison Rape Elimination Commission Report. https://www.ncjrs.gov/pdffiles1/226680.pdf
Penal Reform International. http://www.penalreform.org
Stop Prisoner Rape. http://www.spr.org
United Nations Asia and Far East Institute for the Prevention of Crime and the Treatment of Offenders (UNAFEI). http://www.unafei.or.jp
Vera Justice Institute. http://www.vera.org
Women Coping in Prison. http://curry.edschool.virginia.edu/prisonstudy/

9

THE ETHICS OF CRIMINAL JUSTICE POLICY MAKING

THE ETHICS OF POLICY MAKING

Policy making on criminal justice issues, including crime control, takes place at many different levels in society, ranging from the local community that introduces a neighborhood watch program to the formulation of strategies at the national level after debate in Congress. Policy makers at these different levels must make choices and analyze options, and in determining the approach to follow, they should take into account any ethical aspects involved in their plans and proposals. The policy-making process involves predicting certain future conditions assuming an uninterrupted flow of events, projecting the future implications of a particular course of action, identifying a preferred outcome from a set of available choices, generating a program or policy that will result in the preferred outcome, and creating an adequate monitoring system (Meehan 1990: 41).

Justifying Policy Choices

In considering how particular policies are justified, Frederic Reamer (1986: 224) identifies three grounds, which he calls "ideological," "empirical," and "ethical." Policy made on *ideological* grounds argues that certain policies are desirable because they fit a set of assumptions that may be based on religious beliefs, practice, or even basic intuition. For example, an argument that spending on social services should be decreased may be founded on the ideological assumption that, historically, America has stressed minimum government intervention in the lives of citizens. *Empirical* grounds relate to science and research and to what is known from that research about the likely outcome of a particular policy. For example, a policy concerned with subsidizing child care might draw on research evidence that shows that mothers who are able to take advantage of child care are more likely to seek work, and therefore less likely to want assistance for their dependent children. In contrast to these grounds, those based on *ethical* grounds rely on conclusions drawn from an analysis of what is "right and wrong" or "good or bad" in a moral sense. For example, empirical or research evidence may show that paying subsidies to ailing corporations is less costly than allowing them to fail. Some would argue, however, that it would be ethically wrong for the government to intervene in the workings of a private enterprise in such a fashion. The critical difference between ethical and ideological grounds is that policy making on ethical grounds requires a calculated, philosophical analysis of the morality on which the policy is based. This is not true for ideological grounds.

This chapter will examine some specific criminal justice policies, focus on the ethical issues that are implicated in those policies, and explore the way those ethical implications have been addressed and debated. Of course, criminal justice strategies are not formulated in a vacuum. They take account of ideologies and politics current at the time and, in many cases, are presumed to be giving effect to social movements and public concerns. Policy makers are subjected to many influences in their analysis of policy issues and in their decision-making. For example, elected politicians react to the media, to their constituents, and to the many lobby groups that operate on both sides of all policy issues. Ethical issues, therefore, arise within a pattern of influences, and sometimes the ethical correctness of a particular course of action is used to support an argument that a particular policy action should be followed.

Ethical Policy Making

There are at least two ways of thinking about the ethics of criminal justice policy making:

- First, there is the general issue, applicable to all policy making, that those designing policies should *act ethically* in formulating their plans and projects (Fischer and Forester 1987: 24; Heineman, Bluhm, Peterson, and Kearney 1997: 67).
- Second, specifically in relation to policy making on punishment, it is arguable that punishment itself is a *morality policy* (certainly, capital punishment is such a policy) and that making policy about punishment therefore involves ethics (Studlar 2001: 39).

There is no scope here for an extended discussion of ethical policy making, but Charles Anderson (1987) notes that policy analysis "involves a clarification and ordering of values and any policy analysis inevitably rests on some conception of desirable public purpose," and that "policy analysis that ignores the moral dimensions of public choice and public service is an inadequate pedagogy" (p. 23).

The reasons advanced for the absence of ethical policy making include a reliance on cost–benefit analysis, which tends to be the primary method of policy analysis (Amy 1987: 46). As Rosemarie Tong (1986: 14) explains, cost–benefit analysis comprises several stages, including defining goals, determining the various methods of achieving those goals, determining costs and benefits of the various methods, comparing and ranking the costs and benefits of the various alternatives, and taking account of major uncertainties. In government, some argue that policy makers are prevented from making ethical decisions by a kind of machismo that sees any concern for ethical issues as a sign of political weakness—that is, as an unwillingness to make "tough" policy decisions (Amy 1987: 58). Others argue that "unethical" policy making includes reacting to events and issues that create "moral panics" by making ad hoc, capricious, and arbitrary policies that are not reasoned and not rational. In contrast to unethical policy making of this kind, an ethical piece of policy would involve a reasoned and considered analysis of a particular issue and a rational and informed approach. Where moral panics arise, such as occurred in the war against drugs or the threat of "superpredators," there is a tendency for politicians and others to react viscerally, instinctively, and instantly rather than follow a reasoned and informed policy approach. In fact, many people would think that if politicians did not react instinctively to moral panics, they would be failing to "get tough" on crime and criminals.

Moral Panics and Morality Policy Making

The term *moral panic* was coined by Stanley Cohen (1972) in his work *Folk Devils and Moral Panics*. Cohen described moral panics in terms of the emergence of a condition, event, or group of persons that becomes defined as a threat to the values and interests of society. It is presented in a stylized and stereotypical fashion by the mass media, and groups of experts and "right-thinking people" take moral positions, make judgments, and suggest how the threat should be coped with. Cohen noted that the condition that produced the moral panic then either disappears or becomes more visible. Cohen's argument was that moral panics are generated by the media or special interest groups that use the media to publicize their concerns. In revisiting his theory in later years, Cohen has suggested that in the information society, social networks enable moral panics to be constructed and transmitted with ease and speed. In his view, the subjects of corporate crime, state crime, and environmental crime are strong contenders for future moral panics, but the most important subject is likely to be immigration and associated topics such as border controls, refugees, and migrants, generally (2011: 240, 242).

A second theory of moral panic was developed by Erich Goode and Nachman Ben-Yehuda (1994), who proposed an "elite-engineered model." This theory is further developed by Stuart Hall, Charles Critcher, Tony Jefferson, John Clarke, and Brian Roberts (1978) in their well-known work *Policing the Crisis: Mugging, the State, and Law and Order.* Hall and his colleagues agreed that the media were a powerful force for shaping public consciousness about controversial issues. However, he also argued that typically moral panics about law and order had their origin in statements by the police and judges that were then taken up and elaborated on by the media. (Hall et al. were writing about the situation in England.) Also, Hall and colleagues went further by arguing that the definition of a moral panic included the notion of an irrational response to that panic that was out of all proportion to the actual threat offered. This is in contrast to Cohen's (1972) view that moral panics are a product of "cultural strain and ambiguity."

A third theory advanced by Goode and Ben-Yehuda (1994) stresses the level of popular participation in moral panics; this is termed the *grassroots model.* According to this theory, moral panics are founded on genuine public concern, which is picked up and promoted by the media. In this theory, there is a shift of attention away from politicians and toward the opinions of the general public. It treats moral panic as a cultural phenomenon, as does Stuart Scheingold, who in *The Politics of Law*

and Order (1984) argued that moral panics about street crime had little to do with actual crime, being more concerned about the pervasive presence of violence in contemporary American society.

Theories about moral panic show that the term is problematic, but it has come to represent a situation where, generally speaking, public reaction to an event is disproportionate to the actual problem faced. In other words, there may be a problem, such as street crime, but there is an overreaction about how it should be addressed in terms of crime control.

There is a link between moral panics and morality policy making. Moral panics are often responded to in the form of policy changes and, ultimately, legislation that contains and reflects those policy changes. Clearly, there is a decision-making process by legislators and others that involves policy assessment and analysis and a consideration of policy options to deal with the moral panic. It is during this policy process that irrational, arbitrary, and therefore unethical policy making can occur. Moral panics and morality policy making together form the organizing framework for this discussion on ethics in criminal justice policy making.

Consider the anti-drug movement, which resulted from public, media, and political concern about drug dealing and drug consumption. Responding to this concern, Congress passed legislation that launched a war on drugs. Was this legislation the result of rational, thorough, and informed debate, or did it originate as an instinctive, nonrational response to public fears and concerns? If the latter, then, arguably, legislators in this case promoted and enacted legislation that reflected an unethical decision-making process (see Case Study 9.1).

As discussed in this chapter, specifically in relation to the war against drugs and the three-strikes legislation, policy choices sometimes have a disproportionate impact on minorities. The association between crime, minorities (especially blacks), and criminal justice policy making is underpinned by a substantial body of research that reveals that negative racial stereotypes and collective racial resentment are positively correlated with criminal justice punishment polices favoring punitiveness (Tonry 2011: 7).

Case Study 9.1 An Example of Unethical Policy Making?

Legislation enacted in 1986 shaped the war against drugs by prescribing mandatory minimum penalties for drug trafficking based on the amount of drugs involved and by making a distinction between possession of cocaine and possession of crack cocaine. A penalty was imposed of a minimum of 25 years imprisonment for possession of 5 or more grams of *crack cocaine* (the form of cocaine for which African Americans are disproportionately arrested), and 50 grams meant a 10-year mandatory minimum sentence. In contrast, an offender found guilty of possession of *powder cocaine* (the type commonly used by middle- and upper-class whites) would only be liable for a mandatory minimum sentence of 5 years if the amount of cocaine exceeded or equaled 500 grams. The legislation therefore penalized crack cocaine 100 times more severely than powder cocaine. The legislation was firmly aimed at social control and included provisions that eliminated probation and parole for certain drug offenders and allowed for the forfeiture of assets. Fundamentally, drug abuse had been perceived and defined as a national security issue for the United States, and the war on drugs was portrayed as a matter of national survival. After 1986, however, media and public attention drifted away from the issue of drug abuse.

By the mid-1990s, three out of four persons doing time for drug offenses were African American, and in the federal courts, 94% of persons tried for drug offenses were African American. In 1995, the U.S. Sentencing Commission urged that there be parity in penalties for the different forms of cocaine, explaining that there was no rational basis for this differentiation in sentencing (Glassner 1999: 136). The commission's recommendations had never before been refused, but the White House and Congress aggressively opposed these recommendations, which were struck down in the House of Representatives by a vote of 332 to 83. Rather than give equity to African Americans charged with drug offenses, the White House and Congress preferred to avoid being labeled as "soft on drugs."

(See discussion on the Fair Sentencing Act 2010, which finally reduced the sentencing disparity between crack and powder cocaine.)

Race and Crime Control Policies

In his insightful study of the impact of crime control policies on blacks, Michael Tonry (2011) asks why policy makers and legislators adopted policies that targeted offenses for which blacks were especially likely to be arrested and why those policies were not changed once their racially biased outcomes became known. Tonry identifies what he refers to as the Republican "Southern Strategy" during the late 1980s as a "major precipitator of the severity of modern criminal justice policies and the unfair burdens they place on black Americans" (p. 2). He argues that this strategy sought to weaken traditional support of whites in the South for Democratic candidates by employing public fears and stereotypes and by focusing on issues such as crime, state's rights, welfare fraud, busing, and affirmative action. As Tonry puts

it, "Crime was given a black face"—most specifically in street violence and crack cocaine, where zealous law enforcement greatly impacted blacks (p. 2).

Tonry (2011) points out a second reason underpinning this policy making as one that maintains the culture of racial dominance previously enforced through the practice of slavery. He suggests the third reason is the negative stereotyping that links blacks to crime and thus to policies of retribution and incapacitation. He lists other factors weighing against blacks in criminal justice policy making that count explicitly or implicitly toward bias, including the influence of evangelical Protestantism, which promotes the notion that criminality is morally wrong and criminals are incapable of redemption; political movements that adopt black and white positions with no middle ground, especially in relation to the now almost-constant focus on victim's rights that bars any consideration of the circumstances of the offender; and the peculiarly American practice of electing judges and prosecutors who are influenced by public notions of punitiveness, thereby politicizing the justice system (p. 10).

Tonry provides startling data on the rise in the black imprisonment rate: In 1960, blacks made up 36% of inmates, and the black imprisonment rate was 661: 100,000; civil rights reforms and reform of the law might have been expected to change those figures, and in fact by 1970, the overall black imprisonment rate was 593 (2011: 5). However, this figure increased dramatically from 593 in 1970 to 2,661 in 2006. As Tonry points out, the enormous rise in the prison population is largely a product of the battle against drugs, and for blacks, its effect was wholly disproportionate (p. 27). Given that black street-level drug dealers are easy targets for police arrest, police choose to arrest more blacks, and thus more blacks are imprisoned. However, in policy terms, arresting street-level offenders for drug offenses has almost no effect on drug availability. Such are the rewards of selling drugs, especially in locales such as the inner cities where there are almost no licit employment opportunities available and one jailed dealer is rapidly replaced by another (p. 55).

Today, young black males who have dropped out of high school have an incarceration rate that is almost 50 times the national average, and 68% of black high school dropouts have served time in prison by the age of 34, compared to one third of white high school dropouts (Gottschalk 2015: 122).

Morality Policy

In formulating criminal justice policy on issues of morality (morality policy making), policy makers should act ethically, undertake formal policy analysis, and avoid promoting ad hoc, arbitrary, and irrational policy solutions. However, studies have shown that policy making on issues seen as moral fails to follow this ethical approach to policy making. *Morality policies* are policies that are viewed and constructed by the media, politicians, and sections of the public as involving moral and ethical issues. For example, what should be the policy on capital punishment? What should be the policy on abortion? Thus, the creation

of morality policy depends on how an issue is framed and not on its intrinsic content.

Morality policies share common features: They are driven by public opinion, media coverage, lobbying by interest groups, the political concerns of elected officials, and sometimes ideology. Unlike other policy issues, morality policies are considered easy to understand and require no special expertise for opinions and views to be expressed (Glick and Hutchinson 2001: 56). As Meier puts it, everyone is an "expert" on morality (in Mooney 2001: 116). In designing and legislating policy on morality issues,

> Members of Congress and their staff use more information about constituents' personal experiences and other emotive information than technical policy analysis, they seek out less information, and they use the information they receive more selectively than when they are designing nonmorality policy. (Goggin and Mooney 2001: 131)

As Christopher Mooney (2001: 3–5) points out, morality policy involves a debate in which one party portrays the issue as one of morality and uses moral arguments in support of its view. It is the perceptions of the parties that make a particular policy a morality policy, and in such policies, moral judgment relies more on feelings than on reason. The death penalty is a classic instance of a morality policy because prohibiting the death penalty has the effect of validating a particular value about the sanctity of human life. Issues like the death penalty inevitably invite a higher degree of public participation because democratic theory argues that such policies must incorporate the views of the people (p. 10). It is common for advocacy groups to contest morality policies. Generally, they claim to be supporting some public interest rather than promoting any personal gain. Policy making on issues that call for morality policy usually involves less formal policy analysis than policy making for nonmorality policy (p. 13).

Rationale for Morality Policy Making

Mooney (2001) argues that the United States has a preoccupation with morality policy and suggests that the reasons for this relate to

1. the high adherence to religions in American society, promoting the likelihood of clashes on fundamental values, which are often based in religion;

2. the heterogeneity of society that encourages a clash of values; and
3. the fact that, in contrast to other democratic states, in the United States, "there is a seemingly endless array of alternative venues in which morality policy advocates can pursue political satisfaction" (p. 16).

Those who rely on their intuition to guide their thinking on a particular issue usually take a moral position. However, the danger in following only our intuition is discussed by Jonathan Baron (1998: 18), who points out that while most people take stands on public issues on the basis of intuition about what they consider is right, this approach usually results in only a partial understanding of the issue. Moral panics can sometimes be generated by specific events and lead to instant legislation or policy making. Examples of moral panics include movements to condemn pedophiles, the enactment of mandatory minimum legislation, the war on drugs, and what to do about "juvenile predators." Another way of understanding policy emanating from moral panics is to see them as the expressive side of policy making in that such policies transmit values and intentions. For example, advertisements urging people not to drink and drive reinforce values of sobriety, and capital punishment expresses toughness on criminals (Maynard-Moody and Stull 1987: 249–250). These policies, in fact, are designed to send a message and are intentionally expressive. Of course, not all policy making in criminal justice is expressive, but punishment policy often involves employing the rhetoric engendered by moral panics. This serves to shift policy away from rational, calculating models of policy making toward the expressive forms of policy.

Penal Policies

Penal policies since the late 1970s have resulted in mass imprisonment and have turned the United States into what scholars have termed "the carceral state" (Gottschalk 2015: 1). On December 31, 2014, there were an estimated 1,561,500 state and federal prisoners (down 1% from 2013), and the total state and federal incarceration rate was 612 per 100,000 population (Carson 2015: 1), down from a peak of about 1,615,500 in 2009. The rush to incarcerate has increased the rate of imprisonment from 230 per

100,000 in 1979 to 478 per 100,000 for U.S. residents of all ages, and 612 per 100,000 for U.S. residents aged 18 or older in 2014 (p. 1). In 2013, the adult male imprisonment rate was 1,191 per 100,000 (Carson 2014: 6).

There are wide variations in the rate of imprisonment among the states. For example, Louisiana has a rate of 847 per 100,000, Mississippi 692, and Texas 602, compared to Minnesota 189 and Rhode Island 194 (Carson 2014: 7). Blacks comprised the largest portion of male inmates in 2013 (37%) compared to non-Hispanic whites (32%) and Hispanics (22%). Almost 3% of all black males residing in the U.S. were incarcerated on December 31, 2013, compared to 0.5% of white males (p. 2). In 2013, the total correctional population, including those on probation and parole, was estimated at 6,899,000— that is, about 1 in 35 adults in the country was under some form of correctional supervision (Glaze and Kaeble 2014: 1).

How does the U.S. incarceration rate compare with worldwide imprisonment rates? The 10th edition of the World Prison Population List covering rates of imprisonment between September 2011 and September 2013 revealed that the United States had the highest prison population rate worldwide, comprising 716 per 100,000 persons (Walmsley 2013: 1). This compares to Russia at 475 per 100,000, a median rate for Europe of 98, for Oceania, including Australia and New Zealand, of 151, Japan of 51, England and Wales of 148, and a world prison population rate overall of 144 per 100,000 (pp. 1–3). U.S. justice and crime control policies locate the country well beyond rates of incarceration experienced in the industrialized world.

A full discussion of the suggested explanations for this extraordinary and, in worldwide terms, unique rush to incarcerate is beyond the scope of this book, but numerous factors appear to have played a part. One important element has been what is called "penal populism," as political leaders have adopted policies and programs they believe reflect a punitive turn in public opinion about punishing offenders (see the Public Opinion About Punishment section in this chapter). The mass incarceration of persons has taken place in spite of the fact that crime, especially violent and property crime, has been on the decline since the early 1990s (Clear and Frost 2014: 11), and falling crime rates have been reflected in public opinion polls that indicate less concern about crime and more about national security or the economy.

Changes in crime rates are generally agreed to have had little effect on incarceration rates; for example, the last crime peak occurred in 1994, but despite falling crime rates since then, the incarceration rates increased by two thirds (Clear and Frost 2014: 36). Crime rates do not therefore correlate with punishment. However, rational arguments notwithstanding, punitive justice policies continued to be formulated and implemented long after the crime rate had stabilized, well into the period when crime was diminishing.

In the United States, crime is heavily politicized, sensationalized by the media, frames the exercise of much political and executive action, is subject to powerful vested interests such as prison unions and the corporate owners of private prisons whose economic future is tied to a massive prison system, and has created a culture of fear, causing Simon (2007) to state that "the American elite are governing through crime" (p. 4). Scholars have identified the ideology of neoliberalism[1] as fostering punitive punishment policies, and some regard mass incarceration as a natural development of increasing public indifference or even hostility toward those who commit crimes (Pratt 2001: 304). In general, many agree that the carcerel state is the product of a complex range of historical, institutional, and political events and that no single factor can explain its development (Gottschalk 2015: 10, 14).

In terms of justice policy making, David Garland (2001) points out that "mass imprisonment was not a policy that was proposed, researched, costed, debated and democratically agreed [to]" (p. 2). As he notes, in contrast to the rational and informed policy making of the past in, for example, the New Deal and the Great Society, "mass imprisonment emerged as the overdetermined outcome of a converging series of policies and decisions." Pointing to the war

against drugs, mandatory sentencing, truth in sentencing, and the development of private prisons, Garland emphasizes that these measures did not form a rational and coherent program. Rather, America has drifted into a situation where mass imprisonment has been accepted as the sole method of crime control. He asks the questions, "What does it mean for the United States to be a mass imprisonment society and what are the implications?" For example, "What limits are there to this process and can they be reversed?" and "What is the social impact on communities and neighborhoods?" (p. 2).

The racial implications of crime control and mass imprisonment policies have been discussed earlier in the Race and Crime Control Policies section. A debate about mass imprisonment has begun that highlights the impact of these policies on minorities and their financial cost, but it is too early to say if political leaders are prepared to make the policy changes to the criminal justice system that are required if the rush to incarcerate so many for such lengthy terms is to be halted. In state capitols, legislators and policy makers have been rethinking "tough on crime" policies that have led to overcrowded prisons (see Chapter 7) and inflated corrections budgets; for example, the cost of incarcerating state inmates rose from $12 billion in 1988 to more than $50 billion by 2008.

State proposals to cut prison costs include policy changes, such as reducing sentences for lower-level offenders, placing some offenders in alternative penalty programs, and giving judges more discretion in sentencing.[2] In Texas, which began to implement new sentencing policies in 2005, the state has increased funding of drug treatment programs and used probation for drug abusers and minor offenders, saving more than $2 billion that would otherwise have been spent on building new prisons. The U.S. Supreme Court has recently ruled that California's overcrowded prisons violate the constitutional prohibition against cruel and unusual punishment (Liptak 2011). The state has been ordered to reduce its prison population to 110,000, a figure that is still 137.5% of prison capacity. There are currently about 140,000 inmates, but the figure has been as high as 160,000.

---

1 Gottschalk (2015: 11) explains *neoliberalism* as "an ideology and package of policies that deify low taxes, macroeconomic stabilization (through low inflation and low public debt), financial and trade deregulation, privatization of public assets and services, and a retrenchment of the welfare state. . . . The neoliberal agenda shuns . . . a comprehensive safety net, and strong labor unions." The role of government in solving economic and social problems is also questioned.

2 For a comprehensive discussion of suggested reforms and of reforms already being implemented across the United States, see ACLU 2011.

In 2010, the *Fair Sentencing Act* reformed drug sentencing by repealing the 5-year mandatory sentence for first-time offenders and for repeat offenders with less than 28 grams of cocaine, thereby reducing the sentencing disparity between crack and powder cocaine from 100 to 1 to 18 to 1 (Aviram 2015: 82). In Alabama, prosecutors have been empowered to send more offenders to boot camps or place them in community corrections. As well, minor drug possessions have been reclassified as lower-level felonies that do not qualify for incarceration, and the number of parole officers has been increased. Alabama spent an average of $17,285 for each inmate in 2010, while the expenditure for New York was $60,076 for each of its almost 60,000 inmates in 2010 (Henrichson and Delaney 2012).

Ending Mass Imprisonment?

In her analysis of the new discourse on "cost, frugality and prudence" concerning corrections, Aviram (2015: 4) traces concern about correctional costs to the financial crisis of 2008, when the country went into recession, unemployment was high, mortgages were being foreclosed, and there was a high level of anxiety about the economy. She argues that this new discourse is now to be found in political campaigns and public conversations about corrections generally and that it endorses nonpunitive criminal justice policies that are made viable politically as a measure of fiscal prudence rather than as expressions of any belief in rehabilitation (p. 58). So, for example, it has now become possible to condemn the costs and inefficiency of capital punishment and argue for its abolition without appearing to be "soft on crime." Instead, the new code word for nonpunitive policies is "smart on crime" (p. 84). Similarly, Clear and Frost (2014: 3) confidently believe that "a combination of political shifts, accumulating empirical evidence and fiscal pressures" have replaced the discourse of being tough on crime, with a belief that the penal system cannot be sustained in its present form.

Nevertheless, as Gottschalk (2015: 8) points out, this does not mean that mass imprisonment will soon end because there remain substantial justice policy differences between the political Right and Left, and, as Simon (2014: 3) observes, many of the

laws and policies that produced the carceral state remain in place, along with the public mindset about criminality. While there have been small reductions in the rate of imprisonment over the last 5 years—between 2009 and 2013, the total inmate population fell by 2.5%, or 56,500 persons—there has been no major contraction of the prison population, and in fact there was an increase of 4,300 between 2012 and 2013 (Carson 2014: 1). Given that most corrections costs are fixed in the form of salaries, the only viable path toward reducing spending on corrections is to lay off staff and shut down prison and jails (Gottschalk 2015: 9). However, corrections has become a major employer—1 in 8 state employees work in corrections—and powerful corrections unions would strongly resist such measures (p. 32). In addition, arguments that focus on reducing the costs of imprisonment provide some political leaders with an incentive not to reduce the prison population, but to create more private prisons, which are supposedly more cost effective than state prisons, or to exploit prisoners as cheap labor (p. 19).

Reducing the prison population would require fundamental change in the length of sentences. States have tended to follow the U.S. Sentencing Commission guidelines, which are only advisory and which, until recently, set (by international standards) very lengthy sentences. In fact, length of stay in prison has doubled since 1972, and the rate at which persons are sent to prison for felonies has changed from 25% in 1972 to 75% today (Clear and Frost 2014: 162). The Sentencing Commission gives prominence to retribution and minimizing racial disparities rather than to rehabilitation and has consistently recommended more severe punishments in the form of longer prison sentences for offenses. However, the Commission has begun to question the value of the punitive sentences it recommends and in a 2011 report concludes that federal mandatory minimum sentences are "excessively severe" and are not applied in a consistent manner. In April 2014, it voted to reduce the guideline punishment for some drug trafficking offenses and to make the change take effect retroactively. As a result, about 50,000 federal drug offenders will be eligible for reduced sentences (Gottschalk 2015: 132).

Many states now view the justice system as a revenue generator and want police and the courts to generate increasingly more fines and forfeitures.[3] This means that they have a vested interest in maintaining prisons for those who cannot pay (Gottschalk 2015: 34). States rent out their empty beds in prisons to other states or to the federal prison system, and it is now common for inmates to be required to pay for meals, lodging, and medical visits, as well as inflated charges for telephone calls (p. 36). In 2015, the FCC capped rates for local and in-state long-distance calls in jail or prison by up to 50% (*FCC News* October 22, 2015).

Elderly Inmates

A new major area of concern is the elderly prison population, the fastest growing subpopulation of inmates at state and federal levels. According to the Bureau of Justice Statistics, between 1999 and 2008 the number of incarcerated persons aged 55 and older increased by 76% (from 43,300 to 76,400) compared to an increase of 18% in the entire prison population over that period (Aviram 2015: 123). Estimates of the cost of an elderly inmate range from $60,000 to $72,000 a year compared to around $20,000 for younger inmates because older inmates experience both physical and mental health problems due to low socioeconomic backgrounds, less education, and a greater likelihood of suffering the effects of sustained substance abuse.

States have responded to the issue of elderly inmates by incarcerating them in special low-security housing, supervised by a reduced number of correctional staff, or by geriatric parole releases into the community, using electronic detention (Aviram 2015: 127, 129). It should be noted, however, that while releasing elderly prisoners with significant health needs will save the states some money the costs will likely be displaced to Medicaid, Medicare, and other public programs funded in part by the states (Gottschalk 2015: 27).

Mass Incarceration as the New "Jim Crow"

In her analysis of the mass incarceration policy, Michelle Alexander sees mass incarceration as "a stunningly comprehensive and well-disguised system of racialized social control that functions in a manner strikingly similar to Jim Crow[4]" (2010: 4). Contending that the war against drugs (see also Chapter 4) was not launched to combat increased use of crack cocaine but to perpetuate a "racial caste system" in the same way as slavery and Jim Crow laws, Alexander states that mass incarceration functions to lock "people of color into a permanent second-class citizenship" (p. 3). (Chapter 3 discusses how police interactions with black juveniles and adults can be perceived to operate in the same way and Chapter 2 how police racial profiling in the form of vehicle stops and "stop and frisk" is seen by blacks as consigning them to a lower level of citizenship.) Alexander regards the anti-drug movement as being concerned with race in that it provided a mechanism for the Reagan administration to "crack down on the racially defined 'others'—the undeserving" (p. 49). She explains how the war intensified at the same time as inner-city communities were undergoing an economic collapse, with declining employment opportunities, and how residents turned to drug dealing, specifically in crack cocaine, from around 1985 to earn income (p. 51). According to Alexander, mass imprisonment policies have functioned to create a black undercaste through a network of laws, policies, customs, and institutions that collectively comprise and represent the policy of mass imprisonment, with the aim of ensuring the permanent subordinate status of that group (p. 13).

PUBLIC OPINION ABOUT PUNISHMENT

Should public opinion be the determinant of sentencing and correctional policies? Is it ethical for

---

3   In some counties in Texas, civil forfeitures provide almost 40% of the police budget, and in 2012, the federal government is reported to have seized about $4.2 billion in assets (Gottschalk 2015: 36).

4   The so-called Jim Crow laws were state and local laws that enforced racial segregation following the Reconstruction period (from about 1863 to 1877) and continued in force until about 1965. The 1954 decision of the U.S. Supreme Court in *Brown v. Board of Education* is generally taken to mark the end of segregation and of the Jim Crow laws, but in spite of the Supreme Court decision, five southern states enacted almost 50 new Jim Crow laws in the years following that decision. The Jim Crow laws were modeled on the Black Codes of 1800 to 1866 that had previously restricted the rights of blacks (Alexander 2010: 34–35, 37). The 1964 Civil Rights Act finally ended the Jim Crow laws and their successor laws.

morality policies, in particular, to be formulated solely on the basis of what is perceived to be public opinion on a particular issue? Some argue that public opinion on crime control and punishment fluctuates in response to certain events, such as urban turmoil and escalating crime rates. The alternative view expressed by others, including Scheingold (1984) and Katherine Beckett (1997), is that public opinion does not become shaped by the events of the day but is fashioned and manipulated by politicians and the media. Beckett, for example, investigated how the timing of shifts in public opinion converged with politicians undertaking initiatives such as calling for a "war" on a problem or introducing legislation with media attention focused on an issue. She concludes that changes in public opinion about crime control and drugs most often follow increases in political initiatives and media coverage that emphasizes these issues rather than changes in events in the wider environment. In other words, she suggests that political initiatives and media coverage create moral panics that result in morality policy making.

Since the mid-1970s, there has been a fundamental shift in the ideology of punishment because punitive approaches and the new penology have supplanted the rehabilitative model. Many believe the reasons for this transformation to be complex, but some offer the simple explanation that these new punitive policies merely represent the wishes of the public. For example, John DiIulio (in Cullen, Fisher, and Applegate 2000: 2) argues that citizens have become fed up with crime rates and with offenders victimizing them and have concluded rationally that more offenders should be locked up for longer periods of time. In this style of thinking, getting tough on crime is a manifestation of democracy at work. The discussion of prison and amenities in the "Prison and Amenities" Closer Look box addresses one aspect of this issue—amenities in prison.

A Closer Look

Prison and Amenities

Amenities for Inmates

What standards and conditions should be applied to imprisonment? The topic of what level of amenities should be supplied to prisoners resurfaces in the media periodically. Those politicians who wish to demonstrate a tough-on-crime approach protest that prisoners are provided access to weightlifting equipment, televisions, radios, and "good" food (Banks 2005: 137). In Maricopa County, Arizona, Sheriff Joe Arpia's policies of housing inmates in tents without air conditioning in the more than 110°F summer weather, clothing inmates in pink underwear and striped uniforms, having chain gangs for both men and women, and providing basic and unappealing food such as bologna on dry bread exemplify this attitude. Such politicians argue that if prisoners have standards of incarceration that are superior to the standard of living of the man on the street, then they cannot be said to be suffering punishment. The media fuel this debate by reporting that prisons are "holiday resorts" where prisoners enjoy extravagant amenities and conditions. In response to this political discourse, the No Frills Prison Act was passed in 1996; it bans televisions, coffeepots, and hot plates in the cells of federal prisoners. It also prohibits computers, electronic instruments, certain movies rated above PG, and unmonitored phone calls (Lenz 2002).

The underpinning assumption to this legislation is that a deterrent effect will be achieved "by making a sentence more punitive, that is, making the inmate suffer more" (Banks 2005: 138). Thus, it is assumed that an inmate will be "less inclined to reoffend knowing the harsh conditions in prison." The problem is that there is no existing research that can support this assumption. Some have argued

(Continued)

(Continued)

that state costs are saved to the prison system and to the taxpayers through this approach, but again, this is not supported, given that the 31 states that allow inmates televisions in their cells do not pay for them (prisoners or their relatives pay for them), and cablevision is paid for out of profits from the prison commissary, vending machines, and long-distance telephone charges (Finn 1996: 6–7).

Interestingly, prison administrators are often in favor of permitting amenities in the prisons because staff rely heavily on a system of rewards and punishments to maintain control in their institutions (Lenz 2002: 506). They recognize that keeping inmates busy provides important benefits to inmate order and inmate activities. In other words, bored and unhappy prisoners are more likely to cause security problems that staff in short supply will have to respond to.

Placing telephone calls from prison to wives, husbands, and relatives used to be an inexpensive process, and until the 1990s, inmates could place and receive calls at rates similar to those charged outside. This might be considered a basic amenity for all inmates. Now, however, the prison telephone system has been turned over to private enterprise and is a $1.2 billion-a-year industry. Companies in this business commonly set rates and fees greatly in excess of those charged by commercial providers to persons outside prisons. After a series of complaints, the Federal Communications Commission (FCC) commenced an investigation. The practice is for phone companies to pay hundreds of millions of dollars ($460 million in 2013) in concession fees to state and local correctional systems for exclusive contracts to control the telephone services offered in prisons. According to the FCC, the fees, which are legal, are used to fund a range of prison costs from inmate welfare to salaries, and some end up in the revenue funds of the state concerned. Eliminating the fees has been fiercely opposed by prison and jail officials. In one case a company fee for using its prison phone service included a charge for processing the bill and another charge if the bill was paid over the telephone (Williams 2015).

As Francis Cullen, Bonnie Fisher, and Brandon Applegate (2000: 3) point out, policy making based on what citizens want is unfortunately constrained by the ignorance of the public on many aspects of crime and crime control. Researchers have discovered that in most areas of crime control, there is a widespread lack of knowledge, and this is particularly true for sentencing, where, for example, it is unclear whether citizens are aware of the existence of sanctions other than imprisonment and of the content of community-based sanctions. Research has established that public punitive attitudes about crime do not fluctuate as might be expected as crime rates rise and fall, but instead that punitiveness and favoring harsher penalties remain constant.

Public Attitudes Toward Crime

The views of the public on crime are often investigated through telephone surveys that ask only a limited number of questions about a major policy issue such as capital punishment. However, it is clear that the opinions of the public on crime control often change if multiple questions rather than a single question are used (see Table 9.1). For example, respondents tend to express a less punitive attitude when they are given detailed information about the nature of the offender and his or her criminal offenses. This is also the case if they are given a list of potential sentencing options, including noncustodial sentencing options, to apply to actual offenders. This contrasts with answering broadly worded questions about unspecified criminals (Cullen et al. 2000: 7). In a review of surveys concerning public opinion on crime control and sentencing, Cullen and colleagues (pp. 8–9) developed seven main conclusions:

1. Generally, the public is punitive toward crime.
2. However, their punitiveness is "mushy"; that is, even when they express a punitive opinion, people tend to

be flexible enough to consider a range of sentencing options if provided with adequate information.

3. Members of the public must be given a good reason not to be punitive and are prepared to moderate their punitive attitudes.

4. Violent crime divides the punitive from the nonpunitive because citizens are reluctant not to incarcerate dangerous offenders. However, they are prepared to consider a wide range of sentencing options for nonviolent offenders.

5. Despite attacks on rehabilitation and the treatment of offenders, the public continues to believe in rehabilitation as a goal of corrections.

6. There is strong support for child saving—that is, for the rehabilitation of youthful offenders and for interventions that attempt to divert children at risk away from criminality.

7. The central tendency of the public is to be punitive and progressive—to desire a response to offenders that is balanced and that includes the objectives of achieving justice, protecting society, and reforming offenders.

Research demonstrates widespread support among the public for locking up offenders. As Warr writes,

> Americans overwhelmingly regard imprisonment as the most appropriate form of punishment for most crimes. Although the proportion who prefer prison increases with the seriousness of the crime, imprisonment is by far the most commonly chosen penalty across crimes. (in Cullen et al. 2000: 28)

Michael Tonry (2010: 288) notes that research has revealed that white Americans, "especially politically conservative and fundamentalist

Table 9.1   Public Preferences for the Main Goal of Imprisonment, 1968–1996 (Percentage Agreeing With Each Goal Reported)

Main Emphasis of Prison Should Be	Harris		Gallup	Cincinnati		Ohio	National	
	1968	1982	1982	1986	1995	1996	1995	1996
Rehabilitation	73.0	44.0	59.0	54.7	32.6	41.1	26.1	48.4
Punishment	7.0	19.0	30.0	5.7	27.2	20.3	—	14.6
Protect society	12.0	32.0	—	35.3	36.8	31.9	—	—
Punish and put away	—	—	—	—	—	—	58.2	—
Crime prevention/ Deterrence	—	—	—	—	—	—	—	33.1
Not sure/Don't know/Other	9.0	5.0	11.0	4.3	2.5	6.7	13.4	3.9

Source: Cullen et al. 2000. Reprinted by permission of the University of Chicago Press.

Note: 1968 and 1982 polls reported in Flanagan and Caulfield (1984: 42); 1982 Gallup poll reported in "Public Backs Wholesale Prison Reform" (1982: 16); 1986 and 1995 Cincinnati polls reported in Cullen et al. (1990: 9) and in Sundt et al. (1998: 435); 1996 Ohio poll reported in Applegate, Cullen, and Fisher (1997); 1995 and 1996 national polls reported in Maguire and Pastore (1997: 154–155). The Harris, Cincinnati, and Ohio polls asked "What do you think should be the main emphasis in most prisons—punishing the individual convicted of a crime, trying to rehabilitate the individual so that he might become a productive citizen, or protecting society from future crimes he might commit?" The Gallup poll asked whether it was "more important to punish [men in prison] for their crimes or more important to get them started on the right road" (which was categorized as "rehabilitation"). The 1995 national poll asked whether the government needs to "make a greater effort" to "rehabilitate" or "punish and put away criminals who commit violent crimes." The 1996 national poll asked what should be the main goal "once people who commit crimes are in prison."

Figure 9.1   Percentage of U.S. Population Supporting Punitive Punishment, 1951–2013

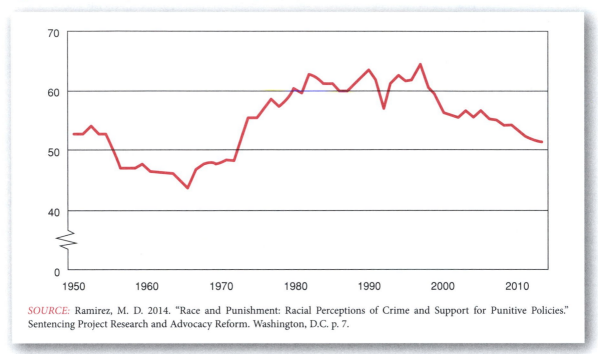

SOURCE: Ramirez, M. D. 2014. "Race and Punishment: Racial Perceptions of Crime and Support for Punitive Policies." Sentencing Project Research and Advocacy Reform. Washington, D.C. p. 7.

Protestant white Americans, tend to support harsh punishments, including the death penalty" whereas blacks support harsh punishments at much lower rates. He attributes this support to "measures of racial animus and resentment" that significantly influence whites' punitive attitudes" (p. 288) and links these attitudes to research that has found that white resentment about the integration of blacks under civil rights programs translated into support for the crime control policies that have criminalized large numbers of blacks.

Surveys have revealed there was wide public support for punitive punishment policies between the 1970s and mid-1990s when crime was rising. Reductions in the level of violent crime since the 1990s (according to FBI data, a decline of 35%, and for property crime, a decline of 25%) have been reflected in public opinion surveys conducted between 1994 and 2013, which show a decline in support for punitive punishment policies such as tough judicial sentencing, capital punishment, and spending on law enforcement (Ramirez 2013: 1007).

A significant new factor influencing public opinion has been the tendency of public officials and the news media to link terrorism with opinions about criminal justice. So, for example, associations have been made between terrorism, transnational crime, drug trafficking, and street violence (the so-called "lone wolf" terrorist), which have inspired greater public fear (p. 1007). While a majority of Americans supported "get tough" sentencing policies in the 1990s, support for this policy declined from 85% in 1994 to 62% by 2012 (p. 1011). While support for capital punishment depends on the form of the question posed, nevertheless, the Gallup poll that asks respondents only whether they favor or oppose the death penalty still shows a decline since 1994 from 80% in favor to 63% in 2012; in fact, support has been in the 60% range since 2004 (p. 1012). As to whether the death penalty should be imposed more frequently, while in 1994 64% believed it should be imposed more often, this support declined to 38% before 9/11. After 9/11, support rose to 47% but by 2011 had fallen to 40%. When given the choice of the death sentence or life imprisonment without parole (LWOP), a majority of those polled between 1985 and 1999 preferred the death sentence, but by 2011, the position had reversed, with 48% supporting the death penalty and 50% supporting LWOP.

In 1999, when asked about attacking social problems or deterring crime with more law enforcement and more prisons and judges, 61% opted to challenge social problems and 32% wanted more crime control, but by 2004, 57% favored attacking social problems and 39% were in support of more crime control. In 1994, in regard to spending on drug abuse, 52% thought too little was being spent on drug rehabilitation, but by 2012, this had fallen to 45%. A significant variation appears in public opinion on the question of whether too much or too little was being spent on halting the rising crime rate. In 2004, 75% thought too little, but by 2012, this had fallen to 59%. The "about right" response scored only 16% in 1994 and had risen to 33% by 2012 (Ramirez 2013: 1018). A similar public perspective is shown by the question of spending on law enforcement: In 1994, 63% thought too little was being spent, but by 2012, this had fallen to 49%.

Overall, while a majority of Americans continue to support punitive crime policies, this support has waned since the punitive years between 1970 and 1994, and there is a consistent decline in support across specific punitive policies such as the death penalty and sentencing.

Public Participation in Sentencing Offenders

Should there be public participation in the sentencing of offenders, and if so, what form might it take? In his summary of the arguments for public involvement in sentencing, Julian Roberts (2014: 228) notes three alternative positions: (a) allow public views to determine sentencing policy and practice, (b) permit some public input into sentencing but keep control of policy within a professional system relying on judges, and (c) do not permit any public participation in sentencing decisions.

In favor of some form of public participation, it is claimed that community involvement in sentencing will ensure greater compliance with the law because if the criminal law functions according to the wishes of the community, this will build confidence in the system and therefore greater compliance with the law. Problems with this view include the fact that, as noted earlier, the public lacks sophistication in their sentencing responses; in addition, this argument lacks empirical validity (Roberts 2014: 232). While it may be correct that confidence would increase if the community sees the systems imposing punishments that mirror their views, it is argued that this is not sufficient justification to allow *all* punishments to be determined in this way.

If public opinion is to be measured and incorporated into policy, one issue is whether this should be "mass" opinion or more educated opinion. If the decision is for mass opinion, this will mean "unprincipled and capricious sentencing," but if people are educated about the system and about sentencing, the group whose views are sought will not be representative of the public (Roberts 2014: 238).

It is possible to have direct community engagement in the sentencing process. As already noted, one approach is through sentencing guidelines and another is by using lay decision-makers in the determination of sentence. A further possibility is through juries who decide both guilt and sentence. However, when juries sentence in death penalty cases, they have already been screened to be "death qualified," so they are no longer truly representative of the community. In addition, studies have shown that in capital cases jurors tend to vote in favor of execution and are nonresponsive to mitigation (Roberts 2014: 242). In a small number of U.S. states, juries sentence offenders in noncapital cases, and research comparing their sentencing with that of a judge reveals the jury sentencing to be more variable and that juries impose significantly longer sentences. One problem for jury sentencing is that the members of a jury would inevitably deliver one-off decisions because they have no knowledge of sentences imposed for similar offenses in the past. This means there would be an absence of consistency and proportionality in sentencing. Far better, it is argued, to leave sentencing decisions to professional judges who have accumulated sentencing knowledge over long periods (p. 243).

This discussion has shown that ethical decision-making is often sacrificed in the interests of expediency and under pressure from cost–benefit analysis, as is common in the case of morality policy making—such as that regarding punishment, moral panics, and ideological stances—as quick fixes prevail over rational, reasoned, and ethical decision-making. The lack of an ethical focus in criminal justice policy making will be illustrated through an analysis of several criminal justice policy issues. These are mandatory minimum sentencing, the war on drugs, truth in sentencing, predators and superpredators, capital punishment, and privatizing prisons.

MANDATORY MINIMUM SENTENCING

The development of policies fixing minimum terms of imprisonment for certain offenses or types of offenders exemplifies the expansion of punitive policies in the criminal justice system. In the 1970s and 1980s, a movement developed away from rehabilitative philosophies that had previously guided criminal justice policy makers toward a more punitive approach involving the creation of a set of policies intended to punish offenders, enhance the status of victims, and placate public fears about crime and criminals. Before this period, crime had not registered in the public mind as a significant issue, and most attribute the emergence of crime as a serious political issue to charges made by Republican Sen. Barry Goldwater, who ran for president in 1964 against Lyndon Johnson. Goldwater criticized Johnson for rising crime rates and accused the president of being "soft on crime" (Robinson 2002: 34). Legislation enacted as part of the war against drugs, as well as habitual felony laws made initially in Washington and California to punish violent felony offenders, are high-profile instances of this new punitive approach toward criminals and crime.

Habitual felony laws, commonly known as *three-strikes legislation,* began in 1993 when an initiative was placed on the ballot in Washington State, mandating the punishment of life imprisonment without parole for offenders convicted for a third time of specified violent or serious felonies (Austin and Irwin 2001: 184). This initiative was promoted by those concerned about the death of a woman murdered by a convicted rapist who had recently been released from prison. Additional impetus was provided by the kidnapping and murder of Polly Klaas in California by a former inmate with an extensive record of violence. Both

Washington and California voters, and later those in other states, passed three-strikes ballot proposals, and by 1997, 24 other states and the federal government had enacted mandatory minimum sentencing legislation.

In California, the three-strikes legislation was drafted independently of government and became law with no significant influence from either the executive or legislative branches (Zimring, Hawkins, and Kamin 2001: 3). In the view of Franklin Zimring, Gordon Hawkins, and Sam Kamin, the legislation "was an extreme example of a populist preemption of criminal justice policy-making" (p. 3). According to these authors, the legislation was heavily promoted by victim's associations, the Prison Guard Union, and the National Rifle Association (p. 11). In relation to victims, they suggest that issues of penal policy, at least in California, have become a contest in which the voter decides a penal issue by choosing between offenders and their victims. There is an assumption that anything bad for offenders must benefit victims; thus, "no punishment seems too extreme if anything that hurts offenders benefits victims" (p. 224). This simplification of policy making on criminal punishment renders expert advice, analysis, and assessment unnecessary and irrelevant in the eyes of the public. In policy terms, the proponents of this type of legislation argue that deterrence will be achieved if severe and certain punishment is imposed on habitual offenders; that is, the offender, aware that the next conviction will result in life imprisonment, will carefully consider the consequences of committing a further offense.

Many argue that this is an unrealistic expectation and bad policy making because it relies not only on offenders being informed of the consequences of further offenses but also on a high probability of their arrest and conviction. It assumes, too, that all offenders make rational, calculating decisions about their future actions, carefully weighing risks and making choices in an informed and measured manner (Austin and Irwin 2001: 185). Proponents of three-strikes legislation also argue that its outcome, incapacitation, has the effect of targeting habitual criminals who must, in their view, be permanently isolated from society. In other words, it is argued that habitual offenders can be identified, and the assumption is made that a habitual offender will continue to offend over time. In fact, studies have shown the difficulty of accurately identifying the so-called habitual offender. Also, the argument ignores the fact that most criminal careers do not continue beyond a certain age. These major policy considerations, however, were ignored, and the initiative proceeded as a morality policy based on a moral panic about habitual violent offenders.

Most legislation imposing three strikes includes the definition of offenses for which a mandatory minimum can be imposed, the number of strikes needed to qualify for the ultimate sanction, and definitions of the ultimate sanction. For example, in California, any felony qualifies as "a strike" if the offender has one prior felony conviction appearing on a list of strikable offenses or if the offender has two prior felony convictions from that list. In the first case, two strikes will result in a mandatory sentence—that is, twice that for the offense involved—and in the second case, the sanction is a mandatory life sentence with no parole for 25 years (Austin and Irwin 2001: 187). The California law is one of the most severe in the country, first, because it provides for a wide number of felonies constituting strikes, and second, because in California, the third strike can be any felony whatsoever, as opposed to a violent felony, a provision found in no other state's law.

In California, this legislation was predicted to more than double the prison population within 5 years; however, those estimates were later adjusted downward. Nevertheless, between the years 1994 and 1998, the total number of cases sentenced to California prisons under the three-strikes law was 45,207 (Austin and Irwin 2001: 197). The types of crimes committed by those subject to three strikes ranged from an offender who attempted to steal a parked truck, held the owner at bay with a knife, fled on the freeway, and was finally placed under arrest and sentenced to 27 years to life with a minimum of 22.95 years to an offender who received a sentence of 27 years to life for attempting to sell stolen batteries to a retailer, where the value of the batteries was $90 (p. 208). In another case in California, a judge ordered the release of a man who was sentenced to 25 years to life for attempting to break into a soup kitchen because he was hungry. He had two prior robbery convictions to support drug addictions, but neither had involved violence or

injury to anyone (Cathcart 2010). In 2010, the California State Auditor reported on the fiscal impact of three strikes, finding that "striker inmates . . . were sentenced on average to an additional nine years of incarceration" and that "these additional years represent $19.2 billion in additional costs over the duration of the sentences of current striker inmates" (Aviram 2015: 143).

The disproportionate punishments imposed in these sample cases highlight the unethical nature of the legislation. According to James Austin and John Irwin (2001: 207), the research data show that in California, most inmates who receive second- and third-strike sentences are not violent or habitual offenders. The courts and prosecutors have generally attempted to find ways to avoid imposing these lengthy sentences, and this has assisted in ameliorating the effect of the legislation (p. 213). As a result, the impact has not been nearly as severe as projected. In effect, bad policy making has been countered by administrative action by the courts and prosecutors.

David Shichor (2000: 1) argues that three-strikes laws have a number of adverse implications. For example, he points to the situation under the California law that gives prosecutors the right to decide whether the third-strike offense should be charged as a felony or a misdemeanor. Also noted is that despite its claims to establish a higher level of uniformity in sentencing the legislation has actually increased punishment disparities both in individual cases and within jurisdictions because punishment policies are shaped by the local district attorneys. For example, by May 1997, Los Angeles County, which contained 29% of the state's population, accounted for 41% of three-strikes prison admissions, whereas San Francisco County, with 5.3% of the population, made up only 0.5% of such admissions (p. 15). Shichor (p. 16) notes that the effect of the legislation was to shift power relationships in sentencing away from the courts and in favor of politically motivated prosecutors. This effect was apparently never considered in the policy making that led to the legislation.

Another criticism leveled at the legislation is its reinforcement of the race bias in punishment by its concentration on street crimes and drug offenses. Gilbert Geis (1996) complains that three-strikes laws fail to meet standards of equal justice for like kinds of criminal wrongdoing because these laws omit white-collar crimes and demonstrate "the strong and ugly strains of race, class, and ethnic bias that have produced these laws" (p. 261). In an important article on penal ideology, Malcolm Feeley and Jonathan Simon (1992) contrast this new trend in penology, a component of which is three-strikes legislation, with the old penology that focused on individuals and individual-based theories of punishment. They emphasize that the new penology is concerned with aspects like "dangerousness" rather than with the question of how to treat and punish an individual offender. Certain groups within society are identified as "career criminals" or "habitual offenders" and are selected for special surveillance, management, and incapacitation. As Stuart Henry and Dragan Milovanovic (1996: 114) put it, this new penology operates on utilitarian considerations rather than moral ones. Shichor (1999: 424) argues that these changes in punishment ideology have flowed from the pessimism experienced since the 1970s about the ability of the criminal justice system to turn offenders into law-abiding citizens. Feeley and Simon argue that penology is now directed toward managing a population of criminals considered to be permanently dangerous and incapable of reform or of being rehabilitated. In this sense, therefore, the labeling of a criminal class through this criminal justice policy parallels the depiction of an underclass—that is, a marginal, unemployable population lacking education and skills.

Shichor (1999: 425) explains that in theory, three-strikes legislation is meant to target violent and dangerous offenders for selective incapacitation. He relates the concept of controlling dangerous offenders to a sociocultural position that encourages the emergence of moral panics. That is, a public perception develops, is reinforced, and is perhaps even engendered by the mass media that dangerous offenders pose a threat to society and the moral order (see Cohen and Young 1973). Where such expressive arguments are advanced, moral considerations about punishment and retribution may tend to overshadow any empirical evidence as to the likely effects of implementing a particular criminal justice policy (Vergari 2001: 202). Mass values, therefore, may override reasoned policy analysis (Heineman et al. 1997: 54).

Does the public support three-strikes laws? In referenda in Washington and California in 1993,

the first three-strikes statute was approved in Washington by a 3-to-1 margin and in California by a margin of 72% for and 28% against (Cullen et al. 2000: 38). Similarly, a *Time/CNN* poll conducted in 1994 reported that 81% of adults favored mandatory life imprisonment for persons convicted of a third serious crime. Nevertheless, it is arguable that citizens do not always wish to apply three strikes to every offender who would be eligible for life without parole because in studies where concrete cases are rated, there is some variation in the impact of prior record on sentencing preferences (p. 39). For example, in a study in 1995 in Cincinnati, where specific offenses were included as three-strikes offenses, the respondents were asked to select a sentence from a range of no punishment and probation to life in prison with and without parole. Only 16.9% chose a life sentence. The results overall suggest that the public can hold views that appear to be incompatible because while they favor three strikes, they do not believe that the principle should be applied indiscriminately to specific offenders under specific circumstances.

THE WAR ON DRUGS

In 1972, President Nixon declared the initial "war" on crime and drugs and in 1973 created the Drug Enforcement Agency (Robinson 2002: 163). In 1982, President Reagan also "declared a war" on drugs. Both "wars" aimed to reduce individual drug use, stop the flow of drugs into the United States, and reduce drug-related crime, but while Nixon had specifically declared a *global war* on drugs, Reagan shifted the focus of the war to *domestic* concerns, namely "big-time organized crime and the drug racketeers who are poisoning our young people" (quoted in Moore 2015: 201). While Nixon considered drug users to be victims, Reagan did not and drew little distinction between traffickers and users (p. 203). Both Democrats and Republicans promoted and supported the initiative—the latter in an effort to win back the "Reagan Democrats" of the South captured by Reagan under the so-called "Southern Strategy" (Alexander 2010: 55).

Not until 1986 and 1988 was actual drug abuse legislation enacted at the federal level. This moved the focus away from major drug dealers and treatment to users and street-level dealers, with an emphasis on those using and dealing crack cocaine (Bush-Baskette 1999: 212). The legislation enacted in 1986 and 1988 came about through an intense media focus on drugs, beginning in 1984 with media accounts about cocaine in California. By the 1986 congressional elections, at least 1,000 newspaper stories had appeared nationally on the issue of crack cocaine, and documentary-style programs representing cocaine use and sales as a national epidemic appeared on television as cocaine, and especially crack cocaine, became campaign issues in the election (p. 213).

Crime Control Politics and the War on Drugs

In her discussion of the origins of this war, Moore (2015: 145) traces its genesis to the politics of crime control, arguing that the federal government of the 1970s wanted to enlarge its role in crime control—normally a matter for the states—and that in seeking a rationale for this, it seized upon a purported drug problem that would justify federal action to criminalize drug abuse. Under the Nixon administration, the 1970 Comprehensive Drug Abuse Prevention and Control Act introduced a classification system for licit and illicit drugs and, based on this, criminalized drug distribution, possession, and use (p. 145). The 1970 act set a mandatory minimum sentence of 10 years for some drug-trafficking offenses and up to 25 years for dangerous drug offenders (p. 147). It also empowered police to forcibly enter homes to search for drugs—the so-called "no-knock" warrant (p. 150).

Drug classification powers under the 1970 act were vested in the attorney general, ensuring that future drug policies would be framed as issues of crime control rather than as issues of prevention and treatment. From this starting point, U.S. drug policy has consistently focused on the supply side and not on the demand for illicit drugs.

The Anti-Drug Abuse Act of 1986 provided mandatory minimum penalties for drug trafficking based on the quantity of drugs involved, and it differentiated between possession of cocaine and possession of crack cocaine. A mandatory minimum of 5 years with a maximum of 20 years was prescribed for those convicted of possessing 5 or more grams of crack cocaine, whereas an offender found guilty of possessing powder cocaine would be liable only to a 5-year mandatory minimum if the amount equaled or

exceeded 500 grams. The legislation therefore extended the reach of anti-drug laws to users as well as traffickers. As well, the act provided that owners of buildings where crack-related offenses occurred were liable on conviction to a sentence of 20 years' imprisonment, and judges were prohibited from ordering probation for a drug offense (Moore 2015: 148). In this legislation, drug abuse was presented as a national security issue, and the drug war was depicted as necessary for the survival of the United States.

In contrast to 1986, the issue of drug control waned in 1987 as the media and public turned their attention to other issues; in fact, one poll in 1987 reported only 3% to 5% of the public considered drugs to be the most pressing social problem (Bush-Baskette 1999: 214). In 1988, another presidential election brought drugs back as a high-profile issue, and about 1.5 weeks before the election, another anti-drug abuse act was passed. This 1988 act included more funding for treatment and prevention, although most of it was still directed toward law enforcement, punishment, and increased penalties for certain crack cocaine offenses. By 1990, media attention to the issue had normalized, and the National Drug Control Strategy of 1991 lacked the intense focus on crack and cocaine of previous years. Nevertheless, the Clinton administration continued to promote the war against drugs with the enactment of the 1994 Violent Crime Control and Enforcement Act that established the "three strikes and you're out" provision that imposes life imprisonment on conviction for a third felony (Moore 2015: 148). Importantly, the 1994 act enabled the designation of areas as drug and violent crime "emergency areas," in which federal and local law enforcement could pool their resources and target specific, usually black, neighborhoods (p. 150). These joint task forces have figured significantly in the militarization of policing throughout the country (see Chapter 2 on police militarization). Alexander argues that the 1994 law enabled the Democrats to show they had finally seized the law and order issue from the Republicans (2010: 56).

Fighting the War on Drugs: Prosecutions and Incentives

The increased and more punitive response to drug abuse over this period has enormously impacted the extent of drug prosecutions and incarceration rates for drug offenses. Prosecution efforts were stepped up, and between 1982 and 1988, there was a 52.17% increase in the number of convictions for drug offenses and an increase of 48.48% of those incarcerated for drug offenses (Bush-Baskette 1999: 215). Federal spending on the "drug war" amounted to $13.2 billion in 1995, two thirds of which was used for law enforcement. If all the costs of incarcerating drug offenders are brought into account, the total expenditure on the drug war would amount to approximately $100 billion every year (p. 215). Huge cash grants were made available to the states under the federal Byrne Program, and in some states, 90% of such grants have funded specialized drug units and task forces, most of which are militarized (Alexander 2010: 73). (See Chapter 2 on police militarization and federal support for weapons and equipment for law enforcement to conduct the fight.) Incentives to states, and especially to law enforcement, to promote the war also included the power to seize cash and assets of drug offenders and retain them for their own use. According to a report commissioned by the Justice Department, drug task forces seized over $1 billion in assets between 1988 and 1992 (pp. 78–79).

Drugs and Incarceration

In 2013, an estimated 16% or 210,200 prisoners were held for drug law violations in state facilities. This compares to violent offenders who comprise about half of all inmates in state prisons (Carson 2014: 15). The figures for female offenders are even more startling. In 1986, 26% of federal female prisoners were incarcerated for drug offenses; by 1991, this figure had risen to 63.9%. In addition, there were significant increases in the mean sentence length for drug offenders. Whereas the mean sentence in 1982 was 54.6 months, by 1991, it had increased to 85.7 months (Bush-Baskette 1999: 220). In 2013, of the 89,000 women serving sentences in state prisons, 21,900 or 24.6% were serving sentences imposed for drug offences (Carson 2014: 15–16). By 2014, the number of women sentenced to more than 1 year increased from 104,300 in 2013 to 106,200 in 2014, an increase of 2% (Carson 2015: 1).

As Alexander (2010: 60) points out, while in the public mind the war was aimed at drug lords and big-time dealers, in practice a majority of drug arrests were for possession, with only one out of five arrests being for selling drugs. Arrests for possession of marijuana accounted for almost 80% of the growth in drug arrests in the 1990s. Between 1980 and 2005, the number of annual arrests for drug offenses more than tripled (p. 72). Copying the federal government, most states enacted similar drug legislation; New York, in particular, became well known for its legislation, enacting the severe "Rockefeller drug laws" in 1973. These imposed mandatory sentences requiring that a convicted offender in possession of 4 ounces of heroin or cocaine or attempting to sell 2 ounces of heroin or cocaine receive a mandatory 15 years to life in prison. Some major components of the Rockefeller laws were repealed following the determination that they had little or no effect on drug use or crime in New York (Bush-Baskette 1999: 221), and in 2009, the New York State legislature enacted a drug reform package that essentially gutted what remained of the Rockefeller drug laws (Gottschalk 2015: 168).

As well as increasing the size of the inmate population generally, the war against drugs has had the effect of disproportionately incarcerating African American men and women. At the state level, there was an 828% increase in the number of African American women incarcerated for drug offenses between 1986 and 1991, whereas the rate for white women was 241% (Bush-Baskette 1999: 222). For the same period, there was an increase of 429% for African American men.

In a reaction to the overwhelming focus of the drug war on incarcerating drug offenders and in a move toward a more treatment-oriented approach, in November 2000 the voters of California approved by a large majority a proposition that would provide drug treatment instead of prison for first- and second-time drug offenders who were not charged with other crimes. This law was expected to divert 36,000 offenders each year away from prison and into treatment programs (Spohn 2002: 250). In a similar shift toward treatment for drug offenders, in June 2000, the chief judge of New York State ordered the commencement of a program that would require nearly all nonviolent criminals who were drug addicts to be offered a treatment option instead of jail time. The objective was to radically reduce the number of repeat drug offenders coming before the courts and the inmate population in the state (Finkelstein 2000).

In February 2001, legislation was introduced into the U.S. Senate, calling for $2.7 billion in spending over 3 years to increase the extent of drug treatment programs in prisons. However, the legislation also proposed more severe sentencing guidelines for those committing drug offenses in the presence of minors or who used children in drug trafficking (Spohn 2002: 250).

Larry Gaines and Peter Kraska (1997), in their critique of the drug war, argue that

> waging war on drugs—as if the drugs themselves constitute our "drug problem"—allows us to overlook the underlying reasons why people abuse these substances. . . . The language of ideology fools us into thinking that we're waging war against drugs themselves, not real people. (p. 4)

In an attempt to correct the sentencing disparities created by the crack cocaine laws, in December 2007 the Supreme Court ruled that judges could hand down lighter punishments in crack cocaine and ecstasy cases than those specified by federal guidelines and that they could depart from sentencing guidelines in cases involving ecstasy distribution. (*Gall v. United States* 2007; *Kimbrough v. United States* 2007; see the "Lighter Sentences Now Possible for Crack Cocaine Cases" Closer Look box.)

Enthusiasm for the fight against drugs appears to have started to wane from the mid-1990s; for example, in 2009 Minneapolis became the first major city to disband its special drug unit as a cost-saving measure. A number of states now give a low degree of priority to enforcing marijuana laws and two states, Colorado and Washington, D.C., have legalized the sale and possession of marijuana. The war on drugs is no longer the paramount force driving the rate of incarceration: From 2000 to 2008, offenses involving violence constituted 60% of the growth in the size of the state prison population, and in this period, the number of sentenced drug offenders declined by 8%.

Nevertheless, at the federal level, the well-entrenched Drug Enforcement Administration continues to conduct the war against drugs, and in 2011, drug charges were the primary reason for the incarceration of almost half of all federal prisoners (Gottschalk 2015: 128–129). States continue to show reluctance in enacting truly reformist penal legislation. For example, in 2012 Massachusetts enacted what the then-governor described as "balanced" penal reform. The legislation comprised a harsh new three-strikes law and some minimal reductions in drug-related punishments at a time when the state's prisons were operating at almost 150% of capacity (p. 167).

The war on drugs is a prime example of morality policy making. The media framed the drug issue as a moral panic, and this was followed by a series of political actions that resulted in the production of an unethical, discriminatory policy that has made a huge contribution to the development of mass imprisonment in the United States. The anti-drug movement demonstrates the perils that can be caused by singling out one subject of criminal activity for special punitive treatment.

A Closer Look

Lighter Sentences Now Possible for Crack Cocaine Cases

Under a 1986 law, first-time offenders convicted of selling 5 grams of crack cocaine receive the same 5-year mandatory prison sentence as dealers of 500 grams of powder cocaine. African Americans account for about 80% of federal crack cocaine convictions (crack cocaine is much cheaper than powder cocaine), and sentencing guidelines set lighter sentences for selling powder cocaine, a substance popular with whites and Hispanics. This divergence in sentencing has provoked criticism that the judicial system is explicitly racially biased in such cases. There has been consistent pressure in

(Continued)

(Continued)

Congress to revise the law, but lawmakers have seemed reluctant to take action for fear of appearing to be "soft on crime," especially on drug offenses.

On April 7, 2008, the Supreme Court addressed this long-standing issue and ruled that judges can impose lighter sentences for crack cocaine and ecstasy cases than are specified in the federal guidelines. The ruling was made by a decisive 7-to-2 margin and comes a day before the U.S. Sentencing Commission is to determine whether or not to make retroactive a reduction in recommended crack cocaine penalties.

The Supreme Court had already decided in 2005 that federal sentencing guidelines were not mandatory and that sentencing judges could therefore apply their discretion in sentencing drug offenders. This most recent ruling involved an African American who received a 15-year prison term for selling crack and powder cocaine, as well as for possessing a firearm, in Virginia. The trial judge rejected as excessive the prison term of 19 to 22 years called for under the guidelines. The Supreme Court did not agree with the appeal court that reducing the sentence to 15 years amounted to "an abuse of discretion."

Finally in 2010, Congress acted to reduce the 100-to-1 disparity in the penalties for powder and crack cocaine to 18 to 1 by enacting the Fair Sentencing Act.

SOURCES: Mikkelsen, Randall. 2007, December 10. "Supreme Court Allows Lighter Crack Cocaine Terms" and ACLU 2012.

TRUTH IN SENTENCING

The new, more punitive penology, together with widespread public concerns about "lies in sentencing," resulted in the enactment of so-called truth-in-sentencing laws. The concern with truth in sentencing relates to offenders being sentenced to prison for substantial periods but being released on parole, in some cases after serving less than one half of their sentences. For example, an article in Alabama's *Birmingham News* from July 2000 referred to two cases—the first involving brothers sentenced to 40 years for kidnapping and rape who were released on parole after serving less than half their sentences, and the second involving a woman sentenced to 25 years for murder and eligible for parole after only 8 years imprisonment (in Spohn 2002: 252).

The policy intent of truth in sentencing was to ensure that a substantial period of a prison sentence was actually served. Through legislation, the federal government set the standard at 85% of the sentence imposed. It is significant that these laws were enacted following the passage of the 1994 Crime Act, which authorized and appropriated grants of nearly $10 billion to the states to build and expand correctional facilities. To be eligible for federal funding, states must require those convicted of violent crimes to serve at least 85% of the court-imposed sentence. By 1999, 27 states and the District of Columbia had adopted laws that met the federal standard, and 13 other states required offenders to serve from 50% to 75% of the sentence imposed (Spohn 2002: 253). Data from states that followed the federal model showed that the average time served by violent offenders increased between 1993 and 1997, as would be expected because of the minimum period of custody required.

Truth-in-sentencing policy and legislation follow the model of mandatory minimum sentencing by basing themselves on the belief that habitual offenders are responsible for a disproportionate amount of crime committed and that incarcerating them for lengthy periods will reduce the crime rate. Joan Petersilia (1999: 497) notes that to satisfy the 85% test, states have limited the powers of parole boards to fix release dates and of prison administrators to award "good time." The effect of truth-in-sentencing policy has therefore been not only to effectively eliminate parole but also to eliminate most "good time." In ethical terms, the conjunction between this policy and the availability of federal funds to construct more prisons is significant. Even if the states had misgivings in policy terms about truth in sentencing, they seemed unable to resist the offer of federal funding. Perhaps this is a good example of the maxim "If you build it, they will come."

PREDATORS AND SUPERPREDATORS

Sexual Predators

During the 1990s, sex offenders emerged as a distinct and dangerous criminal class, associated with a belief that children are more vulnerable to sexual abuse and molestation. In the United States, there now exists a set of assumptions that sexual abuse is pervasive, that it constitutes an issue of immense scope, that child molesters are compulsive individuals, and that their pathologies are resistant to rehabilitation or cure. In addition, it is assumed that sexual molestation generates a cycle of abuse because the original molestation so affects the victim that he or she will ultimately commit the same act against children of the next generation (Jenkins 1998: 1–2).

Philip Jenkins (1998) has explored the history of child abuse and the moral panics connected with child abuse for the period from 1890 until the emergence of the "sexual predator" in the 1990s. He has shown how, over that period, concern about the sexual offender has fluctuated with a series of peaks and dips in the social construction of this issue. The first so-called sexual pervert was identified as deviant and dangerous in the early 1900s, but at the end of the 19th century, sexual perversion was considered akin to defectiveness and degeneracy, and those viewed as perverts could be sterilized to prevent their defective genes being passed on. Policies of that nature for perverts were applied in the 1930s. Later, conceptions about deviancy changed away from biological explanations toward the psychiatric model, and laws were passed requiring indefinite confinement of those considered to be sexual psychopaths. These offenders were evaluated and treated by psychiatrists in mental institutions. Commencing in the late 1950s and continuing until the 1970s, the restrictive measures previously adopted

were eased. Formal legal intervention was now seen as counterproductive because it was inconsistent with greater sensitivity in the courts about racial issues in sex crime prosecutions and procedural rights. During this liberal period, questions were asked about the appropriateness of even criminalizing deviant sexual acts.

The ebb and flow of the social response to sex crimes continued. By the 1980s, there was a surge in concern about sex offenses because feminist activism brought the issue of rape and pornography to the forefront and emphasized the subjugation of women and children. Concern expressed by feminists about women and children as victims of violence fed into a conservative atmosphere that advocated getting tough on crime. Sex offenders became a group highlighted for policy making. As well, Christian fundamentalists linked homosexuality, nontraditional sexual relationships, and the sexual violation of children.

By the 1990s, the general public, politicians, and the media had begun to express a sense of crisis about sex offenders, sexual predators, child rapists, and pedophiles. "Sex offense" came to mean a criminal act involving a pedophile, despite the wide range of acts that constituted sex offenses: Many laws penalized a variety of acts termed *sex offenses*. These ranged from making obscene telephone calls to urinating in public to consensual sex between teenagers and to the rape and murder of a child (Gottschalk 2015: 197). In Washington State, any offense committed "for the purpose of sexual gratification" requires registration and notification. In California, a conviction for "lewd and lascivious conduct" or committing the misdemeanor of indecent exposure has a similar effect. In New York, there are 36 sex offenses, several of which require no actual sexual conduct (Clear and Frost 2014: 96). Federal interest in sex crimes accelerated, and the federal government began to organize joint operations with state and local law enforcement to pursue them, including the Project Safe Childhood, started in 2006, that was aimed at investigating and prosecuting Internet-based crimes against children (Gottschalk 2015: 199).

Laws, Prosecutions, and Punishments

This concern was translated into punitive legislation in some states, despite the fact that data showed that rates of rape and sexual assault were falling rapidly. For example, in 1994 California enacted a law imposing a 25-year sentence with 15 years minimum before eligibility for parole for those convicted of specified sex crimes. In 1996, California enacted a nonvoluntary chemical castration punishment for child molesters that was mandatory following a second conviction and applicable to a first offense if it met certain criteria (Lynch 2002: 532). In 2003, Congress passed the PROTECT Bill (known as Amber Alert) that created a national system of notification of child kidnappings. By an amendment to this bill, Congress also changed the sentencing guidelines for crimes involving pornography, sexual abuse, child sex, and child kidnapping and trafficking by eliminating downward sentencing, departures that would serve to reduce sentences, including family ties, diminished capacity, and educational or vocational skills (Bibas 2004: 295–296).

Between 1993 and 2000, convictions for sex offenses increased by 400%. Between 10% and 20% of state prisoners are now serving sentences for sex offenses, and in some states, the rate is almost 30% and sentence lengths have exploded (Gottschalk 2015: 199). In 2010, the Ninth Circuit Court of Appeals ruled that a life sentence imposed on a Washington man with a previous sex offense conviction who briefly touched a 5-year-old girl between her legs as she was riding down a slide in a play area was not grossly disproportionate, and in 2010, Oklahoma legislators approved a bill that would permit the execution of repeat offenders who sexually abuse children. The bill effectively ignored the Supreme Court decision in *Kennedy v. Louisiana* in 2008 that held unconstitutional the imposition of the death penalty in the case of child rape (p. 199).

In addition, penalties for possessing child pornography[5] have been increased, creating in some cases what amount to life sentences, as mandatory minimum sentences can be imposed for each illegal image possessed—an Arizona teacher with no previous convictions received a sentence of 200 years for possessing 20 images of children judged to be pornographic (Gottschalk 2015: 200).

Registration, Surveillance, and Monitoring of Sex Offenders

Apart from incarceration for their offenses, convicted sex offenders are now subject to a range of identification and surveillance strategies in most states; these laws are often referred to as "Megan's Laws." Although there are variations in different states, the basic format is that specified sex offenders are required to register certain information with local law enforcement, either for several years or even for the rest of their lives. Specific offenders may also be required to have their particulars, such as information about their address, provided to certain community groups and members of the public, such as schools and child care facilities (Lynch 2002: 533). Much of this information, as well as the criminal histories of sexual offenders, is now available on the Internet. In the latest federal iteration of sex offender registration laws, the Adam Walsh Child Protection Act, passed in July 2006, classifies sex offenders into three tiers: Tier 1 and II offenders must keep their registration up-to-date for 15 and 30 years, respectively, and Tier III offenders must register for their lifetime (Grubesic and Murray 2010: 670).

The 2006 act was upheld by the U.S. Supreme Court in the *Comstock* decision, with the Court indicating that state and federal authorities had "virtually unfettered power to preventatively detain sex offenders" (quoted in Gottschalk 2015: 203). The Adam Walsh Act, ostensibly aimed at violent sex offenders, explicitly provides that nothing in the law requires a person to have actually been convicted of such a crime for civil commitment to be invoked (p. 203).

The federal government has increasingly involved itself in the punishment of sexual predators and, in 1994, included in the Jacob Wetterling Act the requirement that funds made available for federal crime fighting be withheld from those states that did not have sex offender registration systems. Naturally, this legislation spawned registration programs, and by 1996, 49 states had registration systems in place. Moreover, in 1996, further legislation was enacted, providing for the nationwide

---

5   Gottschalk (2015: 200) notes that the crime of possession of child pornography has been conflated in the public mind with child abuse "despite weak or inconsistent evidence about the likelihood that people who possess child pornography also sexually abuse children." In 2012, the U.S. Sentencing Commission issued a report calling for a review of the harsh mandatory minimum sentences for possession and receipt of child pornography, but the U.S. Department of Justice has opposed any move to change the law (p. 213).

tracking of convicted sexual predators in a database maintained by the FBI (Lynch 2002: 535).

In at least a dozen states, policy makers are now linking intense supervision of sex offenders with constant GPS monitoring of their location (Lyons 2006). For example, in Florida a 2005 law called the Jessica Lunsford Act, after the abduction and murder of 9-year-old Jessica Lunsford, requires the lifetime GPS monitoring of sex offenders. Most recently, at least 30 states have imposed restrictions on places of residence and employment of all sex offenders, regardless of the seriousness of the crime, and have designated large parts of some localities as off-limits to them. One effect of this has been that there is virtually no lawful place of residence for sex offenders in the city of San Francisco (Gottschalk 2015: 209).

While other countries also require registration of sex offenders, the United States is exceptional in the wide scope of its registration requirements. For example, it is common in other countries to provide for only short registration periods and for the information to be limited to law enforcement and not made available on the Internet. These countries have determined that onerous registration requirements do not enhance public safety but rather promote forms of vigilante violence and adverse public reactions that constrain the reintegration of sex offenders into society (Gottschalk 2015: 205).

Research studies reveal that community attitudes toward sex offenders are more negative than attitudes toward offenders in general. The victims' rights movement, with its strong links to prosecutors, has been a forceful advocate of severe penalties for sex offenders (Gottschalk 2015: 197). Nevertheless, those working with sex offenders, such as probation officers and psychologists, show a more positive attitude. It seems that sex offender stereotypes depicted in the media heavily influence attitudes (Willis, Levenson, and Ward 2010: 548). Studies also indicate that community support for protective measures taken against sex offenders is high probably because of media influences that consistently portray them as unpredictable, evil, dangerous, and inevitable recidivists. Significantly, one study based on interviews with U.S. politicians indicated the media as their primary source of information about sex crimes and that their legislative proposals were shaped by that source (p. 552).

Civil Commitment

The group termed *sexually violent predators* are subject to even more restriction after release from prison. They may be detained in locked facilities for indefinite periods, subject only to a periodic review (see the "States Detain Sex Offenders After Prison" Closer Look box). Even though this gives the appearance of continuing a term of imprisonment that has supposedly terminated, this form of detention is labeled *civil commitment* rather than criminal punishment. In 1997 in the *Hendricks* case, the U.S. Supreme Court upheld civil commitment laws that were "nonpunitive." Civil commitment has been used to commit persons with no prior record of sex offenses. They have been certified to be "sexually dangerous," and offenders serving sentences for crimes such as possession of child pornography or making obscene telephone calls have also been civilly committed (Gottschalk 2015: 210).

As discussed earlier, the moral panic about sexual predators and violent sexual predators (which, according to Gottschalk [2015: 196], has "uncanny parallels with the war on drugs") has employed three distinct mechanisms in the overall response to this criminality—namely, impose harsher sentences; require that sex offenders be registered; that the community be advised of their whereabouts; and impose indefinite civil commitment of those sex offenders who have completed their sentences. As of 2012, about 725,000 persons were registered as sex offenders in the United States, about 1 in 500 persons, constituting approximately double the number from 10 years ago (p. 205). At least 17 states require that registration be for life, and in a number of states, all sex offenders, regardless of the nature of their crime, are listed in publicly accessible registries that give details of place of residence, email addresses, place of employment, and vehicle license plate number (p. 207).

Sexual Predators: A Moral Panic

In her analysis of the debates in Congress during the formulation of sex offender legislation, Mona Lynch (2002: 543) highlights the language of the legislators on sex offenders that has tended to stress the gender of these offenders (always described as male) and their characterization as "stranger" and

A Closer Look

States Detain Sex Offenders After Prison

New York State considers itself at the forefront of a growing national movement to confine sex offenders after their prison terms have expired, using a civil commitment law. These programs have been criticized for not meeting their stated goal of "treating the worst criminals until they no longer pose a threat" (Davey and Goodnough 2007: 1). The number of pedophiles, rapists, and other sexual offenders who are being held indefinitely in special treatment centers in 19 states is estimated at 2,700, with a cost to taxpayers at 4 times the cost of keeping them in prison. Slightly fewer than 3,000 sex offenders have been committed since the law was passed in 1990. Of those, only 81 have been fully discharged from commitment because they are considered ready. Another 115 have been released due to "legal technicalities, court ruling, terminal illness or old age" (p. 1). Texas and Arizona have released an additional 189 and 68, respectively, under supervision or conditions.

Such laws have been upheld by the U.S. Supreme Court on the understanding that offenders will receive treatment in confinement and that it is not a second punishment. However, only a fraction of sexual offenders committed under this legislation "have ever completed the treatment to the point where they could be released free and clear" (Davey and Goodnough 2007: 1). The programs are expensive and unproven, and although they are residents in the programs, patients often accept their lawyers' advice and fail to show up for sessions that require them to confess all their crimes, even those unknown by police. Instead, they spend their time gardening, watching TV, or playing video games.

President Bush signed a law that offers money to states that commit sex offenders to such facilities following their prison sentences. The sex offenders selected for such commitment were not the most violent, according to an investigation of existing programs by *The New York Times*. They discovered that committed offenders included exhibitionists, while some rapists were not included, and some were beyond the age where they are considered dangerous. They found, for example, that one confined person was a 102-year-old man in Wisconsin who had memory loss and poor hearing. The average annual cost per person is $41,845.

SOURCE: Davey, Monica and Abby Goodnough. 2007. "Doubts Rise as States Detain Sex Offenders After Prison." *New York Times*, March 4.

"outsider." This characterization was made despite the fact that only about 3% of sexual abuse offenses against children and about 6% of child murders are committed by strangers. In fact, most children who are sexually abused, neglected, or killed suffer that abuse at the hands of someone in the family (p. 546). When the legislators discussed the Internet and child pornography, they constructed the child sexual predator as a "cyberpredator" "stalking children on the Internet" (p. 547). This enabled some to characterize all material appearing on the Internet as contaminating to children and even to adults, perhaps fulfilling a different agenda than that promoted during debate.

Another aspect of the moral panic engendered by this crime, which is actually very broadly defined, was the legislators' insistence on constructing the sexual predator as uniquely threatening, as compared to an ordinary felon. Speakers referred to unspecified scientific studies showing that those who commit sexual violence against children have the highest rate of recidivism and are unable to exercise any self-control (Lynch 2002: 546). As Lynch puts it, the debates revealed a sense of apprehension by speakers who considered that "the very fiber of traditional family units is under siege by sex offenders" (p. 549). Speakers used language suggesting that families were doing all they could to keep their children safe from pedophiles cruising the Internet and that children had to be protected from inherently vicious child predators.

It is clear that there is a strong current of emotion rather than rationality in the discourse on child predators, which emphasizes risk, danger, and the need to impose punitive measures to manage such monsters. A more rational approach would be for legislators to pursue the predominant group of child abusers—those who offend within families—and develop relevant and rational sentencing policy rather than merely focusing on the stranger pedophiles, who constitute a much smaller group of offenders. Lynch (2002: 558) argues that these emotional reactions reflect issues surrounding sexuality, the family, and gender roles, and they appear to be manifestations of a theme that calls for protecting the "idealized version" of the family from harm.

Jonathan Simon (2000: 15) points out in a discussion of Megan's Law that the use of the terms *predatory* and *prey* connotes forms of danger that are nonhuman. He observes also that this language links with terms such as *monster* to define sexual predators as nonhuman and therefore unworthy of any treatment consistent with human dignity. He notes that Megan's Law contains no provision for the treatment of sexual offenders, its aim being one of surveillance, control, and a long-term continuation of punishment. This process of dehumanizing sex offenders and emphasizing the needs and situation of the victim to the exclusion of everything else has the effect of rendering sexual predators "beyond humanity." They become a species apart from the rest of us, and this legitimizes the kind of legislation embodied in Megan's Law.[6] Jenkins (1998) suggests that moral panics on issues such as sexual predators are a cover for a different agenda. In the case of campaigns to protect children, the agenda often involves attempting to reestablish control over those children and the weakened family, perhaps through political or social

change. In other words, as he puts it, "Preventing sexual acts against the young can be a way of regulating sexual acts by that population" (p. 225).

Juvenile Superpredators

Tonry (2001: 168) argues that repressive crime policies reflect cyclical patterns of increased intolerance for crime and criminals and that a series of moral panics amplified and expounded by the mass media has interacted with each cyclical period. The moral panics and patterns exacerbate the effects of each other and together establish an environment that welcomes symbolic and expressive crime control policies that pay little attention to their direct or collateral effects. During the 1990s, another moral panic emerged, this time in the form of grave public concern about violence, youth, and so-called superpredators. The campaign against superpredators is well illustrated in the following passage from *Body Count* by William Bennett, John DiIulio, and John Walters (1999):

> America is now home to thickening ranks of juvenile "super-predators"—radically impulsive, brutally remorseless youngsters, including ever more pre-teenage boys, who murder, assault, rape, rob, burglarize, deal deadly drugs, join gun-toting gangs and create communal disorders. They do not fear the stigma of arrest, the pains of imprisonment or the pangs of conscience. (p. 27)

This rhetoric was based on an increase in violence committed by and against youth during the late 1980s and early 1990s. Those predicting the coming wave of superpredators projected this increase in juvenile violence as continuing in a straight line into the future. Although it was correct to say that all forms of youth violence had increased significantly in this period, research indicates that this violence remained located in the group most victimized over time—namely, young African American men (Moore and Tonry 1998: 7). Among the explanations advanced for this increase in violence was the notion that youth violence was associated with the epidemic of crack cocaine use and an increased supply of lethal weapons to youth. Philip Cook and John Laub (1998: 27), in their study of youth violence, dismissed notions of superpredators; they found that there was a clear indication of increased

---

6 On May 21, 2011, *The New York Times* (Goode 2011) reported that lawmakers were pushing for online registries, like those for sex offenders, for persons convicted of a variety of offenses, from arson and drunk driving to animal abuse. In Illinois, members of the legislature are considering a registry of first-degree murderers; in Maine, of drunken drivers; and in Virginia, dangerous dogs are already registered. Proponents argue that people have a right to know about potentially dangerous persons living in the community.

gun availability during the so-called epidemic and that every category of homicide and other violent crimes showed an increase in gun use.

The supposed epidemic never eventuated, and statistical data showed that arrests for juveniles for violent crimes, especially juveniles aged 10 to 14, actually declined in 1995 (Brownstein 2000: 122), and that the number of arrests of juveniles for violent crimes had declined by 23% between 1973 and 1995 (p. 128). Significantly, on January 31, 1998, DiIulio published a letter in *The Washington Post* newspaper retracting his earlier statements:

> I have written a number of articles in major newspapers and journals and have testified in Congress, to correct the misperception that a large fraction of juvenile offenders are "super-predators." Also, I have been on record for more than two years now in opposition to efforts to incarcerate violent juveniles in adult facilities. (in Brownstein 2000: 128)

Among the consequences of this particular moral panic has been the movement to have juveniles tried as adults, the call for juveniles older than 16 to be made subject to the death penalty, the call for more punitive punishments for juvenile crime, and moves to ensure that juveniles who "commit the crime, do the time."

CAPITAL PUNISHMENT

The subject of punishment generally is a morality issue. Capital punishment, as a form of punishment, is clearly the preeminent morality issue within the category of punishment. The following discussion will concentrate on the moral arguments advanced about capital punishment, including arguments that are often deployed as part of a policy debate on the subject.

In terms of legal authorization for this particular form of punishment, according to Ernest van den Haag (1985), one of the foremost advocates of capital punishment, the Constitution authorizes the death penalty in the Fifth Amendment when it states that "no person shall be deprived of life, liberty, or property, without due process of law." He argues that the Constitution authorizes deprivation of life, provided that due process of law is made available. A contrary view, however, is expressed by

one of the leading proponents of the abolition of capital punishment, Hugo Bedau (1997), who does not see the Constitution as authorizing the death penalty but as presenting the government with a choice to either repeal the death penalty or carry it out in accordance with the requirements of due process. Whatever may be the correct position on legal authorization, the fact is that in policy terms the decision about whether capital punishment is on the statute books rests with each state. It follows that states that have no capital punishment provision have made a conscious policy decision, perhaps on moral grounds, to prohibit this particular punishment. Equally, those states that retain or have reintroduced capital punishment have made a similar decision in favor of this punishment.

In 1972, the Supreme Court in *Furman v. Georgia* struck down the death penalty in the 35 states that then imposed capital punishment. Some 4 years later, as a result of three other cases, the Supreme Court authorized capital punishment, as long as certain procedural guidelines protecting the accused were adhered to. In response to that ruling, by 1975, 27 states had revised their capital punishment statutes, and by the end of 1997, 29 states in all parts of the country had executed inmates by various means (Culver 1999: 287). Five states accounted for 65% of all executions between 1977 and 1997, and one third of all executions have occurred in the state of Texas. In contrast to the attachment that Texas obviously has to the death penalty, the history of Oregon shows how policy on this issue can change. The death penalty was abolished in Oregon in 1913, restored in 1930, rejected in 1964, and then readopted in 1978 and 1984.

In policy terms, following the Supreme Court's rulings, states have a degree of flexibility in deciding which homicide offenses can be charged as capital offenses. Most states set out a number of special circumstances or aggravating factors that operate to define a murder as capital. For example, there are 18 aggravating circumstances in Alabama, Delaware has 22 special circumstances, and Kansas has 7 "homicide situations" (Culver 1999: 294). This considerable variation in factors and circumstances reflects the policy debate in some states about capital punishment, a debate that, in the view of Jonathan Simon and Christina Spaulding (1999: 96), can be characterized by "populist punitiveness" and as reflecting the extent to which punishment has been democratized at the political level. In a climate where politicians must beware of being accused of being soft on crime, few elected officials within or outside the criminal justice system are prepared to argue against the death penalty (Culver 1999: 289). As Bedau (1996) puts it,

> It is now widely assumed that no political candidate in the United States can hope to run for President, governor, or other high elected office if he or she can successfully be targeted as "soft on crime"; the candidate's position on the death penalty has become the litmus test. . . . The death penalty has become part of partisan political campaigning in a manner impossible to have predicted a generation ago. (p. 50)

John Culver (1999) notes that concerns may arise when the capital punishment debate involves the judiciary because of the likelihood that judicial independence will be compromised by weighing its views to accord with public opinion on the death penalty. In Tennessee, a justice of the Tennessee Supreme Court became the first appellate judge in that state to be defeated in an election for a continuation of her term due largely to her support for the majority opinion in a rape/murder conviction where the death sentence was overturned (p. 289). Being tough on crime and supporting capital punishment until recently included being tough on juveniles because the Supreme Court held in *Stanford v. Kentucky* (1989) that the execution of offenders aged 16 and 17 years is sanctioned by the Constitution. A. James (2001: 184) argues that executing juvenile offenders not only is contrary to fundamental principles of American justice but also violates customary international law. It should be noted that since 1990, only seven countries have reportedly executed juveniles. In 2005, the Supreme Court revisited the issue of the death penalty for juvenile offenders and decided in *Roper v. Simmons* that the Eighth and Fourteenth Amendments of the Constitution forbid the execution of offenders who were under the age of 18 years when their crimes were committed.

A Closer Look

Retentionist and Abolitionist Countries on the Death Penalty in 2013

- Abolition countries, having abolished it for all crimes—98 countries
- Abolitionist for ordinary crimes only, while retaining it for only exceptional crimes, such as under military law—7 countries
- Abolitionist in practice, have not imposed it during the last 10 years, have made an international commitment not to impose it, or have a policy or established practice of not conducting executions—35 countries
- Total abolitionist in law or practice—140 countries
- Retentionist countries who retain it for all crimes—58 countries

SOURCE: Amnesty International 2014: 52.

In March 2014, Amnesty International reported that 98 countries have now abolished the death penalty—almost one half of all nation states. Countries that have restarted executions after having refrained from doing so are Indonesia, Kuwait, Nigeria, and Vietnam. Amnesty reported there had been 778 executions in 22 different countries in 2013, an increase of 15% compared with 2012. This figure takes no account of executions occurring in China, where no official data is available but where Amnesty puts the total in the thousands and greater than the rest of the world combined. Five countries conducted the majority of executions in 2013: China (number not known), Iran (at least 369), Iraq (at least 169), Saudi Arabia (at least 79), and the United States (39).

A Closer Look

United States and the Death Penalty

Why does the United States retain the death penalty in the face of a worldwide abolitionist trend? Many commentators, including Zimring (2003), have pointed out that the U.S. federal system of government allows each state to make its own choice concerning the retention or otherwise of the death penalty, and most executions are performed in a very few states. Consequently, to speak of the United States as a retentionist nation is somewhat misleading. Zimring argues that the attention given to victims of homicides means that the death penalty amounts to a policy response to murder that represents an "undertaking of government to serve the needs of individual citizens for justice and psychological healing" (2003: 49).

In his analysis of the American death penalty, David Garland argues that it is necessary to view the death penalty as being situated in a "complex field of institutional arrangements, social practices and cultural forms" that he calls the "capital punishment complex" (2010: 14). The American form of capital punishment has adapted over time and, according to Garland, has evolved into "an assemblage of practices, discourses, rituals and representations" following the demands of society and the various forces that influence its operation (p. 19).

Like other commentators on this topic, Garland sees links and commonalities between the death penalty and lynching.[7]

- Executions are concentrated in the South.
- The death penalty is a subject of local politics and populism expressed in the election process at various levels and for various offices.
- It disproportionately targets poor blacks who commit crimes against white victims.
- It is energized by heinous crimes and racial hatreds and it continues to provide drama (Garland 2010: 35).

Garland argues that many of the social forces that prompted lynching also promote capital punishment (2010: 35). Accordingly, the death penalty in the United States has some uniquely American features, including the link between capital punishment, the justice system, and due process. The due process protections granted to condemned prisoners by the U.S. Supreme Court mean that the average time spent on death row in the United States is lengthy—in 2007, it was 12 years (p. 45).

Another uniquely American feature, according to Garland, is that "the death penalty is depicted as a vital expression of local community sentiment, as moral outrage authentically expressed, as collective choice, and community justice" (2010: 62). The election of judges, prosecutors, and police chiefs by a popular vote in many states ensures that community views on punishment generally are transmitted to law enforcement and operationalized in its policies and operations. Advocacy for the death penalty signifies being "tough on law and order" generally (pp. 121, 162, 246).

Unlike European nations, the U.S. federal government lacks the centralized control of justice policy that would enable the abolition of the death penalty. Instead, the death penalty is continuously litigated as a constitutional issue with the outcome, as Garland (2010: 191) explains, that the rulings of

---

7   There is some evidence that state officials in the United States associated lynching with hanging and "frontier justice," and as a result, alternative methods of execution were explored (Garland 2010: 119).

the Supreme Court "enhance the perceived lawfulness and legitimacy of capital punishment and thus act as a force for its conservation." Regional differences between the South[8] in terms of the incidence of executions (and the history of slavery, racism, and lynching) and the remainder of the country also provide explanations of U.S. divergence from the mainstream.

In summary, Garland contends that historical and cultural legacies, institutional structures, deeply rooted democratic forms and practices, and a shift to a victim-centric law and order politics, operating collectively, have created constraints to the total abolition of capital punishment throughout the United States. The "capital punishment complex" in the United States now exists independently of any association with crime control, instead serving various partisan and political interests as well as those of the media. Because it exists in a form peculiar to the United States, it is resistant to arguments that have brought about its total abolition in other nations. Accordingly, Garland concludes, capital punishment is an assured element of contemporary U.S. culture (2010: 286).

---

8   Public hanging continued in Kentucky and Missouri up to the 1930s, and southern states allowed the death sentence for rape, robbery, burglary, and arson up to the 1960s, even when the rest of the country had restricted it to first-degree murder (Garland 2010: 124).

Public Opinion on Capital Punishment

In a comprehensive review of public support for capital punishment, Cullen and colleagues (2000: 10) note that Americans are most often polled on their attitude to this form of punishment and that when asked if they support it for convicted murderers, about 7 in 10 respondents reply in the affirmative. This level has remained constant since the early 1970s. However, if respondents are asked not only if they support the death penalty but also whether they would choose the death penalty or life imprisonment without parole, support for capital punishment declines markedly (p. 10). Polling data also reveal that citizens may advocate capital punishment, even when the innocent are executed. For example, a Gallup poll found that 57% of respondents continued to support capital punishment, even when asked to take into account that 1 out of 100 people sentenced to death was actually innocent (pp. 11–12). It is interesting to note that in the 2 decades preceding the 1970s, support for capital punishment was much lower, amounting to 61% in 1936 and 68% in 1953 and declining to 45% in 1965. In 1966, more Americans opposed the death penalty (47%) than favored it (42%; p. 13). Explanations for this change in the public view include the rising crime rate of the 1960s and fear of crime generated by the politicization of crime, the emergence of

racial conflicts, the introduction of tough policies on crime appealing to underlying racist attitudes, a general lack of confidence in the criminal justice system, and a general move away from social causes of offending toward individualistic explanations of crime that emphasize free choice (p. 13).

As to people's motives for supporting the death penalty, research indicates that deterrence and retribution figure highly as justification, along with the notion that it is unfair for taxpayers to keep convicted murderers in prison for life. However, the largest percentage of supporters (74% in one poll) justified the death penalty on the basis that "it removes all possibility that the convicted person can kill again" (Cullen et al. 2000: 19).

Some polls have analyzed how views on the death penalty would be affected if the option of life without parole were available. They have reported that the percentage favoring capital punishment would significantly decline from 71% to 52% (Cullen et al. 2000: 19). Thus, the regular polling showing continued support on this issue gives rise to the possibility that the public may not prefer it to other sentencing options and that people should be asked if they support the death penalty or "other alternative sentences." It is noteworthy that support for an alternative to capital punishment becomes especially strong when respondents are offered the choice of a sentence of life without parole with restitution to the victim. This option was favored by 60.7% compared to 31.6% favoring the death penalty (p. 20). As for those who design the laws, a 1991 survey of New York legislators found that even with the option of life imprisonment without parole and restitution, 58% still preferred the death penalty. In the same survey, it was noted that legislators misconceived the views of the public, reporting that among their constituents they believed 73% would support the death penalty over the alternative of life imprisonment (p. 21). The obvious conclusion is that legislators appear to be a significant barrier to substituting alternatives for capital punishment. It is worth noting that although many Americans continue to support the death penalty, the ability to use DNA to ascertain with certainty the identity of perpetrators and the growing number of persons found to be innocent after years on death row based on DNA evidence has begun to influence the public discourse about the legitimacy of this form of penalty.

What impact does religion have on support for the death penalty?

Polls show that 61% of Americans believe that religion is a "very important" part of their lives (Cullen et al. 2000: 24) and that 96% of Americans say they believe in God. One study found that white fundamentalists (those with fundamentalist religious membership or beliefs) are most supportive of capital punishment, whereas African American fundamentalists are less supportive. Research suggests that religious fundamentalism and biblical literalism are positively related to punitive attitudes, including retribution for crime, support for tough criminal legislation and harsh sentencing, and favoring more severe treatment of juvenile offenders (p. 25).

What are the moral arguments usually advanced against capital punishment in policy debates?

The core moral arguments against capital punishment are usually formulated as follows (Bedau 1997; van den Haag 1985):

1. The death penalty has been distributed in a discriminatory manner because African American or poorer defendants are more likely to be executed than equally guilty others, especially when the victim is white (Russell-Brown 1998: 134).

2. Miscarriages of justice occur and the innocent are executed.
3. The death penalty expresses a desire for vengeance—a motive too volatile and indifferent to the concept of justice to be maintained in a civilized society.
4. Capital punishment is considered to be degrading to human dignity and inconsistent with the principle of the sanctity of life.
5. It is morally wrong to authorize the killing of some criminals when there is an adequate alternative punishment of imprisonment.

Each of these arguments will now be considered:

1. The death penalty has been distributed in a discriminatory manner because African American or poorer defendants are more likely to be executed than equally guilty others, especially when the victim is white (Russell-Brown 1998: 134).

Samuel Walker, Cassia Spohn, and Miriam DeLone (2000: 231) make a case for the existence of racial disparity in the application of the death penalty, pointing to the fact that although African Americans make up only 10% to 12% of the population, they are disproportionately represented among those sentenced to death and executed. In addition, they suggest there is compelling evidence that those who murder whites—and particularly African Americans who murder whites—are disproportionately sentenced to death.

2. Miscarriages of justice occur and the innocent are executed.

The American Bar Association (ABA) has urged the appointment of experienced, competent, and adequately compensated trial counsel for death penalty cases and has lobbied for the adoption of its *Guidelines for the Appointment and Performance of Counsel in Death Penalty Cases*. These guidelines call for the appointment of two experienced attorneys at each stage of a capital case, such appointment to be made by an authority capable of identifying lawyers who possess the necessary professional skills. Clearly, the ABA believes that standard professional qualifications are insufficient for capital cases. No state has fully embraced the ABA recommended system, and it is a notorious fact that unqualified and undercompensated lawyers continue to represent capital clients. In spite of these deficiencies, in 1996 the federal Antiterrorism and Effective Death Penalty Act undermined the ability of death row inmates to use federal habeas corpus procedures to have their cases reviewed in federal courts. It also removed federal funding for postconviction defender organizations that provided legal representation for many prisoners contesting their sentences (Sarat 1999: 9).

The process involved in appealing capital cases varies from state to state, but according to Herbert Haines (1996: 56–57), the process is typically as follows: Death sentences are automatically appealed to the highest state court, with appeals in this first round being limited to the trial record and to procedural errors. If the state court affirms the conviction, the prisoner can appeal to the U.S. Supreme Court for review, but the Supreme Court generally agrees to hear only 2% to 3% of these appeals. If a request for a review is denied, a second cycle of appeals can be brought, in this case not limited to the trial record. These appeals are filed in the lower court, then in the higher state courts, and finally again in the U.S. Supreme Court. During this round of appeals, an inmate is able to argue that he or she was provided with an incompetent defense or, for example, that there is newly discovered evidence showing innocence. If after these two rounds of appeals the prisoner is still under sentence of death, he or she can file for a federal habeas corpus review, during which alleged violations of constitutional rights can be raised. Habeas corpus proceedings work their way through the federal system from the district court to the circuit court of appeals and finally again to the U.S. Supreme Court.

There has been concern about miscarriages of justice in capital cases since at least the 1820s, and in 1987, Bedau and Radelet (in Haines 1996: 88) argued that some 350 persons had been wrongly convicted of potentially capital offenses between 1900 and 1985. There is further evidence in the form of a congressional subcommittee report that at least 45 death sentences were in error in the period 1976 to 1993, and numerous incidents of wrongful convictions have come to the attention of the courts and the media since the advent of DNA testing in 1985. In one case in 1989, a prisoner spent 12 years in a Texas prison and came within 3 days of lethal injection before his conviction was overturned. The court ruled that the prosecutors had used perjured testimony and had knowingly suppressed evidence to obtain a conviction for killing a police officer. In another case, an African American school custodian was wrongly convicted of the rape and murder of a 16-year-old white girl. The errors comprised forensic evidence suggesting the crime was committed by a white man, which was never mentioned to the jury and was "misplaced," as well as evidence pointing to a different suspect, which the police ignored (p. 88).

Those in favor of capital punishment characterize these cases as indicating how well the criminal justice system's procedural safeguards work, but this tends to ignore the fact that not only is the convicted person deprived of years of freedom while waiting on death row, but he or she must also deal with the mental consequences of waiting to be put to death. The activities of the Innocence Project, particularly in DNA testing, have continued to reveal errors and cases of innocence. In *United States v. Quinones* (2002), Judge Rakoff argued that the use of capital punishment is unconstitutional because there is no longer any certainty of a person's guilt in a capital offense. He contended that advances in DNA testing render capital punishment problematic because DNA testing is able to prove absolutely that some condemned persons are actually innocent. In 2004, Congress passed the Justice for All Act, establishing federal prisoners' access to DNA evidence for a minimum of 5 years following their conviction. The act allocates funds to deal with a reported backlog of 350,000 untested DNA samples in rape cases (Sarat 2005: 45).

After many years of hearing death penalty cases, in February 1984 Justice Harry Blackmun of the Supreme Court announced, "From this day forward I no longer shall tinker with the machinery of death." He did not reject the death penalty because of its violence, but rather focused on the procedures applying to death sentences, explaining that

> despite the efforts of the states and the courts to devise legal formulas and procedural rules . . . the death penalty remains fraught with arbitrariness, discrimination, caprice, and mistake. . . .

Experience has taught us that the Constitutional goal of eliminating arbitrariness and discrimination from the administration of death . . . can never be achieved without compromising an equally essential component of fundamental fairness—individualized sentencing. (in Sarat 1999: 7–8)

For all intents and purposes, therefore, Justice Blackmun concluded that the death penalty cannot be administered in accordance with the Constitution and that no procedural rules or regulations can save it from its deficiencies.

3. The death penalty expresses a desire for vengeance—a motive too volatile and indifferent to the concept of justice to be maintained in a civilized society.

The notion that revenge can stand as a motive for official policy on punishment is entirely inconsistent with a rational system of justice conducted by the state on behalf of society (Bedau 1999: 50). Proponents of the death penalty tend to suggest that they favor its application, not for revenge but for retribution. Those against the death penalty respond that if we are to support capital punishment for murder under this retributive principle, we should equally require rapists to be raped and torturers to be tortured, forms of punishment any civilized society would be reluctant to carry out. In addition, they argue that the extreme punishment of life in prison without parole can be imposed for murder, and this in itself is retributive. As explained in Chapter 6, in 1972 and 1976 the U.S. Supreme Court stated that it considers retribution "a legitimate justification for capital punishment" (*Furman v. Georgia* 1972; *Gregg v. Georgia* 1976).

4. Capital punishment is considered to be degrading to human dignity and inconsistent with the principle of the sanctity of life.

The argument is that human life, having infinite value, should be respected and protected and that even murderers' lives should be valued in the same way. Advocates of this position are absolutists and would be against capital punishment, no matter which arguments are put forward about the conduct of a particular murderer. Bedau

(1999: 42) suggests that abolitionists who rely on this argument should insist that the burden of argument lies on those who favor the death sentence. In other words, for the purposes of assessing punishment, society ought to assume that everyone's life is valuable and that all our lives have equal value.

Associated with the value of life argument is the view that we are morally forbidden to take the life of a murderer because he or she has an inalienable right to life that is violated by sentencing a person to death and executing that person. This argument is normative, and again, Bedau (1999) suggests that the burden of argument should be on those who would kill through capital punishment to justify that killing. The notion that this form of punishment violates the fundamental right to life has been endorsed by the Council of Europe and the European Union, which have declared that "the death penalty has no legitimate place in the penal systems of modern civilized societies, and that its application may well be compared with torture and be seen as inhuman and degrading punishment" (Hood 2001: 331).

In relation to human dignity, Bedau (1997) has extended Justice Brennan's concurring opinion in *Furman v. Georgia* (1972), in which the justice identified four principles explaining why the death penalty was an affront to human dignity. The principles expounded in that dissenting decision are that a punishment must not by its severity be degrading to human dignity, that a punishment must never be inflicted in a wholly arbitrary fashion, that a severe punishment must not be unacceptable to contemporary society, and that the unnecessary infliction of suffering is also offensive to human dignity. Bedau supplements these principles by suggesting that it is also an affront to the dignity of a person to be forced to undergo harm at the hands of another when entirely at his or her mercy, as is always the case with legal punishment. He further suggests that it offends a person's dignity when the person imposing punishment is free to arbitrarily choose which offenders are to be punished very severely, when all deserve the same severe punishment if any do. Finally, he proposes that it is offensive to the dignity of a person to be subjected to such a punishment.

A Closer Look

Death by Lethal Injection: Degrading to Human Dignity?

In the case of *Baze v. Rees* (553 U.S. 35) 2008, the U.S. Supreme Court affirmed a particular method of lethal injection for capital punishment. The case concerned the use of a "cocktail" of three drugs in Kentucky—the same one used by virtually all states. The first drug brings unconsciousness, the second paralyzes the muscles, and the third kills by stopping the heart. The third drug is "excruciatingly painful" (Oliver 2015: 95).

It was claimed that the use of the drugs violated the Eighth Amendment's prohibition of cruel and unusual punishment because the drugs carried a risk of inflicting unnecessary pain. The Court found the method to be humane and constitutional and said that an "isolated mishap alone" did not violate the Constitution. It also stated that the first drug in a multidrug cocktail must render the inmate unconscious. Otherwise, there is a "substantial, constitutionally unacceptable risk" that the inmate will suffer a painful suffocation. The Court said that a future challenge to the lethal injection protocol would have to show that the protocol presents "a substantial risk of serious harm" or an "objectively intolerable risk of harm" and that there exists a feasible alternative that can be operationalized that that "would significantly reduce a substantial risk of serious pain" (Gee 2011: 217).

Since 2008, there has been a change in circumstances because one of the three drugs, the first in the cocktail that renders the prisoner unconscious, pentobarbital, is no longer manufactured, and European pharmaceutical companies will no longer sell drugs that are to be used in conducting executions. As a result, states have been forced to revise their lethal drug injection protocols. According to the Death Penalty Information Center, eight states have used a single drug and six more have announced plans to do so but have yet to carry out any executions. Fourteen states have used phenobarbital (commonly used to euthanize animals), with five more planning to do so. Nine states have used or plan to use compounding pharmacies to secure drugs. The unavailability in full of the previous cocktail of drugs has effectively halted executions in several states. States that have tried to use non-FDA approved drug suppliers have had their drugs seized.

One of the first executions using a new combination of drugs occurred in 2014 in Ohio, but the prisoner, Dennis McGuire, was heard making gasping, snorting, and choking sounds during the death process. Witnesses say that he was rendered unconscious but then started moving and gasping a few minutes later. In terms of the Supreme Court decision, it is problematic to state that he was rendered unconscious and therefore could not experience pain. In July 2013, Joseph Wood died in Arizona after nearly 2 hours, following 15 injections of midazolam and hydromorphone, 15 times the amount mandated in the state's execution protocol. Witnesses said that Wood gulped and gasped during this process more than 600 times (Dart 2014).

The sanitizing of death through elaborate regimes of killing by lethal injection is intended to inflict a "clean death" and was said by Chief Justice Roberts to preserve the dignity of the procedure because the second drug prevents involuntary seizures or convulsions during the period of unconsciousness. However, Justice Ginsburg argued that once the second drug that brings paralysis is injected it is impractical to further monitor the prisoner's consciousness without additional equipment and training and that there would be no explicit indication if the prisoner was in fact suffering pain. In other words, when the prisoner is paralyzed, it is not possible to tell visually if he or she is conscious.

(Continued)

(Continued)

In spite of this, the evidence shows that in a number of states the so-called "consciousness check" is performed not by a medical professional, but by a prison staff.

A study of postmortems of prisoners executed by lethal injection found that "prisoners may have been capable of feeling pain in almost 90% of cases and may have actually been conscious when they were put to death." The muscle relaxant component of the drug cocktail effectively masked the ability of the prisoner to indicate he or she was experiencing pain (Oliver 2015: 99).

In April 2015, the Supreme Court heard oral arguments in the case of *Glossip v. Gross* concerning the constitutionality of using the drug midazolam to bring unconsciousness in executions. The plaintiffs, all inmates on Oklahoma's death row, argued that midazolam has no pain-relieving properties and "cannot reliably produce a deep, comatose unconsciousness" to ensure the inmate doesn't experience "intense and needless pain and suffering" when the paralytic and heart-stopping drugs are injected (Howe 2015). In June 2015, the U.S. Supreme Court ruled in this case that the claimants had failed to meet the test that use of the drug entailed a substantial risk of severe pain and had not identified an available and preferable method of execution that would overcome the alleged deficiencies of the drug midazolam (Liptak 2015).

One response to the issues posed by the lethal injection method has been to adopt alternative methods. Rather than go back to hanging or electrocution, the state of Utah passed a law that would make it the only state in the country to carry out a death sentence by firing squad if there is a shortage of execution drugs. The sponsor of the law argued that death by firing squad was a more humane form of execution because a team of trained marksmen would ensure that death was speedy and not long-drawn-out, as has occurred with the lethal injection method. Others disagreed, arguing that firing squads amounted to revisiting and reinventing the Wild West days of the state and would be condemned internationally. Similar legislation has been introduced in Arkansas. In Oklahoma, lawmakers are considering the use of nitrogen gas to execute those sentenced to death (Gambino 2015).

---

5. It is morally wrong to authorize the killing of some criminals when there is an adequate alternative punishment of imprisonment.

Bedau (1997) argues that to do so would be an affront to human dignity. Associated with this argument is that which insists there is no convincing evidence that the rate of murder is consistently lower when the death penalty can be invoked and enforced. The death penalty has not proved to be a more effective deterrent than the alternative sanction of life in prison without parole, and it therefore constitutes an irrational burden within a rational system of criminal justice (Hood 2001: 332). Finally, as Beccaria (in Hood 2001: 332) noted as early as 1764, the death penalty is counterproductive in terms of its moral message because it legitimizes the very behavior—killing—that the law seeks to repress. Its effect, therefore, is to undermine the legitimacy and moral authority of the entire criminal justice system.

In policy terms, as we have seen, retribution as opposed to rehabilitation is now cited as the appropriate justification for punishment, and the intuitive anger felt toward criminals, often now labeled as monsters and predators, can be seen expressed in the notion of capital punishment as an abstract policy. Showing one's support for the death penalty is a symbolic act announcing that one is a supporter of a tough-on-crime policy approach and favors holding criminals morally responsible for their actions. In the political arena, it seems highly unlikely that there will be any widespread movement toward abolition, but abolitionists have recently been comforted by the Supreme Court's decision prohibiting the death penalty when the prisoner can be shown to be mentally challenged or under 18 years of age. Abolitionists must rely on the Supreme Court to continue this approach of eroding the death penalty by stages, as has happened in the case of executing juvenile offenders.

SUMMARY

Policy making in criminal justice usually takes the form of policies and legislation relating to crime control. Justifications for particular policies might be ideological, empirical, or ethical. Those based on ethical grounds result from an analysis of what is "right and wrong" or "good or bad" in a moral sense for a particular issue. Ethics fits into criminal justice policy making in two forms. First, there is a general issue in policy making that those who formulate policies should act ethically; second, there is an ethical responsibility in making policies about subjects like punishment. As Tonry notes, a "legislator or governor who proposes or enacts policy changes he knows will not achieve their purported aims and will, if enacted, cause new injustices, because he hopes it will help him get reelected, is behaving unethically" (2006: 53). This kind of policy making can be termed *morality policy making*. Most policy making results from a cost–benefit analysis that does not include ethical models. A policy that is considered unethical would include reacting to events by formulating irrational, capricious, and arbitrary policies. In the criminal justice policy field, it is possible to link the existence of moral panics and morality policy making. A moral panic occurs when an event arises that is defined as a threat to the values of society—for example, the sale and consumption of drugs or the existence of sexual predators. These events are promoted by the media and engender public concern and political action, usually in the form of legislation. It is here that morality policy and moral panics produce unethical legislation. For example, the present situation of mass imprisonment is not the result of a democratically agreed on and analytically constructed policy but has emerged from a set of converging policies and decisions that do not form a rational and coherent response.

The views of the public about crime and crime control are also linked to moral panics. Surveys show that the public has a general tendency toward punitive measures and that Americans regard imprisonment as the most appropriate form of punishment for most crimes. There has been steady support for capital punishment since the 1970s, and those seeking public elective office are expected by the public to support the continuation of this form of punishment. Political and media attention to certain categories of crime has resulted in mandatory minimum sentencing, a war against drugs, truth-in-sentencing laws, and legislation designed to combat sexual predators and superpredators. Capital punishment is a major issue of morality policy, and the ethical arguments for and against capital punishment are discussed in this chapter.

A significant criminal justice policy issue is the development of private prisons. This raises a set of questions involving ethical issues—should imprisonment be administered by anyone other than the state? Is the profit motive compatible with the state's right to punish through imprisonment? Does the existence of private prisons fuel a demand for further and greater levels of imprisonment? How do private prisons resolve ethical issues concerned with the use of force? These issues are also considered in this chapter.

DISCUSSION QUESTIONS

1. Why is ethics important in criminal justice policy making? How do unethical and ethical policy-making decisions differ?

2. Explain the consequences that have resulted from one policy choice in the field of criminal justice, choosing from the following: the war on drugs, truth in sentencing, or sexual predators.

3. Discuss the ethics of the California law that gives prosecutors the right to decide whether the third-strike offense should be charged as a felony or a misdemeanor while providing no oversight of prosecutor charging decisions.

4. Outline the moral arguments against capital punishment.

5. How important is public opinion in criminal justice policy making? Explain by referencing two examples.

WEB RESOURCES

Center for Criminal Justice Policy Research. http://www.northeastern.edu/cssh/sccj/research/centers/center-for-criminal-justice-policy-research/
Common Sense for Drug Policy. http://www.csdp.org
Criminal Justice Policy Coalition (also includes information on internships). http://www.cjpc.org
Criminal Justice Policy Foundation. http://www.cjpf.org
Families Against Mandatory Sentencing. http://www.famm.org
Prison Policy Initiative. http://www.prisonpolicy.org/reports.html
Justice Policy Institute. http://www.justicepolicy.org/research/index.html
PolicyLink (Leadership for Policy). http://www.policylink.org/
The Sentencing Project. http://www.sentencingproject.org
Stanford Criminal Justice Center. http://www.law.stanford.edu/program/centers/scjc/
Violence Against Women Online Resources. http://ojp.gov/about/ocr/pdfs/vawafaqs.pdf

10

ETHICS AND THE "WAR ON TERRORISM"

The purpose of this chapter is to explore some of the ethical issues associated with the "War on Terrorism" that was declared following the events of 9/11. Establishing a normative and ethical approach toward countering terrorism may not seem to be salient to some in the face of the overwhelming events of 9/11.[1] Nevertheless, as indicated in the first chapter of this volume, ethics is about how we *ought* to live, and "ethical considerations are central to decisions involving discretion, force and due process that require people to make enlightened moral judgments" (Banks 2004: 4). Just as there are normative standards about how to conduct wars (the so-called "just war") and rules about what actions may be taken in time of war against combatants and civilians caught up in the conflict (the Geneva Conventions), so there are normative considerations applicable to the war against terrorism.[2]

This chapter will examine a number of the ethical issues arising out of the war on terrorism that began on September 11, 2001. It will not address the issue of whether terrorism can ever be morally justified, an issue that has been the subject of scholarly comment elsewhere (e.g., see Corlett 2003; Frey and Morris 1991; Held 1991; Narveson 1991; Steinhoff 2005). Rather, the chapter will explore the following issues:

- The meaning of *terrorism*
- Why the United States responded to the events of 9/11 by declaring a war against terrorism instead of treating the terrorist attack as a criminal justice or law enforcement issue
- The issue of the morally justifiable constraints and restrictions that a government should be permitted to impose on its citizens to succeed in the fight against terrorism
- In the context of events post–9/11, the ethics of applying torture to suspected terrorists
- The morality of targeted killing

---

1 Walklate and Mythen (2015: 64) make the important point that 9/11 and other terrorist attacks in Europe should not be seen as isolated events but situated in the context of "antecedent events within a world marked by economic and political flux and historically entrenched faith conflicts."

2 Walklate and Mythen (2015: 68) describe the War on Terror or Terrorism as " a concatenation of security processes and military practices set in train after the terrorist attacks on the United States in 2001" and "constituted by incursions and interventions made against organizations and regimes identified as terroristic in Asia, Africa and the Middle East."

A Closer Look

Explaining "Just War"

The just war tradition is a long-established framework that establishes a basis for judging the morality of a war as a form of violence. The two elements that are applied in judging whether or not a war meets the ethical standard of a "just war"—that is, to say that it is a legitimate and just war—are the *jus ad bellum* (the justice of undertaking a war) and the *jus in bello* (the just conduct of a war). The just war doctrine was developed over the centuries by a series of ethical theorists, including Augustine (CE 354–430), Thomas Aquinas (1225–1274), and Hugo Grotius (1583–1645). Elements of the doctrine of just war are now to be found in international instruments that regulate the conduct of wars, such as the 1949 Geneva Conventions and in the Charter of the United Nations, which stipulates the criteria for a state's use of force against another state (Enemark 2014: 4). Decisions to wage war under the just war doctrine require that the justice of opting for war is determined by whether a proposed war satisfies a number of criteria, including the following:

- The war has a just and proportionate cause.
- It is properly authorized.
- It is motivated by right intention.
- There is a reasonable prospect of success.
- It is a last resort (Enemark 2014: 23).

Therefore, just war doctrine's normative statement is that war is morally and ethically wrong, unless it can be justified according to this criteria.

Just war theory prohibits the intentional harming of civilians but allows for the doctrine of double effect, meaning that an attack on a military target that has the foreseen but unintended effect of harming innocent civilians does not violate just war rules. However, the unintentional harming of civilians must be proportionate to the importance and urgency of the military objective that itself cannot be achieved in any other way. The rules therefore require a positive commitment to save civilian lives (Primoratz 2004: 124).

In the war on terrorism, the United States has deployed armed drones to kill human targets in other countries. To what extent do attacks by armed drones that harm innocent civilians meet these requirements? See later in this chapter for a full discussion of the moral implications of targeted killing using armed drones.

DEFINING TERRORISM

An understanding of the meaning and scope of the term *terrorism* is central to any discussion; however, the definition of terrorism is problematic, and a number of "official" and legal definitions exist, as well as those suggested by researchers and commentators. Some explanations of the meaning of terrorism focus only on terrorism carried out by individuals and groups and ignore state terrorism altogether, others emphasize the political objective of terrorist acts, and still others frame terrorist acts as criminal events and downplay the political motivations. One clearly understood factor among all of these approaches is that terrorism is a method or means of achieving an objective. It is not an aim or objective in itself.

One definition proposed by academic commentator Paul Wilkinson (2001: 12–13) is this:

Terrorism is the systematic use of coercive intimidation, usually to service political ends. It is used to create and exploit a climate of fear among a wider target group than the immediate victims of the violence, and to publicize a cause, as well as to coerce a target to acceding to the terrorists' claims.

Here, there seems to be a clear focus on the political nature of terrorism. By contrast, the United Nations Security Council, in Resolution 1566 of October 2004 condemning terrorist acts, adopts more of a criminal perspective with no explicit mention of political objectives and also co-opts definitions in international agreements on terrorism:

> Criminal acts, including those against civilians, committed with the intent to cause death or serious bodily injury, or taking of hostages, with the purpose to provoke a state of terror in the general public or in a group of persons or particular persons, intimidate a population or compel a government or an international organization to do or to abstain from doing any act, which constitutes offenses within the scope of and as defined in the international conventions and protocols relating to terrorism. (Wilkinson 2006: 2)

Terrorists are motivated by political objectives, and while criminals employ violence (often similar to that of terrorists, including kidnapping, murder, arson) to achieve their ends, their motivation is quite different from that of terrorists because criminals commonly act solely to secure a material gain. As discussed later, the United States regards terrorism not as criminal activity, but as a "form of war" and "as a threat to national security" (Whittaker 2003: 262).

The U.S. Code Title 22, Section 2656, avoids any reference to state terrorism, limits itself to violence, and introduces a separate notion of international terrorism:

> The term terrorism means premeditated politically motivated violence perpetrated against non-combatant targets by sub-national groups or clandestine agents, usually intended to influence an audience. The term international terrorism means terrorism involving citizens or the territory of more than one country. The term terrorist group means any group practicing, or that has significant subgroups that practice, international terrorism. (Wilkinson 2006: 3)

The FBI relies on a definition in the U.S. Code of Federal Regulations that focuses on coercion, unlawfulness, and offenses against property and includes social as well as political objectives: "Terrorism is the unlawful use of force and violence against person or property to intimidate or coerce a government, the civilian population, or any segment thereof, in further of political or social objectives" (Kapitan 2005: 21). The U.S. Defense Department defines terrorism as "the unlawful use or threatened use of force or violence against individuals or property to coerce or intimidate governments or societies, often to achieve political, religious, or ideological objectives" (p. 21). This definition includes a wider range of objectives than that used by the FBI and also encompasses threats as well as actual use of violence.

These multiple definitions demonstrate Michael Freeman's (2005: 44) point that there is no "correct" definition of terrorism and that the term bundles together a multiplicity of acts and motivations. According to Paul Hoffman (2004: 938), the tendency to give a broad and expansive definition to terrorism has caused nonterrorist activity to be caught up within the prohibition and has provided a basis for repressive regimes to conduct so-called antiterrorist campaigns.

Terrorism as a Moral Judgment

As an organizing concept, the term *terrorism* conveys a moral judgment about the illicit activity of a group of persons, and the act of labeling a group *terrorist* transmits moral condemnation. Irrationality and fanaticism are also associated with terrorism, and these connotations tend to enhance the security threat and promote citizen solidarity in response to that threat. When an act is interpreted as terrorism, it fosters public fears about continued unpredictable attacks on civilians. As Card (2010: 125) expresses it, "a terrorist interpretation raises the spectre of more and worse to come" and therefore differentiates acts of terrorism from common criminality, or the acts of mentally disturbed persons who are out of control.

Both the media and government have deployed a new rhetoric of terror constructed from the events of 9/11. They represent and define terrorism as any activity that offends against the rules of legitimate political violence by ignoring the distinction between combatants and civilians and that employs methods that are unsanctioned, such as hijacking commercial airliners and murdering hostages (Kapitan 2005: 23).

Acts of terrorism committed by states are excluded from this discourse, even though, as Tomis Kapitan (p. 27) notes, terrorism by states is a more prevalent and deadly form of terrorism than terrorism by groups. As Walter Laqueur (1987) observes, "Acts of terror carried out by police states and tyrannical governments, in general, have been responsible for a thousand times more victims and more misery than all actions of individual terrorism taken together" (p. 146).

A discourse that demonizes all terrorists, whatever their motivation or strategy, denies an understanding of the terrorist point of view and means that government policies that might have contributed to the grievances of those who have adopted terrorism are not scrutinized. As well, it minimizes the likelihood of negotiating with any terrorists—even the more "traditional" terrorist groups—encourages the use of force and violence to counterterrorists, and enables governments to exploit the fears of the public and overrule any objections to the means employed to respond to and counter terrorists (Kapitan 2005: 27).

Thus, the intricacies of the legal definition of terrorism, the rhetoric associated with terrorism, and the contemporary discourse that shapes and represents terrorism so inadequately illustrate the complexity of explaining terrorism and therefore of developing strategies to counter it.

WARFARE OR CRIME CONTROL?

Soon after 9/11, the United States designated its counterterrorist strategy a "war on terrorism," and its plans and operations have been characterized as warfare rather than law enforcement.[3] More recently, in March 2009 the Obama administration altered the operational name from "Global War on Terror" to "Overseas Contingency Operation" (Walklate and Mythen 2015: 79), but counterterrorist strategies were not substantively changed. Unlike the "wars" against drugs, poverty, and crime proclaimed by various U.S. administrations, the war on terrorism is a real war that incorporates

elements of a conventional war but with significant differences. For example, traditional or conventional conflicts characterized as wars are fought against other states, have a definite duration, and conclude when one of the parties is acknowledged as the victor. In contrast, the war against terrorism is directed not at states but at individuals and groups of persons who practice terrorism as a method of achieving their political and other goals.[4] Also, the U.S. administration has indicated that the war against terrorism will continue until terrorism is ultimately defeated.[5] Thus, it has no defined end point, and the concept of war as employed traditionally gives little guidance about applicable procedures. Richard Wilson (2005: 30) points out that a state of permanent war with no end in sight is not a viable strategy for any nation—it is neither sustainable nor affordable. Importantly, war is also a legal construct associated with numerous rules concerning the use of force, the applicability of which to a battle against terrorism is unclear. In differentiating a war against terrorism from regular warfare, Gabriella Blum and Philip B. Heymann (2010: 28–29) point to

> the nature of the enemy (nonstate, elusive), the location of hostilities (potentially all over the globe), the type of tactics employed (a mix of law enforcement means and combat operations), and the ultimate aim of the relevant parties (the unclear terms of "victory").

---

3 Blum and Heymann (2010: xiv) point out that *war* is a highly charged term morally that "exacerbates the sense of suspicion, hostility, and defensive-offensive posturing on all sides to the conflict."

4 Some argue that the "war on terror" is an incorrect description because terrorism is not an enemy, but a method used by those perceived to be enemies (Van Brunschot and Kennedy 2008: 89).

5 In an address to a joint session of Congress on September 20, 2001, President Bush stated, "Our war on terror begins with al-Qaeda, but it does not end there. It will not end until every terrorist group of global reach has been found, stopped and defeated" (quoted in Walklate and Mythen 2015: 68). In December 2012, the outgoing counsel to the U.S. Defense Department, Jeh Johnson, in an address at the Oxford Union, U.K., asked rhetorically, "Now that efforts by the U.S. military against al-Qaeda are in their 12th year, we must also ask ourselves: How will this conflict end . . . ? War must be regarded as a finite, extraordinary and unnatural state of affairs. We must not accept the current conflict, and all that it entails, as the 'new normal'" (quoted in *The Guardian*, January 2013).

The aims and objectives of al-Qaeda were announced on February 23, 1998, when Osama bin Laden issued a *fatwa* setting up a World Islamic Front for *Jihad,* announcing, "It is the duty of all Muslims to kill U.S. citizens—civilian or military, and their allies—everywhere" (in Wilkinson 2006: 5). Al-Qaeda's objectives are to expel U.S. citizens and other infidels from the Middle East, to topple Muslim governments that they believe fail to practice true Islam, and ultimately, to set up an Islamist caliphate comprised of all Muslims everywhere. Notwithstanding the death of Osama bin Laden on May 2, 2011, at the hands of U.S. Special Forces, al-Qaeda continues to be a functioning terrorist entity. More recently, the creation and growth of the entity known as ISIS or ISIL, the Islamic State of Iraq and the Levant, has posed a new counterterrorist challenge.

Given that the war on terrorism is neither a metaphorical war like those concerning crime, poverty, and drugs, nor a conventional war, it generates a set of moral questions about how it should be conducted.

In considering the strategy of a U.S. war against terrorism, it is appropriate to look at the experience of other states faced with similar threats to national security. In the case of the terror campaign mounted by the Irish Republican Army against the U.K. government in Northern Ireland, the role of the military was to support the police and civil authorities in countering the terrorist threat.[6] John McEldowney notes (2005: 773) that, as in the United States, the effect of tough, new antiterrorist laws in the United Kingdom has been to accrete power to the executive. Similarly, in the United States the content of the criminal law has undergone significant changes reflecting the threat of terrorism, in particular through the Patriot Act. As Zedner (2014: 100, 115) notes, there has been a focus on criminalizing acts that are considered preparatory to the commission of terrorism (precursor offenses) and expanding definitions of terrorism as part of a general preventive strategy.

A Criminal Justice Approach to Terrorism

In his State of the Union speech given on January 20, 2004, President Bush explicitly abandoned a criminal justice strategy to counterterrorism, stating,

> I know that some people question if America is really in a war at all. They view terrorism more as a crime, a problem to be solved mainly with law enforcement and indictments. After the World Trade Center was attacked in 1993, some of the guilty were indicted and tried and convicted and sent to prison. But the matter was not settled. The terrorists were still training and plotting in other nations and drawing up more ambitious plans. After the chaos and carnage of September 11th, it is not enough to serve our enemies with legal papers. The terrorists and their supporters declared war on the United States, and war is what they got. (in Ackerman 2004: 1871)

Clearly, the "war they got" bears no resemblance to the metaphorical wars declared by previous administrations—namely, the wars on drugs, on organized crime and drug racketeers, and on poverty, all of which were preceded by the Cold War.[7] The U.S. administration simply took the position that the events of 9/11 were so horrendous that the appropriate response should be nothing less than a declaration of war, and it viewed the justice system as lacking the capacity to prosecute terrorism.

However, in fact, the war against terrorism has adopted both warlike and law enforcement measures in its overall strategy. For example, while measures have been taken under the Patriot Act to strengthen crime control in the United States with the aim of preventing terrorist acts in the homeland, the Bush administration also conducted wars in Iraq and Afghanistan that employed conventional military forces and military strategies. Nevertheless, wars and criminal justice are distinctly different categories. Clark McCauley (2009: 64–68), in reviewing the two responses to terrorism, suggests they conflict and that the advantage lies in the criminal justice approach:

---

6   In the United Kingdom, the events of 9/11 resulted in the enactment of the Anti-Terrorism, Crime, and Security Act of 2001, granting powers to arrest and detain suspected terrorists without giving reasons and for indefinite periods (McEldowney 2005: 771).

7   Writing about the War on Crime, Alison Young (1996) notes that employing "'a militaristic metaphor' shuts down debate, draws boundaries about which side is morally in the right and incorporates the belief in an ultimate outright winner" (p. 7).

- War and justice commence and cease in different ways—war with a peace treaty while criminal justice is always an ongoing effort.
- They differ in their targeting because a criminal violation is specific and individual, while the target of a war is a group of often numerous enemies in the form of an army and a nation-state.
- They differ in their categorization of the "enemy" because criminals are stereotypically regarded as aberrant and atypical, while military forces are not.
- A declaration of war is a statement that the survival of the nation is at stake, and all resources are devoted to the demands of war, whereas the criminal justice system is a recurrent aspect of government that has to compete for resources with other government agencies.
- Wars tend to call up a harsher and less equitable set of values because survival is at stake, but criminal justice relies on a distinct set of rules developed to govern adversarial contests in the courts.
- Mistakes in criminal law can be corrected through appropriate processes and individuals can be restored to their former status, but in wartime, collateral damage to civilians and erroneously targeting one's own forces are mistakes that cannot be undone or corrected.

Wilson (2005: 30) suggests that a criminal justice approach to terrorism would classify terrorist crimes not as acts of war, but more as crimes against humanity that could be prosecuted both nationally and internationally. In this sense, terrorist crimes would fall into that category of offense coming under international jurisdiction, like migration, the environment, and natural disasters. He notes that it was only when the United Kingdom moved from a military to a law enforcement model in Ireland that the Irish terrorist groups gave up their struggle (p. 33). He suggests that a justice strategy would involve less abuse of detainees' human rights because law enforcement agencies are trained in respecting suspects' rights.

How should the war on terrorism be viewed and conceptualized from the criminal justice perspective? According to David Klinger and Charles Heal (2011), terrorism can be "viewed through prisms that call for both military and criminal responses" (p. 31). John Crank and Patricia Gregor (2005) argue that "issues in counter-terrorism in the U.S. are framed by the conflict between the competing justice perspectives of crime control and due

process" (p. 9) and that the administration has opted for the crime control model. This is said to be evidenced by the enactment of the Patriot Act and its predecessor, the 1996 Antiterrorism and Effective Death Penalty Act. Collectively, these laws have weakened a variety of controls that previously ensured due process and privacy rights (p. 78) and have instead reinforced the kind of punitive crime control strategies outlined in Chapters 7 and 9 of this book. However, it can be argued that Crank and Gregor's perspective on the policy response to 9/11 is too narrow because they locate counterterrorism only within the field of criminal justice and fail to recognize that issues in counterterrorism in the United States are framed by the notion of protecting national security and not by ordinary policies and programs of crime control at all.

For example, in response to the events of 9/11, the Patriot Act sought to enhance national security through what had previously been regarded as generic crime control measures. It introduced more than 1,000 provisions concerning surveillance on financial transactions and border control, as well as new criminal offenses and penalties against terrorism. The act is targeted at non–U.S. citizen terrorists (Mertens 2005: 285), was formulated to augment national security, and both conceptually and in policy terms is outside the conventional parameters of crime control legislation. The act has been described as having been "passed in response to a largely undefined threat from a poorly understood source" (Heymann and Kayyem 2005: 5).

Overall, Wilkinson (2001: 125) favors employing a criminal justice model in countering terrorism and using law enforcement agencies as the spearhead. He notes that these agencies enjoy advantages over the military in handling terrorism, particularly because of their legitimacy in the eyes of the public but also in relation to local knowledge, of their familiarity with the law and with techniques of criminal investigation, and of their access to international sources of assistance and cooperation through agencies such as Interpol.

Other commentators see the merit of the criminal justice approach as a means of ensuring that legal protections and judicial oversight are provided to accused persons through the prosecution process. Therefore, "in place of indefinite preventive detention or extraordinary rendition, the criminal justice model promises a sentence proportionate to the gravity of the offence and prison conditions that accord with prison law and human rights protections" (Zedner 2014: 109). This is especially important when security and intelligence officials are likely to regard suspected persons as sources of intelligence rather than accused persons in criminal trials (p. 107). Nevertheless, as Zedner acknowledges, there are great divergences between intelligence gained through various sources and evidence that will hold up in a criminal trial. It is in such cases that "the tension between the security paradigm and the criminal justice model is acute" (p. 111). The British have met this challenge by introducing "control orders" intended to impede the planning of terrorist attacks by placing restrictions on suspected persons' freedom of movement and association. Such orders operate independently of the criminal justice system (p. 121).

Waging a War on Terrorism

In the fight against terrorism, the criminal justice system has been judged inadequate or inappropriate. Further, while the United States considers itself "at war," it does not regard many of those taken prisoner in that war as prisoners of war who are to be treated in accordance with the rules laid down in the Geneva Conventions (ICRC 2006), especially the Third and Fourth Conventions, which are concerned with the protection and treatment of combatants captured during an international armed conflict and with civilians who are involved in the armed conflict. Article Five of the Third Convention says that if there is a doubt about the status of persons, the issue has to be determined by a competent tribunal, and in the meantime, the persons must enjoy the protection of the convention.

Proponents of the convention approach to the war argue, contrary to the U.S. strategy, that prisoners arrested following 9/11 are to be considered prisoners of war (POWs) until a competent tribunal determines otherwise (Kanstroom 2007). The United States, however, has categorized prisoners as unlawful combatants with no Geneva Convention rights. As noted by Klinger and Heal (2011: 35), the Geneva Conventions establish a regime for warfare conducted between nation-states involving uniformed national militaries. It is improbable that

terrorists will claim to be acting on behalf of any nation-state and equally unlikely they will be wearing uniforms. Thus, in the Overseas Contingency Operation, prisoners captured in Afghanistan or in other countries have been labeled *unlawful combatants*[8] and interned without trial in a prison at Guantanamo Bay, Cuba, or in a selected number of U.S. bases overseas. According to a military order issued on November 13, 2001, prisoners who are not U.S. citizens and who are alleged to be terrorists are not to be tried in the U.S. federal courts, but by a system of military commissions composed of military officers (Wilkinson 2006: 62).[9] Military commissions are rooted in U.S. history and were employed during the American Revolution, the Mexican–American War, and especially during the Civil War. Guantanamo Bay itself, and the special procedures and processes that are being employed to bring suspected terrorists to justice, clearly stand apart from the U.S. criminal justice system.

---

8 Emcke (2005) suggests that terming the prisoners *unlawful combatants* was a device to "avoid all the existing rules, laws, and conventions regarding prisoners of war or other prisoners" and that creating this new category meant that the U.S. administration need not concern itself with rights issues that would have restricted its ability to incarcerate, interrogate, prosecute, or torture those arrested (p. 237).

9 In *Hamdi v. Rumsfeld* (2004), which dealt with the detention of an enemy combatant, the U.S. Supreme Court held that a U.S. citizen who was alleged to have been engaged in supporting forces hostile to the United States must receive adjudication by a neutral tribunal concerning the validity of his classification as an enemy combatant (in Heymann Kayyem 2005: 41). The Court ruled that a citizen who is detained must be provided with notice of the basis for his classification as an "enemy combatant" and given an opportunity to rebut the government's case before an independent decision-maker. Such persons are also entitled to counsel, but the Court suggested that in any proceedings hearsay evidence might be admitted and that there could be a rebuttable presumption in favor of the truth of the government's evidence. This procedure would apply to determine the continued detention of such a person (Scheid 2010: 11). The government argued in Hamdi that a two-page statement on oath by Michael Mobbs (described as an Advisor to the Undersecretary of Defense for Policy) was sufficient evidence to continue to detain Hamdi. The statement was described by the district court judge in the case as "little more than the government's say so." It stated that a series of U.S. military screening teams had concluded that Hamdi was correctly described as an enemy combatant (p. 26).

Detainees held in preventive detention without any criminal charge were described by President Obama in a 2009 major national security address as presenting the greatest difficulty because it is considered they cannot be released or prosecuted and must be held in "prolonged detention" (Scheid 2010: 1). According to Scheid (p. 4), those judged to be "mega-terrorists" can justifiably be held in prolonged detention: He explains a megaterrorist as someone who threatens a level of destruction far beyond ordinary criminal activity and who seeks to challenge the legitimacy of the state. Megaterrorism is therefore akin to warfare or, as Scheid puts it, "quasi-war" (p. 5).

Risks of a Warlike Approach

In discussing a war against terrorism that includes offensive operations and military reprisals against terrorists overseas, as well as their sponsor states, and that does not adopt the criminal justice approach, Wilkinson (2001: 128–129) points out several risks:

- The danger that a military response could provoke a wider conflict involving a diminished focus on the relevant terrorist group in favor of a broader multistate strategy
- The danger that the death of innocent civilians will diminish international sympathy for the victim state and shift the moral high ground away from that state
- The difficulties associated with gaining and ensuring the continuing support of allies when military actions are taken unilaterally
- The danger that military action will give rise to false expectations of a total defeat of terrorism
- The probability of deaths or injury of members of the civilian population given the lethality of modern weaponry and firepower (p. 104).

Wilkinson contends that war constitutes a greater evil than terrorism because of its potential to cause a far greater number of deaths and far greater destruction. This implies that a war against terrorism pursued internationally could potentially generate multiple wars—not only against terrorist groups but also against states alleged to be sponsoring terrorism. Nevertheless, he acknowledges that the military warfare model does carry with it some advantages, including responding to public demands for tough action.

Justifications for Waging War

Why has the U.S. administration elected to wage a war in response to the events of 9/11 rather than pursue a law enforcement approach? Hoffman (2004) argues that the questions of whether the war against terrorism is a war and, if so, what the nature of that war is, are crucial questions in examining counterterrorist activity that challenges the international regime protecting human rights. As he puts it, "One of the characteristics of the war on terrorism is a refusal to accept that any body of law applies to the way this 'war' is waged" (p. 939). He contends that the U.S. response to 9/11 has led to the attrition of rights because by defining the fight against terrorism as a war the United States eliminates many of the protections of international human rights law and international humanitarian law (p. 940). Hoffman further suggests that the war "exists in a parallel legal universe in which compliance with legal norms is a matter of executive grace or is taken out of diplomatic or public relations necessity" (p. 940). He therefore calls into question the morality of the U.S. counterterrorist strategy.

Blum and Heymann (2010: xiii) propose three reasons for adopting the war paradigm: It permitted the employment of warlike measures such as military strikes and battlefield detention concurrently with law enforcement measures such as arrest and extradition; it enabled the executive branch of government to exercise wide powers under the authority of the president as commander-in-chief; and it gave the executive the leverage to demand almost any resources in the furtherance of winning the war.

In support of the warfare approach, some commentators suggest that the kind of terrorism practiced by al-Qaeda is of an entirely different nature than that conducted by more "traditional" terrorist groups, such as the ETA in Spain or FARC in Colombia or the IRA in Northern Ireland. Unlike those groups, al-Qaeda has explicitly embraced a strategy of mass killing, or as Brian Jenkins has written, terrorists in the 1970s and 1980s wanted "a lot of people watching, not a lot of people dead" (in Wilkinson 2006: 5).

Other Responses to Terrorism

How then should a democratic government respond to terrorism if it is inappropriate to wage a war against it? Wilkinson (2001: 94–95) elaborates a "hard-line approach" that nonetheless remains within the boundaries of the criminal justice system. His model includes the following elements:

1. The government must avoid overreaction and repression that could have the effect of eroding or even negating democracy.

2. The government must avoid underreaction, as this would permit terrorists to control territory or otherwise determine the course of events.

3. Both the government and its security forces must adhere to the rule of law because failure to do so will undermine their legitimacy and diminish public confidence in the criminal justice system.

4. The government must conduct a successful intelligence war.

5. Intelligence agencies must be responsible to civilian authorities and fully accountable.

6. Special legislation needed to counter terrorism must be temporary or contain "sunset clauses" that make it subject to renewal by the legislative body.

7. Terrorists should be treated as criminals and not afforded any special status, such as that of a political prisoner.

8. Terrorist propaganda must always be countered to avoid terrorists achieving their aims through political advocacy.

9. The government should avoid granting major concessions to terrorists because this encourages a perception that government is weak in the face of pressure.

Bruce Ackerman (2004) argues that the U.S. response to terrorism is not a war, but a "state of emergency," a concept located in the constitutions of many states in time of war or national emergency that permits derogations from guaranteed human rights provisions, usually for limited periods, to deal with the emergency. In Ackerman's view, public acceptance of a war against "something as amorphous as terrorism" lowers the bar for engaging in more conventional wars against actual states and avoids having to justify each engagement in the "war" as a separate and distinct war of its own. For example, Ackerman argues that the actions taken against Afghanistan and Iraq have been packaged as "battles" subsumed within the entirety of the amorphous war on terrorism. As he points out, it is far easier in constitutional terms for the president to conduct mere battles without congressional authorization because he can argue that he is simply exercising his powers as commander-in-chief.

Blum and Heymann (2010: xvi) suggest that a new paradigm that is neither warfare nor law enforcement is required because international terrorism (along with piracy and action against drug cartels) does not easily fit within either alternative paradigm. They call for an original body of domestic and international law providing powers that can be inserted in the space between traditional warfare and law enforcement. This may be a task for the long term, so in the interim, they propose adopting the paradigm that is most appropriate to the scale of the threat and allow only minimal departures from the war or law enforcement models. For example, if the choice is to supplement domestic powers with wartime powers, this necessarily means accepting also the protections that prevent abuse of powers in wartime. They see the key issue as one of never permitting "a new dark realm of no law, where the powers of killing, interrogating, detaining without trial, or departing from due process procedures are exercised without protections" (p. xviii).

What Are the Morally Justifiable Constraints and Restrictions That a Government Should Be Permitted to Impose on Its Citizens in a War on Terrorism?

Since 9/11, philosophers and terrorism theorists have been debating the extent of the permissible restrictions on rights and freedoms perceived "necessary" to prosecute the war against terrorism. Essentially, the debate has centered on whether any restrictions at all should be imposed, and, if they are, the correct balance between rights and restrictions in a counterterrorist situation. Experience since 9/11 has shown that the U.S. public has become more willing to accept restrictions on rights and freedoms because the emotions generated by acts of terrorism can promote great public insecurity.

Wilkinson (2006) points out the belief that in the battle against terrorism, terrorists must be suppressed "with crushing military force" on the assumption that "the only good terrorist is a dead terrorist" (p. 63). Thus, some advocate that the end justifies the means, that terrorists through their actions have forfeited constitutional and human rights, that the criminal courts are inappropriate for these prisoners, and that even torture can be justified in some circumstances. Others argue that the ends do not justify the means and that abandoning due process protection under U.S. law conflicts with the values and principles that are the foundation of the democracy being defended against terrorist attack. Wilkinson argues that abridging rights corrupts public officials and the military and promotes major injustices in the name of national security.

In support of the notion that it is possible to defeat terrorism without seriously restricting rights, Wilkinson cites the example of measures taken in Italy during the 1970s when that country experienced significant terrorist activity by the Red Brigades. In 1975, the Italian minister for justice introduced legislation giving the police increased powers of arrest and search on suspicion of an offense and expanded the permitted use of firearms (Wilkinson 2006: 65). Additionally, the Italians promoted and established effective coordination between police and intelligence services under a newly created coordination office. This produced high-quality intelligence that enabled the justice system to disrupt and ultimately terminate the activities of the Red Brigades (p. 66). In the early 1980s, judges were empowered to reduce sentences imposed on convicted terrorists who agreed to give testimony for the state under a so-called *pentiti* (repentant) law. This enabled the government to break open the Red Brigades' cells. Whether the events of 9/11 and subsequent events are congruent with the activities of the Red Brigades is perhaps open to question.

Restricting Rights: Patriot Act and Associated Measures

As noted earlier, the U.S. response to terrorism has included the enactment of the Patriot Act, which introduced restrictions on some democratic rights, including giving the FBI wide and unprecedented access to information previously kept private—a power that the FBI employed, using a so-called national security letter, to illegally accumulate intimate information about some 52,000

persons and store it in a database accessible to about 12,000 federal, state, and local law enforcement agencies (Smith 2007). This voluminous law was passed only 6 weeks after 9/11.

As well, a package of measures forming part of the overall counterterrorist strategy impacted rights and freedoms. The measures are noted by Peter Manning (2006: 458) as follows:

- New visa and immigration procedures (which included detaining more than 1,200 immigrants of Middle Eastern descent following 9/11, based on no other factors than their origin)
- New screening procedures for passengers boarding aircraft
- Designing and integrating extensive databases covering visitors to the United States and U.S. citizens
- Consolidating data gathered at immigration and customs locations
- Establishing the Department of Homeland Security with some 170,000 employees
- Establishing the Transport Security Administration (TSA) within the Department of Homeland Security and thereby federalizing the business of airport security
- Establishing a federal directorate of intelligence

These measures were of course supplemented by the use of the U.S. facility at Guantanamo Bay, Cuba, to hold alleged terrorists; the use of extraordinary rendition[10] to move terrorists from country to country for purposes believed to relate to their interrogation (allegedly through torture); and the invasions of Afghanistan and Iraq.

National Security Considerations

Thus, the response to terrorism was represented by a series of measures designed to ensure the security of the nation. However, as John Kleinig (2011: 364) points out, the notion of national security is quite problematic because it is rarely defined in law and, even when it is clarified, tends to be defined very broadly. Kleinig views the concept as linked to

---

10 As Walklate and Mythen (2015: 82) explain, extraordinary rendition "is a strategy of gleaning information from terrorist suspects using a variety of methods of interrogation. . . . In practice it involves the kidnap, detention and movement of terrorist suspects to countries where the threshold for the use of violence by the state is low."

the absence of a threat, fear, or sense of insecurity, associated with more than just securing national borders and as signifying a threat to a way of life. Our understanding of the concept of national security will necessarily shape an assessment of the morality of measures intended to secure it, but, as Kleinig notes, there is a tendency for governments to give the concept a wide meaning and also to "overestimate the actual threat posed by what they consider will endanger it" (p. 366).

Wilson (2005) sees a distinct policy dichotomy between security and rights, contending that following 9/11 "the Bush administration advanced a formulation of international security that detached rights from security concerns" (p. 6). He claims that the U.S. government's hostility to the International Criminal Court is an example of this gulf between human rights and national security, as is the emphasis in Afghanistan and Iraq on fighting terrorism rather than reestablishing the rule of law and human rights.

Luban (in Wilson 2005: 26) suggests it is wrong to focus on whether democratic freedoms should be sacrificed in the interests of national security. This approach assumes that the rights of others are being sacrificed for "our security," that favoring additional security demonstrates a tough-minded response to terrorism, that issues of guilt or innocence have to be decided by the president, and that exceptional measures to counterterrorism are necessary but will only be short term.

Achieving a Balance: Rights or Restrictions?

Some commentators believe it is misconceived to represent the issue of rights and restrictions or security and liberties in terms of achieving a balance. Ronald Dworkin (2006: 286) maintains that the appropriate response is to ask what justice requires. He contends that the government must treat everyone as having equal status and with equal concern because every human life has an equal value. Thus, a system of criminal law should treat all equally in equal cases, and if it denies one category of suspects rights considered essential for others, it acts unfairly. If a system unfairly targets non-U.S. citizens, as does the Patriot Act, Dworkin judges that it must satisfy two requirements. First, it must acknowledge that it is differentiating suspects unjustly for security reasons, and second, it must diminish that injustice by permitting only the minimum curtailment of rights possible. Dworkin argues that the Patriot Act does not satisfy these conditions.

Similarly, Kleinig (2011: 369) questions whether liberty and security are capable of being balanced as suggested, even when taking a consequentialist approach where the appropriate balance is that which maximizes good for the greatest number. He notes that the two values are not equal and that restrictions on liberty are likely to be more certain than dangers to security. Thus, actual restrictions on liberty are to be weighed against *risks* to security. Moreover, as he notes, freedoms of speech and association are not easily susceptible to expansion or contraction along a continuum because they are regarded as core elements for human flourishing (p. 373). He concludes that the notion of balancing is simplistic, as it is based on an underlying belief that what we lose in liberty, we gain in security. What we need, he contends, is some assurance that restrictions will actually increase our security (p. 375).

The notion that security and liberty can be balanced has also been questioned by Waldron (2012: 112), who argues for the need to recognize that there are multiple security issues, including security of the public as opposed to security of the person from unwarranted interference by government agencies. Therefore, the existence of a terrorist threat does not necessarily reduce threats to the person from the state. As he puts it, "The net threat from the state goes up as the power accorded to the state increases" (p. 43).

Freeman (2005: 53) observes that striking a balance between human rights and security in an age of terrorism is a complex matter and that we need to "analyze clearly which human rights are at stake under the threat of terrorism, and which risks we ought to take" (p. 53). Since we, the general public, do not know the risks of terrorism, we rely on government for advice, and our government controls the information. Freeman explains that while we should give the government considerable discretion, "democratic politicians should not be trusted too much." Freeman points out that legislative and judicial oversight may not be sufficient to protect rights and advocates an active civil society as a counterbalance to the power of the state.

In his contribution to the debate on balancing rights and restrictions, Fernando Teson (2005) argues that the balancing test should be that "a security measure is justified if, and only if, the amount of freedom it restricts is necessary to preserve the total system of freedom threatened by internal or external enemies" (p. 64). He contends that threats to security almost never justify restricting personal liberties because human rights are deontological concepts (see Chapter 12) and are conceived as trumping the pursuit of utility or the general welfare. Teson illustrates his argument with the following example (pp. 65–66):

> A villain who asks me to shoot an innocent person says if I refuse he will shoot two innocent persons. If I refuse, I can justify my decision not to kill even with the certain consequence of the death of two others in two ways. Firstly, I may say the right to life is absolute and my duty not to kill an innocent person cannot be overridden by the consequences of complying with that duty even if the consequences are the murder of more innocent persons. Secondly, I can say that I am prohibited from violating the innocent person's right to life by shooting her regardless of what others may do.

Applying this example to restrictions in the interests of national security, Teson (2005: 65–66) notes that a liberal would argue that violating individual rights is a graver issue than the government allowing deaths to occur by terrorist attacks. A second argument is that rights can be categorized in terms of their fundamental importance, so, for example, the freedom against torture or against indefinite detention rank as being more vital than other rights. Thus, in the interests of national security, while other rights might be restricted, those ought not to be sacrificed to the general welfare (p. 67).

Limiting Restrictions

When a terrorist event causes a government to take emergency action such as suspending habeas corpus, it runs the risk of alienating its citizens and playing into the hands of terrorist tactics (Wilkinson 2001: 23). More fundamentally, Wilkinson contends that

> it must be a cardinal principle of a liberal democracy in dealing with the problems of terrorism, however serious these may be, never to be tempted into using methods which are incompatible with the liberal values of humanity, liberty, and justice. (p. 115)

Thus, he argues, a liberal democracy faced with terrorism must follow a path between, on the one hand, the dangers of repression, and, on the other hand, inaction. It is crucial that counterterrorist measures are limited to just that, countering terrorism, and that a government should not take advantage of a terrorist situation to abuse exceptional powers by using them for extraneous purposes. Thus, both politically and morally, a government facing a terrorist threat must avoid repressive overreaction (Wilkinson 2001: 115). As an example of overreaction, Wilkinson cites the use of emergency powers by the British government in Northern Ireland that authorized internment without trial. This measure is now widely regarded as having been counterproductive because although it was originally introduced to protect witnesses, juries, and magistrates from intimidation, it was in practice used by the security forces to arrest large numbers of people who had no connection with terrorist operations.

According to Wilkinson, internment without trial "should only be contemplated in the eventuality of a full-scale civil war, when all other means of curbing the escalation of violence on a massive scale have failed" (2001: 116). In Northern Ireland, using internment promoted recruitment into the Irish Republican Army, motivated many Catholics to give support to the terrorist cause, and greatly increased the level of violence as well as funding support for the IRA from the United States.

Writing post–9/11, Wilkinson (2006) contends that those who claim that the world can no longer afford to ensure that measures to prevent and combat terrorism accord with the rule of law and principles of human rights are themselves "guilty of being soft on terrorism" (p. xvi). He argues that supporting or condoning violations of human rights and liberal democratic principles undermines respect for international and national laws and places those who advocate or support such violations on the same moral level as the terrorists. As he puts it, "By suppressing human rights in the name of protecting national security they play into the hands of terrorists" (p. xvi).

Simpson (2005) agrees with Wilkinson that the justifications offered by the U.S. government for invading personal privacy are self-contradictory and counterproductive. He articulates his concern by asking, "How can the U.S. proclaim its goal in the war on terrorism to be defense of the free and civilized world if its own domestic acts are denials of freedom and civilization?" (p. 204).

In a major contribution to this debate, Michael Ignatieff (2004: viii) explores the issue of how a democracy can respond to terrorism without destroying the values for which it stands. He takes a position between those who argue in absolutist terms that no restrictions on rights ought to be imposed or justified and those advocating a consequentialist approach who judge counterterrorist measures purely by their effectiveness. Ignatieff would prohibit certain torture, illegal detention, and unlawful assassination on the basis that they violate "foundational commitments to justice and dignity" (p. viii). He notes that democracies commonly permit derogations from guaranteed rights and freedoms in emergencies, so rights do not always trump other considerations like national security, but ultimately, in his view, it is the task of the courts, the media, and the legislators to scrutinize such measures for justifiability. Ignatieff points out that in an emergency, such as a terrorist attack, we have to trust our leaders to respond rapidly in our interests but that over the longer term, in determining the balance between security and liberty, we must rely on our democratic institutions to conduct oversight and scrutiny. Ignatieff's overall approach is a "lesser evil position" (p. 8) under which, in a terrorist emergency, rights do not trump necessary measures, but neither do such measures trump rights. Instead, Ignatieff sets a series of tests for leaders as follows:

1. Do the proposed national security measures violate individual dignity? Within the concept of individual dignity, he includes rights against cruel and unusual punishment, torture, penal servitude, extrajudicial execution, and the rendition[11] of prisoners to states that practice torture.

2. The national security measures must pass "the conservative test" (p. 24) that questions the necessity for the proposed measures. Ignatieff argues this test would bar measures such as suspension of habeas

corpus, would require all detention to be subject to review by the courts, and would ensure that prisoners have access to counsel.

3. Applying a consequentialist approach (see Chapter 13) to counterterrorist measures means asking whether they will render citizens more secure in the long term. Necessary measures must function as a last resort in the sense that less coercive means must be judged as inadequate, and all measures should be capable of being sanctioned by the courts at some point in time.

4. Finally, the measures should be congruent with international obligations relating to rights and freedoms.

Ignatieff's view is that if the proposed countermeasures fail the previously described tests, the battle against terrorism will have to be waged without them because, as he puts it, "It is the very nature of a democracy that it not only does, but should, fight with one hand tied behind its back" (2004: 24).

In his critique of Ignatieff's views, Wilson (2005) notes that "Michael Ignatieff's 'lesser evil' ethics and over reliance on a consequentialist ethics places him much closer to the antirights philosophical tradition of utilitarianism than the liberal tradition of human rights" (p. 19). Philosophically and politically, "utilitarian consequentialism is about as far from an ethics of human rights as one can travel." As Wilson explains,

> Lesser evil reasoning makes a virtue out of lowering accepted standards and surrendering safeguards on individual liberties. In the hands of government officials, it enables unrestrained presidential authority and a disregard for long standing restraints on the conduct of war. (p. 19)

Rights, Restrictions and Balancing

In the debate on restrictions on rights and freedoms in the interests of national security and countering terrorism, the differing perspectives all seek the normative framework for government action. While some advocate no restrictions, arguing that governments will abuse special powers and that restrictions on liberty mirror the tactics of the terrorists themselves, others believe that we must place confidence in government and rely on oversight through the legislature and the judiciary. When governments impose restrictions, they can usually rely on public support, at least in the short term, but they must guard against

---

11 As Philip Heymann and Juliette Kayyem (2005) point out, "Highly coercive interrogation methods are all those techniques that fall into the category between those forbidden as torture by treaty or statute and those traditionally allowed in seeking a voluntary confession under the due processes clauses of the U.S. Constitution" (p. 35).

overreacting and becoming too repressive. Thus, striking a balance is seen by many ethicists as a key issue, and many advocate no restrictions on rights they believe to be basic and inviolable such as the prohibition against torture. However these complexities are resolved, it is imperative that a government faced with a terrorist threat or campaign actually addresses the morality of measures that will restrict liberty instead of reacting with no real moral compass.

Waldron (2010) makes the important point that restrictions on rights must amount to a plausible means of avoiding a future catastrophe. As he puts it, "Fear is only half a reason for modifying civil liberties: the other and indispensable half is a well-informed belief that the modification will actually make a difference to the prospect that we fear" (p. 31). It is fitting that the last words on the question of morally justifiable constraints and restrictions should be those of the 9/11 Commission, whose *Final Report* includes the following:

> Recommendation: The burden of proof for retaining a particular governmental power should be on the executive, to explain: (a) that the power actually materially enhances security and (b) that there is adequate supervision of the executive's use of the powers to ensure protection of civil liberties. If the power is granted, there must be adequate guidelines and oversight to properly confine its use. (in Heymann and Kayyem 2005: 1)

Is Torture Morally Permissible as a Counterterrorist Strategy?

Title 18, Section 2340 of the U.S. Code defines *torture* as

> an act committed by a person acting under the color of law specifically intended to inflict severe physical or mental pain or suffering (other than pain or suffering incidental to lawful sanctions) on another person within his custody or physical control. (Massimino 2004: 75)

Torture is a federal crime punishable by up to 20 years in prison and even death if the victim dies following the torture. This law applies to torture committed outside the United States but includes acts by U.S. citizens (Massimino 2004: 74–75).

In the war against terrorism, as well as in allegations of torture in the U.S. detainee facility at Guantanamo Bay, prisoner mistreatment has been identified in reports written after the disclosure of abuses at Abu Ghraib Prison in Baghdad. Instances of acts that could amount to torture included raping a female detainee, raping a 15- to 18-year-old male detainee, beating a detainee with a broom and breaking and pouring a chemical light over his body, followed by sodomizing him with the broom and being assaulted by two female military police (Hooks and Mosher 2005: 1629).

In his written advice to the president, White House Counsel and later Attorney General Gonzales advised that "the war on terrorism is a new kind of war . . . [that] renders obsolete the Geneva's strict limitations on questioning of enemy prisoners and renders quaint some of its provisions" (in Hooks and Mosher 2005: 1634). In August 2002, the Justice Department advised that the Congress had no power to regulate the president's ability to detain and interrogate enemy combatants. In his opinion on the meaning of torture, the assistant attorney general, Jay S. Bybee, advised that the term meant

> extreme acts . . . where the pain is physical it must be of an intensity akin to that which accompanies serious physical injury such as death or organ failure . . . because the acts inflicting torture are extreme, there is [a] significant range of acts that, though they might constitute cruel, inhuman, or degrading treatment or punishment, fail to rise to the level of torture. (in Hooks and Mosher 2005: 1634)

The advice also suggested that mental torture included only acts that resulted in "significant psychological harm of significant duration . . . lasting for months or even years" (quoted in Cohen 2014: 279), even though the notion that mental torture had to be prolonged in order to constitute torture is not reflected in the crime of torture under U.S. law. According to Gregory Hooks and Clayton Mosher, this statement sets a threshold for torture far higher than that established under any international human rights conventions, and specifically under the Convention Against Torture (2005: 1634). Some have argued that there is a moral difference between torture and so-called "torture lite." The latter is argued by its proponents as rendering certain techniques such as sleep deprivation, forced standing, stress positions, noise bombardment, and mock executions permissible because they fall short of torture. However, Rodin (2010: 821) argues, "Not only is the distinction not recognized in law . . . (but) there is no significant moral difference between torture and 'torture lite': Both cause intense suffering and both can have extremely severe long-term physical and mental consequences for victims."

On January 22, 2009, President Obama issued an executive order directing that all interrogations of persons detained as a result of armed conflict be conducted according to the *Army Field Manual* and revoked all previous orders that were in conflict with his order (Scheid 2010: 17).

Torture Methods in the War on Terror

While torture can be viewed as a practice within the framework of coercive interrogation techniques generally, detailed knowledge of such techniques is "cloaked in secrecy" (Lue 2005: 150).[12] However, media reports indicate that in April 2003, some 20 methods involving physical and psychological stress were approved by the Justice Department and the Pentagon for use at Guantanamo Bay Prison (p. 151). Despite a system of authorizations that included requiring the endorsement of the Defense Secretary in the case of some techniques, practices uncovered at Abu Ghraib Prison in Iraq between October 2003 and December 2003 clearly exceeded the limits imposed. For example, in an internal U.S. Army report, Maj. Gen. Antonio M. Taguba found that some acts had involved

[b]reaking chemical lights and pouring the phosphoric liquid on detainees; pouring cold water on naked detainees; beating detainees with a broom handle and a chair; threatening male detainees with rape . . . sodomizing a detainee with a chemical

light and perhaps a broom stick, and using military working dogs to frighten and intimidate detainees with threats of attack, and in one instance actually biting a detainee. (in Lue 2005: 152)

Considerable debate has surrounded the practice of *waterboarding* as applied in the CIA Detention and Interrogation Program with some commentators contending that it does not constitute torture. As explained in Card (2010: 175), waterboarding "has been applied to full body ducking of prisoners strapped to a board and to pouring icy water over a cloth placed over the face of a prisoner who is strapped down with the purpose of simulating the experience of drowning." President Obama stated at one press conference that he believed waterboarding was torture and that whatever legal rationales were applied to justify it, waterboarding was a mistake (Waldron 2010: 16).

Regardless of the U.S.-approved coercive interrogation techniques, as noted previously, there is clear evidence that the United States has secretly "rendered" prisoners to countries such as Egypt and Jordan, which are willing to employ very aggressive techniques, including forms of torture, to secure information relevant to the war on terror (Lue 2005: 150).

Most recently, on December 3, 2014, the Senate Select Committee on Intelligence reported its findings following a study of the CIA Detention and Interrogation Program created as part of the war on terror.

In February 2008, the Congress voted to limit the CIA to using only interrogation techniques authorized by the *Army Field Manual*. The legislation for this was vetoed.

Morality of Torture

Can torture be morally or ethically justified? Before 9/11, the use of torture had been considered impermissible in civilized countries for over a century (Rodin 2010: 820). It was therefore surprising that torture became a subject of debate following 9/11, especially given the prohibitions against torture in U.S. law following the U.S. ratification of the Convention Against Torture.

Khatchadourian (2005: 192) argues that even employing a utilitarianism/consequentialism approach

---

12 International rendition is illustrated by the case of Maher Arar, who was detained at JFK Airport in September 2002 while in transit to Canada, who is a dual Canadian/Syrian citizen, and who was traveling on a Canadian passport. He was held in U.S. custody for 13 days, interrogated about his supposed links to al-Qaeda, and then transported on to Jordan and then Syria without notice to his family or to the Canadian consulate. In Syria, he was held without charge for a year and was tortured and treated in a cruel and inhumane way (Hoffman 2004: 947–948). He was finally released by Syria.

Senate Select Committee on Intelligence

Committee Study of the CIA's Detention and Interrogation Program

Findings and Conclusions

The Committee issued the following findings:

- In July 2002, the CIA asked for Justice Department approval to use a set of coercive interrogation techniques adapted from the training of U.S. military personnel at the U.S. Air Force Survival, Evasion, Resistance, and Escape School, which trains U.S. personnel in conditions that might apply if they were taken prisoner by a non–Geneva Convention country.

- On August 1, 2002, the CIA Office of General Counsel, in a memorandum to the White House on *Standards of Conduct for Interrogation*, advised that "under the current circumstances, necessity or self-defense may justify interrogation methods that might violate" the prohibition against torture in U.S. criminal law.

- On August 1, 2002, CIA lawyers, in a second legal opinion, approved the use of 10 specific interrogation techniques, subsequently referred to as "enhanced interrogation techniques," which were used on detainees held in CIA custody at Guantanamo Bay, Cuba, and in third countries (the names of those countries are redacted in the report).

- The use of these techniques was not an effective means of obtaining accurate information and that the CIA falsely represented to the executive branch of government, specifically the Justice Department and the White House, that the enhanced techniques were effective. In fact, multiple detainees fabricated false information while undergoing enhanced interrogation.

- Interrogations were brutal and far worse in nature than the CIA represented to policy makers and others. The enhanced techniques included slaps and "wallings" (slamming a detainee against a wall), sleep deprivation for up to 180 hours, usually standing or in stress positions with hands shackled above heads, forced nudity, and waterboarding. Waterboarding induced convulsions and vomiting, and repeated waterboardings were equivalent to a "series of near drownings." At least three detainees were threatened with harm to their children, sexual abuse of a detainee's mother, and plans to cut the throat of a detainee's mother.

- On September 6, 2006, President Bush publicly acknowledged the existence of the CIA Detention and Interrogation Program: The CIA had detained 119 persons, of whom at least 39 were subjected to enhanced interrogation.

- By 2006, the CIA program had effectively ended as a result of media disclosures, lack of cooperation from other countries, and legal and oversight issues: The CIA last used enhanced interrogation techniques on November 8, 2007, and ceased holding detainees after April 2008.

(see Chapter 13) would be unable to justify torture in practice and would expressly prohibit torture in principle on the same basis that would cause a state to prohibit the practice of assassination. To torture a human being is to treat him or her not as a moral person, but as an object. According to Dworkin (2006), a "core list of human rights" would include the right not to be tortured; in his view, torture constitutes "the most profound insult to (its victim's) humanity, the most profound outrage of his human rights" (pp. 38–39). Rule utilitarians argue that observing a rule that prohibits torture results in the greatest good because history shows that torture has been employed to silence opposition to a government, and such action adversely impacts democratic principles. As well, it is argued that everyone benefits from a rule against torture because such a rule prevents anyone torturing us at some future time (Bellamy 2009: 35).

Khatchadourian (2005: 192) observes that the double-effect principle[13] cannot justify torture, even by arguing that the pain and suffering inflicted is intended to produce a greater good and with the torturer claiming he intended only the good and not the bad consequences of the torture. The reason is that in the practice of torture it is impossible to isolate the intention from the act itself.

Michael Ignatieff (2004: 137) argues that the prohibition against torture underpins the liberal democratic project and points out that eliminating torture as an affront to human dignity is the aim of a number of international instruments as well as being the domestic law of most states. Other scholars have argued that torture is morally wrong because it violates a norm against attacking those who are defenseless and that it attempts to strip away all the qualities associated with human dignity (Rodin 2010: 822–823). Saul (2009: 57) summarizes the moral absolutist perspective against torture as follows:

> The consequences of forcibly violating the body and the mind are profound and signal an unnecessary return to the blunt techniques of medieval justice. Torture irreparably damages human dignity, devalues human life, and corrupts the institutions and officials of democratic societies.

Justifications for Torture

The events of 9/11 have prompted some to argue that torture is justified as a national security counterterrorist measure in the interests of defending democracy. For example, Alan Dershowitz has suggested that torture might be applied and regulated by the judiciary through a "torture warrant" that would prescribe the kinds of torture to be inflicted

and its limits,[14] and federal judge Richard Posner has written that anyone who doubts that torture "is permissible when the stakes are high enough should not be in a position of responsibility" (in Massimino 2004: 74). Ignatieff rejects this approach on the basis that legalizing torture would effectively render it a routine matter. John Kleinig (2005: 626) also opposes issuing warrants to torture, asking if there is any reason to suppose that judges will be discriminating in torture cases brought before them in light of their wholehearted support for issuing warrants under the Foreign Intelligence Surveillance Act.[15] For Kleinig, as a matter of morality, authorizing torture by judicial warrant would be "pasting a veneer of moral respectability over practices that do not deserve it" (p. 627), and he argues for an absolute ban on torture as a matter of policy.

Stanley Cohen (2014: 273) writes, "It is difficult to imagine, even harder to incorporate into legal and public discourse, anything like a clear definition of 'justified' torture: this amount of pain; using this technique; to these parts of the body; over a certain time."

The "Ticking Bomb" Scenario (TBS)

The TBS has become a standard argument for the policy that torture is justified (Spino and Cummins 2014: 544). A scenario is envisaged where, for example, terrorists have planted a nuclear device that will explode and devastate a huge city area within the hour. There is no possibility of saving many lives in the time available, but one of the terrorists has been captured. The ticking bomb argument goes as follows: Are we not morally justified in using whatever means are appropriate, even torture, to get our captive terrorist to reveal the location of the bomb, so it can be deactivated and save countless lives? Proponents of moral absolutism in relation to torture—that it can never be morally justified—are commonly confronted with the TBS as a counterargument to moral

---

13 According to Solomon (2001), the double-effect principle "aims to provide specific guidelines for determining when it is morally permissible to perform an action in pursuit of a good end in full knowledge that the action will also bring about bad results" (p. 417).

14 Dershowitz goes so far as to identify drilling teeth without anesthetic and injecting air beneath the fingernails as methods that would cause great pain but leave no permanent damage (Bellamy 2009: 25).

15 In 2002, 1,228 warrants were applied for, and all were approved; in 2003, 1,724 out of 1,727 were granted; in 2004, 1,754 out of 1,758 were approved (Kleinig 2005: 626).

absolutism (Spino and Cummins 2014: 544). The TBS presents a scenario appealing to consequentialist notions of the greater good: Torturing one person will save the lives of many. However, as the following critiques show, the TBS is built upon a set of questionable assumptions that can easily be rebutted. In addition, the assumptions that form the foundation of the TBS prejudge the outcome (Bellamy 2009: 22).

Certainly, many would agree that they would personally resort to whatever means are necessary in such a situation, but Kleinig (2005: 616–617), among others, points to some of the issues raised by the ticking bomb argument:

- It suggests there is a known threat—not just a possibility or probability—but in practice, such a high degree of certainty is unlikely to occur.
- There is a need for immediate action because it is certain that the bomb will explode—again, is this degree of certainty likely to be common in practice?
- The magnitude of the danger is enormous, so it is said to be permissible to apply torture, but Kleinig argues that the moral status of any alternative decision is unclear. Similarly, there is no moral clarity about whether or not torture is justified, excusable, or regrettable in these circumstances.
- It is claimed that only the application of torture will secure the necessary information, but we cannot really be sure there are no other alternatives. Also, torture ought not to be regarded as a kind of shortcut that is convenient in such circumstances.
- It would seem essential that the person we intend on torturing be the maker of the threat. This is so because, as Kleinig points out, the moral justification for torture seems much weaker if we encourage him to talk by, for example, torturing his child or his aging mother in front of him.
- It is said that the outcome of the torture will be the removal of the threat. It is assumed, then, that information gained from the torture will almost certainly dispel the danger, but can this be claimed with absolute certainty?

As Kleinig (2005: 623) points out, these assumptions can be given some weight but are unlikely to be found in the real world, and if they cannot be replicated, the case for torture is that much weaker. Even assuming that the TBS is accepted as a basis for torture, Kleinig and others would nevertheless maintain, contrary to Dershowitz and others, that the TBS could never sanction a *policy* authorizing torture. Instead, each case where torture was contemplated would have to be justified by reference to the specific facts and circumstances.

Like Ignatieff, Kleinig (2005) fears the routinization of torture. As he points out, we are on a slippery slope once torture is accepted as a possible course of action because the TBS will inevitably lead to an expansion of the situations where torture is acceptable. For Kleinig, then, torture "threatens and undermines the very characteristics that constitute our human distinctiveness, and attacks them in a way that does not merely extinguish them—as killing does—but in a way that humiliates, degrades and perverts" (p. 619).

The Moral Legitimacy of Torture

In his account of the morality of torture, Ginbar (2008) reviews the moral legitimacy of torture under the TBS and argues as follows:

- Generally, the arguments for and against torture in a TBS divide along deontological/consequentialist lines. A consequentialist would approach the issue by examining the good and bad outcomes—the pain and the pleasure—then choose the action that will result in the maximum pleasure or the minimum pain. In other words, by opting for "the lesser evil." A deontologist, following a Kantian approach, will chose the morally correct course of action by ensuring that the action would be right for all persons to act in that way in similar circumstances; that the action does not amount to using persons as a means but as an end; and that all persons are treated as having their own ends and as being similarly capable of making moral choices (pp. 16–18).

- Consequentialist arguments were adopted by the Landau Commission of Enquiry in Israel in 1987 in the report "Interrogation Methods of the General Security Service Regarding Hostile Terrorist Activity." In discussing the TBS, the commission wrote,

  > The choice, is clearly and simply: must we accept the offence of assault associated with slapping an interrogee's face, or threatening him, to make him speak and expose the hiding place of explosives designed to be used in carrying out a massive terrorist attack against a civilian population, and thus avert the great evil about to happen? The answer for that is obvious. (p. 22)

- While deontologists in general would oppose the use of torture in a TBS, nonabsolutist deontologists would support torture in what are deemed to be "catastrophic" situations or where "horrendous consequences" would likely be the result of following a strict deontological view (pp. 24, 26). The absolutist position—that torture must never be performed whatever the consequences—is not easy to maintain because philosophical and real-life cases show that absolute prohibitions are problematic and even doubtful when applied to specific situations (p. 37). As Maureen Ramsay (2009) notes, in a TBS, there is a tendency to believe that "anyone who does not admit that torture is defensible in these circumstances is morally self-indulgent—placing their own moral integrity over the welfare of others, or at best irresponsible, unrealistic and naïve" (p. 423).

- The "slippery slope" argument against using torture asserts that torture would result in worse consequences overall. Thus, supporters of torture must acknowledge that even the worst imaginable atrocities—for example, torturing a baby—are permissible. Even consequentialists have to acknowledge that some practices are generally considered absolutely prohibited; for example, there is a consensus that petty crimes ought not to be punished with death and that where death is the authorized penalty, it should not involve undue suffering (Ginbar 2008: 47). Similarly, there is an absolute prohibition against waiving informed consent in HIV vaccine trials, whatever may be the consequences (p. 54). These instances show that those who reject the absolutist position would need to justify their stance in the context of the slippery slope. As well, the torturer cannot disregard the possibility that the terrorist attack under the TBS is itself a morally legitimate action. For example, acts of terrorism have been justified where a state makes war against those it terms terrorists but who claim to be fighting for their rights and freedoms (p. 62). These issues and contentions lead Ginbar to conclude that absolutism is a legitimate position and, in fact, one that in practice is taken and implemented.

- The practicalities of performing torture should also be unpacked and made explicit. Here, Ginbar argues that torture is an "absolutely evil act" (p. 65) because if the torture of a person is justified, that then justifies doing anything to the person being tortured, and no act is too harmful or too cruel to exceed a torture boundary. Thus, in a TBS, it follows that any amount of torture is justified to get the information, including the rape of the terrorist and even the torture of an innocent person, such as the terrorist's mother, to ensure that the terrorist talks.

- The position of the torturer must also be considered. Clearly, anyone capable of performing the most extreme forms of torture could never be termed a virtuous person. The torturer must suppress all forms of compassion, ignore screams of pain, and focus only on getting the terrorist to talk (p. 80). In this sense, the torturer is dispensable, and no account need be taken of his or her dignity or moral or religious beliefs or status as a moral agent.

(Continued)

(Continued)

- In considering a TBS where the state faces an act of terrorism and the torturer is an agent of the state, Ginbar (2008) argues that a person acting within the public sphere represents not only himself or herself but also all citizens and the state itself. The state has a moral duty to protect innocent citizens, and using torture as an act of policy will have wide-ranging effects as compared to a single act of torture in the private sphere. Public actions must be impartial and impersonal and may involve forms of violence not found or countenanced in the private sphere (p. 100). Consequentialists and deontologists willing to allow torture will only endorse a state's decision to change its policy to authorize when the consequences of not doing so are far worse than any damage that might be caused by the "slippery slope" argument (p. 159).

- A state that is willing to torture in a TBS will legitimize an act regarded as illegitimate by all civilized nations and will set back worldwide efforts to combat human rights abuses. When the world's leading democracy authorizes torture, this will inevitably be seen as a justification for other states to use it (p. 152).

Bob Brecher (2007) critiques the TBS as a "fantasy derived from philosophers' thought-experiments which are usually designed to test the limits of moral theory" (p. 9). In his view, the TBS is a purely hypothetical case that lacks plausibility in reality. While thought experiments may be useful in considering the limits of philosophical theories, they do not inform us about the real world. Brecher argues that it is not possible to project a person into the position of a torturer in a TBS because obviously he or she will not possess the required skills, and it is highly unlikely that any person would wish to descend to the depths necessary to acquire them. He believes the preponderance of evidence suggests that torture is not an effective method of securing information.

Efficacy of Torture

The *U.S. Military Field Manual* prohibits coercive techniques "because they produce low quality intelligence" (p. 24), and as noted, the Senate Intelligence Committee found that detainees under the CIA program who were subjected to enhanced interrogation techniques regularly fabricated intelligence. Brecher suggests a terrorist held captive in a TBS will adopt a strategy based on several factors: an awareness that unless he or she reveals the location of the bomb, nonlethal torture will occur; the torture will cease once the required information is provided; and

the torture will cease immediately the bomb explodes, so the actual time under torture is likely to be quite brief (it can be assumed that the bomber will leave as short a time as possible between planting a bomb and its detonation). It follows from these factors that a terrorist is likely to adopt a strategy of lying or just holding out and keeping silent. Perhaps he or she has been trained to withstand torture, and denying any knowledge of the location of the bomb and indicating someone else knows the location will be a means of delaying any action (p. 27).

The terrorist might even decide to tell a series of lies about the location, and each lie would have to be checked out. Would the torture be halted while this was done? Presumably, yes, because the purpose of the torture is to aid in interrogation and not to torture "just in case" (p. 28). The time frame associated with the TBS seems therefore in reality inconsistent with its assumptions.

The "Slippery Slope" Argument Against Torture

The "slippery slope" argument is associated with the notion that once permitted in a TBS no line can be drawn against using torture for a wider range of purposes and against an increasing proportion of the population—for example, against drug dealers or organized crime bosses. An example is torture by French armed forces in Algeria in the 1950s, which was justified as a means of halting terrorist bombings.

The outcome was the routine use of torture against every captive, without regard to guilt or innocence or to his or her knowledge of facts relevant to intelligence gathering (Ramsay 2009: 426). Torture, it is argued, will become an institutionalized tool involving an array of social institutions, including the judicial and medical professions. It will become regularized and professionalized, and torturers will undergo training to gain competence in their work as inflictors of pain (Ginbar 2008: 133). When the state elects to use torture, this can be said to constitute a victory for terrorism as the state departs from norms of conduct to become itself a quasi-terrorist (p. 149).

Like Ginbar, Brecher (2007) believes that torture, once authorized, will become institutionalized and a step on the slippery slope to a "tortuous society" that permits the torture of family and friends of terrorists and allows torture to be used for criminal justice purposes to secure confessions and criminal intelligence (pp. 57, 60). Were torture warrants to be introduced, Brecher suggests that judges would have difficulty refusing to issue them and would in any event largely rely on evidence from the government (p. 63). He believes the impact of torture warrants on the criminal justice system would be unimaginable. As well, torturers would be under great pressure to apply for warrants to torture in every situation so as to avoid allegations of not doing everything possible to secure information. Brecher suggests that legitimizing the occupation of torturer would "radically reconfigure peoples conceptions of everyday decency" (p. 69).

Lawful Torture Model

What would a legal model of torture look like? The only legal model of torture that exists is in use in Israel. There, between 1987 and 1999, the first model of legalized torture was applied after the government adopted the recommendations of the Landau Commission.[16] Applications to the Israeli Supreme Court

---

16   The Landau Commission, named after its chair, the former Supreme Court president Moshe Landau, was set up by the Israeli government in 1987 following public concern about the treatment given to prisoners by the security services. The Commission accepted without question the claim by the security services that the use of aggressive measures in interrogating prisoners was an effective means of gaining intelligence (Bellamy 2009: 21).

on behalf of those detained that questioned the treatment accorded to them by the Israeli General Security Service (GSS), or *Shin Bet,* were regularly dismissed as the court accepted GSS justifications and applied a consequentialist approach. In 1999, the court ruled that the defense of necessity to criminal conduct was available to those accused of torture. While it could not be used to authorize torture, it could excuse it (Ginbar 2008: 204).

The court was willing to confer the availability of this defense to all investigators conducting interrogations, even when the bomb in a TBS was not set to explode immediately but in a few days or even weeks in the future (Ginbar 2008: 205). Ginbar notes that there have in fact been no prosecutions against GSS interrogators since the ruling of the court because the attorney general has consistently rejected prosecution on the basis that physical coercion was justified and the necessity defense would mean a prosecution would fail (p. 214). Thus, while the court ruling prohibits torture and therefore no laws or regulations can authorize it, the necessity defense always excuses it.

Is torture permissible in this "new kind of war"? Ignatieff (2004) proposes that the practice of torture cannot be condoned in a war against terrorism, "for torture, when committed by a state, expresses the state's ultimate view that human beings are expendable" (p. 143).

THE MORALITY OF TARGETED KILLING

Assume the United States obtains information that a person is planning a terrorist attack against the country. He is located outside the United States in a country where law enforcement is weak and poorly organized. While U.S. officials can ask local officials of that country to arrest this person with a view to having him extradited, they fear that the weakness of law enforcement and the likely lengthy time frame will result in the terror plot being implemented or, worse, that it may already have taken place. Further, even if the host government were able to ensure the arrest of the person, there is no guarantee that he will continue to be detained. If he is released, clearly, the United States faces more risk. Is it morally acceptable for the United States to kill this person in the host country, or should the United States seek his capture, extradition, and subsequent trial (Blum and Heymann 2010: 69)?

The issue of targeted killing highlights the critical importance of opting for a warfare or law enforcement strategy to counterterrorism. If law enforcement is the policy choice, the use of deadly force is circumscribed by both domestic and international law norms that protect the right to life. Killing a person without going through a trial process that results in an adjudication of guilt and a death sentence is only allowed in very restricted circumstances, such as in self-defense or where the defense of necessity can be invoked. In most other situations, such a killing amounts to an unlawful, extrajudicial execution (Blum and Heymann 2010: 69). Nation-states are required internationally to respect each other's sovereignty and therefore do not ordinarily conduct hunts for criminals in other states, let alone carry out targeted executions within their territory. Rather, an application for extradition is made to the host state using agreed-on legal processes set out in extradition treaties, and the host state arrests the fugitive.

The situation is radically different in time of war. Then, governments may use deadly force against enemy combatants who are easily identified by wearing uniforms designating them as members of the armed forces of a state. Every soldier is a legitimate target and can be targeted for killing with no advance warning, and no attempt to capture or arrest need be made. However, when an individual does not wear a uniform but is suspected to be a terrorist, the issue of targeted killing becomes problematic. The absence of a uniform raises questions about the status of an individual as a member of a hostile force (Blum and Heymann 2010: 70).

Thus, as Michael Gross (2006) asks, "Are targeted killings acts of self-defense or extra-judicial execution?" (p. 323). The question can only be resolved by categorizing the actors and their actions correctly—that is, within a war or law enforcement paradigm. While human rights groups argue that terrorists do not possess combatant status and remain civilians (because they lack the firm status of combatant, they, like others without uniforms, must be civilians), Gross argues that terrorists, once having taken up arms on the battlefield, do not regain their innocence once they leave it;

rather, "they maintain their hostile status off the battlefield as they prepare for battle, lay plans, tend to their weapons and maintain their fighting capability" (p. 324).

Both Israel and the United States have adopted targeted killing, usually through an airstrike—often using unmanned drone aircraft, in the case of the United States—as a specific counterterrorist strategy (Blum and Heymann 2010: 71).

The United States and Targeted Killings

U.S. practice on targeted assassination seems to have begun with the efforts of the CIA to kill Fidel Castro and continued into the Vietnam War with plots to assassinate the president of South Vietnam and with the Phoenix Program, designed to kill Vietcong leaders. In 1986, President Reagan ordered an air raid on the home of the president of Libya. He later signed Executive Order 12333 banning assassinations, but following the 1998 bombings of U.S. embassies in Tanzania and Kenya, President Clinton issued a presidential finding with the status of an executive order, authorizing the use of lethal force in self-defense against al-Qaeda in Afghanistan.[17] Following the 9/11 attack, it was reported that President Bush made another finding, widening the scope of potential targets. Employing the war paradigm as a counterterrorist strategy enabled administration lawyers to differentiate attacks targeting terrorists from banned assassinations and to rationalize such targeting as lawful operations against enemy combatants (Blum and Heymann 2010: 72–73). Under President Obama, there has been an expansion of targeted attacks using Predator drones in a number of countries, including Libya, Pakistan, and Yemen, where no active war is actually being conducted. While it appears the Yemen government approved an attack, the

---

[17] According to Patterson and Casale (2005: 640), President Ford signed Executive Order 11905, stating, "No employee of the United States Government shall engage in, or conspire to engage in, political assassination." President Reagan signed an amended Order 12333 on December 4, 1981, stating, "No person, employee, by or acting on behalf of the United States Government, shall engage in, or conspire to engage in, assassination."

Pakistan government has not approved all attacks within its territory (p. 74).[18]

According to Blum and Heymann (2010), legal advice given to the administration in 1989 asserts that "the targeted killing of enemy combatants in wartime or the killing in self-defense of specific individuals who pose a direct threat to U.S. citizens or national security in peacetime" is permitted and justified (p. 78). Self-defense is authorized under Article 51 of the United Nations Charter, which allows states to use force in self-defense after suffering an "armed attack." Adopting the war paradigm as a counterterrorist strategy has resulted in terrorists—termed *unlawful combatants*—being treated as combatants in that war, justifying their targeted killing on any battlefield because the war against terrorism is said to be a global war.

In contrast to the U.S. approach, Israel has justified targeting terrorists by treating them as civilians taking a direct part in hostilities in wartime (Blum and Heymann 2010: 85). After initially taking a law enforcement approach that viewed terrorists as within the same category as suspected dangerous criminals, Israel changed to the alternative paradigm and invoked self-defense (Gross 2006: 327). Targeted killings were used by Israel against Hezbollah and Hamas in the 1980s and 1990s, and commencing from the mid-2000s, "targeted strikes have become the United States' operational counterterrorism tool of choice" (Blank 2015: 227).

Armed Drones and Targeted Killings

As noted, President Obama expanded the use of armed drones to conduct targeted assassinations with the objective of engaging a less costly military tool than ground troops. The deployment of drones increased threefold between 2008 and 2011 (Walklate and Mythen 2015: 84). The expansion triggered a debate about the use of armed drones and the ethics of this form of killing. An ethical analysis of the use of armed drones identifies numerous issues associated with the deployment of these weapons in the war against terrorism and their association, and that of their operators, with the changing nature of warfare (Enemark 2014). Some of the complex ethical challenges posed by drones are discussed in this section, including whether the targeted drone attacks of suspected terrorists are actions taken in a just war or are simply assassinations.

The best known weaponized drone is the Predator, which, when equipped with Hellfire missiles, is a platform for surveillance and targeted strikes (Enemark 2014: 3). The Predator carries two television cameras (one regular and one infrared); radar that can view through clouds, dust, and smoke; and a laser device that locks on to targets identified by its surveillance apparatus. Drones are used by the U.S., British, and Israeli militaries for surveillance and by the United States for air support to troops in combat zones. They are also operated by the CIA to kill persons designated as terrorists in geographical areas that may or may not constitute actual battlefields (p. 18). Prior to 9/11, the U.S. government opposed targeted killings on the basis that they violated international law (Brunstetter and Braun 2011: 343), but in 2002, the CIA conducted its first targeted drone killing in Yemen. In June 2002, strikes were extended to Somalia, and since then, Pakistan has had the most drone strikes.

The United States conducts a "pattern of life" analysis in a comprehensive surveillance and intelligence collection process as a prelude to a possible drone strike. Commanders are able to use drones to follow a target to a location and the surrounding area for days, gathering intelligence about the civilian population and therefore securing information about the likelihood of civilian casualties if a strike is made (Blank 2015: 232).

Enemark (2014: 3) observes that, arguably, the drone represents a new development in warfare because "the operator of a drone—a platform that combines aircraft and missile technology—is able almost instantaneously to kill another person as far away as the other side of the world." The fact that a drone is uninhabited brings something new to airpower because the armed drone introduces a mode of killing that is risk free (p. 4). Armed drones are regarded as a means of precisely targeting the enemy using minimal force. A key element is that there is no

18 Tom Parker (2005) provides an account of British targeted assassinations, especially in Northern Ireland, concluding that as a result of extensive public enquiries into such activities, numerous prosecutions were instituted but no links were established between the executive and targeted killings. In his view, "for the most part the officials involved took matters into their own hands without direction from the political sphere" (p. 134).

contest between protagonists and, "arguably, if killing occurs in circumstances that cannot plausibly be characterized as a contest, such killing is not in the nature of war" (p. 6). This raises for debate the ethical question of whether drone technology can be located within the moral space that permits killing through the process of warfare. If not sanctioned by the just war principles, killing by drone may amount to extrajudicial killing or assassination.

"Post-Heroic" Warfare

Heroic warfare refers to warfare involving death on a large scale and for some great purpose, such as during the two World Wars. Nowadays, there is a preference for "post–heroic" forms of warfare characterized by a much-reduced physical risk. "New military technologies such as armed drones demonstrate this risk management perspective as does public and political opinion, especially in the U.S. which is not accepting of large numbers of U.S. casualties in armed conflicts" (Enemark 2014: 9). The modern refusal to accept high casualties is evidenced by the fact that while the United States was able to endure almost 50,000 U.S. combat deaths in the war in Vietnam, by the following decade the deaths of 243 Marines in a 1983 bomb attack in Lebanon resulted in the removal of all U.S. operations in that country (p. 11). In 1993, the *U.S. Army Field Manual* declared that "the American people expect decisive victory and abhor unnecessary casualties," and in the 1991 Gulf War, "casualty minimization became from the start an independent operational objective" because of "dread among the . . . leadership that too many American lives lost would implode public and congressional support for the war" (p. 11).

Military technology plays a key role in minimizing casualty rates in modern armed conflicts. Wars, and especially the American mode of warfare, have been characterized by reliance on advanced technology—in particular, airpower. The armed drone is therefore a logical outcome of that doctrine, thought to preclude the need for full-scale war involving large numbers of armed forces.

Drones and Decisions to Use Force

As Enemark (2014: 22) puts it, "From an ethical perspective, the challenge posed by more frequent drone use is to guard against any associated increase in the number of unjust decisions to resort to force at all." International law and practice currently provide only two justifications for states to use force against each other: in self-defense and to prevent or mitigate a large-scale, deliberately-caused humanitarian disaster. The first option does not require UN Security Council approval, but the second does (p. 23). Thus, the increased number of drones and expanded opportunities for their use means there is "an ethical imperative to consider the impact this technology has on political decisions to resort to the use of force" (p. 35). There is a fear then that because drones are regarded as a level of force short of war and because of their ease of use, their deployment is likely to result in an increase in warlike operations or in ethically doubtful political decisions to use force (Brunstetter and Braun 2011: 339; Cook 2015: 220).

Noncombatant Casualties

Under the laws of war, according to the principle of discrimination, combatants may be deliberately targeted and noncombatants are not to be subject to attack in time of war. The coming of precision-guided weapons has increased expectations that civilians will not suffer injury or death in armed conflicts, but the actual balance of civilian and noncivilian casualties resulting from drone strikes is far from clear (Enemark 2014: 44). According to an April 2015 report in *The New York Times*, eight Americans have been killed in drone strikes, and separate counts of drone strikes averaged by three independent organizations found that 522 strikes have killed 3,852 persons, 476 of them civilians.

In the case of the United States, the ethical basis for designating persons as combatants and not noncombatants remains opaque. For example, in Pakistan, where the most drone strikes have been conducted, casualty estimates often rely on vague media reports. According to one source, in Pakistan 5.8% of those killed by drones are noncombatants, but the New America Foundation gives a rate of between 18% and 23% noncombatant deaths. Researchers at the University of Massachusetts, relying on a media database of U.S. and Pakistan drone strikes, report a rate in 2010 of 4.95% civilian deaths. Opposed to these estimates are the limited and sometimes contradictory reports from tribal areas, the high proportion of victims—around 15% whose role or function is unknown—and the uncertainty about which persons are classified as "suspected militants" and therefore considered combatants (Enemark 2014: 47).

In May 2012, it was reported that President Obama had adopted a method of tallying casualties that counted all military-aged males in a strike zone as combatants in the absence of explicit intelligence that proved them "innocent" (Enemark 2014: 48). However, in a May 2013 speech to the National Defense University, President Obama claimed that "before any strike is taken, there must be near-certainty that no civilians will be killed or injured" (quoted in *The Guardian* May 2013).

The International Committee of the Red Cross (ICRC) has recommended that only a person performing a "continuous combat function" should constitute a proper target of attack. To the contrary, the U.S. approach has been characterized as including nonfighters as targets, even to the extent that those known to be donating money to terrorists or functioning as financial officers for terrorist groups would be legitimate targets (Enemark 2014: 49). The American Civil Liberties Union (ACLU) has contended that "financiers and other non-combat 'supporters' of hostile groups cannot lawfully be targeted with lethal force." Nevertheless, a 2009 report from the Senate Foreign Relations Committee disclosed that the target list in Afghanistan included drug lords suspected of aiding the Taliban (p. 50).

Proportionality

The principle of proportionality requires that damage inflicted by a drone attack should not be disproportionate to the benefit to be gained by inflicting it. In terms of civilian casualties, the issue may be whether civilian deaths are *accidental* or are *incidental* to what is considered to be the military advantage (Gregory 2011: 199). In the case of drone strikes, judgments about proportionality may involve the killing of so-called "high value targets," perhaps located in areas where there are many civilians and children. What process is followed by the U.S. administration in applying the proportionality principle? In 2012, *The New York Times* revealed that the president had been personally involved in drone strike decisions. It was reported that when there was an opportunity to strike at a top terrorist but his family was with him, the final decision was the president's. We cannot know how many civilian deaths

are considered proportionate to the targeting of a high-level terrorist. In 2008, the CIA was reportedly authorized to attack in Pakistan not only high-value targets on the "approved list" but also suspected militants having less value whose identity was not known. This represented a dramatic expansion of the drone campaign in that country (Enemark 2014: 54).

Legal and Moral Framework for Drone Strikes

In October 2012, President Obama indicated a need to put in place a legal framework to govern drone strikes. His statement suggested that there existed no rules covering procedures and safeguards to ensure that targeted killings were lawful and justified and that there were no mechanisms to ensure accountability in the case of wrongful killings. The absence of such a framework may indicate that drone attacks constitute assassinations rather than lawful and moral killings in warfare. This is especially the case when targeted killings are carried out by the CIA, which, unlike the U.S. military, publishes no ethical guidelines or rules and is not part of the U.S. armed forces (Enemark 2014: 57; Brunstetter and Braun 2011: 340).

The continued involvement of the CIA and the lack of transparency about drone operations under its command raise "deep ethical concerns about the agency's adherence to the *jus in bello* principles" (Brunstetter and Braun 2011: 353). In addition, nonmilitary personnel such as CIA staff and independent contractors hired by the CIA to conduct or assist in gathering intelligence for drone attacks are not combatants for the purpose of international humanitarian law. They therefore do not possess the right to participate in hostilities or the immunity that is associated with that right and can be prosecuted under domestic law of the countries where the attacks occur and are liable for violations of international humanitarian law, such as the direct targeting of civilians (Blank 2015: 233).

Blum and Heymann (2010: 72) suggest that targeted killings ought to be subject to a set of norms that respect both war and law enforcement values and are justified accordingly. They suggest that an appropriate moral framework would comprise the following elements (p. 90):

- Before considering targeted killings, the host state should be approached to arrest and, if necessary, extradite a suspected person. Thus, assassination would be a last resort, not an initial option, and an extraordinary measure taken in response to noncooperation from the host state.

- Only those actively involved in terrorist activity should be targeted and not every member or suspected member of a terrorist group.
- Accurate identification of targets in the absence of a uniform should be ensured.
- Collateral damage should always be minimized.
- Targeted killing should be reserved for the most urgent and necessary cases, taking full account of all alternative options.

The Disembodied Warrior

"When a drone operator's mind alone goes to war while his or her body remains at home, he or she manifests as a 'disembodied warrior'" (Enemark 2014: 85). Philosopher Peter Singer has said that removing warriors from risk and fear breaks the traditional connection between warriors and soldierly values: There is no relationship of mutual risk between the drone operator and the persons killed. While engaging in warfare, the drone operator suffers no physical risk—something entirely new in warfare—and has no need to display courage, but many ethical claims about combat say that it is only permissible to kill if you yourself run that same risk (Gregory 2011: 205). Arguably, this diminishes the military virtue of the operator (Enemark 2014: 91).

A number of commentators have suggested that the location and functions of the drone operator make operators susceptible to treating killing by drones as if it were merely a game, sometimes referred to as possessing a "Playstation mentality" toward killing (Enemark 2014: 86). This contention has been firmly rebutted by the U.S. Air Force, based on reports that show operators suffer similar psychological stress to soldiers on the battlefield (Brunstetter and Braun 2011: 349). Operators apparently "feel proximate to those with whom they engage" because of the extensive time they spend

surveilling the area and their close view of an actual attack. These factors are said to counteract any dehumanizing tendencies attributable to distance (Wall and Monahan 2011: 249; Blank 2015: 238).

Arguments Against Targeted Killings

In considering the ethical arguments against targeting killing, Eric Patterson and Teresa Casale (2005: 641) note the following:

- Assassination is an immoral act and a form of politically motivated murder outside the bounds of the conventions of war and morality.
- Assassination violates U.S. values and principles because it is done in secret and is a display of the exercise of overbearing state power against individuals. In this sense, it can be said to be "un-American" because it does not honor due process.
- Targeted killing calls into question the morality of U.S. foreign policy, which stresses human rights and democracy.

Concerns about targeted killing, like those relating to torture, often invoke the "slippery slope" argument: that targeted killing can become a strategy of choice against nonterrorists—for example, against drug lords in Afghanistan. Thus, there may develop a temptation to extend the category of persons liable to be subjected to this ultimate penalty simply because of the ease with which it is possible to mount an airstrike inside a territory.

The secrecy and seeming underhandedness associated with targeted killing tends to invoke an instinctive reaction against it as a practice. However, as several commentators have noted, there is a framework, albeit somewhat problematic, that justifies its employment, legally and morally, against terrorists in a time of war on all battlefields and even globally. Setting ethical norms that seek to limit its use and safeguard innocent civilians recognizes the need for counterterrorist nations to respect human rights, human dignity, and the sovereignty of other nations.

SUMMARY

This chapter has explored definitions of terrorism and questioned why, following the events of 9/11, the U.S. administration declared a war against terrorism

instead of allowing the criminal justice system to respond to that act of terrorism. The discussion has revealed the complexity of the moral arguments and debates surrounding the application of torture, the ethical aspects of counterterrorist measures, and the extent to which citizens' rights ought to be restricted in the interests of national security.

A number of major themes have emerged from this discussion. They include, first, that no single "correct" definition of terrorism exists and that the current terrorism discourse, which includes connotations of irrationality and fanaticism, has obscured the fact that most varieties of terror are conducted or sponsored by states that practice far more deadly forms of terrorism than groups or individuals. Second, the war on terrorism is not a conventional war but is shaped almost entirely by the events of 9/11 and is a reaction to those events. Third, post–9/11, terrorism is perceived by U.S. strategists and policy makers as an issue of national security, not crime control, and therefore as calling for a response that is warlike but falls short of a conventional war. As well, protecting U.S. citizens against further terrorist attacks necessitates the creation of special courts and procedures, the abandonment of the U.S. criminal justice system, and probable violations of national and international law. Defending citizens also means that their rights and freedoms can legitimately be restricted, presumably for as long as it takes to "win" the war against terror. Fourth, exceptional measures, including violently assaulting the integrity of the human person through torture, are regarded by many as justified and even imperative in conducting the war.

Antiterrorist strategies have been challenged on moral grounds. Charges have been made of abuse of government powers. It is said that the administration has acted unethically by rejecting customary legal rules and procedures in the pursuit of victory. Devices such as categorizing suspected terrorist prisoners as unlawful combatants have been employed, allegedly to avoid legal rules and enable incarceration and torture.

The morality of the fight against terrorism itself has been called into question on the basis that representing a counterterrorist strategy as warfare lowers the bar for engaging in more conventional wars against actual states. It also enables the United States to conduct events called *battles*, subsumed within the entirety of an amorphous and unending war on terrorism. As well, commentators have pointed out that, ethically, causing death or injury to civilians in countering terrorism seems to mirror the acts of the terrorists themselves.

Thus, the war against terrorism can be seen as constituting a greater evil than terrorism itself. In the face of such charges, is it sufficient to maintain that citizens must rely on judicial and legislative oversight to ensure that the administration's excesses are corrected? Ultimately, the question may be whether condoning breaches of human rights and liberal principles in conducting a war on terrorism also risks undermining respect for national and international laws that destroy foundational commitments to justice and human dignity.

DISCUSSION QUESTIONS

1. The definition of *terrorism* is problematic. How does this affect our view of terrorism?

2. Which is the better approach—to treat terrorism as a criminal activity or to fight terrorists as if they were enemies in a war? Explain.

3. Does the Patriot Act give the executive branch of government too much power in pursuing terrorism? What effect does the exercise of that power have on civil rights in the United States?

4. What measures should a democratic government take to respond to terrorism that are consistent with its ethical responsibilities?

5. Is it ever ethically acceptable to torture a person in the war against terrorism? Explain.

6. What, if any, human rights should be suppressed in the interests of winning the war on terrorism, and how would suppressing these rights contribute toward "victory"?

7. What are the ethical arguments that make it acceptable (or unacceptable) to use drone strikes against persons designated as combatants and strikes against combatants where the potential for harming noncombatants also exists?

11

MEDIA ETHICS
AND CRIMINAL JUSTICE

The influence of the media, both print media and broadcast television—from the networks to cable television—cannot be doubted. The media, as Roger Silverstone (2007) notes, is "tightly and dialectically intertwined with the everyday. We have become dependent on the media for the conduct of everyday life" (p. 5). Numerous studies have shown that most people gain their knowledge of events from the media, and therefore, the selection and shaping of news by the media is a critical element in forming and modeling public opinion on most topics, including criminal justice. Indeed, Silverstone suggests that the worldwide media, in an age of globalization, constitute a "site for the construction of a moral order" (p. 7). Lawrence (2000: 91) agrees, noting that the media police the boundaries of what is considered morally and socially acceptable behavior and identify transgressions as news. The deviant and the unpredictable constitute "social and moral disorder stories" defining propriety, and in this manner, the media articulate public morality. For Jack Katz, crime stories provide the material "for a literal working out of the moral perspectives that must be applied to dilemmas of everyday life" (in Greer 2010: 234).

MEDIA CONSTRUCTIONS OF CRIME

The media decides what is newsworthy, and crime ranks high on that scale. The mediated experience of crime—as opposed to actually experiencing it in reality—represents most Americans' experience of crime. Ray Surette (2011: 25) notes that in modern society the mediated crime event displaces the actual event, and the vicarious pleasure of seeing crime on television or reading about it from a place of safety and security is far preferable to being victimized. Yvonne Jewkes (2011: 41) explains that the media version of reality is determined by two factors: (a) the mediated portrayal of reality fashioned by the news-production processes and (b) agenda setting—that is, the assumptions of media professionals about their audience that cause them to select some items as newsworthy and others not are what determine how a story is framed.

The media construction of crime will define what are thought to be the causes of crime, what acts are regarded as criminal, and what policies of crime control should be adopted because media constructions of reality represent crime for legislators and criminal justice policy makers. For example, the new crime of "road rage" is a media construction (Surette 2011: 45), and the media can elevate the seriousness of the crime as it did with driving under the influence (DUI). As Surette observes (p. 45), prior to the 1980s, DUI was seen as an individual problem, was not zealously prosecuted, and lacked real public interest. Then, new claim makers appeared in the form of Mothers Against Drunk Driving (MADD) to reconstruct DUI as a crime committed by "killer drunks" and to socially stigmatize anyone drinking while driving. With media assistance, MADD succeeded in characterizing drunk drivers as a new menace to society for whom laws had to be made tougher.

Within the context of crime as entertainment, the media promotes the notion that all crimes can be solved using forensic science methods, as in the *CSI* police procedural series and its spin-offs. The construction of the crime scene investigator comprises unlimited resources, impossible forensic test times, and distorted depictions of actual crime scene investigations (Surette 2011: 95). Nevertheless, programs like *CSI* influence juror expectations about evidence. For example, the absence of forensic evidence connotes sloppy police work or even innocence and causes jurors to give less weight to eyewitness evidence. Juror expectations of the evidence that will be presented at trial are shaped by multiple exposures to *CSI* programming, to the extent that forensic evidence becomes reified and cannot be questioned.

Finally, the media represent a distorted picture of the courts as soft on crime and obsessed with technicalities that free the guilty and the dangerous. The legal system is depicted as an obstacle to crime fighting, with complex procedures and trials and dramatic adversarial contests. In reality, there is little drama, few accused actually go to trial, and unexciting plea bargains are the norm (Surette 2011: 106).

Crime, Media, and Ethics

What are the ethical responsibilities of the media in its reporting and presentation of crime and criminal justice? What images of criminality do the media deploy, and how far do they represent the reality of crime and justice? Does media coverage of crime enhance fear of crime, such as in moral panics, and thus lead to greater social control? How does the criminal justice system interact with the media, and to what extent do criminal justice agencies seek to manipulate the news to meet their perceived needs? Do the media act ethically in the representation and reporting of crime? These key issues and associated questions of ethics and media responsibility will be explored in this chapter.

The movement toward ethics in journalism generally began as early as the 1860s when the *Philadelphia Public Ledger* introduced "24 Rules" that stressed accuracy and fairness in reporting on the Civil War. In 1922, the American Society of Newspaper Editors was formed and at its first meeting appointed a committee to formulate a code of ethics. By 1923, seven "Canons of Journalism" had been adopted by the Society. At that time, concerns centered on newspaper responsibility, truthfulness, accuracy, impartiality, fair play, and decency. In 1908, the first school of journalism was established at the University of Missouri, and in 1912, the Columbia University School of Journalism was created (Berry 2008: 80).

Klaidman and Beauchamp's *The Virtuous Journalist* (1987) offers an appropriate framework for this discussion of media ethics and criminal justice. Noting the special position of the media under the U.S. Constitution and the familiar refrain *"freedom of the press,"* the authors argue that in overall ethical terms, the issue of limits to the freedom of the media is determined by competing moral rights—that media freedom is constrained by the rights of others (p. 120). Thus, media freedom may be overridden by the competing moral right not to be defamed or by other rights. Often, there will be controversy about which rights are in the balance and which right has the greater moral weight.

Klaidman and Beauchamp take the view that *journalists ought to make the necessary ethical decisions* themselves instead of adopting the approach that a journalist or broadcaster has absolute freedom to publish anything unless the courts rule otherwise (p. 12). They argue that leaving the issue to be decided by the law amounts to abnegation of responsibility for moral decision-making and designates the issue as one of law rather than morality. Thus, they call on the press to develop procedures to ensure that this balancing of rights and interests will be accomplished wisely. As noted in Chapter 1, it is important not to confuse legal issues with moral issues; as Klaidman and Beauchamp put it, "Although the law is often concerned with moral problems, it is not the basic repository of our moral standards and values"(p. 12). They give the example of a journalist who may not be legally liable for libel but may still bear moral responsibility for that libel. Thus, inventing facts for a media story may not attract a legal penalty but is still morally problematic. This occurred, for example, when Janet Cooke made up a story about juvenile drug abuse; her actions were not illegal, but few argued they were morally correct. In a newspaper article titled "Jimmy's World" that appeared in *The Washington Post* on September 28, 1980, Cooke wrote a gripping profile of the life of an 8-year-old heroin addict. The story generated a high level of sympathy among readers, and the mayor of Washington, D.C., organized an all-out police search for the boy, which was unsuccessful and led to claims that the story was fraudulent. Cooke received a Pulitzer Prize for the story, which she returned after her deception had been uncovered.

Klaidman and Beauchamp (1987) suggest that virtuous traits are critical in a profession such as journalism, where stories are often produced in haste and under pressure of events. They propose that *cultivating moral virtues* ought, therefore, to be an ongoing process within the media so that fundamental virtues such as honesty and trustworthiness are embedded and operationalized in stress situations. They also propose that reporters and editors should foster the virtues of "fairness, truthfulness, trustworthiness and nonmalevolence (avoiding harm)" but do not see a place for "tenderness and compassion" (p. 19; see Chapter 14 for a discussion of virtue ethics). In their account of a "the virtuous journalist," the authors discuss the following virtues: truth, avoiding bias, avoiding harm, serving the public, maintaining trust, escaping manipulation and inviting criticism, and being accountable. They note that in the media, fairness seems to subsume other discrete virtues incorporating impartiality, bias, incompleteness, imbalance, and the like (p. 21). In addition, fairness links to competence because "standards such as fairness and accuracy are moral dimensions of competence" (p. 23).

Competence is a key issue for the media, and its absence—or any weakness in competence—can be revealed when a journalist is unable to separate his or her personal beliefs from the subject matter of the reporting. Failing to separate notes and writing from source materials can also be problematic because it can result in plagiarism. Competence may be general in the sense that a journalist should possess the skills to cover a multitude of different tasks, such as recognizing a story, telling a story through language well enough to convey its importance to readers, organizing and editing copy, checking facts quickly and accurately, and achieving the correct balance in presenting a story. Specific competence, however, relates to a specific context and a defined task (Klaidman and Beauchamp 1987: 24).

Responsibility (e.g., in the use of sources of information) and competence are linked together, and incompetence may be the outcome of a moral failure of responsibility rather than a lack of skill. The journalistic propensity to simplify can also be seen as a mark of competence. As Chibnall observes, news stories must be shaped to meet varying standards of readership ability, and, as he puts it, "good reporting involves 'pruning down' the reality of a situation, trimming its rough edges and moulding its shape to fit the pre-existing forms of news" (in Greer 2010: 207).

REPORTING THE TRUTH

Reporting the truth to the public is fundamental to the role of the media in society, as well as a moral responsibility of the media (Klaidman and Beauchamp 1987: 30). It is an element in all journalism codes of ethics; for example, the *Declaration of Principles on the Conduct of Journalists of the International Federation of Journalists*, adopted in 1954, says, "Respect for truth and for the right of the public to truth is the first duty of the journalist" (EthicNet n.d.). Truth is perceived to be a desired ethical value "and is seen as an end-goal developed by methodological rigour, for once subjective opinion fuses with facts then truth has become infected" (Berry 2008: 111).

However, the concept of the truth in journalism is not unproblematic. For example, there are questions about the scope of truth, about the completeness of truth, and concerning the quality of information that is published or broadcast. What, for example, is the responsibility of a journalist for making sure that information is not alarmist? How much information about a risk such as a health danger is appropriate to give the public?

Characteristics of Stories

Klaidman and Beauchamp (1987: 32–50) argue that in covering stories where the public's right to know is a determining factor, stories should have the following characteristics:

- *Be substantially complete*—This is the point at which a reasonable reader's requirements for information are fulfilled. It is essential to present the broader context when reporting on complex issues of legitimate public interest. The reader should be able to apprehend all the material or important descriptions of an event and the report should avoid framing an issue in a particular way. The process of framing news has been explained as "a central organizing idea for news content that supplies a context and suggests what the issue is through the use of selection, emphasis, exclusion, and elaboration" (Tankard, Hendrickson, Silberman, Bliss, and Ghanem, 1991).

- *Encourage objective understanding*—This entails shaping a story so as not to suggest a preference for one set of values over another, presenting the views of experts on both sides of an issue but at the same time not presenting views that are clearly uninformed or absurd. Thus, objectivity connotes balance in the sense that a process is employed that weighs different accounts and again avoids framing an issue in a particular way that would undermine its objectivity. Thus, objective reporting is seen as a means for achieving truth (Berry 2008: 111). However, the notion that news reporting is not laden with values and is objective is highly questionable. As David Kidd-Hewitt (1995) observes, the media function "as purveyors of particular social constructions of social reality rather than as objective reporters" (p. 13). Lawrence adds that the notion of the objective professional journalist is firmly embedded in American culture, but journalistic objectivity is something of a myth because, as she puts it,

  > this meaning of "objectivity" tells reporters that in a world full of competing sources making competing claims, it is best to report information that can be officially verified and make less use of sources and claims that are most likely to invite charges of bias. "Objectivity" thus becomes reporting "what happened" in a way that is least likely to be criticized by those in power (2000: 52–53).

  > Media objectivity has been described as a matter of "strategic rituals that when followed allow reporters to claim impartiality" (Heeren & Messing 2009: 206). The rituals include references to authoritative sources, presenting opposing claims, and using quotations to create distance between the reporter and the report.

  > *Cost* is also a factor, as noted by Edward Herman and Noam Chomsky (cited in Greer 2010: 37), because taking information from apparently credible sources minimizes investigative expense. Thus, for reporters, the most credible sources are official sources, and therefore news accounts are often biased in their favor.

- *Be balanced and accurate*—This means developing a story from sound evidence and reporting as fact only information in respect of which there is accurate and sufficient evidence. If there is any doubt as to the accuracy of an account, that doubt should be reflected in the story. Inaccurate reporting can arise when a story unproblematically repeats an initially inaccurate report. Such a situation occurred in New Bedford, Massachusetts, in 1984 when a cheering crowd of onlookers in Big Dan's Tavern reportedly witnessed a gang rape. In fact, at the trials of the six alleged rapists, the prosecution alleged that other than the six defendants and the victim, only three people were in the bar and that the bartender and a customer sought to call the police but were prevented from doing so by one of the six. There was no crowd of cheering onlookers.

Figure 11.1   IFJ Declaration of Principles on the Conduct of Journalists

Ethic Net   Journalism ethics

Home   Codes   Search

IFJ Declaration of Principles on the Conduct of Journalists

This international Declaration is proclaimed as a standard of professional conduct for journalists engaged in gathering, transmitting, disseminating and commenting on news and information in describing events.

1. Respect for truth and for the right of the public to truth is the first duty of the journalist.
2. In pursuance of this duty, the journalist shall at all times defend the principles of freedom in the honest collection and publication of news, and of the right of fair comment and criticism.
3. The journalist shall report only in accordance with facts of which he/she knows the origin. The journalist shall not suppress essential information or falsify documents.
4. The journalist shall use only fair methods to obtain news, photographs and documents.
5. The journalist shall do the utmost to rectify any published information which is found to be harmfully inaccurate.
6. The journalist shall observe professional secrecy regarding the source of information obtained in confidence.
7. The journalist shall be aware of the danger of discrimination being furthered by the media, and shall do the utmost to avoid facilitating such discrimination based on, among other things, race, sex, sexual orientation, language, religion, political or other opinions, and national or social origins.
8. The journalist shall regard as grave professional offences the following:
   – plagiarism;
   – malicious misrepresentation;
   – calumny, slander, libel, unfounded accusations;
   – the acceptance of a bribe in any form in consideration of either publication or suppression.
9. Journalists worthy of the name shall deem it their duty to observe faithfully the principles stated above. Within the general law of each country the journalist shall recognize in professional matters the jurisdiction of colleagues only, to the exclusion of every kind of interference by governments or others.

SOURCE: EthicNet n.d. http://ethicnet.uta.fi/international/declaration_of_principles_on_the_conduct_of_journalists

Crime and Media Stereotyping of Young Black Males

Critics charge that the media provides versions of reality that avoid controversy, protect the status quo, and shun complexity and that this approach results in uninformed audiences and stereotyping based on class, gender, and race (Jewkes 2015: 29). Inaccurate reporting is exemplified in media depictions of young black men portrayed as overwhelmingly responsible for crime. Media stereotyping of young black men in this manner has deeply embedded into public consciousness an image of the "young black male as a violent and menacing street thug" (Welch 2007: 276). There is a common perception that most crime is committed by blacks, and it is true that blacks are disproportionately involved in crime. Although making up only about 13% of the population, in 2002 blacks accounted for 38% of arrests for violent crimes and 27% of arrests for property crime (p. 276). As Welch notes, the war against drugs did much to strengthen the association between blacks and crime, as blacks took to crack cocaine as the drug of choice because of its relative cheapness and easy acquisition. The truth, however, is that whites comprise about 75% of illegal drug users and blacks 13%, a fact not usually incorporated in media accounts of drug dealing and the drug war (p. 279). Discussing media coverage of the drug war, Michael Tonry observes, "Newspapers, television, and movies regularly portray trafficking in cocaine and crack as characteristic of inner-city minority neighborhoods. Any mildly informed person in the late 1980s knew that the major fronts in the drug wars were located in minority neighborhoods" (1995: 105).

Stereotyping of black males as criminal was dramatically demonstrated in 1994 when Susan Smith drowned her sons, aged 3 years and 14 months, by strapping them into their car seats and allowing the vehicle to roll slowly into a lake. She reported to police that her car had been stolen by a black male with her children inside it. The story was immediately national news, and a manhunt began for the black male killer. Nine days later Susan Smith confessed to having killed the boys. *The New York Times* commented that she had chosen a black male as the monster killer to generate the most sympathy for herself, especially among whites (Lawson 2015: 340). In a meta-analysis of eight studies of the representation of blacks in local television news in Orlando, Ted Chiricos and Sarah Eschholz (2002: 400) found that while blacks and whites were depicted as criminals at similar rates, when blacks appeared on television in any role, they were more than twice as likely to appear as criminal suspects rather than in positive roles, as compared to whites. The image of the black male as criminal is now so deeply embedded that alleged victims use the persona to enhance fabricated accounts of crimes.

Images of Black Criminality

In 1995, Maryrose Posner claimed to have been robbed by an armed black male while she and her 2-year-old daughter stood at a bank automatic teller machine. She alleged that a laughing man put a gun to her child's head and then ran to a waiting vehicle and left the scene with three other black males. She later admitted in court that her story was a complete fabrication and that she had constructed it to get attention from her busy cardiologist husband. Although she later retracted her confession, she ultimately pled guilty to a second-degree charge of filing a false statement.

SOURCE: Rome 2006: 80.

Dennis Rome (2006) presents a process model showing how media imagery creates and blends with stereotypes to perpetuate the image of the criminal black male:

Step 1 ↓

The media constantly disseminate images and depictions of crime; they are largely images of street crime with poor whites and especially blacks shown to be the perpetrators. When the public communicates about crime, it adopts these images.

Step 2 ↓

The public composes conceptual summaries of media depictions of crime for the sake of convenience, and these become symbolic of all crime and criminality.

(Continued)

(Continued)

Step 3 ↓

As the public communicates its received concept of crime, the concept begins to form a reality.

Step 4 ↓

Once the concept is firmly embedded in the mind, indicators of its existence are searched for in the media.

SOURCE: Rome, Dennis M. 2006. "The Social Construction of the African American Criminal Stereotype." Pp. 78–87 in *Images of Color, Images of Crime*, edited by Coramae Richey Mann, Marjorie S. Zatz, and Nancy Rodriguez. Oxford, England: Oxford University Press.

Jody Miller, Toya Z. Like, and Peter Levin (2006: 112) argue that in the popular media treatment of race and crime whites are presumed noncriminal by nature, and therefore, their crimes have to be explained by reference to life factors such as early childhood traumas, abuse, and psychological factors. A good example is Jeffrey Dahmer, a serial killer who murdered, mutilated, and dismembered 17 people, storing body parts in his apartment. While early media depictions used words such as *evil* and *monster* to describe him, the media soon began to focus on his childhood traumas to explain his behavior and highlighted his religious conversion from the time of his arrest (p. 116). In the case of black criminals, the same questions are not asked because criminality is assumed in their nature.

Media Stereotyping of Gender and Crime

Masculine assumptions are commonly deployed by the media to characterize women's experience of crime, especially crimes of violence which are deemed more newsworthy. Thus, when women come into conflict with the law as perpetrators or victims, the media call upon a set of assumptions that either valorize or demonize them. One such assumption is the "good woman" or the "bad woman" label, which assigns the category of Madonna or virgin to marriageable women and whores and vamps to women who are sexually available (Humphries 2009: 19). This device enables the media to label women so that, for example, in cases of rape the media raise issues of provocation or consent, suggesting the victim was to blame or at least has to explain "questionable conduct." Similarly, in cases of date rape the man is often assumed to have

innocently misread the circumstances or the woman was not sufficiently explicit about her intentions.

A prime instance of media reporting of the "good woman" was the Laci Peterson case in 2003. Laci's husband, Scott Peterson, reported her missing to police on December 24, 2002, when she was 8-months pregnant. He claimed to have been on a fishing trip and did not miss his wife until he returned home late on Christmas Eve. Scott Peterson became a suspect in his wife's disappearance when it became known that he was having an affair with another woman, Amber Frye. While he denied any wrongdoing, police found the decomposed body of Laci and her unborn child near where Scott said he had gone fishing. Scott was charged with murder but fled while on bail; he changed his appearance but was recaptured. He was convicted of first-degree murder on November 12, 2004, and sentenced to death.

The media narrative throughout presented Laci as the epitome of the good woman—as a domestic, stay-home wife and homemaker, as attractive, pregnant, and a schoolteacher. She was described in terms of being the perfect wife and daughter—as part of an attractive couple; as an excited, expectant mother; as a great cook and friend to all—and her death was treated by the media as a "national tragedy" (Meloy and Miller 2009: 34). In contrast, Scott became the "evil husband"—a cheater, liar, and adulterer. The case attracted enormous public attention as the story of the "All-American couple," epitomizing the cultural ideal of homemaking, affluence, and being young, white, and physically attractive. As the story unfolded and the image became tarnished, it became an iconic narrative about the fall from grace (p. 37). The case illustrates how conforming to traditional stereotypes of the good woman brings rewards in the form of respectful media coverage.

In contrast to the story of Laci Peterson, that of missing Hispanic woman Evelyn Hernandez attracted little media attention. Compared to Laci, Evelyn had a troublesome life as a legal immigrant from El Salvador who went missing in May 2002 with her 5-year-old son. No members of her community termed Evelyn *a friend to all*, she lacked education, gave birth when a teenager, and was unmarried. Evelyn's body washed up in San Francisco Bay in July 2003—the same place as Laci's body would be found about a year later. There was no national media coverage of Evelyn—only five stories over the 11 months from when she went missing until her body was found—compared to the hundreds of local stories about Laci (Jirard 2010: 85).

The media read black women through a lens that sees them as "Mammy" or the black matriarch—the former an image that calls up the role of the black woman as a domestic servant in a wealthy white family and as one who socializes her children to meet the demands of white society, the latter as emblematic of the role that such women play in poor black families and as one who lacks parenting skills, commits crime, and cannot hold down a job. Moreover, black women's sexuality is framed differently—as eroticized whore (Humphries 2009: 22).

Women who kill are commonly framed by the media as being extra deviant because they have subverted the conception of the nurturing and emotional mother or passive and cooperative wife. A woman who kills "profoundly challenges deeply held assumptions about women and their capacity to nurture others" (quoted in Easteal, Bartels, Nelson, and Holland 2015: 32). To explain this deviance, the media commonly portray women killers as insane or emotionally unstable, as domestic-violence victims, or as sexual deviants and bad mothers and wives. In other words, they are perceived to be aberrations of true womanhood (p. 32).

The media narrative of Susan Smith—who killed her two young boys by strapping them into their car seats and allowing the car to run into a lake—described her as a "bad mother" who committed "unnatural" acts. The media reported her victimization as a child—sexual abuse by her stepfather, unfaithfulness by her husband, and rejection by her boyfriend—but when the media discovered she had consensual sex with her stepfather 6 months before

killing her children, her personal history was used against her, and she was characterized as a "temptress who invited and enjoyed sexual attention" and as having grown up "to become a promiscuous, sexually exploitive young adult" (Easteal et al. 2015: 25).

In the case of Andrea Yates who drowned her five children in the bathtub in 2001 and then told police she had murdered them to save them from Satan, the media portrayal categorized her as mad, stressing her history of attempted suicides, depression, and frequent hospitalizations. She was convicted of murder but then successfully appealed and was found not guilty by virtue of insanity. The media coverage differed from that of Susan Smith because the media offered reports that attempted to understand why she committed this crime (Easteal et al. 2015: 36).

Media Distortions of Crime and Victims of Crime

Content analyses of crime stories reveal what Surette (2011) terms the *law of opposites* because the nature of crime, criminals, and victims portrayed in the media is generally the complete opposite of the pattern shown through official crime statistics or victim surveys. The following are characteristics of crime stories regularly found in content analyses:

- Crime stories are a prominent feature of all media.
- Crime stories are overwhelmingly about serious violent crime against individuals, with homicide being the primary crime.
- Offenders and victims in media stories are generally of higher status in society and older than those actually involved in crime.
- The risks of crime are presented as more serious than are described as probable in authoritative official statistical reports or victim surveys.
- Police and the criminal justice system are generally represented in a highly favorable manner, and police corruption is often explained using the "bad apples" analogy rather than as a systematic practice.
- Crime stories focus on special and discrete cases, and the wider issues of causation, policy, and trends receive little or no attention (Reiner, Livingstone, and Allen 2003: 15–16).

How can unrealistic and distorted media representations of crime be transformed? Greg Barak (1994: 237) has proposed a project of "news-making criminology" that would aim to

- demystify images of crime and punishment;
- strive to affect public attitudes and discourses about crime and bring about a public policy based on structural and historical analyses of institutional development;
- allow criminologists to deploy their knowledge and show themselves to be credible voices in public policy making on crime; and
- call on criminologists to develop the necessary media skills to participate in dialogues on crime and justice.

Criminologists have been slow to take up this challenge, and as punitive populism has taken the lead on crime control, experts like criminologists have been sidelined in favor of populist narratives that argue against expertise and in favor of so-called common sense approaches.

Robert Elias (1994, 1996) has argued that the media misrepresents the situation of crime victims by distorting the causes and impact of victimization and by presenting victims as passive and vulnerable. There is no doubt that the media has given increasing attention to victims, with the result that victims now constitute one of the key sources through which crime is portrayed and understood in conditions of modernity. The harm caused by crime is equated with the suffering of victims as well as with the potential threat of victimization, and readers are invited to identify with victims. The media has been accused of perpetuating the image of the "ideal victim" by focusing attention only on victims who meet that standard of victimhood (De Mesmaecker 2010). Media decide the relative newsworthiness of victims according to the degree of emotion engendered by a victim's experience. In this way, the media promote a stereotypical victim and discount those who do not fit the typification. Thus, media accounts rarely differentiate victims and provide a false image of victimization and victims (p. 251).

A Closer Look

Comic Books: Constructions of Crime, Justice, and Punishment

Narratives about crime and punishment that do not match lived experience and disregard official data are not exclusive to the news media. In popular culture, comic books have been disseminating crime stories since they were created in the 1930s. While today comic books have a limited readership, their narratives, characters, and constructions of crime and justice are increasingly being translated into films like *Spider-Man, Superman, Batman, Captain America, Iron Man,* and the *X-Men* series and into video games like *The Avengers, Fantastic Four,* and *Wolverine.*

Based on a content analysis of about 200 comic books sold between 2002 and 2010 and the responses of focus groups of readers, Phillips and Strobl in *Comic Book Crime: Truth, Justice and the American Way* examine the depiction of crime and punishment in these popular cultural texts with the aim of understanding how such texts negotiate cultural meanings about crime. The authors explain the moral themes promoted by comic book superheroes and how readers absorb and reproduce the notions of crime, justice, and punishment acted out by comic book characters like Superman, Superwoman, and Batman. The authors contend that comic book narratives communicate messages about the motivations for crime and influence and shape public attitudes and understanding of crime (2013: 83).

Comic books originated in the 1930s as an offshoot of newspaper comic strips. In 1938, the character of Superman was created, and he was tasked to remedy injustice and fight organized and white-collar crime and corrupt city officials (Phillips and Strobl 2013: 22). The Batman character was created in 1939 as a darker, more threatening crime fighter. The period from the 1930s to the 1950s is regarded as comics' Golden Age when numerous superheroes emerged, including the Flash, Green Lantern, Wonder Woman, Green Arrow, and Captain America. During the 1940s, comic books were found in almost every home but experienced a decline after 1945 when they began to depict forms of extreme violence. By the 1950s, they were being attacked by psychiatrists as contributing to juvenile delinquency (p. 25). In 1948, an industry code prohibited sadism, torture, and obscene language, and depictions of law enforcement and justice officials as "stupid or ineffective" were banned. Later iterations of the code required that there should be no depictions of disrespect for established authority, that "in every instance good shall triumph over evil," and that criminals should always receive punishment (p. 27).

During the 1960s and 1970s, comic books ventured into social commentary, and racial diversity was displayed: The 1975 X-Men team included many races, and some black superheroes appeared in the 1970s, including Black Panther (Phillips and Strobl 2013: 33). Comic narratives became more complex during the 1980s as characters began to question their roles as possessors of powers beyond the ordinary. It seemed that the traditional conventions of the superhero were no longer adequate for the times (p. 34). Since the 1990s, the superhero has translated to the motion picture, and the comic book industry continues to experience declining sales.

The dominant themes extracted from the texts are conceptions of crime fighting, justice, and punishment articulated by the comic's writers, artists, and editors and consumed by readers.

Crime Fighting

The heroes and superheroes that dominate this genre are commonly depicted as white males who fight crime to restore a timeless American way of life. They are hypermasculine, often brawny and macho, and project strength and power. Female crime fighters must retain their femininity while also demonstrating competence to fight crime like a man. Race is deployed in complex ways, sometimes stereotypically, but often in multiple constructions, though minorities are rarely displayed as characters. Comic book narratives inform readers when violence is an appropriate response to crime, but violence is often the chosen response. Some characters always use violence in fighting crime, but others (like Superman) use violence that incapacitates but does not actually kill.

Typically, narratives depict the present as a time of crisis and despair, caused by a criminal threat of apocalyptic proportions. The threat may be government corruption, terrorism, organized crime, street crime, and even war crimes such as genocide. Fears of the demise of family, democracy, and freedom are prevalent. Evil looms in the gritty cities, which are populated by strippers, gangs, and corrupt leaders who have collectively collapsed the social order so that the prime objective is now survival. Frank Miller's *Sin City* in movie form expertly expresses this conception, and Gotham City created in the *Batman* series has become the icon of the urban dystopia—"a distorted metropolis that corrupts the souls of good men" (Phillips and Strobl 2013: 76).

Superheroes are tasked to restore stability because law enforcement is commonly depicted as incompetent and incapable of coping with the criminality that challenges it. Many narratives show criminals with psychopathic personalities, and crime is commonly framed as deeply rooted within the personality. Social, economic, and structural factors associated with criminality are ignored. Thus, individualistic explanations are offered to explain criminal origins often signified by physical distinguishing marks indicating the evil contained within the villain—for example, Batman villain Harry Dent is disfigured by acid, leaving the left side of his face deeply scarred (Phillips and Strobl 2013: 88), and the mental instability of the Joker is signified by his white makeup, greenish hair, and red lips (p. 89).

As well, numerous villains are portrayed as having suffered childhood traumas that have shaped their motivations and life choices. While Batman was traumatized as a child by seeing his parents murdered

(Continued)

(Continued)

in front of him, he has directed his rage toward the public good, but his antagonists, such as Scarecrow (who was sadistically punished as a child and locked in a dark room where crows would fly in and attack him), have turned their rage on others, nurturing their victimhood and sometimes becoming psychopathic like the Joker (Phillips and Strobl 2013: 92).

Justice

Criminality is presented as so dire that combating it is beyond the capacity of the community, hence the need for heroes or a team of heroes to restore social order. Superheroes generally shun approaches to justice that employ peaceful means; various forms of "justice" are employed, including decisions to kill antagonists, but within a context where such action is justified by the complete failure of the criminal justice system, including the corruption of justice actors (Phillips and Strobl 2013: 109). The theme of good versus evil predominates with superheroes presented as models of rectitude and righteousness. For example, Batman stands over the Joker and states, "There was good and evil. Red and black. Life and death. The joke and the punchline" (p. 111). These dichotomies simplify moral choices, and while some superheroes often act, in effect, as vigilantes, others maintain a firm "no kill" policy, expressing contrary views of what justice requires. Generally, crime control is the preferred model, and other options as well as due process are disdained, as signified by displays of extreme violence, such as brutal interrogations that are always justified by the severity of the crisis or the imminence of the threat to social order. *The Punisher* series exemplifies the vigilante approach to justice (he routinely seeks the death of his antagonists) in contrast to the *Wonder Woman* series, where violence is eschewed unless necessary to save oneself.

Punishment

Retribution and incapacitation (see Chapter 6 on punishment) are the predominant themes in comic book justice. Treatment and rehabilitation and forms of restorative justice are rare occurrences: The Joker's sidekick, Harley Quinn, declares, "There will always be a Joker. Because there's no cure for him. No cure at all. Just a Batman" (Phillips and Strobl 2013: 198). Deterrence is expressed and endorsed but within a framework of retribution, as, for example, in displays of violence that are intended to communicate the consequences of criminality. Comic book narratives affirm there is pleasure to be gained in punishing those who deserve it. The authors note that some villains are deemed to be "deathworthy" based on the nature of their crimes, the impact on victims, and the personality of the superhero engaged in a particular confrontation; for example, Batman's self-imposed rules limit killing, regardless of the nature of the crime. Phillips and Strobl (2013) found that a villain was deathworthy if: (a) the killing was done in self-defense, (b) the villain had done harm to others, (c) the villain was morally depraved (e.g., a junkie who admits he will do anything to obtain more drugs), and (d) innocents have been killed as collateral damage (p. 129).

A character's dilemma is often presented as a limited choice between killing or incapacitation, the former being an instrument for advancing justice because prisons are revealed as prone to breakouts and riots. Only prisons classed as *maximum-maximum* security where inmates have no human contact and inhabit cells reinforced with steel and "adamantium" (a fictional indestructible metal) will suffice (Phillips and Strobl 2013: 207).

Phillips and Strobl argue that "for fans, one of the major attractions to comic books is the emotional resonance of retributive justice—the visceral response to the violent narratives and graphic imagery" (2013: 216). Comic books are a seductive site where readers may express moral outrage through the characters and participate in crime fighting and dispense harsher justice than is acceptable outside the world of comic book morality.

Media and Moral Panics

Media accounts that engender moral panics, such as stories about school shootings, sex crimes—especially those involving children—and specific and unusual cases like the James Bulger case in the United Kingdom, amplify deviance and function as advocacy for greater levels of social control (Jewkes 2011: 74). The media no longer simply report the facts of the case but take these cases as exemplars and articulations of wider social issues and concerns, raising the level of public anxiety and generating fears about the forces of evil and threats to social order. Thus, crime comes to be read as a warning that society is in danger of being destabilized unless something is done. The "something" is usually a set of measures that enhance levels of social control beyond what is rational or necessary (see Chapter 9). In this way, the media influence crime control policies, as Surette (2011) observes:

> The media therefore supply a large amount of information about specific crimes and convey the impression that criminals threaten the social order and its institutions with imminent collapse. Media provide less information to help the public comprehend the larger society-wide forces that underlie individual crimes and cases. Rare is the thematic interpretive analysis that places criminal information in historical, sociological, or political context. (p. 183)

The media project a consistent message that crime is caused by ruthless predatory individuals who are inherently evil and that they can only be challenged by an unfettered crime fighter. Crime, then, is the product of individual choice, a matter of individual personality, and social and structural factors are irrelevant. The emphasis is on the front end of the justice system: Investigations and arrests promote policies that favor law enforcement. This simplistic portrayal of crime by the media is accompanied by solutions that involve violence and aggression, widespread use of weapons, sophisticated technology, and heavy punishment (Surette 2011: 186). The media tend to deal in what Jewkes (2011: 49) calls *binary oppositions*—that is, to present events as choices between good and evil, guilt and innocence, and deviant, dangerous, or sick as opposed to normal. These processes of simplification obscure and distort the complex reality of life; for example, a terrorist is designated completely evil, and the problematic of terrorism versus freedom fighting is ignored. Thus, criminals have no redeeming features—they are simply bad and dangerous.

In 2013, the media actively promoted a moral panic referred to as the "knockout game" that involved alleged random black-on-white assaults for fun. It became a dominant narrative, drawing on the trope of white fears of black violence. Reports of knockout game attacks in numerous cities were featured daily in the media, with videos showing groups of blacks walking casually down a street and sucker-punching a passing white person for no apparent reason and saying nothing (King 2015: 86). In fact, the videos were "an anecdotal amalgam of footage selected from all over the country over a span of years" (p. 86). The New York City police commissioner publicly refuted the alleged attacks, indicating there was no evidence of any increase in random attacks and asking the media to be more responsible in its reporting. In fact, data from the Department of Justice revealed a decrease in random assaults of whites on blacks and blacks on whites.

It appears the origins of this moral panic were to be found in a 2012 self-published book called *White Girl Bleed a Lot: The Return of Racial Violence to America* written by Colin Flaherty, who was named by the Southern Poverty Law Center, which tracks hate crimes and extremists, as a "White Nationalist propagandist" (King 2015: 88). The cable channel, Fox News, is said to have taken a central role in promoting the story so that its media competitors were also obliged to cover it, thus amplifying the panic. The media coverage not only fostered fears of black-on-white violence, but began to frame the narrative in terms of white victimization and self-defense and the so-called "stand your ground" laws in some states that legitimate the use of lethal force as an act of self-defense in defined circumstances (p. 90). Consistent with the moral-panic thesis, within days of the peaking of the story legislators in a number of states began formulating new laws to target the supposed knockout game, despite the fact that assaulting another person was already punishable under numerous laws. An example was a proposed Washington State law that created the offense of randomly assaulting a stranger and made it a mandatory felony. It is argued that this moral panic was designed to construct and support an argument that whites were subject to racial oppression (p. 92).

A Closer Look

The College Experience: Media Representations of "Binge Drinking" and Unsafe and Violent Campuses

Since about 2000, media reports of crimes, including shootings and sexual assaults, and of alcohol abuse on campuses have become regular occurrences. If the media reports are correctly portraying the situation, then "a dark side" of academia has been revealed. In *The Dark Side of the Ivory Tower: Campus Crime as a Social Problem*, John Sloan and Bonnie Fisher (2011) examine claims about campus crime and alcohol abuse (and other campus-related anxiety and risk issues that will not be discussed here) and argue the following:

- Historical evidence shows that violence and alcohol abuse have long been common on college campuses in the United States, and therefore, recent reports have not revealed some hidden or unknown concern.

- Starting from the 1980s, issues that were treated as private problems for campuses have been rendered public issues of concern so that crime on campus and alcohol abuse—so-called "binge drinking"—have been declared by government agencies, advocates, and the media to be major social problems that require a public policy response.

- Concerns about crime and alcohol abuse have been socially constructed as new social problems. As explained in theories of social construction, this means that crime and alcohol abuse have been "discovered" through the efforts of advocates—called claims makers—with aid and support from the media. Thus, these issues have been labeled *social problems* not through a level of objective evidence, but through a process of social construction (see Chapter 9 for a discussion of moral panics).

Violence and Crime on Campus: Historical Accounts

Since the 1980s, the notion of college as a place set apart for contemplation and study has changed. Some campuses, such as Virginia Tech and Northern Illinois, have suffered shooting incidents, and the 24-hour news cycle has ensured that almost every incident involving crime or violence on a college campus has received media saturation. Campuses have become sites for social problems, even while history shows that since the founding of the first colleges in the United States much campus crime has been a routine fact of college life. The authors map crime and violence from the 1600s through today and conclude that from early times students have always engaged in improper and sometimes illegal behavior. Students were frequently drunk, conducted hazing of other students, and assaulted and even murdered fellow students. In the South during the 19th century, students followed a code of honor that endorsed and encouraged drunkenness, gambling, sexual promiscuity, and general deviant behaviors. In this period, violence was commonplace as students brawled and rioted when angered by the college administration.

Violence and Crime on Campus: Modern Period

During the first part of the 20th century, campuses were described as "play worlds" for mainly middle- and upper-class students, where alcohol consumption was a tradition and alcohol abuse before, during, and after football games, followed by student brawling, was a weekly highlight. During the 1920s, male and female relationships became more flexible, and a survey in 1925 among students ranked "sex irregularity" as first among "what was a sin for college students." With the end of prohibition in 1933, drinking alcohol became less exciting. In the 1940s, students returning from the war were mature veterans who concentrated on completing their education. During the 1950s, various fads were popular, including large-scale panty raids, during which students invaded dormitories to collect lingerie; sometimes women were assaulted or carried outside in their pajamas during these episodes. It was in this period that the spring break became an institutionalized feature of college life. The 1960s was a time of political agitation and engagement on many campuses, associated especially with the Vietnam War, and involved mass takeovers of college buildings, clashes between students and police, relaxed sexual mores, and a culture of drug taking. In the 1970s and 1980s, there occurred a transformational change in the mass media as CNN began continuous news broadcasting, and immediacy became the media priority, with new technologies such as video and satellite assisting the trend toward sensational coverage and simplistic narratives within short-time frames.

Campus Crime: A Social Problem

In the 1980s and 1990s, the media began to run stories suggesting that campus crime had become a social issue and a threat to the well-being of millions of students: Major newspapers asserted that criminal victimization was running at "unprecedented," "startling," or "heretofore unimagined" levels. There were also reports of hazing activities resulting in injury or even death, and the presence of guns on campus was presented as a new danger to students. Overall, reports indicated students were confronted by unprecedented levels of danger, and no student could be regarded as safe on any campus. It was claimed there existed an "epidemic of violence" that was being concealed by college administrators to increase enrollment.

Responding to these concerns and to social anxieties, state courts began to hold institutions liable for student victimizations; the *Student Right-to-Know and Campus Security Act* of 1990 required colleges to report crime data annually, and programs focusing on alcohol abuse and sexual victimization were designed and introduced. Students organized Take Back the Night, an annual candlelight event to raise awareness about violence against college women. Technology also played a role in the form of security measures, such as computer-controlled or key-card access to facilities on campus, closed-circuit television, and general upgrades in security that included formulating "best practices," crime prevention activities, and community policing.

The authors asked what explained this seemingly sudden concern about events that had been commonplace in the history of colleges. Their analysis revealed that claims makers, with assistance from the media and a group of researchers, played major roles in altering perceptions about crime on campus. Once the public had accepted that a social problem existed, other interest groups joined the claims makers and pressed legislators, college administrators, and the courts to devise solutions to these "new" social problems.

The foremost claims maker on campus crime was Security On Campus, Inc. (SOC), a lobbying group founded in 1988 by the parents of a Lehigh University student who was brutally murdered in her dorm room in 1986; it was supported by other crime victims and their families who carried their stories to the media and filed lawsuits. SOC routinely used the student's murder to typify the abundant violence to be found on college campuses. It claimed one murder was being committed every 10 days, that one out of five students was a crime victim, and that "hundreds and thousands" of students were being victimized. The parents appeared on national television talk shows, conducted numerous print media interviews, and testified before the House and the Senate. They were regarded as experts on the problem.

(Continued)

(Continued)

SOC commonly presented campus crime data without any context, issuing "fact sheets" that itemized the number and nature of campus crimes over a time period. Thus, they presented an aggregate figure for crime over a 3-year period, ignoring the context of on which campuses the crimes had occurred or how many students were enrolled. SOC therefore failed to present any rational unit of comparison—for example, the number of reported offenses per 10,000 students. Claims makers preferred not to precisely define the nature of "campus crime," which could therefore mean any act from a minor theft up to homicide.

Social constructionist theories suggest that claims makers are familiar with the role of the media in creating social problems and that they depend on media assistance to bring their cause to the general public. Thus, the media narratives framed crime on campus as "idyllic campuses in a violent world" and contrasted "evil" villains with "innocent" victims, presented disparate instances of campus crime as examples of the larger problem, and broadcast emotionally charged accounts of the problem. It was important also to portray campus crime as a new problem: It would then gain more media attention as an issue that could touch the millions of parents with children in college or of college age.

Binge Drinking on Campuses

Drinking alcohol, moderately or otherwise, is a choice faced by students as they transition into campus life. Some observers identify a core "party culture," said to approve of drinking not only after class in the evenings and on weekends, but before class. This culture is also said to condone drinking alcohol before, during, and after sporting events and is supported by marketing campaigns by the beer, wine, and spirits industry. Alcohol may also play a central role in the annual pledge process, and it may be used as a means of breaking down inhibitions to facilitate social connections on campus. According to this view then, drinking becomes a pervasive part in campus social gatherings.

In 2007, the National Institute of Alcohol Abuse and Alcoholism reported that during that year about 60% of enrolled students at tertiary institutions self-reported they were regular drinkers of alcohol. About 5% reported daily alcohol use, and 40% that they had consumed five or more drinks in a single sitting during the previous 2-week period. The data also showed that 1,700 students aged 18 to 24 die annually form alcohol-related injuries. This behavior was labeled *binge drinking* by the U.S. Surgeon General. The Harvard School of Public Health's *College Alcohol Study* series defined binge drinking as the consumption of five or more alcoholic drinks in a row at one sitting for men and four or more such drinks for women (commonly referred to as the "five/four definition") on more than one occasion during a 2-week period. College researchers have, however, failed to reach a consensus on what constitutes binge drinking.

As noted, the historical record shows that drinking alcohol has always figured in the landscape of the college experience, but it suddenly became a "new problem" during the 1980s and into the 1990s. In the past, as now, alcohol was an element in weekend "tailgating parties," in "mixers" in Ivy League faculty clubs, and as part of weekly "kegger" parties held in dorms and frat houses. Adjacent to campuses, bars would hold "happy hours" with discounted alcohol on sale. All these practices enjoy a long tradition, and consuming alcohol has long been a rite of passage of the college experience.

The authors asked what triggered this claim about binge drinking; the response was that during the 1990s and early 2000s public health researchers and activists, including MADD and SOC, discovered alcohol abuse and claimed that it resulted in serious consequences. Claims makers in the field of public health constructed college binge drinking as a social problem threatening college campuses. Activists also linked claims about binge drinking to the campaign against crime and to claims about sexual assaults on campuses. Researchers used the mass media to broadcast messages that

- a new and dangerous drinking culture had taken hold on American campuses;
- a significant proportion of students, especially those under the legal drinking age, were binge drinkers;
- that the negative consequences of this behavior included poor academic performance, unintentional injuries, criminal victimization, and death; and
- tertiary institutions were not addressing this problem.

During the 1990s, therefore, media reports began to appear of widespread binge drinking and deaths attributable to that behavior. Many media stories identified hazing as a cause, thereby contributing to the construction of a new social problem of fraternity hazing as a threat to academia. Public attitudes to the consumption of alcohol on campus were influenced by public health reports issued during the 1990s describing students' alcohol consumption patterns. The media disseminated the findings of these reports along with messages about the need to control consumption and criticism of college administrators for failing to do more about alcohol abuse. Media headlines included "Sea of Booze Threatens to Engulf America's College Students" and "College Taps Runneth Over." Generally, the media message was that alcohol abuse was widespread and out of control. The notion of binge drinking began to be linked to the alcohol-related deaths of students: Students were not just abusing alcohol, they were binge drinking. Public health reports were picked up by the media as authoritative statements about this new social problem, including findings that 50% of male college students and 39% of female students were binge drinkers.

The outcome of this activism was the creation of a belief that excessive drinking on campuses posed a threat to the health and safety of all students—college drinking on *all* campuses was framed as binge drinking and as a cause of injury and death. The creation of the five/four measure of binge drinking meant that the media and activists could name the problem and give it scientific credence. The five/four measure was now applied across students (regardless of campus) and across campuses (regardless of location). The pattern of activism that followed was similar to that deployed in the case of campus crime and violence: Media reports about binge drinking took individual instances of that behavior and offered them as proof that binge drinking was a widespread and dangerous problem on all college campuses. Fraternities in particular were targeted as cultures that focused on alcohol abuse that led to student deaths as if fraternities were defined by alcohol abuse.

The victims of the "new" social problem of binge drinking on campus were identified as underage drinkers captured by a drinking culture; nondrinking students who were derided for not adhering to college norms about drinking; and crime victims who had to cope with the effects of alcohol abuse. The causative agents of the new social problem of binge drinking on campuses were students who favored drinking and adhered to the drinking culture, fraternities and sororities that condoned drinking as a normal part of the college experience, and institutional administrations who had failed to recognize the problem while at the same time accepting advertising revenue from the beer, wine, and spirit companies. Throughout the 1990s, media narratives portrayed *all* student drinking as binge drinking and *all* student drinking as resulting in injury or even death.

(Continued)

(Continued)

What responses were suggested to cope with this new social problem? Media reports indicated that college administrations ought to exercise better control over student drinking habits, and words such as *ban*, *regulation*, and *laws* began to appear increasingly in media reports during the 1990s. Better enforcement of underage drinking laws was urged, as well as a "get-tough" approach by administrators. Colleges began to respond with educational programs on drinking and increased enforcement of underage drinking laws.

Conclusions

As the authors note, whether campus crime is actually a threat to millions of college students and their families remains unclear. As they put it—we need to ask unsafe and violent compared to what? To communities surrounding the college? To cities of similar size? We also need to decide what metric to apply to determine the question of unsafe and violent. According to the Justice Department Bureau of Statistics, the violent victimization rates of college students during 1995 to 2002 were lower than the rate for nonstudents, and their overall violent victimization rates fell more sharply than rates for nonstudents in this period. Another area of questioning is the campus crime data reported under federal law, which includes only offenses reported to campus police or authorities on campus. Many people do not report they have been victimized, so there may be underreporting of campus crime. In addition, theft is omitted from the list of reportable crimes, even though studies have shown it to be the most prevalent crime on campus. Finally, the authors assert that the role played by the disclosure of crime data is not clear because there are no evaluations of the impact of the Campus Security Act.

As to binge drinking, the authors suggest that we need evidence about students who do not drink or suffer the outcomes of binge drinking: How many are in this group, and how do they avoid harms? What are the long-term trends in college alcohol abuse and use—have levels remained fairly constant or have there been significant changes? If they have changed, what explains the variation? As to the various programs introduced on campuses to respond to the new social problems, how effective have they been? While there are a few case studies from colleges, there is no overall evaluation of these interventions.

The authors stress the importance of understanding how problems that have existed on campuses for more than 300 years were transformed over a period of about 20 years into social problems requiring legislative and judicial action and enhanced administrative management and control.

These accounts of the social problems of crime on campus and binge drinking reveal the role of the media in acting as unquestioning agents for the dissemination of new social problem narratives that were problematic in light of the overall lack of adequate research and contextualization into the claims being made. Legitimate questions arise about whether in these instances the media acted ethically in terms of objectivity and truth in their reporting issues.

Media and Fear of Crime

Fear of crime and fear of being victimized by crime are key influences in criminal justice policy making and in the promotion of punitive policies. The media provide a foundation from which fear of crime can be built with its portrayal of serious individual criminal events, "infotainment" programming that highlights violence and aggression, and the morality tale of the crime fighter battling ruthless criminals intent on savaging you and your home. The media "fuel public fears" (Jewkes 2011: 155), but the public should not been seen as absorbing media influences about crime in isolation of their actual lived experience. Thus, in the inner-city areas, it is fair to say that media coverage of crime tends to reinforce what people already know and what some have actually experienced through having been victimized. It follows that while it is difficult to identify a specific media effect, it is likely that the media play a part in stoking fear of crime simply because our lives are media saturated.

As Jewkes (2011) notes, "Media images of crime perpetually reinforce people's anxieties; we are, at one and the same time, fascinated by representations of crime and alarmed by them" (p. 157). Many studies have found associations between media consumption patterns and measures of fear of crime (Hope and Sparks 2000: 108); for example, heavy viewing of television crime programming is linked to fear of crime and support for "get-tough" crime policies, and readers of newspapers who describe violent crimes more often and more sensationally express more fear of crime when responding to survey questions. Surveys have revealed that the majority of persons confirm they receive their knowledge of the risk of crime from the media. Public perceptions reflect the message given by much of the media—that the crime rate is always rising and the criminal justice system is always too "soft on crime" (Jewkes 2015: 168).

AVOIDING BIAS

According to Klaidman and Beauchamp (1987: 60), bias is represented not simply by a distortion of facts or information, but by a departure from objectivity that is informed by the values of the writer or editor. Thus, bias should be distinguished from error—for example, when, due to a mistake, some part of a story is omitted with the outcome being a bias in the story. Bias is not the same as superficiality and is not necessarily ideological. Being partisan does not always mean that a story is biased because partisanship may be completely justified by the particular story. Partisanship will only equate to bias in cases where the underlying partisan values distort a story. As the authors define it, *bias* is "a distorted or unfair judgment or disposition caused by the values of a reporter, editor, or institution. Bias is not necessarily ideological, partisan or manifest over an extended period; and it need not be introduced intentionally" (p. 61).

Newsworthiness: Shaping News

Given that reporting the news must involve selecting certain events and not others as news, many suggest that the media shows bias because it takes a point of view and shapes the information that constitutes news (Greer 2010). In this sense, news is constructed by the media, which decide what is "newsworthy." Many studies have revealed that this process involves a series of media judgments based on conventions about what constitutes news—for example, the "news values" discussed by Stuart Hall, Chas Critcher, Tony Jefferson, John Clarke, and Brian Roberts (cited in Greer 2010: 241), which provide the criteria for the practices of journalism and enable determinations of what is newsworthy. Wars and disasters, of course, rate highly in newsworthiness, as do certain crime stories, especially those involving children. For example, in a study in Australia of sex offender legislation, noting that requirements for the registration of offenders had often been enacted in response to media accounts of the dangerousness of sex offenders (see Chapter 9), researchers found that newspaper accounts of sex offenders had doubled after the introduction of the legislation. Moreover, the newsworthiness of the subject matter was often enhanced by sensationalist reporting, including the use of dramatic language such as *monster, sex fiend,* or *predator* (Ducat, Thomas, and Blood 2009: 156). High-profile stranger cases were given prominence, suggesting that these individuals posed the highest risk, despite evidence clearly showing that sex offenders are usually known to the victim. Here, therefore, newspapers provided inaccurate and misleading material about a subject they decided was newsworthy.

Homicide is the most likely crime to be reported. One study found that the newsworthiness of a homicide was enhanced when the suspect or victim was white, when a male was the suspect, or when victims were females, children, or the elderly (Pritchard and Hughes 1997: 49). The newsworthiness of a crime can determine the level of police and prosecution resources assigned, and highlighting particular criminals and victims conveys a message about the kind of behavior that matters most in society.

Media and Police

Media representations of police using lethal force undoubtedly influence public perceptions of the police. In their examination of newspaper accounts of police use of deadly force from 1997 to 2000, Paul Hirschfield and Daniella Simon (2010: 156) seek to identify how the media frames such incidents in terms of the threat presented by the victim and the response of police to that threat. Hirschfield and Simon's analysis of press reports shows that 69.5% of articles supported explanations that the lethal force was justified. These mainly officially sanctioned accounts of incidents stressed the threat presented and the reasonableness of the law enforcement response, and only 16% of articles expressed doubts about the justifications for police actions (p. 165). In one case, a lethal shooting was presented as warranted because the victim had 21 prior convictions for stealing. The media often employ euphemisms that are designed to minimize or play down the harm caused by police. For example, the media can frame a lethal police shooting as "a deviation from legitimate procedures rather than as violence" or may refer to an officer having fired at the victim rather than explicitly stating that he was killed by police (p. 170).

Hirschfield and Simon (2010) contend that the media stereotypically construct police as three types: the professional, the vigilante, and the oppressor. The *professional* exercises the power to use deadly force wisely but is circumscribed by endless rules and regulations; the *vigilante* is a figure from popular justice who welcomes and is ready to use deadly force against dangerous criminals; and the *oppressor,* especially salient for African Americans, is one who uses legal violence to repress minorities and whose actions can provoke stories of violations of civil rights, calling up images of the civil rights era (p. 157). The killing of Amadou Diallo, who was shot 19 times by NYPD officers on February 4, 1999, was something of a watershed in media accounts of police violence. It displaced the stereotypical accounts of the professional and the vigilante and evoked a civil rights framing whereby police were oppressors. Hirschfield and Simon reveal that, following the Diallo killing, media accounts more often adopted a race angle and that pro-police media strategies diminished significantly, especially in the first 6 months after his killing. Generally,

post-Diallo, the media began to adopt a more cautious approach to lethal police violence. Victims of police violence are treated less sympathetically by the media than other murder victims, and media accounts tend to present such incidents as a lawful police response to the victim's behavior (p. 176).

Lawrence (2000) reveals how media and police collaborate in making crime news and how media often uncritically accept official police accounts of incidents and reinforce police stereotypes of crime fighting and professionalism. Cooperation between police and the media is now a norm worldwide. For example, in England and Wales all 43 police forces have departments concerned with media relations. These are staffed by civilians, often former journalists or specialists in marketing. Services provided by these units to the media include prepackaged news materials, press conferences, and media access to police raids (Cooke and Sturgis 2009: 407).

Critical citizen voices are significantly absent in media accounts of police violence (Lawrence 2000: 31), and official accounts by police are privileged by the media. As Lawrence puts it,

> Moreover, people who accuse police of brutality are often non-white, are often relatively poor, and often have criminal records. . . . These are not the kinds of people reporters feel most comfortable relying on for "news." Nor are they the audiences for whom many reporters envision producing the news. (p. 55)

The media adopt official claims about use-of-force incidents and frame such incidents as necessary and defensive in nature and as nonproblematic. Of about 8,000 articles on police use of force appearing in *The New York Times* and the *Los Angeles Times* between 1985 and 1994, Lawrence (2000: 43) found that almost 80% relied on official sources for their reporting. Simple news narratives are constructed to omit any complexity, are based on police and official accounts, and are shaped to manage public perceptions (p. 37).

AVOIDING HARM

The "do-no-harm" principle is commonly associated with medical ethics, but Klaidman and Beauchamp (1987: 94) link it to the writing of John Stuart Mill who, they argue, devised the principle as a means of determining the validity of limiting individual freedoms. Immanuel Kant contended that we are duty bound to give to others all the respect consistent with the notion of human dignity—that is, treating others as ends in themselves and not merely as a means to further our own goals (see Chapter 12). Kant also argued that we are under a duty to advance the interests of others when possible because by so doing we can enhance their capacity to exercise free will. For Kant, then, minimizing harm is an element of a fully constituted moral agent (Plaisance 2009: 105). William D. Ross defined seven essential duties we should exercise as moral agents, such as keeping promises, reparation, and expressing gratitude. He also identified a moral duty to not injure others, which he thought ought to carry substantial moral weight as compared to other moral duties (in Plaisance 2009: 106).

The do-no-harm principle says that "a person's liberty may justifiably be restricted to prevent harm that that person's actions would cause to others" (Klaidman and Beauchamp 1987: 94). What is meant by harm? The scope of this is contested, with some arguing that it relates to explicit actions such as violations of liberty or damage to reputation and others that it includes acts like causing a person embarrassment or causing harm by insinuation or innuendo. Some contend that an invasion of privacy constitutes harm, even when, for example, the name of a rape victim is obtained from a public record (p. 94). Relying on Joel Feinberg's (1984) notion[1] that a harm is to be interpreted as thwarting, defeating, or setting back an interest, Klaidman and Beauchamp (p. 98) suggest that the concerns of a journalist should include a concern for the public interest, even when serving that interest results in harm to a public official.

An example of such a story appeared in the *Wall Street Journal* on February 25, 1985, concerning the private life of the director of enforcement at the Securities and Exchange Commission (SEC), John Fedders. The *Journal* reported that he had admitted in divorce proceedings to regularly beating his wife, that he had lived beyond his means, and that his credibility was affected by an alleged cover up of a corporate bribe scheme by a previous client (Jackson 1985). Fedders resigned the day after the story ran, claiming the story would hurt the SEC.

Klaidman and Beauchamp (1987: 98) argue that the *Journal* was justified in publishing the story, despite the harm it caused, as it concerned the integrity of a public official and his fitness to serve in that capacity. In addition, a substantial basis for the *Journal's* story had been established before it published its account. Therefore, acts by the media that infringe privacy must be justified by the need to serve a vital public interest. Using disclosures to increase profits by selling more newspapers or to increase the salacious content of a publication are not ethically justifiable acts.

As David Archard (1998: 90) notes, a clear distinction must be drawn between a story being in the public interest and a story that interests the public. If the public interest justification is relied on for what would otherwise be an unethical act, the media must specify exactly what public interest is being served and why in a particular case the interest should override a claim to privacy.

In another incident, to pursue a newsworthy crime story, the media seems to have overly intruded into a secluded community and caused it harm.

When harm is caused, an assessment of moral responsibility for that harm will usually be made. Moral blame will be ascribed to those who acted carelessly, resulting from failure to discharge a morally imposed duty to take care or behave reasonably toward others.

An example of a lack of due care is found in the case of Brian Taugher, an assistant attorney general in California who, one day in 1985 without warning, was arrested in his front yard and charged with child molestation (Klaidman and Beauchamp 1987: 102). Seven months later, he was acquitted by a jury. His arrest was based on the story of a 9-year-old girl with no supporting evidence. The press coverage of the alleged molestation may have influenced the decision to prosecute, but it is indisputable that the incident caused great harm to Taugher's reputation and cost him $50,000 in legal fees. Klaidman and

---

1 According to social philosopher Joel Feinberg (1984: 45–47), a *harm* is an act that sets back the interest of another, such as a person's reasonable interest in a career, reputation, or privacy. The act of setting back must involve a concrete event that explicitly makes a person's overall state of well-being or his or her ability to achieve reasonable goals worse off than if the event had not occurred. It must also have set back significant desires such as raising a family or achieving a long-term project and not a merely trivial interest.

A Closer Look

Murders in Amish Community

In October 2006, Charles Carl Roberts planned and carried out the murders of five Amish girls, aged 7 to 13. He took them hostage in a schoolhouse and wrote a suicide note explaining how he had been tormented by the desire to molest young girls since the death of his premature daughter 9 years before. When he began to execute the girls, police stormed the school, and he shot himself. Media crews in large numbers invaded the reclusive Amish community, and local media attacked the national reporters for acting disrespectfully and for presenting the community as a spectacle.

SOURCE: Plaisance 2009: 117.

Beauchamp argue that a reasonable standard of care, in line with the do-no-harm principle, would require more evidence than solely the word of a 9-year-old girl before publishing this story.

SERVING THE PUBLIC

The historical account of press freedom in the United States reveals that, in return for the special privileges granted to them, the media are expected to provide public benefit in the form of timely, relevant, accurate information that informs the public understanding. As the *American Society of Newspaper Editors* (n.d.) affirms in its statement of principle, "The primary purpose of gathering and distributing news and opinion is to serve the general welfare by informing the people and enabling them to make judgments on the issues of the time." According to Klaidman and Beauchamp (1987: 131), the effect of the First Amendment is to make the media morally bound to produce public benefits. Nevertheless, they argue that the media are often more concerned with rights than responsibilities.

Serving the public well can also extend to enhancing public knowledge of crimes like homicide and avoiding formulaic approaches in reporting them. In an interesting proposal that would associate homicide reporting with the ethic of care (see Chapter 17), Romayne Smith Fullerton and Maggie Jones Patterson (2006: 304) argue that

formulaic crime coverage promotes cynicism and distances the reader from the actual crime and those involved. If the public understanding of a homicide were strengthened, it is argued, the outcome would be an engagement with issues such as social responsibility, reconciliation, and social justice. In its reporting of homicides, the media tend to employ stereotypical images of the helpless victim and the evil murderer that attempt to confine a story within a predetermined story line.

As Reiner and colleagues put it, "Offenders are portrayed not as parts of social relations or structures that the victims or the public are also embedded in, but as pathologically evil" (2003: 31). Would it not be preferable, the authors ask, to conduct "a deeper and more caring probe in to the causes and consequences of crime?"(Fullerton and Patterson 2006: 307).

Crime and Infotainment

Serving the public with news has shifted in meaning over time and now connotes not simply a news service but also what Surette (2011) calls *infotainment,* defined as "the marketing of edited, highly formatted information about the world in entertainment media vehicles" (p. 19). Infotainment aggregates aspects of news, entertainment, and advertising. Crime as a subject is ideally suited for infotainment because it represents real events that can be presented in an entertaining manner. According to Surette, as the media, with television in the forefront, became more capable technologically, so the viewing audience became more voyeuristic and entertainment focused. Satellite technology enables television to screen riots and wars in real time, and surveillance cameras show crimes as they happen on television shows. Surette (p. 20) observes that beginning from the late 1980s, crime-related infotainment began to appear on television, and the boundary between crime and entertainment dissolved. Consequently, consumers of news now find it difficult to distinguish crime news from crime entertainment, and one dominant model of responding to crime is supreme within the crime and justice infotainment world: the crime control model. Another new infotainment spectacle is the media trial, most famously associated with the prosecution of O. J. Simpson and now a staple item of mixed news and entertainment, characterized by intensive coverage with live coverage and legal punditry commenting on every aspect of the process and evidence. Surette argues that this mixture of news and entertainment creates a "dramatic mini-series developed around a real criminal case"(p. 24).

A Closer Look

"The CSI Effect"

Jurors in a murder trial in Phoenix, Arizona, alerted the judge to the fact that a bloody coat introduced as evidence had not been tested for DNA. In fact, the test was not needed because the defendant had admitted being at the scene of the murder. The judge believed that television had taught jurors about DNA tests but not about when they were needed (Durnal 2010: 2).

The CSI effect refers to the supposed influence of the television show *CSI: Crime Scene Investigation* and its offshoots, *CSI: Miami, CSI: New York,* and *Cold Case,* on jurors in a criminal trial. The images of forensics presented in the drama are said to have significantly shaped perceptions about the real world of forensic science. Prosecutors in particular believe that exposing persons who frequently watch *CSI* and who sit on juries will encourage them to acquit guilty defendants if forensic evidence is not produced in court as it always is in the television show (Kim, Barak, and Shelton 2009: 452).

A number of studies have attempted to establish the truth or otherwise of the CSI effect. A study in 2009 found that jurors reacted differently according to the type of evidence given in a trial. Similar to a previous study, it was found that the CSI effect had no direct effect where the evidence was circumstantial or was that of an eyewitness. However, exposure to the drama had a strong indirect effect on circumstantial evidence because it raised expectations about scientific evidence, and this reduced the jury's willingness to convict when no scientific evidence of any kind was presented (Kim et al. 2009: 458). It appears that jurors may equate the credibility of eyewitness evidence with scientific evidence because there was no direct or indirect effect on that kind of evidence. Other studies have found no specific CSI effect (Ley, Jankowski, and Brewer 2012: 53), but there is some evidence overall that *CSI* viewers do expect prosecutors to present scientific (especially forensic) evidence in trials than do nonviewers (p. 62).

CSI presents DNA evidence as totally reliable, its use in criminal justice to be routine and central to an investigation, and the forensic scientists as absolutely convincing (Brewer and Ley 2010: 98). These expectations about scientific evidence fostered by the drama present problems for police and prosecutors because there are huge backlogs in laboratories, and in the real world, it is impossible for police to collect the kinds of scientific evidence or conduct the kind of forensic tests shown in the drama (Kim et al. 2009: 459).

(Continued)

(Continued)

One outcome of the CSI effect is that the number of students interested in studying forensic science has increased greatly. Students see the quick, simple tests portrayed on the drama and do not understand the training, sample preparation, and data analysis that is involved. The drama represents a DNA test as being performed in a few minutes and a database search as taking only seconds to conduct. These scenes are inconsistent with the reality of such testing, which is much more time-consuming (Durnal 2010: 5).

The myths created by the media in *CSI* have led one forensic scientist to estimate that 40% of the science depicted there does not exist. Scientists complain that the media representation of forensic science in *CSI* is that there is always adequate evidence left behind after a major crime, and the scientist merely has to find it. One adverse outcome of the drama is that it has taught criminals about scientific techniques, and they now take care to leave less evidence (Durnal 2010: 5).

MAINTAINING TRUST

One of the most urgent moral concerns in journalism is securing and keeping the trust of the public. Without that trust, the media's function of providing information for the public benefit cannot be satisfied. Truthfulness is fundamental to trust and is associated with fidelity and loyalty. Trust in the media must also be informed and skeptical, and the public must be sufficiently media literate to make their own judgments concerning what is presented—trust should not be blind nor passive (Silverstone 2007: 127).

The importance of the virtue of trust is illustrated in a story about whether a newspaper and television station should have cooperated with a police operation in what was claimed by police to be the protection of an innocent life (Klaidman and Beauchamp 1987: 156–157). In fact, the cooperation resulted in the media lying in print and in broadcasts, signifying a fundamental breach of trust.

The facts were that a reporter for the *Hattiesburg American* received a call with information that there was to be a "hit" killing in Hattiesburg. After contacting the police, the reporter was asked to stay in contact with the caller, who subsequently asked police if they could supply a person to pose as a hit man. The police provided a poser, and the bogus hit man was contracted to kill the target. By this point, the U.S. attorney, the district attorney,

and the media, in the form of the newspaper and the manager of the local television station, had been asked to cooperate with the authorities. The authorities proposed that the killing be staged with the full cooperation of the media, who would report the incident so that the man hiring the hit man could be trapped when he paid for the hit. The bogus hit man had been told that unless he made the hit by the upcoming weekend, another hit man would be hired. It was clear, therefore, that unless the hoax succeeded, a man might actually be killed.

The media were explicitly asked to deceive the public even though their code of ethics requires them to always present the truth. Ultimately, the newspaper compromised by suggesting in the story that police were seeking information about a suspected murder, while the television station fully cooperated. Despite this, the man who was financing the killing did not believe the murder had taken place and refused to pay the hit man. Later, he tried to hire another hit man and was caught by police, this time without media involvement. This set of events helps demonstrate how some media will adhere to ethical standards, including keeping the public trust, despite the pressures to act otherwise.

It is easy to see how eroding the public trust in the media would result in the public paying less regard to the media and being less well informed. As well, it could be expected that there might be demands for media freedom to be circumscribed. Surveys into media credibility have been taken by organizations such as the Pew Research Center for the People and the Press (2008). The 2008 biannual poll on media credibility found the following:

- Over the preceding 10 years, almost every news organization or program had seen its credibility marks decline.
- In relation to the major broadcast news outlets, the credibility rating ranged between only 22% and 24%.
- For newspapers, *The Wall Street Journal* rated higher (22%) than *The New York Times* (18%) or *USA Today* (16%).

This trend revealing a low level of credibility in the media has been consistent over many years and can be presumed to indicate a long-term inconsistency in media reporting in terms of trust, fairness, and competence. When the public trust is seriously undermined due to deliberate fraud (as in the Cooke 1980 story), the public is harmed, and the media fails to honor the privilege it enjoys under the U.S. Constitution.

Honesty is also in play when the media is thought to be encouraging injustice and unfairness, as occurred when O. J. Simpson sought to profit from the death of his ex-wife.

A Closer Look

Media Promoting Unfairness and Injustice

The former football star O. J. Simpson wrote a book 12 years after his ex-wife and a friend were murdered in Los Angeles. In the book, he described hypothetically how he would have killed them both. The book was titled *If I Did It* and was published by a company owned by the FOX TV parent company, News Corp. The book was distributed to bookstores in 2006, and public outcry forced News Corp CEO Rupert Murdoch to cancel the project, terming it "ill considered." A planned 2-hour interview on FOX TV stations was due to air during November 2006 but was also canceled after advertisers withdrew and a number of affiliates declined to broadcast the program. Simpson earned $3.5 million for the book and TV appearance. While it is true that Simpson was acquitted of the murders, he was later found liable for the deaths in a civil suit and ordered to pay $33.5 million to the families of the victims. Nearly 50,000 people signed a petition on the web, demanding that the media projects be canceled.

SOURCE: Plaisance 2009: 94–95.

MANIPULATION

Media manipulation of public opinion demonstrates the power of the media and the consequences of abuse. Media power is formidable in political, economic, and social fields—a media review of a new product can make it or break it, and plays and films can be destroyed or made by the media (Klaidman and Beauchamp 1987). However, in general, press power is exercised through its selection, treatment, and presentation of information (p. 181).

When media attempt in hard news to persuade using emotional rhetoric rather than fact, this constitutes manipulation. Similarly, when a journalist relies on an unsubstantiated argument without noting its weaknesses to produce a desired conclusion, he or she is employing techniques of manipulation. Reasoned arguments that explain and persuade do not constitute manipulation, but often, media presentations cross a line and inject emotional content. At that point, persuasion can become manipulation.

According to Klaidman and Beauchamp (1987), manipulation is "any intentional and successful influence of a person by noncoercively altering the actual choices available to the person or by nonpersuasively altering the other's perceptions of those choices" (p. 188). The essence of manipulation is the absence of any resort to coercion and to reasoned argument. As well, the employment of techniques of manipulation always requires justification. The media itself are readily and regularly manipulated by those who wish to shape opinion, especially by politicians, interest groups, police, and the like. Journalists rely on sources for information, on quotes and analysis, and therefore individuals can readily use the media as a means of promoting a particular perspective and as a vehicle for influencing the broader public.

Examples of manipulation by journalists include their use of deception to influence others to disclose material they would normally not disclose. For example, in one case, a journalist wanted to write a series of articles about life in prison and believed the only way he could achieve this was by becoming a prisoner himself (Klaidman and Beauchamp 1987: 195). Other than being sent to prison for a crime, the journalist could only resort to deception. He therefore persuaded the local attorney general to allow him to enter a state prison as a transfer inmate from a county prison awaiting a grand jury trial.

Questions arise about whether the story this journalist was seeking was important enough to justify the deception he used to obtain it and what harm the deception caused to those who were deceived— namely, the prison officials and inmates. Klaidman and Beauchamp argue that this deception was not morally wrong even without the compelling account of the journalist's 6 days in the state prison because there was no other way to obtain this important story.

SUMMARY

The articulation between media, crime, and ethics is complex and multifaceted. Ethical standards for the media, similar to the standards explored in this volume for police, judges, and others in the criminal justice field, sometimes give way to the realities of the workplace. There is fierce competition between media outlets to capture market share and retain it, especially among newspaper tabloids, and crime stories can play a determining role in profit making. The nexus between crime and newsworthiness is well established, and the influence of the media in designating what counts as crime to the ordinary citizen promotes racial stereotypes and inverts the real and accurate representation of criminality. Instead of disseminating information that will inform and educate citizens about crime, the media simplifies events and circumstances and creates narratives that present polar opposites and eliminate all complexity.

The media fuel moral panics and public fear of crime and distort policy making so that rational informed strategies are replaced by ad hoc populist responses. In terms of its ethical responsibilities for reporting the truth, avoiding biases, avoiding harm, serving the public, and maintaining trust in the field of crime, the media record is clearly imperfect. When the media play such a significant role in defining crime and criminality, one question that must be asked is, whose interest is being served by such reporting?

PART II

The Application of Ethical Theories to the Criminal Justice System

In Part I of this book, concrete ethical issues within the criminal justice system are presented and contextualized. The role of moral philosophy in answering the questions "What is right behavior?" and "How ought I to live?" has been explored and the meaning of these questions addressed. We saw in Chapters 1 through 11 that professionals working in the criminal justice system may have to confront ethical issues and ethical dilemmas. Part of the process of responding to ethical issues and dilemmas involves reflecting on ethical theories and applying them.

Part II presents various ethical theories that can be applied to the resolution of ethical dilemmas. The leading ethical theories are deontology and consequentialism (utilitarianism), although virtue ethics has found increasing acceptance among moral philosophers, sufficient even to raise its prominence to the level enjoyed by deontology and consequentialism. This theoretical discussion extends beyond these principal theories to include the classical Greek theories of hedonism and Stoicism as well as the theory of ethical egoism. The theories of social justice and feminist ethics are represented in the works of John Rawls and Carol Gilligan, respectively. As explained in the Preface, the format of the book is a deliberate inversion of the usual presentation. The aim is to ensure a grounding in the practical issues before grappling with ethical theory and applying those theories to ethical issues found within the system. Those who prefer to focus on philosophical theory before examining the ethical issues that can arise in the criminal justice system are encouraged to reverse the order of the book to accomplish their purposes.

In Part II of this book, each ethical theory will be examined in some detail, and the leading theories of utilitarianism, deontology, virtue, social justice, and the ethic of care will be incorporated into specific case studies as part of an analysis of criminal justice ethical issues. These analyses will help illustrate the concrete application of these ethical theories in the resolution of ethical issues. Neither the classical Greek theories nor ethical egoism are generally considered viable ethical theories today.

In this introduction to Part II, an attempt will also be made to demonstrate how philosophical notions about ethics have developed and changed over time. This brief discussion of present-day thinking about ethics includes the postmodern perspective. As explained in Chapter 1, humans employ concepts of morality as an approach to trying to make their lives better. The aim is to create a social framework that guarantees the conditions required by human beings to live good lives. Morality formulates the principles that guide our evaluations of individual lives, of human action, and of social institutions as right or wrong, good or bad, as they bear on the goodness of human lives. It involves our attempt to shape a world that is not particularly hospitable to our endeavors, to adjust our endeavors to what is unchangeable in this world, and to harmonize our often conflicting individual endeavors so that we can pursue them with minimal interference from one another (Kekes 2000: 18). Morality is a collection of different ways of performing in different situations; these ways develop as we struggle with the many problems we meet in daily life (Wallace 1996: 14). Morality should not be seen as something separate from specific ways of acting because our knowledge of morality is caught up with our decisions about how to act in our everyday lives. We do not learn how to be a good family member or friend and then learn about the virtues of honesty and loyalty because the two go together.

Consequentialism (utilitarianism) and deontology are contrasting ethical theories. Consequentialist theories contend that the right thing to do always depends on the goodness of consequences. Utilitarianism is a consequentialist moral doctrine because, for the utilitarian, morality is solely a matter of consequences (Hinman 1998: 163). In contrast, deontological theories focus on considerations other than good and bad effects. The term *deontology* is widely used in moral philosophy, yet there is no standard definition of the term. It is more straightforward to simply say that deontologists are those who reject consequentialism. Generally, deontology connotes a constraint, and deontologists, in contrast to consequentialists, believe in constraints or rules that cause moral barriers in the promotion of the good (Kagan 1998: 73). Those who favor a deontological approach tend to believe that acting ethically or morally involves accepting constraints or rules that place limits on how we pursue our own interests as well as on the pursuit of the general good. Deontologists argue that the consequentialists' pursuit of furthering their own interests or pursuing the general good fails to provide morally sufficient reasons for taking action (Davis 1991: 205). They believe that certain acts are wrong in themselves and morally unsupportable and that such acts are an unacceptable way to pursue any ends, even those that are morally good.

Deontologists take the view that to act rightly, persons must first of all refrain from doing things that can be said to be wrong before the fact; these wrong acts are defined by what are variously called *rules, laws,* and *constraints.* For a deontologist, it is not the wrongness of the consequences of a particular lie or of lying in general that makes it wrong to lie. For them, lies are wrong because of what they are, and they are therefore wrong even when they produce good consequences (Davis 1991: 207).

Deontological theorists claim that the rightness or wrongness of an act depends entirely on the kind of act that has occurred and not on its consequences. Accordingly, for example, it is right to keep one's promises because, by its very nature, a promise must be carried out regardless of a person's inclinations or the effects that carrying it out will have. Deontological theories are sometimes called duty ethics because they stress ideas of obligation and duty.

As Geoffrey Scarre (1996: 13) points out, often consequentialist and deontological approaches will, in practice, lead to similar moral conclusions. For example, a deontologist would argue that the act of breaking promises or stealing goods is wrong because such acts break the moral law or because they infringe on people's right to be told the truth or the right of persons to keep their private property. A consequentialist would agree that promise breaking and theft are morally wrong, but his or her judgment would rely on the negative impact of these practices on human welfare, not on the intrinsic wrongness of these acts. A conflict will arise, however, in those exceptional cases where performing an act normally considered to be wrong is likely to increase the utility or benefit achieved in the outcome.

Julia Annas points out that

there has been a growing sense that there is something deeply inadequate about the view that when we systemize theories about our ethical view we are faced with the traditional option, a simple choice between consequentialist and deontological ways of thinking. If this is our option, then we must choose between calculating consequences to discover the right way to act, or rely on moral rules to guide us. (in Kopperi 1999: 1)

In response to this constraint, philosophers have returned to the classical forms of moral thought and especially to the virtue ethics of Aristotle. Virtue theories aim to provide a person with a clear picture of the good life and a means of ordering one's priorities in a way that enables the good life to be realized. In contrast, modern ethics, relying on consequentialist and deontological approaches, does not engage with questions such as, "What aims should I pursue?", "What books should I read?", or "What friends should I have?" As Annas puts it, "A great deal of modern literature and psychology arises and revolves around the way people reflect about their lives, but thought about one's life is no longer seen as central to ethical philosophy, at least to ethical theory" (in Kopperi 1999: 9–10). More recently, a number of philosophers have argued for an approach to ethics that would include all aspects of human life. For example, Nussbaum (p. 10) seeks to replace the distinction between the moral and nonmoral aspects of life with a notion that would include all aspects of that life. R. C. Solomon (p. 11) promotes a virtue ethics approach to business ethics, relating business practice and ethics to individual responsibility and character and not to abstract principles or moral rules.

In his philosophy, Kant criticizes virtue ethics for confusing happiness and morality. He argues that concerns about one's own happiness and broader concerns about morality are entirely different issues, each with their own objectives, and that they should be kept separate (Kopperi 1999: 12):

> Whereas virtues in ancient theories enable a human being to live a good life and to achieve her final goal, in modern ethics they enable her to follow the moral law that is, in turn, independent of the notion of the good life. (p. 15)

Ancient ethics stands in contrast to modern ethics because each advises persons to seek guidance about moral actions from a different direction. Whereas ancient theories call on the notion of the good life when determining the moral worth of particular acts, modern moral theories see morality and the good life as two quite distinct issues. The modern view is that a particular action is not morally right simply because it contributes to the good life or to happiness (Kopperi 1999: 22). The classical moral theorists believed that persons have a specific end given to them by nature and that realizing or achieving this end would constitute their good life and happiness (pp. 26–27). They considered that ethics ought to tell us how to realize our true natures and reach these specific ends. In this way of thinking, a good life is one in which one's potentialities as a human being are fulfilled. Once it is assumed that there is a clearly defined end for a person, it is then possible to work out what kinds of behavior ought to be encouraged and what character traits should be developed to lead a good life. This ancient notion of human nature having a specific end was jettisoned by the modern moral philosophers as modern science developed in the 16th and 17th centuries. According to the new interpretation, there are no final ends or purposes and no conception of the good life.

For Plato, Aristotle, the hedonists, and the Stoics, the questions are "What sort of life is best?" and "What sort of life constitutes 'happiness'?" (Sharples 1996: 84). The Greek conception of the world was of an orderly system where everything had a proper place and where everything in nature existed for a purpose (Rachels 1997). In this ordered system, for example, rain existed for the sake of growing plants, which in turn existed to benefit animals, which in turn existed to benefit people, whose well-being was the prime consideration. After the Greeks came Christian thinkers, who, while accepting this rational orderly system, believed that God was needed to complete the picture. According to their way of thinking, rain helps growing plants because that is what God intended, and animals benefit humans because that is what God made them for (p. 34). This Greek and Christian view of the world generated a number of ethical notions, including those of the importance of human life and the preeminence of humans over animals, as well as over nature. The rational and orderly world gave rise to laws of nature and notions of natural and unnatural acts. In the 16th century, with the advance of science and the knowledge of the earth's position in the universe, humankind's central place in the divine scheme of things was displaced, and Galileo, Newton, and others explored natural phenomena using empirical methods. Now it was found that the rain did not fall to help plants grow, but because of physical causes (p. 35).

Like many disciplines, philosophy has been impacted by postmodernism. In a detailed exploration of postmodern ethics, Zygmunt Bauman (1993: 4) argues that postmodernism has brought about a change in the way we address moral problems. Instead of responding to those problems through a philosophical search for universal principles and universal theories, postmodernism claims that absolute obligations and principles are oppressive, and in the postmodern age, the individual need not seek to attain moral ideals and guard moral values (p. 2). Bauman's contention is that rather than rejecting moral concerns altogether, what is required is a new way of approaching ethics. He identifies a number of aspects associated with the postmodern perspective on ethics, including the following (pp. 10–14):

- The notion that humans are essentially good and are merely in need of moral guidance has been discredited and replaced by the notion that humans are in fact morally ambivalent, and therefore no coherent ethical code can satisfy all needs. The absence of a moral code means we need to learn how to live without those sorts of guarantees.
- The assumption that morality and ethics function like law in trying to define what is proper or improper in given situations substitutes a body of rules for the individual moral self. This notion, says Bauman, leaves no "grey area" of ambivalence and multiple interpretations. In other words, it acts on the assumption that in each life situation, one choice can and should be decreed to be good in opposition to numerous bad ones, and so acting in all situations can be rational while the actors are, as they should be, rational as well. But this assumption leaves out what is properly moral in morality. It shifts moral phenomena from the realm of personal autonomy into that of power-assisted heteronomy. It substitutes the learnable knowledge of rules for the moral self constituted by responsibility.
- Postmodernism holds that few ethical choices can be considered unambiguously good and that the majority of such choices are made on the basis of impulses, which are often contradictory. As Bauman writes, "The moral self moves, feels and acts in the context of ambivalence and is shot through with uncertainty" (p. 11). There is,

therefore, a stress on moral acts seldom providing complete satisfaction and on the uncertainty that accompanies any ethical decision-making.
- Morality is not universalizable.
- Morality is irrational in the sense that attempts to erect a body of rules for ethical conduct meet resistance in the form of the autonomy of the moral self.
- Power plays a role in shaping moral codes because such codes purport to be the final authority on morality. In contrast, the postmodern perspective holds ethical codes to be relative and sees the moral practices they recommend as being the outcome of political exercises of power that claim the status of "universal" for ethical codes. Codes of ethics that deny relativism as well as the local and the particular substitute rule-bound ethics for personal morality.

The postmodern trend in ethics is exemplified in the work of Richard Rorty, who has argued that philosophy in its traditional form is dead and that the privileged position of philosophers as guardians of the truth has ended. Rorty sees a need for philosophy to help individuals and society break free from philosophical vocabularies and attitudes that he regards as outdated and worn out. As Richard Rumana (2000) explains, Rorty does not accept the notion that "truth is something waiting to be discovered; that only Universal claims are to be accepted; or that there are clear boundaries that separate academic disciplines into neat departments" (p. 4). Rorty's statement appears to be correct because an association has developed between ethics and literary and cultural theory that has generated collaboration between these various disciplines (e.g., see Rainsford and Woods 1999). Like Bauman and Rorty, Emmanuel Levinas rejects universal laws and favors a postmodern approach to ethics that emphasizes goodness and responsibility. He sees ethics as shaped by relationships rather than by ethical codes (in Atterton 2002: 231).

The exploration of ethical theories begins with the principal theories of deontology (Chapter 12), consequentialism (Chapter 13), and virtue (Chapter 14); and it continues with Stoicism, hedonism, and ethical egoism (Chapter 15), social justice (Chapter 16), and finally the ethic of care and peacemaking (Chapter 17).

12

DUTY AND PRINCIPLE

Immanuel Kant (1724–1804) is considered one of the greatest of the modern philosophers. He argued that morality depends on following absolute rules. For example, he believed that lying is never right, no matter what the circumstances. The central issue for Kant is "What ought I to do?" and he attempts to determine the rules, maxims, or fundamental principles of action that we should adopt (O'Neill 1991: 176). For Kant, motive is essential, and actions possess moral worth only if they are performed in accordance with what he termed the *categorical imperative* and out of the motive of duty (Benn 1998: 172).

Kant's focus was on the morality of the act and not on its outcome. He relied on rational arguments for his evaluation of morality, arguing, for example, that reason requires that we never lie. He contends that it is important not only to do what is right but also to do it for the right reason or motive and that the only motive that provides us with moral worth is the motive of what he calls duty (Holmes 1998: 113). That is, *we do what is right because it is right, and it is right because it is our duty*. Persons who act from the motive of duty are said to "have a good will." Kant's approach is therefore to focus on an internal orientation. He takes no account of the consequences of a particular act, of preferences, or of any theological framework (O'Neill 1991: 184).

Kant's philosophy does not mean that morality should be based on feelings or emotions but rather on the concepts of duty, obligation, and rationality. Morality requires that we act as fully rational beings would act, and therefore moral conduct is rational conduct (Holmes 1998: 114). In answering the question "What is a moral action as opposed to an unethical action?" Kant would reply that a moral action is one done from a respect for duty, and therefore a moral person is one who acts from a motive of duty and not from inclination or simply in accord with duty. He offers the example of a person who refuses the temptation to commit suicide even though his life is miserable and wretched (Hinman 1998: 212). If the refusal to commit suicide is motivated by duty, it has moral worth, according to Kant. However, if the refusal were motivated by other factors, such as one's fears about the act of killing oneself or from a desire to live, it would not have moral worth. In another example, Kant contrasts two types of people who help others. One type helps others without motives of vanity or self-interest, but simply because he receives inner pleasure from helping others. Kant argues that such actions have no moral worth because they are not done for the sake of duty but out of a desire for "good feelings." The second type of person helps others for the sake of duty alone, even though she has problems of her own, has no inclination to become involved in aiding others, and has no feelings of care or sympathy (p. 214). Kant argues that this person's actions have moral worth for the reason that it is morally valuable for a person to help others because it is the right thing to do, even though she is overwhelmed with her own problems. In Kant's vision of morality, there are some actions we must perform. We impose a moral law on ourselves that creates an obligation to act in certain ways. Kant does not see morality as arising from acts that make us want to help others but instead sees it as a struggle and as the moral strength of our will to overcome the temptations that might lead us to go against the moral law (Schneewind 1992: 310).

HYPOTHETICAL AND CATEGORICAL IMPERATIVES

Kant distinguished hypothetical or conditional imperatives from categorical imperatives. *Hypothetical imperatives* are courses of conduct governed by the word *ought* that establish a pattern that we have a certain wish and recognize that a particular course of action will help us to achieve that wish, and, as a consequence, we decide that we should follow that course of action (Rachels 1999). An example of a hypothetical imperative might be, "If you want to achieve good grades, you will have to study hard."

In contrast, moral obligations do not depend on particular desires but are categorical, taking the form, "You ought to do such and such." A *categorical imperative* commands and lays down a law (Scruton 2001: 85). Such acts are unconditional. For example, the categorical rule is that you should be helpful to people regardless of your particular wants and desires. In contrast, the hypothetical imperative would state that you ought to help people *if* you care for them or *if* you have some other purpose that might be served by helping them. Kant developed two versions of the categorical imperative: the principle of universality and respect for all persons.

These two versions of the categorical imperative are discussed in the following sections.

The Principle of Universality

Kant expounded the principle of the categorical imperative (first version) in 1785 in his work *Groundwork of the Metaphysics of Morals*. He expressed this form of the categorical imperative as follows: "Act only according to the maxim by which you can at the same time will that it should become a universal law" (in Rachels 1999: 124).

Kant suggests that this version of the categorical imperative can determine what one's duty will be in a particular set of circumstances. He contends that because human beings are rational creatures, they ought to behave rationally, and, for Kant, this means that one ought always to behave as if one's course of conduct were to become a universal law. That is to say, every action must be evaluated according to how it would be regarded if it were to be a code of behavior that applied to everyone universally. This principle suggests a procedure that can be used to determine whether an act is morally permissible.

What is a maxim? According to J. B. Schneewind, a maxim "is a personal or subjective plan of action, incorporating the agent's reasons for acting as well as a sufficient indication of what act the reasons call for" (1992: 318). The term *maxim* includes both principle and motive (Scruton 2001: 85). A maxim is a subjective rule, and there are many commonly known rules that can be described as maxims. Some examples include the following:

- Always be loyal to your friends.
- Always watch out for number one.
- Never act in a way that would make your parents ashamed of you (Hinman 1998: 222).

A rational person tests his or her maxims before acting on them. The "maxim of the act" means the rule you would be following if you were to do that act. You must then ask whether you would be willing for that rule (maxim) to be followed by everyone all the time so that it would be a universal law. If this criterion is satisfied, the rule or maxim may be followed, and the act is permissible. If, however, you would not be willing for everyone to follow the rule, you ought not to follow it, and the act would be considered morally impermissible. Thomas Hill suggests that the universal law formula is concerned with our "willingness to reciprocate, to avoid being a free-rider, and to check one's personal policies by reflecting about what would be reasonable from a broader perspective" (2000: 39). However, he also acknowledges the difficulty of working out the details through which this simple formula can operate as a test for determining right and wrong in particular cases. He notes that a significant literature has developed as followers of Kant have constructed devices to make the formula work as an "action guide."

Robert Holmes (1998: 119) calls our attention to the fact that the categorical imperative makes no reference to goodness and does not advocate promoting the good of anyone. In this sense, the imperative is not concerned with consequences or with goodness, and if we follow the categorical imperative, we will be cultivating goodwill purely for the reason that we will be trying to do what is right because it is right. Kant believes people have goodwill in the sense that they act in accordance with the motive of duty; that is, they show respect for the moral law.

Kant provides a number of examples of this maxim in operation, one of which concerns borrowing money. Suppose a man needs to borrow money and is aware that no one will make a loan to him unless he promises to repay (Rachels 1999: 124). He is aware of this, but he also knows that he will not be able to repay the loan. He therefore faces the following issue: Should he promise to repay, knowing he cannot do so, to get someone to make him the loan? If this is what he decides to do, the maxim or rule he would be following can be stated as follows: Whenever you need a loan, promise to repay it, even though you know you will not be able to do so. Applying the principle of the categorical imperative, we would ask ourselves, "Could this rule become a universal law?" The answer is clearly no because it would be self-defeating—no one would believe promises to repay any longer, and no one would make loans.

Kant argues that the categorical imperative binds rational agents because they are rational (Rachels 1999: 130). Therefore, he insists that a person who did not accept the categorical imperative would be not only immoral but also irrational. This means that a moral judgment must be backed by good reasons (it must be rationally arrived at). You may not say that you accept reasons some of the time but not all of the time, and moral reasons must be binding on everyone all the time. The basic idea here is that individuals cannot regard themselves as special from a moral point of view, and they must accept that moral reasons require a consistent approach.

Kant proposed that the rule against lying is a categorical imperative, and he wrote that lying in any circumstances is "the obliteration of one's dignity as a human being" (in Rachels 1999: 125). He argued that the prohibition against lying flowed from the categorical imperative. We cannot will that it be a universal law to lie because such a law would be self-defeating. People would quickly realize they could not rely on what other people said, and lies would not be believed. Thus, one should never lie because if lying became a universal law all relations based on trust and honoring promises would become unworkable.

Respect for All Persons

As well as the formulation of the first version of the categorical imperative already noted, Kant provided a second formulation and stated that the ultimate moral principle can also be expressed as follows: "Act so that you treat humanity, whether in your own person or that of another, always as an end and never as a means only" (in Rachels 1999: 133).

Kant apparently believed that this version of the categorical imperative expressed the same basic idea as the earlier version and was intended to be its equivalent in that it would yield the same moral judgments for particular situations (Holmes 1998: 123). It is a command requiring us to respect other people because they are rational human beings just like us. This respect should not be based on social rank, individual talents, or even moral goodness, but is grounded in the dignity of humanity, a value possessed by everyone who has the capacity to be a moral agent (Hill 2000: 64). If we do not treat others as ends in themselves but only as a means of achieving what we want, we disregard their humanity and treat them as things. Kant proposed a perspective based on the idea that human beings are ultimately the source of all our values, moral and personal (p. 68). As Hill puts it, "The common framework Kant proposes . . . is a basic requirement across cultures and individual differences, to respect every human being as a source of value" (p. 77).

In Kant's view, human beings have an intrinsic worth or dignity that is not enjoyed by other animals. He saw animals merely as a means to an end, with man as the end. In Kant's perspective, therefore, animals could be used any way we liked, but humans could never be used as a means to an end. He thought that humans had intrinsic worth and dignity because they are rational agents—that is, humans are free agents able to make their own decisions, set their own goals, and guide their conduct by reason. He argued that the moral law is an expression of the law of reason, and therefore rational beings embody the moral law itself. Since rational beings have a value beyond all price, they ought always to be treated as an end and never as a means. This means, for example, that we have a strict duty to strive to promote the welfare of others; we must respect their rights and avoid causing them harm. We must also respect their rationality, which means we must never manipulate or use people to achieve our own purposes (Holmes 1998; Rachels 1999).

Kant provides an example of this version of the categorical imperative similar to the borrowing example used to illustrate the first version (Rachels 1999: 134–135). He says, suppose you need money and want a loan but know you cannot repay it. You are desperate and consider giving a false promise to repay to induce a friend to give you the money. You might need the money for a good purpose and be able to convince yourself that lying to a friend would be justified. Nevertheless, Kant argued, if you lied to your friend, you would be manipulating her and using her as a means to an end. Suppose, on the other hand, you told the truth, explaining that you needed the money for a particular purpose and could not repay it. In this case, your friend could make up her own mind about whether to give you the loan, and she could exercise her own powers of reason and make a free choice. If she did decide to give you the money, she would be choosing to make your purpose for the money her own. So in this case, you would not be using her to achieve your goal. This principle has been important in theories of democracy because it supports the notion that all

people are created equal (where this notion signifies that no one should be discriminated against before the law).

In another example, Lawrence Hinman (1998: 229) describes research done in the 1930s in the United States on the long-term effects of syphilis. The researchers decided to take a group of black men who had already been diagnosed with syphilis, not tell them they had syphilis or treat them with penicillin, and simply observe the development of the disease in the group until they died. These men therefore became the unknowing subjects of a medical research project that continued until 1972 and cost them their lives and their well-being. There are a number of objectionable factors in this case, such as the obvious fact that these men were allowed to die when they could easily have been treated to prevent their death from syphilis. We therefore object to the pain and suffering that resulted from this decision. It is also objectionable that they were deceived about their condition, and we recognize that because they were not told about the research, they had no choice about participating in it.

Hill (2000: 114) argues that treating others with basic human respect applies even to the perpetrators of serious crimes, who should not be seen as having forfeited that respect based on the criminal acts they committed. He also argues that the use of force to protect oneself against an opposing force is both a right and a responsibility, but that proportional responses to threats against us should not show contempt for the attacker. Even when self-protection warrants the use of lethal force, Hill suggests that a readiness to kill when absolutely necessary need not include a contemptuous attitude toward the attacker because such an attitude would be indicative of our judgment that the aggressor has forfeited all respect as a human being. Thus, he argues that a self-defender showing respect for human dignity would prefer that aggressors retreat peacefully, that they not suffer permanent pain or humiliation, and that ultimately they would be able to rejoin the law-abiding community.

Basic respect for human dignity is also signified by providing fair trials and access to legal advice, ensuring processes of appeal, taking into account mitigating circumstances, and creating prison conditions that do not degrade the individual who has received the just punishment of society already in the form of deprivation of liberty (Hill 2000: 116). Fundamentally, Hill suggests that punishment and moral censure ought to be just and respectful, consistent with the presumption that all human beings have dignity, a status "that need not be earned and cannot be forfeited" (p. 117).

Kingdom of Ends

A third formulation of the categorical imperative commands that we "act only so that the will through its maxims could regard itself at the same time as universally law giving" (Holmes 1998: 124). The emphasis in this form of the categorical imperative is that when we act morally we fully choose our own moral decisions as autonomous moral agents. When we act on rules or maxims that can be universally accepted by all rational beings, it is as if we are legislating for all rational beings as though we were each of us universal law-givers. We should not, therefore, allow our choices to be made for us by anyone else because we would be compromising our autonomy. Consequently, we cannot rely on society, government, or religious leaders to tell us what our moral decision should be. Also, we must not allow our choices to be determined by our own desires, preferences, or wishes, as this would ultimately reduce all decisions about choices to acts of self-love. On the contrary, we must act from the motive of duty to achieve a goodwill.

This notion that every adult is an autonomous agent broke radically from the views prevailing at the time because the theorists who were influential in the 17th and 18th centuries did not believe that most people had the ability to know what was right without being told what morality required of them (Schneewind 1992: 311–312). The theorists of the time accepted that God had given everyone the ability to know basic principles of morality, but they did not believe that persons were capable of grasping by themselves what moral action was required in particular cases. During that time, most theorists thought of morality as centering on obligations imposed by law and backed by threats of punishment for violations.

CONFLICTING DUTIES

The notion that there are absolute moral rules—such as a rule against lying—that do not allow any exceptions gives rise to a problem in conflict cases (Rachels 1999: 129). These are instances when one is faced with two alternative courses of action, both of which are held to be absolutely wrong. What does a person do when faced with two absolutely wrong choices when she must act and no other alternatives are available? An example occurred during World War II when Dutch fishermen often smuggled Jewish refugees in their boats. These boats would sometimes be stopped by Nazi patrol boats when they had refugees in the hold. The Nazi captain would ask the Dutch captain questions about the boat's route and who was on board, and the Dutch fishermen would lie and bring their refugees to safety. It is clear that in this case, the fishermen had only two alternatives: to lie or to allow themselves and their passengers to be taken and shot. There was no third alternative because they had to answer the questions, and they could not outrun a fast patrol boat. If the two rules "It is wrong to lie" and "It is wrong to allow innocent people to be murdered" are both taken to be absolutes, the Dutch fishermen would have to do one or the other, and so a moral argument that prohibits both absolutely makes no sense. The way out is to argue that in certain circumstances only one of these rules is absolute, although this alternative may not work in every case, and there is always the possibility that two absolute rules will come into conflict.

One way of dealing with this problem of conflict of duties is to argue that moral rules should be treated as generalizations and not as categorical rules without exceptions. Thus, in general, we should tell the truth, but there may be circumstances where we would feel morally obliged to tell lies. *In other words, telling the truth is an obligation that should be kept, provided there are no other overriding factors present.* Another deontological philosopher, W. D. Ross (in Dancy 1991: 219), has referred to those obligations that a person is obliged to perform in the absence of any other overriding factors as *prima facie duties*. His view is that all sorts of things matter, and it is not possible to maintain a neat list of morally significant features. He argues that we have a prima facie duty to help others, to keep promises, to repay past acts of kindness, and to not let down people who rely on us. For Ross, these things matter morally and have to be taken into account in considering what we should do and in assessing whether we have acted rightly in what we choose to do. However, these duties are only prima facie, and other things matter too (p. 221). In other words, we have other prima facie duties as well—for example, to increase the welfare of others. In a particular case, we cannot tell in advance which prima facie duty will turn out to matter most, and all we can do is consider the circumstances and try to decide which course of action is more important. In doing this, no set of rules can answer the question for us.

Nevertheless, as Hill (2000: 52) points out, in Kantian moral theory, strict moral dilemmas are conceptually impossible. Therefore, if it seems a duty forbids Action A and Action B, but we cannot avoid doing one or the other, then the solution is to go back and rethink the issue. This includes, if necessary, reviewing the reasoning that initially led us to think of A and B as strict duties in the first place.

APPLYING DEONTOLOGICAL THEORY

Case Study 12.1 illustrates how deontological theory can be applied to an ethical dilemma within the criminal justice system.

Case Study 12.1 Rough Justice in a Juvenile Institution

Joe is a corrections officer in a juvenile detention center and works on a unit housing 15 young offenders, many of whom suffer mental health problems. Joe has worked at the institution for about 2 months, he feels comfortable with the job, he has been accepted by the other staff, and he admires them for the skills they show. He has not had any significant problems with the juveniles and is generally enjoying the work and is learning skills on the job.

It is lunchtime on Monday, and Joe is in the dining room supervising the juveniles as they eat their lunch. At one table sit six juveniles, one of whom is a 17-year-old named Brian who Joe thinks has a developmental disability. Brian displays offensive table manners, which on this day put Joe off his own meal. Brian keeps adding ketchup in vast quantities to every dish and slurping it from the plate. He also uses his hands instead of his fork, keeps talking while he is eating, and spits food across the table. Joe can see that the other juveniles are repulsed by this behavior in the same way that he is.

Joe is surprised to see his coworker, Daren, suddenly get up from the table, go over to Brian, grab him by the shirt collar, and move him away from the table. Daren takes Brian off to the kitchen and returns with a large mixing bowl. He then tells Brian to scrape out what is left of his meal into the bowl, and, taking Brian to the center of the dining room, he puts the bowl on the floor and tells Brian to eat. He tells him he has disgusting manners, and if he is going to eat like a dog at the table, he might as well get down on the floor like a real dog. He tells him to stay down there until he has licked his bowl clean.

Joe does not react to these events. Later, Daren explains to Joe and other staff members who were present that the reason he acted in that way with Brian was to shock him into understanding that his table manners were highly offensive. He thought that if he used "tough love" on Brian in that way, Brian would be less likely to alienate his co-detainees, and this might help him get through the experience of being in the institution.

SOURCE: Jones and Carlson 2001: 165–166.

In resolving what may be an ethical dilemma, Joe will follow the process of resolving an ethical dilemma set out in Chapter 1:

1. *Is Joe faced with an ethical dilemma?*

   Joe is faced with the dilemma of whether to report Daren's treatment of Brian. He might also consider whether he ought to have intervened to prevent Brian's mistreatment.

2. *What are the facts and circumstances of the incident?*

   Joe needs to review in his mind the facts and circumstances and perhaps write them down in the form of a report so that his memory of the events is quite clear.

3. *What are the facts relevant to the decision he has to make? What are his own values about the issue, and what are the values of his workplace about such an issue?*

   The relevant facts are the following:

   - Joe has worked at the institution for only a short time.
   - He has confidence and trust in the experience and skills of other staff.
   - Brian may be mentally challenged or have a developmental disability.
   - Daren's conduct toward Brian was certainly offensive and unpleasant to watch.
   - Daren's conduct in relation to Brian was surprising to Joe.
   - Joe takes note of Daren's explanation for his conduct.
   - Joe agrees with Daren that it is important for the juvenile detainees to get along with each other during their time in the institution.

Joe is in sympathy with the juveniles detained at the institution and does not have a punitive attitude toward them. He believes his job is worthwhile, and he believes in professionalism in the workplace. In relation to the values of the workplace, he is aware because of his training that there is a code of ethics that regulates his conduct as a correctional officer; he is also aware of various departmental rules and regulations about how he is to conduct himself that make him responsible for the safety and well-being of those in his custody. Informally, he is aware of an institutional culture that he shares with his coworkers. This culture is complex, but it does stress loyalty and support for coworkers generally.

4. *What ethical theories does he call to mind to assist him in resolving the dilemma?*

   In this case, Joe will apply deontological ethical theory to the dilemma.

5. *What are Joe's available courses of action?*

   Joe made no move to intervene at the time of the incident, so the time has passed for decision-making in relation to the actual incident. This leaves him with two alternatives: He can take no further action, or he can prepare a written report of the incident and give it to his supervisor.

6. *Joe will make his decision after applying, in this case, the deontological approach to each alternative course of action, and he will choose the course of action that is the most ethically appropriate for him under deontology.*

A process for assessing an ethical dilemma from a deontological perspective is set out in the "Deontological Evaluations of Ethical Dilemmas" Closer Look box. Applications of the criteria listed are shown in the "Applying Deontology" Closer Look box.

A Closer Look

Deontological Evaluations of Ethical Dilemmas

1. The focus is on the act, and therefore, one must identify the act to be evaluated. The question must then be asked, what is the act?

2. What is the intention underlying the act?

3. What duties are involved in this situation and to whom or what?

(Continued)

(Continued)

4. Do the duties conflict?

5. Will this act show respect for the human dignity of *everyone* involved?

6. Will it use any person as a means to an end?

7. Given that the act must follow the categorical imperative and therefore must be applied universally, can I will this act onto everyone?

A Closer Look

Applying Deontology

1. The focus is on the act, and therefore one must identify the act to be evaluated. The question must therefore be asked, what is the act?

   There are two possible options: to report the incident or to do nothing.

2. What is the intention underlying the act?

   In reporting the incident, the underlying motive is to protect Brian from any further injury, to protect other juveniles from the same kind of treatment, and to deter Daren and possibly other staff from taking such action again.

   In doing nothing, the underlying motive is to support coworkers through a demonstration of loyalty and to agree with Daren that, on balance, Brian's interests are better served by tough love treatment like this, so he can reform his behavior and have good relations with his co-detainees.

3. What duties are involved in this situation and to whom or what?

   Joe and all juvenile workers have a duty to protect those in their custody from mistreatment. At the same time, Joe and his coworkers have a duty to support each other in carrying out their duties within the bounds set by ethical standards and departmental rules and regulations.

4. Do the duties conflict?

   Yes, the duties conflict with each other, and this creates a problem under the deontological approach because Kant offered no way of resolving such conflicts other than to go back and rethink the ethical dilemma and the relevant duties.

5. Will this act show respect for the human dignity of everyone involved?

   Reporting the matter will show respect for the dignity of Brian. Not reporting fails to show respect for the dignity of Brian because it condones a humiliating act and raises the possibility that Daren or others might do the same or similar acts in the future.

6. Will it use any person as a means to an end?

   If Joe reports the incident, he is not using anyone as a means to an end, and in particular, he will not be using Brian or his colleague Daren in making that report because in the process he will be respecting their humanity and dignity.

If Joe does not report the incident, he will be using Brian as a means to an end because his end will be to cover up the incident and protect Daren; in doing this, he will be sacrificing the interests of Brian and his duties toward him.

7. Given that the act must follow the categorical imperative and therefore must be applied universally, can I will this act onto everyone?

If he reports the incident, the maxim would be that "I ought to protect juveniles in my custody from harm and mistreatment," and he can will this maxim as a universal law.

If he does not report the incident, he cannot formulate any universal maxim. The reason for not reporting is either because Joe believes he has a duty to be absolutely loyal to his coworkers or because he accepts Daren's explanation that this particular act was one of tough love and therefore was for the good of the juvenile. It is not possible to have a universal law of absolute loyalty to coworkers because this would allow any act, however harsh or barbaric, to be condoned. Tough love is often used as justification for conduct that is seen by the perpetrator as appropriate in the particular circumstances. Such conduct may vary from case to case. Since it lacks precise definition and because others may not agree with the perpetrator that it is appropriate conduct, it cannot stand as a universal law.

In all the circumstances, it is clear that the appropriate course of action for Joe, applying the deontological perspective, is to report the incident to his supervisor.

SUMMARY

Kant's answer to the question "What ought I to do?" is that one should act in accordance with duty and obligation and in a rational manner. For Kant, the consequences of an act are irrelevant, and duty and the formulation of absolute rules for behavior ought to supersede all other considerations. For deontologists, moral obligations are seen as categorical, and the categorical imperative, as formulated by Kant, lays down the law that must be followed regardless of one's individual wants and desires. It is our duty to follow a categorical imperative.

Kant believed that humans are rational creatures and that every act should be evaluated as if one's behavior were to become a universal law. In other words, this evaluation would determine whether everyone should act this way and therefore whether an act was morally permissible. The test for the categorical imperative is whether an individual is willing for a particular rule to be followed by *all* persons at all times, and if it is, this gives it the status of a universal law. This seems simple on the surface but can give rise to specific problems. For example, Kant proposed that the rule against lying was a categorical imperative and argued that it was

wrong to lie under any circumstances. However, in practice, people will sometimes lie when faced with moral choices about how to act. For example, it is both wrong to lie and wrong to allow innocent people to be murdered, and in some situations, these two rules can conflict. A number of solutions have been suggested to resolve this conflict, including treating moral rules not as absolute categorical rules, but as generalizations. In other words, we should always tell the truth, provided there is no other overriding factor that would morally justify telling a lie.

Another important principle developed by Kant is that we should respect other people because they are rational human beings with dignity, and we should not treat them as a means to an end but as an end in themselves. This means that we should not use people to satisfy our own ends, and we should always respect others' rights, promote their welfare, and avoid causing them harm. In doing so, we promote the worth and dignity of individuals. This concept appears in practice in the criminal justice system in the form of ensuring fair trials, giving access to justice, and treating prisoners with dignity, compassion, and humanity.

DISCUSSION CASE

Consider the following circumstances and the individual ethical duty of Officer Ricardo Colon by applying the deontological criteria.

No Special Treatment?

In the early evening hours of February 12, 1998, Captain James Brady of the homicide division of the Philadelphia Police Department, a 27-year veteran, finished his shift at police headquarters and headed for a popular bar just a few blocks away, where he partied with coworkers, New York police, and some justice professionals. He drank 64 to 80 ounces of alcohol. At about 11 p.m., Brady departed the bar, leaving behind a briefcase containing his pistol, his cell phone, and some case files. He drove off to his home.

That evening an eyewitness filed a report with police. She had heard a loud noise outside her apartment shortly after 11 p.m. A police report recounted that a 1992 blue Honda Civic sedan had been struck at that location, not far from the bar where Brady had been drinking. Brady had hit this vehicle and then left the scene of the accident. The front grill of his car was badly crushed, the left side of the hood jutted straight up, and the air bag had inflated from the force of impact. Brady was driving an unmarked police vehicle, a 1989 Plymouth Grand Fury. Officer Ricardo Colon, who noted the unmarked police car riding slowly by with heavy damage, observed Brady driving away from the scene of the accident. Colon sounded two blasts on his air horn, signaling the driver to stop, but Brady continued driving until Colon switched on his lights and siren. Colon then notified police radio that he had the car stopped, and the dispatcher requested, as was customary, that an officer back up Colon in his investigation.

Without waiting for the backup to arrive, Colon approached the vehicle, and Brady identified himself as a police captain. At this point, Officer Gregory Yatcilla arrived. He, like Colon, had less than a year on the job. By this time, Brady had exited the vehicle and was wobbling as he stood and was slurring his speech. Also, the inseam of Brady's pants was soaked, indicating that he had wet his pants. Colon understood the seriousness of the situation and, as he had been trained to do, radioed for a supervisor, who arrived shortly in the person of Lt. Joseph DiLacqua, a 25-year veteran.

DiLacqua had been disciplined on numerous occasions. He conducted a private conversation with Brady and then ordered Yatcilla to move the damaged car onto the sidewalk. DiLacqua then radioed in an auto accident report that gave the impression that no injuries had occurred and that an oncoming vehicle had invaded Brady's route. When the department's Accident Investigation Division (AID) arrived (called because a city vehicle was involved), they were told the same story by DiLacqua. Brady said nothing. After AID gave its release, DiLacqua drove Brady back to the bar to pick up his briefcase, but it had already been transported back to police headquarters, the return having been organized by a bartender. Brady was then driven home by Yatcilla. No blood alcohol test was administered.

That night, accident investigators photographed the scene, and the photographs revealed a different story than that told to AID. There was no debris underneath the car, and a trail of engine coolant from the radiator stretched for 14 blocks back to the original point of impact. There were no skid marks showing that Brady had swerved or braked when he was allegedly run off the road.

What is Colon's ethical dilemma? What should Colon do, according to a deontological perspective?

SOURCE: "Policing the Brass: A Case Study in Command Malfeasance," by William Giannetti in *Criminal Justice Ethics*, Volume 22, Number 2 (Summer/Fall 2003), pp. 32–50. Reprinted by permission of the Institute for Criminal Justice Ethics, 222 West 57th Street, Suite 607, New York, NY 10019–1029.

DISCUSSION QUESTIONS

1. Do you agree that formulating absolute rules for behavior helps us to live a moral life? Explain with reference to Kant's principles.

2. Explain how acting according to absolute moral rules might present moral conflicts in practice. Provide examples for your explanations.

3. What is the place of emotion and intuition in Kant's thinking? Explain with examples.

4. Respect for other people is a crucial aspect of deontological theories. Discuss with reference to policing and correctional practice.

13

CONSIDERING THE CONSEQUENCES

When we think about the right ethical action to take in a particular situation, we might ask ourselves whether we should always act to bring about the best possible consequences. Consequentialism is an important and widely discussed theory of ethical action, and according to this approach, what makes an act morally right or wrong is its consequences and nothing more (Benn 1998: 60). The motives for the act or the nature of the act itself are not important considerations in consequentialism. The classical utilitarian (consequentialist) theorists were Jeremy Bentham (1748–1832) and John Stuart Mill (1806–1873). Bentham is considered to have originated the doctrine of consequentialism and Mill to have provided a more refined version of it. Bentham led a group of radicals who sought to reform the laws and institutions of England using utilitarian approaches. Mill was the son of James Mill, a distinguished Scottish philosopher and historian and a follower of Bentham (Rachels 1999a: 97).

The utilitarians attempted to lay down an objective principle that would determine whether a particular action was ethically right or wrong; they called this principle the *principle of utility.* Mill referred to the principle of utility as the Greatest Happiness Principle (Rachels 1999a: 97). It states that an action is right insofar as it tends to produce the greatest happiness for everyone affected. In other words, this principle states that if we have a choice about which action or social policy to follow, we ought to choose the one that will give the best overall consequences for all concerned. Therefore, utilitarians reject the idea that actions are right because God says they are or because they are inherently moral in their own right (Benn 1998: 62). Bentham and Mill rejected appeals to intuitive commonsense judgments that justified established practices that were philosophically suspect (Darwall 1998: 110). Mill, for example, who also wrote against the subjugation of women, believed that subjecting women to men's domination and control could not be justified by arguing that such social practices seemed natural and appropriate. Utilitarians argue that morality is simply an attempt to bring about as much happiness as possible (Rachels 1999a: 97).

At the time this idea was first promoted, it was considered revolutionary (Rachels 1999a: 98). Bentham and Mill associated happiness with pleasure, and Bentham believed that mankind was governed by pain and pleasure. He argued that some things give us pleasure, whereas others cause us pain, and this basic fact explains why we behave as we do—we look for pleasure and attempt to avoid pain. It also explains why we determine some things to be good and others evil. Bentham therefore followed the reasoning that morality consists of trying to bring about as much pleasure as possible, for as many people as possible, while at the same time attempting to minimize the amount of pain in the world (Rachels 1999b: 65).

Also connected with the idea of pleasure is the theory of hedonism, which contends that the only ultimate intrinsic good is pleasure. This notion will be discussed more fully as a separate doctrine in Chapter 15. It is considered an attractive theory because it is simple and expresses a notion that we find intuitively right—that things are good or bad because of the way they make us feel (Rachels 1999a: 108).

After publication of his work *Utilitarianism* in 1863, Mill was criticized for the hedonistic aspect of his doctrine, which was categorized by many as being "worthy of swine" (Benn 1998: 62). Applying the idea that happiness equates with pleasure, the principle can be said to state that an action is right if it produces the greatest amount of pleasure for the greatest number affected. If it does not achieve this goal, the action is considered morally wrong. However, many modern philosophers who are utilitarians do not interpret utilitarianism in this hedonistic manner; instead, they take "preference satisfaction" (Hinman 1998: 164) and not happiness as the final goal (Benn 1998: 61). Preference satisfaction refers to satisfying human preferences, interests, or desires (Scarre 1996: 3). The idea is that what should be maximized is not the balance of pleasures over pain, but the satisfaction of preferences more generally (Goodin 1991: 243).

Utilitarianism emphasizes the effects of an action, and if an action produces more beneficial effects than harmful effects, it is considered an ethical action; otherwise, it is not. It is crucial to understand that the consequences of an action determine whether it is right or wrong and not the motive which prompts it to be done. For example, even Hitler may have believed that he was acting from a genuine desire to improve the German State, but his acts generated pain and genocide and ultimately caused the collapse of the German State. A utilitarian would therefore say that Hitler's behavior produced more pain than pleasure, so his acts were wrong for that reason.

In determining whether an action was right or wrong, consequentialists argue that it is possible to measure action. For example, it is possible to find out whether a particular action caused more pleasure than pain for all affected by the situation. We can calculate the amount of pleasure and the amount of pain and then determine whether the act was right or wrong by calculating which is greater. Bentham, in fact, developed a method for this calculation that he called the *hedonistic calculus*. This hedonistic calculus has seven elements, including the intensity of the pleasure and its duration, which allow the amount of pleasure or pain of an act to be measured. He thought that numerical values could in principle be attached to these elements and then an arithmetical operation performed to determine the relative merits of varying courses of action (Scarre 1996: 75). Nevertheless, he did not believe that this process needed to be strictly pursued in the case of every moral judgment, but rather that the notion of a calculus should be kept in mind as an ideal model of moral deliberation to which actual decision-making should conform as closely as possible. It follows from this belief that the main outcome of utilitarianism is to separate the rightness or wrongness of an action from the motivation of the agent performing it—in other words, to distinguish the worth of the action from the worth of the agent. Obvious problems with Bentham's hedonistic calculus are the difficulties in accurately predicting consequences, as well as its time-consuming nature.

It is important to appreciate that utilitarianism does not require us to ignore what may be good for ourselves. It does, however, require that we extend our concern to encompass the good effects on all those people affected by our actions (Holmes 1998: 131). In other words, we should try to bring about the greatest balance of good over bad that we can for *all* people. James Rachels (1999a: 107–108) summarizes utilitarian theories in the following three propositions:

1. Actions are to be determined right or wrong by virtue of their consequences, and right actions are those that produce the best consequences. Nothing else is relevant.
2. In assessing consequences, everything is irrelevant except the amount of happiness or unhappiness that is produced. Accordingly, right actions are those that produce the greatest balance of happiness over unhappiness.

3. In calculating happiness or unhappiness, each person's welfare is equally important, and right actions are those that produce the greatest possible balance of happiness over unhappiness, taking into account each person affected.

According to Lawrence Hinman (1998: 201), utilitarians conduct their lives according to two basic principles. The first is that utilitarians will always be concerned about the actual effects of their choices. They will be continually concerned about the basic facts of moral life, such as who will suffer pain or hurt and who will gain pleasure resulting from a particular decision. They will try to predict outcomes accurately but will also accept, if they are not able to make accurate predictions, that there is an element of luck in leading a moral life. Accepting that luck will play a part may be problematic but does not mean abandoning utilitarianism as an adequate moral theory. Second, because utilitarianism is a "benevolent moral doctrine," utilitarians want to make the world a better place for all and increase the extent of well-being throughout the world. Utilitarians believe that their theory produces a happier world, reducing pain and suffering, and that morality should operate to make the world a better place for all.

PLEASURE AND HAPPINESS

Mill argued hedonistically that the only ultimate value is pleasure or happiness, and he appears to equate the two. Yet, pleasure and happiness are not interchangeable because it is possible to experience pleasure without being happy and vice versa. Also, pleasure is generally linked to a particular activity or feeling in contrast to happiness, which is more a state of mind. Hinman (1998: 165) argues that we think of pleasure in terms of the body and of sensuality and that happiness is less directly related to the body. In response to criticisms of his emphasis on pleasure, Mill expressed the view that some pleasures were higher or more elevated than others; in other words, pleasures can be compared in terms of their quality (Benn 1998: 64; Scarre 1996: 90–92). He thought that a satisfying human life must contain "pleasures of the intellect, of the feelings and imagination, and of the moral sentiments," which he

regarded as having a higher value as pleasures "than those of mere sensation" (Scarre 1996: 92). According to Hinman (1998: 167), there is no one choice for the standard of utility, and there may well be advantages in having utility signify a number of different factors and for consequences therefore to be measured according to various standards.

ACT CONSEQUENTIALISM

Utilitarians who are considered *act consequentialists* argue that we should ask ourselves, in relation to each separate act, whether or not it promotes the greatest good. This means that individual decisions would be made on a case-by-case basis. Act consequentialists equate good with pleasure and believe that we should determine the rightness of individual acts according to whether each act would produce more pleasure than pain (Holmes 1998: 137). If more pleasure is produced, the act will be considered morally right; if less pleasure is produced, the act will be considered morally wrong. These theorists do not consider themselves bound by rules about, for example, stealing or lying, but they might believe that these acts should be avoided because they usually produce bad consequences. Nevertheless, they do not believe that there is a rule that forbids them.

Hinman (1998: 180) notes a number of objections to act consequentialism, including the fact that it is extremely time-consuming to calculate the consequences of every individual action; that it is too difficult to predict the consequences of individual actions, especially in the long term; and that it generally neglects moral rules. In relation to the time-consuming argument, act utilitarians respond that they follow basic rules of thumb that incorporate the past experience of many situations and argue that what society generally considers a good outcome will usually produce the best consequences for everyone. Yet, they insist that such rules are not absolute moral rules and are only summaries of what has occurred previously in relation to individual acts. Concerning the criticism that it is difficult to predict consequences, act utilitarians agree that there are limits to prediction, but they see this as a difficulty with life in general and not their theoretical position. As such, the proper response, according to them, is not to reject their theory, but to attempt to increase our ability to foresee consequences (p. 181).

Rule Consequentialism

In contrast to act consequentialists, this group of utilitarians argues that it is possible to link the consequentialist view of what makes acts right or wrong with moral rules (Holmes 1998: 137). In other words, they believe that keeping to certain rules produces better consequences than trying to determine what consequences will follow from every individual action. For example, most people believe it to be their duty to speak the truth, even when doing so would cause more pain than pleasure. They do not advocate obedience to rules just because they are rules, but because they see following rules as the best way to achieve the general good or the best outcome for all affected. In other words, an act is right only if it is in agreement with a rule that would maximize overall net happiness for all people affected, as any alternative rule (Darwall 1998: 135). Rule consequentialists are subject to criticism for the argument that if they take rules to be absolute and without exception, then they will have abandoned consequentialism (Hinman 1998: 183). If they acknowledge exceptions to rules, then they could really be described as act consequentialists.

Public Policy and Utilitarianism

Since it is consequentialist in nature, a utilitarian strategy and approach to public policy making would require that government officials base their actions and programs on the most accurate and detailed information of particular circumstances and of the likely results of the alternatives and options available to them. Mill maintained that ethical questions could be settled only by empirical investigation. As William Shaw (1999) puts it, "Realism and empiricism are the hallmarks of a utilitarian orientation, not customary practice, unverified abstractions, or wishful thinking" (p. 171). For example, in considering public policy about punishment, a utilitarian would argue that punishment is justified if:

- the pain and suffering to those who are punished is outweighed by the benefits of punishment; and

- those benefits cannot be achieved with less suffering or at a lower cost to those who are being punished (p. 174).

The utilitarian perspective on punishment is more fully considered in Chapter 6.

Arguments Criticizing Utilitarianism

We have seen that utilitarian theory urges us to accept the notion that only consequences matter. Significant arguments against the utilitarian approach propose that there are other considerations, in addition to utility, that are important in determining whether actions are right. Critics argue that utilitarianism is incompatible with the ideal of justice, according to which we should treat people fairly, taking account of their individual needs and merits. Critics say this is not a priority of the utilitarian perspective. The following example is offered by H. J. McCloskey:

> Imagine a utilitarian visiting an area where there is racial strife. During his visit, an African American man rapes a white woman, and this causes race riots with white mobs and the police attacking and killing African Americans. Imagine the utilitarian is in the area when the rape is committed, and his evidence could convict a particular African American man who was innocent.
>
> As a utilitarian, if he knows that an early arrest will stop the race riots, he must surely conclude that he has a duty to give false evidence in order to bring about the punishment of an innocent person. This might have some bad consequences—for example, the innocent African American man might be executed—but a utilitarian would consider that this would be outweighed by the good consequences that the riots would be stopped. Accordingly, applying utilitarianism, the best consequences would be achieved by lying, and lying would be the most ethical act. However, it could be argued that it would be wrong to be the cause of the execution of an innocent man; therefore, in implying that it would be right to bring about that execution, utilitarianism must be an incorrect theory. (in Rachels 1999a: 110–111)

Critics of utilitarianism state that the theory is inconsistent with the notion that people have rights that may not be infringed simply because good results are anticipated:

> In a 1963 case in the U.S. Court of Appeals Ninth Circuit, an appellant, Ms. York, approached the police department in Chino, California, to file charges for an assault committed on her. Officer Story of the police department told her that photographs would have to be taken of her, took her to a room in the police station, and told her to undress. She was also told to adopt various indecent positions, and he photographed her in those positions. Ms. York objected to the undressing, pointing out there was no need to take photographs because the bruises would not show up. Later Officer Story told her that the photographs had not come out and that he had destroyed them, but contrary to what he told her, the officer in fact circulated her photographs amongst police officers at Chino. Later, two other officers made further prints of the original photographs and circulated these amongst police. Ms. York brought proceedings against all three officers for violating her legal rights and won. (in Rachels 1999a: 112–113)

Considering the morality of the conduct of the officers, act utilitarianism would argue that their actions can be defended if they produce a greater balance of happiness over unhappiness. In other words, we should consider the unhappiness caused to Ms. York and compare it with the amount of pleasure created for the officers by viewing the photographs. It is certainly arguable that more happiness than unhappiness was caused, in which case a utilitarian would have to conclude that the police officers' actions were morally correct. In this case, Ms. York's right to privacy has been violated, and most people do not think that our rights should be set aside so easily. The idea of rights includes the notion that there are limits on how others may treat us, regardless of the good purposes that might be accomplished and the happiness that breaching those limits might bring.

Another criticism offered is that utilitarianism is mistaken in claiming that only consequences matter, and this can be illustrated by reference to "backward-looking reasons" (Darwall 1998: 131; Rachels 1999a: 113–114). Imagine you have promised to meet someone this afternoon, but when the time comes to carry out that promise, you don't want to do it because you have judged that your time would be better spent working. What should you do? Imagine you decide that the utility of accomplishing your work slightly outweighs any inconvenience caused by standing up your friend. As a utilitarian, you would then conclude that working is the right course of action, but intuitively, this does not seem correct. This is due to the fact that making a promise imposed an obligation on you that you cannot escape so easily. In other words, a small gain in utility does not overcome the obligation imposed by the promise you gave. This example illustrates the fact that utilitarianism emphasizes that the rightness of an act has to do with the future; that is, it has to do with what will happen as the result of our actions. However, as this case demonstrates, we also think that past considerations are important, and our promise to meet someone is a fact about the past and not the future. Here, therefore, utilitarianism seems inadequate because it takes no account of backward-looking considerations.

Utilitarianism, it is argued, eliminates the distinction between obligatory actions that are morally required and *supererogatory actions*, which, although not strictly required, are still praiseworthy (Goodin 1991: 234; Rachels 1999a: 115). Absolute adherence to the utilitarian standard would require us to give away our resources to the point where economic equality is reached. While we might admire people who are prepared to give away their goods or give up their pleasures to help others, we do not see them as simply doing their duty but as going beyond what is required by duty. In other words, a moral ethic that requires us to subordinate everything to promote the general welfare would have the effect of causing us to give no priority to our own interests and to abandon most of the acts that we do for ourselves that give our life character and meaning. Peter Singer (1979) argues that

> because giving money is regarded as an act of charity, it is not thought that there is anything wrong without giving and . . . people do not feel in any way ashamed or guilty about spending money on new clothes or a new car instead of giving it to famine relief. (pp. 269–270)

Singer contends that we ought to give money away and that it is morally wrong not to do so, rejecting the notion of supererogatory actions and taking the position that if we have the chance to make the world a better place we are morally obliged to take it.

An important element of utilitarian theory is the notion that every person's life and interests rank equally with everyone else's (Rachels 1999a: 115). While this sounds appealing, in practice, it would require that we give up our special relationships with family and friends to whom we show partiality and preference (Goodin 1991: 234). Family and friends are not just members of humanity; they are special to us, and the argument that we should show no more concern for their welfare than for anyone else's is quite counterintuitive. Take the example of a parent who allows his child to burn in a building on the basis that others are in the building who should be saved because their future contribution to the general welfare seems likely to be greater than the child's. That parent would not be considered a hero, but rather regarded with horror and contempt and would be considered to have acted immorally.

Rachels (1999a: 116) explains that utilitarians rebut these criticisms by pointing out that the arguments are unrealistic because they do not describe real-world situations but are imaginary. It is argued that utilitarianism is a guide for making decisions in the real world and for situations we actually face. Rachels suggests that utilitarianism counters these criticisms by modifying the theory to introduce rule utilitarianism and act utilitarianism. In the case of the race riot example, rule utilitarianism would ask which general rules of conduct would promote the greatest happiness. A society that contained a rule against false testimony or one that did not? Would people be better off in the former or the latter society? Clearly, in terms of utility, the former society is to be preferred, and therefore, the rule against giving false evidence would be accepted, and the person should not testify against the innocent man. In contrast, an act utilitarian faced with the same situation would likely give false evidence because the consequences of that particular act would be good.

A final defense against criticisms of utilitarianism is more radical—it essentially asks, so what? It reverses the presumption that utilitarianism is irrational and does not accord with our moral and intuitive common sense by asking "Why should we assume that our feelings are always correct?" and "Why should we reject a rational theory of right conduct just because it conflicts with those feelings?" This defense argues that it is the feelings and not the theory that should be discounted (Rachels 1999a: 119). This defense therefore implies that many of our commonly held moral feelings may be mistaken, and it challenges us to rethink those views and feelings (p. 120).

It is sometimes suggested that consequentialism is a less than efficient way of living and deliberating on issues because it requires long and complicated calculations of utility that tend to make a person overly hesitant and ineffectual (Scarre 1996: 13). Far better for human welfare, it is argued, that people are able to act on simple moral rules, such as keep your promises, pay your debts, and help the needy.

Two examples of the application of utilitarian theory to moral issues are shown in the "A Case of Euthanasia" and "The Treatment of Animals" Closer Look boxes.

A Closer Look

A Case of Euthanasia

Matthew Donnelly, a physicist, worked with X-rays and, perhaps through too much exposure, contracted cancer and became blind. He was told that he had about one year to live and was in constant pain. He decided he did not want to carry on living in that condition and begged his three brothers to kill him. Two refused, but the youngest brother, Harold, brought a pistol into the hospital and shot Matthew to death.

(Continued)

(Continued)

Was Harold's Act Immoral?

We can assume that he was motivated by compassion and love for his brother and wished only to relieve his pain. Also, Matthew had asked each of his brothers to help him die. We therefore feel sympathy toward Harold and feel that we should be lenient toward his acts. However, according to the dominant moral tradition, the Christian tradition, what Harold did was morally wrong. Christianity teaches that intentionally killing innocent people is always wrong.

What Would a Utilitarian Approach Be to This Issue?

A utilitarian would ask, considering the choices available to Harold, what course of action would produce the best overall consequences—the greatest balance of happiness over unhappiness for all concerned? If Harold did not kill Matthew, Matthew would continue to live in pain for a while longer, and this would cause significant unhappiness. How much unhappiness is difficult to calculate, but we do know that Matthew himself preferred death to continuing in that unhappy state. We also know that killing him would allow him to escape his pain and misery. A utilitarian would therefore argue that euthanasia in this case might be morally correct, contending as follows:

- The right action is that which will bring about the greatest balance of happiness over unhappiness.
- Sometimes the greatest balance of happiness over unhappiness can be occasioned by mercy killings.
- Therefore, at least sometimes, mercy killing may be morally correct.

SOURCE: Rachels 1999a: 99–100.

A Closer Look

The Treatment of Animals

The Christian tradition holds that only man is made in the image of God, and animals do not possess souls. This means that, according to the natural order, humans may use animals for whatever purpose they wish. As Saint Thomas Aquinas wrote, "It is not wrong for man to make use of them, either by killing them or in any other way whatever." However, Aquinas agrees that it is wrong to be cruel to animals, not because of the welfare of the animals, but because being cruel to animals impacts human welfare because it has a tendency to encourage men to be cruel to other men. This might seem a rather extreme statement about animals, but, in fact, we do eat animals, use their skins for various purposes, confine them in zoos, and use them for experiments in science. As well, we hunt and kill them.

Utilitarians do not support this view because they believe that what matters is whether an individual is able to experience happiness and unhappiness, pleasure and pain. If an individual is able to experience suffering, then a utilitarian would say we have a duty to take that into account in our acts, even if the individual is an animal and not human. Since both humans and animals can suffer, we ought not to mistreat either, and therefore both are entitled to moral concern.

The philosopher Peter Singer first wrote about animal liberation in 1975, arguing in accordance with utilitarian principles that the way we treat animals is cruel and objectionable. He cites the example of research on the behavior of dogs that involved giving intense electric shocks to dogs, causing them considerable suffering. The question, he argued, was whether there was any compensating gain in happiness for this suffering because if there was not, the experiment was not morally acceptable. The pain caused to the animals requires justification, and we cannot apply Christian doctrine that because they are not humans we may act as we wish. Utilitarianism therefore claims that we must expand the moral community to include all those whose interests are affected by what we do, and we should not consider that human beings alone are worthy of moral consideration.

SOURCE: Rachels 1999a: 102–104.

Case Study 13.1 Good Friends Are Hard to Find

When Ben first joined the police department, a long-standing friend in the same department told him that he would only have cop friends and that no one else understood police except other police. Ben felt uncomfortable about this and, together with his wife, made a conscious effort to find friends outside of the police force. They succeeded in part because Ben's wife, who was a teacher, was able to make friends from that profession. Nevertheless, Ben found that many people treated him differently than an ordinary citizen when they found out he was a policeman. They tended to blame him for all the troubles they encountered and especially for any citations they received from other police officers.

To deal with this problem, Ben and his wife decided not to tell any new acquaintances about his job. He would just say that he worked in public relations in the city, and after they became friends, he would tell them what he really did. This seemed to work quite well, and after a while, Ben and his wife developed a circle of good friends. He found that these friends would alter their schedules to accommodate his shift work. For example, if a party was planned, Ben and his wife were contacted first to make sure that he would be available and could get the night off. Ben thought that some of these friends might be recreational drug users, but they always respected his position as a police officer, and he never observed them taking drugs in his presence.

Two friends, Jim and Sandy, invited Ben and his wife to dinner one Friday night, and when they arrived, Jim immediately gave Ben his favorite drink, which was Scotch on the rocks. Jim put on some music, and Ben's wife went to help Sandy in the kitchen while Ben and Jim sat in the living room. Ben needed something to put under his drink so that it would not leave rings on the coffee table, and he saw a wooden box on the coffee table that looked the right size and shape to hold coasters. He reached out and opened the box. It did not contain coasters but several joints of marijuana. He put the lid back on the box, looked up, and saw fear in Jim's eyes.

SOURCE: Close and Meier 1995: 171.

APPLYING UTILITARIAN THEORY

Case Study 13.1 illustrates how utilitarian theory can be applied to an ethical dilemma within the criminal justice system.

In resolving what may be an ethical dilemma, Ben will follow the process of resolving an ethical dilemma set out in Chapter 1.

1. *Is Ben faced with an ethical dilemma?*

   Ben is faced with the dilemma of whether or not to arrest Jim for possession of an illegal substance.

2. *What are the facts and circumstances of the incident?*

   Ben needs to review in his mind the facts and circumstances so that he is clear about the issue with which he is faced.

3. *What are the facts relevant to the decision he has to make? What are his own values about the issue, and what are the values of his workplace about such an issue?*

   The relevant fact is that Ben has found evidence of an offense, and as a police officer, he has discretion as to whether or not to arrest the alleged offender. His own values are as follows: As a police officer, he believes in upholding the law; he understands that the police culture tends to compel police to have only coworkers as friends, but he values friendships outside law enforcement and does not want to be completely enveloped by the police subculture. In terms of workplace values, he is well aware of police codes of ethics and of standing rules that relate to the exercise of his discretion in making arrests. He is also aware of the informal police subculture, which is more complex than the written rules and regulations and which is ambivalent about incidents like this. Some of his coworkers would not hesitate to arrest in such circumstances, but others would be prepared to overlook the minor infractions of their good friends.

4. *What ethical theories does he call to mind to assist him in resolving the dilemma?*

   In this case, Ben will apply utilitarian ethical theory to the dilemma.

5. *What are Ben's available courses of action?*

   Ben has the choice of arresting Jim or deciding not to arrest him and therefore ignoring the incident. As a police officer with the discretion to arrest or not, he could always tell himself that it was a minor offense and not worth processing all that paperwork anyway and therefore decide not to arrest. He could also give Jim a warning not to repeat the offense.

6. *Ben will make his decision after applying, in this case, the utilitarian approach to each alternative course of action, and he will choose the course of action that is the most ethically appropriate for him under utilitarianism.*

   A process for assessing an ethical dilemma from a utilitarian perspective is set out in the "Utilitarian Evaluation of Ethical Dilemmas" Closer Look box. Applications of these criteria are shown in the "Applying Utilitarianism" Closer Look box.

A Closer Look

Utilitarian Evaluation of Ethical Dilemmas

The focus is on the outcome of the decision in each option—if it is good for all, then it is ethical. Utilitarianism considers the greatest good for *all* those affected by the decision and often uses persons as a means to an end. Whatever means are used to achieve the best outcome are acceptable, as long as the outcome is good for all those affected. This approach to ethics often fails to protect individual rights—the individual experience is sacrificed to the interests of all. Thus, for utilitarians, consequences count; utilitarians always want to know what actual effects their choices will have on real people. Utilitarians want the world to be a better place for everyone affected (including organizations and the community) and therefore seek to increase the amount of well-being in the world and to reduce the amount of pain and suffering.

1. Identify all the options.

2. Identify all those affected by the decision. Consider individuals and organizations as well as the community.

3. Describe the harms and benefits for all those affected under Option 1, then Option 2, and so on.

4. Choose the option that produces the most benefits for all those affected by the decision after calculating the difference between the good and bad effects.

A Closer Look

Applying Utilitarianism

1. *Identify all the options.*

Ben has the options of arresting Jim or of taking no further action.

2. *Identify all those affected by the decision.*

Those likely to be affected by the decision are Jim and Sandy, Ben and his wife, other friends of Ben and his wife who are also friends of Jim and Sandy, the police department, and the local community.

3. *Describe the harms and benefits for all those affected under Option 1, then Option 2, and so on.*

Under Option 1, to arrest, the harms and benefits will be as follows:

Jim and Sandy: They will suffer harm because they will cease to be friends with Ben and his wife, Jim may be convicted of a criminal offense, they will suffer shame in the community, and Jim's job may be affected by a conviction. They will receive no benefits.

Ben and his wife: They will suffer harm because they will lose Jim and Sandy's friendship, they may lose other friendships with those who hear about the arrest, they may end up with no friends other than policemen, and Ben's wife's teaching job may be affected when her coworkers hear about the arrest. In terms of benefits, if he arrests, Ben will be following formal ethical codes and departmental rules, and he will be showing that he is an impartial police officer interested in performing his duty with integrity.

Other friends of Jim and Sandy: They may be harmed because they may cease their friendship with Ben and his wife and perhaps also with Jim and Sandy.

Police department: The department will benefit because it will be aware that Ben is prepared to arrest his friends who commit criminal offenses and therefore that he upholds ethical codes and departmental rules.

(Continued)

(Continued)

Community: The community will benefit because it will be aware that at least one police officer is not willing to turn a blind eye to evidence of criminal offenses, even by his friends, and is willing to apply the law with impartiality.

Under Option 2, which is to do nothing or to give Jim a warning not to repeat the offense, the harms and benefits will be as follows:

Jim and Sandy: The benefit is that they will continue to be friends with Ben and his wife. The harm is that they will know that Ben is prepared to condone criminal conduct by his friends.

Ben and his wife: They will continue to benefit from Jim and Sandy's friendship, and Ben will have demonstrated his loyalty to his friends in that he is prepared to overlook acts of criminal conduct. The harm is that Ben may be placed in the same situation again with either Jim or other friends. Another harm is that Jim and Sandy may tell their other friends about Ben's willingness to compromise his position as a police officer. If this gets back to the department, it might lead to disciplinary action against Ben by the department and will constitute a harm for Ben.

Other friends of Jim and Sandy: They will not be affected except that they may benefit by learning about Ben's willingness to overlook his friend's indiscretions.

Police department: The department will be harmed by not being aware that Ben is prepared to overlook his friends' criminal offenses. It is possible that the department might learn from the community about Ben overlooking the offense. This might harm the department's reputation in the community.

Community: The community might hear about Ben's inaction in not arresting Jim and may think that this action is typical of police in the community. This would be harmful for the community because it would affect their view of the integrity of the police force. It is also possible that some members of the community may tell the police department about Ben's willingness to overlook the offense. This would be a benefit to the community because hopefully the police would take disciplinary action against Ben and restore the police reputation in the community.

4. *Choose the option that produces the most benefits for most of those affected by the decision after calculating the difference.*

According to the utilitarian perspective, it would be necessary to assign values to the harms and benefits and then calculate which option benefited all parties affected by the decision. Assuming a greater value would be given to benefits to the community and to the police department, the option producing the most benefits would be to arrest Jim.

SUMMARY

Consequentialists, also known as *utilitarians,* believe that what makes an act morally right or wrong is its consequences and that all other considerations are irrelevant. Therefore, when they are considering the correct moral approach to an issue, they ask which action would bring about the best possible consequences. This principle, known as the *principle of utility,* requires that utilitarians act so as to produce the greatest happiness for everyone affected; therefore, they reject the idea that duty should determine how people choose to act.

The classical utilitarians, Bentham and Mill, saw happiness as equivalent to pleasure, and they argued that humans look for pleasure and try to avoid pain and that this explains how we make choices about how to act. Nowadays, a more modern approach is to aim for preference satisfaction and not for happiness. The idea is that we should not aim for pleasure over pain but instead should determine how we can best satisfy human preferences, interests, or desires.

Act utilitarians argue that the motive behind an act is irrelevant and that it is possible to measure whether an act causes more pleasure than pain and therefore has more "utility." This would seem a very difficult and time-consuming exercise, and therefore, act utilitarians adjust this basic principle by following rules of thumb that draw on past experience. In contrast, rule utilitarians link consequentialism with moral rules and argue that if we follow certain rules, better consequences are likely to result. In this sense, rule consequentialism may be said to blend with deontology to a limited extent. For example, most of us believe that as a rule we should speak the truth, even when doing so in a specific instance would cause more pain than pleasure and that in the long term telling the truth produces greater benefits overall.

One main criticism of consequentialism is that it puts the outcome of an action above the ideals of justice, such as treating people fairly. It can also be argued that utilitarianism requires us to give away all our resources to others because that would promote the general welfare and pleasure of others. In choosing between duty and consequences, we have to weigh absolute rules about how we should act against the need to calculate which act will provide the most pleasure for the greatest number of people.

Consequentialism is considered an important theory in punishment policy and practice because a major focus of policy making for the punishment of offenders is deterrence—that is, attempting to deter crime by drawing attention to the penalties that will be imposed for criminal acts. This approach assumes that giving certain individuals or groups of offenders more severe punishments to deter others from committing similar crimes is for the benefit of everyone.

DISCUSSION CASE

Punishing a Police Officer for False Testimony

New York police officer James Sullivan, 34, had a distinguished record, having made nearly 100 arrests and earned nearly 2 dozen commendations during his 9-year career. A man he had arrested in 1998, who was subsequently convicted and jailed and then released on parole, was appearing before the U.S. district court in Brooklyn on a parole revocation hearing. Sullivan had received a subpoena to testify at this hearing.

The background to the case was that Sullivan and his partner had arrested Mr. Francis on charges of attempted murder and firearms possession following a shooting. Francis, who had three prior convictions, including one for conspiracy to distribute cocaine, was tried in state court and acquitted on all charges arising from the Sullivan arrest. However, following his acquittal, Francis was indicted by federal prosecutors for firearms possession and convicted and jailed. As a convicted felon, he could not legally possess a firearm.

Sullivan and his partner Melin had both testified in the state trial that they had taken the weapon from Francis, placed it in the trunk of their vehicle, and then driven straight to the police station. The officers also testified that Sullivan had picked the weapon up from the place where Francis had dropped it. However, Sullivan later told a federal prosecutor that, in fact, Melin had picked up the gun, had handed it to him (Sullivan), and that Sullivan had put it on the front seat of the patrol car. During the federal trial of Francis, the prosecutor revealed that Sullivan had given this false testimony in the state trial.

In 1996, New York City Police Commissioner Howard Safir announced a policy of firing any officer for lying to a superior or in an official proceeding. Because of this policy and his false testimony,

(Continued)

(Continued)

Sullivan was told to bring a lawyer to the parole revocation hearing in case any action was taken against him. When asked their intentions regarding Sullivan and his false testimony, the state prosecutors indicated that they had not decided whether or not to pursue perjury charges against Sullivan. The main deciding factor was that the false testimony he had given was not material to the case and would not have affected the verdict. However, despite no decision having been made about Sullivan, some action had already been taken against Officer Melin, who had been placed on modified duty.

It was uncertain whether further action would be taken against Melin and Sullivan.

SOURCE: Adapted from Rashbaum 2000.

After applying the criteria for a utilitarian analysis, should the state prosecutor's office charge the officers with perjury?

DISCUSSION QUESTIONS

1. What are the main principles advocated by consequentialists?

2. How does consequentialism help us to make the right moral choices?

3. What criticisms can be made of a consequentialist approach toward resolving ethical dilemmas?

4. How does consequentialism deal with the rights of individuals in ethical decision-making?

5. Explain how consequentialist theories are applied to policy making on crime control and punishment.

14

THE IMPORTANCE OF CHARACTER

In Chapters 12 and 13, we examined ethical theories based on duty and on consequences. According to deontologists such as Kant, the answer to the question of "How should we act?" is that we should always act for the sake of duty because it is the right thing to do. According to consequentialists, the rightness or wrongness of acts does not depend on intentions but on consequences, and the right action is that which produces the greatest amount of happiness or pleasure. Kantians and consequentialists hold in common the notion that ethics is an answer to the question "What ought I to do?" (Hinman 1998: 323). These modern philosophers ask a different question than did the classical or ancient philosophers, and because of this, their thinking moved in a different direction, developing theories concerned with rightness or obligation rather than virtue. This chapter is concerned with the ethics of virtue, an approach that emphasizes our virtues or moral character as opposed to a theory that emphasizes duties or rules or one stressing the consequences of actions.

Contemporary virtue theory has been inspired by the Greek philosopher Aristotle (384–322 BCE), in particular by his work *Nicomachean Ethics* (see the "Aristotle" Closer Look box). In contrast to Kantian and consequentialist approaches, Aristotle does not seek to uncover a fundamental principle telling us what to do and how to act in an ethical way. Rather, he is concerned about the sort of people we must become if we are to live the good life—in other words, an ethical life. For example, take a case where it is obvious that I ought to help someone who is in need (Hursthouse 1999: 1). A utilitarian or consequentialist will stress the fact that the consequences of helping will maximize well-being. A deontologist will emphasize the fact that in helping that person I will be following a moral rule, such as "Do unto others as you would have done unto you." A virtue ethicist, however, would emphasize the fact that offering help would demonstrate my charitable or benevolent character. Most recently, virtue ethics has been promoted by a number of philosophers as a third way of approaching ethical questions and dilemmas. In 1958, the distinguished British philosopher G. E. M. Anscombe published an article suggesting that modern moral philosophy was misguided and that philosophers should stop thinking about obligation, duty, and rightness and place virtue center stage (Rachels 1999: 177).

According to Stephen Darwall (1998: 191), many philosophers have realized that Aristotle presents a more subtle, rich, and realistic picture of the ethical life, and they have found theories such as Mill's and Kant's to be unrealistically abstract. The proponents of virtue theory join with Aristotle in believing that ethical knowledge involves a degree of wisdom or judgment that cannot be expressed in the form of an absolute rule. Others criticize nonvirtue theories as being too individualistic, arguing that the prominence that Aristotle gave to the social dimension of human life and to community should prevail over individualistic notions of conflict.

For Aristotle, rather than asking the question "What ought I to do?" ethics should be concerned with answering the question "What kind of person should I be?" or, to put it another way, "What character traits should I acquire?" In Aristotle's view, once we have answered this question we may be in a position to answer the question "What ought I to do?" Virtue ethics is primarily concerned with persons and character rather than with duties or with the consequences of actions (Holmes 1998: 32). Aristotle is mainly interested in virtues and vices—in other words, the strengths and weaknesses of character that operate to promote or hinder the flourishing of the human personality.

A Closer Look

Aristotle

Aristotle, one of history's greatest philosophers, was born in 384 BCE in the north of Greece. His father was a medical doctor and a court physician. Due to his father's position at court, Aristotle formed an early association with the ruling elite. In 367 BCE, Aristotle entered Plato's Academy as a student, and he remained there until Plato's death in 347 BCE. While it seems clear that Aristotle respected and admired Plato, he was not a rigid follower of Plato's teachings, and he often used Plato's philosophy as a springboard from which to develop his own views. In 347 BCE, he left Athens for about 12 years, traveling and conducting research. During this time, he married and was also a tutor to the young Alexander the Great. In 335 BCE, he returned to Athens and founded his own school, the Lyceum. Most of the works of Aristotle that we still possess were written during this period.

When Alexander the Great died in 323 BCE, the people of Athens, who were anti-Macedonia, charged Aristotle with impiety because of his friendly relations with Alexander. In response, Aristotle left Athens rather than having to face a trial. He died the following year.

Most of the works of Aristotle that we possess are treatises, which may have been his own notes for lectures given in the Lyceum. Historically, the *Nicomachean Ethics* has been the subject of more study and has become more influential than his other works, and it contains his definitive statement on ethics.

Book 1 of the *Ethics* is an investigation of happiness or the good life; he defines this life in terms of virtue. The notion of virtue is discussed in depth in Book 2. Book 3 examines the concepts of choice or preference, and Books 4 and 5 consider particular moral virtues. He argues that moral virtues require the virtue of practical wisdom for their proper exercise, and he examines this concept in Book 6. Moral weakness, which is a failure of practical wisdom, is examined in Book 7. Books 8 and 9 concern friendship, and Book 10, the concluding book, is concerned with pleasure and a reconsideration of the good life.

SOURCE: Prior 1991: 144–146.

VIRTUES

In considering the nature of virtue, several questions arise: What is a virtue? What character traits (a disposition to act in a certain way; e.g., to tell the truth, to help those in need) constitute virtues? What do these virtues consist of? Why are these qualities good for a person to have? Virtues are personal qualities or traits of character, shown through habitual action, that make us persons of excellent character. They can include natural qualities such as intelligence or strength, learned or acquired qualities, qualities relating to temperament, religious qualities, and qualities of character (Holmes 1998: 32). The repetition of virtuous actions causes a person to develop a virtuous character, and once that character is formed, it becomes the source of that person's virtuous actions. As Aristotle wrote,

> By abstaining from pleasures we become self-controlled, and once we are self-controlled we are best able to abstain from pleasures. So also with courage: by becoming habituated to despise and endure terrors we become courageous, and once we have become courageous we will be able to endure terror. (Book 2, in Prior 1991: 158)

For example, in relation to the virtue of honesty, it is not enough for someone to tell the truth sometimes or only when it is to his or her advantage. An honest person, in the sense of a virtuous person, is a person who is truthful as a matter of course, regardless of the outcome. It is important that virtuous action be habitual because when practices become habitual they make up the fixed character that determines the identity of an individual (Tessitore 1996: 25). In the best case, a person may have a natural inclination to the virtuous, but the additional training of habitually virtuous action must complement this natural disposition. This guidance is usually provided by parents and teachers and through laws.

A virtuous person will ask himself or herself: How will I be good in this situation? What would be the normal course of action? In this way, he or she encourages moral persons to demand of themselves the highest degree of excellence of which they are capable (Tessitore 1996: 46). According to virtue ethics, what is wrong with lying is not that it is unjust because it violates others' right to the truth or their right to be treated with respect, but that it is dishonest, and dishonesty is a vice (Hursthouse 1999: 6). Similarly, what is wrong with wrongful killing is not so much that it is unjust and violates the right to life, but that it is callous and contrary to the virtue of charity.

Which character traits should be cultivated as virtues? Aristotle proposes a much larger list of virtues than did Plato and Socrates, who identified only four or five primary virtues (wisdom, courage, temperance, justice, and piety; Prior 1991: 163). Aristotle discusses a dozen virtues that do not include justice or wisdom. James Rachels (1999: 178) provides the following as Aristotle's list:

Benevolence	Industriousness
Civility	Justice
Compassion	Loyalty
Conscientiousness	Moderation
Cooperativeness	Reasonableness
Courage	Self-Confidence
Courteousness	Self-Control
Dependability	Self-Discipline
Fairness	Self-Reliance
Friendliness	Tactfulness
Generosity	Thoughtfulness
Honesty	Tolerance

Each virtue has its own special features, and some raise distinctive issues. For example, the virtue of *courage* can present troublesome cases. Consider the case of a terrorist who gives his life for a cause, such as the destruction of Israeli society, by blowing himself up with explosives and causing the death of innocent people. Is he courageous? It can be argued that the terrorist does not really possess the virtue of courage because courage in an unworthy cause is not a virtue (Rachels 1999: 179). If his motive was not to destroy another society but to fight for the right of existence of a Palestinian nation, the analysis about whether he is acting out of courage might be altered. Another example is the Nazi soldier who fights bravely but for an evil cause. It does not seem right to say that he is not courageous. An alternative explanation is that he is displaying two qualities, one that is admirable (being brave in the face of danger) and one that is not (being willing to fight for an evil regime that aims to destroy Jews). His courage is deployed in the promotion of an evil cause and on the whole is not virtuous (p. 180).

In considering the virtue of *generosity,* how much is enough to give? Utilitarians would argue that it is your duty to do what will produce the best overall consequences for everyone affected, and this means being generous with our wealth until we reach the point where giving more would be more harmful to us than it would be helpful to others. However, adopting this approach would provide a severe constraint on our normal living, and we would have to abandon our everyday lives, give up our projects and plans, and live in a very different way. Rachels (1999) suggests that a reasonable mean in relation to the virtue of generosity is that "we should be as generous with our resources as is consistent with conducting our ordinary lives in a minimally satisfying way" (p. 181).

In deontological ethics, the imperative is to do what is right, whereas in virtue ethics, the imperative is to be a good person. Usually when we refer to a "good person," we mean a person who is morally good because even though someone may possess many of the qualities referred to earlier, this does not mean that he or she possesses moral integrity. It is important to appreciate that a person can possess good qualities but still not be a good person overall. The critical point is that virtues are necessary for conducting our lives *well* (Rachels 1999: 185).

As already stated, moral virtues are represented by habits, traits, or dispositions of character and, according to Aristotle, must be acquired through practice. For example, to become a generous person, one must carry out generous acts with regularity. Similarly, a person who always acts courageously over a period of time will find that the character trait of courageousness will become habitual.

Aristotle and Happiness

Aristotle adopted an empirical approach to ethical problems, so instead of simply reflecting on ways to discover the nature of the good life, he examined the behavior and ways of people in everyday life. He noticed that some people were regarded as leading good lives and others as leading bad lives. He considered that the so-called good life contained the characteristic of happiness, and in contrast, the life regarded as bad contained unhappiness. In answer to the question of what is a good life for man, he therefore concluded that it is a life of happiness. However, what exactly is meant by the word *happiness?* The word Aristotle uses can also be translated into notions of "flourishing" or "well-being," and virtues and vices should be understood in that context. Aristotle regards happiness as the good to which all human action aims, and he seeks to encourage his students to develop a more satisfying understanding of happiness (Tessitore 1996: 20). According to Aristotle, when we develop as we "ought," we live well, thrive, and flourish, and when we do not, we suffer and decay (Darwall 1998: 195). Therefore, virtues are strengths of character that promote human flourishing and well-being, and vices are weaknesses of character that hinder human flourishing or well-being (Hinman 1998: 326).

Aristotle tries to explain the meaning of the term *happiness.* In a famous definition in his book *Nicomachean Ethics,* he defines happiness as "an activity of the soul in accord with perfect virtue." It is not immediately clear just what this means, and various interpretations of this definition have been offered. One commonly accepted interpretation is that Aristotle is emphasizing that happiness is not static but is rather an activity, something that accompanies activities rather than being a goal of them. Happiness, therefore, becomes a way of doing things—for example, of not being defeated by circumstances. It is a way of engaging in life's various activities in a certain way. When we make choices during our lives, promoting our own happiness ought not to motivate the moral choices we make (Kopperi 1999: 16). Instead, what is a morally right or wrong act is ultimately to be judged in contrast to our final goal of happiness. In this sense, therefore, moral norms should be seen as rules that tell us how to live and direct us toward realizing our own good. Failing to follow these rules or norms will separate us from our own happiness.

Aristotle argues that "flourishing" arises out of virtuous activity. He writes that all things have a function or activity, and he offers the example of playing a musical instrument (Darwall 1998: 199). He contends that not just anything counts as playing that instrument and that the activity of playing has certain standards built into it. If one plays well, one flourishes as a player of that instrument. Similarly, an object like a knife is designed for a certain purpose, and its function determines what it is that makes it perform well. Aristotle concludes from this that human beings also have a function, as does every natural thing. For example, for plants, the function is a life of nutrition and growth. What is distinctive about human beings is the way in which ethical conceptions are located in our thoughts, feelings, or actions and the ways in which we can affect our choices by performing our functions well. Therefore, a flourishing life becomes one of excellent, distinctively human activity—that is, a life of virtuous activity. Aristotle does not think that man's function is simply biological living or perception because plants and animals also live biologically and some animals perceive (Benn 1998: 162). He concludes, therefore, that man's function is that which is unique to us as human beings: "an activity of soul exhibiting excellence" (p. 162).

THE GOLDEN MEAN

Having determined that the good life is a life of happiness, Aristotle went further by proposing that people should behave in ways that will achieve happiness. From this notion developed the idea of the mean or the *golden mean*. In situations where we have to make practical decisions, we can see that there are two extremes and a mean or average between them. Our aim should be to find that mean, and this will enable us to act rightly. How do we find the mean in particular cases? Aristotle advises that "such things depend on particular facts, and the decision rests with perception" (in Holmes 1998: 43).

This suggests that you should look at all the relevant facts of the situation, including the kind of person you are, your strengths and weaknesses, and your tendencies and dispositions. The mean lies between an excess and a deficiency so that, for example, eating too much is an extreme or excess and eating too little is going to the other extreme and is a deficiency. Eating just the right amount is the mean. However, the mean is often relative and varies according to the individual, so, for example, an act of generosity for a millionaire may be quite different from that of a beggar on the street. This leads to the consequence that ethically there are different correct ways of living for different people. What may be good for one person may not be good for another, and it is impossible to tell, using reason alone, which is the correct way of living for a particular person. The correct way can be discovered only by experimentation and trial and error. Aristotle's ethics is therefore relativistic because the right thing to do in a situation may not be the same for different people (Prior 1991: 160). This explains why his ethics may not be reduced to a set of rules to be applied universally.

Therefore, Aristotle argues that the proper way to behave in an ethical or moral sense is in accordance with the mean (Hinman 1998: 333). For example, courage is the mean between cowardice and rashness; pride is the mean between vanity and humility; and generosity is the mean between extravagance and stinginess. Aristotle concludes, therefore, that to achieve happiness, a person ought to act moderately and attempt to find the mean between the two extremes (see Figure 14.1).

Figure 14.1   The Golden Mean

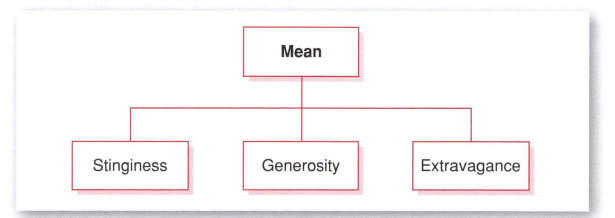

Practical Wisdom

Aristotle emphasizes the way in which well-being and flourishing relate to "practical wisdom," and he argues that people of practical wisdom are those able to effectively deliberate about what is good for their life as a whole as opposed to what may just be expedient. Practical wisdom equates to prudence and forethought as well as intelligence, and this notion is at the very heart of Aristotle's conception of the moral life (Hinman 1998: 355). Essentially, practical wisdom involves applying excellent character to a situation in light of an overall conception of what amounts to a good life. Aristotle makes a distinction between a wise person and a person who is simply clever. He contends that the clever person knows the best means to a particular end but does not have the wisdom to understand which ends are worth pursuing. In contrast, the wise person knows how to achieve a particular end and also understands which ends are worth achieving (p. 356). Applying practical wisdom is therefore a thinking process in which we reflect on circumstances and apply our wisdom to a specific case. As Aristotle explains it, practical wisdom is not constituted by the attribute of cleverness, but practical wisdom does not exist without cleverness.

An individual of practical wisdom is a person able to reason correctly about ethical matters and is someone who has the vision to see which is the correct course of action (Prior 1991: 161). A person who exercises practical wisdom is able to make choices about how to act—that is, to see which specific act would satisfy the goal of acting nobly in a particular situation (Darwall 1998: 211–212). Such a person is able to deliberate well in the sense that she is able to understand what action justice, temperance, and courage calls for. Aristotle proposed that practical wisdom should be seen as a kind of insight or perception, and he contended that it was impossible for individuals to know what to aim for when considering courses of action unless they were already virtuous. Persons who practice ethical wisdom deliberate well and reflect ethically, not just about what is good in a particular sense but also about the good

life in general. Such persons stand apart from their activities to see what makes sense as they reflect; in this process of reflecting, they perform ethical philosophy (p. 213).

How do we acquire practical wisdom? According to Aristotle, it is gained through a good upbringing that includes associating with good people who provide examples of good actions and through acting in a good way. It is important not to just observe or interact with good people, but to imitate them and do the same kinds of things they do.

What's Wrong With Virtue

It is important to keep in mind that Aristotle was writing at a particular time in history in a flourishing Greek civilization where the community (the *polis*) was an essential component of the social life in the city-state of Athens (Hinman 1998: 328–329). His notion of what amounted to a community differs significantly from that used today, and there is a political as well as a social component to community in Aristotle's teachings. For the Greeks, the political realm was an essential part of well-being and flourishing. It is therefore important to locate Aristotle's teachings historically and not to abstract his ideas from the cultural and social environment in which he lived and thought (MacIntyre 1984: 11). Aristotle spoke as an educated Athenian man, addressing the best citizens of the best city-state in the belief that the city-state was the unique political form in which the virtues of human life could be genuinely and fully realized (p. 148). Aristotle regarded the Athenian gentleman as the epitome of human excellence, and he considered that virtues were not available to all because some virtues, such as magnanimity and generosity, were confined to people of great wealth and high social status (p. 182).

Both Aristotle and Alasdair MacIntyre (1984) have linked virtue to particular forms of social life. Lawrence Blum (1996: 232–233) carries on that approach in the modern day in his exploration of possible linkages between virtue and the community. He identifies a number of possible links that are located in the literature on virtue, including notions that virtues can be learned only within forms of social life like families; that virtues can be sustained only in communities because members of the community are able to support moral strengths and identify weaknesses; that since the communities in which we live shape the way we apply our moral principles, without communities, we would not know how to act ethically in our social lives; and that some virtues such as trust and tolerance are particularly appropriately exercised in communities.

The notion of the golden mean has been criticized because, although the idea of finding a mean seems reasonable and plausible initially, there will be situations where this notion does not work. For example, what is the middle course between keeping a promise and not keeping one? It is obvious that there is no middle course because one either keeps a promise or does not, and we tend to feel that those who keep promises are moral and those who do not lack morality. The same argument can be applied to truth telling because one either does or does not tell the truth. Thus, it seems that certain virtues such as promise keeping and truth telling are absolute and not relative to various people and situations. It might be argued, however, that keeping promises and truth telling are actions rather than virtues. The virtues of loyalty, dependability, and honesty could collectively equate to promise keeping and truth telling, and these virtues do have a middle course.

A further criticism of the teachings of Aristotle is that he is, for all intents and purposes, proposing the notion that happiness will result from moderate behavior. While this may be true in some cases, there are other cases in which behavior in excess of the mean is proper for an individual. For example, a man who is by temperament passionate and zealous may find that moderate behavior does not suit him, and that person cannot be happy if forced to exercise control by acting in a moderate way. Therefore, for those who have this temperament, Aristotle has little to offer.

Aristotle has been criticized for his account of virtue ethics because it is said that his is an ethics for the ruling class—that is, for the privileged, free, adult, Greek males whose main concerns were politics, war, and leisure. At the time Aristotle was writing, women, foreigners, and slaves were excluded from many of the activities of life in Athens, despite the fact that the privileged class enjoyed benefits that were largely generated by these excluded groups. Certainly, the audience for his ethics was composed fundamentally of those who had benefited from a noble upbringing, had some experience of life, and had reached a certain level of maturity (Tessitore 1996: 17). Aristotle considered that the good life and the happiness of an adult, male citizen of noble birth differed from that of a woman or a slave (Kopperi 1999: 28). Women's natures as well as slaves' were seen as different from those of men of noble birth, and, therefore, the form of human life appropriate for them also differed. Significantly, what was best for a woman or a slave was not for them to decide for themselves; the appropriate conception of the good life for women and slaves was based on what was thought to be their human nature, and they were expected simply to accept this conception.

It is a common criticism of Aristotle that his list of virtues is arbitrary, and it is certainly constructed by reference to Aristotle's cultural boundaries and shaped by the values prevailing in ancient Athens. However, Lawrence Hinman (1998: 334–335) argues that there are some universal elements in his list of virtues. He suggests that we all need to develop certain attitudes to cope with our lives, such as the way we react to the suffering of others. Here, Hinman suggests that the excess is pity or bleeding heart, the deficiency is acting callously, and the mean compassionately. Similarly, he proposes that we all need to develop an attitude toward our friends where the mean would be loyalty, the excess flattery, and the deficiency indifference. Hinman offers the table shown in Table 14.1 to illustrate the mean (the most virtuous response) to various attitudes or spheres of existence. Hinman draws our attention to the fact that when we attempt to develop virtuous responses to these attitudes we must focus on the patterns in our behavior because these, rather than specific acts, reveal our character (2003: 279).

Table 14.1   Virtues and Spheres of Existence

	Deficiency	Mean	Excess
Attitude Toward Self	Servility Self-deprivation	Proper self-love Proper pride Self-respect	Arrogance Conceit Egoism Narcissism Vanity
Attitude Toward Offenses of Others	Ignoring them Being a doormat	Anger Forgiveness Understanding	Revenge Grudge Resentment
Attitude Toward Good Deeds of Others	Suspicion Envy Ignoring them	Gratitude Admiration	Over-indebtedness
Attitude Toward Our Own Offenses	Indifference Remorselessness Downplaying	Agent regret Remorse Making amends Learning from them Self-forgiveness	Toxic guilt Scrupulosity Shame
Attitude Toward Our Own Good Deeds	Belittling Disappointment	Sense of accomplishment Humility	Self-righteousness
Attitude Toward the Suffering of Others	Callousness	Compassion	Pity "Bleeding heart"
Attitude Toward the Achievements of Others	Self-satisfaction Complacency Competition	Admiration Emulation	Envy
Attitude Toward Death and Danger	Cowardice	Courage	Foolhardiness
Attitude Toward Our Own Desires	Anhedonia	Temperance Moderation	Lust Gluttony
Attitude Toward Our Friends	Indifference	Loyalty	Obsequiousness
Attitude Toward Other People	Exploitation	Respect	Deference

SOURCE: *Ethics: A Pluralistic Approach to Moral Theory,* 3rd ed., by Lawrence M. Hinman. Copyright © 2003 Wadsworth, a part of Cengage Learning, Inc. Reproduced with permission of Thomson Wadsworth.

A central criticism of Aristotle's approach to ethics is that it fails to tell us how to act (Hinman 1998: 359). Notwithstanding what he tells us about good character, Aristotle does not provide us with answers to moral questions like those of the death penalty and euthanasia. Proponents of deontological and consequentialist theories argue that virtue ethics has no ethics of action and is therefore incomplete. In answer to this charge, it can be argued that an ethics of action needs an ethics of character, such as that provided by virtue ethics. For one reason, a person with a morally sensitive character is more likely to apply a moral rule of action with insight, and without good character, there may be a temptation to act insensitively. Rachels (1999: 189) agrees that developing a theory combining the best features of right action theory with aspects of the virtue approach, supplementing a theory of right action, would give a better account of moral character.

Edmund Pincoffs (1998: 442–449), in a general discussion of what he terms *quandary ethics* (ethical dilemmas), suggests that when faced with an ethical dilemma, the approach is to ask what is the right thing to do, emphasizing action rather than character. His contention is that the question of whether or not an act is right is difficult to separate from the question of whether the agent is praiseworthy and that seeing dilemmas only in terms of the elements of the situation that a person is faced with is an inadequate strategy because reference to individual standards and ideals is an essential feature of moral deliberation. Although not specifically addressing virtue ethics as an aspect of resolving ethical dilemmas, Pincoffs does seem to suggest that the development of a notion of the moral self is a necessary prerequisite because the absence of a developed moral self means that moral dilemmas will simply not arise for an individual. He specifically mentions the qualities of "loyalty, generosity (and) courage" as other features of moral character, bringing his argument closer to that of virtue ethics (p. 447).

However, other philosophers argue that virtue ethics can stand alone as an alternative to other ethical theories, and at least one philosopher, Rosalind Hursthouse (1999: 26), argues that virtue ethics can provide action guidance. She proposes that an action is right if it is what a virtuous agent, acting in character, would do in the circumstances and that a virtuous agent is one who has and exercises certain character traits—namely, the virtues (pp. 28–29). As she puts it, "Not only does each virtue generate a prescription—do what is honest, charitable, generous—but each vice a prohibition—do not do what is dishonest, uncharitable, mean" (p. 16). Piers Benn (1998: 168) offers an example. When confronted with the choice between keeping quiet and divulging a friend's confidence to be entertaining, the question is "What would the person with the relevant virtue do?" In this case, loyalty is an integral part of friendship because it is the virtue that makes friendship possible. Therefore, here the question would be "What would a loyal person do?" Rachels

(1999: 190) suggests that one approach is to assess an action as being right or wrong by reference to the reasons that can be given in favor of or against it, but the reasons given must be reasons connected with the virtues. In other words, the reasons in favor of doing an act will relate to whether the act is honest, generous, fair, and so on, and the reasons against doing it will relate to it being dishonest, unfair, and so on.

Hursthouse (1999: 43) argues that the requirements of different virtues can lead us in different directions that conflict with each other. For example, the virtue of charity may prompt me to kill a person who would truly be better off dead, but the virtue of justice forbids it. It follows that virtue ethics gives no guidance over the rightness or wrongness of euthanasia. Another example is the question of whether a doctor should lie to a patient who has a limited time left to live. The virtue of honesty tells doctors that they should tell the truth, even though it may be devastating, but kindness and compassion suggest a course of remaining silent or even of lying. Hursthouse makes the point that deontologists are also faced with this conflict problem. However, it might be argued that one does not do a person any kindness by concealing this sort of truth from him or her, even though the truth may also be devastating.

Susan Moller Okin (1996) offers a critique of virtue ethics from a feminist viewpoint. She contends that the notion of virtue has been constructed as a quality regarded as admirable in free men with high social standing and that Aristotle's account of the virtues is written from the perspective of the "free, educated, and leisured male members of society" (p. 212). Accordingly, his arguments are predicated on the exclusion of women. In fact, Aristotle's views on women assume their inferiority, and he concludes that women—whom he calls "a deformity of nature"—exist only to perform their role of sexually reproducing men (p. 213). Similarly, Okin attacks Aristotle's notion of growth and nurturing because he conceives that process as something each person achieves alone, when in fact it was women and slaves who provided the food and services that made such growth possible (p. 214). Okin points out that Aristotle's discussion of virtues is constructed in terms of men only and is bounded by the social hierarchy and domination present in the society in which he lived. She concludes by arguing that there has been little advance in formulating a specifically feminist account of virtue ethics (p. 229).

For Aristotle, gaining access to ethical ideas and thought is dependent on an upbringing that teaches and fosters maturity and growth and brings about the right habits and character (Darwall 1998: 214). An upbringing and education of this kind is necessary for a person to develop emotional and cognitive knowledge that may lead to the acquisition of ethical knowledge. It follows, then, that ethical knowledge may not be available to everyone and that ultimately judgment and wisdom result from maturity, growth, nurturing, and applying the wisdom of earlier generations. This view of ethics stands in complete contrast to the views argued by Mill and Kant, which are law based. Aristotle's conception of ethics differs in that it is based on a set of ideals. As we practice the virtues, we make choices that demand judgment. It follows that the exercise of virtues requires a capacity to judge and "do the right thing in the right place at the right time in the right way," and the exercise of this judgment does not constitute an application of rules in a routine way (MacIntyre 1984: 150).

APPLYING VIRTUE THEORY

Case Study 14.1 illustrates how virtue theory can be applied to an ethical dilemma within the criminal justice system.

Case Study 14.1 Profiling in the Neighborhood

Rodney is a rookie police officer assigned to a mainly white, middle-class neighborhood. On the evening shift, Rodney and his partner Max, a more senior officer, are patrolling the neighborhood when Max says, "Hey, look at that kid. He doesn't belong here. Let's question him." Rodney stops the patrol car, and he and Max get out and approach the boy, asking him for his identification. The boy produces his identification and asks the two officers, "Why have you stopped me? Is it because I'm black?" They do not respond, and Max just searches him and then arrests him. Later that night, Max tells Rodney that the boy "pissed him off" with his attitude. He tells Rodney to write a report of the incident and charge the boy with loitering.

SOURCE: Adapted from Goodman 1998: 59.

In resolving what may be an ethical dilemma, Rodney will follow the process of resolving an ethical dilemma set out in Chapter 1.

1. *Is Rodney faced with an ethical dilemma?*

   Rodney is faced with the dilemma of whether or not to write a report about the incident when he knows that he is being asked to write a false report and to bring a false charge based on a false arrest.

2. *What are the facts and circumstances of the incident?*

   Rodney needs to review in his mind the facts and circumstances of the stop and arrest and perhaps write them down in the form of a report so that his memory of the events is quite clear.

3. *What are the facts relevant to the decision he has to make? What are his own values about the issue, and what are the values of his workplace about such an issue?*

   Rodney and his partner stopped the boy because he was an African American moving around at night on foot in a white, middle-class neighborhood; he was questioned and provided his identification but protested being stopped, suggesting that the sole reason was that he was black. Rodney and Max had no basis for stopping or making an arrest; Max admitted to Rodney that the boy had "pissed him off" with his attitude, and Max has instructed Rodney to write a false report of the incident to justify the stop and arrest.

Rodney's personal values relate to his position as a rookie cop; that is, he wants to do well in the job and make arrests, and he looks to his more experienced coworkers for guidance. His workplace values comprise the formal police code of ethics and police rules and regulations about stopping and searching and arresting, as well as the police subculture on these issues. In many police departments, racial profiling is a routine event, and police are expected to show loyalty toward each other and to support their partners.

4. *What ethical theories does he call to mind to assist him in resolving the dilemma?*

   In this case, Rodney will apply virtue ethical theory to the dilemma.

5. *What are Rodney's available courses of action?*

   Rodney may comply with his partner's request and complete the false report; he may refuse to fill out the report and tell Max, who instigated the incident, to make the report himself; or he may simply report the whole incident as well as Max's request to his supervisor.

6. *Rodney will make his decision after applying, in this case, the virtue approach to each alternative course of action, and he will choose the course of action that is the most ethically appropriate for him under virtue theory.*

   A process for assessing an ethical dilemma from a virtue perspective is set out in the "Virtue Ethics Evaluation of Ethical Dilemmas" Closer Look box. Applications of these criteria are shown in the "Applying Virtue Ethics" Closer Look box.

A Closer Look

Virtue Ethics Evaluation of Ethical Dilemmas

The focus is on the character of the decision-maker. As a person with moral character, I must assess the knowledge I have or will need to reach my full potential and become a virtuous person.

1. Regardless of the dilemma, I must first ask what kind of person (police officer, prosecutor, correctional officer, judge, etc.) I should become to be the best person I can be in that role.

2. I must then ask which virtues will allow me to become the best person (officer, prosecutor, correctional officer, judge, etc.) I can become. I will identify which virtues I must practice in this situation and explain to myself why they are relevant to my goals of becoming virtuous and developing good moral character, including integrity, honesty, compassion, courage, duty, and so on.

3. Once I have decided what kind of person I will need to become to be a virtuous person and which virtues I will need to practice to achieve that goal, I must ask myself which option in the dilemma allows me to practice these virtues and explain to myself how this option allows me to practice these virtues and why the other options would not.

4. I will then practice these virtues until they become habit and part of my character so that when ethical dilemmas present themselves to me in the future, I will know what to do and will no longer face a dilemma of this kind.

A Closer Look

Applying Virtue Ethics

1. Regardless of the dilemma, I must first ask what kind of person (police officer, prosecutor, correctional officer, etc.) should I become to be the most virtuous person I can be in that role.

   I might say, for example, that a virtuous police officer is one who is honest, has integrity, has respect for the individual and for the dignity of the individual, and is fair, civil, courageous, and self-disciplined.

2. I must then identify which virtues will allow me to become the best person (officer, prosecutor, correctional officer, judge, etc.) I can become in this situation. I need to explain why these virtues are relevant to my goal of becoming a virtuous person.

   I might say that in the given situation, the best person would have the virtues of courage (because as a rookie officer I need to be able to say no to my more experienced partner), honesty (because I am being asked to make a false report), fairness (because I am being asked to treat a person unfairly), and respect for the dignity of the individual (because racial profiling forms the basis of my dilemma, and this practice is inconsistent with the dignity of the individual).

3. Once I have decided what kind of person I will need to become to be a virtuous person and which virtues I will need to practice to achieve that goal, I must ask myself which option in the dilemma allows me to practice these virtues, and explain to myself how this option allows me to practice these virtues and why the other options do not.

   Rodney has the options of writing the report, refusing to write the report, telling Max to write it himself, or reporting the whole incident to his supervisor. Rodney has identified the virtues of courage, honesty, fairness, and respect for human dignity as relevant virtues in this situation.

   The option of writing the report does not satisfy the virtues of courage, honesty, fairness, or respect for human dignity.

   The option of telling Max to write his own report satisfies the virtue of courage only in the sense that Rodney is refusing to write a false report himself. It does not satisfy the virtues of honesty, fairness, or respect for human dignity because the report will be false even though Rodney does not write it—it is based on a false arrest that is in turn based on racial profiling and nothing more.

   The option of reporting the incident to his supervisor satisfies all of the described virtues because it will expose the incident as being an act of racial profiling, it will show that the stop and arrest were based on nothing more than racial profiling, and it will show that the arrest was false and that the officer was merely trying to penalize the African American boy for questioning his authority. It will also show that the charge brought was a false one.

   The most virtuous option for Rodney is to report the entire matter to his supervisor because that action allows him to practice the most virtues in this particular incident.

4. I will then practice these virtues until they become habit and part of my character so that when ethical dilemmas present themselves to me in the future, I will know what to do and will no longer face a dilemma of this kind.

   Rodney will now practice the virtues of honesty, courage, fairness, and respect for human dignity until they are part of his character, and in a similar situation, he will know how to react instinctively.

SUMMARY

Whereas deontology focuses on duty and utilitarianism on consequences, virtue ethics is concerned with virtue and moral character. Virtue ethics began with the Greek philosopher Aristotle, who was interested in the kind of person we must become to lead the good life. Instead of posing the question "What ought I to do?" virtue ethics poses the question "What kind of person should I become?" and contends that it is only when we have answered this question that we can determine what is the right thing to do.

Virtues are personal qualities or character traits that are developed through habitual action and that help us to become, over our lifetime, persons of excellent character. The virtues include both natural and acquired qualities, such as intelligence, honesty, generosity, loyalty, and self-control. Whereas deontology absolutely prohibits lying and consequentialism may permit it if the consequences are beneficial, virtue ethics argues that lying is dishonest and that dishonesty is a vice, not a virtue. Sometimes virtues can raise problems. For example, is the terrorist who gives his life for a cause he believes in by committing suicide acting courageously? If generosity is a virtue, how generous is one required to be?

An important aspect of Aristotle's notion of virtue is the concept of happiness because Aristotle believed that a good life was one that included happiness. By happiness, he meant well-being or flourishing, and Aristotle therefore argued that virtues promote flourishing and well-being. Aristotle's concept of happiness is difficult to define with any precision, but it is generally thought of as an activity rather than a state of mind, and for that reason, it can be thought of as a way of doing things that is positive and as demonstrating an active engagement with life. He argued that we should act in ways that will bring about happiness, and he proposed the idea of the mean or the golden mean. According to the golden mean, when we have to make decisions, we should look for a mean or average between two extremes. For example, we should not eat to excess or insufficiently but consume just the right amount—that is, the mean. It is easy to see how this idea can be applied to everyday ethical behavior.

Another idea promoted by Aristotle is that of practical wisdom, which involves the notion of applying one's excellent character to a situation in the overall context of establishing a good life. Applying practical wisdom means thinking about the circumstances, reasoning correctly, and making the right choices. Individuals who practice practical wisdom have a kind of insight or perception that guides them in making the right decisions.

Virtue ethics as explained by Aristotle has been criticized for being historically specific because it was formulated in the context of Athenian society at a particular point in history, and this society assumed that virtues were confined to those who possessed great wealth and high social status. Nevertheless, modern philosophers have linked virtue ethics to modern social life and the community, emphasizing the virtues that can be learned within the family as well as within communities. Some see Aristotle's list of virtues as arbitrary, but others think that there is a universality about the notion of virtue and that we all need to develop balance and positive attitudes in our lives.

A major criticism is that virtue ethics does not tell us how to act. For example, it gives us no basis for looking at issues like the death penalty. One answer to this charge is that virtue ethics, as an ethics of character, is essential because it supplements and complements approaches that take an ethics of action. Others argue that developing a moral self means first developing a virtuous nature and that it is only possible to resolve ethical dilemmas if one possesses the necessary individual qualities and character. Some modern philosophers take the view that virtue ethics can stand on its own and that a right action is one taken by a virtuous person acting in character in particular circumstances. In thinking about virtue ethics and the criminal justice system, it is easy to see how character is important in law enforcement and in avoiding abuse of authority and corruption.

DISCUSSION CASE

A Virtuous Prosecutor?

U.S. Attorney Thomas Marks is to prosecute three persons charged with distributing 5 kilograms of cocaine and with conspiracy. They were arrested in a sting operation when an undercover police officer sold them the cocaine for $75,000. They were arrested after one of the defendants had given the undercover officer the money and had taken possession of the cocaine.

According to the Federal Sentencing Guidelines, each of the three defendants faces a mandatory minimum jail sentence of 10 years. Each defendant had a different role in the transaction that led to their arrest as follows:

Defendant One: This person appeared to be the primary ringleader, used his business premises for meetings to discuss the drug conspiracy, and had the largest role in negotiating price and terms of sale. According to police, he is the leader of a drug organization that markets about 20 kilograms of cocaine each month and launders the proceeds through his business.

Defendant Two: This person appeared to act as Defendant One's lieutenant; he made several incriminating statements recorded on tape during the sale negotiation, revealing a knowledge of the cocaine business and his plans to resell the drugs. He has no prior criminal record.

Defendant Three: This person basically acted as a lookout during the transaction; he can be convicted as an accomplice but was not a substantial player. He drove the other defendants to meetings and searched the police undercover officer on the date of the sale.

Defendants One and Two have no criminal records, but Defendant Three has a significant record of violent crime that includes assault convictions, domestic violence, firearms possession and use, and stalking.

The lawyer for Defendant Two informs the prosecutor, Marks, that his client will testify against Defendants One and Three if the distribution charges against him are dismissed and if the court is given a recommendation for a short jail term on the conspiracy charge.

Question: After applying the criteria for a virtue approach, should Marks accept the plea bargain offered?

SOURCE: Cassidy, Michael. 2006. "Character and Context: What Virtue Theory Can Teach Us About a Prosecutor's Ethical Duty to 'Seek Justice.'" *Notre Dame Law Review* 82 (2): 100–161.

DISCUSSION QUESTIONS

1. How does one become a virtuous person? Discuss with reference to Aristotle's ideas and theories.

2. Why do modern philosophers regard virtue ethics as an alternative to deontological and consequentialist ethical decision-making approaches?

3. What are the main criticisms leveled against virtue ethics?

4. How do professional codes of ethics relate to virtue ethics, and why are they important in ethical decision-making in criminal justice?

15

EGOISM, PLEASURE, AND INDIFFERENCE

This chapter will present three ethical theories—namely, ethical egoism, hedonism, and Stoicism. Of the three, only Stoicism has any present-day following in the field of moral philosophy (e.g., see Becker 1998).

STOICISM

In its time, particularly after the death of Alexander the Great, Stoicism was a very influential ethical philosophy. It dominated Roman thinking about moral philosophy until Christianity replaced it. Stoicism, as a philosophy, has been refined and developed over time from its initiation by Zeno (3rd century BCE), who is supposed to have lectured from a porch called a *stoa,* from which Stoicism derives its name.

It is important to appreciate Greek history to understand how Stoicism developed. In summary, Phillip, the father of Alexander the Great, placed Greece under Macedonian rule, ending the regime of the Greek city-states (Prior 1991: 194–197). During his life, Alexander the Great extended the Macedonian empire and began the process that dispersed Greek language and civilization throughout the Mediterranean. The period of transition from Greek city-states to an empire is known as the Hellenistic period. These changes to Greek civilization were influential because Greek philosophy became widely available throughout the region. The city-states were replaced by imperial rule. This change seemed to make much of the work of Plato and Aristotle on ethics and politics obsolete because now philosophers began to see themselves as part of a single enterprise rather than as representing the individual city-states.

The classical Greek philosophers shaped their view of virtue and the good life from the community of small city-states, but this form of social organization no longer existed. Questions were now asked about how virtue would apply in this new age. It was thought that the new social structure required a new philosophy. In addition, much of the daily activity of a citizen in classical Athens had changed with the onset of imperial rule. The political and social life of the city continued, but the close relationships between individuals as well as the social life of the city had changed. In response to these dislocations, new religions arose in an attempt to give individuals a new sense of citizenship. As well, some turned to philosophy instead of religion, and this led to the development of the schools of Epicureanism and Stoicism.

The Stoics reacted to the collapse of the closed social system of the city-states by offering advice to individuals in what for them was a crumbling world. Although Stoicism is a complex moral theory, the basic principle advocated by Stoics is that one should learn to be indifferent to external differences. Many of the writings of the early and later Stoics have disappeared, but among those remaining are the writings of Epictetus, who began life as a Roman slave. He advocated a philosophy of *indifference*, believing that this practice would constitute progress for the individual. In the early period, Zeno was succeeded as head of the Stoic school by Cleanthes and later by Chrysippus (Prior 1991: 208). The best-known Stoic philosophers today are the Roman emperor Marcus Aurelius and Epictetus, both of whom focused on the presentation of Stoicism in a popular form.

The Stoics assumed that good or evil depends on the self, and although others have power over events that may affect you, if you can nevertheless be indifferent to those events, others will not be able to exercise power over you. Epictetus writes,

> All existing things are either in our power or not in our power. In our power are thought, impulse, will to get and will to avoid, and, in a word, everything which is our own doing. Things not in our power include the body, property, reputation, office, and, in a word, everything which is not our own doing. (in Prior 1991: 209)

He further explains, "Virtue resides in the will—only the will is good or bad." Therefore, if one has a good will, achieved by remaining indifferent to external events, external events will not destroy one's character, and one will be a free person, independent of the world. In other words, for Stoics, virtue consists of learning to accept whatever happens. Epictetus urged a person to compel or force his or her will to conform to events and to try not to force events to conform to his or her will. This reflects the Stoic teaching about living life in accordance with nature (Prior 1991: 211); that is, we should live in accordance with our own

human nature, and we should live consistently with the nature of the universe of which we are a part. Since our knowledge is inherently limited, we ought to follow the guidance of our own nature, but if things turn out other than we expect, we should accept them as if they turned out for the best (Sharples 1996: 101).

The ethics of the Stoics should be understood in the context of their belief in predestination—that is, *all that happens in the world is fixed according to some preconceived divine plan, and nothing happens by chance* (Prior 1991: 209). Stoics believed that whatever happened had a rational explanation and was for the best. For them, virtue is achieved through a will that operates in accordance with the happenings of nature. Appreciating and accepting that events have been fated allows one to avoid frustration and despair in trying to alter those events, and, conversely, it is the person who struggles to change events who is not free. Similarly, death should not be considered a bad thing because it has been predestined by God and therefore must be considered good. *The aim is to achieve a state of being where one is not susceptible to passion or emotion* (p. 212). One of the main effects of Stoicism is that it places the onus for becoming good or bad directly on the individual, in the sense that cultivating the appropriate frame of mind will lead to virtue. Virtue alone is good. According to Stoics, our health and wealth are not to be taken into account, and we ought to be indifferent to them (Sharples 1996: 102).

The Stoics believed in a commitment to serving the public. This distinguishes Stoicism from hedonism because the latter advocates a withdrawal from public life and living with a circle of like-minded friends (Sharples 1996: 87). The Romans, with their tradition of public service, admired this aspect of the Stoic philosophy (Prior 1991: 214). The goal of the Stoic philosophy is, therefore, a life of complete rationality and of developing oneself so that one remains invulnerable to passion and emotion. The Stoics depicted the person who lived such a life as a "sage" and believed that philosophy was the means of achieving this life. Stoicism is a philosophy that advocates acceptance of life and events and is pessimistic in tone. A good example of this detached attitude appears in the following passage from Epictetus:

> When you go to visit some great man, prepare your mind by thinking that you will not find him in,

that you will be shut out, that the doors will be slammed in your face, and that he will pay no heed to you. And if in spite of all this you find it fitting for you to go, go and bear what happens and never say to yourself "it was not worth all this"; for that shows a vulgar mind and one at odds with outward things. (in Prior 1991: 219)

In contrasting Stoicism and hedonism, William Prior (1991) points out that both assist in providing a means for dealing with events beyond our control. The Stoics explain that certain things may not be within our power, and the strength of both philosophies is that they teach us "how to bear with dignity those events which truly are beyond our control" (p. 223). In addition, both Stoics and hedonists would agree that one cannot become just or courageous if one behaves in an unjust or cowardly manner (Sharples 1996: 82). In other words, character cannot be separated from action.

HEDONISM

Traditionally, hedonism has been expressed as the view that "pleasure alone is intrinsically good," "pleasure is the only thing worth seeking for its own sake," and "pleasure is the good" (Feldman 1997: 80). Hedonism is the doctrine that pleasure is the sole good. The foremost exponent of hedonism was the Greek philosopher Epicurus (see the "Epicurus" Closer Look box). His name appears in the form of the English words *epicure* and *epicurean,* meaning a person whose main enjoyment is derived from exotic and carefully prepared food and wine. In fact, this connotation is far removed from the philosophy expounded by Epicurus himself. He advocated living moderately yet pleasurably and considered pleasure to be the good for which humans aim. Nevertheless, he also appreciated that pursuit of pleasure might itself result in pain (Prior 1991: 200). For example, if, in seeking pleasure, individuals drink to excess, they will suffer headaches and stomachaches. Therefore, in Epicurus's view, the proper way to live is to live "pleasantly" and at the same time not suffer any of the undesirable effects of that pleasant living. Epicurus stated that the aim of human existence was "health of the body and

tranquility of mind" (p. 201). He did not endorse a life of endless pleasure or sensuality because by *pleasure* he meant "the absence of pain in the body and of trouble in the soul." Tranquility is attained by philosophical understanding and through practical wisdom. The former teaches that death should not be feared and the latter advocates living virtuously (p. 203).

There are two forms of hedonism—psychological hedonism and ethical hedonism. The *psychological* form suggests that people pursue pleasure and only pleasure in their lives and that all their activities are directed toward achieving pleasure and avoiding pain (Feldman 1997: 109). *Ethical hedonism* is the view that not only do people seek pleasure, but they also *ought* to seek pleasure because pleasure alone is good. According to psychological hedonism, every action is motivated by a search for pleasure, whereas ethical hedonism goes one step further, seeing the pursuit of pleasure as normative. Hedonism in both its forms can be criticized for attempting to provide a single explanation for every human act. In other words, in psychological hedonism every act is supposedly motivated by a desire for pleasure.

According to proponents of ethical hedonism, the question of how one ought to live is answered by the contention that the good life consists of a life of pleasure and that a person ought to act in such a way as to acquire pleasure. As already noted, Epicurus attempted to find pleasures that did not produce painful consequences, having recognized that some pleasures might be accompanied by pain or might produce pain. For example, some find that smoking cocaine gives pleasure, but it will also produce severe adverse physical and mental effects if continued beyond a certain point.

In practice, it seems difficult to separate pleasure from pain in the way Epicurus advocated. For example, friendship, a pleasure, can be accompanied by depression and sadness at the death of a close friend. It is difficult, therefore, to see how ethical hedonism can function as a guide for behavior in our daily lives because advising a person to seek pleasure is often also advice to seek pain. In addition, although the notion that people ought to conduct themselves in such ways as to acquire pleasure seems reasonable and plausible, it also seems to violate our commonsense views about how we ought to act. Generally, people feel that sometimes it is acceptable to act to gain pleasure, but few would regard this as the sole objective in life. For example, we frequently have to fulfill obligations, even if we receive little or no pleasure in the process.

A Closer Look

Epicurus

Epicurus was born in 341 BCE on the Greek island of Somas, but his father was an Athenian. He moved to Athens and established a school there in 307 BCE called "The Garden" because it met in the garden of his home. Unusually, women and slaves were permitted to become members of the school. Epicurus lived and taught at The Garden until his death in 271 BCE. He is said to have written over 300 scrolls, but only a tiny number have survived. It is thought that many of his works were destroyed because they were considered adverse to Christianity. Epicurus's main aim was to establish a philosophy concerned with the attainment of happiness. He thought that the main constraint to happiness was the fear and unease caused by religion.

SOURCE: Prior 1991:198.

ETHICAL EGOISM

Typically, an egoist is self-centered, inconsiderate, unfeeling, and a pursuer of the good things in life, whatever may be the cost to others. Egoists think only of themselves, and if they think about others at all, it is merely as a means to their own ends. Essentially, egoism involves putting one's own well-being above that of others (Baier 1991: 197). It argues that the right actions are those that promote self-interest, and the wrong actions are those that detract from self-interest (Hinman 1998: 138). This stands in contrast to most other systems of morality, which recommend that we ought to act unselfishly, that we ought to take other people's interests into account, and that we should care for, rather than harm, other people (Rachels 1999: 70). Lawrence Hinman (1998) argues that, in fact, egoism does not amount to a moral theory at all.

Psychological Egoism

There are two theories of egoism: *psychological egoism* and *ethical egoism*. The former theorizes that all persons are egoists in the sense that our actions are *always* motivated by our own best interests. Proponents of psychological egoism suspect that altruistic explanations of behavior are superficial and without substance (Rachels 1999: 71). In other words, they contend that when a person's motives are properly analyzed, although it may seem that he or she is acting unselfishly—for example, by doing volunteer work in a hospital or church or by saving a child from a burning house—his or her actual motives would tell a different story. For example, the hospital volunteer may be making amends for some misdeed in his or her past or may be trying to build a good résumé, and the person saving the child may be motivated by a desire to be recognized as a hero. This approach can be criticized as being based on the assumption that we will never find the real explanation for someone's behavior until we have discovered an appropriate egotistical motivation (Baier 1991: 199). In other words, a way can always be found to set aside acts of altruism and self-sacrifice and see in them a self-centered motive. However, if one is to interpret all acts in terms of their lack of altruism, one must surely distinguish between acts that are done solely out of selfish motives and those done out of a motive to help others but that also produce feelings of satisfaction and enhance our self-perceptions as "good persons." Surely, one has more moral worth than the other.

Thomas Hobbes (1588–1679) was a believer in psychological egoism, and he tried to give a more general account of it by listing motives and showing how each could be read as egoistical acts or intentions (Rachels 1999: 72). For example, in relation to the motive of charity, Hobbes concluded that it constituted the pleasure one takes in demonstrating one's powers; that is, charitable persons confirm to themselves and others that they are more capable than others. Not only can these individuals take care of themselves, but they also have a surplus available for those who are not as accomplished. In demonstrating charity, they are really emphasizing their own superiority.

Another example is pity. Here, Hobbes concluded that the real reason we feel pity for others' misfortunes is that we are reminded that the same thing might happen to us. As James Rachels notes, psychological egoism appeals to a "certain cynicism in us, a suspicion that people are not nearly as noble as they seem" (1999: 73). As he points out, it is not possible to prove psychological egoism because the theory shows only that it is possible to interpret all motives in an egotistical manner.

Ethical Egoism

Ethical egoism claims that promoting one's own greatest good is always to act in accordance with reason and morality (Baier 1991: 201); that is, everyone ought to pursue his or her own self-interest exclusively (Rachels 1999: 83). Whereas psychological egoism is a theory about *how people actually behave,* ethical egoism is a theory about *how we ought to behave.* It says that we have no duty other than to do what is best for ourselves (p. 84). It is important to understand that ethical egoism does not advocate promoting one's own interests in addition to the interests of others. Rather, it stresses that the only duty we have is to promote our own interest. However, at the same time, ethical egoism does not require us to avoid actions that might help others. Therefore, if a particular act would benefit our own self-interest as well as the interests of others, that act will not be considered contrary to the goals of ethical egoism.

Those who support ethical egoism argue that if we all look after our own interests, it is more likely that we will all be better off. In other words, if we want to do the best for others, we should not act altruistically because, for example, while we are fully aware of our own individual wants and needs, we are not completely aware of others' needs. This line of reasoning suggests that we should not set out to act altruistically because we are not in a good position to do so. Some also insist that looking out for others intrudes into their privacy and that giving charity degrades others and robs them of dignity (Rachels 1999: 85). Ayn Rand, for example, proposed that ethical egoism is the only philosophy that respects the integrity of human life. Rand argued that altruism is a destructive idea, devaluing the individual (Hinman 1998: 149; Rachels 1999: 86), because it claims that one's own interests ought to be sacrificed for another's interests. It is in this sense that altruism does not value the individual. In contrast, Rand suggested that ethical egoism does affirm the value of the individual and is the only moral position to do so.

Rachels (1999) explains that although philosophers have rejected ethical egoism, it is nevertheless a theory that has been returned to again and again. He gives three typical arguments that reject this doctrine. The first is that ethical egoism does not assist in resolving conflicts of interest but rather exacerbates them (p. 91). The second is that it is logically inconsistent, and the third is that ethical egoism is unacceptably arbitrary in the same way that racism is arbitrary (p. 94). Like racism, it advocates dividing people into groups where the interests of one group are considered to count more than the interests of others. This is contrary to the general principle that we can only justify treating people differently when there is a factual difference between them that is relevant and justifies a difference in treatment.

In the same way, ethical egoism contends that we should each divide the world into two categories of people—ourselves and the rest—and that we should regard the interests of the first group as more important than those of the second group. However, this division, and therefore ethical egoism itself, is quite arbitrary because there is no general difference between one's self and others. An additional difficulty for ethical egoism is suggested by Hinman (1998: 152): While ethical egoists can have acquaintances, it is not clear that they are able to have deep friendships with others because such friendships are usually founded on the basis of a mutual concern for each other's welfare, and ethical egoism seems to preclude that concern. Hinman also suggests that ethical egoists suffer from moral insensitivity and an unwillingness to help others (p. 154). Compassion and concern for others is completely opposed to self-interest, and therefore these values are prohibited by this philosophy. This means that ethical egoists would respond to issues such as world hunger by claiming that starving people should be helped only when it is in their own self-interest to do so. This seems rather implausible and callous.

APPLYING THE THEORY OF ETHICAL EGOISM

Case Study 15.1 illustrates how ethical egoism can be applied to an ethical dilemma within the criminal justice system.

Case Study 15.1 Giving Your Own Punishment

Harry is a corrections officer at the Grim Correctional Center. He has a reputation among his coworkers for being very strict with inmates and always being ready to issue violations for the slightest breach of prison rules. One of the inmates he has charge over on his wing is George, a career criminal and experienced prisoner. George and Harry do not like each other, and George often tries to challenge Harry's authority by breaking prison rules or threatening to break them. In the past, Harry has reacted to this resistance by issuing many citations for rule violations and having George dealt with through the inmate disciplinary process. Harry has now reached the stage where he is tired of having his authority questioned by George and has decided to show him who is really the boss. He decides that he will use informal methods to punish George and reinforce his own authority over him. One Friday, Harry inspects George's cell and finds that George has two more pictures in his cell than is permitted by the rules, according to his inmate classification. Harry considers whether or not he should seize on this violation to use informal means to impose his will on George or whether he should follow proper prison procedures for dealing with rule violations. He knows that prison officers can use various informal ways of controlling prisoners, even though the rules do not allow these methods to be used. Examples would include not telling an inmate about a scheduled visitor appointment, withholding toilet paper, or shutting off the hot water to an inmate's cell. He decides to think about a possible informal way to deal with George. In his mind, he formulates the following plan. Instead of issuing a disciplinary report for the extra pictures, Harry will not unlock George's cell the next morning during the daily prison routine and will secretly place a "keep lock" tag on George's cell door. This tag will indicate to other correctional officers that George is to remain locked in his cell and will suggest that a formal order has been given to this effect. This also means that George will remain locked in the cell until he can get someone's attention and complain to the deputy superintendent, who will not be on duty until Monday morning. Harry now has to decide whether to act formally or informally.

In resolving what may be an ethical dilemma, Harry will follow the process of resolving an ethical dilemma set out in Chapter 1.

1. *Is Harry faced with an ethical dilemma?*

   Harry is faced with the dilemma of whether to use informal means to reinforce his authority over George or to use the formal inmate disciplinary process.

2. *What are the facts and circumstances of the incident?*

Harry needs to review in his mind the facts and circumstances.

3. *What are the facts relevant to the decision he has to make? What are his own values about the issue, and what are the values of his workplace about such an issue?*

   The relevant facts are as follows:
   - Harry and George have a history of clashes over Harry's exercise of his authority.

- Harry feels he needs to demonstrate to both inmates and other staff that he is always in control, and he sees this as essential for his work as a correctional officer. In his view, those who demonstrate the most power in the prison environment will prevail.
- Harry has always used formal methods to control George before, but it seems to him that this approach has not changed George's attitude toward him.
- Harry wants his coworkers to see that he can control George because this is expected by the prison officer culture, which requires that officers never show leniency toward inmates and that they provide unquestioning support to coworkers, especially in the face of inmate resistance.
- Harry knows that informal methods are sometimes more effective with inmates than formal processes.

4. *What ethical theories does he call to mind to assist him in resolving the dilemma?*

In this case, Harry will apply ethical egoism to the dilemma.

5. *What are Harry's available courses of action?*

Harry can either follow the formal disciplinary process, or he may use informal methods to punish George.

6. *Harry will make his decision after applying, in this case, the ethical egoism approach to each alternative course of action, and he will choose the course of action that is the most ethically appropriate for him under ethical egoism.*

A process for assessing an ethical dilemma from an ethical egoism perspective is set out in the "Ethical Egoism Evaluation of Ethical Dilemmas" Closer Look boxes. Applications of these criteria are shown in the "Applying Ethical Egoism" Closer Look box.

A Closer Look

Ethical Egoism Evaluation of Ethical Dilemmas

1. What act would most benefit me?

2. How will my self-interest best be promoted?

3. The most ethical course of action is that which is best for me.

4. Will others benefit from what would most benefit me?

A Closer Look

Applying Ethical Egoism

1. What act would most benefit me?

In considering whether to use formal or informal methods to punish George, Harry must consider which action will give him the most benefit. If he takes a formal approach, he knows from past experience that George will continue to resist his efforts to bring George under his control. He feels this will make him look bad in the eyes of other inmates as well as his coworkers. If he takes

(Continued)

(Continued)

an informal approach toward controlling George, something he has never done before, he thinks it might be more effective in establishing his control over George. He also thinks he would look better in the eyes of his colleagues if the informal approach works.

2. How will my self-interest best be promoted?

Harry believes his self-interest will be best served by gaining control over George, and therefore, the question is which method, informal or formal, will give him that control over the inmate. He is aware that formal methods have not worked so far, and his inclination is that informal methods will best serve his self-interest.

3. The most ethical action is that which is best for me.

Harry thinks that what is best for him is to adopt the best method to finally get control over George. Again, he has to decide based on his past experience whether formal or informal methods of disciplining George will be best for him. He also has to consider whether the act of breaking prison rules by applying informal disciplinary methods will have a negative affect on him or on his career if his actions are discovered. In this case, he believes that his actions will not be discovered by the administration because the prison officer subculture will ensure that his informal methods of punishment are not revealed to his supervisors. Even if they are discovered, he believes he can claim he just made a mistake.

4. Will others benefit from the action that would most benefit me?

Ethical egoism does not require that one choose an act that will benefit others. It only requires that an act benefit oneself. However, if an act also benefits others in the process of benefiting oneself, that act is still considered ethically correct under an ethical egoist approach. In this case, Harry thinks that gaining control over George using informal methods will also benefit other prison officers because, if he is successful, they will be able to control George more effectively as well and will not have to resort to informal means of controlling him. He also feels that after his demonstration of officer superiority all inmates will show more respect for the prison officers generally in the future.

In all the circumstances, it is clear that the appropriate course of action for Harry, applying the ethical egoist perspective, is to take informal action against George because that will best serve his own self-interest.

SOURCE: Glover 1999.

Recalling that egoists are self-centered, inconsiderate, unfeeling pursuers of the good things in life, whatever may be the cost to others, and that egoists also put themselves above the well-being of others, it is hard to advocate this approach to ethical decision-making as an ethical approach at all. It contrasts with almost all other systems of morality, which take the view that we ought to act unselfishly, that we ought to take other people's interests into account, and that we should care for, rather than harm, other people (Rachels 1999: 70).

SUMMARY

Stoicism, ethical egoism, and hedonism have very little following among moral philosophers, even though egoism and hedonism celebrate self-gratification in ways that seem to accord with the values of modern consumer society. However, in ethical terms, they appear to have little to offer.

Stoicism is a complex ethical theory founded, like virtue ethics, during a particular period in history when one civilization was being replaced with another and when philosophical issues were generated by societal change. Stoics argue that a person should learn to become indifferent to external differences and should cultivate a life of indifference. Essentially, it asks that we accept that some things are within our power to change and influence, and others are not. Stoicism tries to persuade us that we can achieve a good will by remaining indifferent to external events and by learning to accept things we cannot change. This is consistent with the Stoic belief in predestination, which emphasizes that nothing happens by chance, that whatever happens has a rational explanation, and that whatever happens is always for the best. Stoics argue that if we try to resist events that have been predetermined, we simply generate frustration and despair within ourselves. In some respects, Stoicism shares the concern of virtue ethics with individual character because it argues that developing the appropriate stoic frame of mind will lead us to virtue.

Hedonism advocates the pursuit of pleasure as the sole good. There are two types of hedonism: psychological hedonism and ethical hedonism. Psychological hedonism assumes that we all look for pleasure in our lives and that all our actions are aimed at achieving pleasure and avoiding pain. Ethical hedonism is the moral version of hedonism, asserting that people not only seek pleasure but also ought to seek pleasure because pleasure alone is good. Quite simply, the answer to the question "How ought I to act?" is answered by hedonists through their contention that the good life is a life of pleasure and that a person ought to act in ways that will achieve pleasure. However, it is difficult to accept that this notion can form the sole basis for deciding how to act ethically in our lives.

Ethical egoists try to persuade us that the right action is one that promotes our own self-interest, and typically, egoists advocate the pursuit of the good things in life regardless of the feelings or concerns of others. Like hedonism, egoism is divided into two forms—namely, psychological egoism and ethical egoism. Psychological egoism suggests that all humans are motivated and act according to egoist concerns and denies all altruistic explanations of behavior, instead contending that apparently unselfish acts are always carried out for egotistical reasons. Ethical egoists claim that morality and reason are served only by promoting one's own greatest good and self-interest and that we ought to behave in a way that is best for ourselves. This does not mean that we must avoid actions that might help others but rather that we are duty bound to stress the promotion of our own interests.

Among the many criticisms of ethical egoism is the fact that it is quite arbitrary and resembles racism in its regard for the interests of one group as being more important than the interests of others. That is, it divides the world into others and ourselves, and it subordinates all other interests to our own interests. Additionally, it would seem that ethical egoists are unable to develop deep friendships or compassion for others because they are so much focused on their own interests. This would mean, for example, that ethical egoists would deny any assistance or compassion to starving people, unless they could see such assistance as serving their own self-interest. In the criminal justice system, ethical egoism can be used to justify acts that most would consider lacking in compassion or that are corrupt, abusive, or inhumane.

DISCUSSION QUESTIONS

1. Why is ethical egoism not considered a legitimate ethical theory?

2. How can ethical egoism be applied to the criminal justice system, and what are the implications of using this approach in ethical decision-making?

3. Contrast virtue ethics and Stoicism, and explain why you prefer one approach to the other.

4. What parallels do you see between hedonism and ethical egoism?

16

A SENSE OF JUSTICE

John Rawls was a prominent philosopher and theorist who wrote about the concept of justice. In *A Theory of Justice,* Rawls (1973) aims to "work out a theory of justice that represents an alternative to utilitarian thought" (p. 22). He asserts it is the business of moral theory to establish fundamental principles that would govern a morally good society. Rawls favors an emphasis on the rights of individuals rather than the means–end technique of thinking used by utilitarians, and in this respect, he follows a Kantian approach to ethics (Blocker and Smith 1980: xv). For Rawls (1973: 50–51), a theory of justice is a theory of morality that sets out the principles governing our sense of justice. He argues that moral persons have two distinguishing features (p. 505). First, they have an understanding and conception of "the good," and second, they are capable of possessing a sense of justice—that is, a desire to apply and act on principles of justice. Rawls defines principles of justice in his work and sees these principles as playing a crucial part in our moral thought and action (p. 121).

Rawls's conception of justice has an ancient and classical origin (Holmes 1998: 147). For example, Plato emphasized the importance of justice for social living and believed that we all possess a sense of justice. While observing young children at play, the psychologist Jean Piaget noted the presence of a sense of justice in their activities. When justice is thought of in moral terms, rather than in terms of rules and procedures contained in legal systems, it is often perceived as a virtue or as a moral principle by which we can guide our behavior. Aristotle maintained that justice could be thought of as an aspect of morality, and it is in this sense that the contribution of John Rawls toward embedding justice in our daily lives will be explored.

Rawls's argument is complex and detailed and has given rise to a vast secondary literature. In this chapter, the outline of his argument will be presented and some of its implications explored. As noted, Rawls argues that moral persons possess a sense of justice, as well as the capacity to pursue a conception of "the good" in a rational manner. For moral persons to develop these moral capabilities, it is necessary for them to create a society and agree on the principles that will govern it; this agreement should be the result of a fair procedure designed with fair conditions (Alejandro 1998: 20–21). In his model, the persons who must decide and conclude this agreement from what is called the *original position* are men and women of ordinary talents and tastes. They do not know their place in society or their class or social position and are unaware of their natural assets and abilities or of their level of intelligence (Rawls 1973: 12). Rawls contends that we can discover the nature of a just society by ascertaining the kind of society that would be chosen by those in the original position. The persons choose the principles of justice behind a *veil of ignorance*. This ensures that no one will gain an advantage or suffer a disadvantage because of his or her particular circumstances in society (Holmes 1998: 189). For example, a wealthy person might support a principle that favored those with wealth, but under the veil of ignorance, one could not be influenced in this way because the person would not know whether he or she was wealthy in the actual society where the principles apply. Similarly, a poor person would most likely choose principles favoring the poor, but because of the veil of ignorance, that person would not have knowledge of the economic or class conditions in which he or she would be living. After concluding the agreement, these men and women would return to their position in society and make moral judgments based on the principles they have chosen.

Rawls attempts to demonstrate that if the parties are rational and act only in their own self-interest, they will choose the two principles of justice that Rawls puts forward. These principles are the following (Rawls 1973: 60):

- Each person is to have an equal right to the most extensive basic liberty compatible with a similar liberty for others.
- Social and economic inequalities are to be arranged so that they are both (a) reasonably expected to be to everyone's advantage and (b) attached to positions and offices open to all.

Rawls describes these principles as principles of social justice that provide a means of assigning rights and duties in the institutions of society and that define an appropriate distribution of benefits and burdens (Rawls 1973: 4). Rawls maintains that a well-ordered society ought to be regulated by a public conception of justice where everyone accepts and knows that everyone else agrees to the same principles of justice and where basic social institutions follow these principles. For Rawls, a public conception of justice is "the fundamental charter of a well-ordered human association" (p. 5).

Social justice is the crux of Rawls's discussion, and he sees *justice* as the basic structure of society and as the basis for describing how major social institutions distribute fundamental rights and duties. He does not pretend to identify the totality of principles that would satisfy the demands of the basic structure of society. He regards such a conception as a social ideal, and for Rawls, the principles of justice make up only a part—although they are perhaps the most important part—of the complete set of principles needed to define this ideal (1973: 9). Nevertheless, he advocates the notion that a just society would conform to the previously noted two principles by incorporating them into its basic structure. He sees the inclusion of a Bill of Rights within the U.S. Constitution as one significant way in which the first principle of justice could be institutionalized in a given society (Martin 1985: 24).

APPLICATION OF THE PRINCIPLES

Rawls (1973: 46) intends to formulate a set of principles that would help us to make judgments about institutions and actions. Rawls's notion is that if we apply his principles to our beliefs as well as to the facts and circumstances, we will make judgments that will give effect to the principles. If we make judgments in accordance with those principles, we will be acting morally. The principles apply to the basic structure of society. They govern the assignment of rights and duties and regulate the distribution of social and economic benefits (p. 61).

Part (a) of the second principle stated earlier is also known as the *difference principle* (Rawls 1973: 75). The difference principle would seem to apply naturally to inequalities arising from the creation of new jobs, to offices and positions that carry special monetary rewards, or to an increase in income from an existing job. However, the principle's application is much broader because it is to apply to all inequalities in primary social goods. It is not limited to jobs, positions, or offices, but rather the principle is to include all of the general features within a society and its structures that create unequal shares of primary social goods (Scanlon 1989: 192).

The *difference principle* says that although primary goods and services are to be equally distributed, there is nevertheless a way in which certain inequalities can be considered just. Rawls contends that any inequality must benefit everyone, but in particular, it must benefit the least advantaged (Jones 1980: 284). If the least advantaged are better off within an unequal situation than they would be with equality, then the principle argues that there is no injustice. Therefore, equality is a mark of social justice, and any acts promoting equality are justified, provided they do not worsen the situation of the least advantaged.

Conversely, actions that move away from equality are justified only if they benefit the least advantaged. A corollary is that if society wishes to treat all persons equally, it must give greater attention to those victimized by injustice and to those who, because of unfair treatment, have ended up in the less favorable social positions. The difference principle reflects the Kantian principle that people are never to be treated as means to an end but always as ends in themselves (Darwall 1980: 317). In proposing the difference principle, Rawls is promoting the idea that a good society is a society that operates to counteract those natural inequalities that come from birth, ambition, talent, and circumstances, all of which are features that tend to contribute toward the unfair distribution of wealth. For Rawls, the common good is to be assessed by reference to basic benefits to individuals who would otherwise be economically disadvantaged. Overall, the difference principle is egalitarian in nature in the sense that it places a restriction on the amount of inequality that is permitted, and it therefore has a strong appeal to those who favor a close connection between fairness and equality (Benn 1998: 122). Rawls generally defines the basic liberties of citizens as comprising political liberty (meaning the right to vote and stand for public office), freedom of speech and assembly, liberty of conscience and freedom of thought, liberty of the person and the right to hold property, and freedom from arbitrary arrest and seizure.

As to the distribution of wealth and income under the second principle, while the distribution of these need not be equal, it must be to the advantage of all, and positions of authority and offices of command must be accessible to everyone. The first principle must be satisfied before the second; therefore, any departure from equal liberty may not be justified by greater social and economic advantages. Rawls (1973) sees the two principles as part of a more general conception of justice, which he expresses in the following terms: "All social values—liberty and opportunity, income and wealth, and the basis of self respect—are to be distributed equally unless an unequal distribution of any, or all, of these values is to everyone's advantage" (p. 62). Rawls emphasizes that the principles are for institutions to follow and stresses the need to avoid confusing principles of justice that apply to institutions with those that apply to individuals and their actions (p. 54). He clarifies the term *institution* as meaning a "public system of rules which defines offices and positions with their rights and duties, powers and immunities," mentioning specifically parliamentary institutions (p. 55). Jones (1980: 275), in seeking to apply Rawls's theory to a discussion of discrimination, argues that it is possible to extend the principles to individuals, suggesting that the way an individual should act ought at the very least be consistent with the requirements of justice for institutions. He also points out that Rawls makes an explicit statement that individuals should follow the principle of supporting and furthering just institutions.

It is important to keep in mind that the principles and the *original position* concern hypothetical people in a hypothetical situation, and therefore, what is revealed is simply that if there were such people who went through that process, then the principles they agreed on would be justified (Holmes 1998: 191). This is not to say that those principles are actually justified. In other words, it is not clear what application those hypothetical arguments have in the real world. It can be argued, however, that Rawls's model ensures that at least the principles are impartial and that this is a desirable feature of moral principles. At the very least, this might demonstrate that we should give serious consideration to applying these principles to the real world. However, Piers Benn (1998: 125–126) suggests that it is unrealistic to discount talents and abilities, as Rawls proposes in the original position. He argues that any credible theory would have to make reference to the abilities of the parties; nevertheless, he accepts that it is hard to deny that a society would be unfair if it took account of race or parental occupation in deciding life chances.

JUSTICE AS FAIRNESS

Rawls explains that his intention is to present a model of justice that is abstract in nature. There is no intention on his part to establish principles for a particular society or for a particular form of government.

Rather, on a hypothetical basis, the principles previously discussed are those which free and rational persons would accept. They specify the kinds of social cooperation that can take place and the forms of government that can be established. Rawls (1973) describes this way of looking at the principles of justice as "justice as fairness" (p. 11). He explains that it transmits the idea that the principles of justice are agreed to in an initial situation that is considered fair (p. 12).

Moral Development

Rawls discusses moral development particularly in the context of the family (1973: 462). He sees a sense of justice as being gradually acquired by children as they grow and contends that the necessity to teach moral attitudes to children is one of the conditions of human life. He assumes that the well-ordered society includes the family unit and, on the assumption that children are first subject to their parents' authority, sees this first stage of moral development as the *morality of authority* (pp. 462–463). He envisages that parents will love their children and, in so doing, will become the objects of their children's admiration. This, he argues, will influence their children to develop a sense of their own value as well as a desire to emulate the parents. Parents will explain rules of conduct and the reasons justifying them in clear terms and as exemplifying the morality they teach their children.

In the second stage of moral development, which Rawls calls the *morality of association,* the family itself is seen as a small association, with each member having rights and duties and with the child being taught standards of behavior as he or she develops (1973: 467). Similar associations arise through the school and the neighborhood, and through these institutions, the child learns morality. At the same time as the process of attaining morality through association with these institutions develops, an understanding of the principles of justice is acquired (p. 472), and therefore, there is a progression from mere association to actual knowledge of the standards of justice, which Rawls calls the *morality of principles* (p. 473). The idea is that the child, having developed an attachment to certain individuals and communities, is likely to

follow the moral standards that are reinforced by social approval and disapproval. The child complies with moral positions largely because of bonds of friendship and feeling for others and because he or she wishes to gain the approval of the wider society. Rawls sees the well-ordered society as containing citizens who take an interest in political affairs and hold public offices and who therefore are required to apply and interpret the standards of justice.

Susan Moller Okin (2003) notes that, alone among modern theorists of justice, Rawls "treats the family seriously as the earliest school of moral development" (p. 247). However, she contends that Rawls makes an assumption that family institutions are "just" institutions and that he ignores the operation of gender in the family. She explains that in her view a just society would give women the same opportunities as men to exercise political power, develop their talents, and be economically secure within families. In reality, the sexual division of labor has been a fundamental part of the marriage contract. Notions of public and private have penalized women, and this has resulted in neglect of the family by those who theorize about justice.

Rawls suggests that his two principles of social justice will create harmony and cooperation among citizens and will regulate the likelihood that human beings will perform unjust acts. His model places considerable emphasis on the state, and people show solidarity toward each other through the state. At the same time, while the state does not seek to abolish inequalities, it does aim to regulate them through fair bargaining power. This does not mean that employees will always be successful in negotiations with their employers. What is implied, however, is that although employers may be able to cap salaries according to Rawlsian fairness, employees would have opportunities to argue their cases, challenge employers in court, or lobby their congressional representatives—that is, to apply to public institutions that have the capacity to restrain the power of employers. As Roberto Alejandro (1998) puts it, "Rawlsian fairness is constrained power" (p. 25). In other words, in the Rawlsian scheme of things, power, especially that derived from private wealth, can be a danger to a stable, well-ordered society and therefore ought to be regulated, not through individuals, but through public institutions that are themselves representative of the regularity and stability essential to the maintenance of a harmonious society. Alejandro sums up the Rawlsian vision of a good society:

> Rawls wants a society where wealth is distributed widely, people engage in meaningful work, citizens have the opportunity to participate in the political process and political parties advance a vision of the public good. He wants a society where inequalities are not explained away as natural but are justified to least-favored members. (p. 28)

APPLYING RAWLSIAN THEORY

It is clear from this outline of Rawls's complex theory of social justice that Rawlsian conceptions of social justice cannot be applied to individual ethical dilemmas. Rather, his theory is directed at social institutions, at achieving social justice, and at the question of how to construct a well-ordered society. In addition, Rawls emphasizes that his conceptions are abstract and hypothetical and are not intended to be applied in the real world. However, some have applied his conceptions to concrete issues (e.g., see Jones 1980), and it would seem possible to apply some of his broadly formulated principles to aspects of the criminal justice system. Rawls's discussion of inequality, for example, might be linked to the analysis in Chapter 4 of discrimination in the criminal justice system. This might be achieved by posing the questions shown in the "Social Justice Evaluation of Ethical Dilemmas" Closer Look box concerning discrimination drawn from the Rawlsian discussion of social justice. Applications of these criteria are shown in the "Applying Social Justice" Closer Look box.

A Closer Look

Social Justice Evaluation of Ethical Dilemmas

1. Is there fair, equal, and just application of the laws, or are laws applied unfairly, unequally, or unjustly to certain groups by the criminal justice system?

2. Is there discrimination based on race, gender, or socioeconomic status within the criminal justice system?

3. Is there equal and fair access to justice, regardless of race, gender, or socioeconomic status in the criminal justice system?

A Closer Look

Applying Social Justice

1. Is there fair, equal, and just application of the laws, or are laws applied unfairly, unequally, or unjustly to certain groups by the criminal justice system?

   Any examination of questions of inequality, unfairness, and the just application of laws would have to consider the position of marginalized groups, such as the poor, minorities, and those without

(Continued)

(Continued)

power in society. Are such groups treated unjustly by the criminal justice system? For example, are they subject to higher rates of arrest than other groups? Are they policed more intensively? Are they subjected to greater levels of surveillance and control by law enforcement or public institutions generally? Does legislation impose social controls that have the effect of penalizing some groups over others? For example, consider the position of legislation penalizing panhandling, soliciting money from the public, and sex work.

2. Is there discrimination based on race, gender, or socioeconomic status within the criminal justice system?

The discussion in Chapter 4 reveals that criminologists dispute the existence of any systematic discrimination within the criminal justice system but agree that discrimination does occur at specific points in the system. For example, racial origin may influence decisions about whom to arrest, social background may adversely affect an application for bail, and stereotyping certain groups as being more dangerous to society than others may have the effect of denying bail to members of those groups. Jury selection has been a prominent issue historically where explicit discrimination was practiced, and in sentencing decisions, poverty, urbanization, and related factors seem to play a part in determining the length of a prison sentence. Does the criminal justice system treat women differently than men, and has increased policing of drug use affected women disproportionately?

3. Is there equal and fair access to justice, regardless of race, gender, or socioeconomic status in the criminal justice system?

An examination of this issue would have to consider the racial disproportionality of the U.S. prison population, and in particular the effects of the drug war and three-strikes legislation. Questions about the death penalty would also be raised because research has shown that race is a factor in a prosecutor's decision to seek the death penalty and in its actual imposition. In a society where money buys the best legal representation, is it fair for some to have more than competent legal advice and representation when others must rely on often overburdened and inexperienced lawyers in public institutions? How wealth is distributed within U.S. society affects the level of legal representation available to a person who is arrested. If minorities have less wealth, does this mean they are disadvantaged if they come into contact with the criminal justice system? Can access to justice be improved for those without wealth, or must we simply accept the fact that inequalities will continue and that society will not follow Rawls's hypothetical model of surrendering equality in favor of advantaging the disadvantaged?

SUMMARY

Unlike the other ethical approaches discussed in earlier chapters, the work of John Rawls is concerned with establishing fundamental principles that would govern a morally good society rather than with individual ethical choices and acts. His approach is Kantian in nature because his theoretical position favors establishing principles to govern our sense of justice. That is, he sees us acting on principles rather than looking at consequences or at our individual character. Rawls's conception of justice is concerned with justice as a form of morality in the sense of fairness and not with legal rules and procedures found in legal systems. Justice is seen as a principle that can guide the way we behave as a society.

Rawls believes that moral persons possess a sense of justice and the potential to pursue a conception of the good. To realize this potential, we must create a just society and agree on the principles that will govern it. He imagines or hypothesizes an agreement between a group of persons who decide on the nature of this society and who do so from a classless social position and without regard to any natural assets or abilities. Rawls argues that this group of persons would choose two principles of justice–one of which is concerned with the equal right to basic liberties and the other with social and economic inequalities. Under the first principle, persons would enjoy personal liberty such as the right to vote and stand for public office and freedom of speech and assembly. Under the second principle, part of which is known as the *difference principle,* there is to be an equal distribution of primary goods and services. However, certain inequalities will be considered just if they benefit everyone, especially the least advantaged. Thus, if the least advantaged are better off in an unequal situation than they would be with equality, there would be no injustice. This means that if it wishes to treat everyone equally, a just society must give more attention to those who are victimized by injustice or to those who, because of unfair treatment, are placed in a less favorable position. This argument parallels Kant's principle that people should be treated as ends in themselves and not as means to an end.

In his general conception of justice, Rawls emphasizes that the principles he expounds should be followed and applied by social institutions and that the principles are hypothetical and no attempt should be made to apply them to the real world. Nevertheless, Rawls does maintain that his principles would be accepted by free and rational persons and would give effect to the idea of "justice as fairness."

Like Lawrence Kohlberg (discussed in Chapter 17), Rawls sets out three stages of moral development in a person's life, beginning with the *morality of authority* developed by parents, moving to the *morality of association* arising through contact with the school and the neighborhood, and then to the *morality of principles* where individuals follow moral positions as a result of earlier moral development and because they wish to secure the approval of the wider society.

In terms of creating a society that values social justice, Rawls believes his principles will create harmony and cooperation and reduce injustice. The state should regulate inequalities for the good of all and manage its power to create a stable, well-ordered society. As applied to the criminal justice system and its institutions, it can be argued that Rawlsian notions of social justice can assist in overcoming inequalities in access to justice as well as forms of discrimination within the system.

DISCUSSION QUESTIONS

1. What are the merits of Rawls's approach to ethical decision-making within public institutions?

2. Explain Rawls's conception of social justice.

3. How do you think Rawls's approach to social justice can be linked with other ethical theories to produce a just society?

4. How could Rawls's theories be applied to the issue of the racial disproportionality of the U.S. prison population?

5. After applying the criteria for a social justice approach to the war against drugs and the applicable laws, decide whether or not the relevant social and criminal justice institutions (the political process, law enforcement, courts, jails and prisons) can be said to be achieving the principles of social justice. Make sure to provide detailed support for your answer.

17

CARING FOR OTHERS

A number of philosophers have already been considered in this book. It is apparent from this examination that men have historically dominated the study of moral philosophy. While this has changed in recent years, it is nevertheless true that moral philosophy is concerned almost exclusively with men's moral experiences (Hinman 1998: 365). The absence of women's voices has caused contemporary feminist ethical theorists to argue that classical and traditional moral philosophy is distorted. Lawrence Hinman (pp. 367–369) summarizes feminist criticisms of classical and traditional moral philosophies as follows:

- They assume the notion of the isolated individual, independent and separated from everyone else.
- They envisage the objective of moral philosophy as theorizing and explaining how *individuals* ought to treat each other.
- They rely on theories concerning the development of a social contract as a way for the person to enter into moral relationships.
- They emphasize impartiality and universality in their ethical theories.

In contrast, feminist ethical philosophers have drawn attention to the connectedness that exists between human beings, and they argue that basing ethical theory on the isolated individual and relying on social contract approaches does not reflect the reality and centrality of relationships or the notion of trust, which is grounded in relationships. As to impartiality and universality, feminists argue that traditional ethical theory ought to concern itself with the reality of everyday moral experience and detach itself from supposed notions of impartiality and universality, focusing instead on the conditions of life and the particularity of the human experience.

KOHLBERG AND GILLIGAN

The starting point for a dramatic review of the place of women in moral philosophy was the publication in 1982 by Carol Gilligan of *In a Different Voice: Psychological Theory and Women's Development*. Prior to the publication of this book, Gilligan had become interested in psychology and moral development and in Lawrence Kohlberg's work on the psychology of moral development (Hinman 1998: 370).

A THEORY OF MORAL DEVELOPMENT

Kohlberg wanted to understand why people would break a written law for a purpose they held to be a higher good. In particular, this question arose for him from the time when Israel was struggling for statehood and was subject to a strict embargo prohibiting the import of food, medicine, weapons, and people. Some defied this embargo and broke the law to involve themselves in the formation of the State of Israel.

Kohlberg posed a number of questions to the participants in his study, including a problem known as *Heinz's dilemma* (Rachels 1999: 163). He interviewed children of different ages and, after presenting them with various dilemmas, invited their responses with the aim of establishing the nature and content of their moral judgments (Darwall 1998: 219). In the case of Heinz's dilemma, the scenario was presented as follows:

> Heinz's wife was near death, and her only hope for living was a drug being sold by a pharmacist at an excessive price. The drug had cost $200 to make but was being sold for $2,000, and Heinz was only able to pay $1,000. He offered this sum to the pharmacist but his offer was rejected. Heinz said he would pay the rest later but still the druggist would not accept his offer. Now desperate, Heinz considered stealing the drug. Would it be right for him to do that? (p. 219)

Kohlberg discussed the reasoning offered in individual cases. For example, the dilemma had been given to an 11-year-old boy named Jake who considered it obvious that Heinz should steal the drug, explaining that a human life was worth more than money. However, when the dilemma was put to a girl, Amy, also 11 years old, her response was much less emphatic, and she appeared hesitant and evasive. She did not agree that stealing was right, thinking there might be other ways, such as borrowing the money. Rachels quotes from the girl:

> He really shouldn't steal the drug—but his wife shouldn't die either. . . . If he stole the drug, he might save his wife then, but if he did, he might have to go to jail, and then his wife might get sicker

again, and he couldn't get more of the drug, and it might not be good. So, they should really just talk it out and find some other way to make the money. (1999: 165)

Despite attempts by the interviewer to elicit a more positive response from Amy, she would not change her perspective, essentially refusing to accept the terms of the problem itself. She reformulated the issue as a conflict between Heinz and the pharmacist that should be talked out between them. Amy's response tends to focus on personal relationships, whereas Jake appeals to rules and principles— namely, that a human life is worth more than money. Kohlberg concluded that people pass through stages of moral development (see Table 17.1), most achieving the fourth of six stages (Hinman 1998: 371). He assumed these stages are universal, that they operate in sequence, and that they are irreversible.

"IN A DIFFERENT VOICE": CAROL GILLIGAN

Carol Gilligan studied women's moral development and noted that women's responses did not coincide with Kohlberg's moral stages (Rachels 1999: 166). According to Kohlberg's model, women can achieve only the *second level* because they are focused on caring for others. Gilligan (1993) suggests that Kohlberg's model is incorrect in explaining women's moral development because women have different moral stages than men. She interviewed both boys and girls using Kohlberg's theory. Following her study, she specifically attacked Kohlberg's conclusions about Jake and Amy.

Kohlberg argued that Jake had advanced one or two full stages beyond Amy and that he was operating at Stage 4 or 5, while Amy had only achieved Stage 3. Gilligan argued that the two children thought differently, but this did not mean that Amy's way of thinking was inferior. She contended that Jake's response could be located at a higher moral level only on the assumption that an ethic of abstract principle was superior to an ethic that stressed caring and personal relationships. She asked why such an assumption should be made, noting that it seemed to

Table 17.1   Kohlberg's Theory of Moral Development

Level 1: Preconventional Morality	The emphasis is on the self and on self-interest. Morality is based on a hedonistic approach that maximizes pleasure and minimizes pain. The main criteria of morality is seeking reward and avoiding punishment. The rightness and wrongness of an act is assessed by its consequences.
Stage 1: Punishment and Obedience	This is dominated by the desire to avoid punishment. The criterion for morality is avoiding punishment through obedience.
Stage 2: Reciprocity	This stage embodies an attitude of reciprocity; that is, you do a favor for me, and I'll do one for you. We obey to obtain rewards for the favors that can be returned. It is an attitude of "I'll scratch your back if you scratch mine."
Level 2: Conventional Morality	The emphasis is on society and conformity to social rules. At this level, a person tries to do what is expected by others to get the social approval of others and to show respect for legitimate authorities. One is moral if one considers the consequences for others. Morality is defined as conforming to the rules of authorities (including parents and lawmakers).
Stage 3:	This stage is termed the *good boy/nice girl orientation,* where the child aims to be a good person in his or her own eyes and in the eyes of others where personal relationships are paramount.
Stage 4:	This stage shows a law and order mentality where the child/adult follows authority rules. Morality means rigid adherence to social rules and the laws of society for the sake of conformity—guilt is associated with this stage, and we are concerned with what others think of us.
Level 3: Postconventional Morality	We exercise internalized principles of ethics and develop personal conscience. Moral judgments are made on the basis of universal moral principles and impartiality and go beyond social convention. Most don't achieve this level, and if achieved, it is rarely sustained consistently all throughout life. This level involves a concern for a universal principle, such as respect for all humans as individuals, and considers that all humans have inherent dignity.
Stage 5:	In this stage, individual rights are accepted and reviewed in response to critical discussion. Respect for the rights of others takes precedence over rigidly following social rules.
Stage 6:	In this stage, there is an orientation toward the acceptance of universal ethical principles of justice, reciprocity, equality, and respect. Only a few persons of high moral repute, like Gandhi and Martin Luther King Jr., reach this stage. At this stage, we use our conscience to guide moral behavior that values mutual respect and trust. The focus is on universal principles of justice, such as equality, respect, and reciprocity. The key to morality is to respect the rights of others by following our internalized ethical principles. This stage corresponds with Kant's themes of universality and rationality. The test of a just act is whether it can still be considered just after reversing the roles of the actor and the recipient. An act is considered just if it can still be regarded as just when everyone in society acts that way, and this results in its development as a universal principle.

SOURCE: Hinman 1998: 371.

have been made on the basis that most moral philosophers (mostly male) had favored a form of ethics based on rules and principles.

Gilligan concluded that women, as opposed to men, tend to see moral life in terms of care rather than justice and in terms of responsibility rather than rights. Whereas men see treating everyone fairly and impartially as a moral standard, women view caring as a moral imperative and "moral requirements as emerging from the particular needs of others in the context of particular relationships" (Flanagan and Jackson 1993: 70). Therefore, women are more likely to try to resolve issues by seeking solutions that maintain relationships. In contrast, men apply rules fairly, impartially, and equally. Gilligan argues that men's moral decisions are concerned with individual rights and autonomy and that noninterference is highly valued, as is the application of rights and rules to abstract hypothetical dilemmas (Nicholson 1993: 90).

They ask, "Have the rules been properly followed and applied?"

In contrast, Gilligan argues that in their moral decision-making, women focus on relationships and interdependence and on feelings of empathy and compassion, and women are situationally oriented. In Gilligan's view, women's moral decision-making is contextual rather than categorical, often responding to ethical situations with, "It depends" (Nicholson 1993: 90). Women judge moral issues after considering the suffering of other people. In assessing morality, women ask, "Have relationships been maintained or were people hurt?" and focus on the quality of relationships rather than on impartiality. Gilligan also sees women as developing moral appreciation through stages and has identified three full levels or stages and two transitional stages, which are outlined in Table 17.2.

Table 17.2   Gilligan's Theory

Level 1: Orientation to Individual Survival	*Individual survival* is paramount, and moral considerations are relevant only when one's own needs are in conflict. Morality consists of imposed sanctions on the self.
First Transition	*From selfishness to responsibility.* Women begin to become aware of their responsibility for others' well-being. They are aware that morality requires that they become responsible for the well-being of others.
Level 2: Goodness as Self-Sacrifice	*Goodness becomes identified with self-sacrifice*; that is, to be a good person involves taking care of other people (family) at the expense of oneself. Social norms and consensus are the basis for moral judgments and concern for others, especially others' feelings, and the possibility of hurting others is of major concern. Goodness in the form of self-sacrifice is joined with the desire to care for others.
Second Transition	*From goodness to truth.* Women now understand that care includes caring for themselves as well as others. Women begin to struggle when they learn they need to care for themselves as well as for others and may initially see this as a regression to the first stage.
Level 3: Morality of Nonviolence	*Moral goodness is seen as caring both for oneself and for others.* The previous issue between being selfish and showing responsibility to oneself is resolved in a principle of nonviolence, and an injunction against hurting others is established. At this point, care becomes "a universal obligation." This level takes on the ideals of inclusiveness and nonviolence and condemns exploitation and hurt. Morality is primarily about caring.

SOURCE: Gilligan 1993: see Chapter 3.

The conclusion Gilligan reached was that the caring approach is an equally valid moral perspective that has generally been ignored in both moral theory and psychological research because of male bias (Sterba 2001: 52). In 1984, Kohlberg acknowledged, "An orientation of care and response usefully enlarges the moral domain" (in Benhabib 1987: 156). However, Kohlberg still did not consider notions of "care and responsibility" to be a separate track of moral development but rather regarded them as a moral orientation in conjunction with "justice and rights." It was Gilligan's conclusion that there seemed to be two quite different ways of thinking about ethics that led her to depict that difference in terms of voices. She termed this different voice, which did not fit into Kohlberg's categories and was evidenced more among females, the *ethic of care*.

GENDER AND THE ETHIC OF CARE

Gilligan's research was conducted with female participants, but she emphasized in her work that the ethic of care was not differentiated according to gender. It follows, therefore, that the caring approach is not exclusively female, and there may be women who make decisions based on principles and men who make them on the basis of care and relationships. It might also be argued that women might be more attracted to an approach that emphasizes caring because of the social role that they have traditionally performed (Rachels 1999: 168). Thus, women have traditionally been given responsibility for caring for children and for the domestic aspects of life, and therefore, the ethic of care is simply an outcome of women's socialization and lived experience.

An alternative view might be offered that women demonstrate a caring perspective because it is an innate characteristic of their sex. For example, Nel Noddings (1984) claims that "an ethic built on caring is . . . characteristically and essentially feminine . . . [arising] . . . out of our experience as women, just as the traditional logical approach to ethical problems arises more obviously from masculine experience" (p. 8). This view has been derided by feminists who argue that it is social conditioning that constructs and creates gender boundaries

rather than sex roles (Grimshaw 1991: 493). They contend that if this argument were accepted, women would be forever consigned to the domestic sphere and that this would render them permanently oppressed.

Jean Grimshaw (1991: 493) outlines two responses to this question of differential male and female thinking. The first is that there are typical differences in male and female thinking on moral issues but that this difference must not be expressed in terms of a deficiency on the part of women. In other words, the stereotypes of women being incapable of reason, as emotional, and as unable to act on principle must not be reinforced. Grimshaw argues that difference can be recognized without that difference connoting deficiency. The second is that social practices such as caring for others and particularly mothering, which have traditionally been regarded as within the female domain, can be seen as generating forms of virtue that can stand as corrective influences to those domains commonly dominated by men.

An Ethic of Care

Gilligan's conclusions have been adopted by moral philosophers, both male and female, and a number have theorized about the nature and extent of an ethic of care. This form of ethics conceives moral life as a network of relationships with particular persons, and it sees living well as caring for those people within those relationships (Rachels 1999: 170). It affirms the priority we give as a matter of course to our family and close friends and goes beyond the notion that being a loving parent is simply a duty. We are all aware that a loving parent acts from motives beyond that of duty and that a caring relationship with one's children that merely satisfies duty is likely to be construed as an unloving relationship by one's children. Both Gilligan (1993) and Noddings (1984) argue that women resort less to rules and principles than men and are more likely to want concrete rather than abstract reasoning. As well, they argue that women seek a detailed knowledge of a particular situation and to resolve dilemmas by reference to the relationships involved (Grimshaw 1991: 495).

How does the notion of caring for others constitute an ethic? It is first necessary to consider how the ethic of caring differs from traditional ethics. As noted earlier, the ethic of care rejects the idea of relying on rules to assess morality, regarding them as guidelines and not as determinants of right or wrong. It argues that we should respond caringly to those with whom we interact in life. One difficulty is that "acting caringly toward others" gives the appearance of a principle, stating, as it does, that a person ought to enhance notions of caring in oneself and in others (Blum 1994: 208; Holmes 1998: 204–205). If this is true, and the admonishment to care for others is in fact a principle, then the ethic of care does not dispense with principles, as its proponents claim. Lawrence Blum (1994) argues, however, that the ethic of care does not establish a principle but rather expresses certain sensitivities and attitudes toward others that can be promoted as good ways to act and live in particular situations. Robert Holmes (1998) seems to agree with this position, arguing that if it is read as a principle, the ethic is derived from judgments about particular cases. The rightness of particular cases is not resolved by appealing to the principle but rather by referring to particular cases to arrive at the principle.

Another question raised by the ethic of care is, *how do we recognize what is the right or caring thing to do in particular situations?* While it may be easy to determine how we should care when dealing with our family members and friends, it may be more difficult to recognize a caring act when considering world problems and international relations. Holmes (1998: 205) considers that the challenge to the ethic of caring is to decide what is morally correct in cases outside the scope of family and friends. Michael Slote (1998) questions whether the morality of caring can "really provide a total framework for moral thought and action" (p. 171). He points to the fact that to deal with our obligations to those with whom we are not acquainted, as well as to address wider issues in society, a morality of caring seems to need supplementation from notions of rights and justice. He nevertheless argues that the ethic of caring can be sustained in the form of a specifically "virtue-ethical manner" as a form of virtue ethics, where it can be plausibly articulated and defended. In other words, he sees it primarily tied up with virtue ethics. Slote suggests that even if the ethic of caring

calls for a show of greater concern for those who are nearer and dearer to us, it might still condemn indifference to strangers, and he draws a distinction between the depth and breadth of concern or of caring. His suggestion is that the morally most attractive or virtuous individual "is one who has *deep* concern for particular others . . . but who is also *broadly* concerned with the well being . . . of other human beings" (p. 181).

Developing the Ethic of Care

An ethic of care, according to James Rachels (1999: 171), focuses on close personal relationships, and caring cannot occur in the absence of those relationships. Noddings (1984), in *Caring: A Feminine Approach to Ethics and Moral Education,* agrees with Rachels that there can be a caring relationship only if there is a personal one-to-one encounter and that there is no obligation to help "the needy in far regions of the earth" because it is impossible to do so (p. 152). She perceives caring for starving children in Africa as being an impossible task because it would require that she abandon the caring she is obligated to perform here (p. 86). She therefore defines the extent of the caring obligation by looking at the possibility of completing a particular act of caring. Noddings sees two classes of persons eligible for caring by virtue of their relationship with the caregiver. The first class is composed of those related to the caregiver or who will potentially be related, therefore creating an absolute obligation to care. The second class is composed of those with whom there is a "dynamic potential for growth in relation" (p. 86).

In contrast, Virginia Held (1987: 118) argues that particular others with whom a person has relationships can include children starving in Africa and even future children in that situation. Rachels (1999) suggests that a response that ignores starving children in other parts of the world feels uncomfortable and wrong. He proposes that an alternative approach is to state that the ethical life "includes both caring personal relationships and a benevolent concern for people generally" (p. 171). In other words, the ethic of care can be seen as supplementing traditional theories of obligation rather than replacing them. Rachels ultimately concludes that there is a clear nexus between virtue theory, with its emphasis on a moral person possessing certain character traits, and the ethic of care—he sees the ethic of care as one part of virtue ethics. He goes so far as to contend that most feminist philosophers view virtue ethics in this light (p. 174).

Grimshaw (1991: 495), pointing to the difficulty in describing the differences between male and female thinking about moral issues, emphasizes the need to avoid any suggestion that because it may be different, women's thinking is somehow deficient. She suggests that the answer may be not so much that men and women reason differently about moral issues but that they have different ethical priorities, and, therefore, what women see as important in terms of principle, such as maintaining relationships, is viewed by men as a failure of principle. She suggests that if women's life experiences are different from those of men, it is reasonable to assume that ethical priorities will be gendered. She points to the experience of women in pregnancy, in childbirth, and in child rearing as illustrative of this.

Ruddick (in Grimshaw 1991: 496) contends that the act of mothering itself generates a conception of virtue and that this experience is central to women's ethical life (also see Held 1987: 114). Whitbeck (in Grimshaw 1991: 496) has similarly suggested that motherhood is at the very center of the female practice of caring for others and that this caring can provide an ethical model that contrasts with competitive and individualistic norms that inform life experience. Grimshaw (p. 496) cautions, however, that there are dangers in suggesting that female practices are able to generate an alternative form of ethics because such practices are always located in the social sphere and are impacted by issues such as class, race, culture, and well-being. Nevertheless, she sees these practices and life experiences as constituting a source from which to mount a critique on the male-dominated public sphere (p. 498). In agreeing that there is a need for an ethic of care, Held (1987: 120–121), in contrast, calls for a more pluralistic view of ethics, arguing that appealing to one or several simple principles cannot solve all ethical problems. She stresses the experiences open only to women and suggests it is necessary to consider their significance for moral experience and theory. She understands mothering as central and fundamental to social relationships

and argues that morality ought to make room for the social bond between the mothering person and the child (p. 115).

Blum (1994: 108) takes the view that although Gilligan and other writers recognize a notion of care, they do not develop the implications of this theoretically in a way that would sustain a morality of care, and they do not sufficiently articulate the different virtues and sensitivities that make up that notion. He contends that it is necessary to explore whether care may take different forms in different contexts and draw on different virtues and sensitivities. He offers the example that being able to appreciate that someone is depressed and having the ability to lift that person's depression is a different quality than being constantly available to others to perform caring functions. Both may be expressions of caring in a general sense, but they contain components of distinct sensitivities. He argues that an analysis that promotes the contextual nature of caring will ultimately give the ethic of care a greater theoretical power and scope, and he is inclined to extend the boundaries of the ethic of care beyond personal relations and into more public domains such as professional life (p. 111). Even within personal relations, there is differentiation—for example, caring for children is not the same as caring for friends—and appreciating the existence of care in less intimate relationships can have the effect of broadening the scope of the ethic.

Whereas Gilligan understands relationships and caring in terms of concrete persons with whom one stands in specific relationships—such as father, teacher, brother, or friend—Michael Sandel (in Blum 1994: 219) sees a person as "encumbered" and extends encumbrances to forms of communal identity, such as being a member of a particular nation, religious or ethnic group, class, or neighborhood. He therefore suggests that any ethic of care could draw wide boundaries in terms of relationships. Responding to Sandel's point, Blum (p. 249) imagines a situation in which someone utters a racial slur about Kevin, a member of my racial group. To illustrate the differences between individual and group approaches, two possibilities are identified. The first is that in responding to the racial slur, I might be concerned about Kevin as an individual and how the slur has affected him.

I therefore am attentive to his needs, and I help him talk through how he feels about the abuse he has suffered and what we might do together to formulate an appropriate response to what has happened. This represents the individual caring mode.

The second response to this event is that I perceive it from the perspective that a member of my race has been targeted with a racial slur. Here, my moral concern is not on the basis of friend to friend but as a member of a group toward another member. Therefore, my focus will be not only on how Kevin is injured by the racial attack but also on how all members of the group have been harmed. This represents the group and not the individual response to relationships.

Finally, in his presentation of views about the development of the ethic of care and its relationship to traditional moral philosophy, Stephen Darwall (1998) suggests that the ethic of care may not stand in opposition to traditional moral theory but instead can operate as an important supplement and a different path, bringing issues of relationship to the fore that have been relatively neglected in the past. As he puts it, "The ethics of care provides a way of seeing equal concern and respect as themselves rooted in ways of relating to others as particular individuals" (p. 228).

THE ETHIC OF CARE AND JUSTICE

How might the ethic of care be applied to the criminal justice system? In a provocative essay, Robin West (1997: 9) argues that caring should be at the center of an understanding of public and legal virtues as well as private and personal virtues, and specifically, it should be central to the meaning of legal justice. West agrees with those who have suggested that caregiving should be thought of as an ethical activity and goes beyond this to ask whether judges ought to act in accordance with an ethic of care when deciding cases coming before them in the same way that they perform in accordance with an ethic of justice. Noting that care is associated with context, relationships, and the private sphere, she explains that although judicial work has plenty of evidence showing judicial respect for the ethic of justice, there are few signs of an ethic of care. She contends that instead of being oppositional, the ethic of justice and the ethic of care are interdependent and interrelated and are each necessary conditions of the other (p. 24).

West (1997: 30) contrasts the virtue of legal justice with that of compassion or care in a number of cases, using images of legal justice to highlight the differences. She explains that legal justice demands that judges operate according to the rule of law and with respect for precedent, that they demonstrate personal integrity, and that they show impartial universality in the form of an unbiased approach to issues brought before them. The images of care she identifies include the mother's nurturance of the newborn, images of compassion, and the protection and care that a woman shows for her child. She concludes that care images appear to be oppositional to images of justice (p. 32). West underscores the feminist belief, developed since the late 1970s, that care, no less than justice, is a moral activity and not a purely emotional response, and she argues that this should result in a broad-based reexamination of virtually every field of inquiry. She does not see caregiving as confined to family life, arguing that if a caring response is a moral response, then public life and public decision-making should also include this virtue (p. 34). West contends that if the ethic of care were applied in the exercise of justice, injustice would be avoided, for example, through a "more compassionate reading of the applicable law" (p. 48). She provides, as an example of justice and care combined, the decision in 1989's *DeShaney v. Winnebago County* (in West 1997: 49) that ruled it is the task of a juror in death penalty cases to give a decision that does not take into account the life circumstances of the defendant. She considers this ruling as a demonstration of an imbalance between justice and compassion.

Generally, West (1997) sees the ethic of care as a morality that should be followed in the judicial system so that justice, compassion, and care go hand in hand. To this extent, she expands the boundaries set by Gilligan and others beyond the personal and into the field of public administration, law, and dispute settlement. For West, doing justice ought to include showing care and compassion as a matter of moral rightness.

Noddings (1984: 36) also raises the issue of justice. She rejects abstract notions and argues that when women are faced with moral dilemmas, they will follow a process that allows them to envisage and examine a concrete situation. She offers the example of determining the appropriate punishment for a particular crime. She contends that the traditional approach, which she considers a masculine approach, is to identify the principle that applies to the particular case. In contrast, Noddings argues that a feminine approach would require more information about the offender and the victim(s). She suggests that a woman might even begin to analyze a dilemma by thinking, "What if this were my child?" She contrasts the process of legal abstraction, isolated from the complicating factors such as persons, places, and events, with a process that is concrete and based on facts, others' feelings, and life histories. As she puts it, "The father might sacrifice his own child in fulfilling a principle; the mother might sacrifice any principle to preserve her child" (p. 37). She concedes that this approach is too simplistic to be definitive, but she does consider it instructive.

PEACEMAKING

Some criminal justice practitioners advocate an approach that is variously termed *peacemaking criminology* or *peacemaking*. Michael Braswell and Jeffrey Gold (1998: 26) suggest that there are three aspects of peacemaking: *connectiveness*, meaning that we are not simply isolated individuals but rather are connected to all other human beings, animals, and the environment; *caring*, which, as we have seen already, is an element considered critical in ethical decision-making with a focus on "caring for" and "relationships with" others; and *mindfulness*, an aspect that advocates thinking about our actions and the needs of others in the long term and acting in ways that demonstrate our knowledge of the correct thing to do in the long term.

Peacemaking criminologists argue that the ethic of care has linkages with peacemaking because it includes the notions of caring, connectiveness, and mindfulness in its formulation of ethics. For example, the authors of *Corrections, Peacemaking, and Restorative Justice* view peacemaking as a "broad, encompassing process" that draws on ancient philosophical traditions and on spiritual sources as well as "from Nel Noddings' feminist concept of caring" (Braswell, Fuller, and Lozoff 2001: 1). Since these authors describe peacemaking as a process, they may not be claiming that it provides the basis for explaining how we ought to live. As well, the fact that it is linked to the ethic of care may suggest that, if it is a philosophical approach, it is agent based rather than action based.

John Fuller (1998: 55) has designed a pyramid of concepts that he believes constitutes peacemaking criminology (see Figure 17.1). The foundation of the pyramid is *nonviolence*, which he includes due to the status of nonviolence as a fundamental peacemaking principle. The intent here is that violence and coercion, including capital punishment and excessive force, ought to be outlawed from the criminal justice system. The next level is *social justice*, and Fuller argues that criminal justice solutions must take account of social justice so that they do not reflect practices involving racism, sexism, or ageism. The next level, *inclusion*, means that there must be participation by all concerned parties in solutions. Solutions must be arrived at through the next level of *correct means;* these entail nonviolent means, social justice, and inclusion, as well as due process rights. Solutions must be sought that incorporate values of cooperation, nonviolence, and compassion. The next level is referred to as *ascertainable criteria,* and these criteria must be understood, be considered valid, and be trustworthy to all concerned parties so that one party does not hold all the power to define and decide the factors to be considered in the solution (p. 56). The apex is formed by the *categorical imperative* developed by Immanuel Kant. For Fuller, the categorical imperative must be applied because we must act in a way that we can "will" that act onto all others in similar circumstances and so that the action can become a "universal law." Fuller argues for the inclusion of the categorical imperative on the basis that solutions to problems in criminal justice should have as their foundation "underlying moral reasoning" (p. 57).

Figure 17.1   Peacemaking Solutions to Criminal Justice Problems: Peacemaking Pyramid

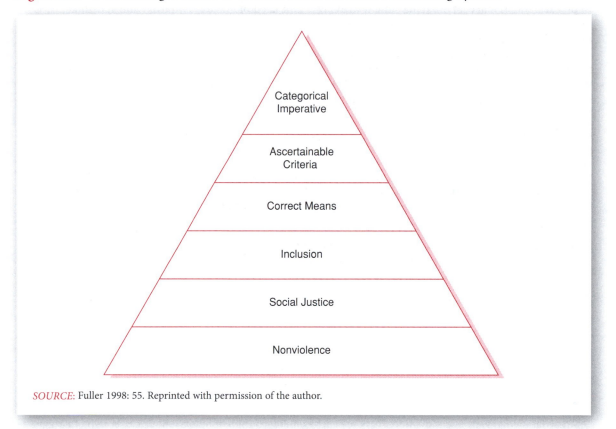

Categorical
Imperative

Ascertainable
Criteria

Correct Means

Inclusion

Social Justice

Nonviolence

SOURCE: Fuller 1998: 55. Reprinted with permission of the author.

Fuller's (1998) multifaceted approach seems to be programmatic rather than theoretical or philosophical because, in his view, the peacemaking model emphasizes "social justice, conflict resolution, rehabilitation, and a belief that people need to cooperate in democratic institutions to develop meaningful communities" (p. 41).

Fuller (1998) stresses that peacemaking ought not to be confused with peacekeeping, but Hal Pepinsky's (1999: 52) notion of "peacemaking criminology" seems to adopt an approach grounded in peacekeeping. Pepinsky is rather more precise about the principles included in his version of peacemaking and conceives peacemaking as being linked to social control. He sees two contrary approaches toward social control in the forms of *war making* and *peacemaking* (p. 56). The four

principles he advocates in social control solutions are, first, taking time to review one's own feelings and impulses in to generate choices for oneself; second, "introducing oneself to the apparently weakest, or quietest victim" (p. 62); third, making a deliberate attempt to draw out victims and hear their stories, especially their fears and pain; and fourth, to join with those who have no voice in confronting those who hold the most power in given situations and who threaten or discount the needs and interests of weaker groups (p. 56). Pepinsky sees these peacemaking steps as being incorporated into social interactions, and he advocates using the four principles as an alternative to blaming and attacking one's enemies (p. 57). Pepinsky's approach seems to stress a kind of nonviolence when confronted with exhibitions of power that threaten one's security. As he puts it, "Peacemaking is the art and science of weaving and reweaving oneself with others into a social fabric of mutual love, respect, and concern" (p. 59).

Currently, writers advocating peacemaking write from many perspectives, ranging from nonviolence to Christian ethics as well as from a Buddhist position. Certainly the notion of peacemaking is attractive in a general sense, although it seems to be in need of greater definition and specificity.

APPLYING THE ETHIC OF CARE

Case Study 17.1 illustrates how the ethic of care can be applied to an ethical dilemma within the criminal justice system.

Case Study 17.1 Tough Love

Jay Barros was a delinquent. He would even admit it freely. He'd done just about everything and had been on probation and in and out of institutions for years. The psychologists had long ago classified him as a typical sociopath: no conscience, never learning from the past, impulsive, and manipulative.

Harold "Red" Chapman was a probation officer. He was also an ex-cop. He didn't counsel his charges; he supervised them with an iron hand. He had one rule: Any misconduct and you get violated. No questions, no excuses. It was odd, though; he didn't violate that many kids. Most of his probationers led pretty straight lives when they were on Red's caseload.

Jay knew he had messed up. He had been cutting classes, had been caught drinking, and didn't come home for three straight days. Jay's mother had called Red to report on Jay's behavior, and Red had called Jay into his office for a conference. Jay figured that it was back to the state's boys' school again as he walked into Red's office.

"Sit down and shut up," Red said in a stern voice. "We're gonna talk. As I see it, you've got two choices. Your first choice is a quick trip to the detention center and an even quicker trip out to the boys' school. But that's a lot of paperwork on my end."

"Yeah, and what's my second choice?" Jay asked, beginning to think if he played his cards right, he might just get out of this. Red reached into his lower drawer and brought out a piece of leather 2.5 inches wide and 3 feet long.

"This is a strop. Barbers use them to sharpen razors. I use this one to adjust attitudes. That's your second choice. Ten with the strop and you walk out of here. It's your choice." Jay stood up and grabbed his ankles.

While this was happening, Mary, another probation officer, walked past Red's door, overheard the whole incident, and saw Jay bend over to receive his punishment while Red was holding the strop.

SOURCE: Adapted from Close and Meier 1995.

In resolving what may be an ethical dilemma, Mary will follow the process of resolving an ethical dilemma set out in Chapter 1.

1. *Is Mary faced with an ethical dilemma?*

   Mary is faced with the dilemma of whether to intervene and stop the corporal punishment and do nothing further, or to allow the incident to occur but report it immediately to her supervisor.

The option of doing nothing is not an ethical option because it would conflict with Mary's duty as a probation officer to protect juvenile probationers from harm and abuse.

2. *What are the facts and circumstances of the incident?*

   Mary needs to review in her mind the facts and circumstances.

3. *What are the facts relevant to the decision she has to make? What are her own values about the issue, and*

what are the values of her workplace about such an issue?

The relevant facts are as follows:

- Red has an unprofessional attitude toward his work as a probation officer.
- He believes in tough love in the form of corporal punishment rather than following the rules relating to violations of probation.
- He adopts a tough-love stance because it saves him work, not because of any genuine belief in its efficacy.
- Jay, the probationer, is prepared to accept corporal punishment to avoid being reincarcerated, but this will inevitably affect his relationship with Red because he will know that Red is prepared to bend the rules to suit his own convenience.
- Mary is a professional probation officer who believes in upholding the rules and standards of probation, including the protection of juveniles.
- The values and culture within probation generally support the notion that a probation officer should back up his or her coworkers. However, where juvenile probation officers are concerned, workplace values do not support actions that harm the probationer and flout the rules.

4. *What ethical theories does she call to mind to assist her in resolving the dilemma?*

In this case, Mary will apply the ethic of care to the dilemma.

5. *What are Mary's available courses of action?*

Mary may intervene and stop the assault on Jay and do nothing further, or she may allow the assault to take place and immediately report it to her supervisor. She does not have the option of doing nothing at all about the assault because that would be unethical in light of her duty to protect the well-being of juvenile probationers.

6. *Mary will make her decision after applying, in this case, the ethic of care approach to each option. She will choose the option that is the most ethically appropriate for her under the ethic of care.*

A process for assessing an ethical dilemma from an ethic of care perspective is set out in the "Ethic of Care and Peacemaking Approaches to Ethical Dilemmas" Closer Look box. Applications of the listed criteria are shown in the "Applying the Ethic of Care" Closer Look box.

A Closer Look

Ethic of Care and Peacemaking Approaches to Ethical Dilemmas

The focus is on developing solutions that maintain relationships and minimize harms and that recognize the connectiveness and interdependency of everyone involved. This approach is supportive of inclusive, nonviolent solutions that take account of social justice. It focuses on personal responsibility within the context of specific situations.

Steps in applying the ethic of care and peacemaking approach include the following:

1. Identify the options involved.

2. Identify all the particular relationships involved and state them as relationships (i.e., offender and the community; victim and her family).

3. Apply the first option and then state how each relationship is affected. Next, state what harm is caused to each relationship by this option, explaining the nature of the harm.

4. Apply the second option and then state how each relationship is affected. Next, state what harm is caused to each relationship by this option, explaining the nature of the harm.

The most ethical option will be that which, while it maintains relationships, minimizes the harm caused by the impact of the dilemma on those relationships. Accordingly, if most relationships are maintained but the harm caused by a particular option is minimized, then this is the most ethical option under an ethic of care.

A Closer Look

Applying the Ethic of Care

1. Identify the options involved.

   Mary may intervene to stop the corporal punishment and do nothing further.

   She may let the incident occur without intervention but immediately report it to her supervisor.

2. Identify the particular relationships involved and state them as relationships (i.e., offender and the community; victim and her family). There are the following relationships:

   Between Red and Jay

   Between Red and Mary

   Between Mary and the probation department

   Between Red and the probation department

   Between the probation department and the community

3. Apply the first option and then state how each relationship is affected. Next, state what harm is caused to each relationship, explaining the nature of the harm.

   Red and Jay: This relationship will continue, and Red will continue to be Jay's probation officer. The relationship will be harmed because Red will be able to repeat his unprofessional abusive behavior toward Jay and toward others unless Mary or someone else intervenes again.

   Red and Mary: Their relationship will continue, but harm will be caused because Mary has become aware of Red's abuse, and she will have no confidence or trust in him as a coworker.

   Mary and the probation department: The relationship will continue as before. It will not be harmed because the department will not have been informed of Red's conduct or Mary's intervention.

   Red and the probation department: The relationship will continue and will not be affected, but harm will result because the department will not be aware of Red's abusive practices, and he will likely continue using them.

   The probation department and the community: The relationship will continue and remain unaffected, but harm will be caused because Red may abuse Jay and other children again, and this will reduce the department's standing in the community due to the fact that no action will be taken to stop Red.

4. Apply the second option and then state how each relationship is affected. Next, state what harm is caused to each relationship, explaining the nature of the harm.

   Red and Jay: This relationship will end because Red will be fired. No harm will result in ending this relationship because Red will not be permitted to act unprofessionally again.

   Red and Mary: Their working relationship will end, but no harm will be caused because Mary will no longer have to work with an unprofessional and abusive coworker.

   Mary and the probation department: The relationship will be strengthened, and no harm will be caused. In fact, this relationship will be enhanced because Mary will be seen to be taking action against abusive probation officers and protecting children, as is her duty under the law.

   Red and the probation department: The relationship will end, but no harm will be caused because the department will now be rid of an abusive probation officer.

The probation department and the community: The relationship will continue and will be enhanced. No harm will result because the community will know that the department is prepared to fire abusive and unprofessional probation officers to protect children, as is its duty.

5. The most ethical option will be that which, while it maintains relationships, minimizes the harm caused by the impact of the dilemma on those relationships. Accordingly, if most relationships are affected but the harm caused is minimized by a particular option, then this is the most ethical option under the ethic of care.

After comparing Options 1 and 2, it is evident that both options affect the relationships involved when action is taken to resolve the dilemma. However, it is evident that harms are maximized under the first option and minimized under the second. Accordingly, Option 2 is the most ethical choice of action because even though most relationships are affected, overall harms are minimized under this option.

SUMMARY

Feminist approaches to moral philosophy have drawn attention to the importance of gender in ethical theory. Feminists have critiqued ethical theories for their emphasis on the individual, impartiality, and universality, arguing that a feminist approach would stress relationships, care, and connectiveness. Research by Gilligan and Kohlberg has shown how moral development varies according to gender and, in particular, how gender shapes the focus of moral inquiry. Thus, women tend to see moral life in terms of care and responsibility, asking whether relationships were maintained or harm suffered, whereas men stress the application of rules in a fair, impartial, and equal manner. As well, men are concerned with individual rights and autonomy and whether the rules have been followed, whereas women are more likely to resolve issues by applying solutions that affirm relationships and minimize harm. It is important to appreciate, however, that women should not be seen as creatures of emotion or as somehow deficient in taking a different moral approach from that of men because it is social conditioning (not sex roles) that creates gender boundaries. Also, women do not claim a monopoly on the ethic of care; men may also follow this ethic rather than applying the ethical perspective generally shared by men.

There are a number of problems with the ethic of care, including in particular whether it is capable of standing on its own as a philosophical theory. Some argue that it is best seen as a supplement to virtue ethics. Another problem with the ethic of care is the extent of the obligation to honor relationships and to show care. While it is easy to see how an ethic of care can be applied in close family relationships, philosophers dispute the boundaries of the ethic, asking, for example, whether the duty can extend to the needy throughout the world. Some see the obligation to the family as absolute and other obligations as secondary if only a potential rather than an actual relationship exists. Others stress the importance of the depth of a relationship and the extent to which the depth varies according to the closeness between the caregiver and a third person. Some argue that the ethic of care can be extended to include one's identity in a communal sense, such as membership of an ethnic group.

West has suggested that caring should be a focus of public and legal virtues and at the core of legal justice. She believes that an ethic of care should be allied with the ethic of justice so that public institutions exercise compassion or care while applying legal justice. According to West, this would avoid injustice because the law would be read and interpreted compassionately so as to take account, for example, of the life circumstances of an accused in a death penalty case.

Peacemaking has close connections with the ethic of care but is advocated as a separate philosophy variously called peacemaking, peacekeeping, or peacemaking criminology. In a general way, all these concepts emphasize relationships, caring, and mindfulness (thinking about our actions and the needs of others in the long term). Peacemaking also identifies nonviolence as a fundamental principle, advocating that violence and coercion in such forms as capital punishment and excessive force should be eradicated from the criminal justice system. Peacemaking advocates come from many different persuasions and positions, including Christian ethics and Buddhism. As a concept, peacemaking, although attractive with its emphasis on connectiveness and caring, seems to lack theoretical rigor and to be in need of greater definitional specificity.

DISCUSSION CASE

Practical Jokes, Initiation, Hazing, or Discrimination?

Mary Bloom is a chief of police. She worked her way up through the ranks, starting as a patrol officer at a time when women police officers were not taken seriously and were allocated tasks such as doing secretarial work, acting as matrons, or working with juveniles. In those days, the idea that a woman police officer could go on patrol like a male officer was considered laughable. Male officers, on the other hand, were assumed capable of being patrolmen, and no one used the term *patrol woman*.

As a new recruit, Mary was the victim of practices that can variously be described as practical jokes, hazing, initiation rituals, or discrimination. One time, her field-training officer (FTO) told her to inventory the contents of a squad car, and when she opened the door, there was a large snake there! She recognized it as a harmless species, picked it up, and brought it to her FTO, whose turn it now was to be startled. She noted that other recruits were also subjected to these antics, such as being sent to the maintenance section for a sawdust pump, being told to fetch a "group tightener" to place on the end of a service weapon to improve aim, or finding shaving cream in their hats just before inspection.

Those officers who just accepted these jokes and didn't complain were accepted, but the complaining officers were not. Mary opted not to make a fuss, and after a while, the jokes diminished and she became accepted. Later, she herself participated in these antics with the rookie police. As she climbed through the ranks, she noticed that these practices did not interfere with the daily police work because they happened during slow periods or after especially stressful events, when officers needed some relaxation and amusement.

Being promoted to police chief put Mary in charge of a large metropolitan area. She was the first female police chief, and one issue that she needed to pay attention to, following a request from the city manager, was the underrepresentation of minorities in the police department— minority officers made up only 3% of the force, and among the 300 officers, only two sergeants were minorities. As well, she was the only female above the rank of patrol officer. Responding to the need to bring in minorities, Mary went on a recruitment drive, and after 4 years, there was adequate minority representation. However, the issue was not dead.

Members of the African-American Law Enforcement Officers Association (AALEOA) and the Hispanic-American Law Enforcement Officers Association (HALEOA) were not satisfied. They claimed there existed an undercurrent of racism among command officers and supervisors, and at least one independent study confirmed this. They wanted this issue addressed, and Mary responded by organizing a series of seminars concerned with cultural diversity and sensitization. Every officer completed at least 16 hours of this training. In spite of this, the AALEOA and HALEOA members continued to voice their concerns and now began to allege being victims of "pranks" organized by senior officers. Mary's command officers told her that these pranks are not racially motivated. They are a ritual that all new recruits undergo, but the minority associations' members remain unconvinced and believe the practices are discriminatory and racially based.

After analyzing this issue applying an ethic of care approach, consider what Chief Bloom can do to resolve the situation.

SOURCE: Adapted from Close and Meier 1995: 531–532.

DISCUSSION QUESTIONS

1. What linkages do you see between an ethic of care and virtue ethics? Explain with examples.

2. Explain how moral development is differentiated according to gender.

3. "Applying the ethic of care to the criminal justice system would bring about a more compassionate system." Discuss three examples of areas within the criminal justice system where compassion might influence decision-making.

4. Explain how a peacemaking approach can be applied to our system of corrections

References

PART I

Chapter 1

"A Bad Shoot." 2010, March 4. *The Economist.* Retrieved October 11, 2011 (http://www.economist.com/node/15610132).

Arrington, Robert. 1983. "A Defense of Ethical Relativism." *Metaphilosophy* 14: 225–239.

BBC. 2010, June 15. "The Islamic Veil Across Europe." Retrieved August 10, 2010 (http://news.bbc.co.uk/2/hi/5414098.stm).

Bell, Dan. 2006, November 11. "Netherlands Moves Toward Total Ban on Muslim Veils." *The Guardian.* Retrieved April 23, 2007 (http://www.guardian.co.uk/religion/Story/0,,1945461,001.html).

Bunting, Harry. 1996. "A Single True Morality? The Challenge of Relativism." Pp. 73–85 in *Philosophy and Pluralism,* edited by David Archard. Cambridge, England: Cambridge University Press.

Bureau, Cain, and Michael Kunzelman. 2012, April 4. "Ex-Cops Sentenced in Katrina Killings Case." *ABC News.* http://lawreport.org/ViewStory.aspx?StoryID=8819.

Clements, Joan. 2006, November 18. "Holland to Ban Burqa as 'Terror Threat.'" *The Telegraph.*

CNN. 2003, December 17. "Chirac: Ban Headscarves in Schools." Retrieved March 23, 2007 (http://www.cnn.com/2003/WORLD/europe/12/17/france.headscarves/index.html).

Cook, John. 1999. *Morality and Cultural Differences.* New York: Oxford University Press.

Death Penalty Information Center. 2007. "Ohio Inmate Becomes the 119th Innocent Person Freed From Death Row." Washington, DC: Death Penalty Information Center. Retrieved April 7, 2007 (http://truthinjustice.org/jamison.htm).

Felkenes, George. 1987. "Ethics in the Graduate Criminal Justice Curriculum." *Teaching Philosophy* 10(1): 23–26.

Glover, Jonathan. 1999. "Capital Punishment." Pp. 245–253 in *The Right Thing to Do: Basic Readings in Moral Philosophy* (2nd ed.), edited by James Rachels. Boston: McGraw-Hill.

Grice, Andrew. 2006, October 18. "Blair: 'Veils Are Mark of Separation and Make Other Uncomfortable.'" *The Independent.* Retrieved November 5, 2011 (http://www.independent.co.uk/news/uk/politics/blair-veils-are-mark-of-separation-and-make-others-uncomfortable-420538.html).

Haakonssen, Knud. 2010. "Early Modern Natural Law." Pp. 76–87 in *The Routledge Companion to Ethics,* edited by John Skorupski. New York: Routledge.

Hare, Richard M. 1987. "Moral Conflicts." Pp. 205–238 in *Moral Dilemmas,* edited by Christopher Gowans. New York: Oxford University Press.

Hinman, Lawrence. 1998. *Ethics: A Pluralistic Approach to Moral Theory.* Fort Worth, TX: Harcourt Brace.

Holmes, Robert. 1998. *Basic Moral Philosophy* (4th ed.). Belmont, CA: Wadsworth.

Human Rights Watch. 1998. "New Orleans: Recent History." New York: Human Rights Watch. Retrieved March 1, 2008 (http://www.hrw.org/reports98/police/usp093.htm#).

Kane, Robert. 1996. *Through the Moral Maze: Searching for Absolute Values in a Pluralistic World.* Armonk, NY: North Castle Books.

Ladd, John. 1973. *Ethical Relativism.* Belmont, CA: Wadsworth.

Rachels, James. 1991. "Subjectivism." Pp. 432–441 in *A Companion to Ethics,* edited by Peter Singer. Cambridge, MA: Blackwell Press.

Roper v. Simmons, 543 U.S. 541 (2005).

Singer, Peter. 1995. *How Are We to Live? Ethics in an Age of Self-Interest.* Amherst, NY: Prometheus Books.

Steffen, Lloyd. 2012. *Ethics and Experience: Moral Theory From Just War to Abortion.* Lanham, MD: Rowman & Littlefield.

Womack, Mari. 1995. "Studying Up and the Issue of Cultural Relativism." *NAPA Bulletin* 16: 48.

Chapter 2

Activist Post. 2015, April 9. "Montana Legislature Passes Bill to Limit Federal Militarization of Local Police." http://

www.activistpost.com/2015/04/montana-legislature-passes-bill-to.html.

Alexander, Michelle. 2010. *The New Jim Crow: Mass Incarceration in the Age of Colorblindness.* New York: The New Press.

Alpert, Geoffrey P., and Roger G. Dunham. 2004. *Understanding Police Use of Force: Officers, Suspects, and Reciprocity.* Cambridge, England: Cambridge University Press.

American Civil Liberties Union (ACLU). June 2014. *War Comes Home: The Excessive Militarization of American Policing.* New York: ACLU Foundation.

Apuzzo, Matt. 2014, June 8. "War Gear Flows to Police Departments." *The New York Times.* http://www.nytimes.com/2014/06/09/us/war-gear-flows-to-police-departments.html?_r=0.

Associated Press. 2010, March 19. "Linked to Police Misconduct, 185 Drug Cases Are Dropped." *The New York Times.* Retrieved August 5, 2011 (http://www.nytimes.com/2010/03/20/nyregion/20camden.html?scp=75&sq=prosecutor+misconduct&st=nyt).

Bacon, Matthew. 2014. "Police Culture and the New Policing Context." Pp. 103–119 in *The Future of Policing*, edited by Jennifer Brown. London: Routledge.

Balko, Radley. 2013, July 13. "Rise of the Warrior Cop." *The Wall Street Journal.* http://www.wsj.com/articles/SB10001424127887323848804578608040780519904.

Bayley, David. 1994. *Police for the Future.* New York: Oxford University Press.

Barker, Tom. 1996. *Police Ethics: Crisis in Law Enforcement.* Springfield, IL: Charles C Thomas.

Beckett, Katherine, and Theodore Sasson. 2000. *The Politics of Injustice: Crime and Punishment in America.* Thousand Oaks, CA: Pine Forge Press.

Berry v. Leslie 767 F.3d 1144.

Bittner, Egon. 1967. "The Capacity to Use Force as the Core of the Police Role." Pp. 36–47 in *The Functions of Police in Modern Society*, edited by Egon Bittner. Washington, DC: National Institute of Mental Health.

Caldero, Michael A., and John P. Crank. 2011. *Police Ethics: The Corruption of Noble Cause.* Boston: Anderson.

Campbell, Donald J., and Kathleen M. Campbell. 2010. "Soldiers as Police Officers/Police Officers as Soldiers: Role Evolution and Revolution in the United States." *Armed Forces and Society* 36(2): 327–350.

Catlin, Dennis, and James R. Maupin. 2004. "A Two Cohort Study of the Ethical Orientations of State Police Officers." *Policing: An International Journal of Police Strategies & Management* 27(3): 289–301.

Chan, Janet. 1997. *Changing Police Culture: Policing in a Multicultural Society.* Cambridge, England: Cambridge University Press.

Chan, Janet. 2007. "Police Stress and Occupational Culture." Pp: 129–152 in *Police Occupational Culture: New Debates and Directions*, edited by Megan O'Neill, Monique Marks, and Anne-Marie Singh. Oxford: Elsevier.

Chevigny, Paul G. 1999. "Police Accountability in Hemispheric Perspective." Pp. 69–88 in *Democratic Policing and Accountability: Global Perspectives*, edited by Errol Mendes, Joaquin Zuckerberg, Susan Lecorre, Anne Gabriel, and Jeffrey Clark. Aldershot, England: Ashgate.

Clemons, John Tyler. 2014. "Blind Injustice: The Supreme Court, Implicit Racial Bias and the Racial Disparity in the Criminal Justice System." *American Criminal Law Review* 51: 689–713.

Closs, William, and Paul McKenna. 2006. "Profiling a Problem in Canadian Police Leadership: The Kingston Police Data Collection Project." *Canadian Public Administration* 49(2): 143–161.

CNN. 2001, October 3. "Airlines, Passengers Confront Racial Profiling." Retrieved April 3, 2007 (http://archives.cnn.com/2001/TRAVEL/NEWS/10/03/rec.air lines.profiling/index.html).

Cohen, Howard. 1996. "Police Discretion and Police Objectivity." Pp. 91–106 in *Handled With Discretion: Ethical Issues in Police Decision Making*, edited by John Kleinig. Lanham, MD: Rowman & Littlefield.

Coleman, Stephen. 2004. "When Police Should Say 'No!' to Gratuities." *Criminal Justice Ethics* Winter/Spring: 33–41.

Crank, John. 1998. *Understanding Police Culture.* Cincinnati, OH: Anderson.

Crank, John, and Michael Caldero. 2000. *Police Ethics: The Corruption of Noble Cause.* Cincinnati, OH: Anderson.

Crank, John P., Colleen Kadleck, and Connie M. Koski. 2010. "The U.S.A.: The Next Big Thing." *Police Practice and Research* 11(5): 405–422.

Davis, Julie Hirschfeld, and Michael D. Shear. 2015, May 18. "Obama Puts Focus on Police Success in Struggling City in New Jersey." *The New York Times.* http://www.nytimes.com/2015/05/19/us/politics/obama-to-limit-military-style-equipment-for-police-forces.html.

Delattre, Edwin. 1989. *Character and Cops: Ethics in Policing.* Washington, DC: American Enterprise Institute for Public Policy Research.

Den Heyer, Garth. 2014. "Mayberry Revisited: A Review of the Influence of Police Paramilitary Units on Policing." *Policing and Society* 24(3): 346–361.

Del Pozo, Brandon. 2005. "One Dogma of Police Ethics: Gratuities and the 'Democratic Ethos' of Policing." *Criminal Justice Ethics* Summer/Fall: 25–46.

Dershowitz, Alan. 1996. *Reasonable Doubts: The O. J. Simpson Case and the Criminal Justice System.* New York: Touchstone Books.

Eck, John E., and Edward R. Maguire. 2005. "Have Changes in Policing Reduced Crime? An Assessment of the Evidence." Pp. 207–265 in *The Crime Drop in America*, edited by Alfred Blumstein and Joel Wallman. New York: Cambridge University Press.

Eijkman, Quirine. 2006. "To Be Held Accountable: Police Accountability in Costa Rica." *Police Practice and Research* 7(5): 411–430.

Epp, Charles R., Steven Maynard-Moody, and Donald Haider-Markel. 2014. *Pulled Over: How Police Stops Define Race and Citizenship.* Chicago: The University of Chicago Press.

Feldberg, Michael. 1985. "Gratuities, Corruption, and the Democratic Ethos of Policing: The Case of the Free Cup of Coffee." Pp. 267–276 in *Moral Issues in Police Work*, edited by Frederick Elliston and Michael Feldberg. Totowa, NJ: Rowman & Allanheld.

Felknes, George. 1984. "Attitudes of Police Officers Toward Their Professional Ethics." *Journal of Criminal Justice* 12(3): 211–220.

Fyfe, James. 1996. "Structuring Police Discretion." Pp. 183–205 in *Handled With Discretion: Ethical Issues in Police Decision Making*, edited by John Kleinig. Lanham, MD: Rowman & Littlefield.

Gershon, Robyn R. M., Briana Barocas, Allison Canton, Xianbin N. Li, and David Vlahov. 2009. "Mental, Physical, and Behavioral Outcomes Associated With Perceived Work Stress in Police Officers." *Criminal Justice and Behavior* 36(3): 275–289.

Giroux, Henry A. 2015, April 7. "Terrorism, Violence, and the Culture of Madness." *Philosophers for Change* [blog]. Para. 19.

Goldsmith, Andrew. 1999. "Better Policing, More Human Rights: Lessons From Civilian Oversight." Pp. 33–68 in *Democratic Policing and Accountability: Global Perspectives*, edited by Errol Mendes, Joaquin Zuckerberg, Susan Lecorre, Anne Gabriel, and Jeffrey Clark. Aldershot, England: Ashgate.

Goldstein, Herman. 1977. *Policing in a Free Society*. Cambridge, MA: Ballinger.

Government Accounting Office. 1998. *Report to the Honorable Charles B. Rangel, House of Representatives, Law Enforcement: Information on Drug-Related Police Corruption*. Washington, DC: Author.

Griffin, Sean P., and Thomas J. Bernard. 2003. "Angry Aggression Among Police Officers." *Police Quarterly* 6(1): 3–21.

Hall, Abigail R., and Christopher J. Coyne. 2013. "The Militarization of U.S. Domestic Policing." *The Independent Review* 17(4): 485–504.

Haller, Mark. 1996. "Historical Roots of Police Behaviors: Chicago, 1890–1925." Pp. 7–26 in *Classics in Policing*, edited by Steven Brandl and David Barlow. Cincinnati, OH: Anderson.

Heitzeg, Nancy A. 2015. "'Whiteness,' Criminality, and the Double Standards of Deviance/Social Control." *Contemporary Justice Review: Issues in Criminal, Social, and Restorative Justice*. 1–18.

Herbert, Steve. 2006. *Citizens, Cops, and Power: Recognizing the Limits of Community*. Chicago: University of Chicago Press.

Hill, Stephen, and Randall Beger. 2009. "A Paramilitary Juggernaut." *Social Justice* 36(1): 25–40.

Huberts, Leo, Terry Lamboo, and Maurice Punch. 2003. "Police Integrity in the Netherlands and the United States: Awareness and Alertness." *Police Practice and Research* 4(3): 217–232.

Ivkovic, Sanja Kutnjak. 2005a. *Fallen Blue Knights: Controlling Police Corruption*. New York: Oxford University Press.

Ivkovic, Sanja Kutnjak. 2005b. "Police (Mis)behavior: A Cross-Cultural Study of Corruption Seriousness." *Policing: An International Journal of Police Strategies & Management* 28(3): 546–566.

Ivkovic, Sanja Kutnjak, and Tara O'Connor Shelley. 2005. "The Bosnian Police and Police Integrity: A Continuing Story." *European Journal of Criminology* 2(4): 428–464.

Jackman, Tom. 2006, February 13. "Spotsylvania Deputies Receive Sex Services in Prostitution Cases." *The Washington Post*. Retrieved April 8, 2007 (http://www.washingtonpost.com/wp-dyn/content/article/2006/02/12/AR2006021200943.html).

Jefferis, Danielle C. 2012. "Battlefield Borders, Threat Rhetoric, and the Militarization of State and Local Law Enforcement." *National Security Law Brief* 3(1): 37–73.

Johnston, M. 1995. "Police Corruption." Pp. 285–313 in *Morality in Criminal Justice: An Introduction to Ethics*, edited by Daryl Close and Nicholas Meier. Belmont, CA: Wadsworth.

Kane, Robert J., and Michael D. White. 2013. *Jammed Up: Bad Cops, Police Misconduct, and the New York City Police Department*. New York: New York University Press.

Kania, Richard. 2004. "The Ethical Acceptability of Gratuities: Still Saying 'Yes' After All These Years." *Criminal Justice Ethics* Winter/Spring: 54–63.

Kelling, George, and Mark Moore. 1996. "The Evolving Strategy of Policing." Pp. 71–95 in *Classics in Policing*, edited by Steven Brandl and David Barlow. Cincinnati, OH: Anderson.

Kennedy, Randall. 1991. *Race, Crime, and the Law*. New York: Vintage Books.

Kiker, Cadman Robb. 2015."From Mayberry to Ferguson: The Militarization of American Policing Equipment, Culture and Mission." *Washington and Lee Law Review*: 282–298.

Kleinig, John. 1996. *The Ethics of Policing*. New York: Cambridge University Press.

Kleinig, John. 2000. *The Blue Wall of Silence: An Ethical Analysis*. Occasional Paper XIII. The Center for Research in Crime and Justice, New York University School of Law.

Klockars, Carl. 1980. "The Dirty Harry Problem." *The Annals of the American Academy of Political and Social Science* 451: 33–47.

Kraska, Peter. 2007a. "The Blurring of War and Law Enforcement." Pp. 161–187 in *Violence, Conflict, and World Order: Critical Conversations on State-Sanctioned Justice*, edited by G. Barak. Lanham, MD: Rowman & Littlefield.

Kraska, Peter. 2007b. "Militarization of the Police." Pp. 790–793 in *The Encyclopedia of Police Science: Vol. 1 A–I* (3rd ed.), edited by Jack Greene. New York: Routledge.

Kraska, Peter B. 2007c. "Militarization and Policing: Its Relevance to 21st-Century Police." *Policing*: 1-13.

Knowles v. Iowa 525 U.S. 133 (1998).

Laird v. Tatum 408 U.S. 1 (1972).

Loftus, Bethan. 2010. "Police Occupational Culture: Classic Themes, Altered Times." *Policing and Society* 20(1): 1–20.

Manning, Peter. 1989. "Occupational Culture." Pp: 360–364 in *The Encyclopedia of Police Science*, edited by William G. Bailey. New York: Garland.

Manning, Peter. 1996. "The Police: Mandate, Strategies Appearances." Pp. 215–243 in *Classics in Policing,* edited by Steven Brandl and David Barlow. Cincinnati, OH: Anderson.

Manning, Peter. 1997. *Police Work: The Social Organization of Policing.* Prospect Heights, IL: Waveland Press.

Manning, Peter. 2007. "A Dialectic of Organizational and Occupational Culture." Pp: 47–84 in *Police Occupational Culture: New Debates and Directions,* edited by Megan O'Neill, Monique Marks, and Anne-Marie Singh. Oxford, England: Elsevier.

Mendes, Errol P. 1999. "Raising the Social Capital of Policing and Nations: How Can Professional Policing and Civilian Oversight Weaken the Circle of Violence." Pp. 13–32 in *Democratic Policing and Accountability: Global Perspectives,* edited by Errol Mendes, Joaquin Zuckerberg, Susan Lecorre, Anne Gabriel, and Jeffrey Clark. Aldershot, England: Ashgate.

Miethe, Terance. 1999. *Whistleblowing at Work: Tough Choices in Exposing Fraud, Waste, and Abuse on the Job.* Boulder, CO: Westview Press.

Miller, Joel. 2003. "Police Corruption in England and Wales: An Assessment of Current Evidence." London: Home Office–Research Development and Statistics Directorate. Retrieved March 19, 2007 (http://www.homeoffice.gov.uk/rds/pdfs2/rdsolr1103.pdf).

Miller, Seumas, John Blackler, and Andrew Alexandra. 1997. *Police Ethics.* Sydney, Australia: Allen and Unwin.

Morash, Merry, Robin Haarr, and Kwak Dae-Hoon. 2006. "Multilevel Influences on Police Stress." *Journal of Contemporary Criminal Justice* 22(1): 26–43.

More, Harry. 1998. *Special Topics in Policing* (2nd ed.). Cincinnati, OH: Anderson.

Muir, William K. 1977. *Police: Streetcorner Politicians.* Chicago: University of Chicago Press.

Newsome, Yvonne. 2003. "Border Patrol: The U.S. Customs Service and the Racial Profiling of African American Women." *Journal of African American Studies* 7(3): 31–57.

New York Civil Liberties Union. "Stop and Frisk Facts." Retrieved June 6, 2015 (http://www.nyclu.org/issues/racial-justice/stop-and-frisk-practices).

Neyroud, Peter, and Alan Beckley. 2001. *Policing, Ethics and Human Rights.* Cullompton, England: Willan.

Peak, Bethany J. 2015. "Militarization of School Police: One Route on the School-to-Prison Pipeline." *Arkansas Law Review* 68: 195–229.

The Pittsburgh Channel. 2000, December 28. "Wilkinsburg Police Officers Punished: Is Move Whistleblowing Retaliation?" Retrieved April 26, 2003 (http://www.thepittsburgchannel.com/station/218765/detail.html).

Pollock-Byrne, Joycelyn. 1998. *Ethics in Crime and Justice: Dilemmas and Decisions.* Pacific Grove, CA: Brooks/Cole.

Prenzler, Tim, and Carol Ronken. 2003. "A Survey of Innovations in the Development and Maintenance of Ethical Standards by Australian Police Departments." *Police Practice and Research* 4(2): 149–161.

Punch, Maurice. 2003. "Rotten Orchards: 'Pestilence,' Police Misconduct and System Failure." *Policing and Society* 13(2): 171–196.

Punch, Maurice. 2007. "Cops With Honours: University Education and Police Culture." Pp: 105–128 in *Police Occupational Culture: New Debates and Directions,* edited by Megan O'Neill, Monique Marks, and Anne-Marie Singh. Oxford, England: Elsevier.

Reiman, Jeffrey. 1996. "Is Police Discretion Justified in a Free Society?" Pp. 71–83 in *Handled With Discretion: Ethical Issues in Police Decision Making,* edited by John Kleinig. Lanham, MD: Rowman & Littlefield.

Reiner, Robert. 1985. "The Police and Race Relations." Pp. 149–187 in *Police: The Constitution and the Community,* edited by John Baxter and Laurence Koffman. London: Professional Books.

Roebuck, Julian, and Thomas Barker. 1974. "A Typology of Police Corruption." *Social Problems* 21(3): 423–437.

Rokeach, Milton, Martin Miller, and John Snyder. 1977. "The Value Gap Between Police and the Policed." *Journal of Social Issues* 27(2): 155–171.

Ruiz, Jim, and Christine Bono. 2004. "At What Price a 'Freebie'? The Real Cost of Police Gratuities." *Criminal Justice Ethics* Winter/Spring: 44–53.

Schafer, Joseph A., Beth M. Huebner, and Timothy Bynum. 2003. "Citizen Perceptions of Police Services: Race, Neighborhood Context, and Community Policing." *Police Quarterly* 6(4): 440–468.

Scheingold, Stuart. 1984. *The Politics of Law and Order.* New York: Longman.

Schmidt, Michael S. 2015, February 12. "F.B.I. Director Speaks Out on Race and Police Bias." *The New York Times.* http://www.nytimes.com/2015/02/13/us/politics/fbi-director-comey-speaks-frankly-about-police-view-of-blacks.html.

Sherman, Lawrence. 1982. "Learning Police Ethics." *Criminal Justice Ethics* 1(1): 10–19.

Sherman, Lawrence. 1985. "Becoming Bent." Pp. 253–266 in *Moral Issues in Police Work,* edited by Frederick A. Elliston and Michael Feldberg. Totowa, NJ: Rowman & Allanheld.

Sklansky, David Alan. 2007. "Seeing Blue: Police Reform, Occupational Culture, and Cognitive Burn-In." Pp. 19–46 in *Police Occupational Culture: New Debates and Directions,* edited by Megan O'Neill, Monique Marks, and Anne-Marie Singh. Oxford, England: Elsevier.

Skolnick, Jerome. 1966. *Justice Without Trial.* New York: Wiley.

Skolnick, Jerome. 2010. "Enduring Issues of Police Culture and Demographics." *Policing and Society* 18(1): 35–45.

Skolnick, Jerome, and James Fyfe. 1993. *Above the Law: Police and the Excessive Use of Force.* New York: The Free Press.

Smith, Erica, and Matthew Durose. June 2006. "Characteristics of Drivers Stopped by Police, 2002." Bureau of Justice Statistics publication NCJ 211471. Washington, DC: Department of Justice.

Stanford, Anthony. 2015. *Copping Out: The Consequences of Police Corruption and Misconduct*. Santa Barbara, CA. Praeger.

Stratton, John G., David A. Parker, and John R. Snibbe. 1984. "Post-Traumatic Stress: Study of Police Officers Involved in Shootings." *Psychological Reports* 55: 127–131.

Sulzberger, A. G. 2010, May 6. "New York Officer Linked to a Violent Robbery Ring." *The New York Times*, A21. Retrieved August 10, 2011 (www.nytimes.com/2010/05/07/nyregion/07officer.html?scp=62&sq=prosecutor+misconduct&st=nyt).

Tankebe, Justice. 2010. "Public Confidence in the Police: Testing the Effects of Public Experiences of Police Corruption in Ghana." *British Journal of Criminology* 50: 296–319.

Terry v. Ohio 392 U.S. 1 (1968).

Tobar, Hector. 1998, December 28. "An Ugly Stain on a City's Bright and Shining Plan." *Los Angeles Times*, A1.

United States v. Arvizu 534 U.S. 266 (2002),

United States Department of Justice. December 2014. *Guidance for Federal Law Enforcement Agencies Regarding the Use of Race, Ethnicity, Gender, National Origin, Religion, Sexual Orientation, or Gender Identity*. Washington, DC: Department of Justice.

Waddington, P. A. J. 1999. "Swatting Police Paramilitarism: A Comment on Kraska and Paulsen." *Policing and Society* 9: 125–140.

Walker, Samuel. 1996. "A Critical History of Police Reform: The Emergence of Professionalism—Introduction." Pp. 27–35 in *Classics in Policing*, edited by Steven Brandl and David Barlow. Cincinnati, OH: Anderson.

Walker, Samuel. 2001. *Police Accountability: The Role of Citizen Oversight*. Belmont, CA: Wadsworth.

Walker, Samuel. 2005. *The New World of Police Accountability*. Thousand Oaks, CA: Sage.

Walker, Samuel, and Betsy Wright Kreisel. 1996. "Varieties of Citizen Review: The Implications of Organizational Features of Complaint Review Procedures for Accountability of the Police." *American Journal of Police* 15(3): 65–88.

Walker, Samuel, Cassia Spohn, and Miriam DeLone. 2000. *The Color of Justice: Race, Ethnicity and Crime in America*. Belmont, CA: Wadsworth.

Warren, Patricia, Donald Tomaskovic-Devey, William Smith, Matthew Zingraff, and Marcinda Mason. 2006. "Driving While Black: Bias Processes and Racial Disparity in Police Stops." *Criminology* 44(3): 709–738.

Waters, Judith A., and William Ussery. 2007. "Police Stress: History, Contributing Factors, Symptoms, and Interventions." *Policing: An International Journal of Police Strategies and Management* 30(2): 169–188.

Westmarland, L. 2005. "Police Ethics and Integrity: Breaking the Blue Code of Silence." *Policing and Society* 15(2): 145–165.

Whren v. United States 517 U.S. 806 (1996).

Wilson, James Q. 1968. *Varieties of Police Behavior*. Cambridge, MA: Harvard University Press.

Withrow, Brian, and Jeffrey Dailey. 2004. "A Model of Circumstantial Corruptibility." *Police Quarterly* 7(2): 159–178.

Wright, Barry. 2010. "Civilianising the 'Blue Code'? An Examination of Attitudes to Misconduct in the Police Extended Family." *International Journal of Police Science and Management* 12(3): 339–356.

Wyatt-Nichol, Heather, and George Franks. 2009. "Ethics Training in Law Enforcement Agencies." *Public Integrity* 12(1): 39–50.

Zhao, Jihong, He Ni, and Nicholas P. Lovrich. 1998. "Individual Value Preferences Among American Police Officers." *Policing: An International Journal of Police Strategies & Management* 21(1): 22–37.

Chapter 3

Alemika, Etannibi E. O. 2003. "Police, Policing and Rule of Law in Transitional Countries." Pp. 63–102 in *Human Rights and the Police in Transitional Countries*, edited by Leone Lindhot, Paulo de Mesquita Neto, Danny Titus, and Etannibi E. Alemika. The Hague: The Danish Institute for Human Rights and Kluwer Law International.

Alpert, Geoffrey P., and Roger G. Dunham. 2004. *Understanding Police Use of Force: Officers, Suspects, and Reciprocity*. Cambridge, England: Cambridge University Press.

Alpert, Geoffrey P., and Jeffrey J. Noble. 2009. "Lies, True Lies and Conscious Deception: Police Officers and the Truth." *Police Quarterly* 12: 237–254.

Amnesty International. June 2015. *Deadly Force: Police Use of Lethal Force in the United States*. Washington, DC: Amnesty International.

Barker, Tom. 1996. *Police Ethics: Crisis in Law Enforcement*. Springfield, IL: Charles C Thomas.

Barker, Tom, and David Carter. 1995. "Police Lies and Perjury: A Motivation-Based Taxonomy." Pp. 254–262 in *Morality in Criminal Justice: An Introduction to Ethics*, edited by Daryl Close and Nicholas Meier. Belmont, CA: Wadsworth.

Bishopp, Stephen A., David A. Klinger, and Robert G. Morris. 2014. "An Examination of the Effect of a Policy Change on Police Use of Tasers." *Criminal Justice Policy Review*: 1–20.

Brown, Gregory R. 2015. "The Blue Line on Thin Ice: Police Use of Force and Modifications in the Era of Cameraphones and YouTube." *British Journal of Criminology* [advanced access], published June 3, 2015.

Brown v. City of Golden Valley, 574 F. 3d 491 (8th Circuit 2011).

Burch, Andrea M. 2011. *Arrest-Related Deaths, 2003–2009: Statistical Tables*. Washington, DC: U.S. Department of Justice, Office of Justice Programs, Bureau of Justice Statistics.

Bryan v. McPherson, 630 F.3d 805 (9th Circuit 2009).

Canton v. Harris, 489 U.S. 378 (1989).

Casey v. City of Fed. Heights, 509 F. 3d 1278 (10th Circuit 2007).

Center for the Study of Ethics in the Professions. 2003. "Law Enforcement Code of Ethics." Chicago: Illinois Institute of

Technology. Retrieved August 31, 2003 (http://www .iit.edu/departments/csep/PublicWWW/codes/coe/ International_Association_of_Chiefs_ of_Police_Law_ Enforcement_Code_of_ Ethics_1989.html).

Clemons, John Tyler. 2014. "Blind Injustice: The Supreme Court, Implicit Racial Bias and the Racial Disparity in the Criminal Justice System." *American Criminal Law Review* 51: 689–713.

Commission to Investigate Allegations of Corruption and Anti-Corruption Procedures of the Police Department, City of New York. 1994. *Commission Report.* New York: Author.

Compton, Michael T., Roger Bakeman, Beth Broussard, Dana Hankerson-Dyson, Letheshia Husbands, Shaily Krishan, Tarianna Stewart-Hutto, Barbara M. D'Orio, Janet R. Olivia, Nancy J. Thompson, and Amy C. Watson. 2014. "The Police-Based Crisis Intervention Team (CIT) Model: Effects on Level of Force and Resolution, Referral and Arrest." *Psychiatric Services* 65(4): 523–529.

Crank, John. 1998. *Understanding Police Culture.* Cincinnati, OH: Anderson.

Crow, Matthew S., and Brittany Adrion. 2011. "Focal Concerns and Police Use of Force: Examining the Factors Associated With Taser Use." *Police Quarterly* 14(4): 366–387.

Dai, Mengyan, James Frank, and Ivan Sun. 2011. "Procedural Justice During Police–Citizen Encounters: The Effects of Process-Based Policing on Citizen Compliance and Demeanor." *Journal of Criminal Justice* 39: 159–168.

Davis, Julie Hirschfeld. 2015, March 2. "Obama Calls for Changes in Policing After Task Force Report." *The New York Times.* http://www.nytimes.com/2015/03/03/us/politics/obama-calls-for-changes-in-policing-after-task-force-report.html.

Dershowitz, Alan. 1983. *The Best Defense.* New York: Vintage Books.

Doyle, Arthur. 2000. "From the Inside Looking Out: Twenty-Nine Years in the New York Police Department." Pp. 171–186 in *Police Brutality: An Anthology,* edited by Jill Nelson. New York: Norton.

Eligon, John. 2010, June 18. "Jurors Watch Video of Officer Hitting Man With a Baton." *The New York Times,* A16.

Ericson, Richard. 1992. "The Police as Reproducers of Order." Pp. 163–208 in *Understanding Policing,* edited by K. R. E. McCormick and L. A. Visano. Toronto, ON: Canadian Scholar's Press.

Ferge v. State, 764 N.E. 2d 268, 270 (Ind. Ct. App. 2002).

Fernando, Basil. 2003. "Police and the Rule of Law in Asia." Pp. 29–49 in *Human Rights and the Police in Transitional Countries,* edited by Leone Lindhot, Paulo de Mesquita Neto, Danny Titus, and Etannibi E. Alemika. The Hague: The Danish Institute for Human Rights, Kluwer Law International.

Federal Bureau of Investigation, New Orleans Division. 2012, April 4. "Five New Orleans Police Officers Sentenced on Civil Rights and Obstruction of Justice Violations in the Danziger Bridge Shooting Case." Press Release. Washington, DC: U.S. Department of Justice.

Franz, Stephanie, and Randy Borum. 2011. "Crisis Intervention Teams May Prevent Arrest of People With Mental Illnesses." *Police Practice and Research* 12(3): 265–272.

Graham v. Connor, 490 U.S. 386 (1989).

Greer, Chris, and Eugene McLaughlin. 2010. "We Predict a Riot? Public Order Policing: New Media Environments and the Rise of the Citizen Journalist." *British Journal of Criminology* 50: 1041–1059.

Harfield, Clive. 2012. "Police Informers and Professional Ethics." *Criminal Justice Ethics* 31(2): 73–95.

Hays, Tom. 2000. "Cop Gets 15 Years in Torture Case." *Infobeat.* Retrieved January 15, 2001 (http://www.infobeat.com/ stories/cgi/story.cgi?id=2567684838-eb5).

Hays, Tom. 2007, January 8. "Would-Be NY Subway Bomber Gets 30 Years." *The Washington Post.* Retrieved April 9, 2007 (http://www.washingtonpost.com/wp-dyn/content/ article/2007/01/08/AR2007010800158.html).

Hickman, Matthew. 2006. *Citizen Complaints About Police Use of Force: Bureau of Justice Statistics Special Report.* Washington, DC: U.S. Department of Justice.

Huggins, Martha K. 2010. "Systemic Police Violence in Brazil in Police Use of Force: A Global Perspective." Pp. 73–82 in *Police Use of Force: A Global Perspective,* edited by Joseph B. Kuhns and Johannes Knutsson. Santa Barbara, CA: Praeger.

Inbau, Fred, and John E. Reid. 1962. *Criminal Interrogation and Confessions.* Baltimore, MD: Williams and Wilkins.

Jackson, Jonathan, Ben Bradford, Mike Hough, Andy Myhill, Paul Quinton, and Tom R. Tyler. 2012. "Why Do People Comply With the Law? Legitimacy and the Influence of Legal Institutions." *British Journal of Criminology* 52: 1051–1071.

James, Doris. J, and Lauren E. Glaze. 2006. *Mental Health Problems of Prison and Jail Inmates.* Washington, DC: U.S. Department of Justice, Office of Justice Programs, Bureau of Justice Statistics.

Jobard, Fabien. 2003. "Counting Violence Committed by the Police: Raw Facts and Narratives." *Policing and Society* 13(4): 423–428.

Johnson, Richard R. 2011. "Suspect Mental Disorder and Police Use of Force." *Criminal Justice and Behavior* 38(2): 127–145.

Kassin, Saul M., Richard A. Leo, Christian A. Meissner, Kimberly D. Richman, Lori H. Colwell, Amy-May Leach, and Dana La Fon. 2007. "Police Interviewing and Interrogation: A Self-Report Survey of Police Practices and Beliefs." *Law and Human Behavior* 31: 381–400.

Keslowitz, Steven. 2009. "The Trial of Jack Bauer: The Televised Trial of America's Favorite Fictional Hero and Its Influence on the Current Debate on Torture." *Cardozo Law Review* 31(4): 1125–1132.

Klahm, Charles F., and R. Tillyer. 2010. "Understanding Police Use of Force: A Review of the Evidence." *Southwest Journal of Criminal Justice* 7(2): 214–239.

Kleinig, John. 1996. *The Ethics of Policing.* New York: Cambridge University Press.

Kleinig, John. 2007. "Ethical Constraints on Taser Use by Police." *Policing* 1(3): 284–292.

Klockars, Carl. 1980. "The Dirty Harry Problem." *The Annals of the American Academy of Political and Social Science* 451: 33–47.

Kochel, Tammy Rinehart. 2011. "Constructing Hot Spots Policing: Unexamined Consequences for Disadvantaged Populations and for Police Legitimacy." *Criminal Justice Policy Review* 22(3): 350–374.

Lassiter, G. Daniel, and Jennifer J. Ratcliff. 2004. "Exposing Coercive Influences in the Criminal Justice System: An Agenda for Legal Psychology in the Twenty-First Century." Pp: 1–8 in *Interrogations, Confessions, and Entrapment*, edited by G. Daniel Lassiter. New York: Kluwer Academic/Plenum.

Lawrence, Regina. 2000. *The Politics of Force: Media and the Construction of Police Brutality*. Berkeley: University of California Press.

Lawson, Kenneth. 2015. "Police Shootings of Black Men and Implicit Racial Bias: Can't We All Just Get Along." *University of Hawaii Law Review* 37: 339–535.

Lee, Hoon, and Michael S. Vaughn. 2010. "Organizational Factors That Contribute to Police Deadly Force Liability." *Journal of Criminal Justice* 38: 193–206.

Leo, Richard A. 2004. "The Third Degree and the Origins of Psychological Interrogation in the United States." Pp: 37–84 in *Interrogations, Confessions, and Entrapment*, edited by G. Daniel Lassiter. New York: Kluwer Academic/Plenum.

Leo, Richard A. 2008. *Police Interrogation and American Justice*. Cambridge, MA: Harvard University Press.

Lersch, Kim Michelle, and Tom Mieczkowski. 2005. "Violent Police Behavior: Past, Present, and Future Research Directions." *Aggression and Violent Behavior* 10: 552–568.

Los Angeles Times. 2001, March 23. "Louima to Settle NYPD Lawsuit for $9 Million." http://articles.latimes.com/2001/mar/23/news/mn-41693.

Marx, Gary. 1985. "'Who Really Gets Stung?' Some Issues Raised by the New York Undercover Work." Pp. 99–128 in *Moral Issues in Police Work*, edited by Frederick A. Elliston and Michael Feldberg. Totowa, NJ: Rowan & Allanheld.

Marx, Gary. 2001. "Under-the-Covers Undercover Investigations: Some Reflections on the State's Use of Sex and Deception in Law Enforcement." Pp. 262–274 in *Criminal Justice Ethics*, edited by Paul Leighton and Jeffrey Reiman. Upper Saddle River, NJ: Prentice Hall.

Mazerolle, Lorraine, Sarah Bennett, Jacqueline Davis, Elise Sargeant, and Matthew Manning. 2013. "Procedural Justice and Police Legitimacy: A Systematic Review of the Research Evidence." *Journal of Experimental Criminology* 9(3): 245–274.

Meissner, Christian A., and Saul M. Kassin. 2004. "'You're Guilty So Just Confess!': Cognitive and Behavioral Confirmation Biases in the Interrogation Room." Pp: 85–106 in *Interrogations, Confessions, and Entrapment*, edited by G. Daniel Lassiter. New York. Kluwer Academic/Plenum.

Mesquita Neto, Paulo, and Adrianna Loche. 2003. "Policing Community Partnerships in Brazil." In *Crime and Violence in Latin America: Citizen Security, Democracy, and the State*, edited by Hugo Fruhling, Joseph Tulchin, and Heather Golding. Washington, DC: Woodrow Wilson Center Press and The John Hopkins University Press.

Miller, Laurence. 2015. "Why Cops Kill: The Psychology of Police Deadly Force Encounters." *Aggression and Violent Behavior* 22: 97–111.

Miller, Seumas, John Blackler, and Andrew Alexandra. 1997. *Police Ethics*. Sydney, Australia: Allen and Unwin.

Miranda v. Arizona, 384 U.S. 436 (1966).

Morabito, Melissa Schaefer. 2007. "Horizons of Context: Understanding the Police Decision to Arrest People With Mental Illness." *Psychiatric Services* 58: 1582–1587.

Morabito, Melissa S., Amy N. Kerr, Amy Watson, Jeffrey Draine, Victor Ottati, and Beth Angell. 2012. "Crisis Intervention Teams and People With Mental Illness: Exploring the Factors That Influence the Use of Force." *Crime and Delinquency* 58(1): 57–77.

Morabito, Melissa Schaefer, and Kelly M. Socia. 2015. "Is Dangerousness a Myth? Injuries and Police Encounters With People With Mental Illnesses." *Criminology and Public Policy* 14(2): 1–24.

Paoline, Eugene A., and William Terrill. 2011. "'Listen to Me!': Police Officers' Views of Appropriate Use of Force." *Journal of Crime and Justice* 34(3): 178–189.

Parent, Rick. 2006. "The Police Use of Deadly Force: International Comparisons." *The Police Journal* 79: 230–237.

Perez-Pena, Richard. 2015, April 8. "Fatal Police Shootings: Accounts Since Ferguson." *The New York Times*. http://www.nytimes.com/interactive/2015/04/08/us/fatal-police-shooting-accounts.html.

Perlmutter, David. 2000. *Policing and the Media: Street Cops and Public Perceptions of Law Enforcement*. Thousand Oaks, CA: Sage.

Planty, Michael, Andrea M. Burch, Duren Banks, Lance Couzens, Caroline Blanton, and Devon Cribb. March 2015. *Arrest-Related Deaths Program: Data Quality Profile*. Washington, DC: U.S. Department of Justice, Office of Justice Programs, Bureau of Justice Statistics.

Prenzler, Tim, Louise Porter, and Geoffrey P. Alpert. 2013. "Reducing Police Use of Force: Case Studies and Prospects." *Aggression and Violent Behavior* 18: 343–356.

Rochin v. California, 342 U.S. 165 (1952).

Rojek Jeff, Geoffrey P. Alpert, and Hayden P. Smith. 2012. "Examining Officer and Citizen Accounts of Police Use-of-Force Incidents." *Crime and Delinquency* 58(2): 301–327.

Ross, Jacqueline. 2008. "Do Rules of Evidence Apply (Only) in the Courtroom? Deceptive Interrogation in the United States and Germany." *Oxford Journal of Legal Studies* 28(3): 443–467.

Scott v. Harris, 550 U.S. 372 (2007).

Sherman v. the United States, 356 U.S. 369 (1958).

Skolnick, Jerome. 1982. "Deception by Police." *Criminal Justice Ethics* 1(2): 40–54.

Skolnick, Jerome, and James Fyfe. 1993. *Above the Law: Police and the Excessive Use of Force.* New York: The Free Press.

Slobogin, Christopher. 1996. "Testilying: Police Perjury and What to Do About It." *University of Colorado Law Review* 67(4): 1037–1060.

Smulovitz, Catalina. 2003. "Citizen Insecurity and Fear: Public and Private Responses in Argentina." In *Crime and Violence in Latin America: Citizen Security, Democracy, and the State,* edited by Hugo Fruhling, Joseph Tulchin, and Heather Golding. Washington, DC: Woodrow Wilson Center Press and The John Hopkins University Press.

Stinson, Philip Matthew, Bradford W. Reyns, and John Liederbach. 2012. "Police Crime and Less-Than-Lethal Coercive Force: A Description of the Criminal Misuse of Tasers." *International Journal of Police Science and Management* 14(1): 1–19.

Stitt, B. Grant, and Gene G. James. 1985. "Entrapment: An Ethical Analysis." Pp. 129–146 in *Moral Issues in Police Work,* edited by Frederick A. Elliston and Michael Feldberg. Totowa, NJ: Rowan & Allanheld.

Taylor, Bruce, Geoffrey Alpert, Bruce Kubu, Daniel Woods, and Roger G. Dunham. 2011. "Changes in Officer Use of Force Over Time: A Descriptive Analysis of a National Survey." *Policing: An International Journal of Police Strategies and Management* 24(2): 211–232.

Tennessee v. Garner, 471 U.S. 1 (1985).

Terrill, William, Eugene A. Paoline, and John Ingram. 2011. *Assessing Police Use of Force Policy and Outcomes: Final Report.* Washington, DC: National Institute of Justice.

The Guardian. 2015, May 26. "Cleveland Announces Historic Second Settlement Over Chronic Police Abuse."

The New York Times. 2015, May 12. "U.S. Justice Department Inquiry Finds Abuses by Cleveland Police."

Tyler, Tom R. 2011. "Trust and Legitimacy: Policing in the USA and Europe." *European Journal of Criminology* 8(4): 254–266.

USA Today. 2014, August 26. "Poll: Whites and Blacks Question Police Accountability."

U.S. Department of Justice and Police Executive Research Forum. 2011. *2011 Electronic Control Weapon Guidelines 12.* Washington, DC: U.S. Department of Justice.

U.S. Department of Justice, Civil Rights Division. 2015, March 4. *Investigation of the Ferguson Police Department.* Washington, DC: U.S. Department of Justice.

Wolf, Brian, and Joseph De Angelis. 2011. "Tasers, Accountability, and Less Lethal Force: Keying In on the Contentious Construction of Police Electroshock Weapons." *International Journal of Criminology and Sociological Theory* 4(2): 657–673.

Chapter 4

Aguirre, Adalberto, and David Baker. 1990. "Empirical Research on Racial Discrimination in the Imposition of the Death Penalty." *Criminal Justice Abstracts* 22: 135–153.

Albonetti, Celesta. 1990. "Race and the Probability of Pleading Guilty." *Journal of Quantitative Criminology* 6: 315–334.

Albonetti, Celesta, Robert Hauser, John Hagan, and Ilene Nagel. 1989. "Criminal Justice Decision Making as a Stratification Process: The Role of Race and Stratification Resources in Pretrial Release." *Journal of Quantitative Criminology* 5: 57–82.

Alexander, Michelle. 2010. *The New Jim Crow: Mass Incarceration in the Age of Colorblindness.* New York: The New Press.

Alvarez, A. 2000. "Unwelcome Citizens: Latinos and the Criminal Justice System." Pp. 85–98 in *Investigating Difference: Human and Cultural Relations in Criminal Justice,* edited by The Criminal Justice Collective of Northern Arizona University. Needham Heights, MA: Allyn & Bacon.

American Anthropological Association. 1997. *Race and Ethnic Standards for Federal Statistics and Administrative Reporting.* Arlington, VA: Author.

Associated Press. 2010, July 28. "Congress Votes to Change Crack vs. Cocaine Sentencing Laws." Retrieved August 5, 2011 (http://newsone.com/nation/associatedpress3/congress-votes-to-change-crack-vs-cocaine-sentencing-laws/).

Baldus, David, George Woodward, and Charles Pulaski. 1990. *Equal Justice and the Death Penalty: A Legal and Empirical Analysis.* Boston: Northeastern University Press.

Banks, Cyndi. 2002. "Doing Time in Alaska: Women, Culture and Crime." Pp. 232–257 in *It's a Crime: Women and Justice* (3rd ed.), edited by R. Muraskin. Upper Saddle River, NJ: Prentice Hall.

Banks, Richard, and Jennifer Eberhardt. 1998. "Social Psychological Processes and the Legal Bases of Racial Categorization." Pp. 54–75 in *Confronting Racism: The Problem and the Response,* edited by Jennifer Eberhardt and Susan Fiske. Thousand Oaks, CA: Sage.

Barkan, Steven, and Steven Cohn. 2005. "On Reducing White Support for the Death Penalty: A Pessimistic Appraisal." *Criminology & Public Policy* 4(1): 39–44.

Batson v. Kentucky, 476 U.S. 79 (1986).

Beckett, Katherine, Kiris Nyrop, and Lori Pfingst. 2006. "Race, Drugs, and Policing: Understanding Disparities in Drug Delivery Arrests." *Criminology* 44(1): 105–137.

Bishop, Donna M., Michael Leiber, and Joseph Johnson. 2010. "Contexts of Decision Making in the Juvenile Justice System: An Organizational Approach to Understanding Minority Overrepresentation." *Youth Violence and Juvenile Justice* 8(3): 213–233.

Black, Donald, and Albert Reiss. 1970. "Police Control of Juveniles." *American Sociological Review* 35: 63–77.

Blumstein, Alfred. 1982. "On the Racial Disproportionality of the U.S. States' Prison Population." *Journal of Criminal Law and Criminology* 73: 1259–1281.

Blumstein, Alfred. 1993. "Racial Disproportionality of U.S. Prison Populations Revisited." *University of Colorado Law Review* 64: 743–760.

Brod, Thomas M. 1975. "Alcoholism as a Mental Health Problem of Native Americans." *Archives of General Psychiatry* 32: 1385–1391.

Brown, Craig, and Barbara Warner. 1995. "The Political Threat of Immigrant Groups and Police Aggressiveness in 1900." Pp. 82–98 in *Ethnicity, Race, and Crime: Perspectives Across Time and Place,* edited by Darnell Hawkins. Albany: State University of New York Press.

Brown, Robert, and James Frank. 2006. "Race and Officer Decision Making: Examining Differences in Arrest Outcomes Between Black and White Officers." *Justice Quarterly* 23(1): 86–126.

Brown v. Board of Education, 347 U.S. 483 (1954).

Building Blocks for Youth. April 2000. *Resources for Disproportionate Minority Confinement/ Overrepresentation of Youth of Color: Key Studies.* Retrieved April 8, 2007 (http://www.buildingblocksforyouth.org/issues/dmc/studies.html).

Byers, Bryan, and Lori Spillane. 2000. "Hate Crime in Contemporary American Society: A Sociological Approach." Pp. 243–270 in *Multicultural Perspectives in Criminal Justice and Criminology,* edited by James Hendricks and Bryan Byers. Springfield, IL: Charles C Thomas.

Carson, E. Ann. 2014. *Prisoners in 2013.* Washington, DC: U.S. Department of Justice, Office of Justice Programs, Bureau of Justice Statistics.

Carson, Ann. September 2015. NCJ 248955. "Prisoners in 2014." Washington, DC: Bureau of Justice Statistics, US Department of Justice.

Chambliss, William. 1995. "Crime Control and Ethnic Minorities: Legitimizing Racial Oppression by Creating Moral Panics." Pp. 235–258 in *Ethnicity, Race, and Crime: Perspectives Across Time and Space,* edited by Darnell Hawkins. Albany: State University of New York Press.

Chambliss, William, and Robert Seidman. 1971. *Law, Order, and Power.* Reading, MA: Addison-Wesley.

Clemons, John Tyler. 2014. "Blind Injustice: The Supreme Court, Implicit Racial Bias and the Racial Disparity in the Criminal Justice System." *American Criminal Law Review* 51: 689–713.

Death Penalty Information Center. December 2010. "The Death Penalty in 2010: Year-End Report." Washington, DC. Retrieved August 5, 2011 (http://www.deathpenaltyinfo.org/documents/2010YearEnd-Final.pdf).

DeNava-Walt, Carmen, Bernadette Proctor, and Cheryl Hill Lee. 2006. *Income, Poverty, and Health Insurance Coverage in the United States: 2005.* Washington, DC: U.S. Census Bureau.

Dilulio, John. 1996. "My Black Crime Problem, and Ours." *City Journal* 6: 14–28.

Doerner, Jill K., and Stephen Demuth. 2009. "The Independent and Joint Effects of Race/Ethnicity, Gender, and Age on Sentencing Outcomes in U.S. Federal Courts." *Justice Quarterly* 27(1): 1–27.

Federal Bureau of Investigation. December 2014. *Hate Crimes Statistics Report.* Washington, DC: FBI. https://www.fbi.gov/news/stories/2014/december/latest-hate-crime-statistics-report-released/.

Fields, Reginald. 2011. "Unequal Crack Cocaine Penalties Cleaned Up as Cost Balances Anti-Crime Pressure." Cleveland.com. Retrieved August 5, 2011 (http://www.cleveland.com/open/index.ssf/2011/07/unequal_crack_cocaine_penaltie.html).

Fienup-Riordan, Ann. 1994. *Boundaries and Passages: Rule and Ritual in Yup'ik Eskimo Oral Tradition.* Norman: University of Oklahoma Press.

Fyfe, James. 1982. "Blind Justice: Police Shootings in Memphis." *Journal of Criminal Law and Criminology* 73: 707–722.

Georges-Abeyie, Daniel. 2001. "Petit Apartheid in Criminal Justice: The More 'Things' Change, the More 'Things' Remain the Same." Pp. ix–xiv in *Petit Apartheid in the U.S. Criminal Justice System,* edited by Dragan Milovanovic and Katheryn Russell. Durham, NC: Carolina Academic Press.

Girgenti, Alicia A. 2015. "The Intersection of Victim Race and Gender: The 'Black Male Victim Effect' and the Death Penalty." *Race and Justice* 2: 1–23.

Gottschalk, Marie. 2015. *Caught: The Prison State and the Lockdown of American Politics.* Princeton, NJ: Princeton University Press.

Greenfeld, Lawrence A., and Steven Smith. 1999. *American Indians and Crime.* Bureau of Justice Statistics Publication NCJ 173386. Washington, DC: U.S. Department of Justice.

Grobsmith, Elizabeth. 1994. *Indians in Prison: Incarcerated Native Americans in Nebraska.* Lincoln: University of Nebraska Press.

Hagan, John, and Kristin Bumiller. 1983. "Making Sense of Sentencing: A Review and Critique of Sentencing Research." Pp. 1–54 in *Research on Sentencing: The Search for Reform,* edited by Alfred Blumstein, Jacqueline Cohen, S. Martin, and Michael Tonry. Washington, DC: National Academy Press.

Hinman, Lawrence. 1998. *Ethics: A Pluralistic Approach to Moral Theory.* Fort Worth, TX: Harcourt Brace.

Holmes, Malcolm D., and Brad W. Smith. 2008. *Race and Police Brutality: Roots of an Urban Dilemma.* Albany: State University of New York Press.

Independent Commission on the Los Angeles Police Department. 1991. *Report of the Independent Commission on the Los Angeles Police Department.* Los Angeles: City of Los Angeles.

Jordan, Kareem L., and Tina L. Freiburger. 2010. "Examining the Impact of Race and Ethnicity on the Sentencing of Juveniles in the Adult Court." *Criminal Justice Policy Review* 21(2): 185–201.

Klein, Stephen, Joan Petersilia, and Susan Turner. 1990. "Race and Imprisonment Decisions in California." *Science* 247: 812–816.

Knepper, Paul. 2000. "The Alchemy of Race and Crime Research." Pp. 15–30 in *The System in Black and White: Exploring the Connections Between Race, Crime, and Justice,* edited by Michael Markowitz and Delores Jones-Brown. Westport, CT: Praeger.

Kraus, Robert, and Patricia Buffler. 1979. "Sociocultural Stress and the American Native in Alaska: An Analysis of Changing Patterns of Psychiatric Illness and Alcohol Abuse Among Alaska Natives." *Culture, Medicine and Psychiatry* 3: 111–151.

Langton, Lynn, and Michael Planty. 2011. "Hate Crime, 2003–2009." Special Report. BJS, NCJ 234085. Washington, DC: U.S. Department of Justice.

Lee, Catherine. 2006. "Hispanics and the Death Penalty: Discriminatory Charging Practices in San Joaquin County, California." *Journal of Criminal Justice* 35: 17–27.

Mast, Brent, Bruce Benson, and David Rasmussen. 2000. "Entrepreneurial Police and Drug Enforcement Policy." *Public Choice* 104: 285–308.

Mauer, Marc. 2006. *Race to Incarcerate*. New York: The New Press.

May, Larry, and Shari Sharratt. 1994. *Applied Ethics: A Multicultural Approach*. Englewood Cliffs, NJ: Prentice-Hall.

McCleskey v. Kemp 481 U.S. 279 (1987).

McDonald, Douglas, and Kenneth Carlson. December 1993. *Sentencing in the Federal Courts: Does Race Matter?* Bureau of Justice Statistics Publication NCJ 145332. Washington, DC: U.S. Department of Justice.

Miethe, Terance, and Charles Moore. 1986. "Racial Differences in Criminal Processing: The Consequences of Model Selection on Conclusions About Differential Treatment." *Sociological Quarterly* 27: 217–237.

Milovanovic, Dragan, and Katheryn Russell (Eds.). 2001. *Petit Apartheid in the U.S. Criminal Justice System: The Dark Figure of Racism*. Durham, NC: Carolina Academic Press.

Minton, Todd D., and Zhen Zheng. 2015. "Jail Inmates at Midyear 2014." Bureau of Justice Statistics NCJ 248629. Washington, DC: U.S. Department of Justice.

Moore, Nina M. 2015. *The Political Roots of Racial Tracking in American Criminal Justice*. New York: Cambridge University Press.

Murakawa, Naomi, and Katherine Beckett. 2010. "The Penology of Racial Innocence: The Erasure of Racism in the Study and Practice of Punishment." *Law and Society Review* 44(3/4): 695–730.

New York State Judicial Commission on Minorities. 1991. "Panel Says New York Courts Are 'Infested With Racism.'" *Criminal Justice Newsletter* 22(12): 1–2.

Paternoster, Raymond, Robert Brame, Sarah Bacon, Andrew Ditchfield, David Biere, Karen Beckman, Deanna Perez, Michael Strauch, Nadine Frederique, Kristin Gawkoski, Daniel Zeigler, and Katheryn Murphy. 2003. "An Empirical Analysis of Maryland's Death Sentencing System With Respect to the Influence of Race and Legal Jurisdiction: Final Report." Retrieved March 21, 2007 (http://www.newsdesk.umd.edu/pdf/exec.pdf).

Perry, Steven. 2004. *American Indians and Crime: A BJS Statistical Profile, 1992–2002*. Bureau of Justice Statistics Publication NCJ 203097. Washington, DC: U.S. Department of Justice.

Petersilia, Joan. 1983. *Racial Disparities in the Criminal Justice System*. Santa Monica, CA: RAND.

Peterson, Ruth, and John Hagan. 1984. "Changing Conceptions of Race: Towards an Account of Anomalous Findings of Sentencing Research." *American Sociological Review* 49: 56–70.

Peterson, Ruth D. 2012. "The Central Place of Race in Crime and Justice: The American Society of Criminology's 2011 Sutherland Address." *Criminology* 50(2): 303–327.

Pew Research Center. 2014, December 12. "Factank." http://www.pewresearch.org/fact-tank/2014/12/12/racial-wealth-gaps-great-recession/.

Phillips, Michael, and Thomas Inui. 1986. "The Interaction of Mental Illness, Criminal Behavior and Culture: Native Alaskan Mentally Ill Criminal Offenders." *Culture, Medicine and Psychiatry* 10: 123–149.

Piliavin, Irving, and Scott Briar. 1964. "Police Encounters With Juveniles." *American Journal of Sociology* 69: 206–214.

Pope, Carl, and William Feyerherm. June and September 1990. "Minority Status and Juvenile Justice Processing: An Assessment of the Research Literature" (Parts 1 and 2). *Criminal Justice Abstracts*: 327–335, 527–542.

Rachels, James. 1999. *The Elements of Moral Philosophy*. Boston: McGraw-Hill College.

Rimer, Sara. 2002, February 13. "In Dallas, Dismissal of Black Jurors Leads to Appeal by Death Row Inmate." *The New York Times*. Retrieved January 15, 2003 (http://www.nytimes.com/2002/02/13/national/13DEAT.html).

Rodriguez, Nancy. 2010. "The Cumulative Effect of Race and Ethnicity in Juvenile Court Outcomes and Why Preadjudication Detention Matters." *Journal of Research in Crime and Delinquency* 47(3): 391–413.

Ross, Luana. 2000. "Imprisoned Native Women and the Importance of Native Traditions." Pp. 132–144 in *States of Confinement: Policing, Detention, and Prisons*, edited by J. James. New York: St. Martin's Press.

Russell-Brown, Katheryn. 1998. *The Color of Crime: Racial Hoaxes, White Fear, Black Protectionism, Police Harassment, and Other Macroaggressions*. New York: New York University Press.

Sampson, Robert, and Janet Lauritsen. 1997. "Racial and Ethnic Disparities in Crime and Criminals in the United States." Pp. 311–374 in *Ethnicity, Crime and Immigration: Comparative and Cross-National Perspectives*, edited by Michael Tonry. Chicago: University of Chicago Press.

Schafer, N. E., Richard Curtis, and Cassie Atwell. 1997. *Disproportionate Representation of Minorities in the Alaska Juvenile Justice System: Phase 1 Report*. Anchorage: Justice Center, University of Alaska.

Smith, Brian. 2000. "Historical Injustices, Contemporary Inequalities: African Americans and Criminal Justice." Pp. 71–84 in *Investigating Difference: Human and Cultural Relations in Criminal Justice*, edited by The Criminal Justice Collective of Northern Arizona University. Boston: Allyn & Bacon.

Smith, Douglas. 1986. "The Neighborhood Context of Police Behavior." Pp. 313–341 in *Crime and Justice: A Review of Research: Vol. 8, Communities and Crime,* edited by Albert Reiss and Michael Tonry. Chicago: University of Chicago Press.

Snell, Tracy. 2010. *Capital Punishment, 2009: Statistical Tables.* Bureau of Justice Statistics Bulletin NCJ 231676. Washington, DC: U.S. Department of Justice.

Snell, Tracy. December 2014. *Capital Punishment, 2013 Statistical Tables.* NCJ 248448. Washington, DC: U.S. Department of Justice, Bureau of Justice Statistics.

Sommers, Samuel R., and Michael I. Norton. 2008. "Race and Jury Selection: Psychological Perspectives on the Peremptory Challenge Debate." *American Psychologist* 63(6): 527–539.

Soss, Joe, Laura Langbein, and Alan Metelko. 2003. "Why Do White Americans Support the Death Penalty?" *Journal of Politics* 65: 397–421.

Spohn, Cassia, John Gruhl, and Susan Welch. 1987. "The Impact of the Ethnicity and Gender of Defendants on the Decision to Reject or Dismiss Felony Charges." *Criminology* 25: 175–192.

Spohn, Cassia. 2015. "Disadvantage and Sentencing of Black Defendants: Evolution of Sentencing Research." *Criminology and Public Policy* 14(2): 1–8.

Strauder v. West Virginia, 100 U.S. 303 (1880).

Tonry, Michael. 1995. *Malign Neglect: Race, Crime, and Punishment in America.* Oxford, England: Oxford University Press.

Tonry, Michael. 1998. "Racial Politics, Racial Disparities, and the War on Crime." Pp. 41–57 in *The Criminal Justice System: Politics and Policies,* edited by George Cole and Marc Gertz. Belmont, CA: West/Wadsworth.

Tonry, Michael. 2010. "The Social, Psychological and Political Causes of Racial Disparities in the American Criminal Justice System." *Crime and Justice* 39(1): 273–312.

Tonry, Michael, 2011. *Punishing Race: A Continuing American Dilemma.* New York: Oxford University Press.

Wacquant, Loic. 2008. "Commentary." Pp. 57–72 in *Race, Incarceration, and American Values,* edited by Glenn Loury. Cambridge, MA: MIT Press.

Walker, Samuel, Cassia Spohn, and Miriam DeLone. 2000. *The Color of Justice: Race, Ethnicity and Crime in America.* Belmont, CA: Wadsworth.

Wilbanks, William. 1987. *The Myth of a Racist Criminal Justice System.* Monterey, CA: Brooks/Cole.

Zatz, Marjorie, and Coramae Mann. 1998. "The Power of Images." Pp. 1–12 in *Images of Color, Images of Crime: Readings,* edited by Coramae Mann and Marjorie Zatz. Los Angeles: Roxbury.

Chapter 5

Allen, Francis. 1985. "A Serendipitous Trek Through the Advance-Sheet Jungle: Criminal Justice in the Courts of Review." *Iowa Law Review:* 311–341.

American Bar Association. 1993. *ABA Standards for Criminal Justice: The Prosecution Function.* Chicago: Author.

American Bar Association and Center for Professional Responsibility. 1998. *Model Rules of Professional Conduct.* Chicago: Author.

American Bar Association Standing Committee on Ethics and Professional Responsibility. 1999. *ABA Model Code of Judicial Conduct.* Chicago: Author.

Associated Press. 2011, August 11. "Pennsylvania Judge Gets 28 Years in 'Kids for Cash' Case." Msnbc News Services. Retrieved August 11, 2011 (http://www.msnbc.msn .com/id/44105072/ns/us_news-crime_and_courts/t/ pennsylvania-judge-gets-years-kids-cash-case/#. TkUib78QuE5).

Averett, Steve. 2004. "Judicial Ethics in Utah." *BYU Journal of Public Law* 18: 695–707.

Babcock, Barbara. 1983. "Defending the Guilty." *Cleveland State Law Review* 32: 175–187.

Baker, Al. 2004, December 11. "Judge Censured for Conduct Unbecoming His Authority." *The New York Times,* B5.

Berger v. United States, 295 U.S. 78 (1935).

Brady v. Maryland, 373 U.S. 83 (1963).

Bureau of Justice Statistics. 2002. *Sourcebook of Criminal Justice Statistics: 2002.* Washington, DC: U.S. Department of Justice.

Chalmers, Henry R. Spring 2010. "Prosecutorial Misconduct Leads to Dismissal of Criminal Charges." *Litigation News* 35(3). Retrieved July 31, 2011 (http://apps.americanbar. org/litigation/litigationnews/top_stories/ruehle- broadcom-prosecutor-misconduct.html).

Comisky, Marvin, Phillip Patterson, and William Taylor. 1987. *The Judiciary—Selection, Compensation, Ethics, and Discipline.* New York: Quorum Books.

Dodd v. Florida Bar, 118 S0.2d 17 (Fla. 1960).

Editorial. "A Judicial Campaign Rule Survives at the Supreme Court." 2015, April 29. *The New York Times.*

Eligon, John. 2011, February 16. "Freed Man's Suit Accuses Brooklyn Prosecutors of Misconduct." *The New York Times,* A26.

Etienne, Margareth. 2005. "The Ethics of Cause Lawyering: An Empirical Examination of Criminal Defense Lawyers as Cause Lawyers." *Journal of Criminal Law & Criminology* 95(4): 1195–1260.

Farelly, Colin, and Lawrence B. Solum. 2007. "An Introduction to Aretaic Theories of Law." Pp: 1–23 in *Virtue Jurisprudence,* edited by Colin Farelly and Lawrence B. Solum. Basingstoke, England: Palgrave Macmillan.

Faretta v. California, 422 U.S. 806 (1975); 95 S. Ct. 2525 (1975).

Fisher, Stanley. 1988. "In Search of the Virtuous Prosecutor: A Conceptual Framework." *American Journal of Criminal Law* 197: 198–199.

Frankel, Marvin. 1975. "The Search for Truth: An Umpireal View." *University of Pennsylvania Law Review* 123: 1031–1059.

Freedman, Monroe. 1966. "Professional Responsibility of the Criminal Defense Lawyer: The Three Hardest Questions." *Michigan Law Review* 64: 1469–1484.

Freedman, Monroe. 1975a. "Judge Frankel's Search for the Truth." *University of Pennsylvania Law Review* 123: 1060–1082.

Freedman, Monroe. 1975b. *Lawyers' Ethics in an Adversary System.* Indianapolis, IN: Bobbs-Merrill.

Fried, Charles. 1994. "The Lawyer as Friend: The Moral Foundations of the Lawyer-Client Relation." Pp. 97–126 in *The Ethics of Lawyers,* edited by David Luban. New York: New York University Press.

Gerber, Rudolph. 1999. *Cruel and Unusual: Our Criminal Injustice System.* Westport, CT: Praeger.

Gershman, Bennett. 1986. "Why Prosecutors Misbehave." *Criminal Law Bulletin* 22(2): 131–143.

Gershman, Bennett. 1987. *Prosecutorial Misconduct.* New York: C. Boardman.

Gershman, Bennett. 2001. "The Prosecutor's Duty to Truth." *Georgetown Journal of Legal Ethics* 14: 309–354.

Gier, Kelly. 2006. "Prosecuting Injustice: Consequences of Misconduct." *American Journal of Criminal Law* 33(2): 191–222.

Gottfredson, Michael, and Don Gottfredson. 1988. *Decision Making in Criminal Justice: Toward the Rational Exercise of Discretion* (2nd ed.). New York: Plenum Press.

Greenhouse, Linda. 2006, September 19. "Federal Judges Take Steps to Improve Accountability." *The New York Times,* A20.

Hansen, Mark. 2005. "Hand It Over." *ABA Journal* 91(12): 30–32.

Haskell, Paul G. 1998. *Why Lawyers Behave as They Do: New Perspectives on Law, Culture, and Society.* Boulder, CO: Westview Press.

Hazard, Geoffrey, and William Hodes. 2002. *The Law of Lawyering: Vol. 1* (3rd ed.). Gaithersburg, MD: Aspen Law & Business.

Herzog, Sergio. 2004. "Plea Bargaining Practices: Less Covert, More Public Support?" *Crime & Delinquency* 50(4): 590–614.

In re Friedman, 392 N.E.2d 1333, 1336 (1979).

"Judges Might Go on Ballot in Maricopa County." 2008, March 24. *East Valley Tribune.* Retrieved March 30, 2008 (http://www.msnbc.msn.com/id/23774435/from/ET/).

Kilgannon, Corey. 2008, October 18. "City to Pay $3.5 Million to Wrongfully Imprisoned Queens Man." *The New York Times,* A21. Retrieved August 5, 2011 (http://www.nytimes.com/2008/10/18/nyregion/18settle.html).

Kipnis, Kenneth. 1986. *Legal Ethics.* Englewood Cliffs, NJ: Prentice-Hall.

Kipnis, Kenneth. 2001. "Criminal Justice and the Negotiated Plea." Pp. 362–371 in *Criminal Justice Ethics,* edited by Paul Leighton and Jeffrey Reiman. Upper Saddle River, NJ: Prentice-Hall.

Levine, Susan, and Lori Montgomery. 2003, January 8. "Large Racial Disparity Found in Study of Md. Death Penalty." *The Washington Post,* A01.

Libby, Eileen. 2009, October 1. "A Higher Law." *American Bar Association Journal.* Retrieved July 31, 2011 (http://www.abajournal.com/magazine/article/a_higher_law/).

Liptak, Adam. 2006, October 27. "Reprimand for a Justice Who Met With Inmates." *The New York Times,* A12.

Luban, David. 1984. "The Sources of Legal Ethics: A German-American Comparison of Lawyers' Professional Duties." *Rabels Zeitschift* 48: 245–288.

Luban, David. 1988. *Lawyers and Justice: An Ethical Study.* Princeton, NJ: Princeton University Press.

Luban, David. 1990. "Partnership, Betrayal and Autonomy in the Lawyer-Client Relationship: A Reply to Stephen Ellmann." *Columbia Law Review* 90: 1004–1043.

Marzulli, John. 2014, August 19. "Exclusive: Jabbar Collin, Who Spent More Than 15 Years in Prison for Wrongful Conviction, Settles Suit With City for $10 Million." *New York Daily News.* http://www.nydailynews.com/new-york/brooklyn/jabbar-collins-settles-suit-city-10-million-article-1.1908675.

McDonough, Chris, Diana McDonough, and Raymond Keenan. 2000. "The Ethical Obligations of the Criminal Prosecutor." Pp. 50–64 in *Morality and the Law,* edited by Roslyn Muraskin and Matthew Muraskin. Upper Saddle River, NJ: Prentice-Hall.

McKissick v. United States, 379 F.2d 754 (5th Cir. 1967).

Miller v. Pate, 386 U.S. 1 (1967).

Mitchell, John. 1980. "The Ethics of the Criminal Defense Attorney—New Answers to Old Questions." *Stanford Law Review* 32: 293–337.

Morrell v. State, P.2d 1200: Alaska Supreme Court (1978).

Newman, Andy. 2004, August 19. "Played in Court, Tapes Show Judge Coaching Lawyer and Taking Cash." *The New York Times,* B1.

Nix v. Whiteside, 475 U.S. 157, 106 S. Ct. 988 (1986).

Noonan, John. 1966. "The Purposes of Advocacy and the Limits of Confidentiality." *Michigan Law Review* 64: 1485–1492.

Papke, David. 1986. "The Legal Profession and Its Legal Responsibilities: A History." Pp. 29–49 in *Ethics and the Legal Profession,* edited by Michael Davis and Frederick Elliston. Buffalo, NY: Prometheus Books.

Pepinsky, Hal. 2000. "Prosecuting for Safety's Sake." Pp. 65–78 in *Morality and the Law,* edited by Roslyn Muraskin and Matthew Muraskin. Upper Saddle River, NJ: Prentice-Hall.

Pepper, Stephen. 1994. "The Lawyer's Amoral Ethical Role: A Defense, A Problem, and Some Possibilities." Pp. 57–80 in *The Ethics of Lawyers,* edited by David Luban. New York: New York University Press.

Philips, Susan. 1998. *Ideology in the Language of Judges: How Judges Practice Law, Politics, and Courtroom Control.* Oxford, England: Oxford University Press.

Politico. March/April 2015. "I Was Alabama's Top Judge. I'm Ashamed by What I Had to Do to Get There." http://www.politico.com/magazine/story/2015/03/judicial-elections-fundraising-115503.

Pool, J. 1979. "Defending the 'Guilty' Client." *Massachusetts Law Review* 64: 11–19.

Remington, Frank. 1993. "The Decision to Charge, the Decision to Convict on a Plea of Guilty, and the Impact of Sentence

Structure on Prosecution Practices." Pp. 73–133 in *Discretion in Criminal Justice: The Tension Between Individualization and Uniformity,* edited by Lloyd Ohlin and Frank Remington. Albany: State University of New York Press.

Ridolfi, Kathleen. 2007, July 11. *Prosecutorial Misconduct: A Systemic Review.* California Commission on the Fair Administration of Justice, Preliminary Report. Retrieved July 30, 2011 (http://apps.americanbar.org/litigation/litigationnews/top_stories/ruehle-broadcom-prosecutor-misconduct.html).

Rimer, Sara. 2002, February 6. "Convict's DNA Sways Labs, Not a Determined Prosecutor. *The New York Times.* Retrieved June 27, 2003 (http://www.nytimes.com/2002/02/06/national/06DNA.html).

Savage, Charlie. 2011, January 18. "A Step to Deal With Prosecutors' Misconduct." *The New York Times.* Retrieved August 7, 2011 (http://thecaucus.blogs.nytimes.com/2011/01/18/a-step-to-deal-with-prosecutors-misconduct/?scp=16&sq=judge+misconduct&st=nyt).

Scheck, Barry, Peter Neufeld, and Jim Dwyer. 2000. *Actual Innocence: When Justice Goes Wrong and How to Make It Right.* New York: Signet.

Schoenfeld, Heather. 2005. "Violated Trust: Conceptualizing Prosecutorial Misconduct." *Journal of Contemporary Criminal Justice* 21(3): 250–271.

Shaffer, Thomas. 1981. *On Being a Christian and a Lawyer.* Provo, UT: Brigham Young University Press.

Shaman, Jeffrey M., Steven Lubet, and James J. Alfini. 2000. *Judicial Conduct and Ethics.* Charlottesville, VA: Lexis Law.

Simon, William. 1988. "Ethical Discretion in Lawyering." *Harvard Law Review* 101(6): 1083–1145.

Simon, William. 1994. "The Ideology of Advocacy: Procedural Justice and Professional Ethics." Pp. 179–296 in *The Ethics of Lawyers,* edited by David Luban. New York: New York University Press.

Subin, Harry. 1987. "The Criminal Lawyer's 'Different Mission': Reflections on the 'Right' to Present a False Defense." *Georgetown Journal of Legal Ethics* 1: 125–153.

"Texas Judge Reprimanded in Death Row Case." 2010, July 17. *The New York Times,* A20.

Truth in Justice. 2001, January 5. "92nd Death Row Inmate Freed Since '73." *The New York Times.* Retrieved March 12, 2008 (http://www.truthinjustice.org/n092.htm).

United States v. Agurs, 427 U.S. 97 (1976).

United States v. Perry, 643 F.2d 38 2d Cir. (1981).

Wasserstrom, Richard. 1975. "Lawyers as Professionals: Some Moral Issues." *Human Rights* 5: 1–24.

Wasserstrom, Richard. 1986. "Lawyers as Professionals: Some Moral Issues." Pp. 114–131 in *Ethics and the Legal Profession,* edited by Michael Davis and Frederick Elliston. Buffalo, NY: Prometheus Books.

Wolfram, Charles. 1986. *Modern Legal Ethics.* St. Paul, MN: West.

Yaroshefsky, Ellen, and Bruce A. Green. 2012. "Prosecutors' Ethics in Context: Influences on Prosecutorial Disclosure."

Pp. 269–292 in *Lawyers in Practice: Ethical Decision Making in Context,* edited by Leslie C. Levin and Lynn Mather. Chicago: University of Chicago Press.

Chapter 6

American Friends Service Committee. 1971. *Struggle for Justice: A Report on Crime and Punishment in America.* New York: Hill and Wang.

Andenaes, Johannes. 1972. "Does Punishment Deter Crime?" Pp. 342–357 in *Philosophical Perspectives on Punishment,* edited by Gertrude Ezorsky. Albany: State University of New York Press.

Bazemore, Gordon, and M. Dooley. 2001. "Restorative Justice and the Offender: The Challenge of Reintegration." Pp. 101–126 in *Restorative Community Justice: Repairing Harm and Transforming Communities,* edited by Gordon Bazemore and Mara Schiff. Cincinnati, OH: Anderson.

Bazemore, Gordon, and Maria Schiff. 2001. "What and Why Now: Understanding Restorative Justice." Pp. 21–46 in *Restorative Community Justice: Repairing Harm and Transforming Communities,* edited by Gordon Bazemore and Mara Schiff. Cincinnati, OH: Anderson.

Bennett, Christopher. 2002. "The Varieties of Retributive Experience." *Philosophical Quarterly* 52(207): 145–163.

Bean, Philip. 1981. *Punishment: A Philosophical and Criminological Inquiry.* Oxford, England: Martin Robertson.

Blumstein, Alfred, Jaqueline Cohen, and Daniel Nagin (Eds.). 1978. *Deterrence and Incapacitation: Estimating the Effects of Criminal Sanctions on Crime Rates.* Washington, DC: Panel on Research on Deterrent and Incapacitative Effects.

Boonin, David. 2008. *The Problem of Punishment.* Cambridge, England. Cambridge University Press.

Braithwaite, John. 1998. "Restorative Justice." Pp. 323–344 in *Handbook of Crime and Punishment,* edited by Michael Tonry. New York: Oxford University Press.

Brooks, Thom. 2012. *Punishment.* London: Routledge.

Carawan, Edwin. 1998. *Rhetoric and the Law of Draco.* Oxford, England: Clarendon Press.

Carlen, Pat. 1994. "Crime, Inequality, and Sentencing." Pp. 306–332 in *A Reader on Punishment,* edited by Antony Duff and David Garland. Oxford, England: Oxford University Press.

Daly, Kathleen, and Julie Stubbs. 2007. "Feminist Theory, Feminist and Anti-Racist Politics, and Restorative Justice." Pp. 149–170 in *Handbook of Restorative Justice,* edited by G. Johnstone and D. W. V. Ness. Portland, OR: Willan.

Day, Andrew. 2011. "Offender Rehabilitation: Current Problems and Ethically Informed Approaches to Intervention." *Ethics and Social Welfare* 5(4): 348–360.

Day, Andrew, Kylie Tucker, and Kevin Howells. 2004. "Coerced Offender Rehabilitation—A Defensible Practice?" *Psychology, Crime & Law* 10(3): 259–269.

Duff, R. A. 1992. "Alternatives to Punishment: Or Alternative Punishments?" Pp. 44–68 in *Retributivism and Its Critics,* edited by W. Cragg. Stuttgart, Germany: Franz Steiner.

Duff, R. A. 1999. "Punishment, Communication, and Community." Pp. 48–68 in *Punishment and Political Theory,* edited by Matt Matravers. Portland, OR: Hart.

Duff, R. A., and David Garland. 1994. "Introduction: Thinking About Punishment." Pp. 1–43 in *A Reader on Punishment,* edited by Antony Duff and David Garland. Oxford, England: Oxford University Press.

Feinberg, Joel. 1965. "The Expressive Theory of Punishment." *Monist* 49: 397–423.

Feinberg, Joel. 1994. "The Expressive Function of Punishment." Pp. 71–91 in *A Reader on Punishment,* edited by Antony Duff and David Garland. Oxford, England: Oxford University Press.

Foucault, Michael. 1977. *Discipline and Punish: The Birth of Prison.* London: Penguin Books.

Frankel, Marvin. 1972. *Criminal Sentences: Law Without Order.* New York: Hill and Wang.

Furman v. Georgia, 408 U.S. 238, 308, 342, 394 (1972).

Gallo, E., and V. Ruggiero. 1991. "The 'Immaterial' Prison: Custody as a Factory for the Manufacture of Handicaps." *International Journal of the Sociology of Law* 19(3): 273–291.

Garland, David. 1990. *Punishment and Modern Society.* Oxford, England: Oxford University Press.

Gregg v. Georgia, 428 U.S. 153, 184 (1976).

Holroyd, Jules. 2010. "The Retributive Emotions: Passions and Pains of Punishment." *Philosophical Papers* 39(3): 343–371.

Hoskins, Zachary. 2011. "Fair Play, Political Obligation, and Punishment." *Criminal Law and Philosophy* 5: 53–71.

Howe, Adrian. 1994. *Punish and Critique: Towards a Feminist Analysis of Penalty.* London: Routledge.

Hudson, Barbara. 1996. *Understanding Justice: An Introduction to Ideas, Perspectives and Controversies in Modern Penal Theory.* Buckingham, England: Open University Press.

Kleinig, John. 1973. *Punishment and Desert.* The Hague, Netherlands: Martinus Nijhoff.

Konigs, Peter. 2013. "The Expressivist Account of Punishment, Retribution, and the Emotions." *Ethical Theory and Moral Practice* 16(5): 1029–1047.

Kramer, Matthew H. 2011. *The Ethics of Capital Punishment: A Philosophical Investigation of Evil and Its Consequences.* Oxford, England: Oxford University Press.

Lipsey, Mark. W., Nana A. Landenberger, and Gabrielle L. Chapman. 2004. "Rehabilitation: An Assessment of Theory and Research." Pp. 211–227 in *The Blackwell Companion to Criminology,* edited by Colin Sumner. Oxford, England: Blackwell.

Lokanan, Mark. 2009. "An Open Model for Restorative Justice: Is There Room for Punishment?" *Contemporary Justice Review* 12(3): 289–307.

Martinson, Robert. 1974 "What Works? Questions and Answers About Prison Reform." *The Public Interest* 35: 22–54.

Matthews, Roger. 1989. "Alternatives to and in Prisons: A Realistic Approach." Pp. 128–150 in *Paying for Crime,* edited by Pat Carlen and D. Cook. Milton Keynes, England: Open University Press.

Morris, Herbert. 1994. "A Paternalistic Theory of Punishment." Pp. 92–111 in *A Reader on Punishment,* edited by Antony Duff and David Garland. Oxford, England: Oxford University Press.

Morris, Norval. 1974. *The Future of Imprisonment.* Chicago: University of Chicago Press.

Murphy, Jeffrie. G. 1994. "Marxism and Retribution." Pp. 44–70 in *A Reader on Punishment,* edited by Antony Duff and David Garland. Oxford, England: Oxford University Press.

Murphy, Jeffrie G. 2012. *Punishment and the Moral Emotions: Essays in Law, Morality and Religion.* Oxford, England: Oxford University Press.

Nadelhoffer, Thomas A. 2013. "Introduction." Pp: xv-xxiv in *The Future of Punishment,* edited by Thomas. A. Nadelhoffer. Oxford, England: Oxford University Press.

Nagin, Daniel. 1998. "Deterrence and Incapacitation." Pp. 345–368 in *The Handbook of Crime and Punishment,* edited by Michael Tonry. Oxford, England: Oxford University Press.

Nozick, Robert. 1981. *Philosophical Explanations.* Cambridge, MA: Harvard University Press.

Nygaard, Richard. 2000. *Sentencing as I See It.* Incline Village, NV: Copperhouse.

Reiman, Jeffrey. 1985. "Justice, Civilization, and the Death Penalty: Answering Van Den Haag." *Philosophy and Public Affairs* 14: 115–148.

Rotman, Edgardo. 1994. "Beyond Punishment." Pp. 281–305 in *A Reader on Punishment,* edited by Antony Duff and David Garland. Oxford, England: Oxford University Press.

Steffen, Lloyd. 2012. *Ethics and Experience: Moral Theory From Just War to Abortion.* Lanham, MD. Rowman & Littlefield.

Ten, C. L. 1987. *Crime, Guilt, and Punishment: A Philosophical Introduction.* Oxford, England: Clarendon Press.

Tonry, Michael. 1994. "Proportionality, Parsimony, and Interchangeability of Punishments." Pp. 133–160 in *A Reader on Punishment,* edited by Antony Duff and David Garland. Oxford, England: Oxford University Press.

Travis, Lawrence III. 2002. "Criminal Sentencing: Honesty, Prediction, Discrimination and Ethics." Pp. 175–187 in *Justice, Crime and Ethics* (4th ed.), edited by M. Braswell, B. R. McCarthy, and B. J. McCarthy. Cincinnati, OH: Anderson.

Tullock, Gordon. 1974. "Does Punishment Deter Crime?" *The Public Interest* 36: 103–111.

Van den Haag, Ernest. 1975. *Punishing Criminals: Concerning a Very Old and Painful Question.* New York: Basic Books.

Van Ness, Dan, and Karen Heetderks Strong. 1997. *Restoring Justice.* Cincinnati, OH: Anderson.

Vasiljevic, Milica, and Viki G. Tendayi. 2013. "Dehumanization, Moral Disengagement, and Public Attitudes to Crime and Punishment." Pp: 129–146 in *Humanness and Dehumanization,* edited by Paul G. Bain, Jeroen Vaes, and Jaques-Philippe Leyens. New York: Psychology Press.

Volpe, Maria R. 1991. "Mediation in the Criminal Justice System: Process, Promises, Problems." Pp. 194–206 in *Criminology as Peacemaking,* edited by H. E. Pepinsky and R. Quinney. Bloomington, IN: University Press.

von Hirsch, Andrew. 1994. "Censure and Proportionality." Pp. 112–132 in *A Reader on Punishment,* edited by Antony Duff and David Garland. Oxford, England: Oxford University Press.

von Hirsch, Andrew. 1998. "Penal Theories." Pp. 659–682 in *The Handbook of Crime and Punishment,* edited by Michael Tonry. New York: Oxford University Press.

von Hirsch, Andrew, and Committee for the Study of Incarceration. 1976. *Doing Justice: The Choice of Punishments.* New York: Hill and Wang.

Walker, Nigel. 1991. *Why Punish?* Oxford, England: Oxford University Press.

Wood, David. 2010a. "Punishment: Nonconsequentialism." *Philosophy Compass* 5(6): 470–482.

Wood, David. 2010b. "Punishment: Consequentialism." *Philosophy Compass* 5(6): 455–469.

Zimring, Franklin. 1976. "Punishing Homicide in Philadelphia: Perspectives on the Death Penalty." *University of Chicago Law Review* 43(2): 227–252.

Zimring, Franklin. 1994. "Making the Punishment Fit the Crime: A Consumer's Guide to Sentencing Reform." Pp. 161–173 in *A Reader on Punishment,* edited by Antony Duff and David Garland. Oxford, England: Oxford University Press.

Chapter 7

Adcox, Seanna. 2007. "S. C. Considers Cutting Prison Time for Inmates Who Donate Organs." *The State.* Retrieved March 13, 2007 (http://www.thestate.com/mld/thestate/news/local/16861780.htm).

Austin, James, and John Irwin. 2001. *It's About Time: America's Imprisonment Binge* (3rd ed.). Belmont, CA: Wadsworth.

Aviram, Hadar. 2015. *Cheap on Crime: Recession-Era Politics and the Transformation of American Punishment.* Oakland: University of California Press.

Beckett, Katherine, and Naomi Murakawa. 2010. "The Penology of Racial Innocence: The Erasure of Racism in the Study and Practice of Punishment." *Law and Society Review* 44(3/4): 695–730.

Brownlee, Kimberley. 2013. "A Human Right Against Social Deprivation." *Philosophical Quarterly* 63(251): 199–222.

Carson, E. Ann. 2014. *Prisoners in 2013.* Washington, DC: U.S. Department of Justice, Office of Justice Programs, Bureau of Justice Statistics.

Carson, Ann. September 2015. NCJ 248955. *Prisoners in 2014.* Washington, DC: Bureau of Justice Statistics, US Department of Justice.

Christie, Nils. 2000. *Crime Control as Industry: Towards Gulags, Western Style?* London: Routledge.

Clemmer, Donald. 1940. *The Prison Community.* New York: Rinehart.

Conover, Ted. 2001. *Newjack: Guarding Sing Sing.* New York: Vintage.

Crouch, Ben. 1980. "The Guard in a Changing Prison World." Pp. 5–48 in *The Keepers: Prison Guards and Contemporary Corrections,* edited by Ben Crouch. Springfield, IL: Charles C Thomas.

Crouch, Ben, and J. Marquart. 1980. "On Becoming a Prison Guard." Pp. 63–110 in *The Keepers: Prison Guards and Contemporary Corrections,* edited by Ben Crouch. Springfield, IL: Charles C Thomas.

DiIulio, John. 1990. "The Duty to Govern: A Critical Perspective on the Private Management of Prisons and Jails." Pp. 155–178 in *Private Prisons and the Public Interest,* edited by D. C. McDonald. New Brunswick, NJ: Rutgers University Press.

Drake, Deborah. 2011. "The 'Dangerous Other' in Maximum Security Prisons." *Criminology and Criminal Justice* 10(1): 1–16.

Gifford, Sidra Lee. 2002. *Justice Expenditure and Employment in the United States, 1999.* Bureau of Justice Statistics Bulletin NCJ 191746. Washington, DC: U.S. Department of Justice.

Glaser, Daniel, and Lincoln Fry. 1987. "Corruption of Prison Staff in Inmate Discipline." *Journal of Offender Counseling, Services and Rehabilitation* 12(1): 27–38.

Glaze, Lauren E., and Danielle Kaeble. 2014. *Correctional Populations in the United States, 2013.* Washington, DC: U.S. Department of Justice, Office of Justice Programs, Bureau of Justice Statistics.

Goffman, Erving. 1959. *Asylums: Essays on the Social Situation of Mental Patients and Other Inmates.* New York: Anchor Books.

Goffman, Erving. 1961. "On the Characteristics of Total Institutions: The Inmate World." Pp. 15–67 in *The Prison: Studies in Institutional Organization and Change,* edited by D. Cressey. New York: Holt, Rinehart, and Winston.

Gottschalk, Marie. 2015. *Caught: The Prison State and the Lockdown of American Politics.* Princeton, NJ: Princeton University Press.

Guenther, Lisa. 2013. *Solitary Confinement: Social Death and Its Afterlives.* Minneapolis: University of Minnesota Press.

Harding, Richard. 1998. "Private Prisons." Pp. 626–655 in *The Handbook of Crime and Punishment,* edited by Michael Tonry. New York: Oxford University Press.

Harrison, Paige, and Allen Beck. November 2006. *Prisoners in 2005.* Bureau of Justice Statistics Bulletin NCJ 215092. Washington, DC: U.S. Department of Justice.

Hepburn, James. 1985. "The Exercise of Power in Coercive Organizations: A Study of Prison Guards." *Criminology* 23(1): 145–164.

Hepburn, James. 1989. "Prison Guards as Agents of Social Control." Pp. 191–206 in *The American Prison: Issues in Research and Policy,* edited by Lynne Goodstein and Doris Layton MacKenzie. New York: Plenum Press.

Hoskins, Zachary. 2013. "Punishment, Contempt, and the Prospect of Moral Reform." *Criminal Justice Ethics* 32(1): 1–18.

Horwitz, Sari. 2015, May 28. "Justice Department acts to end sexual assault at women's prison in Alabama." *The*

Washington Post. https://www.washingtonpost .com/world/national-security/justice-department-acts-to-end-sexual-assault-at-womens-prison-in-alabama/ 2015/05/28/f72e1fcc-055c-11e5-8bda-c7b4e9a8f7ac_story. html.

In Re Medley (1890) 134 U.S. 160, 161.

Institute for Criminal Policy Research (ICPR). 2015. "World Prison Brief." Retrieved November 20, 2015 (http://www. prisonstudies.org/highest-to-lowest/prison-population-total?field_region_taxonomy_tid=All).

Jacobs, J. 1977. *Statesville: The Penitentiary in Mass Society.* Chicago: University of Chicago Press.

Jones 'El and Others v. Berge and Litscher, 164 F.2d 1096 (2001).

Kauffman, Kelsey. 1988. *Prison Officers and Their World.* Cambridge, MA: Harvard University Press.

King, Kate, Benjamin Steiner, and Stephanie Ritchie Breach. 2008. "Violence in the Supermax: A Self-Fulfilling Prophecy." *The Prison Journal* 88: 144–168.

Kleinig, John, and Kevin Murtagh. 2005. "Disenfranchising Felons." *Journal of Applied Philosophy* 22(3): 217–239.

Klofas, John. 1984. "Reconsidering Prison Personnel: New Views of the Correctional Officer Subculture." *International Journal of Offender Therapy and Comparative Criminology* 28(3): 169–175.

Light, S. C. 1991. "Assaults on Prison Officers: International Themes." Pp. 207–224 in *Prison Violence in America,* edited by M. Braswell, R. Montgomery Jr., and L. Lombardo. Cincinnati, OH: Anderson.

Lilly, J. Robert, and Paul Knepper. 1992. "An International Perspective on the Privatization of Corrections." *Howard Journal* 31: 174–191.

Lippke, Richard. 1997. "Thinking About Private Prisons." *Criminal Justice Ethics* 16(1): 26–38.

Logan, Charles. 1990. *Private Prisons: Cons and Pros.* New York: Oxford University Press.

Lombardo, Lucien. 1989. *Guards Imprisoned: Correctional Officers at Work* (2nd ed.). Cincinnati, OH: Anderson.

Madrid v. Gomez 150 F. 3d 1030.

Mauer, Mark. 2006. *Race to Incarcerate: The Sentencing Project.* New York: The New Press.

Minton, Todd D., and Zhen Zheng. 2015. "Jail Inmates at Midyear 2014." Washington, DC: U.S. Department of Justice, Office of Justice Programs, Bureau of Justice Statistics.

Nozick, Robert. 1974. *Anarchy, State, and Utopia.* New York: Basic Books.

Owen, Barbara. 1998. *"In the Mix": Struggle and Survival in a Women's Prison.* Albany: State University of New York Press.

Pew Center on the States. 2008. *One in 100: Behind Bars in America in 2008.* Washington, DC: Pew Charitable Trusts. Retrieved March 27, 2008 (http://www .pewcenteronthestates.org/uploadedFiles/8015PCTS_ Prison08_FINAL_2-1-1_FORWEB.pdf).

Pew Charitable Trusts. 2015, June 17. "Congress Hears From States on Improvements to Public Safety." http://www.

pewtrusts.org/en/research-and-analysis/analysis/ 2015/06/17/congress-hears-from-states-on-improvements-to-public-safety.

Pew Research Center. 2014, December 12. "Factank." http:// www.pewresearch.org/fact-tank/2014/12/12/racial-wealth-gaps-great-recession/.

Poole, Eric, and Robert Regoli. 1980. "Role Stress, Custody Orientation, and Disciplinary Actions: A Study of Prison Guards." *Criminology* 18(2): 215–226.

Porter, Nichole D. 2010. *Expanding the Vote: State Felony Disenfranchisement Reform, 1997–2010.* Washington, DC: The Sentencing Project.

Reisig, Michael, and Travis Pratt. 2000. "The Ethics of Correctional Privatization: A Critical Examination of the Delegation of Coercive Authority." *Prison Journal* 80(2): 210–222.

Schmitt, John, Kris Warner, and Sarika Gupta. June 2010. *The High Budgetary Cost of Incarceration.* Washington, DC: Center for Economic and Policy Research. http://www.cepr. net/documents/publications/incarceration-2010-06.pdf

Shichor, David. 1995. *Punishment for Profit: Private Prisons/ Public Concerns.* Thousand Oaks, CA: Sage.

Shalev, Sharon. 2009. *Supermax: Controlling Risk Through Solitary Confinement.* Devon, England: Willan.

Shalev, Sharon. 2011. "Solitary Confinement and Supermax Prisons: A Human Rights and Ethical Analysis." *Journal of Forensic Psychology Practice* 11: 151–183.

Simon, Jonathan. 2014. *Mass Incarceration on Trial: A Remarkable Court Decision and the Future of Prisons in America.* New York: The New Press.

Sundt, Jody L., Thomas C. Castellano, and Chad S. Briggs. 2008. "The Sociopolitical Context of Prison Violence and Its Control: A Case Study of Supermax and Its Effects in Illinois." *The Prison Journal* 88: 94–122.

Sykes, Gresham. 1999. *The Society of Captives: A Study of a Maximum Security Prison.* Princeton, NJ: Princeton University Press. (Original work published 1958)

The Sentencing Project. 2008. "Felony Disenfranchisement Laws in the United States." Retrieved April 10, 2008 (http://www .sentencingproject.org/Admin/Documents/publications/ fd_bs_fdlawsinus.pdf).

U.S. Department of Justice. 1998, November 25. "Report to the Attorney General Inspection and Review of the Ohio Correctional Center." [Letter to Janet Reno]. http://www. justice.gov/ag/report-attorney-general-inspection-and-review-northeast-ohio-correctional-center.

Webb, G. L., and D. Morris. 1980. "Prison Guard Conceptions." Pp. 150–161 in *The Keepers: Prison Guards and Contemporary Corrections,* edited by Ben Crouch. Springfield, IL: Charles C Thomas.

Weber, Max. 1964. *The Theory of Social and Economic Organization.* New York: Free Press.

Wheeler, Stanton. 1961. "Socialization in Correctional Communities." *American Sociological Association* 26: 697.

Chapter 8

Abadinsky, Howard. 1982. *Probation and Parole: Theory and Practice.* Chicago: Nelson-Hall.

American Correctional Association. 1990. "American Correctional Association Code of Ethics." Retrieved April 3, 2008 (http://www.aca.org/pastpresentfuture/ethics.asp).

American Probation and Parole Association. n.d. "Code of Ethics." Retrieved August 30, 2003 (http://www.appa-net.org/about%20appa/codeof.htm).

Apuzzo, Matt. 2015, April 3. "Transgender Inmate's Hormone Treatment Lawsuit Gets Justice Dept. Backing." *The New York Times.*

BBC News. 2010, January 12. "Italy 'to Open First Prison for Transgender Inmates.'" Retrieved November 5, 2011 (http://news.bbc.co.uk/2/hi/8455191.stm).

Banks, Cyndi, Paul Rector, and Mary Jackson. 2005. *Coconino County Juvenile Court Probation Officer Attitudes Toward Safety and Carrying Weapons Study.* Unpublished Report Prepared for Coconino County Juvenile Court. Flagstaff, Arizona.

Beck, Allen, Marcus Berzofsky, and Christopher Krebs. 2013. "Sexual Victimization in Prisons and Jails Reported by Inmates, 2011–2012." NCJ 241399. Washington, DC: Bureau of Justice Statistics.

Berger, Joseph. 1994. "10 Jail Guards Are Charged in Smuggling." *The New York Times,* April 21, B1.

Brookes, Derek. 2001. "The Possibility of a Correctional Ethic." Pp. 39–68 in *Discretion, Community, and Correctional Ethics,* edited by John Kleinig and Margaret Leland Smith. Lanham, MD: Rowman & Littlefield.

Carroll, Leo. 1998. *Lawful Order: A Case Study of Correctional Crisis and Reform.* New York: Garland.

Champion, Dean. 1996. *Probation, Parole and Community Corrections* (2nd ed.). Upper Saddle River, NJ: Prentice-Hall.

Clark v. Evans, 840 F.2d 876 11th Cir. (1988).

Conover, Ted. 2001. *Newjack: Guarding Sing Sing.* New York: Vintage.

Conrad, John P. 1973. "Corrections and Simple Justice." *Journal of Criminal Law and Criminology* 64: 208–217.

Conrad, John P. 1982. "Can Corrections Be Rehabilitated?" *Federal Probation* 46 (2): 3–8.

Crouch, Ben. 1980. "The Guard in a Changing Prison World." Pp. 5–48 in *The Keepers: Prison Guards and Contemporary Corrections,* edited by Ben Crouch. Springfield, IL: Charles C Thomas.

Crouch, Ben, and J. Marquart. 1980. "On Becoming a Prison Guard." Pp. 63–110 in *The Keepers: Prison Guards and Contemporary Corrections,* edited by Ben Crouch. Springfield, IL: Charles C Thomas.

Deering, John, and Martina Feilzer. 2015, July 7. "Probation Officers Feel Betrayed by 'Shambolic' Part- Privatization." *The Guardian.* http://www.theguardian.com/public-leaders-network/2015/jul/07/probation-officers-betrayed-part-privatisation-service.

del Carmen, Rolando, Maldine Beyh Barnhill, Gene Bonham, Lance Hignite, and Todd Jermstad. 2001. *Civil Liabilities and Other Legal Issues for Probation/Parole Officers and Supervisors* (3rd ed.). Washington, DC: U.S. Department of Justice.

Dolovich, Sharon. 2012. "Creating the Permanent Prisoner." Pp: 96–137 95 in *Life Without Parole: America's New Death Penalty?,* edited by Charles J. Ogletree Jr. and Austin Sarat. New York: University Press.

Domurad, Frank. 2000. "Who Is Killing Our Probation Officers? The Performance Crisis in Community Corrections." *Corrections Management Quarterly* 4(2): 41–51.

Dreyer v. Jalet, 349 F. Supp, 452 S.D. Texas (1972).

"Ex–S.C. Correctional Officer Sentenced." 2001. Retrieved May 7, 2003 (http://database.corrections.com/news/results2.asp?ID?1503).

Farmer v. Brennan, 511 U.S. 825 (1994).

Gilbert, Michael. 1999. "The Illusion of Structure." Pp. 263–277 in *The Administration and Management of Criminal Justice Organizations: A Book of Readings,* edited by Stan Stojkovic, John Klofas, and David Kalinich. Prospect Heights, IL: Waveland Press.

Glaze, Lauren. August 2006. *Probation and Parole in the United States, 2005.* Bureau of Justice Statistics Bulletin NCJ 215091. Washington, DC: U.S. Department of Justice.

Glaze, Lauren E., and Danielle Kaeble. 2014. *Correctional Populations in the United States, 2013.* Washington, DC: U.S. Department of Justice, Office of Justice Programs, Bureau of Justice Statistics.

Gottschalk, Marie. 2015. *Caught: The Prison State and the Lockdown of American Politics.* Princeton, NJ: Princeton University Press.

Graham v. Florida. 560 U.S. 48 (2010).

Hamm, Mark. 1995. "Whistleblowing in Corrections." Pp. 202–209 in *Morality in Criminal Justice: An Introduction to Ethics,* edited by Daryl Close and Nicholas Meier. Belmont, CA: Wadsworth.

Hensley, Christopher, Mary Koscheski, and Richard Tewksbury. 2003. "The Impact of Institutional Factors on Officially Reported Sexual Assaults in Prisons." *Sexuality & Culture* 7(4): 16–26.

Hensley, Christopher, and Richard Tewksbury. 2005. "Wardens' Perceptions of Prison Sex." *The Prison Journal* 85(2): 186–197.

Henriques, Z. W. 2001. "The Path of Least Resistance: Sexual Exploitation of Female Offenders as an Unethical Corollary to Retributive Ideology and Correctional Practice." Pp. 193–201 in *Discretion, Community, and Correctional Ethics,* edited by John Kleinig and Margaret Leland Smith. Lanham, MD: Rowman & Littlefield.

Henry, Jessica S. 2012. "Death-in-Prison Sentences: Overutilized and Underscrutinized." Pp: 68–95 in *Life Without Parole: America's New Death Penalty?,* edited by Charles J. Ogletree Jr. and Austin Sarat. New York: University Press.

Hepburn, James. 1989. "Prison Guards as Agents of Social Control." Pp. 191–206 in *The American Prison: Issues in Research and Policy,* edited by Lynne Goodstein and Doris Layton MacKenzie. New York: Plenum Press.

Herberman, Erinn J., and Thomas P. Bonczar. 2014. *Probation and Parole in the United States, 2013*. Washington, DC: Department of Justice, Office of Justice Programs, Bureau of Justice Statistics.

Hudson v. McMillian, 503 U.S. 1 (1992).

Human Rights Watch. 2001. *No Escape: Male Rape in U.S. Prisons*. New York: Human Rights Watch.

In re Jaime P., 40 Cal, 4th 128, 146 P.3d 965 (2006).

In re Tyrell, 876 P.2d 445 (Cal. 1998).

Jones, James, and Daniel Carlson. 2001. *Reputable Conduct: Ethical Issues in Policing and Corrections*. Upper Saddle River, NJ: Prentice-Hall.

Kauffman, Kelsey. 1988. *Prison Officers and Their World*. Cambridge, MA: Harvard University Press.

Kenny v. Indiana Youth Center, 950 F.2d 462 (1991).

Kleinig, John. 2001. "Professionalizing Incarceration." Pp. 1–15 in *Discretion, Community, and Correctional Ethics*, edited by John Kleinig and Margaret Leland Smith. Lanham, MD: Rowman & Littlefield.

Lippke, Richard. 2007. *Rethinking Imprisonment*. Oxford, England: Oxford University Press.

Lombardo, Lucien. 1989. *Guards Imprisoned: Correctional Officers at Work* (2nd ed.). Cincinnati, OH: Anderson.

Mair, Julie Samia, Shannon Frattaroli, and Stephen Teret. 2003. "New Hope for Victims of Sexual Assault." *Journal of Law: Medicine & Ethics* 31: 602–606.

Mann, Rebecca. 2006. "The Treatment of Transgender Prisoners, Not Just an American Problem: A Comparative Analysis of American, Australian, and Canadian Prison Policies Concerning the Treatment of Transgender Prisoners and a 'Universal' Recommendation to Improve Treatment." *Law and Sexuality* 19: 92–116.

Marquart, James. 1986. "Prison Guards and the Use of Physical Coercion as a Mechanism of Prisoner Control." *Criminology* 24(2): 347–366.

May, Edgar. 1980. "Prison Guards in America—The Inside Story." Pp. 138–149 in *The Keepers: Prison Guards and Contemporary Corrections*, edited by Ben Crouch. Springfield, IL: Charles C Thomas.

McCarthy, Bernard. 1995. "Patterns of Prison Corruption." Pp. 280–285 in *Morality in Criminal Justice: An Introduction to Ethics*, edited by Daryl Close and Nicholas Meier. Belmont, CA: Wadsworth

McCarthy, Bernard. 2002. "Keeping an Eye on the Keeper: Prison Corruption and Its Control." Pp. 253–266 in *Justice, Crime and Ethics* (4th ed.), edited by M. Braswell, B. R. McCarthy, and B. J. McCarthy. Cincinnati, OH: Anderson.

McCullough v. Cady, 640 F. Supp. 1012, E.D. Mich. (1986).

Ministry of Justice. 2011, March 2. *The Care and Management of Transsexual Prisoners* (PSI2011-007). London: National Offender Management Service.

Nader, Christine. 2010. "Correctional Facilities." *The Georgetown Journal of Gender and the Law* 11(1): 77–95

National Center for Lesbian Rights. June 2006. "Rights of Transgender Prisoners." Retrieved August 11, 2011 (www.nclrights.org).

National Institute of Justice. 2006. "NIJ's Response to the Prison Rape Elimination Act." *Corrections Today* 68(1): 60–61.

O'Connor, Anahad. 2010, October 8. "Guard Held in Sexual Attack on Transgender Inmate." *The New York Times,* A24.

Petersilia, Joan. 1999. "Parole and Prisoner Reentry in the United States." Pp. 479–529 in *Prisons*, edited by Michael Tonry and Joan Petersilia. Chicago: University of Chicago Press.

Rosecrance, John. 1986. "Probation Supervision: Mission Impossible." *Federal Probation* 50(1): 25–31.

Rudovsky, D., A. Bronstein, E. Koren, and J. Cade. 1988. *The Rights of Prisoners*. Carbondale: Southern Illinois University Press.

Seville, Lisa Riordan. 2015, June 18. "City Dumps Private Probation Firm Amid Claims It Extorts Poor." *NBC News*. http://www.nbcnews.com/news/us-news/city-dumps-private-probation-firm-amid-claims-it-extorts-poor-n377846.

Shah, Benish. 2010. "Lost in the Gender Maze: Placement of Transgender Inmates in the Prison System." *Journal of Race, Gender and Ethnicity* 5(1): 39–56.

Silverman, Mitchell. 1993. "Ethical Issues in the Field of Probation." *International Journal of Offender Therapy and Comparative Criminology* 37(1): 85–94.

Small, Shawn, and Sam Torres. 2001. "Arming Probation Officers: Enhancing Public Confidence and Officer Safety." *Federal Probation* 65(3): 24–28.

Smith, Margaret Leland. 2001. "The Shimmer of Reform: Prospects for a Correctional Ethic." Pp. 17–37 in *Discretion, Community, and Correctional Ethics*, edited by John Kleinig and Margaret Leland Smith. Lanham, MD: Rowman & Littlefield.

Stop Prisoner Rape. 2006. *In the Shadows: Sexual Violence in U.S. Detention Facilities, A Shadow Report to the U.N. Committee Against Torture*. Los Angeles: Author. Retrieved March 22, 2007 (http://www.spr.org/pdf/in_the_shadows.pdf).

Stop Prisoner Rape. 2007. *Stories From Inside: Prisoner Rape and the War on Drugs*. Los Angeles: Author. Retrieved March 23, 2007 (http://www.spr.org).

Studt, Eliot. 1973. *Surveillance and Service in Parole: A Report of the Parole Action Study*. Washington, DC: National Institute of Corrections.

Tarzwell, Sydney. 2006. "The Gender Lines Are Marked With Razor Wire: Addressing State Prison Policies and Practices for the Management of Transgender Prisoners." *Columbia Human Rights Law Review* 38: 167–219.

Teague, Michael. 2011. "Probation in America: Armed, Private and Unaffordable?" *Probation Journal* 58(4): 317–332.

U.S. v. Nix, 501 F.2d 516 7th Cir. (1974).

U.S. Department of Justice. May 2014. *PREA Data Collection Activities, 2014*. Washington, DC: U.S. Department of Justice, Office of Justice Programs, Bureau of Justice Statistics.

U.S. Department of Justice. 2014, August 4. [Letter to Bill de Blasio, Joseph Ponte, and Zachary Carter.] "CRIPA Investigation of the New York City Department of Correction Jails on Rikers Island." U.S. Attorney, New York.

http://www.justice.gov/sites/default/files/usao-sdny/legacy/2015/03/25/SDNY%20Rikers%20Report.pdf.

U.S. Department of Justice. June 2015. *PREA Data Collection Activities, 2015.* Washington, DC: U.S. Department of Justice, Office of Justice Programs, Bureau of Justice Statistics.

Vargas, Theresa, Ann E. Marimow, and Annys Shin. 2013, May 4. 2013, May 4. "Baltimore Jail Case Depicts a Corrupt Culture Driven by Drugs, Money and Sex." *The Washington Post.*

Vaughn, Michael S. 1996. "Prison Civil Liability for Inmate-Against-Inmate Assault and Breakdown/Disorganization Theory." *Journal of Criminal Justice* 24(2): 139–152.

Walker, Jaffrey. 1996. "Police and Correctional Use of Force: Legal and Policy Standards and Implications." *Crime and Delinquency* 42(1): 144–156.

Webb, G. L., and D. Morris. 1980. "Prison Guard Conceptions." Pp. 150–161 in *The Keepers: Prison Guards and Contemporary Corrections,* edited by Ben Crouch. Springfield, IL: Charles C Thomas.

Wheeler, Stanton. 1961. "Socialization in Correctional Communities." *American Sociological Association*

Whitley v. Albers, 475 U.S. 312 (1986).

Winerip, Michael, and Michael Schwirtz. 2015, January 13. "Rikers to Ban Isolation for Inmates 21 and Younger." *The New York Times.*

Worley, Robert, James Marquart, and Janet Mullings. 2003. "Prison Guard Predators: An Analysis of Inmates Who Established Inappropriate Relations With Prison Staff, 1995–1998." *Deviant Behavior: An Interdisciplinary Journal* 24: 175–194.

Wyatt, Rachel. 2006. "Male Rape in U.S. Prisons: Are Conjugal Visits the Answer?" *Case Western Reserve Journal of International Law* 37: 579–614.

Chapter 9

Alexander, Michelle. 2010. *The New Jim Crow: Mass Incarceration in the Age of Colorblindness.* New York: The New Press.

American Civil Liberties Union (ACLU). 2011. *Smart Reform Is Possible: States Reducing Incarceration Rates and Costs While Protecting Communities.* New York: Author. Retrieved August 13, 2011 (http://www.aclu.org/files/assets/smartreformispossible.pdf).

Amnesty International. March 2014. "Retentionist and Abolitionist Countries on the Death Penalty in 2013." *Death Sentences and Executions, 2013.* London: Author.

Amy, Douglas. 1987. "Can Policy Analysis Be Ethical?" Pp. 45–69 in *Confronting Values in Policy Analysis: The Politics of Criteria,* edited by Frank Fischer and John Forester. Newbury Park, CA: Sage.

Anderson, Charles. 1987. "Political Philosophy, Practical Reason, and Policy Analysis." Pp. 22–44 in *Confronting Values in Policy Analysis: The Politics of Criteria,* edited by Frank Fischer and John Forester. Newbury Park, CA: Sage.

Austin, James, and John Irwin. 2001. *It's About Time: America's Imprisonment Binge* (3rd ed.). Belmont, CA: Wadsworth.

Aviram, Hadar. 2015. *Cheap on Crime: Recession-Era Politics and the Transformation of American Punishment.* Oakland: University of California Press.

Banks, Cyndi. 2005. *Punishment in America: A Reference Handbook.* Santa Barbara, CA: ABC-Clio.

Baron, Jonathan. 1998. *Judgment Misguided: Intuition and Error in Public Decision Making.* New York: Oxford University Press.

Beckett, Katherine. 1997. *Making Crime Pay: Law and Order in Contemporary American Politics.* New York: Oxford University Press.

Bedau, Hugo A. 1996. "The United States of America." Pp. 45–76 in *Capital Punishment: Global Issues and Prospects,* edited by Peter Hodgkinson and Andrew Rutherford. Winchester, England: Waterside Press.

Bedau, Hugo A. 1997. "A Reply to Van Den Haag." Pp. 457–469 in *The Death Penalty in America: Current Controversies,* edited by Hugo Adam Bedau. New York: Oxford University Press.

Bedau, Hugo. A. 1999. "Abolishing the Death Penalty Even for the Worst Murderers." Pp. 40–59 in *The Killing State: Capital Punishment in Law, Politics, and Culture,* edited by Austin Sarat. Oxford, England: Oxford University Press.

Bennett, William, John Dilulio, and John Walters. 1999. *Body Count: Moral Poverty . . . and How to Win America's War Against Crime and Drugs.* New York: Simon & Schuster.

Bibas, Stephanos. 2004. "The Feeney Amendment and the Continuing Rise of Prosecutorial Power to Plea Bargain." *Journal of Criminal Law and Criminology* 94(2): 295–308.

Brownstein, Henry. 2000. *The Social Reality of Violence and Violent Crime.* Boston: Allyn & Bacon.

Bush-Baskette, Stephanie. 1999. "The 'War on Drugs': A War Against Women." Pp. 211–229 in *Harsh Punishment: International Experiences of Women's Imprisonment,* edited by Sandy Cook and Susanne Davies. Boston: Northeastern University Press.

Carson, E. Ann. 2014. *Prisoners in 2013.* Washington, DC: U.S. Department of Justice, Office of Justice Programs, Bureau of Justice Statistics.

Carson, Ann. September 2015. NCJ 248955. *Prisoners in 2014.* Washington, DC: Bureau of Justice Statistics, US Department of Justice.

Cathcart, Rebecca. 2010, August 16. "Judge Order Man Freed in a Three-Strikes Case." *The New York Times,* A18. Retrieved August 10, 2011 (http://www.nytimes.com/2010/08/17/us/17strikes.html).

Clear, Todd R., and Natasha A. Frost. 2014. *The Punishment Imperative: The Rise and Failure of Mass Incarceration in America.* New York: New York University Press.

Cohen, Stanley. 1972. *Folk Devils and Moral Panics: The Creation of the Mods and Rockers.* London: MacGibbon & Kee.

Cohen, Stanley. 2011. "Whose Side Were We On? The Undeclared Politics of Moral Panic Theory." *Crime, Media, Culture* 7(3): 237–243.

Cohen, Stanley, and Jock Young. 1973. *The Manufacture of News: Social Problems, Deviance and the Mass Media.* London: Constable.

Cook, Philip, and John Laub. 1998. "The Unprecedented Epidemic in Youth Violence." Pp. 27–64 in *Youth Violence: Vol. 24*, edited by Michael Tonry and Mark Moore. Chicago: University of Chicago Press.

Cullen, Francis, Bonnie Fisher, and Brandon Applegate. 2000. "Public Opinion About Punishment and Corrections." Pp. 1–79 in *Crime and Justice: A Review of Research*, edited by Michael Tonry. Chicago: University of Chicago Press.

Culver, John. 1999. "Capital Punishment Politics and Policies in the States, 1977–1997." *Crime, Law & Social Change* 32: 287–300.

Dart, Tom. 2014, August 2. "Arizona Inmate Joseph Wood Was Injected 15 Times With Execution Drugs." *The Guardian*.

Davey, Monica, and Abby Goodnough. 2007, March 4. "Doubts Rise as States Detain Sex Offenders After Prison." *The New York Times*. Retrieved March 4, 2007 (http://www.nytimes.com/2007/03/04/us/04civil.html?ei=5088&en=4b5d93af1ae8077f&ex=1330664400&partner=&pagewanted=print).

FCC News. 2015, October 22. "FCC Takes Next Big Steps in Reducing Inmate Calling Rates." Federal Communications Commission. http://apps.fcc.gov/edocs_public/attachmatch/00c-335984A1.pdf.

Feeley, Malcolm, and Jonathan Simon. 1992. "The New Penology: Notes on the Emerging Strategy of Corrections and Its Implications." *Criminology* 30: 449–474.

Finkelstein, Katherine E. 2000, June 23. "New York to Offer Most Addicts Treatment Instead of Jail Terms." *The New York Times*. Retrieved November 11, 2011 (http://www.nytimes.com/2000/06/23/nyregion/new-york-to-offer-most-addicts-treatment-instead-of-jail-terms.html?pagewanted=all&src=pm).

Finn, Peter. 1996. "No-Frills Prisons and Jails: A Movement in Flux." *Federal Probation* 60: 35–44.

Fischer, Frank, and John Forester (Eds.). 1987. *Confronting Values in Policy Analysis: The Politics of Criteria*. Newbury Park, CA: Sage.

Furman v. Georgia, 408 U.S. 238 (1972).

Gaines, Larry, and Peter Kraska (Eds.). 1997. *Drugs, Crime, and Justice*. Prospect Heights, IL: Waveland Press.

Gall v. United States, 200 U.S. 321 (2007).

Gambino, Lauren. 2015, March 11. *The Guardian*. http://www.theguardian.com/world/2015/mar/11/utah-passes-firing-squad-bill.

Garland, David (Ed.). 2001. *Mass Imprisonment: Social Causes and Consequences*. London: Sage.

Gee, Harvey. 2011. "Eighth Amendment Challenges After *Baze v. Rees*: Lethal Injections, Civil Rights Lawsuits and the Death Penalty." *Boston College Third World Law Journal* 31(2): 217–244.

Geis, Gilbert. 1996. "A Base on Balls for White-Collar Criminals." Pp. 244–264 in *Three Strikes and You're Out: Vengeance as Public Policy*, edited by David Shichor and Dale Sechrest. Thousand Oaks, CA: Sage.

Glassner, Barry. 1999. *The Culture of Fear: Why Americans Are Afraid of the Wrong Things*. New York: Basic Books.

Glaze, Lauren E., and Danielle Kaeble. 2014. *Correctional Populations in the United States, 2013*. Washington, DC: U.S. Department of Justice, Office of Justice Programs, Bureau of Justice Statistics.

Glick, Henry, and Amy Hutchinson. 2001. "Physician-Assisted Suicide: Agenda Setting and the Elements of Morality Policy." Pp. 55–70 in *The Public Clash of Private Values: The Politics of Morality Policy*, edited by Christopher Mooney. New York: Chatham House.

Goggin, Malcolm, and Christopher Mooney. 2001. "Congressional Use of Policy Information on Fact and Value Issues." Pp. 130–139 in *The Public Clash of Private Values: The Politics of Morality Policy*, edited by Christopher Mooney. New York: Chatham House.

Goode, Erica. 2011, May 20. "States Seeking New Registries for Criminals." *The New York Times*, A1. Retrieved August 10, 2011 (http://www.nytimes.com/2011/05/21/us/21registry.html?_r=2).

Goode, Erich, and Nachman Ben-Yehuda. 1994. *Moral Panics: The Social Construction of Deviance*. Oxford, England: Blackwell.

Gottschalk, Marie. 2015. *Caught: The Prison State and the Lockdown of American Politics*. Princeton, NJ: Princeton University Press.

Gregg v. Georgia, 428 U.S. 153, 184 (1976).

Grubesic Tony, and Alan Murray. 2010. "Methods to Support Policy Evaluation of Sex Offender Laws." *Papers in Regional Science* 89(3): 669–684.

Haines, Herbert. 1996. *Against Capital Punishment: The Anti–Death Penalty Movement in America, 1972–1994*. New York: Oxford University Press.

Hall, Stuart, Charles Critcher, Tony Jefferson, John Clarke, and Brian Roberts. 1978. *Policing the Crisis: Mugging, the State, and Law and Order*. New York: Holmes & Meier.

Heineman, Robert, William Bluhm, Steven Peterson, and Edward Kearny. 1997. *The World of the Policy Analyst*. Chatham, NJ: Chatham House.

Henrichson, Christian, and Ruth Delaney. 2012, February 29. "The Price of Prisons: What Incarceration Costs Taxpayers." *Vera Institute of Justice*. http://www.vera.org/pubs/special/price-prisons-what-incarceration-costs-taxpayers.

Henry, Stuart, and Dragan Milovanovic. 1996. *Constitutive Criminology: Beyond Postmodernism*. Thousand Oaks, CA: Sage.

Hood, Roger. 2001. "Capital Punishment: A Global Perspective." *Punishment & Society* 3(3): 331–354.

Howe, Amy. 2015, April 30. "Justices Debate Lethal Injection and the Death Penalty: In Plain English." *SCOTUSblog*. http://www.scotusblog.com/2015/04/justices-debate-lethal-injection-and-the-death-penalty-in-plain-english.

James, A. 2001. "Capital Punishment: The Execution of Child Offenders in the United States." *Kluwer Law International* 9: 181–189.

Jenkins, Philip. 1998. *Moral Panic: Changing Concepts of the Child Molester in Modern America*. New Haven, CT: Yale University Press.

Kimbrough v. United States, U.S.—, 128 S. Ct. 558 (2007).

Lenz, Nygel. 2002. "'Luxuries' in Prison: The Relationship Between Amenity Funding and Public Support." *Crime & Delinquency* 48(4): 499–525.

Liptak, Adam. 2011, May 24. "Justices, 5–4, Tell California to Cut Prisoner Population." *The New York Times*, A1. Retrieved August 12, 2011 (http://www.nytimes.com/2011/05/24/us/24scotus.html?pagewanted=1).

Lynch, Mona. 2002. "Pedophiles and Cyber-Predators as Contaminating Forces: The Language of Disgust, Pollution, and Boundary Invasions in Federal Debates on Sex Offender Legislation." *Law & Social Inquiry* 27: 529–566.

Lyons, Donna. 2006. "Where on Earth Are Sex Offenders?" *State Legislatures* 32(3): 14–15.

Maynard-Moody, Steven, and Donald Stull. 1987. "The Symbolic Side of Policy Analysis: Interpreting Policy Change in a Health Department." Pp. 248–265 in *Confronting Values in Policy Analysis: The Politics of Criteria*, edited by Frank Fischer and John Forester. Newbury Park, CA: Sage.

Meehan, Eugene. 1990. *Ethics for Policymaking: A Methodological Analysis*. New York: Greenwood Press.

Mikkelsen, Randall. 2007, December 10. "Supreme Court Allows Lighter Crack Cocaine Terms." *Reuters*. Retrieved April 9, 2008 (http://www.reuters.com/article/domesticNews/idUSN1119916620071210).

Mooney, Christopher. 2001. "Introduction—The Public Clash of Private Values: The Politics of Morality Policy." Pp. 3–18 in *The Public Clash of Private Values: The Politics of Morality Policy*, edited by Christopher Mooney. New York: Chatham House.

Moore, Mark, and Michael Tonry. 1998. "Youth Violence in America." Pp. 1–26 in *Youth Violence: Vol. 24*, edited by Michael Tonry. Chicago: University of Chicago Press.

Moore, Nina M. 2015. *The Political Roots of Racial Tracking in American Criminal Justice*. New York: Cambridge University Press.

Oliver, Kelly. 2015. "Making Death a Penalty: Or, Making 'Good' Death a 'Good' Penalty." Pp. 83–94 in *Death and Other Penalties: Philosophy in a Time of Mass Incarceration*, edited by Geoffrey Adelsberg, Lisa Guenther, and Scott Zeman. New York: Fordham University Press.

Petersilia, Joan. 1999. "Parole and Prisoner Reentry in the United States." Pp. 479–529 in *Prisons*, edited by Michael Tonry and Joan Petersilia. Chicago: University of Chicago Press.

Pratt, John. 2001. "Beyond Gulags Western Style? A Reconsideration of Nils Christie's Crime Control as Industry." *Theoretical Criminology* 5(3): 283–314.

Ramirez, Mark D. 2013. "Americans' Changing Views on Crime and Punishment." *Public Opinion Quarterly* 77(4): 1006–1031.

Ramirez, M. D. 2014. "Race and Punishment: Racial Perceptions of Crime and Support for Punitive Policies." *The Sentencing Project*. Washington, DC: Sentencing Project Research and Advocacy Reform.

Reamer, Frederic. 1986. "Principles of Ethics and the Justification of Policy." Pp. 223–245 in *Policy Analysis: Perspectives, Concepts, and Methods*, edited by William Dunn. Greenwich, CT: Jai Press.

Roberts, Julian, V. 2014. "Clarifying the Significance of Public Opinion for Sentencing Policy and Practice." Pp. 228–252 in *Popular Punishment: On the Normative Significance of Public Opinion*, edited by Jesper Ryberg and Julian. V. Roberts. Oxford, England: Oxford University Press.

Robinson, Matthew. 2002. *Justice Blind? Ideals and Realities of American Criminal Justice*. Upper Saddle River, NJ: Prentice-Hall.

Roper v. Simmons, 543 U.S. 551 (2005).

Russell-Brown, Katheryn. 1998. *The Color of Crime: Racial Hoaxes, White Fear, Black Protectionism, Police Harassment, and Other Macroaggressions*. New York: New York University Press.

Sarat, Austin. 1999. "Capital Punishment as a Legal, Political, and Cultural Fact: An Introduction." Pp. 3–23 in *The Killing State: Capital Punishment in Law, Politics, and Culture*, edited by Austin Sarat. New York: Oxford University Press.

Sarat, Austin. 2005. "Innocence, Error, and the 'New Abolitionism': A Commentary." *Criminology & Public Policy* 4(1): 45–54.

Scheingold, Stuart. 1984. *The Politics of Law and Order*. New York: Longman.

Shichor, David. 1999. "Three Strikes as a Public Policy: The Convergence of the New Penology and the McDonaldization of Punishment." Pp. 421–441 in *The Administration and Management of Criminal Justice Organizations: A Book of Readings*, edited by Stan Stojkovic, John Klofas, and David Kalinich. Prospect Heights, IL: Waveland Press.

Shichor, David. 2000. "Penal Policies at the Threshold of the Twenty-First Century." *Criminal Justice Review* 25(1): 1–30.

Simon, Jonathan. 2000. "Symposium Introduction: Law, Democracy, and Society—Megan's Law: Crime and Democracy in Late Modern America." *Law & Social Inquiry* 25: 1111–1150.

Simon, Jonathan. 2007. *Governing Through Crime: How the War on Crime Transformed American Democracy and Created a Culture of Fear*. New York: Oxford University Press.

Simon, Jonathan, and Christina Spaulding. 1999. "Tokens of Our Esteem: Aggravating Factors in the Era of Deregulated Death Penalties." Pp. 81–116 in *The Killing State: Capital Punishment in Law, Politics, and Culture*, edited by Austin Sarat. New York: Oxford University Press.

Spohn, Cassia. 2002. *How Do Judges Decide? The Search for Fairness and Justice in Punishment*. Thousand Oaks, CA: Sage.

Stanford v. Kentucky, 492 U.S. 361 (1989).

Studlar, Dunley. 2001. "What Constitutes Morality Policy? A Cross-National Analysis." Pp. 38–51 in *The Public Clash of Private Values: The Politics of Morality Policy*, edited by Christopher Mooney. New York: Chatham House.

Tong, Rosemarie. 1986. *Ethics in Policy Analysis*. Englewood Cliffs, NJ: Prentice-Hall.

Tonry, Michael. 2001. "Unthought Thoughts: The Influence of Changing Sensibilities on Penal Policies." *Punishment & Society* 3(1): 167–181.

Tonry, Michael. 2006. "Criminology, Mandatory Minimums, and Public Policy." *Criminology & Public Policy* 5(1): 45–56.

Tonry, Michael. 2010. "The Social, Psychological and Political Causes of Racial Disparities in the American Criminal Justice System." *Crime and Justice* 39(1): 273–312.

Tonry, Michael. 2011. *Punishing Race: A Continuing American Dilemma.* Oxford, England: Oxford University Press.

United States. v. Quinones, 205 F. Supp.2d 256 (S.D.N.Y. 2002).

van den Haag, Ernest. 1985. "The Death Penalty Once More." *U. C. Davis Law Review* 18(4): 957–972.

Vergari, Sheila. 2001. "Morality Politics and the Implementation of Abstinence-Only Sex Education: A Case of Policy Compromise." Pp. 201–210 in *The Public Clash of Private Values: The Politics of Morality Policy,* edited by Christopher Mooney. New York: Chatham House.

Walker, Samuel, Cassia Spohn, and Miriam DeLone. 2000. *The Color of Justice: Race, Ethnicity and Crime in America.* Belmont, CA: Wadsworth.

Walmsley, Roy. 2013. *World Prison Population List* (10th ed.). http://images.derstandard.at/2013/11/21/prison-population.pdf.

Williams, Timothy. 2015, March 30. "Steep Costs of Inmate Phone Calls Are Under Scrutiny." *The New York Times.* http://www.nytimes.com/2015/03/31/us/steep-costs-of-inmate-phone-calls-are-under-scrutiny.html.

Willis, Gwenda M., Jill S. Levenson, and Tony Ward. 2010. "Desistance and Attitudes Towards Sex Offenders: Facilitation or Hindrance?" *Journal of Family Violence* 25: 545–556.

Zimring, Franklin. 2003. *The Contradictions of American Capital Punishment.* New York: Oxford University Press.

Zimring, Franklin, Gordon Hawkins, and Sam Kamin. 2001. *Punishment and Democracy: Three Strikes and You're Out in California.* New York: Oxford University Press.

Chapter 10

Ackerman, Bruce. 2004. "This Is Not a War." *Yale Law Journal* 113: 1871–1908.

Banks, Cyndi. 2004. *Criminal Justice Ethics: Theory and Practice.* Thousand Oaks, CA: Sage.

Bellamy, Alex J. 2009. "Torture, Terrorism and the Moral Prohibition on Killing Non-Combatants." Pp. 18–43 in *Terrorism and Torture: An Interdisciplinary Perspective.* New York: Cambridge University Press.

Blank, Laurie R. 2015. "Targeted Killing." Pp. 227–244 in *The Ashgate Research Companion to Military Ethics,* edited by James Turner Johnson and Eric D. Patterson. Burlington, VT: Ashgate.

Blum, Gabriella, and Philip B. Heymann. 2010. *Laws, Outlaws and Terrorists: Lessons from the War on Terrorism.* Cambridge, MA: MIT Press.

Brecher, Bob. 2007. *Torture and the Ticking Bomb.* Malden, MA: Blackwell.

Brunstetter, Daniel, and Megan Braun. 2011. "The Implications of Drones on the Just War Tradition." *Ethics and International Affairs* 25(3): 337–358.

Card, Claudia. 2010. *Confronting Evils: Terrorism, Torture, Genocide.* New York. Cambridge University Press.

Cohen, Stanley. 2014. "Neither Honesty Nor Hypocrisy: The Legal Reconstruction of Torture." Pp. 267–288 in *The Criminology of War,* edited by Ruth Jamieson. Farnham, England: Ashgate.

Cook, James L. 2015. "The Ethics of Autonomous Unmanned Aerial Vehicles." Pp. 213–226 in *The Ashgate Research Companion to Military Ethics,* edited by James Turner Johnson and Eric D. Patterson. Burlington, VT: Ashgate.

Corlett, J. Angelo. 2003. *Terrorism: A Philosophical Analysis.* Boston: Kluwer.

Crank, John, and Patricia Gregor. 2005. *Counter-Terrorism After 9/11: Justice, Security and Ethics Reconsidered.* Cincinnati, OH: LexisNexis and Anderson.

Dworkin, Ronald. 2006. *Is Democracy Possible Here?* Princeton, NJ: Princeton University Press.

Emcke, Carolyn. 2005. "War on Terrorism and the Crises of the Political." Pp. 227–244 in *Ethics of Terrorism and Counter-Terrorism,* edited by Georg Meggle. Frankfurt, Germany: Ontos.

Enemark, Christian. 2014. *Armed Drones and the Ethics of War: Military Virtue in a Post-Heroic Age.* London: Routledge.

Freeman, Michael. 2005. "Order, Rights and Threats: Terrorism and Global Justice." Pp. 37–56 in *Human Rights in the "War on Terror,"* edited by Richard Wilson. Cambridge, England: Cambridge University Press.

Frey, Raymond G., and Christopher Morris. 1991. "Violence, Terrorism, and Justice." Pp. 1–17 in *Violence, Terrorism, and Justice,* edited by R. G. Frey and Christopher Morris. Cambridge, England: Cambridge University Press.

Ginbar, Yuval. 2008. *Why Not Torture Terrorists? Moral, Practical and Legal Aspects of the "Ticking Bomb" Justification for Torture.* Oxford, England: Oxford University Press.

Gregory, Derek. 2011. "From a View to a Kill: Drones and Late Modern War." *Theory, Culture and Society* 28(7–8): 188–215.

Gross, Michael. 2006. "Assassination and Targeted Killing: Law Enforcement, Execution or Self-Defence." *Journal of Applied Philosophy* 23(3): 323–335.

Hamdi v. Rumsfeld, 542 U.S. 507 (2004).

Held, Virginia. 1991. "Terrorism, Rights, and Political Goals." Pp. 59–85 in *Violence, Terrorism, and Justice,* edited by R. G. Frey and Christopher Morris. Cambridge, England: Cambridge University Press.

Heymann, Philip B., and Juliette N. Kayyem. 2005. *Protecting Liberty in an Age of Terror.* Cambridge, MA: MIT Press.

Hoffman, Paul. 2004. "Human Rights and Terrorism." *Human Rights Quarterly* 26: 932–955.

Hooks, Gregory, and Clayton Mosher. 2005. "Outrages Against Personal Dignity: Rationalizing Abuse and Torture in the War on Terror." *Social Forces* 83(1): 1627–1646.

ICRC. 2006. *The Geneva Conventions: The Core of International Humanitarian Law.* Retrieved June 11, 2007 (http://www.icrc.org/Web/Eng/siteeng0.nsf/htmlall/genevaconventions).

Ignatieff, Michael. 2004. *The Lesser Evil: Political Ethics in an Age of Terror—The Gifford Lectures.* Princeton, NJ: Princeton University Press.

Kanstroom, Daniel. 2007. "'Unlawful Combatants in the United States: Drawing the Fine Line Between Law and War." *Human Rights Magazine.* Retrieved June 12, 2007 (http://www.abanet.org/irr/hr/winter03/unlawful.html).

Kapitan, Tomis. 2005. "'Terrorism' as a Method of Terrorism." Pp. 21–38 in *Ethics of Terrorism and Counter-Terrorism,* edited by G. Meggle. Frankfurt, Germany: Ontos.

Khatchadourian, Haig. 2005. "Counter-Terrorism: Torture and Assassination." Pp. 177–196 in *Ethics of Terrorism and Counter-Terrorism,* edited by Georg Meggle. Frankfurt, Germany: Ontos.

Kleinig, John. 2005. "Ticking Bombs and Torture Warrants." *Deakin Law Review* 10(2): 614–627.

Kleinig, John. 2011. "Liberty and Security in an Era of Terrorism." Pp. 357–382 in *Criminologists on Terrorism and Homeland Security,* edited by Brian Forst, Jack R. Greene, and James P. Lynch. Cambridge, England: Cambridge University Press.

Klinger, David, and Charles "Sid" Heal. 2011. "Manifestations of Aggression: Terrorism, Crime, and War." Pp. 17–39 *Criminologists on Terrorism and Homeland Security,* edited by Brian Forst, Jack R. Greene, and James P. Lynch. Cambridge, England: Cambridge University Press.

Laqueur, Walter. 1987. *The Age of Terrorism.* Boston: Little, Brown.

Lue, Thomas. 2005. "Torture and Coercive Interrogations." Pp. 149–177 in *Protecting Liberty in an Age of Terror,* edited by Philip B. Heymann and Juliette N. Kayyem. Cambridge, MA: MIT Press.

Manning, Peter. 2006. "Reflections on Risk Analysis, Screening, and Contested Rationalities." *Canadian Journal of Criminology and Criminal Justice* 48: 453–469.

Massimino, Elisa. 2004. "Leading by Example? U.S. Interrogation of Prisoners in the War on Terror." *Criminal Justice Ethics* Winter/Spring: 73–76.

McCauley, Clark. 2009. "War Versus Criminal Justice in Response to Terrorism: The Losing Logic of Torture." Pp. 63–85 in *Terrorism and Torture: An Interdisciplinary Perspective,* edited by Werner G. K. Stritzke, Stephan Lewandowsky, David Denemark, Joseph Clare, and Frank Morgan. Cambridge, England: Cambridge University Press.

McEldowney, John. 2005. "Political Security and Democratic Rights." *Democratization* 12(5): 766–782.

Mertens, Thomas. 2005. "Criminal Justice 9–11: ICC or Military Tribunals." Pp. 281–300 in *Ethics of Terrorism and Counter-Terrorism,* edited by Georg Meggle. Frankfurt, Germany: Ontos.

Narveson, Jan. 1991. "Terrorism and Morality." Pp. 116–169 in *Violence, Terrorism, and Justice,* edited by R. G. Frey and Christopher Morris. Cambridge, England: Cambridge University Press.

Parker, Tom. 2005. "Counterterrorism Policies in the United Kingdom." Pp. 119–148 in *Protecting Liberty in an Age of Terror,* edited by Philip B. Heymann and Juliette N. Kayyem. Cambridge, MA: MIT Press.

Primoratz, Igor. 2004. "State Terrorism and Counterterrorism." Pp. 113–127 in *Terrorism: The Philosophical Issues,* edited by Igor Primoratz. New York: Palgrave Macmillan.

Patterson, Eric, and Teresa Casale. 2005. "Implications of Targeted Killing." *International Journal of Intelligence and CounterIntelligence* 18(4): 638–652.

Ramsay, Maureen. 2009. "Saying No to Torture: A Moral Absolute, Self-Righteous or Just Naïve?" Pp. 419–437 in *The Moral Dimension of Asymmetrical Warfare: Counter-Terrorism, Democratic Values and Military Ethics,* edited by Th. A. van Baarda and D. E. M. Verweij. Leiden, The Netherlands: Martinus Nijhoff.

Rodin, David. 2010. "Torture and Terrorism." Pp. 820–831 in *The Routledge Companion to Ethics,* edited by John Skorupski. New York: Routledge.

Saul, Ben. 2009. "The Equivalent Logic of Torture and Terrorism: The Legal Regulation of Moral Monstrosity." Pp: 44–62 in *Terrorism and Torture: An Interdisciplinary Perspective.* New York: Cambridge University Press.

Scheid, Don E. 2010. "Indefinite Detention of Mega-Terrorists in the War on Terror." *Criminal Justice Ethics* 29(1): 1–28.

Senate Select Committee on Intelligence. 2014, December 3. *Committee Study of the CIA's Detention and Interrogation Program: Findings and Conclusions.* Washington, DC: U.S. Senate.

Simpson, Peter. 2005. "The War on Terrorism: Its Justification and Limits." Pp. 197–206 in *Ethics of Terrorism and Counter-Terrorism,* edited by Georg Meggle. Frankfurt, Germany: Ontos.

Smith, Jeffrey. 2007, March 10. "Report Details Missteps in Data Collection." *The Washington Post.* Retrieved April 12, 2007 (http://www.washingtonpost.com/wp-dyn/content/article/2007/03/09/AR2007030902353.html).

Solomon, Wm. David. 2001. "Double Effect." Pp. 418–420 in *The Encyclopedia of Ethics,* edited by Lawrence Becker and Charlotte Becker. London: Routledge.

Spino, Joseph, and Denise Dellarosa Cummins. 2014. "The Ticking Time Bomb: When the Use of Torture Is and Is Not Endorsed." *Review of Philosophy and Psychology* 5(4): 543–563.

Steinhoff, Uwe. 2005. "The Ethics of Terrorism." Pp. 215–224 in *Ethics of Terrorism and Counter-Terrorism,* edited by Georg Meggle. Frankfurt, Germany: Ontos.

Teson, Fernando. 2005. "Liberal Security." Pp. 57–77 in *Human Rights in the "War on Terror,"* edited by Richard Wilson. Cambridge, England: Cambridge University Press.

The Guardian. 2013, May 23. "President Barack Obama's Speech at National Defense University—Full Text." http://www.theguardian.com/world/2013/may/23/obama-drones-guantanamo-speech-text.

Van Brunschot, Erin Gibbs, and Leslie W. Kennedy. 2008. *Risk, Balance and Security.* Thousand Oaks, CA: Sage.

Waldron, Jeremy. 2010. *Torture, Terror, and Trade-Offs: Philosophy for the White House.* New York: Oxford University Press.

Walklate, Sandra, and Gabe Mythen. 2015. *Contradictions of Terrorism: Security, Risk and Resilience.* Abingdon, United Kingdom: Routledge.

Wall, Tyler, and Torin Monahan. 2011. "Surveillance and Violence From Afar: The Politics of Drones and Liminal Security-Scapes." *Theoretical Criminology* 15(3): 239–254.

Whittaker, David. 2003. *The Terrorism Reader* (2nd ed.). London: Routledge.

Wilkinson, Paul. 2001. *Terrorism Versus Democracy: The Liberal State Response.* London: Frank Cass.

Wilkinson, Paul. 2006. *Terrorism Versus Democracy: The Liberal State Response* (2nd ed.). London: Routledge.

Wilson, Richard. 2005. "Human Rights in the 'War on Terror.'" Pp. 1–36 in *Human Rights in the "War on Terror,"* edited by Richard Wilson. Cambridge, England: Cambridge University Press.

Young, Alison. 1996. *Imagining Crime: Textual Outlaws and Criminal Conversations.* Thousand Oaks, CA: Sage.

Zedner, Lucia. 2014. "Terrorizing Criminal Law." *Criminal Law and Philosophy* 8: 99–121.

Chapter 11

American Society of Newspaper Editors. n.d. "ASNE Statement of Principles." Retrieved August 8, 2011 (http://asne.org/kiosk/archive/principl.htm).

Archard, David. 1998. "Privacy, the Public Interest and a Prurient Public in Media Ethics." Pp. 82–94 in *Media Ethics,* edited by Matthew Kieran. London: Routledge.

Barak, Greg. 1994. "Newsmaking Criminology: Reflections on the Media, Intellectuals and Crime." Pp. 237–264 in *Media, Process, and the Social Construction of Crime: Studies in Newsmaking Criminology,* edited by Greg Barak. London: Garland.

Berry, David. 2008. *Journalism, Ethics and Society.* Farnham, England: Ashgate.

Brewer, Paul R., and Barbara L. Ley. 2010. "Media Use and Public Perceptions of DNA Evidence." *Science Communication* 31(1): 93–117.

Chiricos, Ted, and Sarah Eschholz. 2002. "The Racial and Ethnic Typification of Crime and the Criminal Typification of Race and Ethnicity in Local Television News." *Journal of Research in Crime and Delinquency* 39: 400–420.

Cooke, Janet. 1980, September 28. "Jimmy's World." *The Washington Post,* A1. Retrieved August 8, 2011 (http://www.uncp.edu/home/canada/work/markport/lit/litjour/spg2002/cooke.htm).

Cooke, Louise, and Paul Sturgis. 2009. "Police and Media Relations in an Era of Freedom of Information." *Policing and Society* 19(4): 406–424.

De Mesmaecker, Vicky. 2010. "Building Social Support for Restorative Justice Through the Media: Is Taking the Victim Perspective the Most Appropriate Strategy?" *Contemporary Justice Review* 13(3): 239–267.

Ducat, Lauren, Stuart Thomas, and Warwick Blood. 2009. "Sensationalizing Sex Offenders and Sexual Recidivism: Impact of the Serious Sex Offender Monitoring Act 2005 on Media Reportage." *Australian Psychologist* 44(3): 156–165.

Durnal, Evan W. 2010. "Crime Scene Investigation (as seen on TV)." *Forensic Science International* 199:1–5.

Easteal, Patricia, Lorana Bartels, Noni Nelson, and Kate Holland. 2015. "How Are Women Who Kill Portrayed in the Newspaper Media? Connections With Social Values and the Legal System." *Women's Studies International Forum* 51: 31–41.

Elias, Robert. 1994. "Has Victimology Outlived Its Usefulness?" *Journal of Human Justice* 6: 4–25.

Elias, Robert. 1996. "Paradigms and Paradoxes of Victimology." Pp. 9–34 in *International Victimology: Selected Papers From the 8th International Symposium,* edited by Colin M. Israel and M. O'Connell. Canberra: Australian Institute of Criminology.

EthicNet. n.d. "IFJ Declaration of Principles on the Conduct of Journalists." Retrieved August 8, 2011 (http://ethicnet.uta.fi/international/declaration_of_principles_on_the_conduct_of_journalists).

Feinberg, Joel. 1984. *Harm to Others: The Moral Limits of the Criminal Law.* New York: Oxford University Press.

Fullerton, Romayne Smith, and Maggie Jones Patterson. 2006. "Murder in Our Midst: Expanding Coverage to Include Care and Responsibility." *Journal of Mass Media Ethics* 21(4): 304–321.

Greer, C. (Ed.). 2010. *Crime and Media: A Reader.* Abingdon, England: Routledge.

Heeren, John W., and Jill Theresa Messing. 2009. "Victims and Sources: Newspaper Reports of Mass Murder in Domestic Contexts." Pp. 206–223 in *Women, Violence and the Media,* edited by Drew Humphries. Boston: Northeastern University Press.

Hirschfield, Paul J., and Daniella Simon. 2010. "Legitimating Police Violence: Newspaper Narratives of Deadly Force." *Theoretical Criminology* 14: 155–182.

Hope, Tim, and Richard Sparks. 2000. *Crime, Risk and Insecurity.* Abingdon, England: Routledge.

Humphries, Drew. 2009. "Introduction: Toward a Framework for Integrating Women, Violence and the Media." Pp. 1–19 in *Women, Violence and the Media,* edited by Drew Humphries. Boston: Northeastern University Press.

Jackson, Brooks. 1985, February 25. "John Fedders of SEC Is Pummeled by Legal and Personal Problems." *Wall Street Journal,* p. 1.

Jewkes, Yvonne. 2011. *Media and Crime.* London: Sage.

Jewkes, Yvonne. 2015. *Media and Crime* (2nd ed.). London: Sage.

Jirard, Stephanie, A. 2010. "The Missing White Woman Syndrome: Why Missing Women of Color Are Easy for the Media to Ignore." Pp. 85–99 in *Race, Crime and the Media,* edited by Robert L. Bing III. New York: McGraw-Hill.

Kidd-Hewitt, David. 1995. "Crime and the Media: A Criminological Perspective." Pp. 1–24 in *Crime and the Media: The Post-Modern Spectacle,* edited by David Kidd-Hewitt and Richard Osborne. London: Pluto Press.

Kim, Young S., Gregg Barak, and Donald E. Shelton. 2009. "Examining the 'CSI-Effect' in the Cases of Circumstantial Evidence and Eyewitness Testimony: Multivariate and Path Analysis." *Journal of Criminal Justice* 37: 452–460.

King, Mike. 2015. "The 'Knockout Game': Moral Panic and the Politics of White Victimhood." *Race and Class* 56(4): 85–94.

Klaidman, Stephen, and Tom L. Beauchamp. 1987. *The Virtuous Journalist.* Oxford, England: Oxford University Press.

Lawrence, Regina. 2000. *The Politics of Force: Media and the Construction of Police Brutality.* Berkeley: University of California Press.

Lawson, Kenneth. 2015. "Police Shootings of Black Men and Implicit Racial Bias: Can't We All Just Get Along." *University of Hawaii Law Review* 37: 339–535.

Ley, Barbara L., Natalie Jankowski, and Paul R. Brewer. 2012. "Investigating *CSI:* Portrayals of DNA Testing on a Forensic Crime Show and Their Potential Effects." *Public Understanding of Science* 21(1): 51–67.

Meloy, Michelle L., and Susan L. Miller. 2009. "Words That Wound: Print Media's Presentation of Gendered Violence." Pp. 29–56 in *Women, Violence and the Media,* edited by Drew Humphries. Boston: Northeastern University Press.

Miller, Jody, Toya Z. Like, and Peter Levin. 2006. "The Caucasian Evasion: Victims, Exceptions and Defenders of the Faith." Pp. 111–127 in *Images of Color, Images of Crime,* edited by Coramae Richey Mann, Marjorie S. Zatz, and Nancy Rodriguez. Oxford, England: Oxford University Press.

Pew Research Center for the People and the Press. 2008. *News Consumption and Believability Study.* Washington, DC. Retrieved August 24, 2011 (http://www.people-press.org).

Philips, Nickie D., and Staci Strobl. 2013. *Comic Book Crime: Truth, Justice and the American Way.* New York: New York University Press.

Plaisance, Patrick Lee. 2009. *Media Ethics: Key Principles for Responsible Practice.* Thousand Oaks, CA: Sage.

Pritchard, David, and Karen D. Hughes. 1997. "Patterns of Deviance in Crime News." *Journal of Communication* 47(3): 49–67.

Reiner, Rob, Sonia Livingstone, and Jessica Allen. 2003. "From Law and Order to Lynch Mobs: Crime News Since the Second World War." Pp. 13–32 in *Criminal Visions: Media Representations of Crime and Justice,* edited by Paul Mason. Cullompton, England: Willan.

Rome, Dennis M. 2006. "The Social Construction of the African American Criminal Stereotype." Pp. 78–87 in *Images of Color, Images of Crime,* edited by Coramae Richey Mann, Marjorie S. Zatz, and Nancy Rodriguez. Oxford, England: Oxford University Press.

Silverstone, Roger. 2007. *Media and Morality: On the Rise of the Mediapolis.* Cambridge, England: Polity.

Sloan, John J. III, and Bonnie S. Fisher. 2011. *The Dark Side of the Ivory Tower: Campus Crime as a Social Problem.* New York: Cambridge University Press.

Surette, Ray. 2011. *Media, Crime and Criminal Justice.* Belmont, CA: Wadsworth.

Tankard, James, Laura Hendrickson, Jackie Silberman, Kris Bliss, and Salma Ghanem. 1991. *Media Frames: Approaches to Conceptualization and Measurement.* Paper presented at the Association for Education in Journalism and Mass Communication, Boston.

Tonry, Michael. 1995. *Malign Neglect.* New York: Oxford University Press.

Welch, Kelly. 2007. "Black Criminal Stereotypes and Racial Profiling." *Journal of Contemporary Criminal Justice* 23: 276–288.

Part II

Atterton, Peter. 2002. "Emmanuel Levinas." Pp. 231–238 in *Postmodernism: The Key Figures,* edited by Hans Bertens and Joseph Natoli. Oxford, England: Blackwell.

Bauman, Zygmunt. 1993. *Postmodern Ethics.* Oxford, England: Blackwell.

Davis, Nancy. 1991. "Contemporary Deontology." Pp. 205–218 in *A Companion to Ethics,* edited by Peter Singer. Cambridge, MA: Blackwell.

Hinman, Lawrence. 1998. *Ethics: A Pluralistic Approach to Moral Theory.* Fort Worth, TX: Harcourt Brace.

Kagan, Shelly. 1998. *Normative Ethics.* Boulder, CO: Westview Press.

Kekes, John. 2000. *Pluralism in Philosophy: Changing the Subject.* Ithaca, NY: Cornell University Press.

Kopperi, Marjaanna. 1999. *Right Actions and Good Persons: Controversies Between Eudaimonistic and Deontic Moral Theories.* Aldershot, England: Ashgate.

Rachels, James. 1997. *Can Ethics Provide Answers? And Other Essays in Moral Philosophy.* Lanham, MD: Rowman & Littlefield.

Rainsford, Dominic, and Tim Woods (Eds.). 1999. *Critical Ethics: Text, Theory and Responsibility.* London: MacMillan Press.

Rumana, Richard. 2000. *On Rorty.* Belmont, CA: Wadsworth.

Scarre, Geoffrey. 1996. *Utilitarianism.* London: Routledge.

Sharples, Robert W. 1996. *Stoics, Epicureans and Sceptics: An Introduction to Hellenistic Philosophy.* London: Routledge.

Wallace, James. 1996. *Ethical Norms, Particular Cases.* Ithaca, NY: Cornell University Press.

Chapter 12

Benn, Piers. 1998. *Ethics: Fundamentals of Philosophy.* Montreal, QC: McGill-Queen's University Press.

Dancy, Jonathan. 1991. "An Ethic of Prima Facie Duties." Pp. 219–229 in *A Companion to Ethics,* edited by Peter Singer. Cambridge, MA: Blackwell.

Giannetti, William. 2003. "Policing the Brass: A Case Study in Command Malfeasance." *Criminal Justice Ethics* Summer/Fall: 32–50.

Hill, Thomas E. 2000. *Respect, Pluralism, and Justice: Kantian Perspectives.* Oxford, England: Oxford University Press.

Hinman, Lawrence. 1998. *Ethics: A Pluralistic Approach to Moral Theory.* Fort Worth, TX: Harcourt Brace.

Holmes, Robert. 1998. *Basic Moral Philosophy* (2nd ed.). Belmont, CA: Wadsworth.

Jones, John, and Daniel Carlson (Eds.). 2001. *Reputable Conduct: Ethical Issues in Policing and Corrections.* Upper Saddle River, NJ: Prentice-Hall.

O'Neill, Onora. 1991. "Kantian Ethics." Pp. 175–185 in *A Companion to Ethics,* edited by Peter Singer. Cambridge, MA: Blackwell.

Rachels, James. 1999. *The Elements of Moral Philosophy* (3rd ed.). Boston: McGraw-Hill College.

Schneewind, J. B. 1992. "Autonomy, Obligation, and Virtue: An Overview of Kant's Moral Philosophy." Pp. 309–341 in *The Cambridge Companion to Kant,* edited by Paul Guyer. Cambridge, England: Cambridge University Press.

Scruton, Roger. 2001. *Kant: A Very Short Introduction.* Oxford, England: Oxford University Press.

Chapter 13

Benn, Piers. 1998. *Ethics: Fundamentals of Philosophy.* Montreal, QC: McGill-Queen's University Press.

Close, Daryl, and Nicholas Meier. 1995. *Morality in Criminal Justice: An Introduction to Ethics.* Belmont, CA: Wadsworth.

Darwall, Stephen. 1998. *Philosophical Ethics.* Boulder, CO: Westview Press.

Goodin, Robert. 1991. "Utility and the Good." Pp. 241–248 in *A Companion to Ethics,* edited by Peter Singer. Cambridge, MA: Blackwell.

Hinman, Lawrence. 1998. *Ethics: A Pluralistic Approach to Moral Theory.* Fort Worth, TX: Harcourt Brace.

Holmes, Robert. 1998. *Basic Moral Philosophy* (2nd ed.). Belmont, CA: Wadsworth.

Rachels, James. 1999a. *The Elements of Moral Philosophy* (3rd ed.). Boston: McGraw-Hill College.

Rachels, James. 1999b. *The Right Thing to Do: Basic Readings in Moral Philosophy* (2nd ed.). Boston: McGraw-Hill College.

Rashbaum, William. 2000, March 15. "Officer Accused of False Testimony Kills Himself, Police Say." *The New York Times.* Retrieved May 15, 2007 (http://query.nytimes.com/gst/fullpage.html?sec=health&res=9B0CE7DF1E3BF936A25750C0A9669C8B63).

Scarre, Geoffrey. 1996. *Utilitarianism.* London: Routledge.

Shaw, William. 1999. *Contemporary Ethics: Taking Account of Utilitarianism.* Oxford, England: Blackwell.

Singer, Peter. 1979. "Famine, Affluence, and Morality." Pp. 263–278 in *Moral Problems* (3rd ed.), edited by James Rachels. New York: Harper and Row.

Chapter 14

Benn, Piers. 1998. *Ethics: Fundamentals of Philosophy.* Montreal, QC: McGill-Queen's University Press.

Blum, Lawrence. 1996. "Community and Virtue." Pp. 231–250 in *How Should One Live? Essays on the Virtues,* edited by Roger Crisp. Oxford, England: Clarendon Press.

Cassidy, Michael. 2006. "Character and Context: What Virtue Theory Can Teach Us About a Prosecutor's Ethical Duty to 'Seek Justice.'" *Notre Dame Law Review* 82(2): 100–161.

Darwall, Stephen. 1998. *Philosophical Ethics.* Boulder, CO: Westview Press.

Goodman, Debbie. 1998. *Enforcing Ethics: A Scenario-Based Workbook for Police and Corrections Recruits and Officers.* Upper Saddle River, NJ: Prentice-Hall.

Hinman, Lawrence. 1998. *Ethics: A Pluralistic Approach to Moral Theory.* Fort Worth, TX: Harcourt Brace.

Hinman, Lawrence. 2003. *Ethics: A Pluralistic Approach to Moral Theory* (3rd ed.). Belmont, CA: Thomson/Wadsworth.

Holmes, Robert. 1998. *Basic Moral Philosophy* (2nd ed.). Belmont, CA: Wadsworth.

Hursthouse, Rosalind. 1999. *On Virtue Ethics.* Oxford, England: Oxford University Press.

Kopperi, Marjaanna. 1999. *Right Actions and Good Persons: Controversies Between Eudaimonistic and Deontic Moral Theories.* Aldershot, England: Ashgate.

MacIntyre, Alasdair. 1984. *After Virtue: A Study in Moral Theory.* Notre Dame, IN: University of Notre Dame Press.

Okin, Susan Moller. 1996. "Feminism, Moral Development, and the Virtues." Pp. 211–229 in *How Should One Live? Essays on the Virtues,* edited by Roger Crisp. Oxford, England: Clarendon Press.

Pincoffs, Edmund. 1998. "Quandary Ethics." Pp. 435–453 in *Ethical Theory,* edited by James Rachels. Oxford, England: Oxford University Press.

Prior, William. 1991. *Virtue and Knowledge: An Introduction to Ancient Greek Ethics.* London: Routledge.

Rachels, James. 1999. *The Elements of Moral Philosophy* (3rd ed.). Boston: McGraw-Hill College.

Tessitore, Aristide. 1996. *Reading Aristotle's Ethics: Virtue, Rhetoric, and Political Philosophy.* Albany: State University of New York Press.

Chapter 15

Baier, Kurt. 1991. "Egoism." Pp. 197–204 in *A Companion to Ethics,* edited by Peter Singer. Cambridge, MA: Blackwell.

Becker, Lawrence. 1998. *A New Stoicism.* Princeton, NJ: Princeton University Press.

Feldman, Fred. 1997. *Utilitarianism, Hedonism, and Desert: Essays in Moral Philosophy.* New York: Cambridge University Press.

Glover, Jonathan. 1999. "Capital Punishment." Pp. 245–253 in *The Right Thing to Do: Basic Readings in Moral Philosophy* (2nd ed.), edited by James Rachels. Boston: McGraw-Hill.

Hinman, Lawrence. 1998. *Ethics: A Pluralistic Approach to Moral Theory.* Fort Worth, TX: Harcourt Brace.

Prior, William. 1991. *Virtue and Knowledge: An Introduction to Ancient Greek Ethics.* London: Routledge.

Rachels, James. 1999. *The Elements of Moral Philosophy* (3rd ed.). Boston: McGraw-Hill College.

Sharples, Robert W. 1996. *Stoics, Epicureans and Sceptics: An Introduction to Hellenistic Philosophy.* London: Routledge.

Chapter 16

Alejandro, Roberto. 1998. *The Limits of Rawlsian Justice.* Baltimore, MD: John Hopkins University Press.

Benn, Piers. 1998. *Ethics: Fundamentals of Philosophy.* Montreal, QC: McGill-Queen's University Press.

Blocker, H. Gene, and Elisabeth H. Smith (Eds.). 1980. *John Rawls' Theory of Social Justice: An Introduction.* Athens: Ohio University Press.

Darwall, Stephen. 1980. "Is There a Kantian Foundation for Rawlsian Justice?" Pp. 311–345 in *John Rawls' Theory of Social Justice: An Introduction,* edited by H. Gene Blocker and Elisabeth H. Smith. Athens: Ohio University Press.

Holmes, Robert. 1998. *Basic Moral Philosophy* (2nd ed.). Belmont, CA: Wadsworth.

Jones, Hardy. 1980. "A Rawlsian Discussion of Discrimination." Pp. 270–288 in *John Rawls' Theory of Social Justice: An Introduction,* edited by H. Gene Blocker and Elisabeth H. Smith. Athens: Ohio University Press.

Martin, Rex. 1985. *Rawls and Rights.* Lawrence: University Press of Kansas.

Okin, Susan. 2003. "Justice and Gender." Pp. 236–250 in *Justice: Alternative Political Perspectives* (4th ed.), edited by James Sterba. Belmont, CA: Thompson/Wadsworth.

Rawls, John. 1973. *A Theory of Justice.* Oxford, England: Oxford University Press.

Scanlon, T. M. 1989. "Rawls' Theory of Justice." Pp. 169–205 in *Reading Rawls: Critical Studies on Rawls' "A Theory of Justice,"* edited by Norman Daniels. Palo Alto, CA: Stanford University Press.

Chapter 17

Benhabib, Seyla. 1987. "The Generalized and the Concrete Other: The Kohlberg-Gilligan Controversy and Moral Theory." Pp. 154–177 in *Women and Moral Theory,* edited by Eva Feder Kittay and Diana Meyers. Totowa, NJ: Rowman & Littlefield.

Blum, Lawrence. 1994. *Moral Perception and Particularity.* Cambridge, England: Cambridge University Press.

Braswell, Michael, and Jeffrey Gold. 1998. "Peacemaking, Justice and Ethics." Pp. 25–39 in *Justice, Crime and Ethics* (3rd ed.), edited by Michael Braswell, Belinda McCarthy, and Bernard McCarthy. Cincinnati, OH: Anderson.

Braswell, Michael, John Fuller, and Bo Lozoff. 2001. *Corrections, Peacemaking, and Restorative Justice: Transforming Individuals and Institutions.* Cincinnati, OH: Anderson.

Close, Daryl, and Nicholas Meier. 1995. *Morality in Criminal Justice: An Introduction to Ethics.* Belmont, CA: Wadsworth.

Darwall, Stephen. 1998. *Philosophical Ethics.* Boulder, CO: Westview Press.

Flanagan, Owen, and Kathryn Jackson. 1993. "Justice, Care, and Gender: The Kohlberg–Gilligan Debate Revisited." Pp. 69–86 in *An Ethic of Care: Feminist and Interdisciplinary Perspectives,* edited by Mary Jeanne Larrabee. New York: Routledge.

Fuller, John. 1998. *Criminal Justice: A Peacemaking Perspective.* Boston: Allyn & Bacon.

Gilligan, Carol. 1982. *In a Different Voice: Psychological Theory and Women's Development.* Cambridge, MA: Harvard University Press.

Gilligan, Carol. 1993. *In a Different Voice* (2nd ed.). Cambridge, MA: Harvard University Press.

Grimshaw, Jean. 1991. "The Idea of a Female Ethic." Pp. 491–499 in *A Companion to Ethics,* edited by Peter Singer. Cambridge, MA: Blackwell.

Held, Virginia. 1987. "Feminism and Moral Theory." Pp. 111–128 in *Women and Moral Theory,* edited by Eva Kittay and Diana Meyers. Totowa, NJ: Rowman & Littlefield.

Hinman, Lawrence. 1998. *Ethics: A Pluralistic Approach to Moral Theory.* Fort Worth, TX: Harcourt Brace.

Holmes, Robert. 1998. *Basic Moral Philosophy* (2nd ed.). Belmont, CA: Wadsworth.

Nicholson, Linda. 1993. "Women, Morality, and History." Pp. 87–101 in *An Ethic of Care: Feminist and Interdisciplinary Perspectives,* edited by Mary Jeanne Larrabee. New York: Routledge.

Noddings, Nel. 1984. *Caring: A Feminine Approach to Ethics and Education.* Berkeley: University of California Press.

Pepinsky, Hal. 1999. "Peacemaking Criminology and Social Justice." Pp. 51–70 in *Social Justice/Criminal Justice: The Maturation of Critical Theory in Law, Crime, and Deviance,* edited by Bruce Arrigo. Belmont, CA: Wadsworth.

Rachels, James. 1999. *The Elements of Moral Philosophy* (3rd ed.). Boston: McGraw-Hill College.

Slote, Michael. 1998. "The Justice of Caring." Pp. 171–195 in *Virtue and Vice,* edited by Ellen Paul, Fred Miller, and Jeffrey Paul. Cambridge, England: Cambridge University Press.

Sterba, James. 2001. *Three Challenges to Ethics: Environmentalism, Feminism, and Multiculturalism.* Oxford, England: Oxford University Press.

West, Robin. 1997. *Caring for Justice.* New York: New York University Press.

INDEX

Accountability of police, 25, 52
Act consequentialism, 354–355
Adam Walsh Child Protection Act (2006), 270
Administrative segregation, 195
Adversarial system, 128, 132–133, 136
African Americans:
    confidence in police, 62
    conviction rates, 107
    death penalty, 110–111, 114, 117, 278
    driving-while-black, 60–61
    drug enforcement, 104, 110, 119–122, 251, 266, 267–268
    incarceration rates, 109, 253
    Jim Crow laws, 98, 99, 100, 122, 256
    jury selection process, 105–107
    juvenile justice system, 102–103
    media stereotypes, 316–318
    police discretionary power, 103–104
    police use-of-force, 5, 65, 67–68, 69–70, 72, 76–78, 80
    policing procedures, 56–57
    racial bias, 56–57, 65, 67–68, 69–70, 72, 76–78, 80, 101
    racial profiling, 57–62, 77
    sentencing rates, 107, 112t
    separate-but-equal doctrine, 99, 100
    slavery, 99, 122
    socioeconomics, 108
    stop-and-frisk practices, 61–62
Alabama:
    capital punishment, 274
    corrections policy, 255
    prison rape, 191
    probation privatization, 243
Alaska, 131
Alaska Natives, 100
Amber Alert, 270
American Bar Association, 127
American Correctional Association, 199–200
American Indians, 100, 102–103
Amish community, 332
Ancient ethics, 339
Angry aggression theory, 31–32
Anti-Drug Abuse Act:
    1986, 265
    1988, 185
Antiterrorism and Effective Death Penalty Act (1996), 279
Applied ethics, 3
Arbaje-Diaz, Jorge, 50
Archie, Adolph, 5
Argentina:
    police corruption, 53–54
    police use-of-force, 81
Aristotle, 339, 365–366, 368–369
Arizona:
    corrections policy, 257–258
    judicial elections, 149
    racial discrimination, 58
Arpia, Joe, 257–258
Ashcroft, John, 185
Auditors for police corruption, 52–53
Australia:
    incarceration rates, 253
    police corruption, 43–44, 46, 54
    police use-of-force, 65
    transgender inmates, 234
Authority:
    correctional ethics, 202–208
    correctional guards, 203–204, 207–208, 236–238
    legalistic, 207–208
    morality of, 392
    personal, 207
    police, 24–25

Bail, 105
Batson v. Kentucky (1986), 106–107
Baze v. Rees (2008), 281

Beauchamp, T. L., 313
Belgium, 17
Bennett, W., 273
Bentham, Jeremy, 351
Berger v. United States (1935), 136
Berry v. Leslie (2014), 35
Body Count (Bennett, DiIulio, Walters), 273
Bosnia, 46
Brady v. Maryland (1963), 139
Brazil, 81
Brewer, Gerald, 55
Brown, Michael, 67, 77–78
Brown v. Board of Education of Topeka, Kansas (1954), 100
Brown v. City of Golden Valley (2011), 82
Bryan v. McPherson (2009), 82
Building tenders, 238
Burder, Thomas, 72
Bureaucratic rationality, 174
Burnout guards, 202
Burrell, Albert Ronnie, 147
Bush, George H., 185
Bush, George W., 185, 233, 272, 289, 306

Cagle, Houston, 238
California:
    correctional guards, 229, 232–233, 234, 238–239
    law enforcement values, 23–24
    legal ethics, 130, 131
    maximum security prison, 192–193
    police use-of-force, 68, 80, 100–101
    prison overcrowding, 187–188, 254
    prison rape, 229, 232–233, 234
    punishment, 166
    sexual predators, 269, 270
    three-strikes legislation, 262, 263
Canada:
    police corruption, 54
    police use-of-force, 65, 67
    racial profiling, 61
    transgender inmates, 234
Canton v. Harris (1989), 76
Capital punishment. *See* Death penalty
Caring ethic:
    application of, 408–409
    case study, 406–407
    characteristics of, 400–401
    development of, 401–403
    discussion case, 410–411

discussion questions, 411
ethical dilemma approach, 407
gender approach, 400–403
Heinz's dilemma, 397
justice system approach, 403–404
moral development theory, 396, 397, 398t
peacemaking approach, 404–406, 407
women's moral development, 397, 399–400
Caring (Noddings), 401
Casey v. City of Fed. Heights (2007), 82
Castor, Bruce L., Jr., 146
Categorical imperative, 341–345
Censure of punishment, 161–162, 165
Character. *See* Virtue ethics
Ciavarella, Mark, 150–151
Citizen role:
    in police corruption, 53
    in police use-of-force, 66
    See also Public opinion
Civil commitment law, 271, 272
Clark, Bob, 50–51
Clarke, J., 250
Clark v. Evans (1988), 228
Clemmer, D., 200
Clinton, Bill, 157, 185, 306
Cobb, Sue Bell, 148
Code of ethics:
    correctional guards, 199–200
    journalists, 316f
    judges, 147
    lawyers, 127
    parole officers, 239–240
    police, 25–29
    probation officers, 239–240
Code of silence, 4–5, 45–46
Coercive power, 203
Cohen, S., 249
Coleman v. Plata (2009), 187–188
College campus crime, 324–328
Collins, Jabbar, 137
Colon, Ricardo, 350–351
Colorado, 68
Comic book crime, 320–322
Comic Book Crime (Phillips & Strobl), 320
Communicative theory, 163
Comprehensive Crime Act (1984), 104
Comprehensive Drug Abuse Prevention and Control Act (1970), 265
Conahan, Michael, 151

Confessions, 93–94
Conflict theory, 118–119
Consensus theory, 118
Consequentialist theory:
   act consequentialism, 354–355
   defined, 338, 352
   discussion case, 363–364
   Greatest Happiness Principle, 352
   hedonism, 352
   hedonist calculus, 352–353
   lying, 363–364
   pleasure and happiness, 354
   rule consequentialism, 355
   See also Utilitarian theory
Corporal punishment, 157
Correctional ethics:
   case study, 196–198, 200, 212–213
   discussion questions, 216
   elderly inmates, 256
   incarceration rates, 179–191
   inmate amenities, 257–258
   inmate organ donation, 214
   inmate voting rights, 213–214
   Internet resources, 216
   maximum security prison, 191–196
   medium security prison, 196
   minimum security prison, 196
   policy making, 253–256
   power and authority, 202–208
   prison subculture, 200–202
   private prisons, 208–213
   solitary confinement, 194–196, 234
   terminology, 178n1
   See also Incarceration rates; Racial incarceration
     disparity
Correctional guards:
   authority misconduct, 207–208, 236–238
   building tenders, 238
   case study, 220, 225, 232–233, 237, 238
   code of ethics, 199–200
   coercion tactics, 226
   corruption of, 235–238
   discretionary power, 202–203, 220–221, 223
   discussion questions, 247
   ethical challenges, 219–220
   ethical guarding, 218–220
   female inmate rape, 191
   gay inmates, 231, 233
   informal controls, 206

inmate compliance, 204
inmate control, 202–208
inmate power, 207
Internet resources, 247
knowledgeability of, 218
male inmate rape, 220, 229–235
officer authority, 203–204, 207–208
oversight mechanisms, 239
parole, 239, 244–246
prison code, 221–222f
prison conditions, 219
prison experience, 217–218
prison subculture, 200–202
probation, 239, 240–244
punishment system, 204–205, 218–219
reward system, 204–205
role of, 219
rule violations, 205–206
smuggling contraband, 235–236, 237, 238
socialization of, 200–201
strip searches, 219
terminology, 178n1
transgender inmates, 220, 232–233, 234–235
typology of, 202
unethical situations, 223–229
use of force, 223, 224–229
whistle-blowers, 238–239
witnessing violence, 223–224
*Corrections, Peacemaking, and Restorative
   Justice* (Braswell, Fuller, Lozoff), 404
Corrections Corporation of America, 209, 212–213
Costa Rica, 54–55
Crime Act (1994), 268
Crime fighter model, 19
*Criminal Interrogation and
   Confessions* (Inbau & Reid), 95
Crisis intervention team (CIS), 88
Critcher, C., 250
Critical moral thinking, 13–14
Croatia, 46
CSI Effect, 333–334
Cultural relativism, 7–8

Dark Side of the Ivory Tower, The (Sloan & Fisher), 324
Death penalty:
   global practice, 275
   lethal injection, 281–282
   policy making, 274–283
   public opinion on, 277–280, 282–283

racial discrimination, 110–111, 114–117
U.S. practice, 276–277
wrongful convictions, 278–280
Deception of police, 91–96
Defense lawyers, 132–136
Dehumanization theory, 163
Delaware, 274
Denunciation theory, 162
Deontological theory:
    defined, 338
    duty and principle, 346–349
    punishment, 168–169
DeShaney v. Winnebago County (1989), 403
Deterrence, 156, 158–160
Diallo, Amadou, 330
Difference principle, 390–391
DiIulio, J., 273
DiLacqua, Joseph, 350–351
Dillard, Eddie, 232
Dirty-hands analysis, 85
Discipline and Punish (Foucault), 175
Discretionary power:
    correctional guards, 202–203, 220–221, 223
    police, 24–25, 103–104
    prosecutors, 104–105, 138–139
Divine command theory, 10–11
DNA evidence, 142, 145–146, 279, 333–334
Dodd v. Florida Bar (1960), 135
Doing Justice (von Hirsch), 164
Donnelly, Matthew, 357–358
Draconian punishment, 157
Dreyer v. Jalet (1972), 238
Driving-while-black, 60–61
Drone strikes, 306, 307–310
Drug enforcement:
    asset seizure, 104
    incarceration rates, 266–267
    post-release penalties, 108–109
    racial discrimination in, 104, 110, 119–122, 266,
        267–268
    See also War on Drugs
Drug investigations, 48–50
Due process, 133
Duty and principle:
    case study, 346
    categorical imperative, 341–345
    conflicting duties, 345–346
    deontological theory, 346–349
    discussion case, 350–351

discussion questions, 351
hypothetical imperative, 342
kingdom of ends, 345
lying, 341, 343, 345–346
maxims, 342–343
respect for all persons, 343–345
universality, 342–343

Ecuador, 53–54
Eldawoody, Osama, 91
Electronic recordings, 96
Elrod, Daniel, 68
Emergency operator model, 19
England:
    incarceration rates, 253
    police corruption, 47–48, 50–51
Entrapment, 89–91
Epicurus, 382
Equality, 98
*Essay on Professional Ethics,
    An* (Wood), 127
Ethical absolutism, 6, 8–9
Ethical egoism:
    application of, 385–386
    case study, 384–385
    characteristics of, 383–384
    discussion questions, 388
    ethical dilemma evaluation, 385
    psychological egoism, 382–383
Ethical hedonism, 381–382
Ethical pluralism, 9–10
Ethical relativism, 6–7
Ethics:
    applied ethics, 3
    case study, 5, 6, 7
    criminal justice issues, 15–16
    cultural relativism, 7–8
    defined, 3
    discussion case, 16–17
    discussion questions, 17
    divine command theory, 10–11
    ethical absolutism, 6, 8–9
    ethical dilemmas, 12–15
    ethical pluralism, 9–10
    ethical relativism, 6–7
    law, 12
    metaethics, 3
    natural law, 11–12
    normative ethics, 3, 6

religious principles, 10–11
    value of, 4–5
Ethnicity, 98
Expert power, 203
Extreme relativism, 7
Eye-for-an-eye justice, 160–161

Factual guilt, 134
Fair Sentencing Act (2010), 255
Faretta v. California (1975), 130
Farmer, Dee, 220
Farmer v. Brennan (1994), 220
Fay, Michael, 157
Fedders, John, 331
Ferge, James, 90–91
Finland, 46
Fisher, B., 324
Flaherty, C., 323
Fleckney, Evelyn, 50–51
Fleeing felon rule, 57
Florida:
    police use-of-force, 65, 73, 80
    probation privatization, 243
Folk Devils and Moral Panics (Cohen), 249
Foster City Police Department (California), 23–24
Foucault, M., 175
France, 16
Frye, Amber, 318
Functionary guards, 202
Furman v. Georgia (1972), 164, 274, 280

Gall v. United States (2007), 267
Garland, D., 175–176
Gates, Darryl, 35
Gay inmates, 231, 233
Gehring, Genae, 90–91
Georgia:
    death penalty, 110, 274, 280
    military equipment transfers, 38
    police use-of-force, 68
    probation privatization, 243
    transgender inmates, 234–235
Ghana, 46–47
Gilligan, C., 396
Glossip v. Gross (2015), 282
Godschalk, Bruce, 145–146
Goldwater, Barry, 184, 262
Graham, Michael Ray, Jr., 147
Graham v. Connor (1989), 75

Graham v. Florida (2010), 246
Graham v. Sauk Prairie Police Commission (1990), 79
Gratuities, 41–42, 46
Greatest Happiness Principle, 352
Gregg v. Georgia (1976), 164
Groundwork of the Metaphysics of Morals (Kant), 342

Hall, S., 250
Happiness:
    consequentialist theory, 352, 354
    virtue ethics, 368–369, 371
Hard-ass guards, 202
Harvin, Walter, 86
Hate crimes, 114–117
Hate Crimes Statistics Act (1990), 117
Hedonism:
    discussion questions, 388
    ethical hedonism, 381–382
    in consequentialist theory, 352
    psychological hedonism, 381
Hedonist calculus, 352–353
Heinz's dilemma, 397
Hernandez, Evelyn, 318
Heroic warfare, 307–308
Hill, Anthony, 68
Hobbes, Thomas, 383
Holland, 17
Homeland Security Grant Program, 36–38
Hot-spots policing, 74
Howell, Charles, 7
Hudson v. McMillian (1992), 228
Hynes, Charles J., 137
Hypothetical imperative, 342

If I Did It (Simpson), 335
Illinois, 196–198, 200
Impact litigation, 133
In a Different Voice (Gilligan), 396
Inbau, F., 95
Incapacitation punishment, 170–171
Incarceration rates:
    demographic characteristics (2014), 190*t*
    drug enforcement, 266–267
    expansion rates (1980–2013), 182*t*
    expenditures (1980–2013), 181*f*
    explosion timeline, 184–186
    global inmate population, 182–183*t*, 253
    jail population, 180*f*, 187*f*
    mass incarceration policy, 184–191, 253–256

new forms of incarceration, 189, 191
parole rates, 180*f*, 241*t*, 244*f*, 245*f*
prison overcrowding, 186–188
prison system (1880–2008), 186*f*
prison system (1980–2008), 187*f*
prison system (2000–2013), 179*f*
probation rates, 180f, 241*t*
racial discrimination, 99, 109–110, 111*t*, 113*t*,
        254, 256
women, 109–110, 188, 189, 190t, 191
See also Correctional ethics; Correctional guards
Independent Commission on the Los Angeles Police
        Department (1991), 100–101
Indiana, 90–91
Individual relativism, 7
Informants, 92
Infotainment, 313, 328, 332–334
Inquisitorial system, 128, 132
In re Friedman (1979), 144
In re Jaime P (2006), 242
In re Medley (1890), 195
In re Tyrell (1998), 242
Institutional corruption, 42, 45–46
Institutional police culture, 20–24, 21
Institutional policing model, 20
International Association of Chiefs of Police Code
        of Ethics, 26, 27–28
Internet resources:
    correctional guards, 247
    police corruption, 63
    policy making, 284
    racial discrimination, 125
Intuitive moral thinking, 13–14
Italy, 234

Jacob Wetterling Act (1994), 270–271
Jamison, Derrick, 7
Japan, 253
Jefferson, T., 250
Jim Crow laws, 98, 99, 100, 122, 256
Johnson, Lyndon, 262
Jones 'El and Others v. Berge and Litscher (2001), 192
Judicial ethics, 147–152
    code of ethics, 147
    election process, 148, 149
    ethical rules, 149–150
    misconduct, 150–152
    See also Defense lawyers; Prosecutors
Jury selection process, 105–107
Just-deserts theory, 164–167

Justice:
    application of, 393–394
    as fairness, 391–392
    difference principle, 390–391
    discussion questions, 395
    ethical dilemma evaluation, 393
    moral development, 392–393
    morality of association, 392
    morality of authority, 392
    morality of principles, 392
    original position principle, 389–390, 391
    principles of, 389–391
    veil of ignorance, 390
Just punishment, 168
Just-war theory, 286
Juvenile justice system:
    death penalty, 275
    juvenile superpredators, 273–274
    racial discrimination in, 102–103
    sexual assault in, 230

Kansas, 274
Kant, I., 342
Kaufman, Arthur, 6
Keller, Sharon, 152
Kennedy v. Louisiana (2008), 270
Kenny v. Indiana Youth Center (1991), 229
Keunan, Charly Leundeu, 68
Kimbrough v. United States (2007), 267
Kirchheimer, O., 175
Klaidman, S., 313
Knockout game, 323
Knowles v. Iowa (1998), 60
Kocon, Thomas, 55

Laird v. Tatum (1972), 32
Latinos:
    confidence in police, 62
    death penalty, 114*t*
    drug enforcement, 110
    incarceration rates, 109, 253
    juvenile justice system, 102–103
    police use-of-force, 65, 68
    racial profiling, 58, 61–62
    sentencing rates, 112*t*
    socioeconomics, 108
    stereotypes, 100
Law, 12
Lawyers. *See* Defense lawyers; Prosecutors
Legal ethics:

adversarial system, 128, 132–133, 136
case study, 7, 132, 137, 144, 145–146, 147, 150–152
client crime, 131–132
client perjury, 130–131
code of ethics, 127, 147
confidentiality, 130, 131, 132
defense lawyers, 132–136
discussion questions, 153
DNA evidence, 142, 145–146, 279
due process, 133
evidence disclosure, 131, 132, 139, 146
factual guilt, 134
historical context, 126–127
impact litigation, 133
inquisitorial system, 128, 132
judicial ethics, 147–152
lawyer-client relationship, 129–130
legal guilt, 134
neutrality principle, 128–129
partisanship principle, 128
plea bargaining, 139–142
professional ethics, 127–131
prosecutors, 136–147
trust, 128
truth, 134, 135
wrongful convictions, 144, 145–146, 147
Legal guilt, 134
Legalistic authority, 207–208
Legitimate power, 202
Less eligibility principle, 175
Lie detectors, 94
Life imprisonment without parole (LWOP), 245–246
Lohman, Michael, 6
London, David, 86
Louima, Abner, 72
Louisiana:
    incarceration rates, 253
    police use-of-force, 5, 6, 80
Lying:
    consequentialist theory, 363–364
    duty and principle, 341, 343, 345–346
Lying by police:
    accepted lying, 95
    deviant lying, 96
    investigation/interrogation stage, 92, 95–96
    tolerated lying, 95–96

Madison, Lance, 6
Madison, Ronald, 6
Madrid v. Gomez (1995), 195

Mandatory minimum sentencing, 262–264
Manning, Lee Casey, 238
Marks, Thomas, 378
Maryland, 237
Massachusetts:
    correctional guards, 218, 224, 238
    legal ethics, 126
    prison system, 205, 208
Mauer, M., 183–184
Maxims, 342–343
Maximum security prison, 191–196
McCleskey v. Kemp (1987), 110
McCullough v. Cady (1986), 228–229
McGregor, Ruth, 147
McGuire, Dennis, 281
McKissick v. United States (1967), 135
Mead, G. H., 174
Media ethics:
    accuracy, 315
    bias, 329–330
    code of ethics, 316f
    college campus crime, 324–328
    comic book crime, 320–322
    competence, 314
    completeness, 315
    constructions of crime, 312–314
    CSI Effect, 333–334
    distortions of crime, 319
    do-no-harm principle, 330–332
    ethical responsibilities, 313–314
    fear of crime, 323, 328–329
    gender stereotypes, 318–319
    infotainment, 313, 328, 332–334
    injustice, 335
    manipulation, 335–336
    moral panics, 322–323
    newsworthiness, 329
    objectivity, 315
    police portrayals, 329–330
    public service, 332–334
    public trust, 334–335
    racial stereotypes, 316–318
    truth in journalism, 314–329
    victim portrayals, 319–320
Medium security prison, 196
Megan's Laws, 270, 273
Mentally ill offenders, 68, 86–88
Metaethics, 3
Militarization of police. *See* Police militarization

Military Cooperation with Law Enforcement
    Act (1981), 32
Military equipment transfers, 36–38
Mill, John Stuart, 352, 353
Miller-El, Thomas, 106–107
Miller v. Pate (1967), 142
Minimum security prison, 196
Minnesota, 166, 253
Miranda v. Arizona (1966), 92–93
Mississippi, 253
Missouri, 32, 67, 77–78
Mitchell, Gary, 7
Modern ethics, 339
Morales, Roberto, 233
Morality of association, 392
Morality of authority, 392
Morality of principles, 392
Morality policy making, 250, 252–256
Moral panics:
    media ethics, 322–323
    policy making, 249–250
    sexual predators, 271–273
Morrell v. State (1978), 131
Murdoch, Rupert, 335
Muslim clothing ban, 17

Natural law, 11–12
Nebraska, 68, 230
Netherlands, 45–46, 65
New Jersey:
    correctional guards, 237
    maximum security prison, 191–192
    police corruption, 49
New York:
    correctional guards, 224, 225
    drug enforcement policy, 266–267
    entrapment, 91
    media ethics, 330
    military equipment transfers, 37
    police corruption, 45, 49–50
    police use-of-force, 68, 80–81, 86
    prison rape, 229, 233
    racial profiling, 61–62
    sexual predators, 269, 272
New York State Judicial Commission on Minorities
    (1991), 101
New Zealand, 65, 253
Nickerson, Eugene, 72
Nicomachean Ethics (Aristotle), 365, 366, 368–370

Nigeria, 81
Nixon, Richard, 34, 264, 265
Nix v. Whiteside (1986), 135
Noble-cause theory, 42–43, 47–48, 85
Noddings, N., 401
No Frills Prison Act (1996), 257
Normative ethics, 3, 6
North Carolina, 229

Obama, Barack:
    military equipment transfers, 38
    police use-of-force, 66
    War on Terror, 66, 288, 306, 308–309
Occupational culture of police, 20
Occupational stress of police, 29–32
Oceania, 253
Ohio:
    police use-of-force, 67, 84
    prison system, 212–213
    prosecutor misconduct, 7
Oklahoma, 230
Oregon, 81, 274
Organ donation by inmates, 214
Original position principle, 389–390, 391
Overt racism, 99

Paraguay, 53–54
Parole:
    ethical issues, 244–246
    life imprisonment without parole (LWOP),
        245–246, 261
    officer code of ethics, 239–240
    rates of, 180f, 241t, 244f, 245f
    violation rates, 245f
Parry, Kevin, 49
Patriot Act, 289, 290, 294–295
Pearce, Russell, 149
Pennsylvania, 55
Personal authority, 207
Personalistic corruption, 42, 43–45
Peterson, Laci, 318
Peterson, Scott, 318
Petit apartheid, 99
Phillips, N. D., 320
Plea bargaining, 139–142
Police:
    accountability, 25
    angry aggression theory, 31–32
    authority, 24–25

code of ethics, 25–29
crime fighter model, 19
detectives/investigators, 20
discretionary power, 24–25, 103–104
emergency operator model, 19
ethics instruction, 26–27
higher administrators, 20
historical context, 18–19
institutional model, 20
media portrayals, 329–330
middle managers, 20
occupational culture, 20
occupational stress, 29–32
organizational culture, 20–24
patrol officers, 20
policing styles, 19–20
social enforcer model, 19
social peacekeeping model, 19–20
Police corruption, 39–63
    accountability, 52
    auditors, 52–53
    case study, 55
    citizen review board, 53
    code of silence, 45–46
    cross-cultural research, 43–44, 45–46,
        50–51, 53–55
    defined, 39–40
    discussion questions, 63
    drug investigations, 48–50
    explanations for, 42, 43–48
    gratuities, 41–42, 46
    institutional explanation, 42, 45–46
    Internet resources, 63
    new police accountability, 52
    noble-cause explanation, 42–43, 47–48
    personalistic explanation, 42, 43–45
    police personality explanation, 45
    racial discrimination, 56–62
    recruitment perspective, 45
    reduction strategies, 51–52
    restaurant meals, 42
    robbery investigations, 49–50
    rotten-apple explanation, 43
    sex services, 43
    slippery-slope explanation, 42, 47
    societal stress explanation, 48–50
    systemic explanation, 42, 46–47
    typography of, 40–42
    whistle-blowers, 55–56

Police investigation/interrogation, 88–96
    confessions, 93–94
    deception, 91–96
    electronic recordings, 96
    entrapment, 89–91
    informants, 92
    interrogatory deception, 92–93
    investigative deception, 92
    lie detectors, 94
    police lying, 92, 95–96
    polygraph, 94
    privacy, 89
    suspect rights, 88
    testimonial deception, 94
    victim rights, 88
Police militarization, 32–39
    causation factors, 34–35
    consequences of, 35–36
    contemporary context, 32
    historical context, 32
    militarization thesis, 32–33, 36, 38–39
    military equipment transfers, 36–38
    Special Weapons and Tactics (SWAT) teams, 32–34,
        35–36, 38–39
Police personality, 45
Police use-of-force, 64–88
    appropriate circumstances, 70
    arrest-related deaths, 65
    case study, 5, 6, 72, 80, 86
    citizen interactions, 71–75
    citizen journalist role, 66
    code of silence, 4–5
    continuum-of-force policy, 69
    crisis intervention team (CIS), 88
    cross-cultural research, 65, 81, 85
    custody-related deaths, 65–66
    custody-related injuries, 72
    dirty-hands analysis, 85
    ethical assessment of, 79–80
    examples (2014–2015), 67–68
    explanations for, 78–79
    hot-spots policing, 74
    inappropriate circumstances, 69–70
    institutional culture, 21
    mentally ill offenders, 68, 86–88
    noble-cause explanation, 85
    occurrence rate, 64–65
    officer characteristics, 74
    organizational explanations, 78, 79

police perspective on, 70–71
procedural justice, 74–75
process-based policing, 74
racial bias, 5, 65, 67–68, 69–70, 72, 76–78, 80, 101
reduction strategies, 66, 80–81
rotten-apple explanation, 78–79
sociological explanations, 78, 79
Supreme Court decisions, 75–76
tasers, 69, 81–85
torture tactics, 85
Policing the Crisis (Hall, Critcher, Jefferson, Clarke, Roberts), 250
Policy making:
case study, 251
correctional ethics, 253–256
death penalty, 274–283
discussion questions, 284
empirical justification, 248
ethical justification, 248–249
ethics of, 248–252
ideological justification, 248
inmate amenities, 257–258
Internet resources, 284
justification of choices, 248–249
juvenile superpredators, 273–274
mandatory minimum sentencing, 262–264
morality policy, 250, 252–256
moral panics, 249–250
public opinion on crime, 258–261
public opinion on death penalty, 277–280, 282–283
public opinion on punishment, 256–262
public opinion on sentencing, 261–262
racial discrimination, 251–252, 256, 263–264, 266, 267–268
sexual predators, 269–271
three-strikes legislation, 262–264
truth-in-sentencing policy, 268–269
War on Drugs, 264–268
Politics of Law and Order, The (Scheingold), 250
Pollyanna guards, 202
Polygraph, 94
Posner, Maryrose, 317
Posse Comitatus Act (1878), 32
Postmodern ethics, 340
Prison Community, The (Clemmer), 200
Prison Litigation Reform Act (1995), 239
Prison rape:
females, 191, 238
gay inmates, 231, 233

transgenders, 220, 232–233, 234–235
victimization incidents/rates, 229–230, 231*t*
Prison Rape Elimination Act (2003), 233–234
Privacy issues, 89
Private prisons, 208–213
Probation:
ethical issues, 240–244
officer code of ethics, 239–240
officer weapons, 242–243
privatization of, 243–244
rates of, 180*f*, 241*t*
Process-based policing, 74
Proportionate punishment, 165
Prosecutors, 136–147
case study, 7, 137, 144, 145–146, 147
discretionary power, 104–105, 138–139
ensuring justice, 136–138
evidence disclosure, 131, 132, 139, 146
misconduct, 7, 137, 142–147
plea bargaining, 139–142
Protective segregation, 195
Psychological egoism, 382–383
Psychological hedonism, 381
Psychology of Punitive Justice, The (Mead), 174
Public opinion:
on crime, 258–261
on death penalty, 277–280, 282–283
on punishment, 256–262
on racial discrimination, 124–125
on sentencing, 261–262
Public Safety Realignment Act (2009), 188
Punishment:
as revenge, 164
bureaucratic rationality, 174
by correctional guards, 204–205, 218–219
case study, 157
censure, 161–162, 165
communicative theory, 163
corporal punishment, 157
defined, 154–155
dehumanization theory, 163
denunciation theory, 162
deontological theory, 168–169
deterrence, 156, 158–160
discussion questions, 177
draconian punishment, 157
eye-for-an-eye justice, 160–161
historical context, 157
incapacitation approach, 170–171

just-deserts theory, 164–167
just punishment, 168
less eligibility principle, 175
philosophical approach, 156–171
proportionate punishment, 165
rehabilitation, 168–170
restorative detention, 173
restorative justice, 171–173
retributive theory, 156, 160–168
sociological approach, 156, 173–176
state-obligated rehabilitation, 170
tariff sentencing, 165
theoretical approach, 155–156
unfair advantage theory, 163–164
utilitarian theory, 156, 158–160, 167–168
Punishment and Modern Society (Garland), 175–176
Punishment and Social Structure (Rusche & Kirchheimer), 175
Punitive segregation, 195

Quandary ethics, 373

Race, 98, 102
Race to Incarcerate (Mauer), 183–184
Racial bias:
    explicit bias, 76
    implicit bias, 76–77
    police use-of-force, 5, 65, 67–68, 69–70, 72, 76–78, 80, 101
    policing procedures, 56–57, 101
Racial discrimination:
    as police corruption, 56–62
    bail, 105
    case study, 58–59, 106–107
    conflict theory of, 118–119
    consensus theory of, 118
    conviction rates, 107
    decision-making points, 101–102
    determination factors, 100–109
    discussion questions, 125
    driving-while-black, 60–61
    drug enforcement, 104, 110, 119–122, 266, 267–268
    economic factors, 108–109
    equality, 98
    ethical background, 98–99
    ethnicity defined, 98
    explanations for, 118–125
    fleeing felon rule, 57
    hate crimes, 114–117

historical context, 99–100
Internet resources, 125
Jim Crow laws, 98, 99, 100, 122, 256
jury selection process, 105–107
juvenile justice system, 102–103
overt racism, 99
petit apartheid, 99
police discretionary power, 103–104
policy making, 251–252, 256, 263–264, 266, 267–268
political factors, 123–124
prosecutor discretion, 104–105
public opinion on, 124–125
race defined, 98, 102
racial bias, 56–57, 101
racial profiling, 57–62
racism, 98–99
selective law enforcement, 62
sentencing rates, 107–108, 112*t*
separate-but-equal doctrine, 99, 100
social factors, 108–109, 122–123
stereotypes, 100, 124, 316–318
stop-and-frisk practices, 61–62
War on Drugs, 110, 119–122, 251, 266, 267–268
See also specific group
Racial imprisonment disparity, 109–117
    death penalty, 110–111, 114, 117
    incarceration rates, 99, 109–110, 111*t*, 113*t*, 254, 256
    incidents by bias motivation, 115t, 116–117*t*
    new "Jim Crow," 256
Racial profiling, 57–62, 77
Racial stereotypes, 100, 124, 316–318
Ragen, Joe, 197
Rawls, John, 389–390
Reagan, Ronald, 184–185, 264, 306
Referent power, 203
Rehabilitation, 168–170
Reid, J. E., 95
Religion:
    death penalty impact, 278
    ethics of, 10–11
Respect for all persons, 343–345
Restaurant meals, 42
Restorative detention, 173
Restorative justice, 171–173
Retributive theory, 156, 160–168
Revenge as punishment, 164
Reward power, 203

Rhode Island, 253
Rice, Tamir, 67
Richard, Michael W., 152
Roberston, Wayne, 232
Roberts, B., 250
Roberts, Charles Carl, 332
Robinson, Tony, 68
Rochin v. California (1952), 79
Roper v. Simmons (2005), 9n1, 275
Rosero, Linda, 144
Rotten-apple theory, 43, 78–79
Rule consequentialism, 355
Rusche, G., 175
Russia, 253
Safe Streets Act (1967), 184
Safir, Howard, 363–364
Scheingold, S., 250
Schwarz, Charles, 72
Scot v. Harris (2007), 76
Sentencing rates:
    life imprisonment without parole (LWOP),
        245–246
    racial discrimination, 107–108, 112*t*
    women, 111*t*, 112*t*, 113*t*
Sentencing Reform Act (1984), 185
Separate-but-equal doctrine, 99, 100
Sex services for police, 43
Sexual assault of inmates. *See* Prison rape
Sexual predators:
    Amber Alert, 270
    child pornography, 270, 272
    civil commitment law, 271, 272
    Megan's Laws, 270, 273
    monitoring of, 271
    moral panics, 271–273
    policy making, 269–271
    prosecution of, 269–270
    registration system, 270–271
Sherman v. United States (1958), 90
Simpson, O. J., 335
Siraj, Shahawar Matin, 91
Slippery-slope corruption, 42, 47
Sloan, J., 324
Smith, Susan, 238, 316–317, 319
Smuggling contraband in prison, 235–236,
    237, 238
Social enforcer model, 19
Social peacekeeping model, 19–20
Solitary confinement, 194–196, 234

South Carolina:
    correctional guards, 238
    military equipment transfers, 38
    police use-of-force, 73
Spain, 17
Special Weapons and Tactics (SWAT) teams, 32–34,
    35–36, 38–39
Stand-your-ground defense, 323
Stanford v. Kentucky (1989), 275
State-obligated rehabilitation, 170
Stateville Prison (Illinois), 196–198, 200
Stoicism, 379–381, 388
Stop-and-frisk practices, 61–62
Strauder v. West Virginia (1880), 105
Strip searches, 219
Strobl, S., 320
Struggle for Justice (American Friends Service
    Committee), 174
Su, Shih-Wei, 144
Sullivan, James, 363–364
Superogatory actions, 356–357
Systemic corruption, 42, 46–47
Targeted killing, 305–310
Tariff sentencing, 165
Tasers, 69, 81–85
Tates, Jackie, 232–233
Taugher, Brian, 331–332
Tavarez, Emmanuel, 49–50
Tennessee, 75, 243
Tennessee v. Garner (1985), 75
1033 Program, 36–38
Terry v. Ohio (1968), 61
Texas:
    correctional guards, 224, 236
    corrections policy, 254
    death penalty, 274
    incarceration rates, 253
    police use-of-force, 65, 83
Theory of Justice, A (Rawls), 389–390
Three-strikes legislation, 262–264
Torture:
    as counterterrorist strategy, 298–305
    efficacy of, 304
    interrogation techniques, 299–301
    justification of, 301–302
    lawful torture model, 305
    morality of, 301
    police use-of-force, 85
    slippery-slope argument, 304–305

ticking-bomb scenario, 301–304
waterboarding, 299
Transgender inmates, 220, 232–233, 234–235
Truth:
   in journalism, 314–329
   in sentencing policy, 268–269
Tuite, Robert, 55

Unfair advantage theory, 163–164
United Kingdom:
   Muslim clothing ban, 17
   police corruption, 43–46, 47–48, 50–51
   police use-of-force, 65
   probation privatization, 244
   transgender inmates, 234
United States v. Agurs (1976), 139
United States v. Arvizu (2002), 60
United States v. Nix (1974), 228
United States v. Perry (1981), 142
United States v. Quinones (2002), 279
United States v. Ruehle (2009), 143
Universality, 342–343
Use-of-force by correctional guards, 223,
   224–229
Use-of-force by police. *See* Police use-of-force
Utilitarianism (Mill), 353
Utilitarian theory:
   animal rights, 358–359
   application of, 361–362
   case study, 359–360
   defined, 338, 353
   ethical dilemma evaluation, 360–361
   euthanasia, 355–358
   limitations of, 355–357
   principle of utility, 352
   public policy, 355
   punishment, 156, 158–160, 167–168
   superogatory actions, 356–357
   See also Consequentialist theory

Veil of ignorance, 390
Victim Crime Control and Law Enforcement
   Act (1994), 77
Vinzant, Naeschylus, 68
Violent Crime Control and Enforcement
   Act (1994), 265
Violent Crime Control and Law Enforcement
   Act (1994), 185
Virginia, 43, 126

Virtue ethics:
   application of, 376
   case study, 374–375
   defined, 339, 365
   discussion case, 378
   discussion questions, 378
   ethical dilemma evaluation, 375
   golden mean, 369, 371
   happiness, 368–369, 371
   limitations of, 370–374
   practical wisdom, 370
   quandary ethics, 373
   spheres of existence, 372*t*
   virtues, 367–368
Virtuous Journalist, The (Klaidman &
   Beauchamp), 313
Volpe, Justin, 72
Von Hirsch, A., 164
Vose, George, Jr., 238
Voting rights of inmates, 213–214

Wales, 253
Walters, J., 273
War on Drugs:
   case study, 251
   crime control politics, 265
   mass incarceration policy, 184, 185, 186
   police militarization, 34–35
   policy making, 264–268
   prosecution incentives, 265–266
   racial discrimination, 110, 119–122, 251, 266,
      267–268
   See also Drug enforcement; Drug investigations
War on Terror:
   citizen restrictions, 293–298
   criminal justice approach, 289–291
   discussion questions, 311
   drone strikes, 306, 307–310
   heroic warfare, 308
   just-war theory, 286
   military approach, 288–289, 291–293
   national security considerations, 295
   noncombatant casualties, 308–309
   Patriot Act, 289, 290, 294–295
   police militarization, 34–35
   prisoners of war, 291–292
   targeted killing, 305–310
   terrorism defined, 286–288
   torture, 298–305

Washington:
    police use-of-force, 68
    probation privatization, 243
    sexual predators, 269
Whistle-blowers:
    correctional guards, 238–239
    police, 55–56
White, Tavon, 237
White Girl Bleed a Lot (Flaherty), 323
White-hat guards, 202
Whitley v. Albers (1986), 228
Whren v. United States (1996), 60
Wiese, Thomas, 72
Willis, Ernest Ray, 146
Wilson, Darren, 67
Wisconsin:
    maximum security prison, 192
    military equipment transfers, 37

    police use-of-force, 68
    transgender inmates, 235
Women:
    caring ethic, 397, 399–403
    death penalty, 114*t*
    incarceration rates, 109–110, 188, 189, 190*t*, 191
    media stereotypes, 318–319
    mentally ill offenders, 87
    prison rape, 191, 238
    sentencing rates, 111*t*, 112*t*, 113*t*
Wood, G. S., 127
Wood, Joseph, 281
Woodfork, Warren, 5

Yatcilla, Gregory, 350–351
Yates, Andrea, 319
Young, Wilbert, 55

Zambrano-Montes, Antonio, 68